M 1 098 16925 6

D1634984

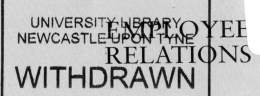

EMPLOYEE RELATIONS

EMPLOYEE RELATIONS

Edited by

Graham Hollinshead

Peter Nicholls

Stephanie Tailby

FINANCIAL TIMES
PITMAN PUBLISHING

FINANCIAL TIMES

MANAGEMENT

LONDON · SAN FRANCISCO
KUALA LUMPUR · JOHANNESBURG

*Financial Times Management delivers the knowledge,
skills and understanding that enable students,
managers and organisations to achieve their ambitions,
whatever their needs, wherever they are.*

London Office:
128 Long Acre, London WC2E 9AN
Tel: +44 (0)171 447 2000
Fax: +44 (0)171 240 5771
Website: www.ftmanagement.com

A Division of Financial Times Professional Limited

First published in Great Britain 1999

© Financial Times Professional Limited 1999

The right of Graham Hollinshead, Peter Nicholls and
Dr Stephanie Tailby to be identified as authors of this
work has been asserted by them in accordance with the
Copyright, Designs, and Patents Act 1988.

ISBN 0 273 62525 X

British Library Cataloguing in Publication Data
A CIP catalogue record for this book can be obtained from the British Library.

10 9 8 7 6 5 4 3 2 1

Typeset by Pantek Arts, Maidstone, Kent.
Printed and bound in China
SWTC/01

The Publishers' policy is to use paper manufactured from sustainable forests.

CONTENTS

Contributor details *ix*

Preface *xi*

Plan of the book *xiv*

Part I
INTRODUCTION

1 INTRODUCTION TO EMPLOYEE RELATIONS 3
Graham Hollinshead, Peter Nicholls and Stephanie Tailby
The study of employee relations 3
The context of employee relations 7
Structure and content of the book 9

2 CONTEXT AND THEORY IN EMPLOYEE RELATIONS 11
Peter Nicholls
Introduction 11
Employee relations and theoretical interpretation 16
Unitary theory 17
Pluralist theory 21
Systems theory 25
Marxist theory 31
Feminist theory 36
Comparative theory 41
Post-modernism 45
Conclusion 49
Chapter summary 49

Part II
PARTIES

3 MANAGEMENT 57
Graham Hollinshead
Introduction 58
The international context for British management 60
The status and calibre of British management 62

Challenges facing management: survival of the fittest? 64
The structuring and restructuring of industry 68
Approaches to the management of employee relations 72
Markets and approaches to managing the employment relationship: investors in people and cost cutters? 74
Management styles: the dimensions of individualism and collectivism 76
Management with or without unions 79
Non-union employee relations 80
Human resource management and employee relations 83
The future: a new partnership approach? 87
Chapter summary 89

4 MULTINATIONALS AND EMPLOYEE RELATIONS 93
Mike Leat and Jill Woolley
Introduction 95
What is a multinational company? 96
Multinationals and the internationalisation of business 97
The scale of MNCs and FDI 97
Reasons for investing abroad, becoming MNCs and locational determinants 99
Different types, forms and approaches 100
MNCs and national cultures 104
The multinational company: a force for good? 105
MNCs and national employee relations systems 107
Employee relations policies and practices within MNCs 112
MNCs and trade unions 114
International regulation and control of MNCs 120
European Works Councils MNCs, collective bargaining and convergence 122
Chapter summary 126

5 TRADE UNIONS 132

Jackie Sinclair

Trade union functions and powers 132
Trade union structure and early development 141
International bodies 148
Trade union internal organisation and democracy 151
Trade union membership and density 159
Employer recognition and non-recognition of trade unions 170
Conclusions: future prospects 172

6 THE STATE IN EMPLOYEE RELATIONS 179

Mike Salamon

Introduction 179
The UK since 1960: a case study in changing government philosophy 181
Government approaches to employee relations 185
The labour market 189
Social justice 194
Industrial conflict 199
Chapter summary 204

Part III
EUROPE AND THE CHANGING REGULATIONS

7 THE EUROPEAN UNION 211

Mike Leat

Introduction 213
Membership, institutions and the decision-making processes 214
Social policy initiatives 229
The Europeanisation of industrial relations 256
Chapter summary 264

8 LEGAL REGULATION OF EMPLOYMENT 268

Richard Snape

Introduction: the collective and individual ambits of law 268
Discrimination in employment 275
Dismissal from employment 283
Conclusion 297

Part IV
PATTERNS AND PRACTICES

9 COLLECTIVE BARGAINING 301

Mike Salamon

Introduction 301
The process of collective bargaining 305
Changes in the structural framework 309
Changes in the bargaining relationship 319
Chapter summary 327

10 PAY 332

Jane Evans

Introduction 332
Contemporary contextual factors 333
The functions of pay within the employment relationship 340
The implications for pay of changing employee relations frameworks 344
The process of pay determination 348
The constituent elements of pay and pay systems 360
Conclusions 372
Chapter summary 372

11 EMPLOYEE PARTICIPATION AND INVOLVEMENT 378

Mike Richardson

Introduction 379
Theoretical origins of EPI in Britain 381
What is EPI? 382
Theoretical approaches to industrial relations 385
Theories of EPI 389
EPI in practice 393
Conclusion 401

12 DISCRIMINATION 408

Sally Howe

Introduction 408
What is discrimination? 410
The psychological/sociological basis of discrimination 411
Historical trends in attitudes to discrimination 412
Structural/economic factors affecting discrimination 421

Political/ethical issues affecting discrimination 425
The legislative approach to discrimination and equal opportunities 427
National initiatives and educational programmes 430
More radical approaches: affirmative action (positive discrimination) programmes 432
Managing diversity 434
Management 438
Trade unions 443
Individuals 446
Conclusions 447
Chapter summary 448

13 FLEXIBLE LABOUR MARKETS, FIRMS AND WORKERS 457
Stephanie Tailby
Introduction 457
The flexibility debates 459
Functional flexibility 468
Working-time flexibility 479
Non-standard labour contracts: an employer's strategy of numerical flexibility? 485
Conclusion 496

14 PUBLIC SECTOR EMPLOYMENT 505
John Black and Martin Upchurch
Introduction 505

From 'model employer' to 'winter of discontent' 506
Monetarism, Thatcherism and public spending cuts 511
'Marketisation' and new public management 513
Pay determination in the 1980s and 1990s 517
Assessment: employee relations or industrial relations? 520
The future? 526

15 VALUES AND THEIR IMPACT ON THE CHANGING EMPLOYMENT RELATIONSHIP 535
Philip Cox and Ann Parkinson
Introduction 537
Scenario 537
Setting the context: the shift from industrial relations to employee relations 544
The organisational perspective 548
The individual perspective 558
Conclusion 562

Afterword 567
Index 569

CONTRIBUTOR DETAILS

Editors

Graham Hollinshead, Peter Nicholls and **Stephanie Tailby** are all members of the School of Human Resource Management, Bristol Business School, University of the West of England.

Contributors

Philip Cox, Jane Evans, Sally Howe, Mike Richardson and **Martin Upchurch** are also members of the School of Human Resource Management, Bristol Business School, University of the West of England.

Mike Salamon is Visiting Fellow at Bristol Business School, University of the West of England.

John Black (currently at the Open University) and **Jill Woolley** are former members of this School.

Richard Snape is in the Faculty of Law at the University of the West of England.

Mike Leat lectures in Human Resource Studies at the University of Plymouth Business School.

Jackie Sinclair is College Lecturer in the Department of Industrial Relations at University College Dublin.

Ann Parkinson is a freelance consultant whose clients include Henley Management College.

PREFACE

A prominent trade union leader stated recently that 'Many young workers have never even heard of trade unions, let alone been asked to join one'.* Many of those entering into the study and practice of employee relations for the first time are now familiar with a political and economic script in which the employer appears centre stage, and the representatives of organised labour, banished from the fabric of popular culture, look on forlornly from the wings. At a societal level, much has been made of the emergence of 'selfish' and individualistic values, at the expense of a more caring collectivist ethos. Undoubtedly, this has had resonances in the field of employee relations where important employment policies – for example, in the areas of pay and discrimination – not only serve to protect the position of the individual employee, but also to engender individual accountability for performance in an insecure set of labour and product market circumstances. The new Labour government elected in May 1997, while espousing community values at a societal level, has promised little to alter the status quo in the sphere of employment, at least in the short term. Thus, the bulk of the anti-union legal infrastructure inherited from its predecessor has been retained, and, despite the government's intention to foster partnerships between employers and unions, union members have been impelled to accept flexible employment practices in the interests of economic competitiveness.

Yet, behind the facade of a fundamental shift in the defining features of employee relations, observers of the subject continue to recognise the influence of collectivist interest groups, so prominent in both public and academic arenas in the pre-Thatcherite era, on the dynamics of the employment relationship. A large proportion of employers continue to recognise the legitimacy of trade unions as *de facto* representatives of the workforce, while the state retains a potent role in employee relations as economic manager, law maker, employer and provider of services for conciliation and arbitration.

In this text our approach is underpinned by analysis and theoretical insights derived not only from the literature in this field but also from adjoining disciplines such as sociology, politics, economics and psychology. By taking a critical, and more profound, view of the dynamics of the employment relationship, the student is better equipped to evaluate the contemporary employment agenda, and to discount more alarmist scenarios concerning, for example, the demise of labour organisations. Even for the new generation of workers referred to above, work remains a central aspect of human experience, and the workplace continues to represent a major source of tension and conflict, as well as satisfaction. It is with the causes of, and attempts to resolve, such conflict that the field of employee relations continues to be associated.

The aim of this book is to convey, in an accessible and stimulating form, an understanding of the prominent features and dynamics of employee relations in Britain. While

---

* Tony Burke, GPMU Deputy General Secretary, reported in (1997) 'Soundbites', *People Management*, 3 (19), 19.

Scholarly investigation of this disciplinary area has enjoyed a considerable history in the UK, and in other countries, debates concerning relationships between management and organised labour are now enjoying something of a renaissance following the election of a Labour government in May 1997. It is likely that the intentions of this government to promote initiatives, such as participation in industry, and to introduce minimum employment standards will engender qualitative changes in the landscape and climate of employee relations in the future. The text is aimed primarily at student readers, who are likely to be engaged on undergraduate courses in business studies or related areas, or on postgraduate programmes embracing this field of study. While up-to-date analyses and descriptions of recognised employee relations institutions and processes are provided, a discursive approach is taken, highlighting contemporary issues, in the public and commercial domain, and analysis is underpinned by relevant theoretical and conceptual frameworks.

The book has a number of key distinguishing features.

- A 'user friendly' style has been adopted which includes clear chapter objectives, illustrative case study material and newspaper articles, chapter summaries, exercises and further reading.

- It is written by a team of authors who are mainly teachers or former teachers from the School of Human Resource Management at Bristol Business School. The approach therefore draws upon the specialist areas of staff while retaining the coherence of a fully collaborative project. The relevance and accessibility of the material are also bolstered by the involvement of the authors, over a period of years, in teaching constituencies of the book's target audience.

- The book, while adhering to many traditional conceptions of the disciplinary area, aims to take a fresh look at some of these, and also aims to emphasise some areas of growing significance. Consequently, particular attention is given to coverage of, for example, international influences and the European employment agenda, non-union employee relations, emerging areas of policy and law, and the transformation of the public sector of industry.

Briefly, **Part I** charts the evolving territory of employee relations, establishes its context, and highlights major theoretical perspectives on the subject matter. **Part II** addresses factors pertaining to the organisation and the role of the acknowledged collective participants in employee relations – management, trade unions and the state – and also considers the emerging and important role of multinational companies. **Part III** examines broader regulatory influences on employment by considering domestic legal provision and European institutional mechanisms. **Part IV** turns to a more detailed analysis of the modes of interaction between the parties, and an investigation of substance and phenomena surrounding the employment relationship. This section addresses the evolving nature of collective bargaining, the growth in arrangements for employee involvement, debates on work flexibility, the prominence of pay as a policy area, concerns about discrimination in employment and the emergent field of values and ethics in the sphere of employment.

We list a number of suggested routes through the book for readers following particular courses of study. It should be noted, however, that these suggestions are merely an indication of potentially relevant chapters.

BA Business Studies and similar programmes

Introduction
Chapters 1 and 2

Core
Chapters 3, 5, 6, 7, 8, 9, 11, 12

Elective
Chapters 3, 4, 7, 8, 10, 13, 14, 15

MA/MSc

Introduction
Chapters 1 and 2

Core
Chapters 3, 5, 6, 7, 8, 9, 11, 12, 14

Options
Chapters 5, 7, 8, 10, 13, 14, 15

IPD Professional Education Scheme

Introduction
Chapters 1 and 2

Core
Personnel and Development: Chapters 3, 8, 9, 10, 11, 12, 15
Employee Relations: Chapters 3, 5, 6, 7, 8, 9, 10, 11, 14
Employee Reward: Chapters 10, 12, 13, 9, 4
Employee Resourcing/HRM: Chapters 3, 10, 9, 12, 15, 8
Employment Law: Chapters 8, 7, 9, 12, 6
International/Global Employee Relations: Chapters 3, 4, 6, 7, 9, 11, 13
Employee Involvement and Communications: Chapters 11, 9, 14, 7
International Personnel and Development: Chapters 3, 4, 7, 11, 13
Equality Management: Chapters 12, 8, 7, 10, 15

Graham Hollinshead
Peter Nicholls
Stephanie Tailby

September 1998

PLAN OF THE BOOK

PART I · INTRODUCTION

Chapter 1
Introduction to
employee relations

Chapter 2
Context and theory in
employee relations

PART II · PARTIES

Chapter 3
Management

Chapter 4
Multinationals
and employee
relations

Chapter 5
Trade unions

Chapter 6
The state in
employee relations

PART III · EUROPE AND THE CHANGING REGULATIONS

Chapter 7
The European Union

Chapter 8
Legal regulation of employment

PART IV · PATTERNS AND PRACTICES

Chapter 9
Collective
bargaining

Chapter 10
Pay

Chapter 11
Employee
participation and
involvement

Chapter 12
Discrimination

Chapter 13
Flexible labour markets,
firms and workers

Chapter 14
Public sector
employment

Chapter 15
Values and their impact
on the changing
employment relationship

Part I

INTRODUCTION

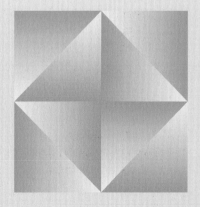

Chapter 1

INTRODUCTION TO EMPLOYEE RELATIONS

Graham Hollinshead, Peter Nicholls and Stephanie Tailby

Work and employment relations are important for any economy and society. In Britain, as in other industrialised countries, most people spend a significant amount of their adult lives in paid employment, or seeking paid work. Employment provides an income and the attraction of other rewards, such as status, friendship, and satisfaction, although stress and frustration may be part of the actual package. Employers have to recruit, deploy and motivate employees in order to achieve their broader business objectives and goals. The maxim that 'human resources are the company's most valuable asset' is sometimes difficult to square with corporate employment practice. Nevertheless, it is true that the ways in which work is organised, and the terms and conditions under which it is performed, are critical. They influence employees' living standards and their quality of life, and they impact upon the competitiveness of employing organisations, and the performance of the wider economy.

This chapter sketches the development of academic interest in employee relations in Britain, and introduces the structure and content of the book. Definitions of the focus and scope of the study of employee relations have shifted over time, from an emphasis on collective bargaining structures and institutions to workplace relations and, in the 1980s, the management of the employment relationship. As discussed below, these shifts of emphasis reflect the subject's intellectual development, changing economic and social conditions, and public policy concerns.

THE STUDY OF EMPLOYEE RELATIONS

In Britain in the late nineteenth and early twentieth centuries, a wave of industrial militancy and a rapid upturn in trade union membership were associated with technological change and the concentration of employment in large workplaces and factories in urban centres. For many workers in mines, docks and factories, and most especially for the semi-skilled and unskilled trades, the conditions of work were difficult, dangerous and degraded. Employment security was minimal. Social reformers such as Charles Booth and Beatrice Webb drew to the attention of the public and politicians the poverty among broad sections of the working class, and in the process established the intimate connection between the two sides of the 'labour question' – social order (the stability of society) and social welfare. These were inseparable; without advances in the latter the former would constantly be threatened. The academic study of employee relations (or industrial relations as the subject was known until fairly recently) emerged initially from a concern with these twin issues (Hyman, 1989).

Many of the social reformers advocated legislative intervention to improve employment terms and conditions. Public policy in Britain, however, identified voluntary collective bargaining as the preferred means of securing order in labour–management relations. Collective bargaining is a process in which workers' representatives and employers or employers' associations negotiate the substantive terms and conditions of employment (pay, hours and so on) and procedural agreements delineating the ways in which disputes are to be handled. Since in Britain there was no statutory support for union recognition, employers were not legally obliged to bargain with trade unions, and collective agreements were not legally binding. The system of industrial relations was described as 'voluntarist'. In many other industrialising countries, the state came to play a more direct role in employment regulation, intervening to set certain rules of work and to give legal support to collectively bargained union–management agreements. In Britain, the distinctive, voluntarist tradition was maintained until the 1960s and 1970s, although the periods of the two World Wars saw substantial modification and much more interventionist government.

Academic analysis of industrial relations in Britain for many years centred largely on the institutions of collective bargaining – in particular, the structures and policies of trade unions and employers' associations. Professorial chairs in industrial relations had been established in a number of universities in the inter-war years, although the expansion of teaching and research really dates from the 1960s. Leading scholars, based at Oxford University, sought to establish the subject on an appropriate theoretical basis. Allan Flanders defined industrial relations as the study of the 'institutions of job regulation' (1965: 10). By this he meant that there were formal and informal rules governing employment. The subject was concerned, therefore, with the ways in which these rules were created, interpreted, administered and changed – that is, with the organisations involved in the rule-making process. In principle, the substantive and procedural rules of work could be determined jointly (through collective bargaining), unilaterally (by management prerogative) or by statute (by government and the legislature).

Statutory regulation, as suggested, had been relatively restricted in Britain. In this light, the attention given in academic industrial relations to joint regulation and collective bargaining is understandable. This focus had certain limitations, however. Trade union membership in Britain peaked at 13.3 million in the late 1970s. Yet over two-fifths of the workforce were not union members and many employees worked in establishments where trade unions were not recognised by management for the purposes of negotiating pay and conditions. The coverage of collective bargaining was wider than these figures suggest: collective agreements negotiated at the national level were applied by most firms in many industries, including those that had not participated directly in the negotiations, and the wages council system – a form of statutorily supported joint regulation – covered industries and occupations where trade unions were very weak. Nevertheless, even in this period the coverage of collective bargaining was incomplete, and the scope of collective bargaining was often quite narrow. Unilateral employer regulation was important, although relatively neglected in mainstream industrial relations (Edwards, 1995: 7).

Industrial relations moved to centre stage in public policy debates in the 1960s and 1970s. On a number of measures, Britain's economic performance had failed to match that of its major competitors. Much attention centred on 'disorder' in workplace industrial relations. Business leaders and the press argued that sluggish rates of productivity growth and inflationary pressures could be attributed to the rising level of unofficial strikes, the drift of wages above nationally bargained rates and 'restrictive' work practices. These 'problems' were attributed to 'unfettered' union power in an era of relatively full employment.

Leading industrial relations scholars offered a more balanced account. Represented in a variety of roles on the Royal Commission, chaired by Lord Donovan and established in the mid-1960s to examine union–management relations, they drew into the analysis management's role and apparent lack of vision and strategy in handling workplace relations. They rejected as unhelpful the calls for a more elaborate legal framework designed to restrict union influence and activity. Nevertheless, their analysis served to perpetuate the view that there was a direct link between the 'industrial relations system' and Britain's relatively weak industrial performance (for a critique *see* Nolan, 1996: 107). They argued that the regulative force of the established system of national, or industry-level, collective bargaining had declined. Furthermore, they proposed that in order to 'regain control', managements should initiate a process of voluntary reform, and conclude with union representatives detailed, comprehensive and formal procedural agreements regulating industrial relations at company and establishment level.

Much industrial relations research in the 1970s followed the contours of this 'reform' agenda. However, a number of developments combined to shift the focus and broaden the scope of the subject (*see* Edwards 1995). First, the preoccupation with the institutions of collective bargaining was challenged, at a theoretical level, by writers who urged that bargaining relationships and conflict should be seen as a reflection of more fundamental power relations in capitalist economies. Wealth and the ownership of industry are concentrated in the hands of the few. The majority of the adult population are obliged to seek paid work in order to secure an income. They enter the labour market in order to find an employer with whom they can trade their labour services for a wage or a salary. The employment relationship is therefore an economic exchange, but is unlike other forms of economic transaction. It involves people, rather than the exchange of non-human commodities, and the parties do not have access to equivalent power resources. Moreover, the commodity bought and sold at the time of hiring is the employee's capacity to work, or labour power. The employer's interest is in the exercise of this capacity in the production of goods and services, and in the generation of a surplus from the employee's endeavours. There is therefore an inherent antagonism in the employment relationship and ample scope for conflict as the employer seeks to organise work in ways that will ensure the generation of a surplus, realised as profit through the sale of the goods and services produced. From this perspective, the proper focus of the study of industrial relations appeared to be the 'study of processes of control over work relations' (Hyman, 1975: 12).

Second, management's role was subjected to more systematic and rigorous analysis; hitherto, the importance of management had been assumed rather than explored through detailed investigation. The increased attention to management reflected also the recognition that industry structures had altered. Large, diversified corporations had emerged through the processes of acquisitions and mergers, and many now operated on an international scale. Some industrial relations analysts urged that if management's role in structuring collective bargaining relationships was to be understood fully, empirical analysis would have to broaden to include top-level management decision making and business strategy (e.g. Purcell, 1983). It seemed evident that higher level management decisions (on product market strategy, the location of investment and so on) set the parameters within which 'lower order' decisions (on business structure and, in turn, the level of bargaining relationships with trade unions) were made. Other researchers were concerned to explore management strategies of labour control – that is, strategies for ensuring the effective translation of labour power into performed work.

Third, the role of government and state, and the changing role of the law in industrial relations, became a more explicit focus of enquiry. Again, this reflected the theoretical evolution of the subject as well as actual developments in the conduct of industrial relations. In Britain, the 'tradition of voluntarism' had been eroded gradually from the 1960s as both Labour and Conservative governments intervened more frequently. Voluntary and statutory incomes policies were introduced with the aim of influencing the outcomes of collective bargaining, and in particular wage settlements. Such measures typically had short-term success but led to an explosion of pent-up pay demands as the controls were relaxed. Their more rigorous application in the public sector, where government holds the 'purse-strings', was widely regarded as the main factor fuelling wage militancy among formerly quiescent employee groups (for example, *see* Winchester and Bach, 1995).

Efforts were made to restrict union power by the Conservative government led by Edward Heath in the early 1970s. The attempt to reform comprehensively the legal framework through a single Act proved unsuccessful, however, and met with employer uncertainty as well as union opposition. Labour governments in 1974–9 sought a 'social contract' with the unions, promising more favourable union legislation and an extension of employee rights, in return for union leaders' cooperation in pay restraint. At the time, the social contract was seen by some commentators as an example of a new 'corporatist' state approach to the regulation of labour–management relations. However, the tensions and conflicts which this approach entailed in Britain exploded in the 'winter of discontent' in 1978–9, when widespread disputes occurred throughout the public services.

Finally, feminist theoretical perspectives highlighted the limitations of any analysis based either on an exclusive preoccupation with class relations, or taking voluntary collective bargaining as its empirical focus. Women's participation in the labour force increased over the post-war period, largely because of the increased participation of married women (most single women had always participated in paid work). Many married women were employed part-time in areas of the economy that were poorly regulated by voluntary collective bargaining, in particular the private services (e.g. hotels, shops, hairdressing). Even in unionised workplaces, women's concerns and demands were often inadequately represented. The passage of equal pay legislation in the 1970s improved women's earnings relative to men's, but failed to close the gender pay gap. In large part this resulted from the gendered segregation of work, which confined a majority of women to low paying industries and occupations. The circumstances producing this segregation had to be incorporated as part of the subject matter of industrial relations.

These theoretical concerns, and developments in industry and labour markets, served to shift the focus of academic industrial relations from bargaining relationships to the nature of the underlying employment relationship, and broadened the scope of empirical enquiry. Earlier studies had tended to focus on those groups of workers most likely to be unionised – that is, male, manual workers in manufacturing and in the nationalised industries. By the 1980s, attention was broadening to include employees in non-unionised workplaces and industries. The changing economic, political and legal context served to accelerate this shift. Definitions of the subject were framed in more inclusive terms; for example, Gospel and Palmer delineate the study of industrial relations as the study of the 'processes of control over the employment relationship, the organisation of work, and relations between employers and employees' (1993: 3). Increasingly the label of employee relations came to be substituted for that of industrial relations. This was often to emphasise the subject's broad concern with all types of employment relationship and with non-union as well as unionised workplaces. However, employee relations has also been used to signify a shift of focus, from the collective to the individual aspects of work relations. Used in the first sense, employee relations denotes much the same field of enquiry as 'contemporary' industrial relations. Used in the second sense it suggests a narrower and more managerialist set of concerns.

THE CONTEXT OF EMPLOYEE RELATIONS

The political, legal and economic context of the 1980s and early 1990s focused attention on the pace and direction of change in British industrial relations. Conservative governments in office from 1979 pursued a radical agenda of economic and social reforms. Institutions formerly accepted as part of the economic and social infrastructure were identified as barriers to change and economic success, not least employee relations and labour market institutions. Government ministers characterised the established, collective structures of employment regulation as barriers to the effective operation of labour markets and constraints on economic growth. The public policy commitment to voluntary collective bargaining as the desired means of regulating relations in industry that had survived for a century was ended. The government's legislative programme, and its policies in the public sector, were designed to undermine trade union power and to encourage the decentralisation and individualisation of employee relations. Labour market deregulation also embraced the weakening of legislative and administrative constraints on employers' use of labour and, in particular, the ability to adjust employment levels in line with product market fluctuations. For example, the qualifying period of service required by employees to accrue the right to claim unfair dismissal was lengthened from six months to two years. European Union (EU) social and employment legislation was perceived as obstructing the operation of market forces and was vigorously opposed.

Coinciding with an expansion of the labour force, the deep recession of the early 1980s resulted in a sharp upturn in unemployment and accelerated the pace of longer-term shifts in the sectoral composition of employment. Job losses were concentrated in manufacturing and among full-time, male manual workers, who traditionally had formed the core of trade union membership. Employment growth was concentrated largely on the services, which by the mid 1990s accounted for over 70 per cent of employees in employment. Many of the new jobs created were part-time jobs for women. The expansion of public sector employment during the 1960s and 1970s was reversed as the government developed its programme of privatisation and the commercialisation of public services. The recession of the early 1990s was more widespread in its impact, affecting a number of the areas of rapid employment growth in the 1980s (for example, the financial services). Full-time employment declined, only recovering after 1994. Part-time employment continued to expand, and in this period employers increased their use of temporary employment contracts. Broadly, the areas of employment growth in the 1980s and early 1990s were those which the trade unions historically had found most difficult to organise.

Against this background, academic attention centred increasingly on employers' policies and practices. Many firms, especially those operating in export markets, had experienced intensified competition in the more turbulent economic conditions prevailing internationally from the 1970s. Competition was fuelled by the 'globalisation' of markets as multinational corporations extended their activities, the diffusion of new technologies, and by the liberalisation of trade (as, for example, through the creation of the Single European Market). In some product markets, established producer nations were challenged by the industrialising economies of the Pacific Rim.

The experience of Japanese competition and the success of Japanese 'transplants' in Britain, Europe and the United States focused attention on Japanese methods of work organisation and the rate of diffusion of these practices in the West. Equally, it prompted business analysts in the United States to consider wider sources of competitive success. Exemplar firms were said to be those which competed on the basis of innovation, design and quality, and invested to achieve a particular configuration of employee relations. The idea of human resource management (HRM) was rapidly taken up in discussions of a 'new industrial relations' in Britain.

While there is no universally accepted definition of HRM, most accounts suggest that its core principles challenge both the traditional practice of personnel management in Britain, and the traditional focus of academic industrial relations on collective employee relations. HRM is said to be a central management activity which should be integrated fully with business planning, and in its practice focused on employees as individuals. One of the aims of HRM is to generate a strong employee attachment to enterprise objectives and goals through extensive employee consultation, communication and involvement.

The weight of the survey data and case study evidence amassed by the early 1990s, however, suggested that HRM might be more developed at the level of rhetoric than of practice. The third national Workplace Industrial Relations Survey in 1990, for example, found that elements of HRM (in particular, mechanisms for employee involvement and participation) were most in evidence in unionised, rather than non-union plants, and that in the growing non-unionised sector of the economy it was managerial unilateralism that was in the ascendancy (Millward *et al.*, 1992). Further evidence casts doubt on the idea that there has been a fundamental transformation of employee relations in Britain. Certainly the recorded incidence of strikes and industrial stoppages shows a steep decline. But many of the issues of concern to the late nineteenth century social reformers are still pertinent. Job insecurity and work-related stress, among both 'white-collar' and manual employees, have been widely reported in the 1980s and 1990s. These have arisen from more intensive work regimes and employers' demands for greater 'labour flexibility'. The gap between high and low income earners widened in the 1980s to dimensions only previously recorded at the end of the nineteenth century.

The 1980s are widely seen as a watershed in British political history and in British industrial relations – the divide between a post-war pluralist consensus and a more overtly individualist and business-orientated regime. Whether a new epoch is in the making in the late 1990s remains to be seen. The new Labour government, elected to power in May 1997, has persisted with a number of the policy objectives of its immediate Conservative predecessors; labour market flexibility remains a priority and much of the industrial relations legislation of the 1980s is to be retained. However, New Labour has promised legislation to promote 'fairness at work' and a new 'partnership approach' to employee relations. To date the government has reversed Britain's 'opt-out' of the European Union Social Chapter, established a Low Pay Commission to make recommendations on the level and scope of a statutory national minimum wage, and published a 'Fairness at Work' White Paper. The latter includes measures which will oblige employers to recognise a trade union where 40 per cent of the workforce ballot in favour of this proposal, or where a majority of employees are union members. Many of these proposals have yet to reach the statute book and their impact remains to be assessed. Nevertheless, chapters in this book outline the proposals and, where possible, discuss their likely implications.

STRUCTURE AND CONTENT OF THE BOOK

This book aims to present a contemporary picture of employee relations and one that is accessible to those coming newly to the subject area. It is organised around four themes: the theory of employee relations; the parties to employee relations; European and legal regulation; and the procedures, practices and patterns of employee relations. The primary focus is on the British context. However, no contemporary text can ignore the influence of developments in the international economy, and our book gives these due weight.

As suggested in the Preface, employee relations is an area of study in which various perspectives are permissible. A strike, for example, will inevitably be viewed in different ways by the strikers themselves, their families, the media, politicians and so on. In Part I, therefore, in addition to setting out the history and current focus of the subject, we attempt to make sense of the range of views that impinge on the subject area and the theories that have been applied in the analysis of employee relations. These perspectives, which range from those viewing the employment relationship as essentially harmonious to those outlining a structural antagonism between the employer and employee, are discussed and located historically in Chapter 2.

Part II introduces the principal parties in employee relations: management, trade unions, the state and government. Chapter 3 considers management's key role in structuring work and employment relations, and assesses the extent to which management approaches in the 1980s and '90s marked a significant departure from the past. Industry structures have changed over recent decades, and increasingly firms operate on an international plane. Chapter 4 looks at the ways in which multinationals manage internal employment relations and their broader impact on the development of work relations in particular national contexts. Chapter 5 considers employee organisations, and specifically trade union organisation, structure and policies. It assesses the impact of the economic and political environment of the 1980s on trade union membership, trade union responses to membership decline and the prospects for a renewal of union influence in the late 1990s. Chapter 6 examines the role of state and government in employee relations, as economic manager, legislator and employer in the public sector.

Part III is concerned with the legal regulation of employment. Chapter 7 outlines the development, dimensions and impact of European Union social and employment legislation. Chapter 8 centres on the aims and impact of the employment legislation originating from the British parliament and judiciary.

Part IV deals with the interaction between the parties to employee relations and the procedures that have been developed to regulate their relations. Chapter 9 considers developments in the coverage, scope and nature of collective bargaining in the 1980s and '90s, and Chapter 10 looks at employer approaches to pay and payment systems. Chapter 11 is concerned with the theory and practice of employee involvement and participation, and considers the depth of employers' initiatives in these areas over the past twenty years. The origins and manifestations of discrimination at work are discussed in Chapter 12, which considers the reasons why firms should counteract such practices, in the interests of securing full use of their labour resources. Chapter 13 explores the academic and public policy debates on the meaning, and means of achieving, greater 'labour flexibility'. Chapter 14 focuses on changing patterns of public sector employment relations, and Chapter 15 centres on values and ethics in the practice of employee relations. In reflecting the more subjectively determined and psychologically driven interpretations of the employment relationship and its broader context, this chapter returns to the theme introduced in Chapter 2 that the values attached to the discipline as a whole, or its constituent parts, are neither absolute nor constant. In charting various epochs within employee relations history, it is argued that the domain of work and employment is not only shrouded in ambiguity but also influenced by the shifting values of each generation.

Each chapter includes features designed to assist the reader in assimilating the theoretical arguments and empirical evidence. In particular, each includes a statement of chapter objectives, illustrative case study materials and extracts from newspaper and academic journal articles, charts and figures, a chapter summary, points for discussion, suggested seminar activities and exercises. The key issues, debates and developments in employee relations identified in the various chapters are brought together in the concluding Afterword.

REFERENCES

Edwards, P. (1995) 'The employment relationship' in Edwards, P. (ed.) *Industrial Relations, Theory and Practice in Britain*. Oxford: Blackwell, pp. 3–26.

Flanders, A. (1965) *Industrial Relations: What Is Wrong with the System?* London: Faber.

Gospel, H. and Palmer, G. (1993) *British Industrial Relations*. 2nd edn. London: Routledge.

Hyman, R. (1975) *Industrial Relations, A Marxist Introduction*. Basingstoke: Macmillan.

Hyman, R. (1989) 'Why industrial relations?' in Hyman, R. *The Political Economy of Industrial Relations*. Basingstoke: Macmillan, pp. 3–19.

Millward, N., Stevens, M., Smart, D. and Hawes, W.R. (1992) *Workplace Industrial Relations in Transition*, the ED/ESRC/PSI/ACAS survey. Aldershot: Dartmouth.

Nolan, P. (1996) 'Industrial relations and performance since 1945' in Beardwell, I. (ed.) *Contemporary Industrial Relations, A Critical Analysis*. Oxford: Oxford University Press, pp. 99–120.

Purcell, J. (1983) 'The management of industrial relations in the modern corporation', *British Journal of Industrial Relations*, 21 (1), 1–16.

Winchester, D. and Bach, S. (1995) 'The state: the public sector' in Edwards, P. (ed.) *Industrial Relations, Theory and Practice in Britain*. Oxford: Blackwell, pp. 304–334.

Chapter 2

CONTEXT AND THEORY IN EMPLOYEE RELATIONS

Peter Nicholls

Learning objectives

By the end of this chapter, readers should be able to:

- appreciate the role of theory in providing a method for organising and making sense of knowledge and information within the discipline of employee relations;

- outline the differing theoretical frameworks to have emerged during the lifetime of the discipline, noting their major features, contributions and limitations;

- make connections between the impetus for particular theoretical frameworks, their intellectual origins and their social context;

- explore these theoretical frameworks, recognising the ability of all theories to sustain their utility for particular social groups over time;

- appreciate the 'architecture' of a theory for informing and influencing the definition of an employee relations problem and subsequently the design of appropriate policies to resolve such problems.

INTRODUCTION

Following the election of a new Labour government in 1997, it is an interesting time to be questioning the role of theory within this discipline and to query whether the very theories used to interpret this changing area of employment have themselves altered to reflect a different set of concerns. These and many other questions related to the role of theory and the context within which employment is located form the main areas of concern for this chapter (*see* the debate between Dunn (1990) and Keenoy (1991) in the *British Journal of Industrial Relations*).

Perhaps to reflect this growing concern for establishing the significance and direction of change, many writing in this discipline now talk of 'New Industrial Relations' (Beardwell (ed), 1996; Farnham and Pimlott, 1990; Marchington and

■ **Exhibit 2.1**

British Airways (aircrew and ground staff) strike

On 30 June 1997, the ground staff and cabin crews of British Airways voted in favour of strike action. Trying to interpret this event in terms of the 'facts of the situation' to arrive at an explanation of the causes of this strike is not easy.

According to one newspaper, the *Daily Telegraph* (2 July 1997):

Robert Ayling, the embattled chief executive of British Airways is said to be one of the new Labour government's model corporate leaders, just as his former chairman, Lord King of Wartnaby, was once 'Mrs Thatcher's favourite businessman'. Like his former boss,   Mr Ayling is trying to bring about a revolution in BA's competitiveness, and all revolutions call for brutal tactics.

On the other hand, an article in *The Times* concluded (2 July 1997):

Regrettable as some of Mr Ayling's tactics may be, BA deserves public support. The alternative is regression to an even unhappier era in the air. Government and industry have a shared interest here – in the new recognition by trade unions that a new administration cannot repeal the laws of supply and demand. A 'new mood' in industrial relations which allows trade unions to frustrate necessary corporate modernisation would be a retrograde step. Amicable agreement between the two sides is desirable.

From the *Morning Star* on the same day:

Transport and General Workers' Union general secretary, Bill Morris, authorised the strike earlier in the day after making a last-ditch bid to hold talks with the airline. ... The tough stance followed a briefing between BA unions and the TUC general secretary, John Monks. Mr Morris said 'I appealed to British Airways again this morning to start negotiations with a view to resolving both disputes. However BA have made it clear they are only prepared to talk about the ground staff issue'.

The *Financial Times* on 1 July 1997 pointed to the basis of the strike:

Both these disputes are essentially about change. The new pay packages offered to the BA cabin crews are not fundamentally contentious. The dispute, according to the Transport and General Workers' Union which represents the disaffected staff, is over the imposition of a deal without negotiation. ... The real issue is whether BA, and indeed other British companies, can go through another round of restructuring without the support of the workforce.

Finally in an article in the *Guardian* on 2 July 1997 a number of questions and answers were listed to provide a brief synopsis of the logic and outcomes of the strike:

Why are the cabin crew striking?

BA has imposed sweeping changes to pay and conditions on the majority, who belong to the Transport and General Workers' Union – including a 19% cut in basic pay for new recruits. Management did a deal with a breakaway group called Cabin Crew 89.

But aren't cabin crew getting big increases in basic pay?

Yes, but only by incorporating overtime and other allowances. BA says no existing steward or stewardess will have their income cut for three years – which the union believes will become a pay freeze, combined with the likelihood of longer hours. BA says the package will save £43 million.

▶

■ **Exhibit 2.1 continued**

> So what is the cause of this strike at BA? Surely the facts speak for themselves and with suffi-
> cient close attention to collecting detailed information we can come to an objective explana-
> tion of the real causes of this strike.
>
> **Questions**
>
> 1 Take each of these newspaper extracts and note the 'key' factor identified in each of these
>   statements, noting the type of language used to depict the situation.
>
> 2 How far do these statements about the situation at BA reflect a set of common causal fac-
>   tors?
>
> 3 How would you categorise the underlying emphasis of each of the different newspapers?

Parker, 1990) and substitute industrial relations with employee relations to indicate a significant shift in the context and content of the employment relationship. The very existence of this debate indicates the contentious nature of the discipline.

As if to underscore this change in the political context of employee relations, only
shortly after the election of the new Labour government, a major industrial dispute
unfolded in an industry which, though unionised, has also displayed high levels of loyalty (Exhibit 2.1). How do we interpret this event? How do we evaluate the different arguments put forward for understanding the reasons that led up to this strike?

The brief extracts in Exhibit 2.1 reflect a variety of competing explanations which exist
not only in the British press, but equally in academic studies of industrial relations. Self-
evidently, the facts do not speak for themselves.

That a set of events becomes classed as a 'problem' is in itself a complex process which
is not at all obvious. Once outside parties become involved, such as the press and academic commentators, we move on from establishing the situation as an 'issue' to trying to
explain the events as they unfold and to account for this particular sequence of events.

Exhibit 2.1 demonstrates that there is wide room for interpretation. Which interpretation is adopted will determine how an issue might be researched or what particular policy options might be chosen. (For an earlier study, *see* Blyton and Turnbull, 1992: 63–73).

If such a modest example as one potential strike evokes so much controversy then it is
not difficult to appreciate that in a subject such as employee relations, a considerable
variety of frameworks exists, some of which might claim the title of theories while others might remain frames of reference or perspectives.

What is implied here is a continuum, from a frame of reference that contains a series
of related factors, to theories that rely upon the interrelationship of concepts, themselves
reflecting well-established definitions, and the existence of indicators with which to measure these. In this chapter a distinction is made between those theories that might be classified as integral to the discipline – unitary, pluralist, systems and Marxist theories – and
those that have been significant for influencing and modifying these core theories and
their variants, including feminist theory, comparative theory and post-modernist theory.
Figure 2.1 summarises some of the distinguishing features of the chapter.

■ Theories and explanations in employee relations

Understanding and operationalising theories can sound a threatening prospect for those newly arrived at the discipline of employee relations, yet in our day-to-day lives we engage in very similar activities without even stopping to consider the process. For instance, we all gather information, evaluate and analyse it and make decisions on the basis of that imperfect procedure.

Our individual social lives are composed of an appreciation that we just cannot know for certain that the answers to most of our questions are comprehensive. What makes our

Perspectives	Genealogy	Status	Features in workplace	Manifestations
Unitary	Now post-industrial associated with ascendancy of management power	Stereotypical integration of unilateral management control of employment relationship	Omnipotent management exercising unilateral control	Unilateral PRP (Performance Related Pay), emphasis on communication and performance evaluation
Pluralist	Reflects ideas of modern democracy legitimating trade union recognition	Stereotypical view of managerial acceptance of limited power-sharing in certain areas of decision making	Limited power sharing between major interested parties	Negotiated with interest groups, latterly stakeholder perspective
Marxist	Mid 19th century analysis of gross inequalities creating capitalism	Theory of society emphasising opposing interests within workplace and beyond	Focus on exploitation and structured inequalities	Conflict absenteeism. Sabotage, false consciousness and consumerism
Systems	Inter-war. Importance of pseudo-scientific conceptual analysis underpinning discipline	A conceptualisation in order to classify the discipline	Institutions in equilibrium governed by rules. Open systems, inputs and outputs affected by environment	Refinement of descriptive tools. Scope for international comparisons
Feminist	Two stages. Earlier recognition of the existence of patriarchy. Latterly, industrial relations recognising male domination	Theory of society emphasising structural inequalities between sexes in workplace and beyond	Male advantages embedded in institutions, culture and hence workplace	Agitation to improve policies and conditions of employment
Post-modern	Disputes nature of knowledge. Emphasis on subjective individual. Interpretation and verification of meaning	Reaction to scientific/empirical explanations of the world. Emphasis on individual experience and meaning	Belief in post-industrial world of work where meanings disputed by ambiguity and ambivalence	Adopts a rhetoric of Human Resource Management plus associated ideologies

■ Fig. 2.1 Theories in employee relations

life possible and manageable is the continuous use of theories, which we are forced to create as a way of organising ourselves to cope with the pressures of our daily lives. In the workplace, for example, management would collapse if it were not the case that we were able to utilise our own theories. For instance, we learn to adopt a whole repertoire of behaviour to deal with individuals at different levels of the organisational hierarchy. From one job to another, we carry patterns of behaviour that 'have worked for us'. In doing so, we have, in a simple sense, generated our own theory based upon observation, interpretation and experience. This is often called 'common sense' (Berger and Luckman, 1966).

When it comes to employee relations, academics need to organise knowledge to enable them to generalise rather than remain in the detail of specific instances, in the detail of common sense. The contribution of the discipline is to make sense of the employment relationship and understand this relationship within the complexity of its context.

Theories are therefore helpful in thinking beyond particular cases and enabling us to summarise and generalise. From this activity we can start to make sense of a wide range of instances and establish common themes and guidelines for interpreting the world of work and employment. Not surprisingly, the existence of competing explanations can result in continuous debate and discussion, leading to particular groupings of academics around particular theoretical positions.

That such debates exist in employee relations explains the 'health' of the discipline. Theories therefore provide a more rigorous analysis than common sense and can be distinguished from it in two principal ways.

■ Breadth of coverage: how broad is the application of that theory? If it relates to a wide variety of situations, will it measure up to being an academic theory?

■ Coherence of its concepts: do the different concepts, which are the building blocks of the theory, logically relate to each other and remain consistent in a variety of different situations?

As we constantly transfer knowledge and experience from one setting to another and select from a wide diversity of facts and situations that which is relevant to our own tasks and activities, we generate our own theories.

In this chapter we are looking at theories created and refined by a wide variety of authors who have used them to interpret the information and data related to work and employment. As various commentators have noted, this information does not speak for itself. How it is collected, and subsequently analysed, means that there is considerable variety in interpretations within the discipline. This dynamic nature of the discipline is part of its intrigue but also part of its problem.

If no one theory is 'right' then what causes one theory to be replaced by another? This is what Kuhn calls a 'shift in the dominant paradigm' – that is, an established set of explanations and research procedures which become established as the 'normal' way of creating knowledge in a given area (Kuhn, 1970). Furthermore, if several major theories emerge, how can they co-exist within the same discipline at the same time?

Outlining the major features of the more significant theories, perspectives and frameworks of employee relations, it is argued, and referring back to these related questions is important for understanding not just the 'content' of employee relations but something of the character of the discipline and its changing concerns.

EMPLOYEE RELATIONS AND THEORETICAL INTERPRETATION

In the Introduction we alluded to the specific meanings associated with the title 'employee relations' as compared to 'industrial relations'. Such distinctions have been discussed in the previous chapter and so to avoid reworking those arguments, the two terms will be treated as synonymous in this chapter.

Clearly, employee relations can be seen as distinctive from industrial relations as a way of describing the employment relationship. Authors like Gospel (1992) and Beardwell (1996) make the claim for such a distinction; they argue that a difference of level of analysis exists between the two and that employee relations clearly suggests a value orientation and therefore leans towards a modern form of managerialism.

How far the discipline has changed as a result of changes in its context is a point of considerable debate (Undy, 1997). Agreement upon the existence of changes in the context of employee relations is extensive; what is harder to establish is the degree of consensus associated with the changes in interpretation adopted by researchers in the area (Keenoy, 1991).

Some of the contextual changes are associated, for example, with the growing role of the state, which influences and shapes employment through fiscal policy and changes in employment law and privatisation. Alongside state influences, discussed in Chapter 6, the private sector continues to change the shape and level of influence through size, scale and increasing global practices (Eldridge *et al.*, 1991).

Management itself continues to refine its technologies whether through manufacturing, financial, marketing or human resource policies, as discussed in Chapter 3. Unions, too, have looked again at their *raison d'être* and entered into many new areas and activities to maintain their position within the employment relationship (*see* Chapter 5). To understand and interpret employee relations in the late-1990s, therefore, requires by definition an analysis guided by theoretical insights.

Understanding and utilising a variety of theories should constitute some of the basic skills of any social science student and yet according to Hyman in the case of industrial relations, the development and cultivation of theory have been limited (Hyman, 1989).

In more detail, a concern to demonstrate the need for a greater awareness of the role of theory is linked to a point raised by Gospel and Palmer, when they discuss the bias towards description and prescription in many explanations within the discipline (1993: 11):

> Prescription lies at the centre of government and trade union debates on the subject. Over the last quarter-century there has been a succession of prescriptions for changes in industrial relations, for new ways of managing resources and for the introduction of industrial legislation of various kinds. In industrial relations, the existence of contentious and conflicting proposals from the different participants suggest that, whatever the assumptions are, they are certainly not 'common to all'.

As Gospel and Palmer go on to explain, there is considerable overlap within the discipline among academic theories, policy prescriptions and descriptive accounts. With so much attention focused upon the employment relationship in an advanced competitive industrial nation, the mixture of these forms of explanation is inevitable. Added to this, the media has an inbuilt interest in portraying the substance of the employment relationship in the most dramatic fashion for generating public interest (Philo *et al.*, 1977).

To start to make sense of theories in employee relations the next section outlines one of the earlier explanations, which like so many of these theories has continued to provide management with a useful analysis of work and employment since its inception.

UNITARY THEORY Individual

> In any executive work which involves the co-operation of two different men or parties, where both parties have anything like equal power or voice in its direction, there is almost sure to be a certain amount of bickering, quarrelling, and vacillation, and the success of the enterprise suffers accordingly. If, however, either one of the parties has the entire direction, the enterprise will progress consistently and probably harmoniously, even although the wrong one of the two parties may be in control. The essence of task (scientific) management lies in the fact that the control of the speed problem rests entirely with management. (Taylor, 1903, quoted by Clawson, 1980)

The story of scientific management has been told by many, but the essential point for us is Taylor's unquestioning assumption that management should maintain control of the organisation and control of work to ensure that business objectives are met. That belief in the 'right to manage' or the managerial prerogative provides an important assumption for those adopting a unitary perspective.

In essence, the unitary theory portrays the employment relationship as harmonious, with employer and employed working together to achieve success. It assumes a common set of values which bind the two parties together and ensure there is no potential source of conflict. Although this might be considered the earliest theory used to describe the employment relationship, it clearly connects with many of the contemporary ideas associated with corporate culture and the use of human resource management (HRM). For this harmonious relationship to exist requires a high level of consensus between the two parties in the employment relationship (*see* Chapter 3).

This begs the question as to how that consensus is achieved, which starts to explain how this theory – which was inspired by a set of conditions in the nineteenth century – can appear to sustain considerable currency in the mid-1990s. Clearly, consensus about the objectives of an organisation can be produced by:

■ ideas and values between employers and employees being absolutely identical as a result of a happy coincidence;

■ ideas and values being a condition of entry to the organisation, their existence therefore being established at the recruitment and selection stage of employment;

■ ideas and values originating with management being learnt by those entering the organisation on a voluntary basis and subsequently adopted by employees;

■ ideas and values being part of a socialisation programme and, through corporate induction courses and other training activities, being involuntarily learnt and adopted;

■ employees being confronted with these ideas and values and their adoption being a condition of their continuing employment. They are then adopted or not by employees, depending on their own circumstances.

Seen in this light, the consensus needs to be understood in a dynamic way and not as an unproblematic given. How it is reached, if it is reached at all, really depends on a whole series of factors existing within the employment relationship at that time.

In the nineteenth century when workers were, for example, forced to move to the cities in search of jobs or join companies like the railways, they had no reference points to evaluate their employment conditions, and in many circumstances they were not sufficiently well informed to question the authority of the employer (Pollard, 1958). The unitary approach, as its name suggests, is therefore emphasising the existence of employers and employees working together, collaborating in the pursuit of these shared objectives. In these circumstances there appears to be little point in allowing a third party to intervene on behalf of either of the two parties.

Systems of ideas like Social Darwinism provided a strong moral justification for these arrangements at this time. It suggested that what took place in nature provided a compelling justification for many in positions of power and privilege in society. The process of natural selection and the survival of the fittest appeared to accord with life at this time and further legitimated the absolute control of employers backed up by the law. It provided a ready-made explanation for those who might wonder why such inequalities in the workplace persisted (Hofstader, 1955).

Trade unions were therefore of no value to either management or employees; it is as if some unnatural force had inserted itself into a natural arrangement. This 'natural' quality to the theory is interesting and today some employers who adopt this theory appear to speak about it as 'good business sense' or even 'common sense', in much the same way as earlier economists talked about the natural and inevitable need for the 'hidden hand' of the market to exist (Hayek, 1960). In other words, the labour market is depicted as a natural structure composed of an omnipotent management backed up by the state and labour dependent on those two parties for its well-being (Gospel, 1992).

If trade unions are considered unnecessary by the theory then we have to explain how the consensus outlined above is maintained. Employees might accept a set of objectives when they start a new job but the long-term cooperation of a workforce is unlikely. So what cements these employees into their jobs and sustains that consensus?

In the nineteenth century paternalism played an important role in binding individual workers to their employers. Accounts of nineteenth century work practices constantly refer to the personalised manner in which work and thereby employees were organised (*see*, for example, Bendix, 1974; Landes, 1972; Laslett, 1971). Employers treated their employees as if they belonged to them. Sometimes this was conducted in such a way that they were treated more like children and had to obey their 'parents'; in other circumstances they were made to feel that they 'belonged' to a family (Laslett, 1971). Clearly, a whole continuum of experiences existed but they all held the potential for overlaying the employment relationship with a sense of obligation to a person in authority.

■ Nineteenth century business and employment

The railways in the mid-nineteenth century provide an interesting example of systematic management of employee relations. Their employment policies reflected many ideas originating in the navy at this time, which provided a suitable training for those confronting the coordination of an uneducated workforce with the demands of a modern technology itself set within a complex organisational structure, dependent upon a series of policies to provide both cooperation and control (Gourvish, 1972; McKenna, 1980). Added together, the experience of these practices clearly led many employees to believe that their needs and those of the company were not far apart. As McKenna describes in an excellent account of employment conditions on the early railways (1980: 45):

> The railwaymen were from the beginning ruled by instructions as detailed as the Koran. They were the first 'organisation men', stitched firmly into the fabric of their company, noted for punctuality, cleanliness and the smart execution of orders. A railway worker was 'in the service'. He reported for duty, and left it only after being relieved. Failure to report for duty meant he was absent without leave. He took unpaid leave only after written permission had been granted; unauthorised leave could lead to suspension, fines, dismissal and even prosecution.

The railway workers very much 'belonged' to the company, which would usually demand testimonials; if accepted, individual employees would be assigned to particular directors, who then became responsible for the future behaviour and performance at work.

This type of employment relationship, which ensured that there was no strike on the railways for the first 50 years of their operation, established practices and assumptions about employee relations that were bound to inform those trying to develop general explanations and theories of employment. So where did the ideas for the unitary theory come from?

Of course it is impossible to trace exactly the genealogy of such ideas but ultimately they may become the parts/concepts that form a theory. Here the historical context provided evidence of the structure and practices of employment, which could provide observers with inspiration for generalising the organisation of work about employment practices.

As Pollard suggests, the biggest worry for entrepreneurs and employers generally in the nineteenth century was the management of labour (Pollard, 1958). Most firms were family firms or partnerships, with very few joint stock companies in existence. Firms were based upon small to medium-sized employment units for most of the nineteenth century guided by family members (Hobsbawn, 1974). In other words, most employees' experience of employment was contained within relatively intimate arrangements with close contact with their 'masters', whether they were family entrepreneurs or leading craftsmen – what Burawoy called the 'despotic regime' displaying a strong relationship of dependence and coercion between employers and employees (Burawoy, 1979, 1985).

In these circumstances employees' experience of work was of constantly being exposed to the organisation's objectives and where employment legislation was very much in favour of employers – for example, the requirements contained within the Master and Servants Act 1867. It was apparent that employees were under considerable pressure to submit themselves to the requirements of the law to ensure their survival.

Unitary theory is associated in the first instance with a version of employment as it existed in the nineteenth century and reflects a set of interests that clearly expresses employers' concerns and not those of employees – in other words, a managerialist perspective. It is based on an idealised employment relationship reflecting a set of desirable arrangements for management which, if operationalised, would ensure that management could maximise its objectives at the cost of its employees, as in the case of the early railway companies.

■ Some shortcomings of unitary theory

As an explanation of employment, unitary theory certainly does not take account of the real needs of the employees nor does it recognise the very real differences in objectives that exist between employers and employees.

To summarise its weaknesses:

■ It fails to recognise the existence of differing interests between management and labour. The assumption is made that managers' decisions are rational and contain within them the interests of all employees.

■ The explanation for the existence of a countervailing force, whether in the form of an individual, group or trade union, rests on the failure to understand the objectives of management. Better means of communication are often exhorted as the cure for such ills.

■ Where this conflict persists, it is explained by what Palmer calls 'deviance' (Palmer, 1983). The behaviour of those acting against management has to be dealt with by dismissal or the law (Palmer, 1983).

■ With ever more sophisticated management techniques, many modern managers point to the existence of a conflict of interests resulting from a failure to establish a sufficiently clear corporate culture against which potential employees' qualities can be established.

Although few would admit to such a simple view of management today, it retains an attraction – as Palmer suggests – resulting from its prescriptive connotations and an ideological stance that has mirrored many of the management nostrums of the 1980s and 1990s (Palmer, 1983).

Farnham calls unitary theory's latest form 'neo-unitary' theory and suggests that since the 1980s it appears to correspond closely with many features associated with the 'new', more aggressive styles of management (Farnham and Pimlott, 1990). This 'new' management is associated with the decline of union power and the ascendancy of the managerial prerogative, by which we mean management's increasing ability to shape and control employment relations. That the unitary theory should once again appear to provide a way of understanding the employment relationship is not surprising. If the context of the 1990s has many features in common with that of the nineteenth century, then why shouldn't the theory inspired by those arrangements re-emerge now to correspond to employment relations, which, for many researchers, have more than a passing resemblance to those earlier conditions when management power was in the ascendant resulting in polarities and divisions within the workforce? Not only do some of the same conditions relate to the earlier period but clearly, for those adopting the theory, it defines the employment relationship in such a way as to ensure that management retains a privileged position and can continue to claim a defining role in the management of labour.

In summary, unitary theory was originally linked to a type of nineteenth-century employment that seems to reflect employers' managerial interests rather than those of the employees. It is based on a kind of idealised relationship at work which suits the management and which, if put into practice, would ensure that management could usually achieve all its objectives at the expense of employees.

More sophisticated versions of the theory have since emerged to create images of consensus, teams and a shared vision of company objectives. Its managerialist bias is unmistakable, however, and its account of employee relations one-sided.

If we took this approach and looked at the original case study of the BA strike (Exhibit 2.1), it would not be difficult to see such a theory concentrating on the business needs of the company articulated by management. In such circumstances, the claim by management that the company must restructure would reflect a unitary analysis.

PLURALIST THEORY

With the growing complexity and scale of business units, however, a more appropriate explanation was required which might move beyond the simplicity of the unitary approach and more accurately reflect the experience of those working in larger and complex employment units. The exponents of pluralists theory acknowledged the existence of a limited level of conflicting interests in the workplace and the need for all parties to work towards achieveing consensus.

In a recent policy document published by the Trade Union Congress (TUC) (the umbrella organisation of the trade union movement), a description of the employment relationship is outlined which clearly acknowledges the differing interests of management and employees.

> The theme of this statement is partnership, a recognition that trade unions must not be seen as part of Britain's problems. At the workplace social partnership means employers and trade unions working together to achieve common goals such as fairness and competitiveness; it is recognition that, although they have different constituencies; it is a recognition that although they have different interests, they can serve these best by making common cause wherever possible. (TUC, 1997)

Although the potential for a conflict of interests exists, a very strong emphasis on a common purpose is evident.

If we could connect pluralist theories in employee relations to a particular historical juncture it would have to be the post-war period leading up to the high-point in the 1970s when such theories provided an explicit framework for government policy. Equally, they had a profound effect on the development of the discipline and its public role.

From this time onwards, no government of any complexion could allow employers and employees to settle things for themselves. As time went on, policies – whether explicit or not – such as incomes policies and the increasing use of the law and other institutional mechanisms, combined to demonstrate the growing level of intervention in employee relations (*see* Chapter 6).

Pluralist theory emerged in Britain at a time when post-war economic growth had led to a level of prosperity which, 20 years after the war, had started to spawn a number of cultural forms that were to challenge established ideas and assumptions and in a sense the 'establishment' of British society. Ideas of power vested in privileged positions and the right of old élites to dictate standards and values to the rest of society were under challenge as a new generation with greater disposable income and opportunities for employment set out with less reverence for the established ways of British society (Halsey, 1995). If the 'pop' and 'rock' culture in Britain signified some of these changes, the adoption of pluralist theory in industrial relations demonstrated to authors like Fox (1973) that the unitary theory had lost its credibility. As a consequence, the significance of pluralism grew and a change in emphasis within industrial relations theory ensued, as Fox confirms (1973: 192):

> One alternative perspective which has developed, however, asserts the unitary view to be diminishingly useful. The increasing size and complexity of work organisations; shifts in the power relations within politics and industry; changes in social values; rising aspirations; weakening of traditional attitudes towards officially constituted governance: these are among the factors which are sometimes said to require managers to develop a new ideology and new sources of legitimisation if they are to maintain effective control.

Under the influence of Dahl (1957) and other political theorists, the idea that any form of governance should acknowledge the competing interests of the groups engaged in the process came to be recognised. As Fox points out, it was Cyert and March (1963) who talked about the existence of 'coalitions' where groups agreed to abide by a set of procedures to ensure the resolution of competing and often conflicting interests (Fox, 1973).

The implication of using this analysis was, unlike unitary theory, that it drew from accounts based upon a political heritage in democratic theory that portrayed decision making as a process of reconciling the different claims made by a variety of competing groups.

In other words, it acknowledged the existence of a variety of competing interest groups, but in addition it accepted this variety as legitimate and normal. At the centre of this conception of the employment relationship was a fluid world where competing interests expended energy vying for the acknowledgement of their arguments and, ultimately, the successful adoption of their policies or proposals.

This fluidity stood in stark contrast to the unitary approach, which had always portrayed management policies as the only legitimate ideas for employment. In unitary theory, a consensus would result because of the common value system that was held to exist. Here, the existence of conflict was allowed for, and to an extent encouraged. Conflict led to creative tension, which encouraged effective arguments and debate. However, this could only be allowed as long as it remained within the 'creative' end of the continuum. As Fox suggests, 'A certain amount of overt conflict and disputation is welcomed as evidence that not all aspirations are being either sapped by hopelessness or suppressed by power. On the other hand, conflict above a certain level is felt to be evidence that the ground rules need changing' (1973: 193). Therefore conflict exists in a way other theories find it hard to account for, yet there is still a restricted definition of conflict, one which sees the basis of that conflict resting in a clash over the means by which objectives are achieved. Further discussion of this feature of the theory will be explored in the section dealing with Marxist theory.

What the theory appears to offer is an account of the nature of industrial relations which achieves greater realism by reflecting the political realities of the situation at that time. This is hardly surprising when the details of that historical period are considered, along with the level of trade union activity and the incidence of industrial disputes in evidence at that time. Conflict was very much in evidence (Bassett, 1987).

If the theory appeared to provide a more realistic account of this period of employment history by acknowledging the wider constituency of factors shaping the world of employment, it also had interesting consequences for the role of management.

1 It reconfirmed management at the centre of this complex world of competing interests. The only group that possessed the capacity to ensure reconciliation between the different parties was management – not unlike the argument that Burnham had earlier espoused to place management at the middle of a 'new' technicist age (Burnham, 1957).

2 If managers were the only group able to resolve the differences between the competing interests, then in the future they would have to develop logical and reasoned arguments to justify their final decisions; otherwise they would be unable to sustain the 'loose coalition'.

This was in stark contrast to the unitarist theory, which indicated that management had a duty to impose their decisions on other groups.

■ Some shortcomings of pluralism

As with unitary theory, pluralism was ultimately premised upon the existence of a consensus, but differed from it in that it allowed for the existence of limited conflict to achieve that consensus. What is interesting to note in this theory, however, is the nature of that consensus and where it operates within the theory.

In the unitary approach the consensus is assumed and left as unproblematic; in the pluralist model it exists as a result of the acknowledged process of socialisation and the sustaining of roles – in other words, it is an active process which at times can fail the system. In the case of pluralist theory, it is given an active role although it becomes a more hidden process, in the sense that it is assumed to exist at a fundamental level, as described by Fox (1973: 197):

> The assumption is being made that while, to be sure, conflicts arise over terms of economic collaboration, values and norms are not so divergent that workable compromises cannot be achieved. Underlying the cut and thrust of marketplace and organisational encounters, in other words, lies the rock-firm foundation of a stable and agreed social system.

Once again, the theory considered by some to provide a more realistic account of employment suffers from a series of assumptions for which there are serious misgivings:

■ it believes in the existence of democracy, which through the franchise ensures that individual rights are recognised;

- it assumes that the institutions of democracy operate to resolve what differences do occur between management and labour;

- it relies on the existence of a common set of rules and procedures which guide subsequent behaviour in the workplace;

- it depicts the differing parties to the employment relationship possessing a rough equivalence of power and influence, competing for power on the basis of similar levels of influence;

- it relies on the power and success of negotiation and bargaining to overcome fundamental differences between management and labour;

- its analytical focus is upon a continuous description of the 'given' institutions of modern capitalism and thereby fails to reveal the inbuilt biases and inequalities of such structures.

Such an emphasis on the institutions of modern capitalism for providing an understanding of the employment relationship plays down the political reality of employment and the very different worlds within which management and labour reside.

Salamon says of collective bargaining, 'the relationship is founded on mutual dependence. So too with pluralism – it relies upon the ability of both sides to appear to retain independent positions with room to maintain their independence of each other (Salamon, 1998: 315).

From a more critical perspective, this misses the point that by entering into such collective agreements or negotiations, employees are unwittingly losing sight of the fact that the institutional arrangement in which they are operating is itself malformed or distorted in favour of those in powerful positions. As Crouch suggests, 'Management have usually succeeded in conceding pluralism over a limited range of issues (wage bargaining, low-level aspects of control of the work process), while maintaining intact a monist position on the more strategic issues of company or industry-level action' (Crouch, 1977: 47).

▮ Post-war democracy and economic growth

This 'post-industrial' theory of employee relations is clearly associated with many features of the post-war period, when Harold Wilson could talk about the 'white heat of technology' coming to the aid of UK plc.

Britain, although declining in terms of position in the world economy, had not yet been consigned to the remedial class. The discussion in social policy and the debates within various Labour governments had revealed a concern for the 'distribution of resources'. Inner city problems had been seen as necessitating the design of better delivery systems; the ideal of equality of access was still considered worth while.

In the world of employment, questions were being asked about the role and influence of trade unions as Britain's performance started to falter. The accepted architecture of pluralism – a modest role for the state, the continuation of voluntarism, trade unions as regulators of labour and an overall consensus over the existence of the pluralist coalition – was also under threat (Armstrong *et al.*, 1991).

One particular event – the Donovan Commission – stands out as the epitome of the influence of the pluralist theory. This had been expressly set up to investigate what many saw as the uncontrolled growth of trade union disorder in 1968. The use of a pluralist frame of reference (sometimes known as the 'Oxford School' or the 'institutional approach' of industrial relations, involving Alan Flanders, Alan Fox and Hugh Clegg) had a major role in shaping this report, and in that capacity depicted the various elements of industrial relations in a way that was to have far-reaching consequences (Eldridge *et al.*, 1991).

As a result of adopting this theoretical perspective, Eldridge *et al.* suggest (1991: 97):

> The Donovan Commission in its attribution of cause and effect was itself taking part in this elaboration of trade union culpability but against a background where its recommendations could not directly address the roots of the 'disorder'.

Such developments tended to concentrate on achieving superficial adjustments to the distribution of work and rewards (Hyman and Brough, 1975). Like other areas of social policy, the coalition that comprised the area of employment had become ineffective and the balance of power needed to be recast. In this process it was the Donovan Commission that pointed to the imbalance between management and the unions as the cause of the breakdown in the coalition of interests. It was therefore the role of management within the relationship that needed redefining. The very theory that was intended to achieve a more realistic account of modern employee relations when operationalised by this commission had the effect of reinforcing the existence of unequal interests.

Pluralist theory confronted the question of competing interests in employment relations. It went beyond unitary theory and captured the political realities of the experience of employment in modern democracies. Ultimately it still portrayed the world of employment as resting upon a sufficient consensus to ensure that all parties would participate in resolving their restricted differences of interests.

If we consider again the case of BA (Exhibit 2.1), it is not difficult to see those accounts that acknowledge the potential for conflict between the two sides and consider the way forward to reside with the process of negotiation and conciliation, leading ultimately to a resolution of the conflict of interests.

To address some of the shortcomings identified above, we now turn to systems theory and its account of the organisation of employment, which, because of its ability to portray employment in a logical manner, did so much to enhance the role of the discipline.

SYSTEMS THEORY

Under a pluralist banner there appeared to be very few attempts to question the underlying distribution of power and construction of hierarchies in work or employment. Alongside the growing influence of pluralist theory in employee relations in the post-war period, systems theory provided a version of pluralist thinking that sought to systematise knowledge of employee relations and establish the discipline as an equal to other areas of social science.

Systems theory, which is identified with the American writer John Dunlop and his landmark book *The Industrial Relations Systems* (1958), could be said to have provided one of the most dominant paradigms in the field of employee relations. But why systems theory, why in 1958, and what has been the consequence of this virtual monopoly of the theoretical field for employee relations?

To answer the first question we need to establish what we mean by systems theory. General systems theory had been popularised by von Bertalanffy, who had established the theory within the field of biology (von Bertalanffy, 1950). The existence of systems has a seemingly natural base within biology. What we know about the operation of biological systems within an ecological context indicates that, for example, a cell requires inputs in the form of food, combines this with its own chemistry and converts this into energy, allowing it to survive in its environment. At the completion of this cycle the waste products of the process are expelled from the cell through its cell lining. Should the cell need more energy, then it absorbs more food from its environment and the whole cycle starts all over again. The logic of the entire system is guided by the need to survive. What was observed in nature appeared to correspond well with the world of work organisations. As Clegg suggests, in relation to the impact of systems ideas on organisations (1990: 68):

> Not only did they produce a major reconceptualisation of organisations striving for orderliness in an otherwise chaotic world; they also successfully reinterpreted the past development of organisation theory. Reading backwards from the open systems perspective, much earlier conceptions could now be interpreted as an excessively internalist and closed system account of organisation structure and process.

What was true for organisations was certainly true of industrial relations at this time. Systems theory appeared to hold the prospect of making sense of a disparate set of phenomena composed of social movements, government organisations and a set of loosely structured procedures at a time of rapid industrial growth within the US economy in the immediate post-war era.

The attraction of systems theory has always been its ability to create an orderly description of its object of study, to provide an account of the variety of parts and connect them all together through the logic of the function each appears to play in sustaining the whole system. Dunlop, searching for a theory that could make sense of an apparently diverse set of factors, could see the opportunity of finding a device that could locate all of these factors within a single framework.

At that time in the US, one of the most powerful exponents of general systems theory was the sociologist, Talcott Parsons. His work used the analogy of systems thinking as an entire framework for accounting for the nature and direction of American society (Parsons, 1952). Itself a system made up of subsystems with boundaries, his theory of society rested on the premise which maintained that society's structure was designed in such a way as to ensure its continued existence. The different subsystems had different jobs to fulfil and all complemented each other to help society to survive; they made it 'function'. That use of systems thinking could be applied to Dunlop's project; industrial relations could now be developed as a viable separate academic discipline and its disparate elements could be presented as logical components of a rational and ordered whole. For Dunlop, industrial relations could be established as a separate subsystem of the Parsons society, possessing identifiable inputs travelling across boundaries where they would engage in the process of transformation which ultimately would lead to outputs in the forms of rules that would subsequently guide the subsystem to its next stage (Fig. 2.2).

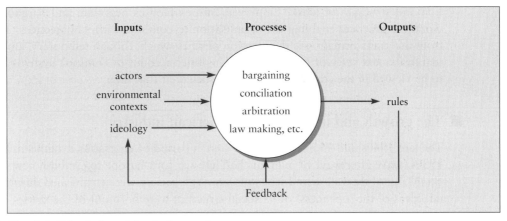

■ Fig. 2.2 The industrial relations subsystem
Source: Dunlop (1958)

One of the consequences of adopting this model was the creation of a set of terms that have become embedded in the language of employee relations. Inputs, as Fig. 2.2 indicates, are composed of actors, environmental contexts and ideology. *Actors* refer to the employers and employees and representative organisations, while the *contexts* are composed of technological regimes, such as the type of production system itself, shaping the patterns of work and the composition of the workforce. Debates on whether the current production regime is 'fordist' (conforming to the dominant pattern of work organisation associated with the early production systems of Ford car plants), 'neo-fordist' (production similar to the Ford archetype but with the possibility of modifications and variations) or 'post-fordist' (production regimes that have passed on to different forms which display far greater flexibility in their arrangements as compared to the rigid control structures associated with the mass production of Ford) would determine the type of environmental input identified by the model, and, depending on which is identified, would have clear consequences for what effects this particular environmental factor might have on the transformation process (Allen, 1992).

The nature of markets and financial factors would also be regarded as contextual factors. With the emphasis over the past 15 years on the impact of markets on business performance and the capacity of firms to shape markets, markets and financial factors are bound to be significant for the model.

Finally, *ideological factors* play a key role in explaining how the different parties in the industrial relations subsystem come to behave in a manner that sustains the desire to reconcile any differences in values and objectives. In Britain, with its strong tradition of voluntarism and an absence of strict legal constraints, an ideological system has emerged that is accessible to all of the different parties. Whether they are trade unions or employers' groups, they have been able to establish within the larger ideological system a set of ideas that sustains their own role and independence. At the heart of the model is the transformation process akin to the biological organism transforming food into energy for its continued existence.

In the same way, the different inputs mentioned above combine within a necessity to ensure that workplaces continue to operate and achieve agreements about the organisation and structure of work. Employers and employees negotiate and bargain to create workable practices enabling the organisation to continue with its objectives. The output from this transformation is the creation of rules which, though temporary, guide the system to its next stage of development. This brief account of Dunlop's systems theory has to be viewed in the context of American society at that time.

■ The growth and integration of American industry

The late 1940s and 1950s in America were a period of enormous dynamism. During the 1930s, wave after wave of migrants had left war-torn Europe to establish new lives in the US. Many of the values and icons of American society were established during this period. Ideas of the 'openness' of its social structure were born out of the stories of migrant success, climbing the economic ladder from the ghettos and achieving the American dream. With the energy deriving from this 'new' impetus, the institutions and practices of American society had to find new ways of integrating this population into the mainstream of American life. Something of this restless energy and opportunity is captured by Jon Dos Passos (1952: 1) in his extraordinary novel spanning this period of American history:

> The young man walks fast by himself through the crowd that thins into the night streets; feet are tired from hours of walking; eyes greedy for warm curve faces, answering flicker of eyes, the set of a head, the lift of a shoulder, the ways the hands spread and clench; blood tingles with wants; mind is a beehive of hopes buzzing and stinging; muscles ache for the knowledge of jobs, the roadmender's pick and shovel work, the fisherman's knack with a hook when he hauls on the slithery net from the rail of the lurching trawler, the swing of the bridgeman's arm as he slings down the white hot rivet, the engineer's slow grip wise on the throttle, the dirtfarmer's use of his whole body when, whoaing the mules, he yanks the plow from the furrow. The young man walks by himself searching through the crowd with greedy ears taught to hear, by himself, alone.

In this immigrants' world, the American cities were a melting pot for those newly arrived as they searched for work and a place in the 'new' society. An earlier researcher had also seen this diversity and sought to establish a theory that might hold the potential to confront this restless and dynamic working population. Elton Mayo, and what was to become labelled the 'human relations school', had seen the need to find a theory that could point to some process of integration. To be able to conceptualise the employment relationship in a way that could lead to integration through the creation of a 'system', held great value for those who might be considering the problem at a national political level.

The journey of systems theory from its biological starting point to the world of industrial relations did much the same. It suggested a framework for making sense of the rapidly changing world of employment, it labelled all manner of different phenomena and it provided an explanation that connected all these different parts (Carey, 1980; Roethlisberger and Dickinson, 1939).

■ Some shortcomings of systems theory

At this stage it is important to step back and assess this major theory in employee relations and perhaps start to understand its long life in the orthodoxy of the discipline. If employee relations is going to be accounted for in terms of a systems analogy we need to get right to the heart of the theory to assess its capacity to explain that subsystem. Its main assumptions include the following:

- The term system implies something that is orderly and capable of description, as we mentioned above. It means more than this, however; it suggests that if the world of employment is a system, it displays a common set of values that binds it together and makes it a system. This is what Parsons called the 'central value system'. A belief in the existence of such a common value system appears at odds particularly with the experience of contemporary American society.

- An equilibrium – or, using the biological language, homeostasis (a point of balance within a biological system) – is achieved. That is, the employee relations subsystem reaches a point of balance within itself and its internal constituencies while at the same time reflecting the needs of the wider society of which it is a part. To use the modern idiom, it 'delivers' the world of employment in a way that is consonant with the requirements of that society at that time. As a result the entire society continues to function and survive. With such a massive experience of social dislocation resulting in mass unemployment, skills shortages and industrial collapse in manufacturing sectors it is hard to see such equilibrium in operation.

- If all of these subsystems are to survive, the individuals within them must reflect as closely as possible the objectives of the organisation. How does this occur? According to systems theory it is produced by the socialisation of individuals into roles which, as individuals, we all learn to adopt. We learn to become a junior management trainee by observing others in that role, reading the relevant training literature and absorbing all manner of clues and information that will aid us in achieving a set of values and behaviours that are considered to correspond with the dominant definitions of that role at that time. For those who do not learn the right values and adopt the correct behaviour, their chance of achieving either access to work or success if they possess a job is limited.

In Dunlop's theory, the emphasis on rules starts to make sense. These outcomes from the industrial relations system are the product of those reconciliations between all the individual employees and their managers – or in systems language, all the values expressed by the workforce are reconciled with the organisation's objectives. The rules in whatever form, whether in what has been termed 'custom and practice' or some other form of collective agreement, express this process. In turn, these agreements come to be highly influential and shape employee relations from that moment into the future, until they are once again negotiated or allowed to be displaced by an entirely new set of agreements or rules.

This theory, although modified at times (Bain and Clegg, 1974; Clegg, 1979), has been dominant in the explanation of employee relations over the years.

Systems theory, which has a reputation for remaining extremely remote and abstract, has persisted in this area although it is claimed that many writers fail to acknowledge its nature and distinctiveness. In this sense it is important for us to ask about the limitations of this particular theory. Clegg and Dunkerley in their book *Organisation, Class and*

Control (1980) provide an excellent review of the major criticisms of general systems theory. They, with Silverman (1970) and Hyman (1989), provide a useful set of critiques that raise enough concerns about systems theory to make one wonder how it has survived so long (unless of course we start to appreciate its operational utility, which is a point we will come to later). Of the many criticisms, we need only outline those that explain the reservations certain authors have regarding the adoption of this particular theory. Its derivation from pluralist theory means that systems theory shares several of its features.

Some of the more significant limitations include:

■ At the centre of the problem is the same question that was raised in relation to the unitary theory, that of consensus. The focus on values, socialisation and the resulting roles adopted by individuals all add up to a workplace where fairly passive individuals appear to sense the need to conform, collaborate and reconcile any differences that might exist between them. The theory appears to concentrate on the need to achieve equilibrium through the resolution of conflict.

■ All of this further assumes that organisation members in the workplace read and interpret the rules in a similar manner and arrive at a rational and predictable answer.

■ Conflict in employment is largely missing; in learning our roles we come to adopt the objectives of the firm according to this account, which implies conformity and cooperation.

■ Related to this point is the question of unequal power. In the present context, with senior management in Britain accruing ever larger shares of the profits to their own reward schemes, it appears hard not to recognise the increasing gulf in pay and conditions, between those employing workers and those who are employed. Owners of enterprises clearly do not have the same level of influence on the system as ordinary employees.

■ As far as the description of the inputs is concerned, it neither explains how they came into existence nor how they might change over time.

■ At the most general level, the theory does not account for change, nor does it reflect the contradictions and failures of either the industrial relations system or the larger society. The fact that we have youth unemployment, a segregated workforce divided on grounds of race and gender, and many other divisions implies that we live in a society where conflict is normal and consensus is, at best, partial.

In systems theory, certainly at its inception in employee relations, we had a theory which once again appeared to reflect managerial concerns, but in this case they were very real problems facing American managers in the early post-war period. Like the unitary theory, systems theory in its earlier forms appeared to hold a method of analysis that contained within it a description of the problems of employee relations that were amenable to managerial initiatives and gave management a chance of sustaining their position in the employment relationship.

Finally, we should also note that, having contributed to the establishment of a whole new world of employee relations by providing a comprehensive theory to underpin what had been a fairly pragmatic discipline based upon 'fact-finding and description rather than theoretical generalisations' (Winchester, 1983: 101), it also opened up the floodgates to empirical research. Its assumptions rooted in structural functionalism (a type of analysis that dwells on the role that the constituent elements of a system have in sustaining the function of that entity) meant that once all of the different pieces of the system had been identified, empirical verification of the relationship between the parts would become a major task for those engaging in the discipline.

Looking back to Exhibit 2.1, we can see how a systems analysis could focus on the imbalance between the financial and human resource subsystems and label this a significant problem for management. In the circumstances, an adjustment would have to be reached through the process of collective bargaining with each side establishing its own agenda. With the proper procedures followed, governed by the established rules and procedures, an outcome would be possible that would contain a new set of conditions and employment practices, reflecting a new point of balance within the organisation. We would not claim that each of the theories discussed here follows some evolutionary path of advancement. Each has arisen at a particular time in a particular context, often with a particular purpose in the mind of its author. Over time they relate to particular policy practices and become modified to reflect the shifting patterns of interests pervading at any one time. Of course, not all theories are as clear cut as systems theory, where a single author can be connected initially to its development, as in the case of Dunlop.

Systems theory confronted the question of the changing shape of industry and employment and created a means of describing the specific arrangements and underlying processes identified as determining the employment relationship. With its emphasis upon the creation of rules and procedures it established the employment relationship as a central issue for research and policy development.

Marxist theory does not follow the foregoing theories in a neat and orderly progression; it too emerged in the nineteenth century but with an agenda to question the existing structure of society with a concern to understand the nature and direction of the 'then' new capitalist economy. In that sense, employment and the employment relationship, though of central concern to Marx's analysis of capitalism, are the focus of an explanation which seeks to understand the mechanism by which the 'whole' capitalist system operates. In that sense, they are not considered to be significant as separate elements within an 'academic' debate.

MARXIST THEORY

For many, the fall of the Iron Curtain, the collapse of the Berlin Wall and recent attempts to introduce market-based policies into Eastern Bloc countries were all evidence of the end of socialism and the final proof of the lack of utility for Marxist-inspired theories. Here we need to make a distinction between the 'theories' inspired by Marx's writing and the actual forms that took shape on the ground as a result of these theories.

The theories themselves clearly emerged from Marx's observations at a time when capitalism was still in its infancy and employment was very much a matter of survival in a world where huge disparities of wealth and power existed. Faced with such a dramatic period of change, Marx set out to understand and identify the logic that drove the economic system to unfold in the way it did. Attached to this project was his ambition to explain how this understanding could in turn account for other features of capitalist society. If the dramatic features of the Industrial Revolution inspired Marx to seek a theory to explain the nature of capitalism, then, like all the other theories we have mentioned, it appears that Marxism continues to provide an important analytical device for understanding the employment relationship.

What is central in making sense of Marxist theory is therefore the connection between theory and practice. For Marx there was no distinction; theory existed to provide an account of society that, in the process of revealing the inner contradictions of the system, would lead to action to overcome these contradictions. In the process of elaborating a theory of capitalism he pointed to the constant exploitation of workers under capitalist employment conditions. Revealing the mechanisms by which these inequalities were generated through debate and policies of political movements, he believed, would lead to radical opposition to those in power and hence overthrow the capitalist class. First and foremost, his theory was a product of the nineteenth century, a period of enormous social upheaval, as the 'new' capitalist society started to take shape (Mandel, 1978).

■ Industrialisation and inequality

The Industrial Revolution provided Marx with the evidence for his theory of capitalism, and most of us are familiar with its main features. What Marx saw was an industrial society in which divisions were being driven by the inevitable competition between classes. His particular insights and originality lay in his ability to connect so many of the different parts of that society within one overriding logic. At the heart of his analysis was the existence of the pursuit of profit by the entrepreneur; this was an 'inevitable' requirement of the capitalist system. This inevitable demand explained much about all the other features of that early society. This logic resulted in a system of work that invariably set one side of the employment relationship against the other. Entrepreneurs needed to maximise their return on investments and employees were bound to defend their standard of living by fighting for a 'decent' wage (Hobsbawm, 1974).

The conditions of work were very often appalling, and employers had little regard for the well-being of their employees (Bendix, 1974). Hours were long, work was often dangerous and unhealthy, and pay, at least for the first half of the nineteenth century, was based on the principle of subsistence (Briggs and Saville, 1967).

In the earliest days it was hardly surprising that in the textile industry, 'only twenty-three per cent of textile factory workers were adult men' (Hobsbawm, 1974). Women and children were forced to work to survive but men were reluctant to enter early factory life because of such conditions. Such accounts of this early industrial society are well-established and it is therefore not difficult to conceive of the inspiration for Marx's theory of capitalist society. What is perhaps more difficult is to provide a brief account of this theory of capitalist society and establish connections between it and the matter of employee relations.

■ Marxist theory and employment relations

Writing when he did, Marx inhabited a world in which the subtleties of capitalist 'exploitation' were still not fully apparent. The role of education, the media, other agencies of government, the attractions of consumerism and the 'need' for recognition all combine to confront what Marx thought would be outright opposition to capitalist controls.

For example, the work produced by some of the more recent critical writers on psychology demonstrates just how difficult it is to see through a whole set of agencies and their practices when it comes to understanding what meanings are attached to us and our behaviour (Kamin 1976; Rose, 1989; Hollway, 1991).

Social workers, welfare workers and personnel practitioners, with many others, all work to identify 'individual problems', which can only be overcome with the aid of their therapeutic methods. Since the Second World War, much research has been conducted with the explicit purpose of ensuring maximum compliance and worker performance, and a whole therapeutic industry has emerged to analyse us, categorise us and direct us. In other words our 'identities' are now the site at which these new professional groups exercise their skills; they define our identity and label our personalities. With such powerful technologies it is hardly surprising that for many of us, the locus of so many contradictions of capitalism appears to be inside the individual and not in the 'structures' of society (Holloway, 1991).

We become the 'problem' of capitalism, not the 'system' we inhabit. Expecting radical reaction to the experience of modern capitalism is, therefore, far less straightforward than at the time when Marx was observing the newly forming capitalist work relations (Carey, 1980).

Today there are entire industries based on redefining our ideas of ourselves, whether this is directly through consumption or through employees adopting patterns of 'emotional labour' which require them to adopt values, attitudes and forms of behaviour (Fineman, 1993; Du Gray, 1995; Sturdy, 1998).

This leaves us with a belief that the theory generated by Marx has many analytical advantages and insights for unravelling features of contemporary employee relations. Whether or not particular action results from these observations is a product of social and political forces, which are beyond the scope of the present analysis. So how can we depict the core of Marx's theory and apply this to the world of employee relations?

The following schema provides some of those connections:

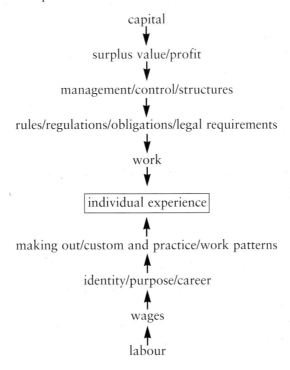

Under capitalism, the employee relationship is founded upon inequality, according to Marx. The very nature of the capitalist labour process is premised upon the extraction from labour of a surplus which can form the basis of profits for the employer.

At the heart of Marx's analysis is a belief that work, however designed, returns to the two sides of the employment relationship unequal portions of reward. Not only is this true economically, but the experience of working for wages or a salary leads workers to experience a loss of control over their natural abilities to control the process of work with which they are involved. Although Marx would never have detached the study of employment from the broader social, political and economic contexts, the employment relationship was to him one of the central features for understanding modern capitalism, for, as we have suggested above, work returns profits to the owners of capital but only wages to those who have to sell their capacity to work. This means workers not only experience economic inequalities but perhaps the even more insidious experience of executing work that more often than not is meaningless and disconnected from their own level of understanding. This sense of the 'partial' nature of many jobs leads in turn to low self-esteem and demoralisation – what Marx called alienation. By this he meant that we become fractured as individuals and separated from our real selves. The work we do and the conditions under which we conduct it can have the effect of turning us into seemingly happy and compliant employees, bearing no relation to the people we really are. Some might argue that this is precisely what modern management seeks to achieve through practices like HRM and total quality management (TQM) (Holloway, 1991; Sewell and Wilkinson, 1992).

In the contemporary labour market it is possible to see how these two sources of inequality become inescapable when experienced within a labour market that is becoming increasingly competitive, unstable and surrounded by a sea of unemployment.

Whatever the inequality experienced, most workers in today's labour market would be far more likely to put up with it than risk the loss of their job. The ability to locate the employment relationship within this broader set of social relationships provides a persuasive account of how people at work come to behave, respond, act or acquiesce. People's responses are not just a function of the determinants of their workplace, but of a whole set of factors and outcomes themselves produced by external contextual and historical forces.

More recently, interest in the Marxist analysis of employment in the 1970s and 1980s has centred around the labour process debate rekindled by Harry Braverman's book *Labor and Monopoly Capital* (1974).

In short, Braverman outlined a theory of degradation of work which resulted from the continuous decline of skill among the workforce leading to a weakening of bargaining power and a loss of control. He illustrated this process by referring to Taylor's system of Scientific Management, which, according to Braverman, inevitably led to the continuous reduction in skill levels as work became increasingly reorganised to satisfy the logic of managerial efficiency. Braverman's central contention of inevitable deskilling unleashed a substantial quantity of research to establish the likelihood of such trends. Today commentators would probably conclude that such 'inevitability' elevates management to a very sophisticated level, and as such reject such an all-embracing account (*see* Chapter 3). Research suggests that management, and particularly British management, tends to 'muddle through' (Sisson, 1994).

Braverman was therefore far too generous to the capacity of management to 'manage' in a rational fashion. Not only do managers deploy all manner of strategies, not just those that deskill (Friedman, 1977), but, as the complexity of capitalism grows, their choice of options expands. Whether or not the central tenets of his argument are misguided, Braverman's concern for the intersection of management practice and the experience of employment has generated a rich layer of theory, entitled 'labour process theory', and an ever-expanding empirical research programme to set against this.

What we are left with is a theory that continues to provide a rich source of analysis by making connections between areas of social life excluded from the theories discussed earlier. In a world of employment where work appears less secure for the majority of the workforce and the pressures for performance are increasingly experienced at the level of the individual, it provides a framework for understanding many significant contemporary phenomena which are closely connected to the employment relationship, whether experienced as pressure from the broader context or within the direct experience of the job.

Although Marxist analysis can include a variety of positions (*see* Gospel and Palmer, 1993: 25), it clearly emphasises the employment relationship and sets it within a discussion of the current stage of capitalist development. Unlike the earlier theories, it draws on a series of fundamental processes which, though changed in form, continue to exert a strong influence on shaping the employment relationship.

As we indicated at the outset of this chapter, for many the insights derived from this theory do not appear to fit comfortably within the world of HRM, high performance teams, business process re-engineering or many of the other latest management practices, and yet we would contend that its capacity to look wider than an immediate problem and relate this to historical antecedents and contextual factors provides a richness of explanation that holds the potential for a more comprehensive understanding of the issue under discussion.

Although this approach remedies many of the earlier criticisms, it too has its limitations, many of which reside in the concentration on the 'structure' of capitalism, which fails to address some of the inbuilt assumptions about those structures. With the 'economic' base of society influencing the direction and shape of the economic system, it is often hard to see the connections between this level of analysis and the changing experiences of those within the employment relationship. For instance, the fact that half the workforce is composed of women and that their experience of modern work is very different from that of men requires more than an explanation that relies upon male views of male structures and processes. Feminist critiques of the workplace have therefore grown to represent a significant body of knowledge, and in many cases have spent a considerable effort in trying to develop new theories that provide important insights into the employment relationship, which for so long has implied men at work.

Marxist theory emerged to explain the problems associated with the growth of capitalism. Unlike the other theories, it does not believe in a consensus based upon shared interests. Classes in society exist in opposition to one another. In employment relations, this is represented by the opposing interests of labour and management. Conflict is therefore endemic in the workplace and is hidden only by active programmes of obscuring the realities of gross inequalities of power, control and reward.

Turning back to the BA case study in Exhibit 2.1, we can say that adopting a Marxist analysis would lead to concentration on the permanent antagonism between classes which can come to be represented in the workplace. Employees are at the mercy of international business, which is constantly seeking to cheapen labour resources, increase exploitation and ensure profit maximisation.

The competition between airlines, themselves multinational corporations, will lead to a constant search for tighter operating margins, as they merge and take each other over in the inevitable route to globalisation.

If Marxist theory set out to explain the workings of the capitalist system it did so at a time when ideas about equality between men and women were only formative. In this sense the analysis missed the subtleties of the divisions which existed within that system. With so many changes in the nature and composition of employment, feminist theories have done much to expose the inequalities between men and women at work.

FEMINIST THEORY

Feminist theory, like many other critical theories, emerged towards the end of the nineteenth century to confront the deteriorating condition in which the majority of women found themselves. As the features of modern capitalism crystallised in the form of large-scale industry and the creation of an urban workforce, women were increasingly located in areas of work that were badly paid, related to definitions of their domestic role and for the most part blocked any chance of achieving a full career to senior positions. With women excluded from the vote and considered inferior to men, the early feminist movement provided a different account of the situation confronting the majority of women (Rowbotham, 1974).

Today we are told that women comprise nearly 50 per cent of the workforce but when we come to look at the study of employee relations there still appears to be a reluctance to account adequately for women's position in the employment relationship.

As Linda Dickens (1989) notes in a special issue of the *Industrial Relations Journal* devoted to feminist analysis:

> The predominant focus of industrial relations academic study, and of related disciplines, had tended to neglect the fact and nature of 'women's work', giving the impression that industrial relations academics were either gender-blind or, like industrial relations practitioners, held the view that 'if it's only women, it doesn't matter that much'.

This 'rediscovery' of women raises important questions about the understanding of women in the workforce and in particular the employment relationship. As she says:

> The question arises, then, whether this rediscovery of women as a potential valuable resource for the 1990s heralds the end of their disadvantaged position in employment. It is a 'rediscovery' of women in that women have been discovered before in times of male labour shortage, as in wartime. This observation must immediately engender some caution, given the achievements of that time.

These two extracts raise several important points for us:

■ If academic theories of industrial relations have only recently acknowledged the contribution of feminist analysis, we need to outline those that can act as a corrective to this shortcoming.

■ If women now make up nearly half the workforce, the implications of the different feminist theories will hold considerable significance for explaining how women understand their position in the employment relationship and the wider labour market.

■ The existence of a variety of feminist theories has important consequences for the selection of appropriate policies to deal with the organisation of women's work.

■ Finally, we need to be able to establish an understanding of the general nature of feminist theories to distinguish them from industrial relations theory.

■ Features of feminist theories

Feminist theory starts from the premise that if you wish to understand how women and men behave in the workplace, the analysis must commence with a description of capitalism which is informed by a discussion of the role of patriarchy. In other words, the overriding feature of modern society is the existence of a set of arrangements that have been designed by men with the effect of constantly defining women in an inferior position. Feminist theory therefore sets out to reveal the true nature of this form of domination of men over women, but in that analysis to provide policy options for overcoming the various forms of domination. Each particular variant of feminist theory will emphasise its particular explanation of this dominance and indicate the favoured path of action to help resolve it (Calas and Smirich, 1996).

Patriarchy and gender are central terms in all feminist theories. The former means an arrangement of society and its institutions to reflect men's interests, while the latter indicates that ideas of behaviour attached to biological sex are a product of socialisation and therefore change over time and reflect different political systems and cultures.

Like Marxist theory, the intention of feminist theory is not just to contribute to academic developments, but to provide understanding, which can inform policy design and implementation.

■ Feminist theory and employee relations

Although it is hard to see examples of feminist theories within traditional industrial relations, such theories have clearly come to influence research and debate in the area (Dickens, 1989). Looking through publications like the *British Journal of Industrial Relations*, it is apparent that articles devoted to women's work or by those claiming to adopt a feminist analysis are infrequent. This becomes all the more surprising when the majority of projections for job growth in the UK suggest that female employment will be favoured.

The justification for including feminist theories within a discussion of theories within employee relations appears incontrovertible.

■ Different theories, different policies

In a short section such as this it is impossible to reflect the range and subtleties of all the different theories. Our intention is therefore to outline three of the main feminist theories and establish their contribution to the understanding of the employment relationship.

Liberal feminism

'Liberal feminist' theory is probably the oldest analysis, developing out of the period of transition to modern capitalism. Its major concern was to establish that women were equal and not inferior to men. As early industrialisation saw the gulf between men and women at work expand (Cockburn, 1975), liberal feminists sought to:

- argue for equality between men and women
- create policies for reform
- reveal the 'cultural' factors that created sex stereotypes
- focus on removing barriers to advancement, e.g. more women managers.

The overall feature of this approach is to take the institutions of society as given and devise ways of improving the position of women through reform. This can take a variety of forms, such as equal opportunity policies, affirmative action plans and assertiveness training.

Essentially, from this viewpoint women as individuals can overcome inequality through the removal of barriers and prejudice through appropriate policies.

Much of the writing in HRM and other management and business practices relies upon this type of analysis, where answers exist and management can take the initiative and respond to the call for greater equality for women (Kanter, 1983).

Some argue that liberal feminism provides a simplistic account which fails to recognise the entrenched nature of inequality between men and women in modern capitalist societies. The radical feminists argue that patriarchy and gender are arrangements that are deeply embedded in our society. To pursue a reformist strategy merely reinforces existing inequalities, albeit in a different guise.

Radical feminism

For the radical feminists, like the Marxist analysis above, the structure of modern capitalist society is patriarchal and no amount of reform will change arrangements when each generation of men reinvents institutions and practices that reconfirm male power and privilege.

Radical feminism has the following core features:

- It believes that women's oppression results from comprehensive and systematic inequalities, which are elements of modern capitalist society.
- Unlike in liberal feminism, therefore, the problems women confront at the workplace, for example, are not individual nor psychological.
- Policies like equal opportunities, although they might carry the prospect of improvement for women in the workforce, do not guarantee it, because the institutions that design and implement policies are themselves integral parts of an unequal capitalist society.
- To overcome men's domination over women in both society and the workplace, fundamental change has to take place to transform unequal and hierarchical institutions, organisations and workplaces and replace these with organisations that allow women to regain their true identity.

The goal of radical feminist theory is therefore very much at odds with the 'male' world of work as it is experienced. In a period of transition to this new set of arrangements, women would pursue a policy of separateness and establish ways of organising work to include 'participatory decision-making, a system of rotating leadership, flexible and inter-active job designs, an equitable distribution of income and an interpersonal and political accountability' (Koen, quoted in Calas and Smircich, 1996). Examples of this can be seen in cases where women have established separate workplaces and avoided the influence of male working practices.

Such theories have done much to redirect our focus away from the particular and local cases of inequality at work and their persistence in the face of political pressure, policies of reform and heightened awareness. Radical feminist theory has revealed the entrenched nature of inequality and sexism in our society. Transforming this situation has been prob-lematic, however, when faced with the enormous weight of existing institutions and assumed 'normal' patterns of work and the relative values attached to the different types of work within the labour market.

Post-modernism

In an attempt to explain how inequality between men and women can be sustained through the 'meanings' attached to our day-to-day lives, the post-modern or post-struc-turalist feminist theories provide a bewildering array of explanations.

Very briefly, these theories start from the view that the very basis of knowledge upon which we guide our lives is highly problematic; that our assumptions about truth, reali-ty and objective science cannot be taken for granted. How we understand the world around us is very much a product of language, or to use their term, 'discourse'. This dis-course contains meanings that reflect assumptions and ideas about the organisation of power in a society (Legge, 1995). The impact of a particular discourse upon individuals has profound effects on how they think about themselves and, for example, how they experience the workplace.

For women this means that by their very involvement in the use of language they are drawn into a world of meanings that can reflect and justify their unequal position in the labour market. By concentrating on meanings and an individual's identity, post-modernism does appear to have important things to say about the more recent techniques used to influ-ence and shape behaviour which belong to the world of management and HRM.

As a theory for explaining women at work, post-modernism:

- rejects ideas of scientific objectivity
- suggests that how an individual behaves is a relative and contradictory process and therefore not easily inferred from conventional research
- dwells on how the subjective individual establishes meanings through engaging with language, which subsequently shape behaviour.

For example, this analysis might argue that in the area of 'skills' in the workplace, mean-ings attached to conventional definitions of skill are not the result of some neutral defini-tional process. Rather, they are the outcome of men claiming status for their skill hierarchies while attaching negative attributes to female skills. In turn, women can come to 'accept' these negative attributes which over time, it would be argued, have led to women being seg-regated into the lower levels of the labour market (Cockburn, 1983; Collinson et al., 1990).

How far such a subjectivist account of employee relations will be adopted by main-stream employee relations writers is yet to be established. Post-modernism, as we discuss in the next section, has many critics due to the features outlined above. Conventional employee relations, whether it assumes a unitary, pluralist, Marxist or systems approach, does have the luxury of sharing in a vocabulary that allows for a fairly straightforward exchange and comparison. Where the very language that we use becomes the focal point of the theoretical analysis, attempts to make comparisons become much more difficult.

■ Feminist theory and the labour market

Returning to the line of argument offered by Dickens at the beginning of this section, it is hard not to appreciate just how significant the feminist approach has become. With such fundamental inequalities still existing between men and women in the workplace (*see* Chapters 10 and 12), an analysis that accepts the statistics demonstrating this situation and provides ideas for reform and policy, appears to be addressing the problems women confront daily in their workplaces.

The sheer scale of the task as depicted in many of these accounts is therefore plain for all to see. Furthermore, those in positions of power can ascribe virtue to themselves should they choose to support one or several of these reforms as either politicians, administrators or managers. As Cockburn (1989) admits, 'Equal opportunities is widely seen as a tool of management. That has sanitised and contained the struggle for equality'. She goes on to argue for a new approach to equal opportunities that relies far more on the radical feminist approach, which sees women uniting with other groups through becoming active in a political sense and by bringing trade union power behind equal opportunity initiatives. By adopting a very different theoretical position she argues that equal opportunities can be used by women to achieve greater power and influence.

Such an illustration serves to demonstrate the variety of feminist theories in use and indicates that each has an important contribution to make when starting to challenge the conventional theories of employee relations, which continue to rely on accounts of the organisation and management of employment that depict men's work as the norm and structures and practices designed by men as neutral. In addition, it has started to address the role of women in trade unions and the problematic nature of women's representation within the official trade union bureaucracy (Heery and Kelly, 1989; Fosh and Heery, 1990).

If we adopted a feminist analysis of the BA case study it would very clearly demonstrate that women within that industry have experienced considerable inequalities compared to their male counterparts. Women hold more of the junior positions and are used by management precisely because of their gendered characteristics for caring, food preparation and dealing with emotional difficulties (Blyton and Turnbull, 1992).

Depending on which particular theory is adopted, the analyses could lead, for example, to:

1 encouraging greater representation at senior levels and assertiveness training (liberal feminist);

2 seeking to exclude men from the industry and perhaps setting up an all-female airline, which would be based on flatter organisation structures, reduced hierarchies of pay and a greater level of participation in decision making (radical feminist);

3 an analysis of the meanings and identity of being an air hostess, perhaps revealing how through prior socialisation women come to think of themselves as 'naturally inclined' to those occupations that demand service, caring and the range of tasks associated with

the traditional domestic role (post-modernism). In their training such qualities might be seen to be reinforced through the language used and the codes of practice adopted in the job (Legge, 1995).

If feminist theory has started to extend the remit of employee relations theory then so too has the development of comparative theory. In a period in which so many changes in employment and employment practices are explained by the pressures of increasing international competition, then it would be surprising not to acknowledge the contribution from comparative theories of employee relations.

COMPARATIVE THEORY

> The growing internationalisation of economic and political life is questioning the very basis of a sub-discipline whose conceptual and explanatory frameworks have been, until now, overwhelmingly national. (Clark, 1995)

As Clark argued in reviewing a series of new texts all adopting a comparative approach to this discipline, employee relations has taken longer than many other disciplines in looking to comparative research to evaluate developments in British employment.

Not only is British industry being increasingly drawn into international business but firms within Britain are competing with overseas companies with very different employment traditions. In addition, British managers, who reflected a fairly insular approach to business, are increasingly confronted with overseas practice peddled by management consultants as the latest panacea (Bean, 1992; Bamber and Lansbury, 1993). How do we come to know about these practices, whether from Japan, the US, Europe or beyond? Over the years interest in each of these countries has reflected reports based on overseas research. Some of this research could be said to come from international studies of industrial relations while some comes from truly comparative studies. The former are associated with research looking at international bodies or developments which span a whole series of countries such as multinational corporations (MNCs) or the role of the General Agreement on Tariffs and Trade (GATT), while comparative studies of industrial relations seek to analyse specific aspects of the employment relationship between two or more countries (Bean, 1992).

Like any area of comparative studies, comparing factors in one country with those of another can have a series of benefits:

■ It helps to establish the relative significance of particular factors in determining aspects of the employment relationship. For example, assessing the impact of two similar pieces of employment legislation might demonstrate other relevant factors that should be considered. For example, do relatively high labour costs in France really stimulate multinationals like Hoover to move operations to the UK?

■ It generates knowledge about overseas examples that can provide alternative forms for conducting aspects of the employment relationship. Many current management practices are brought into this country by academics and consultants using data and evidence from comparative survey work overseas; for example, the practice of quality assurance teams in Japan has been popularised in the UK. The role of the Organization for Economic Cooperation and Development (OECD) is a case in point, where comparative data is used to exhort member countries to pursue similar policy options

- By understanding the stage of development of another industrial system we can better predict the patterns of management, control and employment. Dore's (1973) study of Japanese and British factory regimes pointed to the late emergence of industrialisation in Japan as an important factor in explaining the different regimes of control in the two countries (Hyman and Ferner, 1994).

- A clearer understanding of overseas systems and practices can provide a useful resource for those involved in designing social policy or legislation in the area of employment. In the case of Britain, this occurred in 1971 when the Conservative government attempted to introduce a form of employment legislation modelled on a US statute. As it turned out, what was designed to reduce industrial conflict actually achieved the opposite effect due to the adoption of a piece of legislation designed for one industrial system and transferred to another that was quite different (Bamber and Lansbury, 1993).

- By comparing factors from one country with those of another, new explanations and theories can emerge that can contribute to the growth of the discipline of employee relations.

■ Background assumptions

Most of the work conducted under the title of comparative employee relations continues to rely upon a modest use of theory in the quest to generate descriptively interesting and informative accounts of all manner of employment practices in overseas settings. Many of the leading current texts commence with a chapter on theory and then get on with the business of covering a substantial range of countries and all their particular idiosyncrasies related to employment. This approach is quite understandable when the complexity of the issues raised by the theoretical questions start to emerge.

What follows is a very brief account of some of these difficult questions, which, though they might be played down at present because of the pressures to understand comparative data, nonetheless come back to haunt us when what we use as *bona fide* overseas data turns out to be inaccurate or inappropriate.

■ Theories of comparative employee relations

If different overseas patterns of employee relations are to be compared, then there must exist a series of assumptions about what is being compared. A number of existing theories raise some interesting questions about the context within which those systems exist.

In the 1960s, Kerr and his colleagues popularised the expression 'convergence'. In their book *Industrialism and Industrial Man*, (Kerr *et al.*, 1974) suggested that under the influence of modern technology, national systems of employee relations were being drawn together. The pressures of organising modern workplaces based upon collective bargaining ensured that requirements for education and training unleashed a whole series of related institutional pressures, which, when combined, had the effect of establishing common patterns of institutional life. These in turn led to pluralistic employee relations systems contributing to a range of democratic societal systems.

This optimistic view of Western capitalist countries was informed by the conditions of the time, where the US, in a period of global expansion, sought to see itself as a benign harbinger of modern capitalism. Nobody mentioned the fact that it was the US that so often benefited from the economic expansion by providing the inward investment and a whole series of trading opportunities. Since that period in the late 1950s, the convergence theory of economic development has gained further credibility by the pressures of globalisation and the development of powerful trading blocks supported by the increasing role of multinational corporations. Perhaps the collapse of the Soviet Union and the Eastern Bloc countries and the recent demise of Yugoslavia all provide spectacular examples of the globalising pressures from the capitalist countries. With such powerful evidence it is not difficult to see how authors like Amin and Thrift are able to conclude that we have reached a point where we now have a world economic system (Amin and Thrift, 1994). With the EU playing an ever increasing role in the labour market in the UK, it is not hard to see much of the research related to comparative studies of employee relations 'assuming' an underlying belief in convergence theories.

A different, though related theory, comes from a more critical perspective, which does owe some allegiance to the Marxist theories of economic development. *Development theories* tend to explain the changes taking place within the economic system as a series of stages that are difficult to avoid. Britain's capitalist growth was based upon a pre-capitalist stage where the formative structures of capitalism were being established. For example, early capitalism in the first half of the nineteenth century is represented by the existence of a system of elaborate rules to shape the behaviour of early workers unused to work and time discipline (Pollard, 1958; Thompson, 1968; Bendix, 1974; Landes, 1972). The Master and Servants Legislation encapsulated this 'authoritarian' period during which the 'discipline' of early capitalism was established. As different 'periods' emerge, it is argued, so the character of the entire system becomes modified and a new set of social relations is established in the workplace.

If this is correct, then trying to engage in comparative research will pose some difficult questions, such as whether the two countries being compared are at a similar 'stage' of development (*see* Figs 2.3 and 2.4). If they are not at a similar stage of development, then whether you are studying employment policies, the reasons for unemployment or the different systems for collective bargaining, it is far from comparing like with like. In turn the range of variables to isolate in the attempt to explain which are the causal variables to account for the particular factor under study becomes impossibly complex.

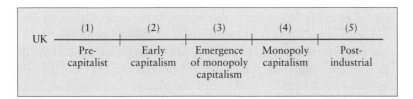

■ Fig. 2.3 Stages of development

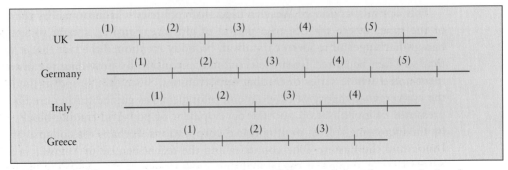

■ Fig. 2.4 Problems with comparing countries at different stages of economic development

If we wish to undertake comparative research between the UK and a variety of other countries then we might end up with the situation shown in Fig. 2.4. Conducting comparative research could well lead to the stage of economic development being the single most important distinguishing feature between the countries rather than the characteristics of a particular factor. An emphasis on 'stages of development' is therefore an important corrective to those accounts that feel able to descriptively compare the inherent features of a particular aspect of the employment relationship without acknowledging its context.

As Cronin and Schneer (1982) point out:

> It is not unreasonable to argue against comparison altogether. Comparison, after all, presupposes some degree of comparability and thus similarity, and it may well be a mistake to assume that the experience of workers at different times and places is similar. Similarities might, of course, emerge empirically, but the assumption of similarity may pre-empt the discovery of crucial differences.

This then brings us to the final theory in this section; it may underlie the majority of approaches in this area. It can be referred to as the '*internal theory*' of the comparative approach. Quite simply, the approach here is to play down the contextual/ historical factors, take the features of the employment relationship and collect data about those features in a variety of different nation states. Data verifying the existence and extent of a particular phenomenon are then compared and explained according to some internal logic. For example, problems of poor productivity comparing Polish and French workers might be explained with reference to some set of organisational arrangements or poor levels of motivation within their respective workplaces. Such an account might be the starting point for an explanation but barely moves beyond the surface of the underlying reasons to be found in the context of employment in the two countries.

In one sense this type of comparative theory can act as a first stage in the development of a more rigorous understanding, which will require the insights from the other two theories discussed above. Whatever the level of theoretical sophistication, it is clear that comparative research in the area of employee relations will continue to expand as all the pressures of internationalisation push business to become increasingly global in its design and implementation (Waters, 1995).

In that sense, as the pressures continue to build, it will become increasingly important to recognise the details of divergence to ensure that in areas of employment particular national characteristics are understood for what they are. As Shalev (1980, quoted in Bean, 1992: 8) indicates, however 'Whatever the ultimate objectives, the fact remains that a good deal of the existing work, although often rich and insightful, has not so far been explicitly theoretical in either its purpose or method.'

As the internationalisation of business grows, so the need to understand overseas systems of employment becomes more urgent. Comparative research in employment relations will inevitably expand as an area of study. However, the theoretical difficulties are substantial, and many researchers and commentators avoid confronting the difficult questions raised in this chapter and settle for descriptive accounts, which do act as a first step to understanding overseas examples but may well lead to false optimism and confidence about our level of comprehension.

For those in search of the latest theorising in the study of employment, post-modernism claims to provide a fundamental break with earlier explanations and emphasises a very different set of factors for explaining the employment relationship.

POST-MODERNISM

To conform to the structure adopted so far, we should have entitled this section 'Post-modernist theory', but unlike earlier discussions there is a wide variety of explanations within this domain which claim to represent the 'true' approach to producing a post-modernist explanation. For the study of employee relations, post-modernism has had significant implications, which are perhaps reflected for some in the change in name from industrial relations to employee relations. Before providing a brief review of some of these changes we need to clarify just what is meant by this term for this is closely related to our earlier discussions when identifying the existence of eras, epochs and stages. As other authors have pointed out, not only is post-modernism a theory about the world around us but it also acts as an account of a particular stage in its development (Legge, 1995).

Advanced capitalism, eras, epochs or change?

To argue for the existence of a post-modernist era in the case of employee relations is to argue that major transformations in the workplace and the management and experience of employment have transpired (*see* Chapter 13). This 'new' era is counterposed to the pre-existing industrial order, which was known as the 'fordist' period or just the 'modernist' era. The generic feature defining employment in this period was the existence of mass production responding to the needs of mass consumption. During this period large manufacturing enterprises employing large workforces, often highly unionised, working to set repetitive methods and producing standardised products were the norm. This period, some would argue, lasted fifty years and required great stability to ensure that the mass and scale of the activities were realised and produced the economies of scale necessary for such substantial initial investments.

As well as an account of a particular 'period', it was itself an outcome of a way of understanding and explaining the world of work, which relied on research from the experimental method based on assumptions of positivism – that is, that the world was out there to be measured and the results to be accumulated to enable those connected to the world of employment to organise work according to the criterion of efficiency and maximise the use of resources, whether inanimate or animate.

■ Contrasting 'modernist' and 'post-modernist' theories of employment

If, then, modernist theories looked at the world of work and employment and believed that a 'scientific method' was the appropriate manner for conducting research into employment, what did this mean in practice?

Perhaps the clearest exponent of the modernist theory of employment was Frederick Taylor. Growing up at the turn of the century in the US, he believed that it was quite appropriate to use the methods of the physical sciences to study work. The fact that he called his theory 'Scientific Management' indicates that he believed that it was based upon 'objective' methods of studying work. If measurement was a straightforward non-problematic procedure in the physical sciences, then it was appropriate for the study of work and employment.

As Baritz points out so clearly, at this time in the US the success of the physical sciences was such that those trying to study social phenomena, like business, management and employment, were hard pressed to resist what appeared to be 'answers' to difficult questions facing managers and industrialists (Baritz, 1960).

Taylor conducted his research on work organisation and claimed to have discovered a 'science' of work which revealed 'laws' about the nature of work organisation. He was so convinced that he had discovered these 'laws', akin to the laws of nature, he felt quite justified in suggesting that trade unions, for example, were totally unnecessary. What was the point of discussing work arrangements when he had discovered the 'one best way'? His was a quintessential statement of the modernist theory of work and employment.

That tradition of 'measuring' the details of work continues, so much of the 'positivist' tradition remains within employee relations, albeit in a much more sophisticated form. Accumulating data to obtain an 'accurate' account of employment practices, trends and developments has become a central, if not the most central, concern for the subject. This has been exaggerated over the past decade or so as research resources have become increasingly tied to the production of 'hard data'.

In contrast to this theory, post-modernist theories of work and employment have tended to concern themselves with more subjective dimensions of work. Post-modernist theory involves expressing a concern for language and symbols. This concern for understanding behaviour in the workplace requires an understanding of the creation of the subjective state of mind of that individual. This is in stark contrast to Taylor's 'external' explanation of the worker. To understand the worker, Taylor literally measured the individual with stop-watches, movie cameras and tape measures – the individual worker was a physical object to be understood in terms of her or his external behaviours and actions. The post-modernist explanation starts from a belief that to understand the external actions of individuals requires a method of research that captures the earlier stages of the process of creating meaning. An individual worker acts in a particular way as a result of a combination of ideas, beliefs and values, which are themselves produced by the language, meaning systems and symbols of the world he or she inhabits. To unravel the process by which these subjective factors come to shape the individual worker requires us to understand the language and symbols surrounding that individual.

For those adopting this position, it means studying the language used in the workplace, the culture, rituals, symbols and pattern of communication, all of which influence and shape the individual's behaviour. If these are the variables that determine behaviour, it comes as no surprise that management development and other arms of applied psychology have devoted so much energy to creating languages and techniques with the intention of achieving a role in the motivation and control of the new, subjective, individualised worker (Peters and Waterman, 1982).

This concern for the subjective individual brings us back to the opening comment about the change of name from industrial relations to employee relations. What is implied by the name change is not just a reflection of a different context of employment which includes a labour market dominated by the service sector, a reduction in trade union density, the growth of female employment, the reduction in full-time jobs and the corresponding explosion in part-time and non-standard work, but also the emphasis on individualism implied by the rhetoric of HRM. The insertion of HRM into the world of employment since the early 1980s has, in some minds, confirmed a transformation to a post-modern era and in turn supports its theoretical utility, adopting as it does a concern for culture, symbols, language and an individualised approach to accounting for worker behaviour. In other words, it depicts the worker as a subjective individual (Storey, 1992a). Table 2.1 contrasts these two theoretical approaches and emphasises the lack of 'connection' between them.

■ Table 2.1 Comparing modernism with post-modernism (after Storey)

Modernism	Post-modernism
Adopts a positivistic position:	Adopts a relativist position:
■ Objective measurement possible and necessary	■ Subjective research possible/desirable
■ Research data/knowledge universal	■ Research knowledge relative
■ General laws allow for universal laws	■ Relative nature of knowledge
Restricted use:	
■ Power located in positions of authority and capacity to control	■ Power exercised through relationships/influence and meanings
■ Employee relations knowledge attends to explaining trends and developments for producing appropriate responses	■ Employee relations knowledge to understand how cultural and linguistic variables shape individual behaviour

In the modernist approach the theory is hard at work generating useful knowledge, which in turn can be utilised for a wide range of policies and actions, whether managerial, organisational or governmental. In the case of post-modernism, knowledge is subjective and hence its application is more problematic due to the accounts being singular and not necessarily of general application. In other words, unravelling the culture and meaning systems in one particular organisation might well lead to a set of understandings that appear local to that particular organisation.

It does not require a huge leap of logic to appreciate how this depiction of the contemporary worker allows or even encourages an argument in which the function of management becomes enhanced by the perceived need to harness the potential of these 'individualised' and isolated workers. Understood in this light, the role, necessity and performance of management become central to all aspects of organisational performance. The particular form of HRM then comes to supply a set of ideas and practices that perfectly correspond to the requirements of the situation.

■ What next?

If post-modernism creates a world of workers who are seen as a relative phenomenon, where individuals are both shaped by their environment and surrounding culture and in turn define the world of work according to these meanings, it is difficult to see what overarching theory can unfold to make sense of the overall patterns of employment.

With such relativism built in to explanations of individual behaviour, we are left not knowing whether the whole post-modernist project is a further elaboration obscuring the realities of, in this case, the world of work and employment. Maybe there is no 'new' era of post-modernism, post-industrialism; perhaps there has been a failure to understand the subjective individual. Some might suggest that the post-modernist theory has certainly corrected an overconcern for a belief in a 'hard measurable' world of workers and employment, but it has overcorrected this form of positivism and now obscured the reality of work and employment, where management function and status have proliferated to the point where they have become an end in themselves, supported by new information technologies and psychological technologies of measurement all aimed at heightening the belief in individualism and hence creating further opportunities for those occupations and professions offering to integrate the mass of atomised individuals into the 'ways of their organisations' (Rose, 1989; Hollway, 1991).

Post-modernism has captured considerable interest from commentators seeking to identify trends in employment. For those in the Conservative government of the mid-1990s there was concern to establish the existence of significant changes in the employment relationship and the labour market. The existence of flexibility, deregulation of the labour market, decline in trade union membership and the growth and effectiveness of HRM can all be interpreted as evidence for policies enacted in the early 1980s. Post-modernism's concern for individualism fits neatly into this 'new' world of employment. If we note, however, that like all the other theories it is also trapped in the limitations of its own epoch, we might be left thinking that it fails to recognise many of the abiding features of the employment relationship which continue to shape the experience of work for most of the employed population.

CONCLUSION

Each new theory of employee relations can claim to correct the failure of earlier explanations but, like all accounts dealing with a complex set of variables associated with individual and collective behaviour, theories are inevitably partial and represent concerns and interests springing from the period in which they are generated. Academics, consultants and commentators involved in studying employee relations cannot escape the confines of their social context. By understanding something of these different contexts of employment, the theories that are the product of these different periods can be understood as imperfect tools that we must use to try to make sense of the complex area of employment, hence understanding something of the features of the historical context helps us to make sense of the interpretations located within it.

When Hyman (1994) discusses the issue of theory in industrial relations he recognises the impartial and incomplete nature of these theories. In his mind there are three reasons for this poor understanding and treatment by most authors in the field:

1 The existence of theory in employee relations is considered important only in as much as it signifies the level of maturity of the discipline.

2 If employee relations rests on the substantial achievements of industrial relations research, itself based on the concerns of practising managers, government policy makers and perhaps union leaders, then theory is seen as an 'intellectual sticking plaster', which somehow binds all these disparate 'facts' together.

3 Related to the point we alluded to above is the belief that theory is seen as a separate activity from concrete research – that is, it can be developed almost as a *post hoc* device to make sense of the data previously collected.

Understanding, explaining and operationalising theories and perspectives are therefore not straightforward tasks in this emergent discipline, and in this sense they cannot be considered absolute truths nor complete systems of explanation that can be regarded as failsafe. Each theory makes sense of some portion of the employment relationship; an understanding of social, political and historical contexts provides us with a set of lenses to make sense of the differing aspects of the employment relationship. With a new set of concerns emerging, including talk of social partnership, minimum wage, works councils and many other developments, the employment relationship is set to change again and those seeking to interpret these developments will no doubt draw upon the theory that accords with their priorities.

CHAPTER SUMMARY

This chapter has discussed a number of theories and frameworks which were developed at a particular historical juncture to explain the employment relationship. As the industrial relations system has changed alongside the vicissitudes of modern capitalism, these explanations have been harnessed to the interests of a number of different groups ranging from academics of different intellectual persuasions, politicians seeking to impose a particular set of arrangements on the employment relationship, and other parties such as trade unionists, employers or consultants, and no doubt many others. Each group has seen the employment relationship from their own perspective situated within the particular context of that moment in history. The resulting diversity of interpretations has created a variety of explanations for the same phenomena, a situation which should ensure debate and development of the academic area.

Over time many of these theories and frameworks are modified and altered to take account of the changing content and context of the employment relationship.

For those studying the employment relationship, an understanding of the existence of these explanations is an important prelude to achieving a degree of realism about the nature of and changes to that relationship. This variety expresses the volatile and uncertain nature of the employment relationship, where employers and employees continue to exchange work for rewards within a dynamic and unstable environment. To appreciate the existence, nature and purpose of the different forms of theories and frameworks is, therefore, to glimpse at the realities of how, on the one hand, people construct work and, on the other, experience that work.

QUESTIONS

1 Take one of the theories discussed in the chapter and explain how its 'context' helps account for its particular features.

2 Why should unitary theory have emerged towards the end of the nineteenth century?

3 Can you explain the connection between the use of systems theory in the natural sciences and in the case of employee relations?

4 What particular features and 'problems' of American society appear to explain the construction of systems theory?

5 Pluralist theory was designed to account for the new institutions of democracy. How is the task of explaining political institutions connected to the world of employee relations?

6 Outline the major flaws in the unitary, systems and pluralist theories.

7 Although a variety of positions exist within the overall project of feminism, outline what you consider to be the common themes adopted by a feminist analysis of the employment relationship.

8 If comparative theory is so useful in understanding overseas examples of employment, why should researchers be wary of the validity of the data they generate?

9 Post-modernism takes account of the 'individual' in the employment relationship. Outline some of the shortcomings of adopting this type of analysis.

EXERCISES

1 Identify a selection of newspapers, and over a few days see if you can identify one event/incident connected to employment and establish the differing interpretations reflected in each of the newspapers.

2 Design six questions that seek to explore the issue of senior management remuneration.

3 Ask interviewees about their explanations for the rapid growth in remuneration packages over the past five to ten years. Write up your results and compare the different explanations.

4 If theories are a method for organising knowledge and providing a way of making sense of employment, identify which theory you consider is most helpful for explaining the current condition of employee relations.

5 With reference to recent statements in the media, identify a current policy related to employee relations and locate the competing statements made by the different political parties and representative groups (e.g. the TUC and the CBI). Locate the different positional statements alongside the different theories of employee relations.

ACTIVITY

In the *Financial Times* of 3 March 1997, Andrew Bolger, the employment correspondent, talked about:

> the 'startling discrepancy' between the reasons that employees give for absence from work and what managers believe to be the true causes, according to the Industrial Society, the independent training and advisory body. The survey of personnel managers in 327 businesses and organisations found there was general agreement that colds and flu were the prime cause of absence ... the next most frequent reasons given in employees' certification forms were: stomach upsets, headaches, back problems and stress/personal problems. Managers however believed the reasons to be stress/personal problems; sickness of family member/childcare; low morale/boring job; Monday morning blues. The survey said: 'management may hold the key to the problems they themselves identify as causes.' Employers who accommodated working from home, flexible hours and flexible annual leave all enjoyed lower than average absence rates.

Questions

1 Take one of the theories outlined in this chapter and analyse the prevalence of absenteeism, itemising the factors it would identify as significant for explaining this phenomenon.

2 Take the unitary theory and provide an explanation of absenteeism followed by a set of policies that might naturally flow from the analysis.

3 Take each of the theories discussed in the chapter and generate a chart defining the major cause of absenteeism.

REFERENCES

Allen, J. (1992) 'Fordism in modern industry' in Allen, P. Braton, P. and Lewis, P. (eds) *Political and Economic Forms of Modernity*. Milton Keynes: Open University Press.

Amin, A. and Thrift, N. (eds) (1994) *Globalisation, Institutions and Regional Development in France*. Oxford: Oxford University Press.

Armstrong, P., Glynn, N. and Harrison, P. (1991) *Capitalism Since 1945*. Oxford: Blackwell.

Bain, G. and Clegg, S. (1974) 'Strategy for industrial relations research in Great Britain', *British Journal of Industrial Relations*, 12 (1), 91–113

 Bamber, G. and Lansbury, R. (1993) *International and Comparative Industrial Relations*. 2nd edn. London: Routledge.

Baritz, L. (1960) *The Servants of Power*. New York: Wiley.

Bassett, P. (1987) *Strike Free. New Industrial Relations in Britain*. London: Papermac.

Bean, R. (1992) *Comparative Industrial Relations: An Introduction to Cross-National Perspectives*. London: Routledge.

Beardwell, I. (ed.) (1996) *Contemporary Industrial Relations: A Critical Analysis*. Oxford: Oxford University Press.

Bendix, R. (1974) *Work and Authority in Industry*. Berkeley, CA: University of California Press.

Berger, T. and Luckman, S. (1966) *The Social Construction of Reality: A Treatise in the Sociology of Knowledge*. New York: Doubleday.

Blyton, P. and Turnbull, P. (1992) *The Dynamics of Employee Relations*. Basingstoke: Macmillan.

Braverman, H. (1974) *Labour and Monopoly Capital. The Degradation of Work in the Twentieth Century*. New York: Monthly Review Press.

Briggs, A. and Saville, J. (1967) *Essays in Labour History*. London: Papermac.

Burawoy, M. (1979) *Manufacturing Consent*. Chicago, IL: University of Chicago Press.

Burawoy, M. (1985) *The Politics of Production*. London: Verso.

Burnham, J. (1957) *The Management Revolution*. Harmondsworth: Penguin.

Calas, M. and Smircich, L. (1996) 'From the women's point of view: feminist approaches to organisation studies' in Clegg, S., Hardy, C. and Nord, W. (eds) *Handbook of Organisation Studies*. London: Sage.

Carey, A. (1980) 'Social science propaganda and democracy' in Boreham, P. and Dow, G. (eds) *Work and the Inequality*, Vol. 2. Basingstoke: Macmillan.

Clark, J. (1995) 'Is there a future for industrial relations?', *Work, Employment and Society*, 9 (3), 593–605.

Clawson, D. (1980) *Bureaucracy and the Labour Process: The Transformation of US Industry 1860–1920*. New York: Monthly Review Press.

Clegg, H. A. (1979) *The Changing System of Industrial Relations in Great Britain*. Oxford: Blackwell.

Clegg, S. (1990) *Modern Organisations: Organisation Studies in a Post-Modern World*. London: Sage.

Clegg, S. and Dunkerley, D. (1980) *Organisation, Class and Control*. London: Routledge, Kegan Paul.

Cockburn, C. (1983) *Brothers: Male Dominance and Technological Change*. London: Pluto Press.

Cockburn, C. (1989) 'Equal opportunities: the short and long agenda', *Industrial Relations Journal*, 44 (1).

Collinson, D. L., Knights, D. and Collinson, M. (1990) *Managing to Discriminate*. London: Routledge.

Cronin, J. and Schneer, J. (1982) *Social Conflict and the Political Order in Modern Britain*. London: Croon Helm.

Crouch, C. (1977) *Class Conflict and the Industrial Relations Crisis*. London: Heinemann.

Cyert, R. M. and March, J. G. (1963) *A Behavioural Theory of the Firm*. Englewood Cliffs, NJ: Prentice Hall.

Dahl, R. (1957) 'The concept of power', *Behavioural Science*, 2, 201–15.

Dickens, L. (1989) 'Editorial women – a rediscovered resource?', *Industrial Relations Journal*, 44 (1).

Dore, R. (1973) *British Factory – Japanese Factory*. London: Allen & Unwin.

Dos Passos, J. (1952) *USA*. Harmondsworth: Penguin.

Du Gray, P. (1995) *Consumption and Identity at Work*. Milton Keynes: Open University Press.

Dunlop, J. T. (1958) *The Industrial Relations System*. New York: Holt.

Dunn, S. (1990) 'Root metaphor in the old and new industrial relations', *British Journal of Industrial Relations*, 28 (1).

Eldridge, J., Cressey, P. and McInnes, J. (1991) *Industrial Sociology and Economic Crisis*. Hemel Hempstead: Harvester Wheatsheaf.

Farnham, D. and Pimlott, J. (1995) *Understanding Industrial Relations*. London: Cassell.

Fineman, S. (1993) *Emotion in Organisations*. London: Sage.

Fosh, P. and Heery, E. (eds) (1990) *Trade Unions and their Members: Studies in Union Democracy and Organisation*. London: Macmillan.

Fox, A. (1973) '*Industrial relations: a social critique of pluralist ideology*' in Child, J. (ed.) *Man and Organisation*. London: Allen and Unwin.

Friedman, A. (1977) *Industry and Labour*. Basingstoke: Macmillan.

Gospel, H. (1992) *Markets, Firms and the Management of Labour in Modern Britain*. Cambridge: Cambridge University Press.

Gospel, H. and Palmer, G. (1993) *British Industrial Relations*. 2nd edn. London: Routledge.

Gourvish, T. (1972) *Mark Huish and The London North Western Railway*. Leicester: Leicester University Press.

Halsey, A. H. (1995) *Change in British Society from 1900 to the Present Day*. Oxford: Oxford University Press.

Hayek, F. (1960) *The Constitution of Liberty*. London: Routledge, Kegan Paul.

Heery, E. & Kelly, J. (1989) 'A cracking job for a woman: a profile of women trade union officers', *Industrial Relations Journal*, 20 (3).

Hobsbawm, E. (1974) *Industry and Empire*. Harmondsworth: Pelican.

Hofstader, R. (1955) *Social Darwinism in American Thought*. University of Virginia.

Hollway, W. (1991) *Work Psychology and Organisational Behaviour: Managing the Individual at Work*. London: Sage.

Hyman, R. (1989) 'Why industrial relations?' in Hyman, R. (ed.) *The Political Economy of Industrial Relations Theory and Practice in a Cold Climate*. Basingstoke: Macmillan.

Hyman, R. (1994) 'Theory and industrial relations', *British Journal of Industrial Relations*, 32 (2).

Hyman, R. and Brough, I. (1975) *Social Values and Industrial Relations*. Oxford: Blackwell.

Hyman, R. and Ferner, A. (1994) *New Frontiers in European Industrial Relations*. Oxford: Blackwell.

Kamin, L. (1976) 'Heredity, intelligence, politics and psychology' in Block, N. and Dworkin, G. (eds) *The IQ Controversy*. New York: Quartet Books.

Kanter, R. M. (1983) *The Change Masters: Corporate Entrepreneurs at Work*. London: Allen & Unwin.

Keenoy, T. (1991) 'The roots of metaphor in the old and new industrial relations', *British Journal of Industrial Relations*, 29 (2).

Kerr, C., Dunlop, J. and Harbison, F. (1974) *Indstrialisation and Industrial Man*. Harmondsworth: Penguin.

Kuhn, T. (1970) *The Structure of Scientific Revolutions*. 2nd edn. Chicago, IL: University of Chicago Press.

Landes, D. (1972) *The Unbound Prometheus*. Cambridge: Cambridge University Press.

Laslett, P. (1971) *The World We Have Lost*. London: Methuen.

Legge, K. (1995) *Human Resource Management: Rhetorics and Realities*. London: Macmillan.

Mandel, E. (1978) *Late Capitalism*. London: Verso.

Marchington, M. and Parker, S. (1990) *Changing Patterns of Employee Relations*. Hemel Hempstead: Harvester Wheatsheaf.

McKenna, F. (1980) *The Railway Workers*. London: Faber & Faber.

Palmer, G. (1983) *British Industrial Relations*. London: Unwin Hyman.

Parsons, T. (1952) *The Social System Theory*. London: Tavistock.

Peters, T. J. and Waterman, R. H. (1982) *In Search of Excellence*. New York: Harper & Row.

Philo, G., Beharrell, P. and Hewitt, C. (eds) (1977) *One-dimensional Views: Television and the Control of Information in Trade Unions and Media*. Basingstoke: Macmillan.

Pollard, S. (1958) *The Genesis of Modern Management*. Harmondsworth: Penguin.

Roethlisberger, F. J. and Dickinson, W. J. (1939) *Management and The Worker*. Cambridge, MA: Harvard University Press.

Rose, N. (1989) *Governing the Soul:The Shaping of the Private Self*. London: Routledge.

Rowbotham, S. (1974) *Hidden from History*. Harmondsworth: Penguin.

Salamon, M. (1998) *Industrial Relations Theory and Practice*, 3rd edn. Englewood Cliffs, NJ: Prentice Hall.

Saul, G. and Wilkinson, B. (1991) '"Someone to watch over me": surveillance, discipline and the just-in-time labour process', *Sociology*, 26 (2).

Silverman, D. (1970) *The Theory of Organisation*. London: Heinemann.

Sisson, K. (1994) *Personnel Management in Britain: A Comprehensive Guide to Theory and Practice*. Oxford: Blackwell.

Storey, J. (1992a) *Management of Human Resources*. Oxford: Blackwell.

Storey, J. (1992b) *New Perspective on HRM*. London: Routledge.

Sturdy, A. (1998) *Customer Care in the Consumer Society in Organisations*. London: Macmillan.

Thompson, E. P. (1968) *The Making of the English Working Class*. Harmondsworth: Penguin.

TUC (1997) *Partners for Progress: Next Steps for the New Unionism*. London: TUC.

Undy, R. (1997) *Book review, British Journal of Industrial Relations*, 35 (1).

von Bertalanffy, L. (1950) 'The theory of open systems', *Physics and Biology Science*, III, 23–9.

Waters, M. (1995) *Globalisation*. London: Routledge.

Winchester, D. (1983) 'Industrial relations research in Britain', *British Journal of Industrial Relations*, XX, 100.

Part II
PARTIES

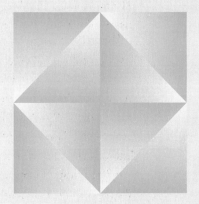

Chapter 3

MANAGEMENT

Graham Hollinshead

Learning objectives

By the end of this chapter, readers should be able to:

- appreciate the contextual influences impinging upon the nature of British management, and how management structures in the UK vary from those in some other countries;
- gain insights into who managers are, the calibre and status of British management, and current tensions in the managerial role;
- gain an overview of the structure of British industry, and key developments in organisational forms;
- understand, by using selected models and concepts, the influence of market forces on approaches to management;
- discern major styles of employee relations management, identifying and explaining preferences towards, and away from, the recognition of trade unions;
- be aware of how the emergence of human resource management and new ideas of partnership between management and trade unions are impacting upon the employment relationship.

Attempts to make organisations 'leaner' through downsizing are failing because too many companies fail to recognise that these new management trends depend on staff support for their success, according to the Institute of Personnel and Development, in a report out today. The IPD says short-sighted cost cutting may damage competitiveness in the medium to long term. 'Too many organisations are unable to differentiate "fat" from muscle' it says 'the result is that the organisation becomes anorexic rather than fit, with a workforce unable and even unwilling to make the most of new opportunities as they arise'.

Source: Financial Times, 9 June 1996.

INTRODUCTION

In the 1990s, managers have both initiated and been affected by rapid and possibly irreversible change. In the UK and beyond, the position of management appears to have been in the ascendancy relative to that of organised labour. Moreover, the interplay of factors outside enterprises at both national and international level has served to set management 'free to manage'. The era of 'Thatcherism' commencing in the late 1970s signalled a move away from familiar tripartite forms of decision making in the sphere of employment and in the broader economic domain, which had involved a process of negotiation and compromise between representatives of organised labour, employers and statutory agencies. Instead, the driving force underlying political and economic transformation in the 1980s was the conviction that a spirit of entrepreneurialism should be injected into both the private and public sectors of industry in order to promote greater market responsiveness and competitiveness. A key dynamic of change has therefore been the promotion of the position of management as an instigator of employee relations policies in conjunction with other corporate policies, as opposed to the previous emphasis on either passing responsibility to appropriate institutions outside the enterprise, or aiming for consensus among the vested interests within it.

This process has been aided and abetted by a set of either deliberately orchestrated or more coincidental developments in the wider society which have served to bolster the position of management. These would include:

- changes in the composition of industry, with diminution of the heavier manufacturing sectors in which unions have had their strongholds and growth of the less unionised and less adversarial white-collar sector;

- restrictive legislation, which has made it more difficult for unions and their members to establish autonomous organisation and to take industrial action;

- the privatisation of previously publicly owned utilities, which has catalysed the replacement of committee structures with business models of management;

- the pervasive effects of the agenda of economic deregulation and the prominence of a 'free market' ideology, which implies non-interference from government, or indeed any other external agency, into the machinations of corporate decision making.

The election of the new Labour government in May 1997 may herald greater conciliation between management and trade unions through the establishment of 'partnership arrangements', which will be discussed later, and a more positive UK position towards the EU social agenda to provide minimum employment standards and employee rights on consultation. Nevertheless, initial indications are that there will not be a sea change in the comparatively restrictive view taken by government of trade union rights and obligations, and on the emphasis placed upon allowing management to operate within deregulated and flexible labour markets.

It has been within the climate of economic deregulation that many new ideas surrounding management proliferated, and notions of 'human resource management' (HRM) emerged with considerable gusto in the US, and subsequently in the UK in the early 1980s. These are based on the premise that adept manipulation of personnel policy 'levers' by management, to include the implementation of appropriate measures on employee consultation, job design and staff procurement, development and reward, would be directly linked to competitive advantage. Organisations aspiring towards HRM would frequently aim to gain a full commitment of individuals or teams of employees to the achievement of organisational goals. The approach tends to emphasise the importance of interconnecting the policy aims of personnel management within a guiding strategic framework. The more idealistic conceptions of HRM equate high quality employees with high quality products or services, and aim to promote flexibly deployed employees within fluid and adaptable organisational structures. Desirable though the picture of the employment relationship viewed through the lens of HRM may be, it would seem at odds with the observed reality of how organisations are managed in 1990s' Britain. A Workplace Industrial Relations Survey (Millward *et al.*, 1992), for example, found in a growing number of non-unionised workplaces: fewer procedures and fewer Health and Safety representatives, fewer channels of information and consultation, less information from management and fewer personnel specialists, more dismissals, more compulsory redundancies, more labour turnover, and more low pay alongside greater dispersion of pay, that is more often performance related and market determined.

Blyton and Turnbull (1994) chart how privatisation, deregulation and ensuing competition in the world airline industry led British Airways to embark upon a programme of radical cost cutting, involving massive job losses at BA itself, while union derecognition and pay cutting occurred in subsidiary carriers. The lowering of costs took place alongside the parallel, but apparently irreconcilable, objective of improving service quality through 'culture change' programmes and the like. The climate of uncertainty and change at work has also been recognised by the mass media; a television documentary (BBC, 1995) revealed that a number of household name companies were competing on the basis of cost reduction, this involving practices such as dismissing staff and replacing them with new workers with less secure and financially inferior contracts, and senior management acquiescing with *de facto* corporate policies that allowed or even encouraged management staff to work up to 60 hours per week.

The world in which management is operating is, then, a complex and ambiguous one. Unprecedented scope exists for management to experiment with new and innovative approaches to employment management, yet many companies are locked into a spiral of cost cutting, which apparently carries with it the inevitability of management action to undermine job security and conditions of employment. Top management themselves have benefited from the liberalisation of the labour market through being the recipients (and sometimes also the donors!) of phenomenal pay increases, raising eyebrows in the spheres of public policy and ethics, while on every rung of the corporate ladder, British managers are reputed to work some of the most extensive hours in Europe. In this chapter, it is recognised that the distinctive approaches towards managing the employment relationship apparent in Britain are not only conditioned by a broader range of institutional arrangements in society, including the state and the financial system, but also that the nature and calibre of British managers themselves have determined management styles and levels of sophistication inherent in employee relations strategies. It is for this reason that the first part of the chapter considers not only the international context for British management, but also reflects upon its comparative level of maturity, and stresses its function.

THE INTERNATIONAL CONTEXT FOR BRITISH MANAGEMENT

Management does not operate in a vacuum. The social, economic and political context for managerial decision making can affect whether it is enlightened and forward looking or short-termist and pragmatic, whether there is a predisposition towards investment in staff, or minimising labour costs and regarding humans as disposable resources. In this respect, it is instructive to engage in international comparisons (keeping in mind the reservations expressed in Chapter 2), as examination of different societies leads to the discovery that the nature of management can assume varied shapes and forms, according to the structural facets of the national system in which it has been moulded.

In a comparative international study of the UK, Germany and France, Christel Lane (1994) uses the notion of 'industrial order' to demonstrate the interdependence between the structure and behaviour of firms, and the broader social and institutional patterns of the societies in which they operate. Lane argues that the major constituent elements of industrial order are present in all advanced capitalist countries, and include the following institutional complexes:

■ **Exhibit 3.1**

DMG managers get bonuses

Deutsche Morgan Grenfell, the London-based investment bank, is likely to disclose that a group of its senior managers became entitled to multi-million pound bonuses last year although the group recorded a loss in its UK subsidiary.

A number of directors are thought to have accumulated gains of several million pounds from a phantom option scheme which pays bonuses according to internal financial performance measures. Mr Michael Dobson, DMG chief executive, is believed by some executives to have become entitled to about £7.5m.

Deutsche Morgan Grenfell Group, the London company that is the main corporate vehicle for DMG, is expected to report a downturn in 1996 as a result of losses on hidden investments in its asset management arm made by Mr Peter Young.

DMG Group's accounts will include the substantial cost of building an equity broking arm from scratch. Its bond division, which is the most profitable part of its operations, is included in the accounts of Deutsche Bank.

The disclosure could ignite controversy among investment banks, and within Deutsche Bank, over the salaries and bonuses paid by DMG to recruit and retain investment bankers.

It is also potentially awkward because of the background of disruption and losses in its fund management arm. Deutsche has estimated the total cost of the Peter Young affair at DM 1.2bn (£450m) including losses and compensation.

The phantom option scheme is being included in the 1996 accounts for tax reasons. The individual gains likely to be shown include rewards for several years, some of which date back to the scheme's first year in 1990.

The bonuses will be paid out over several years and cannot be claimed immediately. DMG is thought to have taken legal advice on what it will have to disclose in the accounts, which have to be filed soon at Companies House.

Mr Dobson, who would not comment on his own gain, said the phantom option scheme rewarded 'about 200' senior Managers in DMG according to measures including return on equity, which averaged 40 per cent between 1993 and 1995.

'There may be a presentational issue for us, but there is a long-term incentive scheme that has served the bank well over several years,' he said. The accounts of Morgan Grenfell & Co, its merchant banking arm, show that a dozen employees earned more than £1m each in 1995, compared with one in 1994.

Source: John Gapper (1996) *Financial Times*, 12 May.

- **the state** – both as a direct economic rule maker, and as an institution that prominently shapes the rules of other important institutions;

- **the financial system** – linked with the system of education and training, particularly the training of industrial managers and employees;

- **the system of industrial relations** – various intermediate associations, such as trade associations, chambers, etc. which influence the ways in which firms acquire, maintain and coordinate resources.

Specific organisational forms, and the significance attached to each component, will vary from country to country, and yet the effect of the institutional complexes defined is to shape the actors' capacity for action. Lane asserts that in the UK a prominent feature is the 'arms' length' distance kept by both the state and the financial system from industry. Harking back to the imperial past, it is argued that the organisation of the City of London and other key financial institutions places demands on management for high, short-term returns on capital. Exacerbated by fear of takeover, this perpetuates a prevalence of financial values at corporate level, and a pre-eminence of accountants in the upper echelons of business. In consequence, under-investment in capital equipment, particularly technologically advanced products and processes, ensues, as well as neglect of human resources. According to Lane, many training and development decisions have been left only to the discretion of managers and needs in this area have frequently been overtaken by pressures to satisfy immediate business objectives. Concern has been expressed about the low level and quality of technical and vocational training since the 1960s.

In contrast, in Germany, closer ties have historically existed between the larger financial institutions and firms, with training and other business decisions being given a higher priority through the tripartite deliberations of the social partners (i.e. representatives of management, trade unions and state). This, according to Lane, engenders longer term perspectives, more cooperative attitudes, and a desire to compete on grounds of superior quality and service, rather than low price.

Lane goes on to assert that in the UK from the late 1970s onwards, successive Conservative governments attempted to reverse lack of national competitiveness through pursuing radical institutional change, which has involved curbing the power of unions and restructuring the system of vocational training under the more complete control of management. Far from engendering a modernised and more forward-looking institutional framework, it is argued that these changes have, counterproductively, only served to accentuate traditional short-termist approaches in the UK, and to undervalue investment in skills (Exhibit 3.2).

In seeking to establish the distinctive features of British managers within the broad international context, it is instructive to briefly reflect upon the question 'Who are the managers?'. A traditional view of management would present it as a 'bowler-hatted' occupation, constituting a privileged (mainly male) cadre, who are closely associated with the owners of business. As the following sections indicate, the current reality of management scarcely bears out the stereotypical picture. Undoubtedly a very affluent stratum of upper management continues to exist, and even grows more wealthy compared to the rest of the population. Yet recent surveys have shown that not only are middle and lower grades proliferating, but that they may be becoming detached from the ruling élites of industry, and that their lives are becoming blighted by tension and insecurity.

■ Exhibit 3.2

Weaknesses in industry highlighted ░FT░

The competitiveness of British manufacturers is being seriously weakened by their failure to organise long-term development programmes for staff and liaise properly with suppliers, a report published today says.

The study, by Ingersoll Engineers, a UK consultancy, of 325 UK-based companies also says many engineering-based processes in these businesses, involving such areas as tendering for new contracts and providing effective links between designers and production staff, are 'not performing satisfactorily'.

The overall conclusion is that manufacturers are 'running fast to stand still' in trying to gain ground on international competitors. Companies also score badly on the general business skills summed up as 'operational management'.

Ingersoll's study is based on ratings by chief executives and other senior executives of how their organisations perform in a number of business areas.

It amounts to a snapshot of how managers feel they are functioning across a swathe of important industries, including automotive, chemicals, electronics, food production, aerospace and general engineering.

Positive findings from the report are that UK companies in these sectors rank themselves highly in financial management and sales and marketing.

They have also made significant progress in reorganising production processes to tackle such areas as quality and delivery times.

Many of these gains have been made through wholesale changes to companies' corporate structures, built around refocusing management to solve customer problems and to use 'teamworking' methods on the shop floor.

However, the overall impact of these changes in raising competitiveness is patchy. 'Long-term issues such as development of the organisation, people and manufacturing technology are ... unsatisfactory,' the report says.

These failings, which spill over to such areas as market research and overall business planning, represent a 'significant weakness' in efforts by UK manufacturers to attain 'world class' status.

The failings possibly reflect 'the British preoccupation with maximising today's returns ... in contrast with the approach of many European and global competitors'.

Source: Peter Marsh (1996) *Financial Times*, 18 November.

THE STATUS AND CALIBRE OF BRITISH MANAGEMENT

■ Who are the managers?

A popular dictionary definition of an employer is 'One who employs for wages, user', while manager is defined as 'one who controls or directs'. Such definitions separate the power derived from ownership of capital to employ (or discharge) people, from the administrative and day-to-day activity of regulating the performance of those at work. Undoubtedly, in many small concerns, the proprietor still takes responsibility for running the business. Yet, beyond the small business sector, which employs only a minority of the labour force, the pattern of business ownership is complex and diffuse, this having been accentuated by the influx of foreign-owned concerns and the dispersal of share holdings for previously publicly owned concerns into the hands of institutional and private investors.

A question that arises from the separation of ownership and control in many business enterprises, and which is central to the 'managerial revolution' thesis (Burnham, 1945), is whether control of large enterprises now resides with professional managers as opposed to owners. Related to this is the issue of whether a cadre of professional managers would possess a distinct orientation and set of priorities. Gospel and Palmer (1993) are sceptical as to whether the existence of a separate nucleus of management has made any fundamental difference to business objectives. According to them, 'top managers adopt the same ideology and objectives as shareholders because they tended to come from the same background, share the same social relations and have a high proportion of their wealth in shares' (1993: 64). Farnham and Pimlott (1995), however, state that, within public limited companies, a 'professional managerial élite' has been established which is responsible for their financial profitability, corporate effectiveness and control of resources, including people. Drawing on the work of Scott (1986), they assert that the owners of large modern enterprises are other enterprises with institutional holdings such as banks, pension funds and insurance companies. According to Scott, various innovations are creating a form of management that is increasingly technical, thus creating its own professional identity, distinct from that of corporate ownership.

It is clear that in recent years, economic recessions, and a wave of corporate downsizing exercises have frequently rendered the managerial position, particularly at middle and junior levels, precarious and highly demanding in terms of work volume. This may give lie to the notion that, for many, management is experienced as an élitist occupation.

■ The managerial legacy

Within the domain of British management, those charting the history of its development have commented upon the rudimentary nature of management structures, and, at least until recently, upon low levels of technical and specialist expertise. Some have attributed this to underlying cultural aversions to managerial values. Eric Hobsbawn (1968: 154), a prominent historian, states:

> The aristocratic scale of values, which included amateur status and not apparently trying too hard among the criteria of the 'gentlemen', and inculcated them in the 'public schools' which indoctrinated the sons of the risen middle class, was indeed dominant. Being 'in trade' was indeed an awful social stigma; although 'trade' in this sense meant small scale shopkeeping much more than any activity in which any really big money, and therefore social acceptance could be gained.

Howard Gospel (1992) finds that in the first half of the twentieth century, at a time when a growing proportion of American, German and Japanese managers were receiving training in applied technical and business subjects, only a small minority of British managers were similarly qualified. 'At the higher reaches of management in large firms the "gentlemen amateur" was a common type, while at middle and lower levels the "practical man" who possessed little in the way of formal qualifications remained dominant' (1992: 48). Gospel suggests that management ineptitude at this early, but formative, stage of development served to entrench a pattern whereby managements would react opportunistically to market forces, as opposed to formulating internal corporate strategies for the management of labour. He states: 'Thus, in Britain, the nvisible hand of the market dominated labour management, and the visible handshake of closer and more lasting relations between employers and employees made only slow progress' (1992: 48).

There is evidence that professionalisation has occurred in recent years, although the legacy of late development is still that underqualified generalists predominate, and those with technical and product quality skills are poorly represented (Lane, 1994).

Furthermore, it has been argued that the British class structure continues to exert an influence on managerial hierarchies, 'pecking orders' not only being determined through principles of merit. Martin Joseph (1989), in examining the social background of senior British managers, finds that they are drawn from a narrow class base. He finds, for example, that all of the eighteen governors of the Bank of England in 1982 went either to a public school, or Oxford or Cambridge, or both, and that directors of banks, insurance companies and other financial institutions also come in higher proportions from élite educational backgrounds. The implication here is that a self-perpetuating system of élitism, in which highly paid, high status individuals can afford to direct their descendants or relatives into similar occupations, is not necessarily guaranteeing that the most able or appropriate people will rise to the top levels of industry and commerce, or that the possession of vital technical, as opposed to social, skills will be fully rewarded.

CHALLENGES FACING MANAGEMENT: SURVIVAL OF THE FITTEST?

So, the picture of British management that is emerging is one in which, compared to some of its major competitors, it is at a comparatively retarded stage of development in terms of possession of technical skills and competence in strategy formulation. A major feature of this faultline has been the apparent predisposition towards reliance on external institutions for regulating employment matters, and allowing the exigencies of product and labour markets to prevail over internalised policy formulation. Over the past few decades, it has been recognised that global and domestic market pressures are exerting an ever more potent influence not only on managerial activity, but more generally on employment security. This section considers how British managers have fared throughout a time of change and crisis (Exhibit 3.4).

Managers and professional workers now constitute a significant proportion of the UK labour force. According to the Institute for Employment Research (Wilson, 1993), this group constitutes around 30 per cent of the total labour force in the UK and it is projected that the overall pattern of growth will continue. Yet, as Hendry (1995) points out, managers have been subjected to turbulences caused by severe product market competition and globalisation of production. In the recession of the 1990s, linked with overcapacity in some industrial sectors, it was middle management that bore the brunt of rationalisation and downsizing, with the traditional pyramidal organisational structure becoming bell- or pear-shaped. The problems besetting middle managers have been exacerbated by technological advances that facilitate data capture at lower levels within organisational hierarchies, potentially rendering superfluous skills and knowledge of managers. This development is well illustrated in the banking and finance sector, where the personal judgement of branch managers on matters such as overdrafts and loans has in many cases given way to spontaneous technological responses to customer enquiries, conveyed to them automatically or by clerical staff. Privatisation of the former public sector has been particularly extensive in the UK, and it has exposed managers in newly privatised organisations to the pressures of the marketplace, and to more rigorous performance criteria. Across both public and private sectors the requirement for customer responsiveness and the assertion of customer rights are stretching conflicting managerial priorities near to breaking point within a cost reduction agenda. In the light of the previous analysis of the lagging state of British managerial sophistication compared to some of its international counterparts, and the historic preference for externalising employment decisions beyond the level of the enterprise, it is questionable whether corporate hierarchies can be sufficiently adept and versatile to respond to the array of economic, political and social uncertainties that confront them.

In a postal survey of around 1300 managers, across a range of sectors and positions, carried out in 1995, by the Institute of Management (Benbow, 1995), the personal experiences and attitudes are charted of those operating within the fallout of seismic economic events (Exhibit 3.3). Presenting an intriguing picture of the 'survivor syndrome', it was somewhat surprisingly reported that most respondents (around 72 per cent) remained on full-time, permanent contracts. However, in a climate where many managers were anxious to keep their jobs, considerable increases in workload were apparent, with 55 per cent of respondents always working in excess of the working week, and one in eight always working at weekends. A majority found work to be a source of stress, this being most pronounced in cases where individuals experienced tensions in balancing work and domestic commitments, particularly when they had young dependants. An interesting, and potentially counterproductive, change in job content was the growing obligation on those with responsibility for the management of people to spend more time monitoring the performance of subordinates, and on counselling and mentoring activities.

Fear of age discrimination was widespread, as restructuring exercises had tended to be at the expense of middle-aged and older workers (which also has implications for the longer term knowledge base of organisations) and such workers were likely to find it problematic to re-enter the labour market. More generally, around a half of the sample felt that they were not in control of their own future career development, and that traditional upward progression had been slowed. This problem was particularly pronounced in the public sector where the effects of the government policy of deregulation and injection of market forces were evident.

In conclusion, it is clear from the survey outlined, and other similar investigations (for example, Herriot, 1992) that many of the espoused principles of mutuality between organisational and individual career needs, as encapsulated in the notion of the 'psychological contract', are merely rhetorical in nature. The reality of much managerial life would seem instead to be characterised by the need for individual survival and material gain in organisational climates of change and uncertainty. Remuneration shows considerable variability according to personal performance criteria for middle and junior ranges, while many directors remained the beneficiaries of ever-polarising pay structures as well as comparative job security.

Perhaps the most alarming fact emerging from the Institute of Management Survey, however, was that the majority of the sample felt confident that they did not lack appropriate skills for survival. Given the declining scope for progression within corporate hierarchies, it is evident that the need for management to acquire transferable skills is paramount. Yet, complacency in this respect would seem to again reflect the historical predisposition towards pragmatism and possibly amateurism.

In conclusion, it may be observed that the heterogeneous group that is referred to as management has, starting from a low base in terms of relative technical competence and sophistication, at its middle and lower reaches at least experienced considerable instability in recent years, which has led to further questioning of its own identity and worth. A theme that has pervaded this chapter to this point has been the major emphasis placed on the role of market forces in the UK compared to many other countries. This has not only promoted an *ad hoc* approach to the formulation of employee relations policies, but has, relatedly, imbued much managerial consciousness itself with a sense of short-termism. We will return to these themes when we consider approaches to the management of employee relations.

■ Two facets of the new competitive world of management

■ Exhibit 3.3

The new culture shock

FT

Most senior to middle managers 'often or always' work longer than their official hours, according to a survey by the Institute of Management – 81 per cent of the 1300 that took part in the survey, Survival of the Fittest. Fifty-five per cent 'always' work extra hours; 54 per cent 'often or always' work at weekends. The institute concludes that 'longer working hours do not necessarily result in enhanced productivity. Excessive hours may reduce efficiency and effectiveness.'

There is another price to pay – at home. Personal relationships are undermined by our culture of long working days. By 1991 the UK had the highest divorce rate in Europe with more than 171 000 divorces, according to the BT Forum's report on the Cost of Communication Breakdown. Between 1961 and 1991 the proportion of people living in one-parent families increased fourfold and by 2000 the UK will have 3m children and young people in stepfamilies.

The Institute's report may provide some solutions. Although most UK managers found their work stressful, the hours long and the demands of their jobs on their personal relationships intrusive, their overriding anxiety concerned the future nature of work.

While 72 percent of managers see themselves as 'core employees', many consider themselves to be on a short-term contract or part-timers or selling their services to organisations. Also, more than 40 per cent 'do not feel in control of their future career development'.

Nearly 30 per cent said they see their future elsewhere. One in four 'thought it highly likely they would be responsible for a dispersed workforce supported by IT by the year 2000'.

The nature of our work seems to be changing profoundly. More organisations are introducing outsourcing, market-testing, interim management and teleworking, which in effect means many more of us will be selling our services on a freelance or short-term basis. And this trend is growing faster in the UK than any other industrialised country.

A contract, freelance, complementary, portfolio or self-employed culture is likely to have several consequences. More people will work from home

as sophisticated information technology helps create and support the 'virtual organisation'. The problem of who does what in the family, and the conflicts surrounding work and domestic space, will upset an already delicate work–home balance. If employers increasingly look for and recruit flexible workers, the likelihood is that women will displace men as the main breadwinner.

According to the Institute of Employment, women will take almost all jobs created between now and 2000. Women already account for half of the entrants to business schools and professions such as accountancy and law.

Andrew Garner, chairman of Boyden, the international headhunters, argues that with their experience of flexible working, job-sharing and career breaks, women are already 'match-fit' for the new workforce. Today's leaner and more flexible organisations seems to favour 'feminine values' such as co-operation, teamworking, intuition and lateral thinking.

A key issue for companies is to rebuild morale and reach a new understanding with employees. As The Economist recently observed, 'Job-sharing, sabbaticals, subsidised education, flexible hours, telecommuting, crèches, paternity as well as maternity leave – today's frills will become the ingredients of any new understanding between employees and companies.'

The challenge will be to place more emphasis on training – or as Jack Welch, chief executive of General Electric Company put it: 'We can't offer you permanent employment, but we will make you more employable.'

Other progressive companies such as Microsoft are bringing in external advisers to help employees define their career aims and provide opportunities to develop their skills.

The culture change to develop a business and operate on a self-employed basis requires help to analyse abilities, update knowledge, develop interpersonal skills, and understand time management and self-marketing.

For companies aiming to encourage employees to work from home, there are undoubted benefits. These include savings on accommodation, complying with health and safety legislation and unproduc-

■ **Exhibit 3.3 continued**

tive staff time; for the employee, there is increased flexibility, no travel time and increased productivity.

Individuals may question their need to commit to organisations that do not commit to them. At stake are also quality-of-life issues, such as workloads, hours of work, family time, control over one's career and some sense of job security. It is important for an effective and less stressful work environment that organisations think about their structures, policies and practices relating to employees and external resources.

Cary L. Cooper is professor of organisational psychology and pro vice-chancellor, University of Manchester Institute of Science and Technology. Wilf Altman is a consultant and business writer.

Source: Cary L. Cooper and Wilf Altman (1996) *Financial Times*, 11 November.

■ **Exhibit 3.4**

Bullies rife in management playground

Managerial and professional staff are more likely to be victims of workplace bullying than junior staff, according to a survey conducted for the Institute for Personnel and Development.

The survey found that one in eight employees had been bullied at work in the last five years.

However, almost 25 per cent of middle managers and 18 per cent of professionals surveyed said they had been bullied – in most cases by the head of department or the managing director.

More than half of those who experienced bullying said it was commonplace in their organisation and a quarter said the situation had worsened in the past year.

'These results confirm that bullying doesn't stop in the school playground, but is a genuine problem in the UK workplace,' said Ms Melissa Compton-Edwards, the IPD policy adviser who led the research.

'A disturbing number of senior executives are abusing their power.'

'When those at the top adopt bullying tactics, it is a green light to everyone else in the organisation to behave likewise.'

Bullying behaviour typically consisted of unfair or excessive criticism, publicly insulting the victim, ignoring their point of view and constantly changing or setting unrealistic work targets.

Other common tactics included shouting or abusive behaviour.

Actual physical violence was less commonly reported by just 8 per cent of victims.

When asked to volunteer an explanation for the bully's behaviour, most victims believed it was because the bully could not cope with their own job or was motivated by jealousy or resentment.

Many also attributed it to the bully being under pressure from a superior or under pressure to meet deadlines.

'Although a tough competitive environment doesn't create bullies, it may aggravate their behaviour,' said Ms Compton-Edwards.

The pressure felt by senior executives to meet performance targets with fewer resources could be encouraging them to bully their managers into delivering results.

'What they fail to recognise is that this kind of macho management can backfire, resulting in demoralisation, stress-related absenteeism, and high staff turnover.'

The survey of 1000 employees found that 19 per cent of those who experienced bullying said they performed less well at work as a result.

Almost a third said they lost confidence and 20 per cent became depressed.

Source: Andrew Bolger (1996) *Financial Times*, 18 November.

■ **Summary**

From a low starting point of technical and professional expertise, British management has needed to establish its worth on grounds of merit. Currently, there is evidence of the 'survivor syndrome', particularly at middle management level. Associated with this is a high level of anxiety concerning job security, intensification in work itself, and correspondingly high levels of stress, promoting a climate of 'survival of the fittest'.

THE STRUCTURING AND RESTRUCTURING OF INDUSTRY

In this section, a brief, factual overview of the major employment sectors in Britain is presented, in order to detail the scenarios in which managers find themselves. In pointing towards a backcloth of structural changes in the UK economy over recent years, the section highlights the theme of rationalisation in both the private and public sectors, reflecting a change in emphasis from supply-orientated, sometimes monopolistic, modes of production, towards the 'new imperative' of consumer responsiveness and flexible organisational form.

Employers in the UK would normally fall into one of three main categories: private businesses, public corporations and public services (Table 3.1). Private businesses employ about 19 million people, and recently there has been a trend towards amalgamation and merger. At the beginning of the twentieth century, the largest hundred firms in Britain produced 15 per cent of net output. This figure is now in excess of 50 per cent (Hannah and Kay, 1977). In the 1980s and 1990s, there has been a further wave of rationalisation in the wake of two major recessions, and the removal of protective trade barriers in the inception of the Single European Market. A further significant trend in the private sector has been the internationalisation of business and the increasing profile of multinational companies, 25 per cent of the largest private companies in Britain being foreign-owned subsidiaries. Britain has long been a favoured base for Japanese and North American enterprises wishing to gain a foothold in Europe. The completion of the Single European Market in 1992, with its potential to exclude external producers, has acted as a catalyst for further inward investment and has spurred internationalisation through cross-border alliances. As an apparent countertrend, a number of British-owned multinationals, including ICI, GKN, Turner and Newall, Glaxo, BOC, Lonrho, Beecham and RTZ, now employ more than 50 per cent of their workforce overseas.

Another notable trend has been the the restructuring of industry towards services and away from manufacturing. This has been associated with the expansion of non-manual occupation and female participation rates, so that the total labour market is now virtually equally divided between females and males. There has also been a growth in part-time working and other flexible forms of contract.

■ **Table 3.1 Types of employer**

Private businesses	Public corporations	Public services	Voluntary bodies
■ Employ over 19 million people	■ Employ around 1 million people	■ Employ around 5 million people	■ Usually small, privately owned organisations providing specialised services to their own members
■ Most common form is registered company (over 1 million)	■ Include nationalised industries such as coal and the Post Office, and public bodies including the Bank of England, British Broadcasting Corporation, Royal Mint and UK Atomic Energy Authority	■ Major public services are the National Health Service (1.2 million employees), education (1.4 million), the Civil Service (1.1 million), including government agencies, and local authority services (1.5 million), including the police	■ Include professional bodies, trade unions, employers associations, political pressure groups and worker/producer cooperatives
■ Sector comprises private and public limited companies; this status affects the number of shareholders and whether shares can be issued to the general public	■ Over 30 public corporations were privatised in the 1980s and 1990s		

Source: After Farnham and Pimlott (1995: 64).

The manufacturing sector, which had been losing capacity for some time, reached a state of collapse in the recession of the early 1980s. According to Hendry (1995), the older industries such as steel, textiles, engineering and shipbuilding suffered the most adverse effects, yet this was presented in a positive light by ministers at the time, who regarded the crisis in manufacturing as a necessary shock to British firms, encouraging them to modernise plant and work practices. Hendry states that the collapse had a number of effects:

1 It produced large-scale unemployment at well over 3 million for almost five years, with large regional imbalances.

2 In making forced redundancies and closing marginal units of production, firms greatly improved their productivity and unit cost situation in the medium term.

3 It stimulated many firms to seek greater flexibility in working practices in order to be able to operate with fewer employees.

4 It encouraged investment in labour-saving technology, including the widespread adoption of technology based on micro-electronics.

5 It led firms to more efficient ways of managing materials, including Just-In-Time (JIT) approaches.

6 It led many firms to fundamentally reassess their products and markets, turning away from low added value towards areas where they could earn higher profits. This reflected a more pervasive concern with profits.

It is within this broad picture of organisational evolution, and the apparently ever intensifying need to respond effectively to the pressures of the product market, that the modern 'M-form' or multidivisional company is providing the ideal type for private, and even public, organisations. Purcell and Ahlstrand (1994), on the basis of extensive data, state that M-form companies dominate the economies on both sides of the Atlantic and that 'at least, for the largest firms, the product division form of organisation is now the dominant form of organisation' (1994: 16). This means that the functional U-form type organisation, whose pyramidal hierarchy is the assumed norm for much personnel literature, has been superseded in many respects by this more versatile organisational form (see Table 3.2).

In essence, the M-form set-up has a three-tier structure comprising corporate office, divisions and operating plant. Divisions will normally possess freedom of operation in respect of a particular array of products, and each division will be 'self-contained' with its own executive. The corporate office possesses an extensive set of controls for monitoring and regulating divisional behaviour, and will be responsible for all aspects of business policy and planning, as well as identifying investment priorities. Divisional freedom of operation will exist so long as divisions or operating units fulfil corporate needs and expectations.

The strategic advantages of the multidivisional establishment are that product market volatility can be counteracted through switching production from site to site, and that the company itself can gain the 'upper hand' over the marketplace by determining price structures in an oligopolistic or monopolistic manner.

The ability of these organisations to gain market leadership positions also provides them with the resources to take a proactive stance in corporate strategy formulation, and to develop sophisticated human resources policies and practice. The principles of the M-form organisation are applicable to many multinational concerns, as well as to domestic multi-site operations. Furthermore, the principles of establishing semi-autonomous business units is a familiar one among the newly privatised ex-public utilities – for example, British Rail.

Public corporations employ about 1 million people. These are managed by government-appointed executives, and include nationalised industries such as coal and the Post Office, as well as public organisations such as the BBC. The policy of transferring previously nationalised industries into private ownership has meant that erstwhile monopolistic producers are now subject to the rigours of the marketplace. For privatised concerns, the government loses direct control over organisational objectives and, instead, the requirements of shareholders and and financial markets gain priority (Blyton and Turnbull, 1994).

Public services employ about 5 million people and include local government, the National Health Service and the Civil Service. Funds for these bodies are raised through National Insurance, taxation and local community charges. The monopolistic position of these organisations, too, has been challenged in recent years through their subjection to internal and external market principles. In a number of instances in the public sector, this has led to forms of organisational restructuring analogous to developments in the private sector. So, for example, an internal market has been created in the National Health Service through devolving budgets to Trusts. Under the provisions of the Local Government Act 1988 certain important local government services, such as refuse collection, street cleaning, school catering, the maintenance of grounds and vehicles, leisure

■ **Table 3.2 Organisational form and structural typologies**

S-form	H-form	U-form	M-form
■ Prevalent in the nineteenth century ■ Small, single plant, single product or product range ■ Owner-controlled, little or no hierarchy ■ Relied on subcontracting, foreman responsible for labour management control and motivation strategies based on personal, direct and close supervision	■ Often developed through merging of S-forms over time, growing into large multiplant enterprises ■ Holding companies loosely controlled and coordinated constituent plants, small HQ ■ Limited and weak management hierarchies ■ Industrial relations matters determined at plant level, consequently diversity and inconsistency within firms ■ Reliance on external support for industrial relations management, from employers' associations ■ Example: British Leyland from the 1950s	■ Growing/merging companies which became unified/centralised ■ Extensive and specialised management hierarchies, duplicated at plant level, larger HQ ■ Formulation of internal, centralised and bureaucratic industrial relations systems and styles, less reliance on employers' associations ■ Examples: (historically) ICI, Ford, Pilkington, the Post Office, British Rail	■ Prevalent in post-Second World War era ■ Multidivisional structures, establishing semi-autonomous divisions usually based on product lines ■ HQ management retains responsibility for strategic decisions and monitoring of lower-level activities, operational decisions left to divisions ■ Deliberately decentralised industrial relations, with various and diverse systems for each division ■ Common in the 1990s example: Unilever

Source: After Gospel and Palmer (1993: 67–9).

services and sports field upkeep, were forced out to tender. In education, local budgeting has been introduced, and institutions are subject to a form of competition for pupils (Hendry, 1995). The effect of encouraging competition on grounds of cost has been to undermine job security and earnings in the sectors open to subcontracting, as well as contributing to a decline in trade union organisation. Such structural changes have been accompanied by shifts in perceived status, which have tended to be at the expense of professional groups (for example, teachers and doctors). According to Keat and Abercrombie (1991), 'the interests of these professional public employees have been portrayed as being pitched against those of parents, pupils, patients and the public. Thus a transference of power has occurred from "privileged producers" to "sovereign consumers"'.

■ Summary

There have been radical changes in business structure over the past few decades, with the growth in large-scale multinational enterprises and the privatisation of the public sector being major trends.

APPROACHES TO THE MANAGEMENT OF EMPLOYEE RELATIONS

■ Introduction: the influence of product markets

In the 1990s, the increasingly competitive and volatile nature of global and national product markets is being used by governments and management teams alike as the justification for the new and radical styles of managing the employment relationship. The quest for flexible organisational responses to increasingly discriminating, demanding and empowered consumers has been particularly pronounced in the UK. Here, as we have seen, the protections of statutory regulation of the economy and employment have been progressively removed, and large sections of the public sector of industry, which previously enjoyed monopoly status, are now subject to the rigours of competition from new service providers. Within this climate, some employers have questioned the 'pluralist' articles of faith that have characterised British industrial relations for much of its history. It may be considered by managements that engaging in negotiations and compromises with the representatives of organised labour will stifle the ability of management to assert a strategy to keep competitors at bay, and to directly gain commitment from the workforce to that strategy. Moreover, the market itself may represent a central catalyst for change in employment practice as standard job definitions, or indeed hours of work, are viewed as being unnecessarily restrictive (the latter being an obvious phenomenon in the retail sector in the mid-1990s). Similarly, collectively determined and standardised pay is viewed as not sustainable in a culture that establishes individual performance as the crucial variable in formulae to determine reward. Although, in certain circumstances, it may be convenient for management to maintain a degree of detachment from the introduction of potentially unpopular policies, we shall see that, in practice, there are variations in the extent to which corporate management teams possess autonomy in defining the direction of employee relations strategy and style. As was mentioned in earlier sections of this chapter, the somewhat rudimentary structures of British management have been associated with a tendency to rely on forces and institutions external to the organisation to determine employment matters. This theme and the consequent detail of the management of employment are pursued below. The next section examines some notable theoretical contributions towards understanding the links between markets and management strategy in employee relations.

Charting the evolution of British approaches to the management of labour from a historical perspective, Gospel (1992) provides an in-depth explanation of the effects of product and labour markets on management systems. It is argued that market transactions are, by their nature, relatively impersonal and short term, but that the insecurities of the marketplace can be superseded by the establishment of firms that comprise longer-term relationships between participants, and which can allocate resources internally in an effective manner. In managing labour, depending on what is economically most advantageous, firms may opt to rely on external regulation of employment matters, they may prefer to internalise responsibility for the management of employment within their own boundaries, or they may decide to combine policies of internalisation and externalisation. The concepts of internalisation and externalisation may be applied to the three broad areas of work organisation, employment relations and management–employee relations (Table 3.3).

■ **Table 3.3   Internalisation and externalisation policies applied to three broad areas**

	External strategy	*Internal strategy*
Work organisation (the way work is organised around products and processes)	■ Reliance on subcontracting	■ Directly organising own workforce
Employment relations (recruitment arrangements, job tenure and promotion, wage and benefit arrangements)	■ Poaching or recruiting labour in the market which others have trained ■ Relying on occupationally orientated apprenticeship arrangements ■ Making extensive use of state training agencies which train in externally marketable skills ■ Reliance on external market for labour ■ Recruiting and laying off as demand changes ■ Filling higher positions with external as well as internal candidates	■ Providing own, firm-specific training ■ More systematically screening and recruiting workers ■ Aiming to make staff permanent ■ Developing job ladders and using internal promotion
Management–employee relations (systems of representation, relations with employees and trade unions, and the process of collective bargaining)	■ Fixing wages according to external market signals ■ Minimal contracts of employment ■ Relies on external employers association to deal with trade unions ■ Accepts external market criteria for the setting of wages, and the processing of grievances through external procedures	■ Fixing wages more according to internal administrative procedures than market forces ■ Developing more extensive fringe benefits, often based on seniority ■ More elaborate contracts of employment ■ Aims to promote in-company form of employee representation, e.g. works council or company union ■ Establishes internal grievance and disputes procedure, even if dealing with 'external' union

Source: After Gospel and Palmer (1993: 55–6).

As we have seen, a long-standing tradition in the UK has been for employers to rely on external regulation of employment matters. This means that, in the context of relative underdevelopment in the field of employee relations management, responsibility for many of the operational aspects of employee relations was passed to the external agencies of employers associations. Such bodies, which frequently acted on behalf of all major employers within industrial sectors, entered into negotiations with industry-level trade union organisation to establish at least minimum terms and conditions across industries. The passing of responsibility for employee relations management to external institutions was accompanied by an acceptance that the short-term interactions of both product and labour markets would set the tenor for policy making in the important areas of recruitment, reward and training. This contrasted with developments in, among other countries, Japan and Germany, where considerable proactivity has been evidenced at corporate level. This has accompanied the recognition that a longer term, and a more sustained, level of corporate and national performance could be achieved through investment in, and development of, the skills of internal staff.

In the UK since the mid-1960s, it has been possible to identify moves towards 'internalisation', which was formally signalled by the majority report of the Donovan Commission (1968) in its clear prescription that company managements could assert control over the informality of workplace behaviour through 'grasping the nettle' and initiating more finely tuned and proactive policies and procedures. This transition in management philosophy may be viewed as an important prelude to the onset of the principles of human resource management (HRM), which are discussed later. It should be noted, however, that in the 1990s, many small concerns still find their survival depends on the interplay of market forces beyond their control, and that broader trends towards subcontracting and part-time working may reflect a continuing preference in the UK for the principles of externalisation.

MARKETS AND APPROACHES TO MANAGING THE EMPLOYMENT RELATIONSHIP: INVESTORS IN PEOPLE AND COST CUTTERS?

Marchington and Parker (1990), in a valuable study of four unionised multiplant organisations in the mid-1980s, find that product markets do not exert a homogenous influence on all organisations, and that there will be degrees of difference in the extent to which companies themselves possess the autonomy and ability to devise employee relations strategies designed to enhance their own competitive advantage. According to Marchington and Parker, who themselves warn against overgeneralising from their case results, organisations that possess monopoly or near monopoly power and a pattern of demand for their products and services that is predictable and stable enjoy considerable latitude and autonomy in deciding the type of employee relations policies to be implemented. On the other hand, those organisations that are confronted by much competition, vulnerable market share and powerful, possibly co-ordinated, customers with much choice (monopsony power) may well find themselves restricted to cost minimising strategies in employee relations. If unionism exists in such concerns, it is likely that the tenor of labour relations will be adversarial. Suggesting self-perpetuating 'virtuous' and 'vicious' circles in the linkage between employee relations strategies and product markets, Marchington and Parker argue that the market leaders that opt to *invest* in their human resources are more likely to enjoy a partnership relationship with union(s), if recognised. Higher levels of collaboration between workforce and management are likely to be consistent with greater reliability of production and quality of output, which will, in turn, bolster the company's market position. In contrast, those concerns that seem constrained to take a *cost minimising/commodity* view of their workers are more likely to encounter disturbed and poor quality of production, and will inevitably continue to occupy the lower end of the market (*see* Table 3.4).

■ **Table 3.4 Types of employment relations policies**

Investment approach	*Cost-minimising approach*
■ Partnership arrangement with trade union/employee representatives	■ Adversarial relationship with union(s), non-recognition or derecognition
■ Job security	■ Job insecurity/hiring and firing
■ Longer-term policies	■ *Ad hoc*/fire fighting employee relations policies
■ More selectivity in recruitment, higher pay, investment in training	■ Casual approach to recruitment, low pay, little investment in training
■ More sophisticated/two-way communications	■ One-way communication (if any) from management
■ Application of procedures, e.g. discipline	■ Procedures not implemented, 'macho' management

Source: After Marchington and Parker (1990).

Adding a further dimension to the analysis of the influence of the market on the behaviour of employees, it is found that, in some companies, direct exposure of employees to market indicators, such as customers, flow of work through a department or other factors, may serve to prompt them to accept management-preferred prescriptions for changes in work practice. In other words, market-based information can represent an important piece of ammunition in the armoury of management as it can be used to convey a stark picture of the precariousness of jobs within a highly competitive economic environment.

In conclusion, these theories suggest that the relationship between markets and management strategy is a complex one. Together they would imply the potential existence of a 'dual economy', in which market-leading concerns are able to internalise employee relations management processes, embarking on longer-term, investment-orientated approaches, while smaller, more vulnerable enterprises live with instability and inability to control their own destiny.

MANAGEMENT STYLES: THE DIMENSIONS OF INDIVIDUALISM AND COLLECTIVISM

We can observe contrasting corporate styles towards the management of employment, which are conditioned by a plethora of factors such as the market position of the organisation, its size and sector of activity, the competence of its management, and so on. A fundamental question in the field of employee relations is, however, whether the organisation wishes to conduct its affairs by recognising one or more trade unions to represent staff, or whether, for market-based or other, more ideological, reasons, it wishes to deny the legitimacy of such modes of collective organisation.

In the UK, it appears that orientation towards collectivism has waxed and waned according to macro political and economic factors, and, notably, the climate set by the prevailing government. However, at corporate level, what is emerging is that patterns of collectivism and individualism in employment relations comprise a multilayered fabric. Thus, the non-unionised sector comprises not only the familiar Dickensian 'sweat shops', but also the 'sophisticated' US multinational concern. Even where unions are recognised, the nature and form of recognition can give greater or lesser prominence to union representatives, and there can be large pockets of non-unionism in unionised enterprises, with parallel mechanisms of communication and consultation applied directly to the workplace. In this section an attempt is made to make sense of the range of observable styles of employee relations management by introducing recognised stereotypical classifications or 'models'.

Drawing upon and elaborating on the 'unitary' and 'pluralistic' frames of reference developed by Alan Fox in 1966, Purcell and Sisson (1983) identify five ideal typical styles of managing the employment relationship. Describing style as a guiding set of principles which delineate the boundaries and direction of acceptable management action in dealing with employees which is 'firm specific, ubiquitous and continuous', the following corporate classifications are presented.

In the *traditional* organisation, labour is viewed as a factor of production, and an authoritarian, often overtly exploitative, attitude is taken towards staff, with employee subordination assumed to be part of the 'natural order' of the employment relationship. Unions are either forcefully opposed, or kept at arms length. Companies associated with this category are likely to be small and owner managed, or franchised, operating in highly competitive product markets, and placing an emphasis on cost control.

The *sophisticated human relations* or *paternalistic employer* again is likely to resist unionisation. However, in contrast to the first category, considerable time and expense is invested in engendering high levels of employee commitment to corporate goals and fostering a cooperative and entrepreneurial culture. Recruitment and training policies are finely tuned to ensure the 'right kind' of people are employed, and market rates of pay are exceeded as a disincentive for employees to combine collectively. Examples of this typology could well be large single-industry companies (frequently American owned), with high market share in growth industries. IBM, Hewlett Packard and Kodak may be fitted in this category.

The *sophisticated modern (consultative)* operation would accept the union role in specified areas of joint decision making with the purpose of encouraging employee participation and consent. A 'partnership' is forged between management and unions, and a problem solving approach characterises interaction between the parties. In common with the above category, a proactive and planned approach is taken to the management of people, with union representatives pivotal in communication processes. This style could well be adopted by large British- or Japanese-owned single-industry companies with high market share operating in process industries. ICI could fit into this category.

The *sophisticated modern (constitutional)* concern has much in common with the previous category in taking a planned and proactive approach to managing the employment relationship. However, this style places a greater emphasis on the formal regulation and institutionalisation of conflict between the parties, with strong partners negotiating codified agreements at workplace level. This 'legalistic' approach, which clearly delineates areas of managerial prerogative, is quite common in North America, with single industries using mass production, such as Ford, being associated with it. For such companies, product market conditions are likely to be highly competitive and labour costs relatively high.

The *standard modern (opportunistic)* organisation is essentially pragmatic, with the position of trade unions within the enterprise fluctuating according to their perceived power base. Where labour/product market circumstances, or perhaps employment legislation, bolsters the position of unions, negotiation and consultation are likely to occur. In more adverse circumstances, managerial prerogatives will be re-asserted. This approach is typical for conglomerate, multiproduct concerns, which allow operating units to react to local circumstances within broad parameters set by senior management. Heavy manufacturing and engineering companies are likely to provide examples of this category, such as GKN.

Although 'ideal types' present an oversimplified and caricatured view of reality, with many organisations in practice possibly straddling a number of these categories, the classifications are useful in helping us to understand why diverse employee relations climates exist in various organisational settings. Clearly, a key explanatory factor in establishing why a particular organisation decides to opt for a sophisticated approach to the management of labour is whether it can afford to invest in its employee relations policies. Thus, the product market position of many small businesses may preclude their paying above average rates of pay, while this may be an option for many larger market leaders. According to Marchington and Wilkinson (1996), organisations selling high-quality products to industrial, as opposed to domestic, consumers in a stable or growing market occupied by a small number of competitors will have greater discretion in establishing an appropriate style than those operating in highly competitive, fashion-orientated and declining markets. However, it is not only product markets that will determine the style of employee relations management an organisation will adopt. Marchington and Wilkinson state that there are four further significant sets of factors. First, the *prevalent form of technology* will be significant, with capital-intensive organisations that have phased-in new technology, and that have quite technologically independent internal operating units being most able to adopt consultative approaches. Second, the *labour market* will determine factors such as the pool of skills available and traditions of unionisation in the area. Third, *organisational characteristics* relate to the size of the enterprise, its structure in terms particularly of degree of centralisation or decentralisation, and the nature of its ownership. Finally, the *social, legal and political environment*, incorporating factors such as levels of unemployment and employment legislation, will establish the parameters for constraints upon employers and opportunities. It is argued that, together, such factors will serve to influence preferred employee relations styles of management. It is possible, too, that management may find it difficult to harness these various and complex influences, as there are areas of potential irreconcilability within them. An example would be a company that wishes to engage in high quality production, but has inadequate supplies of skilled labour available.

Central to Purcell's and Sisson's (1983) distinctions between managerial styles are the dimensions of *individualism* and *collectivism*. While individualism concerns 'policies based on the belief in the value of the individual and his or her right to advancement and fulfilment at work', collectivism, on the other hand, has been described as 'a recognition by the management of the collective interests of groups of employees within the decision making process' (Purcell and Gray, 1986: 2). In practice, this is manifested in the existence of structures for collective bargaining or participation, and concerns the degree of legitimacy management attaches to such structures.

Although constitutionalists, consultors and standard moderns would each manifest a form of collectivism, there are clearly differences between them in the degree of legitimacy attached to collective bargaining, and, indeed, the nature of the relationship between management and union representatives. As we have indicated, the 'consultor' emphasises a partnership approach with trade unions, while in other organisations the recognition of trade unions may be grudging, and an adversarial approach evident in negotiations between the parties. Equally, while 'traditionalists' and 'sophisticated paternalists' both resist trade unionism within their enterprises there would seem to be stark differences in the quality of relationships (at least at a superficial level) between management and employees. Consequently, it would be oversimplistic to argue that collectivism can be directly correlated with more benign 'investment-orientated' managements, while 'individualism' is inevitably associated with cost-cutting authoritarian employers. Considerable debate has surrounded this subject, yet it may be concluded that within both unionised and non-unionised categories, there is scope for a range of corporate profiles to exist.

In a study that highlights the strategy of M-form concerns, which, as we have previously indicated, are becoming increasing dominant players in the economic scene, Purcell and Ahlstrand (1994) cast further light upon the dynamics underlying the formulation of employee relations styles and strategies. This organisational form is regarded as an exemplar of 'internalisation', the authors stating that for the M-form conglomerate 'the invisible hand of the market is replaced by the visible hand of corporate office' (1994: 14). Within this structure, it is suggested that employee relations strategies can only be understood in the context of the business in which they operate, and that employee relations decisions are dependent upon, and derivative of, superordinate 'first order' corporate strategy. Using case study data to observe the evolution of style, and relating this study back to Purcell's previous work in this area, it is concluded that the positions of sophisticated paternalism and constitutionalism are being squeezed out by parallel trends towards cost minimisation (more associated with the traditional model) and investment (more associated with the consultative model). In other words, a dichotomy is becoming apparent between those more affluent concerns whose policies are more in tune with the 'European' consultative agenda, and that are placing an emphasis on the acquisition and development of a skilled workforce, and those preoccupied with short-term payback on investment, which are destined to operate on the basis of low cost and low skill. This perception has been reflected in the work of other authorities. Marchington (1995: 83), for example, observes that 'employee relations is becoming increasingly bifurcated, not so much between union and non-union organisations, but within each of these broad categories'.

MANAGEMENT WITH OR WITHOUT UNIONS?

There has been considerable debate in the 1980s and 1990s about the future role of trade unions, with certain commentators on the right of the political spectrum suggesting that unions are are part of the 'archaeology' of the British industrial relations landscape. Certainly the climate of the past two decades has not been favourable to trade unions, with somewhat intangible, yet commonly observed, shifts in national norms and values away from 'collectivism' and towards the assertion of individual rights and self-interest. More directly, the Thatcher government derecognised unions at GCHQ (recognition rights having been reinstated subsequently by the Labour government), taking a hard line against public sector unions, and progressively undermining trade union rights through its legislative programme. In line with free market orientated thinking, the view has been taken, supported by prominent economists (for example, Minford, 1996), that unions represent a monopoly force, artificially inflating market rates of pay, and that they should return to their former role as 'friendly societies'.

Perhaps surprisingly, in this context, it was found in the third Workplace Industrial Relations survey (Millward *et al.*, 1992: 128) that 'among workplaces with a strong union presence management support for trade unionism remained high throughout the latter part of the 1980s'. According to the survey, trade unions are still recognised by employers in about half of all workplaces employing 25 or more people, and over ten million employees work in unionised establishments. So although there has been a decline in trade union membership (this is pursued in the subsequent chapter on trade unions), the unions remain important participants in many major enterprises. Marchington and Wilkinson (1996) suggest a number of reasons for this:

1 In larger workplaces management may regard trade unions as an essential part of the communication process. Rather than deal with each employee individually, or set up direct communication systems with staff, trade unions may provide a channel that is particularly useful in respect of issues associated with pay bargaining and grievance handling. The involvement of unions may also help to legitimise decisions in the eyes of the workforce.

2 Unions can assist with providing order and stability in the workplace, especially in persuading employees of the need to use procedures in resolving industrial disputes. If all sides adhere to rules and procedures this should foster an air of compromise rather than one of aggression and retaliation.

3 It is likely that in some industrial sectors or regions the need to recognise a union will be virtually inevitable due to past traditions and current expectations. In these circumstances it may be better for management to select the union it wishes to recognise and the form of desired agreement – for example, a single-union agreement.

4 Management may not attach priority to diminishing the role of unions as a corporate objective, and indeed may not be able to achieve this even if they wanted to. Local factors may constrain management and tilt the power balance in favour of the unions – for example, a skill shortage of a particular grade of labour.

Nevertheless, in a growing number of organisations, the perceived advantages of moving towards the derecognition of trade unions have taken precedence over the above factors. It should be noted that derecognition does not always involve complete withdrawal of union rights, but rather some 'halfway houses'. So, for example, derecognition may occur for particular *grades* of staff, or in respect of a set of previously nego-tiable *issues* (Claydon, 1989). Where there are shifts towards marginalisation of unions, by narrowing the negotiable agenda, typically systems of communication will be introduced by management which bypass unions and are directly channelled towards employees. In observing this phenomenon, Marchington and Parker (1990) quote a food factory manager: 'it's pushing negotiations down to consultation and, consultation down to communication'.

The most straightforward scenario, however, is where an employer decides that it wish-es to completely terminate relations with a union or set of unions. In the UK, this has not been a widespread phenomenon, with the third Workplace Industrial Relations survey (Millward *et al.*, 1992) estimating that just 3 per cent of workplaces that recognised unions in 1984 no longer did so by 1990. Blyton and Turnbull (1998: 120) note, howev-er, that instances of 'purposeful' recognition could be growing, citing companies such as Esso, Mobil, Shell and Scottish Agricultural Industries. A much more common occur-rence, and one that represents a serious challenge for unions, is for newly establishing companies to seldom wish to enter into bargaining arrangements with trade unions.

In seeking to understand management motives for derecognition, it should be noted that initiatives in this direction have commonly been associated with changes in corporate ownership, particularly when an enterprise has been passed into overseas (notably American) hands (Beaumont and Harris, 1992). Observation of well-publi-cised cases, such as Tioxide UK or Unipart, would suggest that derecognition is not normally the result of offensiveness, but rather that unions are regarded by manage-ment as having outlived their usefulness in the wake of the onset of new HRM-inspired employment initiatives.

NON-UNION EMPLOYEE RELATIONS

There has always been a large proportion of non-unionised enterprises in the UK, where, even at the zenith of trade union membership in 1979, 45 per cent of the workforce were not trade union members.

Most studies in industrial relations have been geared, however, towards the unionised sector, and consequently, it seems, that perceptions of non-union enterprises have been over-simplified and stereotypical. What is now emerging is that a range of organisation-al typologies and strategies are evident under the banner of non-unionism, which can be more or less favourable to the position of employees within such enterprises.

What is clear is that the 1980s and early '90s provided a favourable climate for employ-ers who wished to work without trade unions. The industrial relations 'lead' established by successive Conservative governments was one that marginalised national trade union institutions from the forums of national economic decision making, diminished the posi-tion of unions in many reaches of the public sector, and undermined the organisational ability of unions through the enactment of a series of adverse statutes. As well as these direct forms of action, the receptiveness of the Thatcher governments towards the entre-preneurial spirit generated by small enterprises as the 'engine room' of the economy estab-lished a model for emulation which was essentially non-unionist, as did the enthusiastic welcome extended by government to Japanese concerns locating in the UK, which were either non-union or were placing relations with unions on a radically new footing.

At a corporate level, the union movement has been challenged by the growing influence of overseas policies and practices through multinational concerns, opening new sites in geographical areas where it may be difficult for trade unions to gain a foothold, or operating in sectors (for example 'sunrise' industries or services) that have weak traditions of collective awareness and action on the part of employees. The potent North American influence on management thinking and practice in the UK, which is most directly asserted through the operations of the many US-owned multinationals locating on British soil, has in general been detrimental to the interests of trade unions. It is instructive to note that in the US, itself approaching 85 per cent of the workforce is not unionised, and there are well-documented traditions of both hostile (sometimes violent) treatment of union organisers by employers or their agents and 'welfare capitalism', whereby companies such as IBM, Delta Airlines and Motorola have provided employees with an impressive array of terms and conditions and established direct channels of communication to management, as a strategic deterrent to trade union organisation. In the US, a growing and lucrative line of consultancy is advising employers as to how they may avoid union recognition.

From the trade unions' point of view, it has been difficult to halt the spread of non-unionism, which now applies to around two-thirds of the UK labour force, due to a general position of relative weakness. As described elsewhere in this volume, this can be attributed to factors such as structural changes in employment, an adverse economic and political climate over the 1980s and much of the 1990s, bad publicity and internal structural and policy difficulties. In some enterprises, a 'vicious circle' has been apparent, in which lack of confidence in a union, or apathy, has led to withering away of membership, which in turn has provided the opportunity for *de facto* derecognition (Claydon, 1989).

In seeking to understand the nature of non-union enterprises, it should be pointed out that non-unionism is not necessarily always total, and may take intermediate forms. Some enterprises – for example, in the finance sector – are prepared to allow internal staff associations or consultative committees, but resist what are viewed as external interferences into the business from trade union officials and institutional arrangements. In other organisations, non-unionism may exist for certain groups of staff, e.g. senior management, but not others. In examining the phenomenon of complete non-unionism, however, it should be noted that it is most prevalent in certain regions (notably the south-east) and in certain sectors of the economy (for example, in retail and hotels and catering). It is also the case that younger and smaller enterprises are more likely to be non-union (Beaumont, 1990). As suggested by the Purcell and Sisson classification of management styles, the preference for non-unionism may be shared by organisations with apparently contrasting employment management philosophies. In order to assist understanding the diversity of characteristics and approaches associated with the non-union enterprise, Guest and Hoque (1995) provide a typology of non-union enterprises. The 'good' employer is likely to be large and a product market leader. Possessing a clear strategy towards the management of its human resources, a range of personnel policies will be adopted to ensure that employee reward packages exceed market rates, that employees' behavioural and attitudinal characteristics comply with company norms and values, that levels of job security and satisfaction are high, and that effective systems exist for the sharing of information and communication. According to Marchington and Wilkinson (1996), the leading food retailers, J. Sainsbury and Safeway, may be placed in this category, having, in recent years, improved their recruitment and induction programmes, placed a greater stress on involvement and communications, and established management development programmes that emphasise open styles of supervision.

Although characterised as '*good*', these organisations, which are concerned to invest in their staff, are certainly not beyond criticism. It would seem that the enlightened approach to the management of people is conditional upon retaining a product market leadership position, and if these organisations fall upon hard economic times, the continuation of the investment orientation may be subject to question. The example of IBM would seem to illustrate poignantly the contradictions surrounding the 'good' non-union employer. Up until the early 1990s the company had provided high levels of job security, commitment to training and development, and much-heralded 'upward' systems of communication, including attitude surveys, 'speak up', and open door policies. Encountering severe competition in the early 1990s, the company was forced to abandon its plank of policies founded upon notions of job security, and to cut almost one-third of the British workforce. From the employees' point of view, although 'good' non-union organisations provide a set of benefits that may well be in excess of those offered in the more traditional unionised concern, the workforce is ultimately denied the ability to bring to bear a countervailing and independent influence on management decision making. The continuation of a relatively protected and favoured employment position for those who are prepared to identify with the 'good' ethos is dependent upon the continued ability and willingness of their employers to maintain a position of enlightened self-interest.

'*Bad*' and '*ugly*' stereotypes refer to the smaller, single-site, more traditional non-union employer. Frequently these types of organisations would be the satellite providers of the more sophisticated and well-established concerns outlined above. The insecure product market position of these firms and the high level of dependency they have on supplying a few major customers mean that they are particularly susceptible to competition on grounds of cost. In consequence, a premium is placed on flexible deployment of staff, involving high levels of job insecurity. Pay is likely to be low, and formal protection of employment rights through the application of procedures overridden by oppressive, management styles, which are highly personalised in nature, involving arbitrary forms of discrimination and favouritism (Scott *et al.*, 1989). Within such enterprises, the recognition of unions is likely to be viewed as something that will impede their ability to meet the primary goal of short-term survival. It is argued that for many of these concerns, the volatility of their product market position means that, in contrast to more sophisticated organisations, their approach to employment management is reactive and unplanned, inevitability surrounding the necessity to implement flexible practices and cut costs. 'Bad' employers are characterised as those who have little choice but to offer poor terms and conditions, while 'ugly' ones deliberately deprive workers of their rights.

'*Lucky*' organisations are likely to have poorly developed personnel policies and procedures, and pay packages are likely to be relatively low, reflecting what can be afforded by the employer in prevailing business circumstances. Operating in an opportunistic and pragmatic manner, owners or managers are unlikely to forcefully oppose trade unions, but rather disregard or ignore them as an irrelevance. The prevailing ethos will encapsulate unitary 'team spirit' values, within a paternalistic managerial style. Channels of communication between management and employees are likely to be open.

In examining non-union concerns, there are echoes of the broader bifurcation, or duality, within employment identified earlier. A distinction is apparent between those benefiting from the relatively protected employ of sophisticated market leaders and those working for smaller, dependent organisations whose employment is characterised by unfavourable terms and conditions and insecurity (*see* Table 3.5).

■ **Table 3.5 Employee relations policies in non-union concerns**

> ■ Workers in unionised companies received more information about their conditions of work than employees in non-union companies.
>
> ■ 'Financial participation' was as common in unionised as in non-unionised firms.
>
> ■ Harmonised conditions of employment were found as frequently in unionised as in non-union companies.
>
> ■ Unionised employers were more likely to collect information on the composition of their workplace and to pursue equal opportunities policies.
>
> ■ Management styles in non-union concerns were found to be more authoritarian.

Source: A summary of the *Third Workplace Industrial Relations Survey* (Millward *et al.*, 1992).

HUMAN RESOURCE MANAGEMENT AND EMPLOYEE RELATIONS

In the early to mid-1980s, considerable attention was given to the possibility of a sea change in thinking and practice surrounding the management of employment. The terminology of HRM emerged initially in the US, where the climate of entrepreneurialism engendered by the free market economic policies of the Reagan administration, paralleled by the waning union movement and compositional changes in the labour market towards the service sector, provided management with the scope for experimentation with new initiatives. The impetus to reconsider the strategic significance of employment practices derived also from the decline in US economic competitiveness relative to Far Eastern economies, and the then 'positive lesson' emerging from Japan of a correlation between the establishment of techniques to engender highly committed employees and strong economic performance. Ideas associated with HRM resonated subsequently in the UK, where an analogous set of contextual political and economic conditions set the scene for enthusiastic debate, among academics and practitioners, alike about the possibilities of reversing what appeared to be long-term economic decline by more spirited and strategic approaches to management. Debates about the definition and character of HRM have been rehearsed at some length elsewhere, but suffice it to say here that there has been considerable ambivalence and even confusion surrounding the concept. The various definitions of HRM, and prescriptions for employment practice emerging from them, betray conflicting views on the part of their advocates of the ultimate value of the 'human resource' itself. '*Soft*' versions of HRM (for example, Guest, 1987) envisage employees to be 'valued assets', which hold the key to competitive advantage. It is argued that human resources policies, which are orientated towards staff development and involvement, should be formulated in such a way that they deliver 'resourceful humans' (Morris and Burgoyne, 1973). A premium is placed on engendering high levels of employee commitment, adaptability and competence, which is in keeping with high quality production, and upon establishing direct linkages between human resource policies and broader corporate goals. '*Hard*' HRM also stresses the importance of integration between human resource activities and corporate strategy, with human resource systems being used 'to drive the strategic objectives of the organisation' (Fombrun *et al.*, 1984: 37). In contrast to softer conceptions, however, human resources are viewed as being passive and as constituting a business expense along with the other factors of production (land and capital). Although clearly benign in intention, there is doubt about the extent to which softer statements of HRM represent anything more than rhetorical gestures on the part of employers. Certainly, beyond a relatively small sample of 'exemplar' organisations, evidence to support widespread adoption of development-orientated policies on the part of employers is singularly lacking. Indeed, the results of the third Workplace Industrial Relations survey (Millward *et al.*, 1992) and comparative international data on rewards and investment in training (Smithers, 1993) would, *prima facie*, suggest a counter-trend towards the cost-cutting and skill reduction policies associated with 'hard' HRM.

The evident 'slipperyness' of the HRM concept thus makes if difficult to judge how it may be translated into a discernible management style or strategy, and how HRM approaches may impact upon trade unions. Taking 'softer' approaches at face value, a central thrust underlying such approaches is the desirability of engendering high levels of employee commitment to organisational goals by management, frequently through the implementation of a set of communications initiatives which operate directly between management and employees, *not* through the intermediary of a third party acting as a representative of the workforce. In this way, employee support can be obtained for preferred managerial courses of action. Indeed, there is survey evidence in this area (Storey, 1987) that a prominent development has been an increased flow of information from management to employees (and vice versa). This places trade union representatives in an insidious position, as some apparently long-standing goals (for example, staff consultation, improvement of terms and conditions) are being realised with active management consent, yet unions themselves may be on the margins of this process. Further, the question may be asked as to whether dual loyalty is possible on the part of employees, simultaneously to the union and the employer (Guest, 1995). On the other hand, the perhaps more realistic 'hard' approach may be more likely to directly undermine the union role through marginalisation, non-recognition or derecognition. Actual areas of policy and practice associated with (softer) conceptions of HRM would, according to Storey (1992), include:

- staff selection as an integrated and key process
- performance-related pay and single status conditions for all staff
- an emphasis on training and adaptive, growing organisations
- teamwork approaches to job design.

According to the doctrine of HRM, the implementation of these, and related areas of practice, should be custom made to satisfy the broader goal of obtaining maximum responsiveness to customer requirements, essentially by exhorting staff to work 'beyond contract'. Referring back to our distinctions between internalisation and externalisation, it is clear that policies associated with *softer* HRM broadly correlate with an internalised view of the enterprise, an emphasis being placed on those employment policies that augment the indigenous skill base, employee commitment and versatility. This in turn promotes a need for a high level of competence within managerial grades, and the location of key managerial tasks would be with well-equipped general, business or line managers. In the light of the previous analysis of the relatively immature and unsophisticated status of British management, this clearly points to a developmental need. By way of contrast, *harder* HRM may retain a reliance on the externalised interplay of market forces.

In seeking to provide understanding of company practice with regard to the interface between industrial relations and human resource management, Guest (1995) defines four potential policy options:

1 *New realism*: a high emphasis on HRM and industrial relations

This represents a joint approach from management and unions, and emphasises mutuality between the parties. Systems for union representation and direct communications between management and employees may coexist, as has been found from Storey's (1992) survey evidence. Ultimately, however, there are doubts, according to Guest, as to whether robust trade unionism can survive in the context of enthusiastic HRM.

2 *Traditional collectivism*: industrial relations without HRM

Here, traditional pluralist industrial relations arrangements are retained, with management negotiating with union representatives across a range of issues. Such a system still exists within British Coal, the privatised docks and large parts of the public sector. According to the third Workplace Industrial Relations survey (Millward *et al.*, 1992) preparedness of management to utilise traditional union channels is dwindling, although some more encouraging data was presented for unions, demonstrating a clear correlation between union recognition and greater wage equality, more disclosure of information, better, channels of communication and greater job security than in non-union concerns.

3 *Individualised HRM*: HRM without industrial relations

As indicated above, there has not been evidence of comprehensive union derecognition in the UK, with traditional bargaining arrangements being systematically supplanted by a new range of policy initiatives. North American owned concerns are most likely to promote a strongly 'HRM' non-union approach, developing policies such as independently determined, relatively high wages and benefits, sophisticated communications, single status conditions of employment, employment security related to training provision and careful screening of potential recruits (Beaumont, 1987) More generally, it would seem that changes in personnel practices (for example, in recruitment, reward and training) have not been introduced in a coherent and planned manner as would be expected if the *strategic* significance of HRM were to be taken seriously, but rather in a reactive and piecemeal fashion (Storey, 1992).

4 *The black hole*: no HRM or industrial relations

According to Guest, this is becoming a more prevalent option, as the practices of union derecognition and not recognising unions on new sites gather momentum. In non-union environments, as has been suggested above, 'traditional' styles of employment management are gaining ground, which, far from establishing strategic connections with corporate objectives, or establishing patterns for employee involvement, are characterised by pragmatic and authoritarian cost-cutting approaches, presenting their employees with bleak and insecure conditions. At best, this would represent a severe strain of 'hard' HRM.

In conclusion, it is difficult to establish coherent strategic thinking underlying the recent vogue towards HRM. In relating the various constructs of HRM to the Purcell and Sisson classifications of management styles, there are clear resonances between 'softer' conceptions of HRM and 'sophisticated' models as these each place an emphasis on investment-orientated approaches. As noted, the 'sophisticated paternalist' attempts to deter trade unionism through the implementation of a set of personnel policies that are favourable to staff, while the 'modern' aims to develop a constructive relationship with trade union 'partners' on a range of issues. Purcell and Ahlstrand (1994) have indicated that a current trend is for the 'paternalist' organisation to be superseded by the 'modern', this implying an active future role for unions with the apparent proviso that the unions themselves are prepared to engage in a 'partnership' agenda. This is likely to entail a continued review of union objectives, possibly to take on board the European and American Quality of Working Life agenda, and active collaboration with employers on 'quality' initiatives, or re-establishing aspects of the 'friendly society' role to incorporate a welfarist agenda in the union portfolio at workplace level (Lucio and Weston, 1992). On the other hand, if harsher styles of management and the 'bleak house' scenario prevail, then the organisational base of unions will be fundamentally threatened, and where unions are organised, 'hard' HRM approaches are likely to produce adversarial industrial relations (as has been the case in the public sector during restructuring, e.g. in railways, steel and coal mining). What would seem to be certain is that fashionable management doctrines, even though they gain the status of orthodoxies, retain limited 'shelf lives'. The newer moves towards process re-engineering could well have radical effects on work organisation and on existing structures of management and employment.

■ Summary

Various management styles relating to employee relations can be discerned according to factors such as the economic position of companies, their labour markets and the dominant mode of technology. It is clear, however, that 'investment' approaches towards staff and sophisticated forms of employee relations management vary within unionised and non-unionised sectors as well as between them. The recent vogue for HRM has proven to be an ambiguous concept, although application of HRM-related techniques is not necessarily at the expense of more traditional union channels and structures.

THE FUTURE: A NEW PARTNERSHIP APPROACH?

The new Labour government, which took office in May 1997, aimed to put into place a 'stakeholder society', implying a revision of the individualist values associated with the previous era of Conservatism and an intention to draw affected interest groups into aspects of decision making in all walks of national life. In the field of employment, a legislative programme including provisions to assist in trade union recognition, union representation rights for non-union employees during discipline and grievance procedures, and improved individual rights in areas such as unfair dismissal and parental leave, would create the legal framework for a new balance in the relationships between the representatives of labour and management. Optimism has been apparent in trade union circles that a change in corporate priorities could emerge at organisational level, replacing short-term decisions on investment (associated with the 'industrial order' discussed under the international context of British management earlier in this Chapter) with organic growth strategies involving employees, customers, suppliers and the local community (Monks, 1998). The case for closer working relationships between the major industrial interest group has been put forward by some prominent advocates reflecting the more favourable stance taken by the new UK government to the European 'Social partnership' model (*see* Chapter 7). The Involvement and Participation Association has anticipated greater receptiveness to the fundamental principles it has been advocating for over a century (IPA, 1995), albeit placing a new emphasis on attitudes and culture, rather than previous forms of institutionised participation or tripartite decision making (Coupar and Stevens, 1998). The Advisory, Conciliation and Arbitration Service (ACAS), in encouraging Labour Management partnerships (LMPs), has endorsed the idea that engendering high trust relations between the parties representing labour and management creates an important avenue towards corporate success (ACAS Occasional Paper 52).

In the UK, a number of companies have experimented with partnership arrangements. For example, Rover's 'New Deal' (*see* Chapter 10) has received considerable publicity. A collaborative labour relations footing has also been introduced in organisations as diverse as Blue Circle, Dwr Cymru/Welsh Water, Rhône Poulenc, Scottish Power, Royal Mail, Baxi and Granada Service, and such arrangements are persisting within organisations associated with participative arrangements over a longer period, notably the John Lewis Partnership (which is actually a non-union organisation). The essence of the partnership concept evident in the more recent initiatives is a commitment towards *job security* for employees by the organisation, in return for employee agreement to *work more flexibly*, frequently in response to customer requirements, by staff. At Welsh Water, for example, major components of the deal struck between the company and its trade unions have included:

- single status conditions for staff and a unified pay structure with pay determination through a mutually acceptable pay formula;

- the establishment of a single table representative council with particular projects delegated to 'issue groups';

- changed working time, involving a reduction in working time with a re-organisation of the working year into a form which is more responsive to customer needs;

- productivity enhancements through flexibility between work groups, skill enhancements, and delegation of responsibilities previously carried out by supervisors; and

- a 'no compulsory redundancy' agreement (Thomas and Wallis, 1998).

It can be seen from the elements of the agreement that partnerships not only concern the *substance* of the employment relationship, particularly in the fields of pay, deployment and staffing, and job security, but also the *mode of interaction* between the parties. This purports to emphasise collaboration and trust building rather than 'old style' adversarial methods. Using terminology originally developed by Walton and McKersie (1965) the partnership approach is based on an *integrative* bargaining ideology, characterised by information sharing between the parties so that a joint and factually grounded approach is taken towards matters such as pay determination. It is implicit that union representatives (and members) are involved in the corporate machinations surrounding the resolution of employment issues. In contrast, the *distributive* model, which has been used to represent more traditional approaches to bargaining, is characterised by conflict and low trust relationships between the parties in dividing fixed sums.

From the managerial point of view, it is clear that partnership can assist the achievement of overriding corporate objectives, perhaps most notably gaining staff acquiescence to changing conditions of employment in order to promote customer responsiveness. Nevertheless, it is likely to be incumbent upon management to display openness and to be prepared to adopt a participative style. From the perspective of employees, there are ostensibly solid benefits associated with partnership, including the elusive prize of employment security as well as greater predictability in the determination of pay, and possible enhancement in the design of work (Thomas and Wallis, 1998). Trade unions are likely to be presented with some ambiguity as a result of the onset of partnership arrangements. On the one hand, it may be that unions will benefit from moving away from the adversarial postures they are widely believed to have adopted in the past which will enable them to engage with management agendas in a more constructive fashion, thus winning the endorsement of employers and increased support from members and the public. On the other hand, some commentators, for example, Claydon (1998), think that partnership may represent another 'union Trojan horse'. He cites trade unionists and academics who 'remain sceptical the possibility of genuine partnership on a broad scale and/or who question the desirability of partnership on the grounds that it will render unions less rather than more able to defend and advance workers' interests'. A simplified view of Claydon's argument asserts that unions run the risk of being disenfranchised through the process of being incorporated into management forums for decision making, and by being presented with an agenda for discourse which has been primarily determined by management. Thus the sacrifice from the union perspective is the time-honoured and proven ability to forcefully oppose management decisions in areas which are most unpalatable to their membership. Returning to the theoretical perspectives discussed in Chapter 2, it may be asserted that the practice of partnership in the 1990s implies a forfeiting of pluralistic principles in the direction of mutual, yet ultimately unitary, approaches towards the formulation of corporate employment policies. At Welsh Water it is instructive to note that, despite the involvement of trade unions, the stated benefits to the organisation are closely aligned with the HRM paradigm discussed earlier, implying, at face value, a limited shifting of managerial ground. The stated benefits (Thomas and Wallis, 1998) include:

- Flexible working arrangements which allow customers to contact the company at their convenience. This has occurred by means of the establishment of a 24-hour call centre.

- Improved quality of service, achieved by training work teams and 'empowering' them to take quality initiatives in the running of water and sewerage treatment plants.

- Cost reductions, created by savings in staffing which have been passed on to the consumer.

- Organisational change (which is now, importantly, agreed by employees) necessitating redeployment of labour and working with contractors and temporary staff.

In seeking to evaluate the development of partnership at corporate level, we should conclude first that, at the end of the 1990s there is little evidence that this form of arrangement, although practised by some high profile 'exemplars', is widely established across the landscape of the British economy. Indeed, it may be argued that the ability to offer job security as part of a broader package of change measures is scarcely a viable option beyond those organisations which possess the resources to engage in a higher degree of strategic thinking in employee relations than is the norm, and to invest in their employment policies. It should also be noted that a number of the organisations entering partnership arrangements did so at a time of organisational turbulence, sometimes involving staff cuts. In the light of such adverse circumstances for the inception of the arrangement, observers may interpret the coming together of the parties as manifesting strong elements of convenience as well as choice. Trade union involvement in the process of rationalisation and restructuring is not only a legal requirement if redundancies are involved, but can also be of assistance in gaining the commitment of survivors to the management of subsequent change. If the reasons for entering into partnership are primarily pragmatic, in keeping with the 'standard modern' model mentioned above, one may question the durability of such arrangements into the longer term.

As mentioned at the outset of this chapter, the management of employee relations occurs within a broader economic, social and political framework. In the UK, the new Labour government has signalled an intention to introduce further basic protection for individual employees, and for trade unions and their members. Nevertheless, it is clear that there will be no attempt to dismantle wholesale the employment edifice established under the previous Conservative era. This emphasises the prevalence of market forces and deregulation of the processes by which terms and conditions of employment are arrived at, in aiming to attract investment from overseas and create a climate for entrepreneurialism. In reality, the concept of partnership fits uneasily with the low skill base, low pay and insecure conditions still found in many workplaces which is a concomitant of such macro-level policies. Whether the 'virtuous circle' of investment in staff leading to high quality output and economic competivenesss can be accomplished in the UK could hinge to a considerable extent on whether the stated intentions of government and some employers concerning the management of employment turn out to be real or rhetorical.

CHAPTER SUMMARY

This chapter has demonstrated that British managers do not operate 'in a vacuum' but are powerfully conditioned not only by the political, social and economic environment in which they operate, but also by historical influences upon their evolution. There has been a tendency in the past for non-professionalised managers to abrogate responsibility for employee relations matters, and to place considerable reliance on the external interplay of product and labour market factors to settle employment conditions. It is only in more recent years that more serious attempts have been made to internalise strategic decision making in this area, and the recent vogue towards HRM may be viewed as a manifestation of this. Currently, two powerful and possibly contradictory trends are apparent in approaches towards employee relations management. On the one hand, larger, market leading concerns are adopting 'investment'-orientated styles, possibly entering into new partnerships with union representatives. On the other, harder, short-termist, cost-cutting approaches are being taken by organisations in more vulnerable market positions. Britain's future role in Europe may hold the key to which approach becomes prevalent.

QUESTIONS

1 What effect is signing the Social Chapter likely to have upon British approaches to managing employee relations?

2 How would you view managerial competency in employment relations? How would you improve it?

3 Why are (i) the growth of multinationals and (ii) the privatisation of major parts of the (previously) public sector important influences on employee relations in the UK?

4 How does a company's market position affect its employment relations policies?

5 What variations exist in types of non-union concern, and how do their employment relations 'climates' vary?

6 How does HRM affect the preparedness of employers to deal with trade unions?

EXERCISE

Carry out a PEST (political, economic, social and technical factors) analysis of changes in the context for employment relations in the UK. Locate major styles of employment relations management within this context.

REFERENCES

Advisory Conciliation and Arbritration Service (undated) *Time for a Change, Forging Labour–Management Partnerships*, Occasional Paper No. 52.

Beaumont, P. (1987) *The Decline of Union Organisation*. London: Croom Helm.

Beaumont, P. (1990) *Change in Industrial Relations: The Organisation and its Environment*. London: Routledge.

Beaumont, P. B. and Harris, R. I. D. (1992) 'Double-breasted recognition arrangements in Britain', *The International Journal of HRM*, 3 (2) 267–83.

Benbow, N. (1995) *Survival of the Fittest, A Survey of Managers' Experiences of, and Attitudes to, Work in the Post Recession Economy*. London: Institute of Management.

Blyton, P. and Turnbull, P. (1998) *The Dynamics of Employee Relations*. 2nd edn. Basingstoke: Macmillan, pp. 73–6.

BBC (1995) *Working All Hours – Uncertain Times* (television programme), BBC2, 23 September.

Burnham, J. (1945) *The Managerial Revolution*, Harmondsworth: Penguin.

Claydon, T. (1989) 'Trade union derecognition in Britain in the 1980s', *British Journal of Industrial Relations*, 27 (2).

Claydon, T. (1998) 'Problematising partnership: the prospects for a co-operative bargaining agenda', in Sparrow, P. R. and Marchington, M. *Human Resources Management: The New Agenda*. London: Financial Times Pitman Publishing, p. 181.

Coupar, W. and Stevens, B. (1998) 'Towards a new model of industrial partnership: beyond the "HRM versus industrial relations" argument', in Sparrow, P. R. and Marchington, M. *Human Resource Management: The New Agenda*. London: Financial Times Pitman Publishing, p. 143.

Donovan Commission (1968) *Report of the Royal Commission on Trade Unions and Employers Organisations 1965–68*. Cmnd 3623. London: HMSO.

Farnham, D. and Pimlott, J. (1995) *Understanding Industrial Relations*. London: Cassell.

Fombrun, C., Tichy, N. M. and Devanna, M. A. (eds) (1984) *Strategic Human Resource Management*, New York: Wiley, p. 37.

Fox, A. (1966) *Industrial Sociology and Industrial Relations*, research paper 3, Royal Commission on Trade Unions and Employers Associations, Cmnd 3623. London: HMSO.

Gospel, H. (1992) *Markets, Firms and the Management of Labour in Modern Britain*. Cambridge: Cambridge University Press.

Gospel, H. F. and Palmer, G. (1993) *British Industrial Relations*. 2nd edn. London: Routledge.

Guest, D. (1987) 'Human resource management and industrial relations', *Journal of Management Studies*, 24 (5), 503–21.

Guest, D. (1993) 'Current perspectives on HRM in the UK' in Brewster, C. (ed.) *Current Trends in HRM in Europe*. London: Kogan Page.

Guest, D. (1995) 'Trade unions and industrial relations', in Storey, J. (ed.) *Human Resource Management: A Critical Text*. London: Routledge, pp. 119–37.

Guest, D. and Hoque, K. (1995) 'The good, the bad and the ugly – employment relations in non-union workplaces', *Human Resource Management Journal*, 5 (1), 1–14.

Hannah, L. and Kay, J. (1977) *The Concentration of Modern Industry*, Basingstoke: Macmillan.

Hendry, C. (1995) *Human Resource Management: A Strategic Approach to Employment*. Oxford: Butterworth Heinemann.

Herriot, P. (1992) *The Career Management Challenge: Balancing Organisational and Individual Needs*. London: Sage.

Hobsbawm, E. J. (1968) *Industry and Empire*, London: Weidenfeld and Nicolson.

Involvement and Participation Association (1995) *Towards Industrial Partnership: Putting it into Practice – Rhône Poulenc Staveley Chemicals: A case study in moving to single status*. London: Industrial Participation Association.

Joseph, M. (1989) *Sociology for Business: A Practical Approach*. Cambridge: Polity Press, pp. 42–3.

Keat, R. and Abercrombie, N. (eds) (1991) *Enterprise Culture*. London: Routledge.

Lane, C. (1994) 'Industrial order and the transformation of industrial Britain, Germany and France compared' in Hyman, R. and Ferner, A. (eds) *New Frontiers in European Industrial Relations*. Oxford: Blackwell, pp. 168–90.

Lucio, M. M. and Weston, S. (1992) 'Human resource management and trade union responses: bringing the politics of the workplace back into the debate' in Blyton, P. and Turnbull, P. (eds) *Reassessing Human Resource Management*. London: Sage.

Marchington, M. (1995) 'Employee relations' in Tyson, S. (ed.) *Strategic Prospects for HRM*. London: Institute for Personnel and Development.

Marchington, M. and Parker, P. (1990) *Changing Patterns of Employee Relations*. Hemel Hempstead: Harvester Wheatsheaf.

Marchington, M. and Wilkinson, A. (1996) *Core Personnel and Development*. London: Institute for Personnel and Development.

Millward, N., Stevens, M., Smart, D., and Hawes, W. (1992) *Workplace Industrial Relations in Transition*, the ED/ESRC/PSI/ACAS survey. Aldershot: Dartmouth.

Minford, P. (1996) *Analysis* (radio programme), BBC Radio 4, 13 December.

Monks, J. (1998) 'Trade unions, enterprise and the future', in Sparrow, P. R. and Marchington, M. *Human Resource Management: The New Agenda*. London: Financial Times Pitman Publishing, p. 173.

Morris, J. and Burgoyne, J. G. (1973) *Developing Resourceful Managers*. London: Institute of Personnel Management.

Purcell, J. (1987) 'Mapping management styles in employee relations', *Journal of Management Studies*, 24 (5), 235.

Purcell, J. and Ahlstrand, B. (1994) *Human Resource Management in the Multi-Divisional Company*, Oxford: Oxford University Press.

Purcell, J. and Gray, A. (1986) 'Corporate personnel departments and the management of industrial relations: two case studies in the management of ambiguity', *Journal of Management Studies*, 23 (2).

Purcell, J. and Sisson, K. (1983) 'Strategies and practice in the management of industrial relations, in Bain, G. S. (ed.) *Industrial Relations in Britain*. Oxford: Blackwell.

Scott, J. (1986) *Capitalist Property and Financial Power*. Brighton: Wheatsheaf.

Scott, M., Roberts, L., Holroyd, G. and Sawbridge, D. (1989) *Management and Industrial Relations in Small Firms*, Department of Employment research paper no. 70. London: HMSO, p. 42.

Smithers, A. (1993) *All our Futures – Britain's Educational Revolution* (television programme), Channel 4.

Storey, J. (1987) *Developments in the Management of Human Resources. an Interim Report*, Warwick Papers in Industrial Relations, 17, IRRU, School of Industrial and Business Studies, University of Warwick, November, p. 6.

Storey, J. (1992) *Developments in the Management of Human Resources*. Oxford: Blackwell.

Thomas, C. and Wallis, B. (1998) 'Dwr Cymru/Welsh Water: a case study in partnership', in Sparrow, P. R. and Marchington, M. *Human Resource Management: The New Agenda*. London: Financial Times Pitman Publishing, p. 163–69.

Turner, L. (1991) *Democracy at Work: Changing World Markets and the Future of Labor Unions*. Ithaca, NY: Cornell University Press.

Walton, R. and McKersie, R. (1965) *A Behavioral Theory of Labor Negotiations*. New York: McGraw Hill.

Wilson, R. A. (1993) *Review of the Economy and Employment 1992/3: Occupational Assessment*. University of Warwick: Institute for Employment Research.

FURTHER READING

Gospel, H. (1992) *Markets, Firms and the Management of Labour in Modern Britain*. Cambridge: Cambridge University Press.

Legge, K. (1998) *Human Resource Management; Rhetorics and Realities*. Basingstoke: Macmillan.

Purcell, J. and Ahlstrand, B. (1994) *Human Resource Management in the Multidivisional Company*. Oxford: Oxford University Press.

Chapter 4

MULTINATIONALS AND EMPLOYEE RELATIONS

Mike Leat and Jill Woolley

Learning objectives

By the end of this chapter, readers should be able to:

- understand the development of modern multinationals (MNCs) and the scale of their activity;

- distinguish and compare different models of the MNC;

- discuss the main criticisms of MNCs ;

- explain the employee relations difficulties and implications that MNCs may have to deal with as a result of operating in different countries and cultures;

- understand how MNCs may encourage change within national systems;

- identify common features of MNC employee relations policies and practices;

- understand the need for and role of international organisations in checking the power of MNCs and the difficulties of enforcement;

- analyse the ability of trade unions at national and international level to respond to MNCs;

- examine the potential of the European Works Council to encourage the development of MNC-wide collective bargaining.

The agreement to establish two sites for the South Korean electronics manufacturer LG, described in Exhibit 4.1, was greeted by British government ministers as further vindication of their policies in deregulating the labour market, for the purpose of attracting foreign inward investment and creating jobs in areas of high unemployment. The intention was that LG would eventually employ around 8000 people in their new South Wales production facilities. The South Korean industrial combine ('*chaebol*') expressed its satisfaction in establishing a significant foothold in Europe.

■ Exhibit 4.1

EU is the lure for Koreans in regions

The decision by LG Group, the industrial combine, to build a £1.5bn electronics complex in Wales will double South Korean industrial investments in the UK to more than US$4bn.

It will also confirm that the UK is the favoured investment destination in the EU among Korean companies, surpassing such challengers as Germany and Spain.

The UK's popularity has gained momentum since 1994 when Samsung Electronics, the electronics affiliate of the Samsung chaebol, or industrial grouping, decided to build a £450m consumer electronics plant at Wynward Park, in north-east England. It opened last year.

'The Samsung decision was the turning point that encouraged other Korean companies to invest in the UK,' said a UK official in Seoul.

At least 13 other investment projects in the UK have been announced by Korean companies since March 1995, including component suppliers to Samsung.

There are over 100 Korean companies altogether – financial and trading companies as well as manufacturers – and some 15 000 Korean residents.

Although Korean companies have preferred England or Northern Ireland, the past year has seen a Korean expansion into Wales and Scotland for the first time. The Halla group, a smaller chaebol, plans to build fork lift trucks and other heavy equipment in Wales, while Shinho Tech, an electronics maker, recently announced a computer monitor factory in Scotland.

More Korean investments appear to be on the way. Daewoo is considering a joint venture semiconductor plant with Texas Instruments in Northern Ireland, where Daewoo already manufactures consumer electronics.

The sudden move by Korean companies into the UK reflects their need to escape increasingly high wage costs in South Korea. Its companies also want to establish a manufacturing base in the EU to avoid possible trade barriers. Mr Daniel O'Brien, managing director of Samsung Electronics' UK manufacturing operations, says: 'The most important attraction is access to the European marketplace.'

Government grants play a big – often decisive – role in domestic competition among British regions. According to a House of Commons trade and industry committee report into regional policy last year, 50 per cent of manufacturing jobs created by inward investors in the 10 years to 1992 went to Scotland, Wales and England's northern region. But these regions, all large aid recipients, accounted for only 18 per cent of existing manufacturing jobs.

The £200m aid for LG is the equivalent of nearly £30 000 a job.

This would seem to set a new record for a large project outside Northern Ireland. Siemens, the German electronics group, received under Pounds 20 000 for the semiconductor plant it is building in the north-east.

Government officials say the grants to LG, covering funds for training and site preparation as well as direct grants, do not breach UK Treasury guidelines. They also deny that LG encouraged any kind of auction between competing regions.

However, since details of the negotiations are confidential, the scale of the award is bound to attract close attention, not least from those regions which lost out to Wales.

Source: John Burton and Stefan Wagstyl (1996) *Financial Times*, 10 July.

At the same time as the agreement was being concluded, South Korea was itself experiencing a series of strikes and riots by its unionised labour force. These were aimed at the government, which had pushed through changes to the existing regulatory legislation in secret, in the middle of the night and without giving opposition members of parliament the opportunity to oppose the proposals. The main thrust of these changes was to deregulate the labour market, reduce employee protection and thereby facilitate a reduction in labour costs.

LG is one of a long line of Multinational Corporations (MNCs) that have established operations in the UK. At first the MNCs were mostly American, followed by the Europeans and the Japanese. As can be seen from Exhibit 4.1, some 100 Korean companies had established operations in the UK by the beginning of 1997. Towards the end of 1997 these plans were thrown into confusion by the financial crisis in South Korea, which encompassed a significant decline in the value of the currency, a number of major bankruptcies and a general review of the scale and direction of multinational activity. It seemed inevitable that there would, at the least, be delay to the implementation of the plans referred to in Exhibit 4.1. There were fears in South Wales that the Korean-based crisis might result in a scaling down of the proposals and that the company might be encouraged to locate more production at home. These developments and concerns illustrate some of the particular risks associated with attracting investment by MNCs for they may abort or close down projects in particular countries for reasons largely unrelated to the success of the endeavour itself.

The proposals to establish the LG factories in South Wales on new 'greenfield' sites also point up a number of the many issues and questions regarding the nature of the employment relationship, working conditions and the management of employee relations within MNCs. These questions and issues are quite likely to arise irrespective of the location of the investment and country of origin of the MNC and we return to some of them at various points within the chapter. Examples of issues and questions are:

- Will the managers and key workers be South Korean, British or some other nationality?
- Will the company adopt and import specifically South Korean or more universal management practices, or seek to adapt their management of employee relations to the traditions, customs and practice of the host country?
- What will be the company's attitude towards recognition of trade unions and the establishment of collective bargaining?
- How and where will pay and other working conditions be determined – within the units in Wales or at some other and higher level of the organisation?
- Is there a distinctive South Korean management approach to employee relations that can be identified in the same way as a stereotypical American or Japanese approach?
- How vulnerable are the operations in the UK country to the results and activities of the company elsewhere?

INTRODUCTION

Given that there are over 1000 MNCs in the UK and that nearly 50 per cent of the working population is employed by them, it is important to acknowledge MNCs as an important influence on empoyee relations.

This chapter falls into two main parts, the first of which is concerned primarily with establishing the scale of international trade and the significance of the MNC, some of the characteristics and stages of development of the modern MNC, including the reasons why companies become MNCs, and some of the more influential models or typologies. We also in this first part identify national culture as an important contextual influence and identify some of the more common benefits claimed for, and criticisms made of, MNCs.

In the second part of the chapter the relationship between the MNC and employee relations is examined further, and in particular a number of main themes, including the relevance of national contextual differences the activities and organisation of MNCs' employee relations policies and practices, and the impact that MNCs can have upon employee relations within national systems. In particular, the phenomenon of 'Japanisation' is discussed, the attitudes of MNCs towards trade unions and the trade union response, the role played by some of the supranational regulatory organisations in seeking to influence the employee relations policies and practices, and the role of the MNC in the internationalisation of employee relations, including an assessment of the likely impact of the European Works Council (EWC) Directive.

WHAT IS A MULTINATIONAL COMPANY?

Many terms are used to refer to MNCs including global, transnational, and international. Some observers have sought to assign specific meanings to each of these and to distinguish between them. Some of these definitions and distinctions are considered later. In this chapter the term multinational issued generically.

At this stage it is necessary to try to define the MNC, or at least to distinguish it from other organisations that trade internationally, but which do not fall into this category.

The simplest of definitions, is that MNCs are enterprises that *in more than one country own or control production or service facilities and activities that add value*. It is the dimension of ownership and control of value adding activity that sets the MNC apart from the organisation that simply trades internationally.

The distinction between organisations that trade internationally and those that fall within the definition of a MNC is demonstrated by Wilkins (1970), who suggests that it is possible to identify four typical stages in the development of American MNCs:

1 The US concern sold items abroad through independent agents or, on occasion, filled orders directly from abroad.

2 The company appointed a salaried export manager and/or acquired an existing export agency and its contacts. This stage might also involve the appointment of independent agencies in foreign countries to represent the company. The foreign agent would sell on its own account or handle shipments on consignment.

3 The company either installed one or more salaried representatives, a sales branch or a distribution subsidiary abroad, or it purchased a formerly independent agent located in a foreign country. At this point, for the first time, the company made a foreign investment; *it is only at this point that the company becomes an MNC.*

4 A finishing, assembly or manufacturing plant might be built abroad to fill the needs of a foreign market.

This element of ownership or control tends to bring with it the challenge of managing human resources and employee relations in different national contexts and poses for the organisation's management problems associated with international human resource management.

MULTINATIONALS AND THE INTERNATIONALISATION OF BUSINESS

Recent decades have witnessed a significant internationalisation of business and an explosion in the number of companies operating as MNCs. Economies are becoming more financially interdependent, and, as Hodgetts and Luthans (1994) assert, this interdependence is not unidirectional, from developed to underdeveloped. Industrialised economies are investing in those that are developing, but the developing economies are also investing in those that are already more advanced.

There are a number of different dimensions and components to this internationalisation of business:

- a significant expansion of international trade;
- the development of more global product markets;
- the extension of free trade agreements and the initiation of more free trade areas, such as the North American Free Trade Agreement (NAFTA);
- an expansion in the number of joint ventures, cross-national acquisitions and mergers and foreign direct investment (FDI), such as that described in Exhibit 4.1.

This globalisation or internationalisation of business has been significantly enabled by the development and use of new technologies, particularly in the arena of information transfer and communications.

Also the increase in the size and extent of free trade agreements incorporating the free movement of capital inevitably facilitates cross-border investment of all kinds.

Ietto-Gillies (1997) suggests that 80 per cent of world trade and all FDI is attributable to MNCs. FDI can take a number of forms, the most significant being the total or partial acquisition of existing operations in other countries, which may themselves already be operating as MNCs, or the establishment of a completely new operation in another country, commonly referred to as investment of a greenfield nature, such as that referred to in Exhibit 4.1.

THE SCALE OF MNCs AND FDI

We have already noted the estimate that some 80 per cent of world trade is attributable to MNCs, of which there are approximately 37 000 with over 206 000 foreign subsidiaries (United Nations Conference on Trade and Development (UNCTAD), 1994).

The top 200 MNCs control approximately one-third of global production. Griffiths and Wall (1996) point out that some MNCs have annual turnovers that exceed the Gross Domestic Product (GDP) of the majority of countries. According to their estimates, only 14 countries had a GDP that exceeded the annual turnover of companies such as General Motors, Ford and Exxon. Hodgetts and Luthans (1997) list the 25 largest MNCs by sales in 1994 and these three companies were fifth, seventh and eighth, respectively. The top four and the sixth corporations (by sales) were all Japanese in origin: Mitsubishi, Mitsui, Itochu, Sumitomo and Marubeni. All of these corporations had sales running in excess of

$101 000 million. The largest European corporation in these terms was Royal Dutch/ Shell, which was tenth in the list with sales figures of nearly $95 000 million.

About one-third of the world's private sector productive assets are owned by MNCs (UNCTAD, 1994).

■ The UK

Traditionally, UK companies have invested more overseas than any other country except the USA, although in the period 1989–94 Japanese outward investment increased substantially. In terms of the world totals of outward FDI in this period, Japan's share was 13 per cent compared to the USA at 19 per cent, France at 12 per cent, the UK at 11 per cent and Germany at 10 per cent. These figures also demonstrate the extent to which the source of outward FDI is concentrated. The Organisation for Economic Cooperation and Development (OECD) Financial Market Trends (1997) indicates that UK outflows for the year 1996 were $43.7 billion, putting it second behind the USA and confirming that the UK is a net investor abroad: outflows exceed inflows.

Eurostat figures for 1997 show that the UK was still a net investor abroad, investing a total of £35.1 billion compared to received investment of £21 billion.

As a home for FDI the UK has by far the largest stock of the world total when compared with any other EU country. In 1994 the total stock in the UK stood at $214 billion, whereas the figures for France and Germany were $142 billion and $132 billion, respectively (United Nations World Investment Report, 1995).

The OECD (1997) asserts that in recent years the UK has been the single greatest recipient of foreign direct investment into the EU. The figures for 1996 show that the UK's share of inward FDI into the EU was in the region of 40 per cent and this amounted to $32.8 billion. This was more than double the inflow into France, which was the next most popular destination. These figures place the UK as the second most popular destination in the world behind the USA. For the period 1991–5 the UK total was $81 billion, putting it third behind the USA and China over the same period.

The Eurostat figures for 1997 also confirm these trends and again show the UK to be the recipient of more FDI than any other EU member state, and in particular the most popular EU source for investment from outside the EU.

Barrell and Pain (1997) refer to IMF data suggesting that in the period 1991–5 the yearly average FDI inflows into the UK were $17.2 billion, slightly higher than the OECD figures quoted above.

In August 1998, Dunn and Bradstreet produced evidence that 23 300 plus companies in the UK were at least partially owned by non-UK interests, approximately one third of them were off-shoots of US organisations and, from within the EU, Dutch, German and French organisations also have substantial ownership involvment. Griffiths and Wall (1996) suggested that multinationals account for some 30 per cent of UK GDP.

These figures for FDI inflow into the UK, which show the UK as a major home for such investment and which indicate that within the EU the UK is *the* major destination, were used by UK governments in the early 1990s as evidence of the wisdom of their 1980s policies to reduce the power and influence of the trade union movement and deregulate labour markets, thereby providing inward investors with the prospect of a compliant and flexible labour force. It is probable that these factors were an influence in some of the investment and locational decisions made, but they were by no means the only or even the major ones. As the next section demonstrates, many factors contribute to such decisions.

REASONS FOR INVESTING ABROAD, BECOMING MNCs AND LOCATIONAL DETERMINANTS

Ghertman and Allen (1984) do not cover the full range of forms of overseas investment (for example, the acquisition of a share in an existing company), but they suggest the following reasons why companies decide to establish their own manufacturing or extraction units in foreign countries:

1 In certain industries there are production limits in any one factory. These may be due to the perishability of the product or, for example, its weight and the transportation costs involved. Examples would be in industries such as the production of milk derivatives or liquid gas. It is not advisable to build huge factories in these industries, since the economies of scale in production are not sufficient to offset higher transport or wastage costs. It is far better to set up new factories in the countries where the customers are based. In contrast, in other industries like chemicals or steelmaking, it is possible to make such economies of scale that a large production unit in a single country is justified on the grounds of profitability.

2 Local governments often prefer to have the MNCs invest in their countries rather than export to them. There are benefits in terms of local employment and an outflow of foreign currency can be avoided, resulting in a better trade balance for the host country.

3 Within MNCs, local managements obviously prefer the parent company to set up a manufacturing plant in the host country because this makes the subsidiary more important within the group and at the same time facilitates relations with the host country.

4 Production in only one country leaves the company open to risks of war, nationalisation or confiscation, or vulnerable to increases in duties or the establishment of import quotas or fluctuations in rates of exchange. Similarly, strikes in a single factory could halt sales to several countries at the same time.

Barrell and Pain (1997) take a somewhat different approach and have suggested that cross-border production activity takes place for a number of reasons:

■ Market size.

■ Cost differentials: relatively low production costs (incorporating the impact of real exchange rates) are an incentive.

■ The role played by knowledge-based firm-specific assets. This term refers to assets such as managerial or marketing skills or reputation (including such factors as brand images) and/or process or product innovations that are firm-specific and may be patented. Barrell and Pain suggest that such assets give economies of scale at the level of the firm rather than at the level of the plant and this may enable single-firm multiplant operations (some overseas) to have a cost advantage over the alternative of two single-plant firms. They also suggest that innovating companies, in possession of patents, are more likely to invest overseas themselves than to license others in foreign markets to provide the product or service.

■ To improve market access and bypass trade barriers such as those that surround the EU. There are potentially great advantages to the organisation if it sets up a production or service facility within such a free trade area since it gives access to the whole of the new market and avoids the tariffs and other barriers that confront products and services from outside.

In the specific EU context, Barrell and Pain argue that the fact that the UK is a net outward investor within Europe and elsewhere casts doubt upon the supposed attractiveness of low labour costs and deregulated labour markets. They suggest that once an organisation has decided to invest within the EU in order to obtain the benefits referred to above, then the decisions regarding the precise location of the investment within the EU are influenced by national or regional variables such as:

- corporate tax burdens;
- the skills and training, the quality of the labour force;
- the quality of the infrastructure;
- language and cultural factors;
- the cost of labour: the more high-tech the operation, the less do labour costs play a significant part in the investment and location decision.

Individual national regimes and infrastructure are therefore relevant at this stage.

DIFFERENT TYPES, FORMS AND APPROACHES

We mentioned earlier that there are a number of different definitions and interpretations of what constitutes a MNC and that different terms are sometimes used. We adopted the term MNC as the generic and a relatively simple definition, but it is important to be aware of at least two of the most prominent typologies of forms of MNC and their approaches to the conduct of multinational activity and the attendant responsibilities. These are the models of Perlmutter (1969) and Bartlett and Ghoshal (1989).

Perlmutter's typology

Perlmutter (1969) classified a variety of attitudes towards management of increasingly globalised companies, or, in his words, the 'tortuous evolution of the multi-national corporation'. He describes four major approaches to the management of overseas subsidiaries.

Ethnocentric

The values, culture and strategic decisions are determined by the outlook of the parent company, which gives very little power or autonomy to the overseas subsidiaries. Subsidiaries are largely managed and controlled by expatriates or former headquarters (HQ) staff and locals have very little input into the way things are carried out in their own country. Lines of communication are often one way as directives are issued by HQ. The host country subsidiary has a tactical rather than strategic role to play and is dominated by the concerns and culture of the parent company. It is often suggested that this commonly represents the first stage in the development of the MNC and that only after time has elapsed will management at the centre be prepared to move in an alternative direction. Many Japanese and American companies have been accused over the years of trying to introduce employee relations policies and practices that may work at home but that are inconsistent with the traditions of the UK. This approach is sometimes characterised as a belief at the centre of the organisation that the ways of the home country are not only the best but also the only way of proceeding.

Polycentric

Each overseas subsidiary is regarded as an autonomous business unit, controlled and managed by local managers. Key decisions, financial investment and overall strategic goals are still maintained by HQ and, generally speaking, at this stage, the key HQ positions are still held by people from the parent company. It is assumed that local managers are most likely to have an understanding of marketing, production and human resource management (HRM) strategies and, indeed, of the requirements of the local regulatory regime. Subsidiaries are therefore allowed a larger measure of autonomy, although there is likely to be strong financial control by the parent company. This approach is much more likely to facilitate the maintenance of policies and practices in the field of employee relations that are consistent with the culture and regulatory regime of the host country. This is discussed further in the following sections.

Regiocentric

Control of both staff and decisions are carried out on a regional or geographical basis, but key, top positions are still held by nationals of the parent company's country. Regional managers, however, have greater discretionary powers and autonomy, but are constrained by the boundaries of the region in which they operate.

Geocentric

These companies can be described as having the best of all worlds and deploying a mix of both home country and parent company managers in overseas subsidiaries. The exchange of ideas, values, information and working methods is seen as a key activity.

In the last two instances the approach to employee relations is likely to be less conditioned by a particular national culture or regulatory regime, either of the home country or of the host country. National regulatory regimes still have to be complied with where plants and other activities are located, but in such companies one would also expect the development of regional or worldwide approaches, policies and practices.

There have been suggestions that the Perlmutter typology – and, indeed, the following Bartlett and Ghoshal model – can be perceived as stages in the development and maturation of the MNC. However, it is a mistake to take too rigid an approach to the interpretation of these models. As Hendry (1994) says:

a normally regiocentric or geocentric organisation may adopt an ethnocentric approach on occasion if, for example, it establishes itself in a new country that, for the moment, does not have appropriate skills. More generally, regional units may take on an ethnocentric stance within their own territory.

Edwards *et al.* (1996) make a similar point in reporting that the stereotypes depicted in the model may be useful as indicators of different approaches and tendencies but should not be regarded as exclusive. In their research they found that MNCs exhibited various of these characteristics simultaneously.

■ The Bartlett and Ghoshal typology

Bartlett and Ghoshal (1989) categorised MNCs into four main types, each type being determined by how far it had developed over time.

Multinational

They tend to build a strong local presence in each of the countries in which they invest, and therefore tend towards being decentralised, with local autonomy and little strategic direction from HQ. Spivey and Thomas (1990) described them as essentially decentralised federations in which overseas operations are regarded as a portfolio of largely independent, nationally orientated businesses. They have sometimes been characterised as 'multidomestics'.

Global

These companies have a more centralised and global approach to markets and in such firms the HQ would adopt a strong role in determining policy for each of the subsidiaries. Levitt (1983) described conditions whereby markets were crossing boundaries and becoming more like one another as different nationalities developed similar consumer tastes, which contributes to the global perception of markets. As Hendry (1994) argues, these firms require a high degree of integration and need to be managed from a corporate centre.

Porter (1985) described the way in which such 'global' companies could extract economies of scale and scope from worldwide activities and exploit national factor differences. Ford of Europe is said to have typified this kind of operation.

International

This form of MNC has a more federal structure; the centre co-ordinates rather than imposes or instructs. The suggestion is that as markets become more sophisticated and diffuse, companies depart from the notion that competitive market advantage can be derived by having standardised products and thereby achieving significant economies of scale. These are firms that need to have a high degree of flexibility. Hendry (1994) quotes the different kinds of washing powder (often claimed to be a uniform product) sold in different countries on account of a variance of views held as how best to wash clothes. Different nationalities have different preferences for temperatures and speeds. The variance in pharmaceutical preferences is another example of this trend away from standardisation.

Firms gain competitive advantage not by producing more goods at a cheaper rate, but by being able to apply their knowledge and skills gained worldwide to local circumstances. Such firms can quite easily move resources such as cash into different markets. Hendry (1994) describes their actions as mobilising people, resources of skill and knowledge, on an international scale.

Transnational

This type of company is in a sense a response to the difficulties that the previous three forms all have in dealing with the increasing complexities of global markets. The stereotypical transnational exhibits more flexible structures than the traditional hierarchy, responsibility is devolved to lower levels and to national teams, knowledge is shared and co-ordination is achieved through the sharing of values, cooperation and teamwork. These are organisations able to respond to the forces of globalisation, local differentiation and worldwide innovation in technologies and products. Innovation, together with the ability to harness it, is perceived as the primary source of competitive advantage and innovation is spread throughout the company. To Bartlett and Ghoshal (1989) this means:

> developing simultaneously the characteristics associated with the MNC, the global firm and the international company – that is, responsiveness to local conditions, efficiency and the ability to handle continuous innovation and learning. Competitive advantage will come from sensing needs in one market, responding with capabilities perhaps developed in a second and diffusing any resulting innovations to markets and facilities around the globe.

They further accept that the 'transnational' company exists more in conceptual form than in actuality and suggest that the transnational represents a new management mentality. Flexibility is a key to managing such forms, and Bartlett and Ghoshal observe that managers seemed to understand very clearly the nature of the strategic challenge but that they had greater difficulty developing and managing the organisational capability to implement the new and more complex global strategies.

ABB (Asea Brown Boveri) is claimed to be one of the very few examples of a transnational company. As Edwards *et al.* (1996) state the characteristics supposedly include horizontal networking through *ad hoc* task groups, which then transfer knowledge among the decentralised operating units, each of which enjoys considerable financial autonomy.

The difficulties of finding companies that conform with the transnational stereotype encouraged Edwards *et al.* to distinguish more simply between nationally (includes the Bartlett and Ghoshal multinational) and globally orientated approaches. The research upon which they report, which covered 101 MNCs, 58 UK-owned, led them to conclude that while there is evidence of globalism it seems that it tends to be more evident in respect of some aspects of the firm's organisation and activity than in others, and that examples of organisations in which globalism pervades relatively rare. The aspects of the firms where globalism was most common included: the global movement of managers, handing profits over to global headquarters, computerised communications and giving board members global responsibility for a particular function.

One of the implications of this is that we should not be surprised to find firms that operate in a broadly geocentric and transnational manner with respect to some aspects of their activity but nevertheless operate in an essentially polycentric manner when it comes to dealing with employee relations matters, thereby demonstrating their flexibility and responsiveness to local circumstance, tradition and culture.

MNCS AND NATIONAL CULTURES

In much the same way as each of these stereotypes or approaches can be seen to imply perceptions of the differentiated local or coherent global nature of markets, so also do they have implications for the way in which differences in national cultures are dealt with within the organisation.

As noted earlier, the ethnocentric is an approach that is also consistent with the belief that 'our way is the only way', and many MNCs have been criticised over the years for operating in a manner consistent with this belief, whereby they seek to impose parent company and country practices in countries in which they may be alien. It is an approach that takes little, if any, notice of local cultures in matters of staffing or employee relations and it may well be that the organisation lays claim to an organisational culture that is reflective of the home country and universal throughout the company. Hewlett Packard has been an example of such an approach; the 'HP Way' was promulgated throughout the company worldwide but was itself reflective of the culture of southern California and the attitudes and beliefs of the two founders of the company.

Where product design, marketing and production are matched closely to different national and cultural preferences, the attitudes of management would be depicted as shifting from ethnocentricity towards polycentricity. In these circumstances, where production is often transferred to the relevant region or country, local managers, sensitive to local tastes and local work practices, are commonly employed.

There are two main schools of thought, according to Schulten, regarding the extent to which MNCs have a polycentric attitude. Maurice *et al.* (1980), in what is known as the 'Aix-en-Provence' school of organisational theory, posited that 'every organisation is embedded in a specific "national culture" and set of "social institutions" ... which have a systematic influence on a foreign owned subsidiary's organisational practices'.

This was known as the 'societal effect theory'. It became very popular in the 1970s and 1980s and sought to explain both the absence of a universal convergence of organisation structures and a continuing existence of national diversity. This position is supported by the extensive survey carried out by the Price Waterhouse Cranfield project (1991) which showed that employee relations in foreign-owned subsidiaries showed no significant differences from locally owned companies. Almost all of the transnational corporations (TNCs) seemed to follow a polycentric approach. However, Boyer (1993) suggests that the increasing 'globalisation' of capital and the emergence of transnationally integrated production networks have also produced a kind of renewal of convergence theory. Where there really are undifferentiated global markets being served by a transnational organisation, it is possible to perceive the company operating with a geocentric perspective, developing within a geocentric culture that is not an imitation of any particular national culture, and the attitude towards staffing and employee relations matters is such that country of origin and location have no significance.

THE MULTINATIONAL COMPANY: A FORCE FOR GOOD?

In his book *The Real Power Game* (1979), Jack Peel argued:

> Is the multinational an instrument of economic imperialism or a beneficial carrier of advanced management, science and technology? ... They reflect man's technological ingenuity, the ruthlessness of the board room power game, the inability of national governments to cope adequately with international business problems and the need to relate the profit motive more closely to social responsibility. But to denounce multinationals in general, is as unrealistic as to present them as benign institutions working for the public good. The truth is probably between the two positions. They bring considerable benefits to society but create a plethora of problems. They are a pertinent example of the gap between man's technological brilliance and society's ramshackle social machinery. In a nutshell, multinationals have been trapped by the speed of their own advance. They have far outdistanced their running mates, governments and trade unions, who have to work in a more ponderous, participative – some would say devious – way.

This extract refers to and implies many of the issues surrounding the formulation of an answer to the question posed by the title to this section. Peel himself suggests that there are different viewpoints and answers and that in his view an honest appraisal is likely to result in a mixed response.

Generally MNCs are attractive to those countries in which they invest for a number of reasons. It is usually anticipated that the investment will:

- create jobs and thereby improve the working conditions, living standards and prospects of the host country inhabitants;
- assist with the necessary process of industrialisation in developing countries;
- assist the host country's development through the process of technology and knowledge transfer;
- generate tax revenues and foreign exchange receipts for the host country government.

The attitude and approach of the multinational are important here, in that if it adopts an ethnocentric approach the impact upon employee relations may be greater than if the approach is polycentric. While it seems obvious that the impact of such investment upon employment levels is likely to be beneficial, it is important to be careful in assessing this impact.

The impact of multinational investment upon net employment depends upon the combined effect of three factors:

1 Direct job creation: this depends upon both the size and the capital–labour mix in the production process. Highly capital-intensive investment will have relatively poor returns in terms of direct job creation.

2 Indirect job creation: this depends upon links with local suppliers and the extent to which the company imports components and other factors of production.

3 The Trojan horse or displacement effect of the investment. If the investment merely means that other local producers are forced out of the market then the overall effect upon employment may not be what it first seemed.

FDI that takes the form of a merger with or acquisition of a going concern may have no beneficial impact upon employment at all and, indeed, it may in the long term lead to employment decline as activities and structures are rationalised and reorganised on a European or transnational basis. UNCTAD (1994) estimated that in the second half of the 1980s some 70 per cent of FDI into developed countries fell into this category of cross-border acquisitions.

Within multinational trade alliances and markets, such as the EU, an additional potential complication to these calculations is that investment in one country may have beneficial net effects upon employment there at the expense of employment in one of the other member states. Within the EU there have been instances of this occurring, and the concept referred to as *social dumping* encapsulates these concerns. This is dealt with at greater length in Chapter 7, but, briefly one of the major concerns associated with the creation of the single market and the implementation of the principle of freedom of movement of capital and labour was that capital was very much more mobile than labour and that consequently capital would be relocated within the market to those areas, regions and countries where the costs of production were the cheapest. This would result in jobs being created in one area, such as Spain or Portugal where labour costs are relatively cheap, at the expense of employment levels in places such as Germany and France. The UK, with a government that was keen to create flexible and deregulated labour markets and which saw lower labour costs as a source of competitive advantage, was seen as a potential beneficiary.

MNCs have been accused of all sorts of 'crimes', and it is alleged that rather than benefiting the development of the recipient country they actually harm it by:

■ causing massive environmental damage through their extraction and exploitation of raw materials and their cynical attitudes towards the land and agriculture;

■ distorting and destroying traditional cultures;

■ cynically exploiting labour.

The following allegations have also been made:

■ While MNCs claim to be investing capital and technology in Third World countries, many extract a large outflow of capital and never relinquish control of their technology.

■ They are able to create artificially low profits in high tax countries and high profits in low tax countries by 'transfer pricing'. These techniques can also be used in negotiations with trade unions, whereby a plant may be shown to be 'unprofitable' by the use of creative accounting and a harder bargain may be driven.

■ Their great global size enables them to interfere in the political affairs of smaller host countries.

■ Having been attracted to regions or countries offering financial inducements such as investment grants, tax concessions, training grants and cheap labour, it is not unknown for the MNC to uproot and depart when these inducements are no longer available. This phenomenon is known as the 'runaway firm' and if that firm is the main employer in the region, the whole community suffers when the company withdraws.

■ In times of high unemployment national governments are particularly prone to seek to attract MNCs to invest, as in the example in Exhibit 4.1, and this gives the MNC considerable bargaining power to persuade both governments and employees and their representatives to make concessions.

■ By dint of widespread and glamorous advertising and promotion, their products often swamp locally produced goods and put local manufacturers out of business.

There certainly is evidence to support these allegations but, as Peel suggests critics of multinationals should be aware of their ambivalent role in host countries, and should bear in mind that they seldom set out with purely altruistic motives.

MNCs AND NATIONAL EMPLOYEE RELATIONS SYSTEMS

Whether an MNC is in the very first stages of setting up an overseas subsidiary or (using Bartlett and Ghoshal's model) is at the global stage of internationalisation, one of the problems that it has to confront is managing operations and staff in different cultures and in different national employment relations systems. There is an inevitable relationship between these two. As Schregle (1981) observed:

> A comparative study of industrial relations shows that industrial relations phenomena are a very faithful expression of the society in which they operate, of its characteristic features and of the power relationships between different interest groups. Industrial relations cannot be understood without an understanding of the way in which rules are established and implemented and decisions are made in the society concerned.

This is not the place for a comparative analysis of employee relations systems. There are several texts that do this; for example, Hollinshead and Leat (1995) discuss the systems in a range of different countries and also compare them on a number of important themes, including trades unions, employers, the role of government and the various processes for the resolution of conflict. Nevertheless, it is important to remember that each employment relations system arises from a different history, legal system and sociopolitical/cultural context.

Dowling and Schuler (1990) emphasise that because employment relations are so diverse across national borders, it is imperative that MNCs employ a polycentric approach when appointing employment relations managers, while Prahalad and Doz (1987) assert that 'The lack of familiarity of MNC managers with local industrial and political conditions has sometimes needlessly worsened conflict that a local firm would have been likely to resolve'.

It is common for MNCs to have to deal with issues arising from national differences. These can pose company-wide problems of consistency of treatment between subsidiaries – for example, on working hours or rates of pay. While internal organisation and arrangements vary considerably from one MNC to another, it is feasible that even in the multidomestic form of MNC, where local autonomy may be high, control/advice from the centre may be prompted by:

- the perceived need to achieve a degree of internal consistency;
- the need to ensure that there is consistency between policies being pursued at a corporate level and those pursued locally.

An example of the latter may be an overseas subsidiary that signs an agreement with a trade union about job security for its members which may then prove an embarrassment to the corporate HQ, which is planning a downsizing or cost-cutting exercise.

The significance of local traditions, customs and knowledge of the national employment relations system has often encouraged MNCs to employ local knowledge and give the role of managing employee relations to a host country national.

However, there is another dimension to the interaction between MNCs and national systems of employee relations. In a very simplistic sense, one can see the foregoing comments and, indeed, much of the discussion in the previous sections as concerned with the impact of national systems upon the MNC and the extent to which the MNC does or does not adapt its approach, policies and practices to these national differences.

The second dimension to this relationship concerns the impact that MNCs themselves might have upon and within national systems. It was noted earlier how by the mid 1990s Japanese companies had come to dominate the ranks of the largest MNCs. Undoubtedly one of the major employee relations phenomena of the past two decades has been the influence within Europe, of Japanese inspired systems, attitudes and values relating to the design and nature of work and the attitudes and behaviour expected of employees.

It is easy to overemphasise the scale of this influence and the coherence with which changes have been implemented but 'Japanisation' cannot be ignored and to some extent it is likely that Japanese MNCs locating within the UK and other European countries are responsible for it. It would be unrealistic to ascribe the whole of this influence to the presence and example of Japanese MNCs in Europe; the demonstrable success of the Japanese economy and the persuasive influence of international organisations such as the International Monetary Fund (IMF) and the OECD, academics and management consultants cannot be discounted.

While the intention here is to concentrate upon Japanisation as the dominant example of the ability of MNCs to influence the nature of a national system, it is not the only example. American and other European MNCs can also be seen to have had an impact. For example, organisations such as Phillips, Volvo, McDonald's, Disney and IBM have all at various times been influential as models of excellence in the development of particular organisational cultures or systems of production and job design with their respective implications for the management and conduct of employee relations.

■ Japanisation: quality, involvement and commitment as competitive advantage

The perceived essence of the Japanese method, the recipe for global success, is an emphasis upon labour, service and product quality, which is to be achieved through a continuous search for improvement that pervades all aspects of the organisation's activity and recognises their interdependence, a system of apparent consensual decision making and an emphasis upon employee involvement in and commitment to the company.

Organisations within the UK have tried to follow this lead and imitate the success of Japanese organisations. Organisations with mechanisms such as quality circles and other forms of problem solving groups and team working. The emphasis upon quality has been additionally pursued through various other mechanisms including total quality management processes and Kaizan or continuous improvement. Just-in-time (JIT) and lean production policies and systems have also been adopted by some organisations and their emphasis upon minimising waste also imposes a concern with quality. All of these have implications for the nature of work and the employment relationship, terms and conditions of employment and the traditions and practice of employee relations.

In the remainder of this section attention is given to the nature of the more common of these 'methods and techniques' and then attempt some assessment of the extent to which their adoption in the UK has impacted upon employee relations, and the nature of such impact is assessed.

The quality circle

This – probably the most famous technique associated with 'Japanisation' – became popular in the UK and some other parts of Europe in the 1970s and 1980s. The popularity of this concept in Europe was linked to the perceived need for European manufacturers to compete on the grounds of zero defects. Quality circles are intended to contribute to the process of reducing defects and the need for repair, as well as providing a vehicle through which employees become more valued by, and involved within, the organisation.

They comprise relatively small numbers of employees (6–10) meeting voluntarily on a regular basis to identify, examine and resolve quality or other operational problems concerned with their own work and immediate environment. Their remit may primarily be to deal with quality problems but they are commonly also expected to devise ways of reducing costs and means for improving the design of work. These groups rarely have the authority to implement their own recommendations and as the problems are resolved there is a danger that there may be a loss of momentum. Experience has also tended to reinforce the view that these groups need to be both guided and led, and it is quite common for the participants to need training and some access to resources. It is important that management are seen to take note and implement at least some of the recommendations of such groups; the effective continuation of problem solving groups, whether quality circles or others, tends to depend upon evidence that their work is valued.

The success of quality circles has been the subject of debate over the years, with some commentators acting as protagonists and others openly critical. They certainly were introduced into some hundreds of companies in the UK and some success was claimed in terms of quality improvements, increased in job satisfaction and employee involvement.

Much of the criticism of the adoption and application of the concept in Europe has focused upon ambiguity about the true purpose of such schemes, with the view being expressed by some (Batstone and Gourley, 1986: 117–29) that the true purpose of these experiments was not so much to secure improvements in quality and employee involvement as to provide a means by which management were able to circumvent and bypass the traditional collective and unionised mechanisms of industrial relations and develop a more individual relationship with their employees.

Total quality management

The TQM approach encompasses a number of the techniques typically associated with Japanese organisations. The essence of the approach is a comprehensive and continuous search for improvement – the production of goods and services with zero defects – which involves most employees and knows few boundaries in terms of organisational activity.

In many respects it is an approach that seeks to generate a culture of quality throughout the organisation.

The driver for this attention to TQM is the internal and external customers. Internally, customers are the employees involved in the next stage of the process. This may be the next individual or team in the assembly process, or the next person to receive a report or the recipient of advice from a service function internal to the organisation.

The focal point for improvements in quality should be the employees doing the job. A fear of failure should be replaced with a search for failure. If people are blamed for failure, they are unlikely to take risks and unlikely to search for them and put them right – they are more likely to try to hide them (Marchington and Wilkinson, 1996: 353–4).

The customer-driven nature of such initiatives and programmes and the implications for employees are illustrated in the Guiding Principles governing a programme initiated within Ford in the UK and quoted by Storey (1992: 57):

- Quality comes first.
- Customers are the focus of everything we do.
- Continuous improvement is essential to our success.
- Employee involvement is our way of life.
- Dealers and suppliers are our partners.
- Integrity is never compromised.

Just-in-time

The essence of the JIT approach and associated systems is to eliminate waste. At all stages of the production of a good or the provision of a service consideration should be given to minimising the time between a resource being needed and its acquisition and between the production of a good and its purchase or consumption. Thus, systems should be designed which result in the final product being produced just before it is required in the marketplace, sub-assemblies being produced just before final assembly, and bought components being acquired just before they are needed. This enables the company to respond more quickly to market demand and it confirms demand as the driver of the production process.

Carried to its logical conclusion, labour would also be acquired just prior to need, implying a degree of flexibility in labour supply and usage that maybe inconsistent with regulatory frameworks designed to promote security of employment and employment protection. (*See* Chapter 7.) Nevertheless, this concept of JIT does give credence and impetus to the models of labour flexibility identified in the 1980s, which distinguish between core and peripheral labour and which have encouraged outsourcing and subcontracting, part-time working and other forms of a typical contract.

These organisational and technical systems give purchasers considerable power. For example, large companies such as Rover, Ford and BT, which are likely to be the major customer of any supplier of components, can exert great pressure upon the supplier to deliver on time a product of the desired quality.

From an employee relations perspective these systems place an emphasis upon trust because the relationship between management and employees is one of high dependency since the system operates without stocks at both ends of the process.

Both TQM and JIT have implied comprehensive change within UK organisations. The emphasis of the former is upon cultural change whereas the latter is more directly concerned with organisational and technical systems. There is likely to be an interrelationship, however, since massive change associated with the introduction of JIT is likely to imply cultural change as a prerequisite to its successful implementation.

■ Incidence and impact of TQM and JIT

There are different sets of views and conclusions about the extent and impact of these comprehensive and culture-changing approaches to the challenge of competitiveness in the global market, which can be seen to be at least partly a product of the influence of Japanese MNCs in Europe.

Legge (1995) summarises the conclusions of many researchers into the impact of these change programmes as evidence of:

- much enthusiasm among managers;
- variable success in implementation;
- the suspicion that in all but a few companies the magnitude of the cultural change and the time over which the enthusiasm and commitment need to be maintained combine to mitigate effective implementation.

There is the suspicion that the notorious short-termism of British business is not suited to these kinds of change programmes. As Legge describes it, a lack of stamina is associated with endemic short-termism.

An alternative and more critical view is presented by Parker and Slaughter (1988), who coined the term 'management by stress' to describe the consequences for labour of these initiatives. Team working and an emphasis upon zero defects are perceived as mechanisms through which both a culture of blame is introduced (rather than eradicated, as the theory proclaims is essential (*see* earlier) and there is more effective control of the labour resource through peer surveillance.

Perhaps what these various assessments indicate are the difficulties associated with seeking to transplant systems that have been successful in one particular socio-political/cultural context to another, even where there are MNC examples to draw upon and imitate. Nevertheless, the attention that has been paid to this phenomenon of Japanisation and the notions of quality and flexibility that are integral to it, is in itself reflective of the potential for MNCs to have an impact in and upon national systems.

Indeed, for many working in organisations, the late 1980s and 1990s have been characterised by a massively increased emphasis upon 'quality', even where those responsible seem unclear as to what quality looks like, and where the drive for quality appears to apply to everything except the nature of the employment relationship, working life and employee relations.

EMPLOYEE RELATIONS POLICIES AND PRACTICES WITHIN MNCs

There has been relatively little research on the employee relations policies and practices of MNCs and even less of a directly comparative nature. The early work was primarily directed at a comparison of American and European MNCs, although more recently the target population has been extended to include MNCs that originate from all parts of the world. The increasing tendency towards cross-border merger and amalgamation has in any event served to dilute and confuse the question of ownership and country of origin.

One of the most influential of these early studies was by Hamill (1983). In a series of studies in the 1980s Hamill studied MNCs in the UK owned by US corporations and UK corporations to compare their employment relations practices. He surveyed 84 US-owned and 50 UK-owned MNCs operating in three different industries so as to compare their practices in regard to:

- union recognition
- employer association membership
- management organisation for labour relations purposes
- the state of their negotiating arrangements
- the level and nature of collective agreements
- grievance procedures
- wage payment systems
- level of wages and employee fringe benefits.

He found that subsidiaries of US MNCs were not so likely to recognise trade unions or to join employer associations. They were more likely to employ specialist employment relations personnel at plant level, and have higher wages and better employee benefits than UK companies.

In another study on decision-making processes in which Hamill interviewed 30 personnel directors from MNCs in the UK (Hamill, 1984b), the findings included a large variety of practices. In the main, they were either totally centralised or totally decentralised, and the following factors were important in determining the extent to which the parent company intervened in employment relations at a local level:

- The degree of inter-subsidiary product integration. A high degree of integration was found to be the most important factor leading to the centralisation of the labour relations function within the MNCs studied.

- Whether the subsidiary was US-owned or European-owned. The former were found to be much more centralised in labour relations decision making than the latter.

- Whether subsidiaries were well-established indigenous firms acquired by an MNC or greenfield sites set up by an MNC. The former tended to be given much more autonomy over labour relations than the latter.

- Whether subsidiaries were performing well or poorly. Poor performance tended to be accompanied by increased investment in labour relations. When poor performance was due to labour relations problems, the MNC tended to attempt to introduce parent-country labour relations practices aimed at reducing industrial unrest or increasing productivity.

- Whether or not the MNC was a significant source of operating or investment funds for the subsidiary. If this was the case, there was increased corporate involvement in labour relations.

Hamill concluded that because US MNCs tended to be more integrated there was more centralisation. He further found greater similarities between UK- and European-owned firms than between UK- and US-owned companies.

Hamill (1984a) also undertook a comparative study of strikes in UK companies and in UK-based subsidiaries of MNCs, concentrating upon the following variables:

- frequency
- extent of strike
- duration of strike.

There was little difference between the two categories of firms as regards strike frequency. Subsidiaries, however, did experience larger and longer strikes than did UK-owned companies. Hamill suggests that this difference may be attributed to the fact that MNCs had greater resources, which enabled them to hold out against a striking workforce, and were more able to switch production to another country, thereby avoiding the impact of the strike.

As an overall conclusion to his research, Hamill stated that different MNCs adopt different labour relations strategies and that it is the type of MNC under consideration that is important rather than multinationality itself.

In another early comment on MNCs, Bean (1985) suggests that:

- European MNCs have tended to deal with labour unions at industry level (frequently through employer associations) rather than at company level. The opposite is more typical for US firms. In America, employer associations have not played a key role in the industrial relations system, and company-based labour relations policies are the norm.

■ The comparative sizes of the domestic and overseas markets and activity is a factor that influences the extent to which the parent company seeks to control overseas operations. If domestic sales are large, relative to overseas operations (as is the case with many US companies), it is more likely that overseas operations will be regarded by the parent company as an extension of domestic operations. This is not the case for many European MNCs, whose international operations represent the major part of their business. Lack of a large home market is a strong incentive to adapt to host-country institutions and norms. Bean also notes that in European MNCs, the overseas subsidiaries are considerably larger than the parent company and cites this fact as a possible reason for greater autonomy in employment relations given to European MNC subsidiaries than in US ones.

More recent research has been undertaken in the UK, as reported by Edwards *et al.* (1996). Their research included 101 MNCs of which 58 were UK-owned and 43 foreign-owned. As noted earlier, one of the objectives of the research was to ascertain the extent to which the transnational model is realistic, but other objectives were to investigate the degree to which the MNCs monitored the activities of subsidiaries, the degree of autonomy of the subsidiaries and the implications for the recognition of trade unions. Their conclusions were that:

■ the collection and use of data that facilitated central monitoring was associated with a global rather than a national or multidomestic orientation;

■ the use and comparison of labour performance data seemed more important in those MNCs operating in markets for standardised products, but where a global orientation was adopted and products were highly specialised, often only being made at one plant, and where it was crucial to be close to the customer, a comparison of such data would be either meaningless or academic;

■ the degree of central co-ordination was greater than might be apparent, this being achieved through a mix of financial mechanisms, expectations, contacts and culture;

■ there was some central direction of pay policy in over half the firms and this demonstrated a degree of co-ordination that was greater than the researchers had expected. As a matter of interest this policy included a policy to pay above the local market rate in only a few companies.

MNCs AND TRADE UNIONS

Unions have long feared the size, growth and spread of MNCs, not only because of their apparent preference for avoiding union recognition where they can (*see* below). MNCs have a range of means by which they may be able to thwart the interests and efforts of employees and their unions *organised on a national basis*. Kennedy (1980) suggested a number of ways in which this could be done:

■ They have formidable financial resources, which may enable them to absorb losses in a particular foreign subsidiary that is in dispute with a national union and still show a profit on overall worldwide operations.

- They may well have alternative sources of supply, and this may take the form of an explicit 'dual sourcing' policy to reduce the vulnerability of the corporation to a strike by a national union.

- They may be able to temporarily move production to facilities in other countries, and there is also the permanent threat of closure of facilities in a particular country or region.

- They may be able to hide from the unions by having a remote locus of authority (the corporate HQ management of an MNC), which is quite likely to be in a different part of the world.

- They have the capacity to stage an 'investment strike' in which the MNC refuses to invest any additional funds in a plant, thus ensuring that the plant will become obsolete and economically uncompetitive, which can be used as a threat to achieve compliance.

- They can exert considerable pressures upon governments to regulate or deregulate in their favour.

■ MNC attitudes towards trade unionism

We noted above that Hamill found that subsidiaries of US MNCs were not so likely to recognise trade unions or to join employer associations. Dowling and Schuler (1990) assert that an MNC's initial attitude and ideology is an important factor in consolidating its position regarding trade unions and employee ralations. For example, trade unionism seems to be an alien concept to many US MNCs. Trade union density in the USA is much lower than in most European countries (not France), although it is interesting to note that because of the North American Free Trade Agreement (NAFTA), many US companies are moving into Mexico, a country with pervasive trades unionism. Edwards *et al.* (1996) concluded that:

- The prospects for trade union recognition appear to diminish as globalism advances. Over half of the UK and just under half of the European respondents asserted that it was their general policy to avoid bargaining with trade unions.

- Where companies were organised on multidomestic lines 40 per cent avoided unions whereas the figure for those companies dominated by global organisation rose to 63 per cent.

- Avoiding unions also seemed to be associated with a strategic emphasis upon market penetration and the existence of advanced organisational systems of management development, a mechanism through which contacts and culture can be reinforced.

- The avoidance of trade unions was something that many of the companies would choose to do but it was not of sufficient importance in most of the companies that they would base location decisions on this factor.

- If nation state governments or the EU strengthen the rights of labour and trade unions it is unlikely to cause an immediate flight of capital from the country or region concerned.

The influence of trades unions on MNCs

Dowling and Schuler (1990) suggested that trade unions may have the ability to constrain the choices of MNCs in three main ways:

1 by influencing wage levels
2 by limiting employment level variation
3 by hindering global integration.

They suggest that labour costs, although decreasing in significance, still play a major part in determining cost competitiveness. Any influence that unions have on wage levels is therefore potentially significant and may influence employment levels. However, Dowling and Schuler (1990) further state that the ability of unions to restrict hours of work and patterns of employment may have a more serious effect on profitability than spiralling labour costs.

Trades unions in Europe have traditionally had significant input into the political process, and national regulatory systems are inevitably the product of interaction at this political level. Many countries have legislation that specifies a minimum wage or that prohibits redundancies or changes in working practices unless the company can show that structural conditions make these labour losses unavoidable. Often such procedures are long and drawn out and involve the employer in high redundancy costs. Payments for involuntary redundancy in some countries can be substantial, especially when compared to the USA.

Dowling and Schuler (1990) observed that 'many MNCs make a conscious decision not to integrate and rationalise their operations to the most effective degree, because to do so could cause industrial and political problems'. They use as an example Prahalad and Doz's (1987) description of General Motors' sub-optimisation of integration. The latter alleged that in the early 1980s GM made substantial investments in Germany (matching its new investments in Austria and Spain) at the demand of the German Metalworkers Union (IG Metal – one of the largest industrial unions in the western world) in order to foster good labour relations in Germany. They conclude:

Union influence thus not only delays the rationalisation and integration of MNC's manufacturing networks and increases the cost of such adjustments (not so much in the visible severance payments and 'golden handshake' provisions as through economic losses incurred in the meantime), but also, at least in such industries as automobiles, permanently reduces the efficiency of the integrated MNC network. Therefore, treating labour relations as incidental and relegating them to the specialists in the various countries is inappropriate. In the same way as government policies need to be integrated into strategic choices, so do labour relations.

However, recent developments that have enhanced the power and influence of MNCs and diminished the power of both the trade union movement and national governments to control and limit their activities cast serious doubts upon the abilities of trade unions to continue to influence the objectives and activities of MNCs in the ways and to the extent that is suggested in these earlier studies. The research findings of Edwards *et al.* would tend to confirm that the influence of the unions upon MNCs diminishes the more the MNCs move along the road of global integration and adopt a global orientation.

Ietto-Gillies (1997) argues that TNCs derive power from their multinational interests, which they can wield against uni-nationals, governments, labour organisations and consumers and that there is a need to try to reverse this trend and give countervailing power to these other players. Governments should use their control over the quality of both the physical infrastructure and the labour force as bargaining weapons to give support to those players that do not themselves have transnational power.

■ Trade union responses

At a fairly early stage it became apparent that effective opposition to the power of the MNC demanded from the worldwide trade union movement cooperation and organisation. However, this has not proved to be an easy objective to achieve.

Study of trade union movements in different countries demonstrates the diversity of trade unions: their membership bases, their structures, their objectives and orientations and their political affiliations differ substantially both within and between countries. (*See* Hollinshead and Leat (1995) for a comparison of trade union movements in a number of countries on these and other criteria.)

There are many countries in which various union factions and confederations exist and in which effective cooperation on a national scale has been largely unattainable (France and Italy are examples of this in Europe), let alone cooperation on an international scale. In some respects the decline of communism as practised in the Soviet bloc has helped the process of integration and cooperation in the past decade as confederations that viewed the Communists as their political and ideological allies have been forced to reappraise their objectives and organisation.

It is also important to bear in mind that when dealing with MNCs, unions may have conflicting national interests. When one country is suffering an economic downturn, trade union officials may put national interests – the interests of their own constituency – before those of international worker solidarity. An example of this occurred in the early 1970s, when the Ford Motor Company, exasperated by the labour climate in its UK plants, decided to make no further investment in them and the media at the time hinted darkly that Ford was about to pull out of the UK and make further investments in the Netherlands. The UK unions were highly critical of Ford but the unions in the Netherlands made no attempt to express solidarity with them. In fact, they expressed full support for the Netherlands businesspeople who were trying to woo Ford away from the UK.

The primacy of national interests is also demonstrated by the following interview:

Milne (1991), in an interview with the German IG Metall leader at Ford, Wilfred Kuckelkorn indicates that there are still significant difficulties facing joint union action: Kuckelkorn says: 'We want the British unions to win a 35 hour week and they will get practical solidarity from Germany, including overtime bans and working to rule.' But with another breath Kuckelkorn rejects out of hand any thought of joint European collective bargaining with Ford: 'the national unions cannot accept European negotiations. If you take away the power of the national unions they will go down.'

Nevertheless, there have been instances over the years of spontaneous and *ad hoc* international trade union solidarity and activity against particular multinationals. An example of this latter form of cooperation was in 1997 over the decision of Renault to close one of its more productive plants in Belgium in favour of the retention of plants in France. This was made worse by the revelation at the time that the company was seeking grants and other forms of assistance from both the Spanish government and the European Commission to build a new plant in Spain. This occasioned marches and demonstrations of support involving union members and delegations from Belgium, France, Germany, Italy, Spain, the UK, the Netherlands, Portugal, Greece and Austria, but to no avail. Renault demonstrated the power of the MNC to exercise its autonomy and ignore the views of the international trade union movement as represented and also to ignore the requirements of the EU Directive that provides employee representatives with rights to prior consultation in the event of collective redundancies.

■ International trade union organisation

Attempts are being made to consolidate international trade union links and to mount worldwide campaigns against global capitalism.

In some industrial sectors there is a long history of attempts to build international links and organisation. In 1864, the first International Workingmen's Association brought together in London a mix of Socialists and trade unionists. The 1890s saw international organisations founded by industrial sectors, such as dockers, steel workers, miners, engineers and garment workers. By 1914, 28 international bodies (latterly known as International Trade Secretariats) were in operation.

One of the long-term goals of each International Trade Secretariat is to achieve transnational bargaining with each of the MNCs in its industry. The elements of the programme are:

- research and information
- organisation of a company conference
- establishment of a company council
- company-wide union and management discussion
- co-ordinated bargaining.

However, attempts by the Industry Trade Secretariats to become the basis for international collective bargaining have been largely unsuccessful although they have established world company councils to link together trade unionists in different branches of MNCs. Within the EU there are examples of social dialogue at sectoral level. Many have argued that the European Works Council (EWC) Directive of 1994 will provide the necessary opportunity for these secretariats to gain a foothold in many MNCs that have previously been able to resist them. This is discussed in more detail in Chapter 7 and there certainly is early evidence that these secretariats were involved in the formation of a number of voluntary EWCs agreed subsequent to the adoption of the Directive (Rivest, 1996).

Global organisations

On a global level, transnational union organisations have tended to be aligned with political and ideological interests. That is to say, in the West, the International Confederation of Free Trade Unions (ICFTU) emerged, with its counterpart in the Communist bloc being the World Federation of Trade Unions (WFTU). There is also a smaller Christian-based World Confederation of Labour (WCL).

The ICFTU has been the most influential of these organisations and this has been perpetuated by the impact upon the WFTU of the break-up of the Soviet bloc.

None of these world confederations succeeded in developing a collective bargaining role and their activities have tended to be dominated by political interests and action and, in the case of the ICFTU, the encouragement of trade unionism and representation in developing countries.

The European Trade Union Confederation

The most influential international trade union organisation within Europe is undoubtedly the ETUC. Membership is not confined to federations from member states of the EU; over 20 countries within Europe have federations and unions in membership. In membership are the vast majority of national level federations within Europe, including most of the former Communist ones, and also affiliated are the 14 sectoral European Industry Committees (EIC). Estimates indicate that about 95 per cent of organised workers are affiliated to the ETUC (European Trade Union Institute, 1995).

The ETUC has long been accustomed to lobbying on a wide variety of issues within the EU. Issues include gender equality, employee protection closure in the event of plant or transfer of ownership, Health and Safety at work and also broader issues such as social policy and macro economic policy.

However, the ETUC is a diverse organisation and it would be wrong to give the impression that there is much cohesion within the movement. The size, nature, traditions and interests of the many union confederations and unions in membership vary considerably, as do their autonomy and authority in respect of their own membership. Visser and Ebbinghaus (1992) described the ETUC as 'united but fragmented and with little internal cohesion'.

The ETUC has been designated by the EU Commission as the representative social partner of European employees and it is in this role that it is likely to have its greatest effect and impact upon the regulatory environment for both MNCs and employees in Europe. The treaties agreed at Maastricht in 1991 and at Amsterdam in 1997 provide an extension of the role and the influence of the Social Partners, in particular via the Social Protocol procedures (*see* Chapter 7 for more detail).

It is worth noting that the first measure adopted via these Protocol procedures was the EWC Directive and this is very much an attempt to regulate and contain the activities of the MNC, to provide employee representatives with rights to information and consultation with respect to a wide range of subjects (*see* Chapter 7).

INTERNATIONAL REGULATION AND CONTROL OF MNCs

We have noted earlier that there are various grounds for and perspectives on the issue of the need to regulate MNCs. It is now questionable whether effective regulation is really possible but nevertheless several international organisations have tried to address this issue, although with varying degrees of influence.

The first major Code of Conduct regarding the operation of MNCs was established by the International Chambers of Commerce in 1972, mostly in response to the fears expressed by developing countries. The code incorporated recommendations that:

1 Host countries adopt a policy of collaboration rather than control, local shareholders should be encouraged and there should be no restrictions on the repatriation of capital, on loans and dividends, or on royalties for technology.

2 MNCs should inform the host country of their plans, so that they can fit into the development objectives of the host country, try to choose local partners and offer them a share in the equity of their subsidiaries, volunteer information about their profits and be aware that sources of local financing may give priority to indigenous industrials.

3 MNCs should also use local labour and give priority to local suppliers, above all, in the developing countries.

It should be stressed that the Code is not compulsory and is solely a question of recommendations for the governments of the countries and the companies involved. There are also further recommendations applying to double taxation, repatriation of dividends and proposed guarantees against non-commercial, administrative and political risks.

Guidelines that deal more directly with employee relations issues are those posited by the Organization for Economic Cooperation and Development (OECD) in 1975. The recommendations of this Code, or so-called 'Guidelines', cover six categories:

■ disclosure of information

■ competition

■ financing

■ taxation

■ science and technology

■ employment and industrial relations.

As with the Code established by the International Chamber of Commerce, the OECD Code is a series of non-obligatory recommendations, but it has, in fact, taken on an obligatory character through the Committee on International Investment and Multinational Enterprises (IME), an organisation made up of representatives of the governments of the OECD member countries. The trade unions cannot refer a complaint to the Committee (IME) directly; they must go through representatives of their country serving on the Committee. The opinion expressed by the Committee is not necessarily followed by the country seeking clarification and therefore the Committee is not seen as a court which judges the actions of the MNCs.

A good example of the work of the IME, occurring on 30 March 1977, concerned a dispute brought about by the actions of the American multinational Raytheon. Its Belgian subsidiary, Badger, was unprofitable and Raytheon decided to close it down. As

Belgian redundancy payments are among the highest in the world, the local Raytheon management balked at the prospect of paying redundancy payments to some 250 workers as the subsidiary was technically bankrupt. The Belgian government and unions felt that the onus for the redundancy payments lay with the American parent Raytheon and that it should make the payments. The case was referred to the IME and although its recommendations were somewhat ambiguous, the American parent eventually made the redundancy payments. In this particular case it is reasonable to assume that the OECD's Code of Conduct was used to pressurise the multinational to act in the way it did.

In 1994, Volkswagen AG (VW) carried out restructuring at its Belgian subsidiary, in order to make it more competitive. Although this incurred the immediate loss of around 2000 jobs with a further 850 job losses to come, production was maintained at pre-restructuring levels. The fact that production was not affected caused the remaining workforce to resist fiercely the necessary increase in the rhythm of work, needed to maintain production levels. The result was a series of strikes. During the negotiations between the unions and management in Belgium, VW's HQ in Germany announced that all production lost by the strikes (around 1000 cars a day) would be transferred from Belgium to other VW production units elsewhere in Europe.

The Belgian unions argued that the action taken by VW's HQ breached the OECD's 1976 Declaration on Investment and Multinational Enterprises, which states that companies should not threaten to transfer all or part of their operations from one country to another in order to influence negotiations (including disputes). This is an example of the difficulties facing employees and management of an MNC subsidiary, when the unions, on the one hand, are under strong pressure from a disaffected workforce and the management, on the other, are under strong pressure from HQ to increase competitiveness and productivity in order to retain current allocated production levels.

The International Labour Organization (ILO), established in 1919, became a part of the United Nations, which itself emerged from the League of Nations. (*See* Chapter 18 of Hollinshead and Leat (1995) for a detailed account of the origin, development and initiatives of the ILO.) The ILO has been influential in setting world standards in Health and Safety and in industrial relations. However once again enforcement is difficult. The ILO did issue a Code in 1977 that was concerned with the social policy of MNCs and in particular sought to deal with matters such as:

- employment
- training
- working conditions
- living conditions
- professional relations.

Any assessment of the impact of such guidelines and Codes of Conduct must recognise that while they may have been useful as means for establishing standards of 'proper' behaviour, ultimately compliance cannot be enforced; persuasive pressures may be brought to bear but at the end of the day there is little that even these international organisations can do to make an MNC do what it does not intend to. Associations of countries in free trade arrangements may have greater success if they have the ability to hurt the MNC financially by refusing entry or using their ability to impose tariff barriers or provide tax benefits. However, the speed and ease of capital transfer, the ability of the MNC to relocate into more favourable regimes and the economic and political power of many MNCs render problematic attempts to counterbalance them.

EUROPEAN WORKS COUNCILS, MNCS, COLLECTIVE BARGAINING AND CONVERGENCE?

Details of the Directive on EWCs are given in Chapter 7. We noted earlier that progress towards collective bargaining at the level of the organisation within MNCs has been slow. However, it has been argued that this particular Directive, in that it creates what might be regarded as an embryonic bargaining structure, will in time encourage the development of collective bargaining at this level. We have also already identified many of the obstacles in the way of such a development; for example, the trade unions might find it desirable but have problems with their national constituencies and the MNCs would clearly appear not to welcome such a development.

We noted earlier that the late 1980s and the 1990s have been a period characterised by considerable restructuring of European capital and expansion of cross-border amalgamations and mergers.

The scale of this restructuring seems to be gathering pace rather than abating. In mid-October 1997 the financial pages of the UK newspapers on one day reported alliances and mergers involving organisations worth in excess of £70 billion.

- A merger between Reed Elsevier, an Anglo-Dutch publishing company, and Wolters Kluwer. The resulting company was to be the largest professional and scientific information group in the world with a market capitalisation of £21 billion. The announcement was accompanied by projections of massive cost savings. The workforce of the combined group would be 42 000.

- A merger worth £22 billion between BAT industries and Zurich Insurance, which would merge the financial service and insurance interests of both groups and create a separate tobacco division. The combined total workforce would be 55 000.

- A bid by the French aggregates group Lafarge for its British rival Redland. The market value of the combined group would be in the region of £6 billion and the combined workforce between 55 000 and 60 000 people.

- A British merger between Guinness and Grand Metropolitan which would create a combined group value of £22 billion with a workforce of 87 000.

This capital restructuring has been accompanied in some instances by organisational restructuring and rationalisation. This is reflected in the development and strengthening of management structures at a European level, which serve to integrate the business functions across Europe. As a result production or marketing strategies are no longer the province of national subsidiaries but are determined and integrated at a European level even when the unit is a division rather than the whole company. These structural developments are consistent with genuine transnationalism.

Marginson and Sisson (1994) in describing this process refer to the emergence of the Euro-company. They also point out the converse trend towards the decentralisation and devolution of operational responsibility and financial accountability to individual business units and cost and profit centres within the larger transnational or Euro-company.

Marginson and Sisson (1996) argue that there are trends in most companies involving increasing decentralisation to individual business units and at the same time centralisation to the European level. They argue that the greater the degree of devolution to individual business units within national systems the greater are the needs for internal co-ordination and control and that this is achieved through the tendency towards centralisation at the Euro-company level. The concentration of strategic integration at the level of the company and control of the decentralised operations are both aided by the new communication and information technologies.

These developments have considerable implications for the conduct and structure of industrial relations within the companies. Where there is a centralisation of certain strategic activities to the corporate or Euro-company level, or the creation of Euro-divisions, a potential exists for the development of company-level or division-specific, and therefore transnational or European, employment and industrial relations policies, structures and institutions also at this level. Marginson and Sisson (1994) refer to this as the 'strategic potential to establish a pan-European approach to employee and industrial relations management'.

Schulten (1996) adapts Perlmutter's (1969) typology in referring to this as the development of a Eurocentric approach towards industrial relations, and suggests that there is some evidence of this emerging in some of these Euro-companies, particularly in the areas of work organisation and working conditions.

There are also some examples, as we have noted earlier, of such organisations voluntarily developing EWC or similar arrangements prior to the adoption of the EWC Directive although in the main these were companies that had originated in a country with a national system that encompassed a legislative requirement for Works Councils, namely France.

The emergence of such company- or division-specific structures would tend to undermine existing sectoral or national and multi-employer systems of joint regulation.

As noted above, however, this tendency towards a centralisation of employee relations policy, strategy and institutions may be accompanied by operational decentralisation. The decentralisation of operational responsibilities and financial accountability referred to above is likely to necessitate the interaction of management and employees and the determination of the terms of the employment relationship at this decentralised level. If the managements of the decentralised units, whether these be specific subsidiaries, particular divisions or cost or profit centres, are to be responsible for costs and profits they need to be able to control the business or unit's labour and associated costs. They will arguably be unable to do this if major constituents of these costs are determined at a completely different level, whether this be at the level of the Euro-company or the national system.

Transnational companies may not want or need to take part in multi-employer arrangements but they cannot ignore the regulatory systems of the countries in which they have undertakings and whatever that imposes in terms of rights, outcomes and structures. MNCs may try to mitigate the effects of particular national regulatory regimes but they are rarely able to ignore them totally.

Nevertheless, the opportunity does exist for many of these companies to go 'regime shopping', meaning that they may decide on the location of their activities on the basis of low employment costs and deregulatory regimes, shifting their resources so as to take advantage of what they perceive as favourable national systems.

This approach is characterised as the 'social dumping' approach (see earlier) and, as Schulten (1996) points out, there are means by which such organisations can press their employees into concession bargaining arrangements through which they encourage competition for work within the company, between locations and groups of employees. This exerts a downward pressure on terms and conditions of employment, and hence costs, as employees compete against each other for the available work. This may be one way to achieve a convergence of industrial relations across national boundaries within the one multinational.

In their study of the European automotive industry, Mueller and Purcell (1992) found that 'management systematically played one subsidiary against another to introduce nightshifts and to extend operating time in capital intensive areas (gear box and engine production, press shops). After the first subsidiary agreed to a relaxation of existing working time regulations, a kind of "domino-effect" was set in motion. Sooner or later, all the other subsidiaries followed the same pattern.' In this situation a phenomenon called 'information asymmetry' occurs. Information is not uniformly available, so local negotiators threatened with social dumping may not be in a position to check the figures of other subsidiaries. The development of the EWC may change this situation.

Sengenberger (1992) suggests that if each subsidiary bargains away its wages and conditions, there could be a 'negative convergence' in which all subsidiaries are caught in a race to undermine existing social standards and the result is the negative convergence of labour relations at a low level of social regulation.

It is for these and similar reasons that the European Commission and some of the member states have been keen to impose regulatory requirements upon the multinationals. The EWC Directive is the first such example, imposing as it does upon the company the requirement that a corporate European level forum be established which provides employees with the right, through their representatives, to be informed and consulted on a range of issues and subject matter.

Schulten (1996) does identify another way in which the emergence of these powerful multinational/Euro-companies may lead to a convergence of industrial relations across national boundaries within the organisation, and that is the 'best practice' alternative, whereby the management search out and implement across the organisation instances and practices that fall into this category. He suggests that this is most likely to occur in organisations that are actively and continuously seeking to improve quality and 'searching for a more productive and innovative production model' in the 'post-Fordist' scenario that is now supposed to inhabit Europe.

It seems unlikely that the development of these Euro and other transnational companies within Europe will enhance the frequency of the interaction of management and employees in a collective bargaining relationship at Euro-company level. The EWC Directive certainly does not require such bargaining and there are no mechanisms at EU level that can be used to force it.

As noted in the opening paragraph of this section, it has been suggested that the EWC Directive will over time enhance the likelihood of the development of collective bargaining at Euro level, the feeling being that it will:

- provide an embryonic and adaptable structure;
- lead to the development of working relationships between employee representatives from different plants and countries;
- enhance the passage of information and knowledge and cross-national comparisons between them;

■ perhaps most importantly, enhance the development of trust between the parties.

It is possible that the information and consultation arrangements associated with the establishment of EWC or equivalent machinery could provide a base for such developments but this seems unlikely.

Assuming that the process of economic integration and the applications of new technology continue to encourage the development of Euro-companies and that they seek to centralise strategy determination in conjunction with a decentralisation of operational and financial decision making and accountability, there would appear to be little scope for such collective bargaining.

There is little if any evidence to suggest that employers are keen to give employees and their representative organisations a role in strategy formulation, and if other decision making and responsibilities are decentralised it is unclear what the bargaining would be about.

To have labour costs determined at the level of the Euro-company makes little sense to operational and line management, in much the same way as multi-employer bargaining within national systems or at a EU level makes little sense to the management of a Euro-company keen to develop its own distinctive employment structures and strategies.

Carley (1993) refers to a study by Gold and Hall (1992) in which managers involved in existing European information arrangements were implacably opposed to the development of European-level collective bargaining. Marginson and Sisson (1994) argue that collective bargaining at the Euro-company level is something that managements of transnational companies 'will oppose especially vigorously' and they assert that this seems to apply as much in those companies that have set up voluntary EWC arrangements as in those that have not. They suggest that the reasons for this include:

■ reducing the capacity of companies to go regime shopping;

■ runing counter to the logic of decentralised decision making and responsibility;

■ there is a preference on the part of many European employers to maintain the traditional separation of consultative and bargaining arrangements and forums.

Nevertheless, Schulten (1996) does identify some companies that have established what he refers to as a 'quite sophisticated arrangement' of European-level industrial relations. He gives particular attention to the case of Danône, the French food manufacturer. In this company a European level joint forum has existed since 1986 and its history has been one of developing cooperation and trust leading to four European-level framework agreements on the subjects of training, equality for women, basic information rights for employees and trade union rights in every Danône subsidiary. He suggests that the company 'seems to be the first case of a move towards a company specific "European collective bargaining system"'.

In examining the prospects for Euro-company level collective bargaining, Marginson and Sisson (1996) postulate that where it does happen such bargaining may take a very different form from the creation of contractual relations that has been the norm in most national systems, and suggest that it might develop along the path of the agreement of 'joint opinions' or 'framework agreements'. They quote the Danône experience as an example of what might happen.

Keller (1991) suggests that more and more European MNCs will use the EWC as a method of collective bargaining 'over a number of non-monetary industrial relations issues (e.g. work organisation, working time, training, equality between men and women)'.

Schulten (1996) also suggests that the EWC, may actually be of great benefit to management as a mechanism through which best practice can be ascertained and the message spread to other units and locations. EWCs may be used as the conduit by which management seek to achieve convergence and a form of transnational human resource management. There is little evidence to suggest that companies will forgo regime shopping and the social dumping approach referred to earlier simply because the EWC provides a mechanism for the transfer of best practice, and it is quite likely that managements will seek to utilise both approaches as means by which they can enhance efficiency, productivity, competitive advantage and profit.

Employee representatives to the EWC will need to guard against being used in this way, and awareness of this threat may, and should, encourage the formation among them of networks and alliances of a transnational nature. However, they will need to be aware that employee representatives from one country or location may be tempted by the rewards held out to them to pursue their 'individual' interests as opposed to the collective interests of all employees. Even within the forum of the EWC it may be possible for employers to exploit the different national constituencies and interests to their own advantage.

Mueller and Purcell (1992) suggest that EWCs could lead to 'a new segmentation into two broadly independent systems of Industrial Relations in Europe: the one for large integrated companies where the focus is on plant activity and active Works Councils; the others serving the smaller domestic producers and those firms in sheltered markets based on the varied traditions and practices of national Industrial Relations arrangements'.

CHAPTER SUMMARY

The 1980s and 1990s have been a period of rapid and great economic integration and expansion in the volume of world trade. Associated with these developments, there has been a considerable increase in the tendency for companies to become MNCs. There are a number of different models of the MNC and their approaches to issues such as the management of employee relations. MNCs have to take some note of national regimes and cultures but the way in which they approach this varies. They are also potential sources of influence for change within national systems.

MNCs are powerful economic force which affect the capital–labour relationship throughout the world. Their need to supply differentiated markets, yet at the same time have integrated systems and management practices, means that they must have an overall employee relations policy, tempered by recognition of localised norms, cultures, laws and practices.

One of the important features of an MNC's approach to employee relations is its attitude towards trade unions. In the main, MNCs seem to prefer to avoid them if they can.

The trade unions themselves have had little effective input so far upon the development of the MNC and upon its employee relations policies and practices. The unions need to respond at the national and international level to defend themselves against possible effects of social dumping and regime shopping. They also need to operate effectively within the company to ensure a homogeneous response across national boundaries with their fellow trade unionists, in order to combat possible attrition and the device known as concession bargaining.

Regulation of the activities of the MNC is both necessary and difficult. International organisations have tried, but with little impact. The EWC Directive is another attempt at regulation; it is still too early to assess the impact. Some have argued that the EWC is a possible example, in embryonic form, of how, at the European level, trade unionists and employee representatives from different countries can meet together with their MNC employer to discuss matters of mutual interest. The prospects for collective bargaining at the level of the MNC seem remote.

■ **Exhibit 4.2**

Ford puts on the brakes

The loss of 1300 jobs in Merseyside is a matter of great regret. So many redundancies in such a depressed region of Britain will be a sad reverse for those who are trying to breathe new life into the Merseyside economy.

It may seem an especially unfair blow to the workers at Ford's Halewood plant, because they have made great efforts in the recent past to reform working practices and become more efficient. But it is important to draw the right conclusions.

New Labour, for example, looked very much like silly old Labour when it laid routine blame on the Conservatives' free market economic policies. It is wrong. Tory economic policies, including the reform of labour markets, have in the past 15 years contributed to a dramatic revival of the British motor industry. Ford is responding mainly to competitive pressures, which have pushed its European operations deep into the red. Stuck with over-capacity, it has decided to concentrate output of the new Escort model, which comes into production next year, in two of the three existing Escort plants – Saarlouis in Germany and Valencia in Spain.

Halewood has lost out mainly because it is a smaller plant which has received considerably less investment in its assembly lines in recent years. (Investment has been concentrated in the transmission plant at the site.) Productivity is therefore somewhat lower, despite the big gains made since the 1970s when Halewood was a by-word for poor industrial relations.

Job cutting

The relative ease with which it is possible to cut jobs in the UK, compared with Germany and Spain, played a part in Ford's decision. Mr Ian McCartney, Labour's employment spokesman, and trade union officials at Halewood have emphasised this fact when suggesting the government is partly to blame for the job cuts.

One can sympathise with the Halewood shop stewards. But Labour should take care with its pronouncements. The fact is that Conservative labour market reforms have contributed a great deal to encouraging foreign car makers to set up plants and invest in Britain. Japanese companies, particularly, could have chosen other EU countries for European plants. They said one reason for picking the UK was its flexible labour market. They did not come intending to sack staff – but they wished to retain the option in case their plans did not work out.

Car output

Existing car makers – including Ford – restructured their businesses to meet the challenge from the east. Employment in the motor industry has fallen by about two thirds since the 1970s and will almost certainly fall further. But car output last year hit its highest level for 21 years and is rising. Britain makes 12 per cent of the EU's cars, compared with 9 per cent in 1986.

Ford has played a significant part in this revival, investing nearly £3.5bn in the UK in 1990–95, including almost £500m at Halewood. Ford's British plants are a key element of its European network.

It would be wrong to see only the job cuts which resulted from competitive pressures and technological changes in the motor industry. These pressures also created new jobs.

There is no room for complacency, however. While the top British plants can match the best in the world in quality, the industry still has too many second-rate factories. The country is behind others in training those working in motors, as in other industries. It is here that the government can make the biggest contribution to the industry's success – raising the quality of school and university education.

Future reforms in the training of workers will be of little help to Halewood today. But it will be the best guarantee of future jobs at the plant. A slide back to restrictive labour markets would have the opposite effect.

Source: Financial Times, 17 January 1997.

■ **Exhibit 4.2 continued**

Ford and unions agree Halewood jobs deal

Ford yesterday agreed to scale down its plans for job losses at the Halewood plant on Merseyside from 1,300 to 980 in return for union agreement to call off a ballot on industrial action.

The company, which last month raised the threat of closure at Halewood in a drive to staunch massive European losses, assured union leaders that it wanted to keep the plant open after production of the current Escort model ends in 2000. The company also confirmed it would build the next generation of the Transit van at Southampton after 2000. The Transit will require linked investments, in transmissions at Halewood and body stamping at the Dagenham plant in east London.

The company also said Dagenham, rather than Cologne in Germany, would be its main plant in Europe for the next-generation Fiesta, due early in the next decade. An unspecified new investment will be made at Halewood to raise stamping capacity to cope with expansion at Ford's Jaguar subsidiary.

Union leaders committed themselves to working with Ford to strengthen the company's role in car-making in Britain. However, the agreement, reached after two days of talks between union bosses and Mr Jac Nasser, chairman of Ford of Europe, looked like a clear win for the company. Many of the "new" investment decisions had been expected.

Ford's main concession, apart from cutting the number of redundancies, was the commitment to build a new multi-purpose version of the next-generation Escort to keep the plant alive after 2000.

The company's willingness to back the project appeared largely based on assurances from the government that it would receive satisfactory subsidies. Neither Ford nor the unions indicated the sum sought. However, both sides seemed confident the project would go ahead. Ford said it would produce another vehicle at the plant if it did not.

The reduction in redundancies is being achieved by switching production of the station-wagon version of the Escort to Halewood from late 1998 and prolonging the life of the Escort van, which is already built at the plant, beyond the end of this year. Production of the next-generation Escort car is being concentrated at Ford's plants in Spain and Germany.

Mr Nasser hailed the deal as "a historic agreement" for Ford, the unions and Britain. It is likely to increase the competition for subsidies as car-makers use each new product to lobby governments for aid for factories in sensitive areas.

In Ford's case, the focus may soon switch to Germany, where the company has so far refused to commit itself to building the next-generation Scorpio executive model at Cologne. Demand for the current Scorpio has slumped, prompting local fears that Ford may be tempted to import the successor model from the US.

Source: Haig Simonian (1997) *Financial Times*, Weekend 8/9 February 1997.

QUESTIONS

1 Examine Exhibit 4.2 and identify and discuss how this exhibit illustrates the strengths and weaknesses of MNC employers and employees.

2 Discuss whether MNCs at corporate level need to understand the historical and cultural contexts of the employee relations system of the countries in which they operate.

3 What are features of MNCs that trade unionists and employee representatives may find undesirable?

4 Describe the ways in which trade unions have responded to MNCs. To what extent have these responses been successful?

5 Discuss the prospects for collective bargaining at a European level within MNCs.

6 Discuss whether the MNC is now out of reach of national regimes and what options there may be for international regulation.

REFERENCES

Barrell, R. and Pain, N. (1997) 'EU: an attractive investment. Being part of the EU is good for FDI and being out of EMU may be bad', *New Economy*, 4 (1).

Bartlett, C. A. and Ghoshal, S. (1989) *Managing Across Borders: The Transnational Solution*. Cambridge, MA: Harvard Business School Press.

Batstone, E. and Gourley, S. (1986) *Unions, Unemployment and Innovation*. Oxford: Blackwell.

Bean, R. (1985) *Comparative Industrial Relations: an Introduction to Cross-National Perspectives*. New York: St Martin's Press.

Boyer, R. (1993) *The Convergence Hypothesis Revisited: Globalisation but still the Century of Nations?* Couvertures Oranges de CEPREMAP No. 9403, Paris.

Carley, M. (1993) 'Social dialogue' in Gold, M. (ed.) *The Social Dimension – Employment Policy in the European Community*. Basingstoke: Macmillan.

Dowling, P. and Schuler, R. (1990) *International Dimensions of Human Resource Management*. Bosten, MA: PWS-Kent.

Edwards, P., Marginson, P., Armstrong, P. and Purcell, J. (1996) 'Towards the transnational company? The global structure and organisation of multinational firms', in Crompton, R., Gallie, D. and Purcell, K. (eds) *Changing Forms of Employment*. London: Routledge.

ETUI (1995) *Les comités d'entreprises européens: inventaire des entreprises concernées*. Brussels: European Trade Union Institute.

Ghertman, M. and Allen, M. (1984) *An Introduction to the Multinationals*. Basingstoke: Macmillan.

Gold, M. and Hall, M. (1992) *Report on European Level Information and Consultation in Multinational Companies – An Evaluation of Practice*. EFILWC.

Griffiths, A. and Wall, S. (1996) *Applied Economics*. London: Longman.

Hamill, J. (1983) 'The labour relations practices of foreign owned and indigenous firms', *Employee Relations* 5 (1), 14–16.

Hamill, J. (1984a) 'Multinational corporations and industrial relations in the UK', *Employee Relations*, 6 (3), 12–16.

Hamill, J. (1984b) 'Labour relations decision making within multinational corporations'. *Industrial Relations Journal*, 15 (2), 30–4.

Hendry, C. (1994) *Human Resource Strategies for International Growth*. London: Routledge.

Hodgetts, R. M. and Luthans, F. (1994) *International Management*. 2nd edn. Maidenhead: McGraw-Hill.

Hodgetts, R. M. and Luthans, F. (1997) *International Management*. 3rd edn. Maidenhead: McGraw-Hill.

Hollinshead, G. and Leat, M. (1995) *Human Resource Management: An International and Comparative Perspective on the Employment Relationship*. London: Financial Times Pitman Publishing.

Ietto-Gillies, G. (1997) 'Working with the big guys: hostility to transnationals must be replaced by co-operation', *New Economy*, 4 (1).

Jones, A.K.V. (1990) 'Quality management the Nissan way', in Dale, B. and Plunkett, J. (eds) *Managing Quality*. London: Philip Allan, pp. 44–51.

Keller, B. (1991) 'The role of the State as a corporate actor in industrial relations system' in Adams, R. *Comparative Industrial Relations: Contemporary Research and Theory*. London: HarperCollins.

Kennedy, T. (1980) *European Labour Relations*. Lexington Books.

Legge, K. (1995) *Human Resource Management: Rhetorics and Realities*. Basingstoke: Macmillan.

Levitt, T. (1983) 'The globalisation of markets', *Harvard Business Review*, May/June, 92–102.

Marchington, M. and Wilkinson A. (1996) *Core Personnel and Development*. London: Institute for Personnel and Development.

Marginson, P. and Sisson, K. (1994) 'The structure of transnational capital in Europe: the emerging Euro-company and its implications for industrial relations', in Hyman, R. and Ferner, A. (eds) *New Frontiers in European Industrial Relations*. Oxford: Blackwell.

Marginson, P. and Sisson, K. (1996) 'Multi-national companies and the future of collective bargaining: a review of the research issues', *European Journal of Industrial Relations*, 2 (2), 173–97.

Maurice, M., Silvestre, J. J. and Sellier, F. (1980) 'Societal differences in organising manufacturing units: a comparison of France, West Germany and Great Britain', *Organisational Studies* 1, 59–86.

Milne, S. (1991) 'Germany 37, Britain 39', *The Guardian*, 25 October.

Mueller, F. and Purcell, J. (1992) 'The Europeanisation of manufacturing and the decentralisation of bargaining: multinational management strategies in the European automobile industry', *International Journal of Human Resource Management*, 3 (1).

OECD (1997) *Financial Market Trends*. June. Paris: Organization for Economic Cooperation and Development.

Parker, M. and Slaughter, J. (1988) *Choosing Sides: Unions and the Team Concept*. Boston, MA: Labour Notes.

Peel, J. (1979) *The Real Power Game*. New York: McGraw-Hill.

Perlmutter, H. (1969) 'The tortuous evolution of the multi-national corporation', *Columbus Journal of World Business*, 4 (1), 9–18.

Porter, M. E. (1985) *Competitive Advantage*. New York: Free Press.

Prahalad, C. K. and Doz, Y.L. (1987) *The Multinational Mission*. New York: Free Press.

Rivest, C. (1996) 'Voluntary European Works Councils', *European Journal of Industrial Relations*, 2 (2), 235–53.

Schregle, J. (1981) 'Comparative industrial relations: pitfalls and potential', *International Labour Review*, 120 (1).

Schulten, T. (1996) 'European Works Councils: prospects of a new system of European industrial relations', *European Journal of Industrial Relations*, 2 (3), 303–24.

Sengenberger, W. (1992) 'Intensified competition, industrial restructuring and industrial relations', *International Labour Review*, 131.

Spivey, W. and Thomas, L. (1990) 'Global management concepts, themes, problems and research issues', *Human Resource Management*, 29 (1).

Storey, J. (1992) *Developments in the Management of Human Resources*. Oxford: Blackwell.

UNCTAD (1994). *World Investment Report 1994: Transnational Corporations, Employment and the Workplace*. United Nations Conference on Trade and Development.

UNCTAD (1995) *World Investment Report 1995*. United Nations Conference on Trade and Development.

Visser, J. and Ebbinghaus, B. (1992) 'Making the most of diversity? European integration and transnational organisation of labour', in Greenwood, J., Grote, J.R. and Ronit, K. (eds) *Organised Interests and the European Community.* London: Sage, pp. 206–37.

Wickens, P. (1987) *The Road to Nissan.* Basingstoke: Macmillan.

Wilkins, M. (1970) *The Emergence of the Multinational Enterprise.* Cambridge: Cambridge University Press.

Chapter 5

TRADE UNIONS

Jackie Sinclair

Learning objectives

By the end of this chapter, readers should be able to:

- provide a definition of trade unions and employee associations, and to trace their early development;
- examine the origins, functions, structure, internal organisation and powers of trade unions;
- examine trends in union membership and explanations for variation;
- analyse the challenges facing trade unions in the 1990s.

TRADE UNION FUNCTIONS AND POWERS

No longer is major prominence afforded by the media or some other commentators to trade unions and their activities during the 1990s; yet in practice they are a reality in many of Britain's workplaces, with 238 registered trade unions, a combined membership of over 8 million, and almost half the population of Britain employed in workplaces where trade unions are recognised for negotiating pay and conditions. They are central to employee relations in Britain and other countries. They have nevertheless suffered varying fortunes, including a loss of membership and other challenges, particularly throughout the 1980s and early 1990s. However, they do remain a significant force in Britain, with membership and trade union presence bearing up well in comparison with other Western countries such as France and the USA. This chapter examines the development of trade unionism, the principles of collective organisation and the fortunes of trade unions in recent years.

What trade unions are, and what they do

Unions or other employee organisations are essentially 'reactive' bodies, since their existence depends on an already existing group of workers, employed by the same employer or in the same location, occupation or industry. Trade unions are essentially 'secondary' organisations, since, as Hyman puts it, 'they are associations of workers who are already "organised" by those to whom they sell their labour power and whose actions they are designed to influence' (quoted in Bain, 1983:61). This characteristic is significant since it is crucial in reaching an understanding of the powers available to trade unions at a particular time, and their ability to be proactive or reactive in response to the various challenges facing them not only in recent years, but throughout their development. The history of the trade union movement is littered with examples of struggles against not only employers over pay and conditions of work, but against the state, for the right to exist. Such struggles, and resultant victories and defeats, have shaped and been shaped by the political, economic and social context of each particular era, as well as by the circumstances of individual employers or industries. Thus, what trade unions *are*, is inseparable from what they do.

The most well-known definition of a trade union was coined by the historians, Sidney and Beatrice Webb (1920):

> A continuous association of wage earners for the purpose of maintaining or improving the conditions of their working lives.

This conveys two significant features of trade unions: the notion of a collective organisation, and that the composition must be of wage earners – employees rather than owners of enterprises. There are also legal definitions, such as that in the Trade Union and Labour Relations (Consolidation) Act of 1992, which similarly conveys the notion of collectivism but does not insist on the organisation being a permanent one. This refers to an organisation, whether permanent or temporary, which consists wholly or mainly of workers of one or more description and is an organisation whose principal purposes include the regulation of relations between workers of that description, and employers or employers' associations.

Both definitions refer to the key functions of a trade union, which in general terms, denote protection of its members with respect to pay and conditions, and the rules governing the employment relationship. However, such definitions are limited since they fail to capture the complexity and variability of trade unions as organisations; this also has implications for tracing how trade unions developed, and in considering how they are organised democratically.

Defining trade unions and describing their functions are normally subject to a qualitative analysis which utilises the concept of *unionateness* (Blackburn, 1967). This has been used to try to capture the degree to which the organisation is committed to the broad aims and ideology of the trade union movement, based on the following principles:

1 whether the body declares itself a trade union;

2 whether it is registered as a trade union;

3 whether it is affiliated to the Trades Union Congress (TUC);

4 whether it is affiliated to the Labour Party;

5 whether it is independent of employers for the purposes of negotiation;

6 whether it regards collective bargaining and the protection of the interests of its members, as employees, as a major function;

7 whether it is prepared to be militant, using all forms of industrial action which may be effective.

The more of these elements are embodied by the organisation, the more 'unionate' it is regarded, although not all of these elements are of equal importance for unionateness. There is significant variation among trade unions in Britain and in Europe and elsewhere, particularly as to the means by which they seek to perform their functions, and some demonstrate a high or low degree of unionateness. Some trade unions, for example, have been prepared to take industrial action in pursuit of their members' interests, as in element 7, while others historically have not (e.g. the nurses' union, the Royal College of Nursing, until recently) or are legally prohibited from doing so (e.g. police). Some do not declare themselves as trade unions as in 1, but are more akin to professional associations which regulate not only relations with employers, but the professional standards of their members (e.g. some health service professional unions such as the Royal College of Midwives). In other trade unions, collective bargaining may not be paramount; the early craft unions were opposed to it, and favoured unilateral regulation with rates of pay dictated to employers, while in recent years, some teachers' trade unions (e.g. National Association of Schoolmasters/Union of Women Teachers) have abandoned collective bargaining and pursued Pay Review Bodies as a form of pay determination, a method which does not involve face-to-face bargaining with the employer. Nevertheless, a strong presence of other 'unionate' characteristics may be detected among such unions. Some unionate elements may be present in order to retain legal or other protections. For example, all except a small number of staff associations are registered as trade unions, by the Certification Officer, who must be satisfied that a trade union is truly independent of the employer, or other external agencies such as the state, before granting a certificate of independence.

The functions of trade unions do focus mainly on their 'bread and butter' role. Unions do normally negotiate on behalf of their members for pay and conditions, and an important function is the policing or monitoring of agreements. They seek to prevent employers from imposing arbitrary treatment on their members by negotiating rules that govern the employment relationship, and they represent their members on an individual basis in cases of disciplinary action, potential dismissal or discrimination.

Crouch outlines the goals of unions as organisations, emphasising the protection of the worker as the vulnerable party within an unequal employment relationship; such goals however are inherently defensive and reactive as opposed to initiating (Crouch, 1982: 121). Even the miners, traditionally viewed as the most militant of trade unions in Britain, in a major dispute prior to the 1926 General Strike were simply engaged in resisting increased working hours and cuts in pay, hence the slogan 'not a penny off the pay, not a second off the day' (Crouch, 1982: 122). This defensiveness has been a source of frustration for some radicals and Marxists, in that working class movements, in particular the trade unions, have often limited themselves to short-term gains within the wages system.

However, these basic defensive functions *are* supplemented often by wider objectives; the unionate characteristics do refer to affiliation by unions to political bodies or commitment to the labour movement and other social aims. Most larger trade unions affiliate to the umbrella organisation of the trade union movement, the TUC and this implies some degree of identification with the broader labour movement. Unions such as the National Union of Teachers (NUT) affiliated late, and one of the largest ten unions, the Royal College of Nursing, is non-affiliated. However, other health services unions have very recently taken up TUC affiliation, such as the Chartered Society of Physiotherapy and the Society of Radiographers. Labour Party affiliation is less widespread among trade unions; by 1992, 30 of the 70 TUC-affiliated unions were also affiliated to the Labour Party, while 45 unions maintained a political fund for spending on political objectives, which can include campaigning or lobbying Parliament.

■ What should unions do?

Defending members' interests is essential, as described above, but priorities will change from time to time in accordance with particular circumstances. A British Social Attitudes Survey conducted among those with a recognised union at their workplace reveals that employees' views on what trade unions should aim to do varied significantly on key issues, in the years 1989 and 1994 (Table 5.1).

■ Table 5.1 Employees' views of what trade unions should try to do, 1989 and 1994

Unions should...	1989 (%)	1994 (%)
Protect existing jobs	28	37
Improve working conditions	21	20
Improve pay	28	15
Have more say over management's long-term plans	6	14
Reduce pay differences at the workplace	6	4
Work for equal opportunities for women	3	2

Source: *Social Trends* 26 (1996: 92).

By 1994 more than twice as many wanted their union to protect jobs as wanted them to improve pay, although these were considered of equal importance in the 1989 survey. No doubt influential was that inflation was at a low level during the 1990s, while job insecurity and unemployment had risen as major concerns.

These various goals, and the priorities of trade unions are not static and unchanging as the issues facing the membership will depend on the specific historical context. However, Hyman and Fryer (1975; cf. McIlroy, 1995) point to the institutional goals that trade unions may develop as organisations, and which may from time to time conflict with members' concerns. For example, a fundamental goal will be the survival of the organisation, implying the need to sustain itself through an unfavourable economic or political climate or survive the pressure on resources during a lengthy dispute.

Financial stability and efficiency may also be key goals, required to maintain the functioning and day-to-day business of the union, yet these may conflict with the goals
of union democracy, or inhibit the members' wish to take strike action, which is often
costly to a trade union.

Furthermore, there may be long-term goals that relate not just to the union as an
organisation in its own right, but to the broad functions of the labour movement. Trade
unions, as part of this movement, always had a commitment to economic, political and
social changes, and the advancement of workers, across national boundaries. Hyman
makes this explicit (1975: 87):

> Trade unionists have often proclaimed far more radical aims: the reconstruction of the
> social order; the abolition of the dominating role of profit; the establishment of workers'
> control of industry; the reorganisation of the economy to serve directly the needs of the
> producers and the general members of society; the humanisation of work; the elimination
> of gross inequalities in standards of living and conditions of life; the transformation of
> cultural richness from the privilege of a minority to the property of all.

Such aspirations are often reflected in the rule books of individual unions, and TUC statements and those of federations of labour.

◼ Unionateness and other employee organisations

While trade unions are the most usual arrangement in which employees combine together, there are other forms of employee organisation. In the UK it has been convention that
trade unions are created by the members on behalf of the members (or occasionally
through merger) rather than through an external agency such as the state. This in itself is
essential as a requirement by the Certification Officer, who must be satisfied that an
employee organisation is truly independent of employers or other external intervention
before it can be registered as a trade union or receive legal protections and immunities
under the law. This has had implications for the small number of staff associations evident
in Britain. Some are seen as akin to the Japanese 'in-house' unions, which typically have
been company sponsored. In Britain these have been limited to the finance or insurance
industries, and to white-collar or managerial employees within these sectors; the total
membership is not counted separately by the Certification Officer, but up to 2 million people may be members (Gospel and Palmer, 1993: 141). These various employee institutions
do not remain unchanging, however. As Farnham and Pimlott report (1995: 106) some
staff associations, such as the Banking, Insurance, and Finance Union, and the National
and Local Government Officers' Association, began life as non-unionate staff associations
and became more unionate and independent over time, now existing as independent trade
unions through mergers or through their own development.

In recent years employees in the finance sectors appear more 'unionate' as demonstrated by affiliation to the TUC of the Independent Union of Halifax Staff, the Nat West
Staff Association and the former Barclays Group Staff Union, Unifi. These developments,
according to Storey, reflect the enormous changes in the industry, namely restructuring
and 'downsizing', and the abandonment of paternalist practices by employers (Storey,
1995 cited in Heery, 1997).

An interesting example emerged during the 1990s of a staff association being refused a certificate of independence by the government-appointed Certification Officer. Following the banning of existing trade unions at the government's spy headquarters at Cheltenham, Government Communication Headquarters (GCHQ), by the Conservative government in 1984, the GCHQ Staff Federation applied for the certificate and was refused in 1989 by the CO, and in 1992 by the Employment Appeal Tribunal, and again in November 1996 by the CO. This was on the grounds that the GCSF was vulnerable to interference by the employer at GCHQ (Certification Officer, 1996):

- The Federation's freedom to affiliate with other organisations was significantly restricted; it could not merge with another union nor could it recruit voting members from elsewhere to broaden its membership base.

- The withdrawal of employer-provided facilities could produce severe disruption to the Federation's activities.

- The Federation was faced with an effective ban on taking or inducing industrial action.

Other organisations which have been refused a certificate of independence by the Certification Officer are the Association of Premier League and Football League Referees and Linesmen, and the Clerical Medical Staff Association. Clearly, some key characteristics of unionateness, in particular independence from the employer, are essential to ensure that the union is genuinely able to act on behalf of its members. This is in contrast with so-called 'sweetheart unions' in the USA, which were used to prevent the spread of independent unionism, or the company-based Japanese unions, which are often considerably constrained by the employer.

The rationale for collective organisation among employees

Why is it considered important for employees to have an independent body to act on their behalf, to regulate the employment relationship? Why is it important for employees to combine into a collective organisation, rather than individually deal with their employer? First, not all workers do join trade unions, and it is worth exploring the reasons for this, prior to considering the rationale for collective organisation.

Crouch (1982: 47) cites a series of reasons why an individual, or a group of employees should choose not to join in combination to form a trade union. A key feature, both historically and in more recent times, is employer or government hostility. If the costs of joining or forming a trade union may be sackings, imprisonment or deportation to the other side of the world, clearly this is likely to present a major dilemma for many employees, even if others still have taken that risk. While trade union organisation became legally permissible, or even encouraged, in European countries, at least from the early part of the twentieth century, their suppression continued in other parts of the world, in newly industrialised or developing countries such as South Korea, Brazil, South Africa and Singapore. Suppression or avoidance of trade union organisation was, and remains, common also in certain regions of the USA, such as the south and west, or certain firms such as those associated with 'Silicon Valley', in hi-tech, computer-related industries. Indeed, employer tactics for discouraging union organisation have been categorised by Donald Roy as 'fear stuff, sweet stuff and evil stuff' (cf. Crouch, 1982: 48). In other words, they could be punitive, with employees threatened with dismissal for attempting union organisation (fear); they could be designed to entice workers away from trade unions by offering generous benefits (sweet); or they could involve methods of propaganda such as allegations of unions' links to communism, witchcraft, (evil), etc.

Legal or employer suppression of trade unions, therefore, can act as a disincentive for workers to take such a risk, even though many still do. However, even in Western countries such as Britain, where the climate was more favourable to union organisation at least in many industries after the Second World War, groups of employees or individuals still can be reluctant to join. In the absence of a statutory obligation on employers to recognise a trade union, the employees still rely on employers' willingness to recognise and bargain with unions.

In other instances the trade unions themselves may have done little to attract the membership of groups that have traditionally been hard to organise such as young people, part-time women workers, or employees in industries such as hotels and catering. On the other hand, unions could historically, in some industries, ensure through a pre- or post-entry closed shop, that only members of a particular trade union could be employed in a particular occupation, hence increasing the likelihood of an individual or group taking up membership.

Apart from these structural factors, which may inhibit the formation or spread of trade unionism, or encourage them, there are still 'lone' individuals who choose not to join a trade union, even if membership is widespread at their organisation. This can be for a number of reasons such as ideological opposition to trade unions, or even indifference or a failure to appreciate any discernible benefits. However, a further explanation relates to the so-called *'freerider'*, who does not join, simply because he or she receives the benefits of union membership regardless of whether he or she actually joins. The individual need not pay a subscription to the trade union, because on a rational calculation, the employer negotiates a pay increase with the trade union, but this is awarded to all employees within a particular occupation, section or industry. Such individuals are often presented as harmlessly exercising their individual freedom not to join or contribute to a trade union if they do not wish to. This is to miss the point, however, since only through collective voice can most individuals receive protection in the first place. As discussed below, union strength and solidarity are based on cohesion and a claim to represent at least a significant proportion of workers in a particular grouping. Their strength relies on numbers, and their ability to organise on a collective basis; this is qualitatively as well as quantitatively different from being simply a collection of individuals. It is this notion whether, conscious or unconscious, which informs the impetus for collective organisation.

Many writers (Hyman; 1975; Crouch; 1982; McIlroy, 1995) have as their starting point the disadvantage of the individual worker when facing his or her employer, due to the imbalance of power in the employment relationship. This hinges on the nature of employment under capitalism; the employee has simply his or her labour to sell in return for wages, while the employer has the advantage of ownership of the business, or the enterprise, and the capital which is invested within it. Colin Crouch investigates this rationale, the drive to combine, which is derived from attempting to redress the balance (Crouch, 1982: 45):

> Is it rational for workers to combine together in unions at all? The simplest answer is to point to the weakness of the isolated individual worker in his relations with his employer (sic). While the labour contract pretends to be an even-handed relationship between two equal partners, this is purely a legal fiction. The individual employee is always precisely that, an individual man or woman; but the 'individual employer' is probably a company, including among its employees those working on problems of how to control labour and keep its costs down. ... Combination appears as a rational strategy for workers because it offers the chance of reducing, though never of overcoming, this inequality.

By forming combinations, the individual has the protection of the whole group of workers, who by acting collectively can limit the employer's ability to, for example, offer very low rates of pay; they can threaten to withdraw their labour unless certain conditions improve, and they can exert some control over the labour market which is available to employers, by controlling entry to a trade or profession through apprenticeship or training requirements. The ability to do these depends on a variety of factors, which hinge on the relative power relations between management and trade unions that exist in a given situation. However, the general imbalance between workers and management is not just based on the position of the former in relation to the latter. It is the nature of capitalism, in which employers themselves have to struggle to retain competitiveness, by keeping up with ever-changing market demands and processes such as new production methods. In this struggle, management are under pressure to alter the 'wage-effort' bargain in their favour, by intensifying the pace of work, through, for example, the use of machinery, or increasing the length of time that workers spend at work. Indeed, jobs themselves are threatened by changes in technology and market conditions, from time to time. Such conditions are always in a state of flux, and the factors that influence unions' and employers' powers will include the nature of the labour market and product market, the current legislative climate, i.e. whether state policy encourages or undermines trade unions and collective bargaining, and the union membership itself, its cohesion and the degree of solidarity among the workforce (Coates, 1983:60).

There exists, therefore, an 'invisible frontier' of control in every workplace (Hyman, 1975: 26) whereby a power struggle takes place on a continuous basis. The notion of power in the workplace means 'the ability of an individual or group to control his (their) physical and social environment; and, as part of this process, the ability to influence the decisions which are taken and are not taken by others' (Hyman, 1975: 26). Yet how are these powers specifically manifest in the workplace? What are the limits of these powers?

Trade union power

The combination of employees within a trade union forms the basis for protecting the individual via collective action. However, this act of combining does not in itself guarantee that they will have the ability to resist the actions of employers. This depends on their power as an organisation. There is much myth and legend concerning the power of trade unions, particularly during the 1960s and 1970s: for example, Jack Jones, leader of the TGWU, was in 1975 described by opinion polls to be 'the most powerful man in Britain' (McIlroy, 1995: 188). Certainly, union leaders wielded some political influence during the years of so-called 'corporatist' governance. Just prior to this period however, trade union-ists such as the 'Shrewsbury Pickets' received harsh penal sectences from the courts. The power of ordinary union members, and of shop stewards or workplace representatives, some of whom did have considerable leverage in some key industries, was in fact vari-able. Claims that trade unions, as a single monolithic body, had powers in excess of those of capital were at best exaggerated and any analysis needs to account for varying cir-cumstances for different groups of workers.

Coates (1983) insists that an analysis of union power should be considered in a wider context, posing the question just how does the power of the trade unions compare with that of the owners of capital, the machinery of the state, such as the courts or police, and which is supported by the prevalent ideology perpetuated by the media? Despite the enor-mous constraints imposed on unions' powers and activities, it was conventional wisdom, at least until recent years, that unions 'have too much power' both in terms of the indus-trial setting and politically. In the case of the former, the power was apparently illustrat-ed by their ability to call strike action, halt production and retain 'rigid' work practices. Yet Coates argues that it was only the high visibility of strikes, picket lines, etc. which fed this notion. Decisions by the owners of capital are taken privately without the high pro-file that often accompanies union demands – such as a resort to picket lines or strikes. This high visibility is often mistaken for a measure of power, rather than a lack of it.

In the case of political powers, the trade unions have traditionally given priority to industrial rather than political methods to exert their influence, by contrast with conti-nental movements where working class political parties preceded the development of trade unions. British trade unions sought limited influence over government policy, except for periods of 'corporatism' during the 1960s and 1970s when they were repre-sented, along with employers' organisations and state representatives, on tripartite bod-ies such as the National Economic Development Office. Historically, they have been sus-picious of state involvement, relying instead on the system of voluntarism. Although the trade unions set up and continue to fund the Labour Party, there was traditionally a rigid separation between political and industrial activities, a demarcation which Hyman is crit-ical of since the two cannot easily be separated (Hyman, 1975: 147). Flanders has also argued that while over-ambitious political aims may damage the unity of a trade union, since the membership will have diverse political views, some minimal political interest must exist, to ensure the unions' have some legal protections or influence on other nation-al policies (Flanders, 1970: 27).

Union powers do exist, Coates concedes, over a range of limited issues such as work-ing conditions, wages, or the speed of work, but these are negative powers to inhibit those of employers or to jointly negotiate over these issues. Negotiation does not extend to the location of factories, levels of investment, the size of the labour force or other strategic decisions (Coates, 1983: 67). Coates therefore is critical of the traditional measures of union power, based on their participation on workplace or state bodies, or even by their effects, which have not been to redistribute wealth or challenge the fundamentals of the economic and social structure. The measures should be based on 'unions' place in the whole structure of social, economic, cultural and political relationships in the society' (Coates, 1983: 75).

Furthermore, not all unions are equal in powers and strength, but much will depend on the strategic importance of the members for the industry or the economy as a whole, or their immediate powers vis-à-vis employers such as the perishability of the product. For example, newspaper printers traditionally relied on their power to stop production of newspapers, which obviously must be sold each day, to gain leverage over their employers. Other groups may have the ability to cause damage to the economy (e.g. transport workers) or risk to human life (e.g. emergency services) should they withdraw their labour but the sensitivity of such action for the 'public interest' has meant that unions are reluctant to take industrial action, or indeed governments have sought to exercise more legalistic controls in terms of disputes in this area – for example, by banning the military and police from taking strike action or forming trade unions.

There are various indicators of trade union power which can provide an idea of the prevailing climate, at national or international and workplace levels. These are:

- union membership in its totality, and membership density, i.e. the proportion of members out of the potential membership and a willingness to act collectively;
- the general economic and business climate, e.g. level of unemployment/employment, product market conditions prevailing in an industry;
- the labour market position of the workers in terms of skills, disposability, ability to disrupt production or services;
- the general political and legal climate which is more or less favourably disposed to encouraging or supporting trade unions, and the level of political influence they might have with regard to political policies;
- the legitimacy offered by employers to trade unions, and their willingness to recognise and negotiate with unions;
- the degree of union activity and facilities at workplace level, e.g. the number, proportions or activities of shop stewards or workplace representatives.

Some of these key influences have produced a less favourable environment for the trade unions generally from the 1980s, although in historical terms, unions faced a harsh climate, with state and employer resistance, from their earliest formation.

TRADE UNION STRUCTURE AND EARLY DEVELOPMENT

Early developments

The formation of employee-based institutions to advance the interests of groups of workers with particular marketable skills originated as far back as feudal times, when guilds, organised around the preservation and protection of skilled journeymen and 'masters' had a fair degree of power in relation to the regulation of apprenticeships, pay and the rules covering work methods, including preventing the dilution of skills. The trade unions developed during the early part of the eighteenth century, and were known as Friendly Societies. Their function was to provide mutual insurance and other benefits such as sickness and unemployment benefit, for those members who made contributions. In the case of trade unions in their more recognisable form and exclusively based on employee organisation, the Webbs (1920) trace their development from the eighteenth and nineteenth centuries, when the state and employers were united in their opposition to combinations of workmen. The Combination Acts of 1799 and 1800 outlawed them until the repeal of these laws in 1824 and 1825, but similar laws were applied on the continent. Even with the lifting of an outright ban, however, employers were still able to victimise trade unionists or dismiss workers who were members or activists in trade unions. Those trade unions that emerged first and managed to retain a foothold were those where the members had skills that were rare or valuable to the employer, compared to general labourers who would have been more easily replaceable.

The earliest unions, in Britain as well as in other European countries, were the craft-based bodies based on small-scale enterprises at district, local level, typically in engineering but also in carpentry, printing and textiles. The source of their strength was the control of external and internal labour markets, through the imposition of the closed shop, or compulsory union membership, the control of apprenticeships, and rules and regulations related to their skills and craft. These bodies continued to provide social insurance benefits such as unemployment and death benefits. Unilateral insistence on rates of pay was preferred to collective bargaining, and was locally based, with employers who refused to comply being boycotted; eventually leading to employers themselves becoming organised into employers' associations. Eventually, by the 1850s the craft unions became organised on a national basis and were to become known as 'new models unions' with the Amalgamated Engineering Union (AEU) as the classic model union. Full-time officers were employed, and administrative procedures and processes set up. These unions remained 'élite' bodies, excluding women and unskilled labourers from membership, and were politically conservative bodies. It was their 'exclusive' characteristics which led to their being known as the 'aristocrats of labour'. Their success depended on their continuing ability to maintain the unions' coverage on a sectional basis, across different industries, although it was equally dependent on employers' demand for their skills and labour. These enviable controls have been whittled away in many crafts, due to changes in the craft occupations themselves, including the impact of technology, which have served to undermine the workers' monopoly on expertise (Gospel and Palmer, 1993: 122). Gospel and Palmer maintain the craft unions' powers were no match for those of the 'ancient professions' of law or medicine, whose professional bodies have wide-ranging powers often backed up by law (Gospel and Palmer, 1993: 122).

It was partly in response to the élitism of the new model unions that the unskilled, general labourers and others began to set up their own organisations whose strength was based on numbers, rather than specific skills, and their aim was to pursue collective bargaining with employers. There was increased momentum, during the 1830s, for 'one great union' which would unite all workers and present a powerful structure to face employers, this aim being achieved briefly by Robert Owen's Grand National Consolidated Trades Union in 1834. This and other trade unions faced a series of setbacks in this period. They still faced persecution by the state, and courts used conspiracy laws in order to defeat them. The famous case of the Tolpuddle Martyrs was one such example, when six Dorset labourers were deported to Australia on charges relating to the 'administering or taking of unlawful oaths', representing a major defeat for the trade union movement in this period (Pelling, 1974: 41). The 'Grand National' was unable to adequately support sections of its membership who took strike action, and the union broke up within a year. It was later, during the 1880s when economic conditions were more favourable for workers, that organisation of relatively unskilled labourers, and particularly women, was successful in some areas, often following strike action against exploitative conditions and starvation wages. The famous 'match girls' strike by women and girls at the Bryant and May factory in 1888 was followed by action by London dockers and gas workers. Successful organisation around issues of casualisation, whereby workers turned up at the dockside in the hope of a day's work, and low pay meant that large groups of unskilled workers now made some impact, and these unions became the forerunners of the large, general unions such as the TGWU and the GMB, which remain highly significant and sizeable unions today.

■ Union classification

Most continental unions tend to be influenced by political and/or religious affiliations. For example, the Catholic church has played a role in the formation of trade unions in Italy, but so too did Socialist or Communist movements. Religious affiliation is also significant in the Netherlands, while the 16 German unions are industry based (Hollinshead and Leat, 1995: 99).

In Britain, the classification of unions normally refers to job territories, but is a complex process and often unsystematic, being constantly undermined by changes in skill and technology, with distinctions gradually becoming less relevant as occupational boundaries have blurred – for example, between 'blue collar' or manual work, and 'white collar' work. In general terms, however, they included the following categories:

- Craft unions, organising a particular trade or skill, e.g. Amalgamated Engineering Union, Royal College of Nursing. Entry would be restricted, and homogenous membership based on qualifications and training.

- Industrial and occupational unions, organising in a specific industry, e.g. National Union of Mineworkers, National Union of Railway, Maritime and Transport Workers. These would often cover numerous grades within an industry, and have less restricted entry than the craft unions. Such forms of organisation developed partly in response to the realisation that the formation of one large union of working class organisation would in all probability not be realised or sustainable.

- General unions, organising across numerous industries. Their original source of membership was unskilled groups who were not organised elsewhere. No restricted entry would operate, subject to inter-union regulations on poaching of members.

While these classifications are useful to the extent that they denote the origins of the trade unions' formation and character, increasingly the characteristics have altered over time. The notion of solidarity with other groups of workers has historically brought trade unions together in alliances or federations. The Triple Alliance of miners, railway and transport workers was formed in 1914 as much to exert pressure on the government of the day, as on employers (Pelling, 1974: 142). The Iron and Steel Trades' Confederation, which developed in 1917, represented part of the general shift towards consolidation and amalgamation of trade unions during that period of financial and membership difficulties.

Furthermore, union structure was complicated by the emergence of white collar and public sector unions beginning after the First World War, and their rapid growth after the Second World War when the expansion of public services meant that trade unions such as the National and Local Government Officers' Association and the large civil service unions became increasingly important. Currently the largest British union, Unison, represents over 1.3 million members in the public sector, having overtaken the Transport and General Workers' Union, which was traditionally the largest. Privatisation of many public sector industries and the tendering of jobs such as school cleaning to private sector companies have affected the membership profile and numbers of the public sector unions.

H.A. Turner, during the 1960s, distinguished between 'open' and 'closed' unions rather than craft or general unions and this serves as a useful reminder that shifts in union structure are not specific to recent years (McIlroy, 1995). Their degree of openness or closedness represented, to some extent, a deliberate strategy for recruitment and consolidating the powers of the membership. The open unions tended to be expansionist, aiming to increase the range of members and expand recruitment into new areas, while closed unions concentrated on the expansion of job controls, status and wages for groups of workers within demarcated areas of skill. McIlroy notes that the current trend is towards openness, while the category of closed unionism is in decline as unions re-adapt their chosen strategies periodically (McIlroy, 1995: 13). In relation to changes in occupational structure, trade union classifications have been reshaped due to the disappearance of some unions and the creation of new ones, often through merger. Craft trade unions such as SLADE and the NGA merged during the 1980s to form the Graphical, Paper, and Media Union and the engineers merged with the electricians in 1992 to form the Amalgamated Engineering and Electrical Union. The pace of mergers accelerated from the 1980s in what McIlroy describes as 'merger mania', with 149 taking place between 1980 and 1991. This is reflected in Table 5.2, which demonstrates the decline in the total

■ Table 5.2 Number of unions, 1979–92, Great Britain

Year	Total number	TUC affiliated unions
1979	453	109
1980	438	108
1981	414	105
1982	408	102
1983	394	98
1984	375	91
1985	370	88
1986	335	87
1987	330	83
1988	314	83
1989	309	78
1990	287	74
1991	275	70
1992	268	69
1993	254	
1994	243	
1995	238	

Source: McIlroy (1995: 19) and *Labour Market Trends*, Statistical update, February (1997: 39).

number of unions since the late 1970s. An outcome of this is the increase in the size of unions, although many do remain small, with some 58 per cent having fewer than 2500 members. Two forms of merger can be used legally. One is a transfer of engagement, normally involving an absorption of one organisation by another – for example, the transfer of the Scottish Health Visitors' Association to the existing public sector union Unison in 1996. The other form of merger involves amalgamation, which usually produces a new organisation. During 1996 one amalgamation and six transfers of engagement took place, the largest involving the amalgamation of the Inland Revenue Staff Federation, and the National Union of Civil and Public Servants, to form the Public Services Tax and Commerce Union.

Table 5.3 shows Britain's major unions by the mid-1990s, compared with the 1989 list of 'top ten' unions, illustrating how the dominance has changed from the large general unions such as the TGWU and the GMB, with a membership based predominantly in manual occupations, towards white collar and public sector unions being in the top positions. The largest eight unions combined account for 62 per cent of all union membership, however (Labour Market Trends, February 1997).

■ **Table 5.3 Membership of top ten unions in 1989 and 1995 compared**

	Top Ten Unions	Membership* (000s)
1989	Transport and General Workers' Union	1271
	GMB	823
	National and Local Government Officers' Association	751
	Amalgamated Engineering Union	742
	Manufacturing, Science, and Finance Union	653
	National Union of Public Employees	605
	Union of Shop, Distributive, and Allied Workers	376
	Electrical, Electronic, Telecommunications, and Plumbing Union	367
	Royal College of Nursing of the UK	286
	Union of Construction, Allied Trades, and Technicians	258
1995	Unison	1355
	Transport and General Workers' Union	897
	GMB	740
	Amalgamated Engineering and Electrical Union	726
	Manufacturing, Science, and Finance Union	446
	Royal College of Nursing of the UK	303
	Union of Shop, Distributive, and Allied Workers	283
	Communication Workers' Union	275
	National Union of Teachers	248
	National Association of Schoolmasters / Union of Women Teachers	234

* Figures rounded up or down to nearest 1000.

Source: Certification Officer's Report (1995), and Sweeney, K. (1996) 'Membership of trade unions in 1994: an analysis based on information from the Certification Officer', *Labour Market Trends*, February, 49–54.

■ Multi-unionism in Britain

The evolution of the British trade union movement has resulted in a complex structure in which unions often compete for members based around the same or similar job territories, and within the same industries and workplaces. This is in contrast to the German structure of union organisation along industry lines, or the Japanese 'in-house' single unions.

Although Britain has seen a decline in the number of unions, there is still a much larger number than exist in other European countries. It is not simply a matter of a large number of unions at national level however; many workplaces have a multi-union presence with different unions representing different grades of staff within the various bargaining units. Millward *et al.* make the point that 'compared with most other European countries the number is enormous and the sheer complexity of negotiating arrangements in Britain is almost incomprehensible to Europeans' (1992: 77). In the public sector multi-unionism is common; teachers in England and Wales, for example have four trade unions representing classroom teachers and two for headteachers, although the majority of teachers are members of the three largest teacher unions.

Table 5.4 illustrates that in 1990 more than 30 per cent of establishments recognised two or more unions for manual workers, while 40 per cent of establishments recognised two or more unions for non-manual workers.

■ **Table 5.4** Percentage of establishments that recognise one or more trade unions, by broad sector

	Number of recognised unions	All establishments (%)		
		1980	1984	1990
Manual	1	65	65	66
	2	18	21	19
	3	9	8	9
	4 or more	8	6	6
Non-manual	1	43	39	45
	2	29	28	31
	3	12	15	9
	4 or more	16	18	14

Source: Millward *et al.* (1992: 78).

Multi-unionism has often been seen as problematic by employers, although McIlroy notes that such criticisms are essentially managerialist (Hyman, cf. McIlroy, 1995: 20). Employers in a small number of new plants on greenfield sites have sought to reduce multi-unionism through the pursuit of 'single-union agreements' or failing that, single table bargaining whereby the trade unions are dealt with on one joint committee, to negotiate a single agreement. From the trade union point of view, inter-union conflict can undermine bargaining tactics and solidarity, or encourage competition and divisions within an industry. In 1990, around a quarter of workplace representatives who reported that there were groups with members in more than one union said there was some active inter-union competition, although this was not prevalent where multi-unionism was already established (Millward *et al.*, 1982: 85).

It is common for the various trade unions to work together and co-ordinate their efforts and bargaining tactics where multi-unionism exists at national or local levels, often on a formal basis through federations such as the Confederation of Shipbuilding and Engineering Unions (CSEU).

The structure of British trade unions and their forms of workplace organisation, which is ever changing and complex, has seen a reduction in smaller bodies, an increased blurring of the distinctiveness of occupational groupings, and occasional inter-union rivalries.

The Trades Union Congress

The TUC, established in 1868, represents the political arm of the trade union movement, existing as a loose affiliation of member unions. Originally it was formed to give trade unions a political voice, and an organisation whereby unions could debate the affairs of the trade union movement as a whole. Its functions are administrative, providing a range of services such as shop steward training, and political, in terms of its pressure group activity. Mediation in inter-union disputes and involvement in strikes are occasional functions. The TUC has a near monopoly of representation, with high levels of union affiliation at over 80 per cent of trade unionists (McIlroy, 1995: 45). In terms of representation, the TUC elects the General Council of approximately 40 members to run its affairs and carry out policy between each annual congress. Membership is related to the size of the affiliated unions, the largest, with between 1.2 million and 1.5 million members being entitled to six seats. There are special provisions or Conferences for groups that have been traditionally under-represented within the trade union movement – for example, reserved seats for women on the General Council, an Annual Women's TUC Conference as well as a Black Workers' Conference. There is some geographical organisation: Scotland has its own TUC, as does Wales, and eight regional councils exist; at local area level the 435 trades councils operate on the basis of affiliation by local union branches, to provide a focal point for unions within a particular area.

The key functions of the TUC are fourfold:

1 As a regulator of trade unions in terms of inter-union conflicts. Traditionally this activity was governed by the Bridlington Agreement of 1939 whereby adjudication between unions was conducted.

2 Service provision for affiliates, particularly in the areas of education and research but also financial and legal services.

3 As the spokesperson of the trade union movement as a whole, particularly in representations with governments, and in seeking to influence economic or employment policies.

4 As a spokesperson for affiliates in the international arena – for example, within the European Union or solidarity links with trade unionists in other countries.

From time to time attempts have been made to provide a stronger role for the TUC – for example in the co-ordination of trade unions or in major disputes with employers – but it remains politically weak and fragmented in comparison with its equivalent in the neighbouring Republic of Ireland (the Irish Congress of Trade Unions) and with other continental bodies. This is particularly so since the TUC's marginalisation by Conservative governments throughout the 1980s. While it did have a significant role at times during the 1970s, on various tripartite bodies such as those set up under the National Economic Development Office, the TUC was criticised for supporting pay restraint in return for walking the 'corridors of power'. In addition, difficulties for a more interventionist role by the TUC are presented by individual trade unions who still value autonomy and few disciplinary measures can be imposed on a dissenter. The ultimate sanction of expulsion is rarely used, although the electricians' union, the EETPU, was expelled in 1988 over the 'poaching' of union members during agreements with employers over 'single-union deals' on greenfield sites. The weaknesses of the TUC were exposed after the 1979 election when the government adopted a hostile stance towards trade unions. Criticisms of the TUC as ineffectual were furthered by its inability to resist anti-union laws introduced throughout the 1980s, but more specific criticisms came over the lack of vigorous support for the miners during the strike over pit closures in 1983/4, and more recently over the dockers' lock-out on Merseyside.

In the period up to and since the election of a Labour government in 1997, the TUC has expressed a desire to develop 'a social partnership' arrangement with the government. John Monks, the General Secretary, hoped to develop a 'social dialogue' with the Confederation of British Industry, on matters such as the influence of European Union rules, and he hoped that 'the problems of competitiveness' for Britain would be up for discussion (*Financial Times*, 22 May 1997). This approach confirms the TUC's desire to be seen to distance itself from the associations of the 1970s, and the 'adversarial' attitude long associated with British trade unionism. Its statement on the future direction for trade unionism in Britain, in the anticipation of an election victory for New Labour, has the following as its preamble (TUC, 1997):

> Just as the nation needs a new Government committed to fairness, so we need a New Unionism so that unions and employers can work together in partnership to make Britain's industries and services more efficient and competitive and to protect people at work. The TUC does not simply look to government for action; it works with unions and employers for the common good.

Just how far such a 'partnership' approach along continental lines could be adopted appears limited; it may not attract great enthusiasm from management, and some trade unions may also be lukewarm, bearing in mind the dominance of the 'voluntarist' approach, the memory of corporatism in the 1970s, the subsequent deregulation of employee and trade union rights, the shift towards increasingly managerial prerogatives which has characterised the recent period, and the continued emphasis by employers and New Labour on deregulation and 'flexible' labour markets. However, structures such as work councils at the workplace, where applicable, may be welcomed by some employees, in the absence of collective bargaining rights.

INTERNATIONAL BODIES

There are several federations of labour organised on an international basis, to which national union bodies normally affiliate. These appeared during the nineteenth century, and had much the same rationale as nationally based confederations: that is, their functions included exchanging information, prevention of strike-breaking by employers and other solidarity measures. Organisations of miners and printers affiliated to their own international bodies in the late 1880s and the first International working men's association was established under the auspices of Karl Marx (Gospel and Palmer, 1993: 152). Currently, the main international confederation for Western countries is the International Confederation of Free Trade Unions, with membership in over 100 countries. It was formed in 1949 following a split from the World Federation of Trade Unions, which obviously became dominated by the (former) Communist bloc of the Soviet Union and Eastern European countries, although its affiliates included European Communist-led union confederations in Italy and France (Bridgford and Stirling, 1994: 91). Since the demise of the Communist bloc, the ICFTU now dominates at international level, although some smaller organisations also exist, such as the World Confederation of Labour (WCL) which has a religious base. The Commonwealth Trade Union Council aims to provide assistance to trade unions in 40 Commonwealth countries, covering some 25 million workers (McIlroy, 1995: 51).

The International Labour Organization was founded as a United Nations agency in 1919, formed due to a recognition by nation states that the fair treatment of labour was significant in terms of preventing social unrest. To this end, the prevention of gross exploitation of employees was a broad aim, but other objectives exist alongside this, as the ILO recognised that social reforms such as the elimination of child labour, would have a likely impact on production costs to employers (Hollinshead and Leat, 1995: 292). The ILO attempts to put its 'wish list' into practice through two instruments: conventions, which are legally binding, and recommendations, which nation states may ratify and adopt into their own domestic law. ILO standards exist in many areas related to the protection of workers – for example, equality of treatment and equal opportunity, freedom of workers to associate, conditions of work such as health and safety, and the protection of young workers.

At a European level, the European Trade Union Confederation (ETUC) was formed in 1972 and has 40 affiliated national union confederations representing some 45 million employees. Its functions include research and education but its main role is as one of the 'Social Partners' at EU level, representing its affiliated membership in talks with the employer body, UNICE, and in relation to the 'Social Dialogue' on various committees and other bodies. Its powers, however, do not extend to collective bargaining, and severe obstacles appear likely to prevent the prospect of transnational bargaining, not least employer opposition voiced by the CBI, and the tendency in Britain for the location of bargaining to be moving downwards, rather than upwards (McIlroy, 1995: 340). Yet, the free mobility of capital and the influence of multinational companies, across the EU as well as worldwide, may make these developments appear more urgent to the trade union side. Exhibit 5.1 illustrates how growing numbers of trade unions are taking a more proactive rather than reactive stance in mobilising across global frontiers. Links between trade unions have been set up and maintained across frontiers. For example, the AEU has established links with the German metalworkers, and meetings and contacts are maintained by unions in similar industries across Europe. However, the prospect of transnational mergers seems some way off, in part due to the British unions' acceptance of inferior conditions in the competition for jobs (McIlroy, 1995: 341).

■ Exhibit 5.1

Labour unions go global

Think global, act local was once the slogan of corporations and environmentalists but it is fast becoming a rallying cry of international labour. In the past, trade unions found it hard to work in unity across national frontiers: now they have started to mobilise in campaigns applying pressure on some of the world's large companies.

There is a growing number of examples of trade unions taking the offensive. Last week the Geneva-based International Federation of Commercial, Technical and Clerical Employees launched a campaign aimed at unionising employees in Toys R Us, the US-based retailer, in 20 countries.

The Teamsters, the US's largest trade union, have taken their protest over what they see as an unfair distribution policy by Ahold, the supermarket multi-national, to the company's home country of the Netherlands, placing advertisements in local newspapers which claim it is hurting the 'poor and elderly' in the US by building hypermarkets outside inner cities.

The Postal, Telegraph and Telephone International, which represents unions in the sector around the world, is involved in international action against Sprint, the US company, after it dismissed Hispanic workers trying to organise a union at its La Conexion Familiar subsidiary in San Francisco.

Deutsche Postgewerkschaft, the German telecommunications union, has indirectly pressurised Sprint to negotiate with its fired US workers by demanding that Deutsche Telekom should introduce a code of basic labour standards as part of its deal to launch a £2.7bn joint venture with Sprint.

French telecoms workers are holding up a similar deal between France Télécom and Sprint while STRM, the Mexican telecoms company, has drawn up charges against the US company which it alleges is in breach of the labour agreements of the North Atlantic Free Trade Agreement.

There is also widespread trade union mobilisation through the International Metalworker's Federation against the anti-union behaviour of Bridgestone, the Japanese tyremaker at its US Firestone subsidiary where striking employees were replaced with a substitute workforce.

This involved a recent protest visit to Japan by leaders of the US Steelworker's union who picketed the company's headquarters.

Officials from the same union visited the UK recently to lobby against British Steel's decision to close its unionised operations in Cleveland and open non-union steel-making facilities in Alabama. Solidarity action is not just being organised by established union organisations. In the current unofficial strike on Merseyside in the UK, dockers are in direct contact with the Longshoreman's union on the US west coast. Support is also coming from union activists in Australia, Israel and Spain.

Nor is all international union action confrontation. Last year, two French companies – Accor, the world's largest hotel chain, and Danône, the food group – signed agreements with IUF, the Hotels and Catering International union that upholds basic labour rights for their employees.

Such diversity of union activity suggests a belated awareness of the impact the new global economy is having on international labour and this looks set to grow in 1996.

In June, at its world congress in Brussels, the International Confederation of Free Trade Unions will adopt a strategy to challenge the power of the trans-national companies especially around the Pacific rim.

The organisation, claiming to represent 127m workers in 190 trade union centres across the world, plans an integrated information network in alliance with the 15 trade secretariats that cover trade unions in different industrial sectors.

'We are building a practical partnership for the first time in response to globalisation,' says Mr Bill Jordan, the ICFTU's general secretary.

Such labour assertiveness against global corporations must not be exaggerated but it appears to reflect a new militancy.

'In the past, international labour was about meetings of top union leaders exchanging platitudes. Now it involves shop stewards and union officials in a practical way as a normal and not an exceptional part of their work,' says Mr Denis MacShane, UK Labour MP for Rotherham and the author of a forthcoming book on global labour.

He believes the unions have taken '15 years to catch up' with the 'globalisation of capital'.

But, with the spread of the Internet and use of information technology, workers and unions are forging corporate strategies that go beyond resolutions.

▶

■ **Exhibit 5.1 continued**

The new mood has been helped by the recent change of leadership at the head of the AFL-CIO union federation. Under its new president, Mr John Sweeney, the US labour movement looks set to take the offensive against what it sees as the excesses of corporate America in the global economy.

But international labour still lacks the clout consumer pressure groups can wield against corporate power such as that used last year by Greenpeace against Shell's threat to dump its Brent Spar oil platform in the north Atlantic.

Source: Robert Taylor (1996) *Financial Times*, 16 January.

TRADE UNION INTERNAL ORGANISATION AND DEMOCRACY

■ Union organisation

Typically, British unions are formally organised geographically: the most basic unit is the branch, which may cover the membership in a particular area such as a town or district.

Alternatively, the branch may operate at the workplace (or the chapel, as it is known in some industries such as print and journalism) and all membership are generally entitled to attend, and participate in branch business, usually electing a committee to administer the branch. The next tier of organisation is often a regional or divisional committee, attended by members or delegates who are elected by members of the branch. The key decision-making body of most trade unions at national level is the National Executive Committee (NEC), often having the responsibility for making policy decisions in between annual or biennial conferences which would normally constitute the supreme decision-making and policy-forming body of a trade union (Fig. 5.1). The NECs and principal officers must be elected by postal ballot of individual members, at least every five years, since legislation during the 1980s overrode the unions' own rules on electing their officers. Prior to this, officers could be elected at branch level, or by ballot at annual conference. The principal officers of the union, whose role is to execute policy and administer the affairs of the union, report to the NEC. Of the paid officials, the General Secretary would normally be the most senior officer and since the legal reforms of the 1980s, must be elected by postal ballot. Full-time officials are appointed and salaried, often starting life, particularly in some craft unions such as the AEU, as lay activists or shop stewards. The full-time officers handle negotiations, grievances, disputes and advice on employment rights, and often deal with matters such as union recruitment as well. Specialist local officers may be employed from time to time also, such as field officers with responsibility for recruitment drives, or for providing advice or services to membership in various geographical locations. Other salaried staff of a trade union may include legal staff, researchers, equality officers, press or publicity officers and education or training officers, and support staff such as clerks and administrators.

The ratio of full-time officers to members was traditionally low compared to that in continental unions, with one employed for every 3800 members during the 1960s (McIlroy, 1995: 39) and since then fluctuating only in line with declining or rising membership levels.

It is evident that unions need considerable resources to run their affairs, and the larger unions have assets comparable with those of a small business, derived overwhelmingly from membership subscriptions. Unison had a total income of £105 318 000 for 1995,

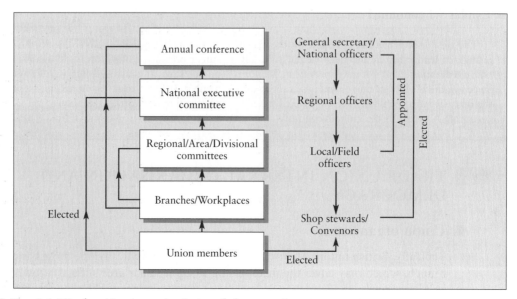

Fig. 5.1 Trade union organisation and democratic structure

while that for the TGWU, the largest general union, was £64 139 000 (Certification Officer, 1996: 52). However, considerable expenditure is required to service the membership; despite mergers, which have accelerated in recent years in part for financial reasons, and economies made in personnel and administration during the 1990s, 'overall unions are poorer in the 1990s than they were in the 1950s' (McIlroy, 1995: 45).

Shop stewards are the workplace representatives who act on behalf of their members in the department, section or workplace as a whole. Joint committees of shop stewards can be set up on multi-union sites in order to coordinate bargaining or other activities. The shop steward, as the nearest point of contact for the 'rank and file' union members, is normally the first to communicate on their behalf with management although stewards' duties vary from routine administration and collection of members' subscriptions, to organising branch activity or industrial disputes. Shop steward organisation became significant during the First World War; the priority of government was to maximise production for the war effort, and this involved curbing the spread of shop steward militancy by seeking to shift bargaining away from the workplace, to national level. The role of stewards gained impetus after the Second World War also, when stewards and work groups were able to build on the fragmented 'informal' systems of bargaining, which had begun to supplement, or even undermine, national arrangements. The development of 'domestic bargaining', conducted between stewards and local management, was largely fragmented and informal, and based on 'custom and practice' enabling stewards to take advantage of local bonus or piecework schemes, in order to improve conditions for their membership. Such bargaining was often outside the control not only of full-time union officers, but even senior management, leading the Royal Commission on Trade Unions and Employers' Associations of 1968 (the Donovan Commission) to conclude that 'two systems' of industrial relations were in operation in Britain, and recommend that more official and orderly collective bargaining should be instigated to make industry more competitive.

Despite this picture of shop stewards during the post-war period, as an active and relatively autonomous group with the ability to undermine national, multi-employer agreements, this form of domestic bargaining was rare outside certain sectors of manufacturing, engineering and construction. In the public sector and among much of white-collar work, for example, it was virtually non-existent (McIlroy, 1995: 99). Even within those sectors where it was prevalent, the image of shop stewards as militants and troublemakers gained currency in the media and elsewhere, while on the left they were often viewed romantically as 'standard bearers' of working class emancipation. Yet their normally mundane duties of collecting members' subscriptions, and dealing with day-to-day welfare issues as well as individual and collective grievances, meant that their role served a useful function for management, not least as a channel for their members' discontent (McIlroy, 1995: 103). The Donovan Commission portrayed them as 'lubricants' rather than 'irritants' and they were to play a key role in the formalisation of agreements in the post-Donovan era of reform. During the 'social contract' period of the 1970s when pay restraint was the *quid pro quo* for an increase in employment rights, these included facilities for shop stewards such as office facilities, time off for training, etc. Such facilities have led to accusations of 'bureaucratisation' among shop stewards, undermining their independence and their main function of organising the rank-and-file members, and of distancing stewards from their members while concentrating on procedures and paper-chasing. Supporters note, however, that significant levels of 'bureaucracy' existed prior to the 1970s, and that shop stewards' activities, including the degree of conflict and accommodation with management were always variable by industry (McIlroy, 1995).

The image often portrayed of shop stewards as distanced from both full-time officials and indeed the 'moderate' rank-and-file members, no matter how simplistic, has nevertheless been influential in debates on the issue of trade unions' internal organisation and democratic structures; such debates have by no means been reducible to a left–right ideological split. The original meaning of democracy as 'rule by the people' was realised within the earliest trade unions, which exercised 'primitive democracy' (Clegg, 1972: 95). Indeed, some trade union leaders, among others, believed themselves to be best placed to run the affairs of the union due to their own expertise, with the ordinary member 'supplementing this work' (Allen, 1957, quoted by McIlroy, 1995: 150). The difficulty of identifying union objectives and functions has been discussed, and it is in part the recognition of trade unions as a campaigning force that has generated controversy over the need for their internal democracy. Yet they are essentially voluntary organisations, such bodies normally enjoying relative freedom from state interference. The TUC has pointed out that unions are 'more democratic than the city, the civil service or the media' (McIlroy, 1995: 145). The expectation is often that trade unions should be democratic because they were created by and for the 'grassroots' membership, albeit with all the associated difficulties of agreement on the nature and function of unions. However, even if the problem of identifying the various goals, both short term and long term, is less pressing, there remains the problem of acting upon them, or identifying the mechanisms for realising these goals. Roberto Michels, concerned with the 'problem' of bureaucracy, developed his thesis of the 'iron law of oligarchy' which argued that in any complex organisation, regardless of the so-called democratic machinery or rhetoric, working class organisations would always be subject to domination by the leadership (Crouch, 1982: 161). This was by virtue of its reliance on leaders who have a specialist role and expertise. It is inevitable that control passes to a small élite or oligarchy, who become distanced from the ordinary members by virtue of a more privileged lifestyle. Crouch finds it surprising that Michels could develop a general theory of labour movement democracy based on the experience of the German labour movement prior to the First World War, which existed under an authoritarian regime (Crouch, 1982: 164). Other writers contest the assumption of the iron law as applicable to trade unions since countervailing pressures exist that contest the oligarchic tendency, such as the shop stewards' movement, and members' expectations of democracy (McIlroy, 1995: 156).

Nevertheless, many union members and leaders are aware of the potential for oligarchic tendencies that may arise, and they aim to counter them by adopting structures and procedures that militate against them, and facilitate control from the bottom up. Debate on union democracy is linked to the relationship between three agencies: the national or regional union leadership who are paid their salaries from union funds and thus indirectly through the membership, the lay activists, delegates or shop stewards, who play a key role in union affairs but in an unpaid capacity, and the so-called 'ordinary members' who pay subscriptions but otherwise have a minimal role in union affairs. Issues of control, participation by membership, and accountability of those in elected or influential positions within trade unions are central to the debate, with claims made by both right- and left-wing commentators that it is union leaders who are out of touch with their members, and who need to be made more accountable to the wider membership. Ambiguities do arise in the different levels of a trade union, from what Hyman refers to as the 'two way system of control' by which disciplinary action can be exercised over a member by a union official, who in turn is employed by the membership (Hyman, 1975: 73). This results in a sometimes contradictory relationship in which union officials are subject to very real pressures to exercise control over their members, e.g. during a dispute. Yet they are paid for by the members whom they serve.

How trade unions are judged in terms of democratic credentials depends on which definition or perspective is adopted. Two main models of union democracy are prevalent, and these illustrate how politicians and union leaders have approached the issue; Fairbrother (1983) describes these as the participatory and parliamentary models. The former emphasises membership participation in decision making. Interaction between the various layers of union government is considered essential, via a process of dialogue, debate, discussion and constant examination of policies and decisions. Maximum participation of the membership is important for control of the leadership, emphasising the latter's accountability to those they serve, and collective interests rather than individual preferences are given priority. By contrast, the parliamentary model focuses on the rights of individual members to elect representatives but who will act on their behalf without necessarily consulting with them. Participation is periodic, and the views of the membership made to the leadership on an individual basis, often through ballot papers. As with a Member of Parliament, discretion in the activities of the union leader is exercised, and structures and voting procedures are established to ensure periodic accountability.

It is crucial that the values and assumptions that are implied in these two models of union democracy are considered. The parliamentary model is favoured by some union leaders and/or members but was also favoured by the Conservative governments of the 1980s. For example, the introduction of individual secret ballots prior to industrial action and for the election of union leaders was central to the Trade Union Act of 1984. Such a procedure dispenses with the need for dialogue and continuous involvement by an active membership, but simply voting on a one-off basis is the sum total of membership participation. Critics of this approach argue that the legislation fails to recognise trade unions as cooperative organisations that exist to advance the collective interests of the whole membership; rather, a trade union becomes a collection of aggregate individuals. Collective organisations are formed in order to increase the power of individual employees. Therefore, the adherence to common decisions, involving if necessary the subordination of individual, self-interested goals, is a prerequisite for union effectiveness (Hyman, 1975). Voting at home, in the absence of debate and discussion, is said therefore to make a mockery of union democracy, especially since the influence of the media over how individuals vote can be brought to bear without the counterbalancing influence of union meetings.

Historically, various constraints have in reality been in operation with regard to the activities of union officials. The diversity of the trade unions and the particular characteristics of the membership will influence the propensity of the members to form factions or to participate in union decision making. For example, occupational homogeneity, where a workforce is concentrated within one industry, tends to facilitate high participation and opposition, since it is not felt that such actions threaten the cohesion of the union. In Lipset's study of union democracy in 1956, the parliamentary model utilised by the International Typographical Union involved rival groups competing for office via elections. Opposition by 'factions' or 'parties' need not be recognised officially, and often is not necessarily seeking power so much as ensuring the aspirations of the grassroots membership are addressed. A more diverse union membership, covering a wide range of industries, by contrast, such as that of the TGWU, may be characterised by 'popular bossdom', since the emphasis is more often on sectionalism, with the necessity for a strong leader who can hold the union together.

In the absence of well-organised opposition, other countervailing tendencies can be seen in unions such as the National Union of Mineworkers and the GMB, whereby decentralised regions or districts have relatively autonomous decision-making powers. Another issue that has been controversial is the issue of ballots in decision making, particularly over strike action. One such controversy raged throughout the miners' strike of 1984/5, when under Rule 41, the National Union of Mineworkers allowed individual areas to call strikes without holding a national ballot (McIlroy, 1995: 152). Ballots were held in Scotland and Yorkshire in favour of strike action over pit closures, but other areas, particularly Nottingham, whose members would have been unaffected by the threatened closures, voted against. The NUM Executive Committee was accused of manipulating the rules in order to avoid holding a ballot for what was in effect, a call for a national strike. The NUM had always had a strong tradition of ballots, both area and national, and found itself taken to court by dissident miners (not for the first time) for allegedly breaking its own rules, and its assets were eventually seized. This episode illustrates how unions' own rules and procedures, far from providing a coherent framework for guiding the relationship between different levels of membership and officers of the union, can be used by dissidents or the judiciary, and can appear as significant as the issue at the heart of a dispute.

■ Legislation and reform of union democracy

The Conservative governments of the 1980s introduced legislation to regulate the internal affairs of the trade unions, such as their decision-making mechanisms for elections and for taking industrial action (Table 5.5). Such activities had traditionally been left to the unions themselves, through their own rule books and procedures, although periodically, state intervention in this area would be attempted. The programme of legislation introduced throughout the 1980s and continuing into the 1990s was based on the assumption that unions were run by militant union leaders who often manipulated their members into taking strike action against their will, and that legislation which forced unions to ballot individual members for the election of such officers would enable the views of the 'moderate majority' to surface.

The 1984 Trade Union Act, for example, required trade unions to hold secret ballots prior to taking official industrial action; only those directly involved were to be balloted, and a majority had to specify that they wished to take the action. Cautionary wording on the ballot paper should warn the voter, it was specified, that he or she may be in breach of contract by taking industrial action.

Further ballots were introduced for the election at least every five years, of union officers, who were to serve on the main executive body of the trade union, and in 1988 this was extended to include all national executive members whether or not they were entitled to vote.

The 1984 Act required that trade unions hold secret ballots at least every ten years if they wished to set up or retain a 'political fund' which allows the union to spend money on 'political objects', which were also redefined by the Act. The Labour Party receives most of its funding through this source, although the fund can be used for activities such as political campaigns. Several unions, such as NALGO and the CPSA, held such ballots and set up political funds for the first time during the 1980s. All other unions have repeatedly achieved substantial votes in favour of retaining such funds.

The programme of legislation produced real and potential problems for the trade union movement, including arguably, inability to discipline its own members for breaches of rules such as strike breaking, but also presented challenges that were overcome and even used to their advantage.

■ Table 5.5 Legislation on union democracy and internal organisation

Act	Provisions
Employment Acts 1980 and 1982	Provision of funds for secret ballots
Trade Union Act 1984, amended by Trade Union and Labour Relations (Consolidation) Act 1992	Ballots for election of union officers Ballots for set up/retention of political funds Ballots prior to industrial action
Employment Acts 1988, 1990 and 1993	Rights for individual 'strike breakers' not to be disciplined by trade union. More complex ballot procedures, e.g. independent scrutineers to be appointed Individual member to confirm, every three years, continuation of 'check off' scheme for deduction of union subscriptions by employer

Administration and cost

Initially there were problems facing the unions in the administration and costs of ballots. Union members' records were required to be updated regularly, a difficult task for unions such as USDAW or the TGWU which have high turnover of members in any case. Part of the cost could be recovered under the Employment Acts of 1980 and 1982, although the TUC urged trade unions to boycott these funds in the first few years and this facility was phased out by 1996. However, costs of some £12.5 million were recovered between 1981 and 1991, mainly for the costs of Executive Committee elections.

Strike ballots and negotiations

Assumptions that the views of a silent majority would produce 'moderation' have not been borne out by the experience of union ballots, since the majority of such ballots have produced votes in favour of taking industrial action. ACAS report that 3704 separate ballot exercises were conducted by the two independent balloting organisations during 1995, of which 76 per cent were in favour of industrial action (ACAS, 1995: 39). Postal ballots are notorious for producing low turnouts, while the highest turnouts generally are those ballots held at the workplace, but these no longer afford trade unions immunity under the law.

Ballots, however, came to be considered part and parcel of negotiations, and often a high number of votes in favour of industrial action brought the employers to the negotiation table. Severe problems occurred, however, with regard to legal manoeuvres over ballots, some of which relate to the burdensome administrative requirements placed upon trade unions. For example, the Civil and Public Servants Association sent ballots to workplace addresses, when the members concerned had not given written authority for their addresses to be used. The Certification Officer, on receiving a complaint, ruled that the legislation had been breached (Certification Officer, 1996: 32). Employers have used the laws on strike ballots to delay or prevent industrial action primarily through the use of injunctions, but in some instances, legal constraints were highly significant politically. When the Conservative government, as part of a commitment to the removal of obstacles to the workings of the free market, proposed abolition of the National Dock Labour Scheme in the late 1980s, the legal constraints imposed by the courts prevented the TGWU from successfully calling for a strike in time to save the scheme. This had been introduced 40 years earlier in response to the problems of degradation and casualisation in dockland areas (Blyton and Turnbull, 1994: 132).

It is evident that the government and judicial interventions into the internal affairs of unions were problematic in various ways, but in general unions have learned to live with the legal provisions, and in some instances use them to their advantage. Whether or not the outcome has been 'to return the unions to their members' is debatable.

Union democracy – widening participation and representation

Nevertheless, many trade unions are aware that in terms of participation and representation, there are some areas where they are less than ideal. In particular, with respect to women and ethnic minorities, both groups have been under-represented in the executive and senior committees of trade unions, and among full-time officers. Women were barred from joining the early craft unions (Cockburn, 1991) in Britain and in other countries, and, facing this exclusion, women workers set up their own forms of organisation. Upon acceptance to the movement, women's membership grew significantly in the post-war period, but still their numbers are not reflected in the trade union hierarchy. While women constitute one-third of trade union members, there were just four female general secretaries of trade unions in 1994, and women were represented on National Executive Committees in proportion to their numbers in membership in just one-third of trade unions (Ledwith and Colgan, 1996: 152). Table 5.6 shows the proportions of women in membership in the largest ten TUC affiliated unions. Explanations for this under-representation are cited by Colgan and Ledwith as related to women's inequality at work generally, patriarchal attitudes, union rules on office holding, inconvenient times and locations of union meetings, unequal sharing of domestic responsibilities and lack of childcare provision (Ledwith and Colgan, 1996: 155). It is not just women's lack of representation in the union hierarchy that is recognised by many unions to be problematic, but that issues of concern to women are largely absent from the bargaining agenda; indeed the priorities of traditional collective bargaining themselves perpetuate women's disadvantage in paid employment (Dickens and Colling, 1990). Women dominate part-time work and are over-represented in smaller workplaces or in jobs with low pay and status which are hard to organise, but trade unions have until recently often neglected to address the specific issues affecting women at the workplace.

Women themselves, and some men, have challenged the unions' traditional attitudes and structural barriers towards participation. There is an awareness among the trade unions that with the increased levels of participation by women in the workforce, they need to recruit women members.

Union membership and density figures also show that ethnic minorities are just as likely to join trade unions as whites, despite sometimes racist tendencies within the trade union movement itself, which historically were always challenged by anti-racist campaigners within and outside the movement (Phizacklea and Miles, 1993). In 1991 the election of the first

■ **Table 5.6 Women in trade unions – the largest TUC affiliates, 1994**

	UNISON	TGWU	AEEU	GMB	MSF	USDAW	GPMU	UCW	NUT	UCATT
Total membership	1 400 000	958 834	546 000	800 000	552 000	316 491	250 230	180 586	162 192	157 000
Women (%)	68	18	9	37	27	60	17	20	74	2
On NEC (%)	42*	5	0	36	24	61	5	20	27	0
At Conference (%)	46[†]	10	8	25	25	42	11	Not known	48	1
TUC delegates (1993) (%)	54	20	6	33	33	12	5	20	35	1
National officers (%)	20	9	11	13	18	19	5	17	16	0
Regional officers (%)	31	7	0	0	12[‡]	21[‡]	2[†§]	0[‡]	11	0[‡]

* 1993 figures; the Executive elections in 1995 achieved proportionality for women.
[†] 1995 figures.
[‡] 1993 figures.
[§] Branches covering geographical areas are roughly the equivalent of regions

Sources: SERTUC (1994) 'Women's Special – women in unions: still too few at the top', *Labour Research*, March; Colgan and Ledwith (1995, quoted in Ledwith and Colgan, 1996: 155).

black trade union leader in Britain, Bill Morris of the TGWU, marked a turning point, and the TUC General Council has three seats reserved for black trade unionists (McIlroy, 1995: 179). Various strategies to counter racism and sexism, and to encourage a wider participation and representation, have been introduced since the 1980s, including positive action policies, the appointment of equality officers, and specialist black members' and women members' conferences. Unison was launched specifically with a constitution based on proportionality, i.e. fair representation within the union's structures. This was applicable for all groups who had traditionally been under-represented, namely women, black members, disabled members, lesbians and gay men (Colgan and Ledwith, 1996: 169).

TRADE UNION MEMBERSHIP AND DENSITY

There are major difficulties in collecting and compiling accurate information on trade union membership. The two key sources for measuring trade union membership in Britain come from the Labour Force Survey (LFS), which collects information from individuals, and the Certification Officer for Trade Unions and Employers' Associations. Each of these has different methods for compiling data. For example, the LFS excludes those not in employment, but does include some detail on the individual's characteristics and workplace details. The CO collects information from trade unions themselves, and does include the unemployed, retired and overseas members of trade unions.

By 1995 there were 238 trade unions in the UK, with a combined membership of 8.1 million members. This amounts to the lowest number of union members since 1945, and represents a continuing decline in membership from the peak of 13.3 million in 1979 (*Labour Market Trends*, February 1997). The recent decline in membership has averaged approximately 3 per cent per year since 1989 (Table 5.7).

Union membership figures overall relate to total numbers who are members, but a more useful figure, that of union 'density', is often used alongside the aggregate figures. Density refers to the percentage of members out of the potential of trade union membership, either of the labour force in total, which includes the unemployed, or of those in employment.

Union density varies significantly by industry. For example, public sector workplaces exhibit higher union density than do those in the private sector; there are also regional variations, with employees in the north of England being more likely to be union members than those in the south. Variations in density are also shown in terms of characteristics of individuals, such as gender, ethnic origin, marital status, and qualifications and status. Job-related characteristics such as whether full-time or part-time, and the size of the workplace, will also show differences in the union density of employees. Table 5.8 shows union density according to the personal characteristics of employees. Union members are more likely to be in their 40s than in their teens, and union density among young people is particularly low, at 6 per cent. Among males, union density is 35 per cent, compared to 44 per cent in 1989, and among females density is 30 per cent, declining from 36 per cent in the same period. This is despite growing female employment during the 1990s. However, women's union membership has not stood still, but has grown significantly among white-collar professional workers, especially public sector unions such as teachers' and nurses' unions.

Internationally, women's numerical representation in unions is generally in proportion to their participation in paid employment, although it is significantly lower in France, Greece and the Netherlands, but proportionately higher in Finland and Denmark (EIRO, 1997: Comparative Supplement).

■ Table 5.7 Trade unions: numbers and membership, 1970–95

Year	Number of unions at end of year	Total membership, end of year (000s)	Percentage change in membership since previous year
1970	543	11 187	6.8
1971	525	11 135	−0.5
1972	507	11 359	2.0
1973	519	11 456	0.9
1974	507	11 764	2.7
1975	470	12 026	2.2
1976	473	12 386	3.0
1977	481	12 846	3.7
1978	462	13 112	2.1
1979	453	13 289	1.3
1980	438	12 947	−2.6
1981	414	12 106	−6.5
1982	408	11 593	−4.2
1983	394	11 236	−3.1
1984	375	10 994	−2.2
1985	370	10 821	−1.6
1986	335	10 539	−2.6
1987	330	10 475	−0.6
1988	315	10 376	−0.9
1989	309	10 158	−2.1
1990	287	9 947	−2.1
1991	275	9 585	−3.6
1992	268	9 048	−5.6
1993	254	8 700	−3.8
1994	243	8 278	−4.9
1995	238	8 089	−2.3

Source: Labour Market Trends, February 1996, February 1997

Ethnic minority groups are almost as likely as white employees to belong to trade unions, although there is variation among ethnic groups. Blacks are more likely than any other ethnic group, including whites, to belong to a trade union, while the converse applies for women of Pakistani or Bangladeshi origin, who are less likely to belong to a trade union than any other ethnic group. These variations reflect the different employment patterns of the different groups, with some groups more likely to work in unionised environments such as the public sector, compared to small enterprises which are non-unionised, or in self-employment. Fifty-one per cent of employed black women work in the public sector compared to 31 per cent of employed white women; while 19 per cent of employed Asian women are self-employed compared with 7 per cent of all employed women (Sly, 1995: 251). Such differing labour market experience does feed through to union density figures.

With respect to the qualifications of employees, it can be seen that those with degrees or other higher education qualifications are more likely than any other group to be union members, while those with GCSEs as their highest qualification are less likely to be union members.

■ Table 5.8 Union density by individual characteristics, 1995

	All (%)	Men (%)	Women (%)
All employees	32	35	30
Age group			
Under 20 years	6	6	6
20–29 years	24	24	24
30–39 years	35	37	33
40–49 years	40	45	35
50 years and over	36	40	31
Ethnic origin			
White	32	35	29
Non-white	31	30	33
Black	41	39	42
Indian	28	30	27
Pakistani/Bangladeshi	18	20	*
Other	29	25	32
Highest qualification			
Degree or equivalent	40	35	47
Other higher education	49	37	58
A-level or equivalent	32	37	23
GCSE or equivalent	24	27	22
Other	29	35	23
No qualifications	28	34	24
Marital status			
Single, never married	22	23	22
Married or cohabiting	35	39	32
Divorced/separated	33	39	30
Widowed	33	38	31

* Base too low to provide reliable estimate.
Note: includes all employees except those in the armed forces.
Source: Labour Force Survey, in *Labour Market Trends*, May 1996.

Table 5.9 illustrates how the employment status of the employee and the type of employment contract tends to produce significant variations in union density of employees. For example, temporary workers and part-time workers are less likely to be union members; the predominant pattern of work for women is of part-time employment, and they are more likely than men to work in establishments that have a lower propensity to be unionised such as small workplaces and private service.

The public sector is more highly unionised than the private sector; Table 5.10 shows union density of 61 per cent for the former compared to 21 per cent for the private sector. When compared by industry, however, the difference is even more stark. Union density is almost three quarters of employees in public sector construction compared to just 16 per cent in private sector construction.

■ Table 5.9 Union density by employment status of employee

	All (%)	Full-time (%)	Part-time (%)
All employees	32	36	21
Length of service			
Less than 1 year	13	15	8
1–2 years	17	20	11
2–5 years	24	27	17
5–10 years	37	39	28
10–20 years	50	52	41
20 years or more	60	63	40
Occupational group			
Managers/administrators	21	22	17
Professional	52	53	46
Associate/professional/technical	47	45	54
Clerical and secretarial	27	30	19
Craft and related	37	38	13
Personal and protective	29	39	17
Sales	12	13	10
Plant and machine operatives	43	45	20
Other occupations	28	39	18
Managerial status			
Manager	27	28	25
Foreman or supervisor	42	43	36
No managerial duties	32	38	19
Employment status			
Permanent	33	37	22
Temporary	21	24	16
Special working arrangements			
Flexitime	43	48	25
Job sharing	33	*	33
Term-time working	45	72	25
Annualised hours contract	50	56	30
9 day fortnight/4.5 day week	48	49	*
Work mainly in own home	6	7	5

* Base too low to provide reliable estimate.
Note: includes all employees except those in the armed forces.
Source: Labour Force Survey, in *Labour Market Trends*, May 1996.

Industry variations are themselves significant although there are considerable variations within sectors; for example in manufacturing, where union density is 32 per cent overall, but 53 per cent in motor vehicle manufacture, and 21 per cent in electrical equipment manufacturing (Cully and Woodland, 1996: 220). However, taking the broad industry classifications, union density is highest in electricity, gas and water supply at 66 per cent, and lowest in agriculture, forestry and fishing with just 7 per cent, and hotels and restaurants with 8 per cent density (Cully and Woodland, 1996: 220).

■ **Table 5.10 Union density by workplace characteristics, 1995**

	All %	Private %	Public %
All employees	32	21	61
Industry			
Agriculture, forestry and fishing	7	5	*
Mining and quarrying	36	36	*
Manufacturing	32	32	61
Electricity, gas and water supply	66	65	*
Construction	26	16	74
Wholesale and retail trade	11	11	*
Hotels and restaurants	8	6	39
Transport and communication	49	39	79
Financial intermediation	37	37	47
Real estate and business services	13	8	62
Public administration	59	31	60
Education	56	28	60
Health	48	15	64
Other services	25	12	48
Region or country			
Greater London	30	17	62
Rest of south-east	23	15	49
East Anglia	26	19	48
South-west	27	18	54
West Midlands	33	23	63
East Midlands	32	22	62
Yorkshire and Humberside	35	24	64
North-west	39	27	70
North	42	30	72
Wales	44	31	72
Scotland	39	24	68
Northern Ireland	39	25	65
Workplace size			
Fewer than 25 employees	16	9	52
25 employees or more	40	29	64

* Base too low to provide a reliable estimate.
Note: includes all employees, except those in the armed forces.
Source: Labour Force Survey, in *Labour Market Trends*, May 1996

Regional variations reveal that the highest union density is in Wales, with 44 per cent of employees in membership, followed by the north of England with 42 per cent, the north-west of England, Scotland and Northern Ireland with 39 per cent. The lowest density by region is in the south-east of England excluding Greater London, with just 23 per cent union density, and East Anglia with 26 per cent, marginally higher than the south-west of England with 27 per cent.

The same table also demonstrates that the smaller the workplace, the less likely employees are to be unionised. Among workplaces employing fewer than 25 employees union density is just 16 per cent compared to 40 per cent in those employing more than

25 employees. Among smaller workplaces in the public sector, however, density rises to 52 per cent although density is 64 per cent among public sector workplaces employing more than 25 people.

■ Decline in union membership and density from the 1980s

Union membership peaked in 1979 with over 13 million members and 55 per cent density, having expanded during the 1960s and 1970s especially with the growth in the public sector and white-collar work. After 1979 this was reversed as union membership declined by 4 million members between 1979 and 1992, although decline was more rapid between 1980 and 1983 (Waddington, 1992: 301) (*see* Fig. 5.2). By 1995 approximately 32 per cent of all UK workers were members of trade unions. Density had declined by 20 per cent over the previous seven years, but the rate of decline then slowed from 3 per cent per year from 1989 to 1 per cent in 1995. The decline is more marked, however, among men compared to women, and among manual workers compared to non-manual workers.

There are several explanations for union membership variation, which is certainly not a recent phenomenon. Rapid growth of union members occurred from the period preceding the First World War until the early 1920s, rising to 8 million, fuelled by wartime production and the large intake of union members among 'unskilled' groups of workers. Decline in membership to 4 million occurred in the 1930s at a time of depression, with numbers being regained, and stabilising at around $9\frac{1}{2}$ million until the late 1960s. The post-war boom and expansion of the public sector saw a period of exceptional growth in union membership and density until their peak in 1979. It is in the recent period since the late 1970s, however, that the losses to trade unions have been substantial. Not only have explanations been prolific, but a key concern has been whether or not this decline is reversible. Most accounts have hinged on such factors as changing workforce composition, labour laws and other state policies, economic variables affecting levels of inflation, wages and unemployment, and employer and union behaviour.

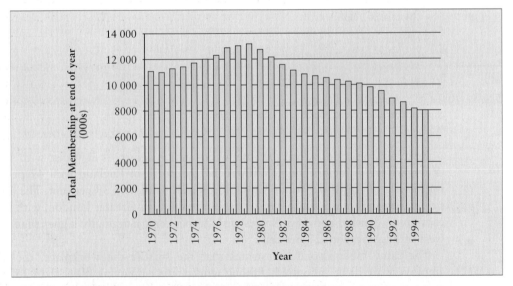

■ Fig. 5.2 Changes in trade union membership since 1970

Business cycle

Bain and Elsheikh (1976) produced a model of union growth and decline which suggests a positive effect of rising inflation on union membership levels since workers have an incentive to join in order to protect their standard of living. If rising wages are correlated with union membership then this will produce a positive effect on the union. By contrast, a rise in unemployment will threaten union membership overall, since unemployed people have little incentive to remain in membership, and in addition, unions' bargaining power is decreased since management is in a better position to resist their claims. The relatively low inflation of the 1980s and high unemployment may thus have acted as a disincentive to workers to pursue unionisation. The periods of incomes policy of the 1970s, during which time white-collar workers' differentials with manual workers were squeezed, gave them an incentive to unionise throughout this period to maintain their living standards. In the 1980s, however, their earnings rose relative to those of manual workers, thus impacting on union recruitment (Waddington, 1992). While 'business cycle' explanations appear credible, such models tend to over-predict levels of unionisation (Waddington and Whitston, 1995: 170).

Compositional changes in employment

A massive rise in unemployment, to over 3 million within the Conservative government's first eighteen months of office, was significant in reducing the highly unionised sectors in the north of England and Scotland, and among male manual workers, who were traditionally heavily unionised. However, the shift in the composition of the workforce, particularly marked from the late 1970s, including changes in gender composition, has had a negative impact on union membership. Employment contracted in those areas where union members were most concentrated, and expanded in areas where they were relatively sparse. The decline in manufacturing employment and rise of service sector employment led to the removal of whole sections of relatively highly unionised workforces employing predominantly males. As discussed above, density among women is traditionally lower than among men, itself a reflection of women's employment in services which unions find difficult to organise, and in part-time enclaves. Where manufacturing plants did open up, new establishments were less likely to be unionised, as were smaller establishments, which also became more numerous (Millward *et al.*, 1992).

Yet there are several reasons for not relying on compositional effects as the main explanatory cause of union decline. The composition of the workforce also underwent significant changes during the 1970s, most of which were disinclined to conditions for union growth such as a reduction in the manufacturing sector (Waddington and Whitston, 1995: 171). In addition, there is a problem for analysis of disentangling some compositional effects, such as the increase in private services and the increase in female and part-time employment (Waddington and Whitson, 1995: 171).

Legal reforms/state policy

Legal reforms under the Conservatives, which made it more difficult for unions to organise, to take industrial action or solidarity activities, or to form a closed shop, were considered by some to be the key causes of trade union decline in this period (e.g. Freeman and Pelletier, 1990). Other aspects of state policy that have had a negative impact on trade union membership have been the privatisation and competitive tendering of jobs formerly held in the public sector, such as the water, steel, coal and electricity industries, and services provided by local government, producing job losses in these highly unionised sectors. The government also withdrew the statutory union recognition procedure, which operated under the auspices of ACAS, and marginalised trade unions at the national level. The withdrawal by the state of such institutional support for trade unionism and collective bargaining has been a key element in weakening them (Purcell, 1993). The state's active encouragement of legislative and other measures designed to create difficulties for the trade union movement served also as an ideological offensive, and encouraged employers to adopt a similar stance.

Employer policies and the 'threat' of HRM

The assertion of managerial prerogative has been manifest in a number of ways, from 'macho management' at British Leyland, P&O and News International during the 1980s, to the less dramatic but gradual reduction in the scope of collective bargaining, and the enforcement of changed working practices reported in the third Workplace Industrial Relation Survey (Millward *et al.*, 1992). Furthermore, where collective bargaining remained, the tendency was a decline in national agreements and towards decentralisation to establishment level, itself often a form of derecognition since shop stewards are denied a platform for the raising of company-level issues (Clark and Winchester, 1994: 713). In both the private and public sectors, management techniques often associated with HRM, such as individual performance-related payment methods and individual contracts, have emerged. These managerial techniques, although piecemeal and limited in their extent, can be viewed as a threat to the collective traditions of trade unionism in terms of workplace organisation. The thrust of HRM is essentially individualistic, promotes 'flexibility' rather than 'demarcation', and the emphasis is on techniques aimed at eliciting employee commitment to company goals. Other elements of HRM may nevertheless be perceived as beneficial for trade union members, e.g. training; yet it is questionable how far such changes have been introduced. The changes that there have been have left largely undisturbed many of the institutions of collective bargaining, and tend to be more widespread in unionised environments than non-union (Millward *et al.*, 1992; Guest, 1995). Such employer-led reforms as have taken place, often viewed as *ad hoc* rather than strategic, were introduced to assert controls that the political climate afforded them (Sisson and Marginson, 1995: 113) and their impact has been variable on trade unions' ability to organise, bargain on behalf of their members, or take effective industrial action.

Commentators have suggested the likelihood that no single causal explanation will suffice, but an interplay of factors will be influential on membership figures over a given period (Metcalf, 1991; Waddington, 1992). The problem, however, is one of weighting the various explanatory factors; some commentators suggest it is the cyclical character of such factors, in terms of economic and political changes, which provides a more satisfactory explanation for union decline, rather than the individual factors themselves (Blyton and Turnbull, 1994: 109), the suggestion being that such decline need not be permanent. Furthermore, decline in union membership and density is by no means unique to Britain, and international comparisons suggest at least some similar conditions are present elsewhere. Economic and compositional forces have also had a negative impact on union membership and density in most industrialised countries (*see* Table 5.11), most of which have not had the extensive legislative reforms to which British unions have been subject. Indeed, several of the countries saw declining membership while governments were in power which were sympathetic to unions, such as France, Spain and Australia, leading commentators to play down the significance of legislative change in Britain (Brown *et al.*, 1997).

■ International comparisons

As with all comparative data, caution should be taken when making international comparisons of union membership and collective bargaining, since methods of collection vary or data quickly becomes out of date. The OECD publishes estimates within Europe, on unionisation rates in a range of countries, which indicate that Britain's rate is higher than that in Germany, France, the Netherlands and Spain, but lower than Austria, Belgium, Finland, Norway and Sweden.

Moreover, the coverage of collective bargaining is more extensive in most other EU states than the UK, with normally 70 per cent or more of workers covered by collective agreements compared to 47 per cent in the UK, by 1990.

■ Table 5.11 Trade union membership by country, as a percentage of all employees, 1970–95

Country	1970	1980	1990	1995
UK	45 (9th)	50 (10th)	39 (10th)	32 (11th)
Australia	50	48	40	33
Austria	62	56	46	43
Belgium	45	56	51	53
Canada	31	36	36	34
Denmark	60	76	71	82
Finland	51	70	72	81
France	22	17	10	9
Germany (W)	33	36	33	29*
Greece	36	37	34	n.a.
Ireland	53	57	50	38†
Italy	36	49	39	38
Japan	35	31	25	24
Netherlands	38	35	25	26
New Zealand	41	56	45	22
Norway	51	57	56	56
Portugal	61	61	32	32
Spain	27	25	11	15
Sweden	68	80	82	83
Switzerland	30	31	27	26
USA	23	22	16	15

*1993: UK rank order of highness of density.
† Estimates using LFS data indicate union density of 43 per cent.
Source for 1970–90: OECD *Employment Outlook*, July 1994.
Sources for 1995: ILO unpublished; various, including Ebbinghaus and Visser; Ferner and Hyman, both forthcoming.
Source for all above: Brown *et al.*, (1997).

Table 5.11 illustrates trade union membership within various countries, including Britain's rank order in terms of density, which has slipped only slightly from ninth to eleventh place since 1970.

Although similar problems have affected European and North American union movements – a decline in union membership and density, weakening of corporatist arrangements, problems of unemployment and casualisation of labour markets – there is still enormous diversity among trade unions in terms of membership, density, bargaining arrangements, and ideological and political attachments. For example, bargaining arrangements for most European countries are at industry level, while Denmark and the Netherlands have strong centralised framework agreements and Britain, Spain and Portugal have tended to decentralise bargaining.

■ Trade unions' responses to the challenges of the 1980s and 1990s

There were two main types of response to the problems of loss of membership and employer policies, which were emphasised from the early 1980s. The first of these centred on business unionism and 'new realism', which was taken up enthusiastically by the EETPU although other unions have increasingly adopted such an approach. This emphasises cooperation with management in accepting 'reality', and is associated with single-union and/or 'no strike' agreements. Some initiatives in the 1980s and 1990s involved a variation of business unionism, namely the professionalism of union management – for example, the use of business planning models involving targets for recruitment and other objectives, appropriate training including the establishment by the TUC of a National Vocational Qualification (NVQ) for trade union officials, and a Cranfield University course for trade union leaders to learn modern management techniques (Heery, 1997). These and other initiatives which resembled a managerial model became more commonplace and have caused controversy. The implication of these measures is that unions are seen as organisations operating in a marketplace, which must provide potential consumers with a range of services, while union officials persuade them into membership to sell the union's product (Heery, 1997). There has been no shortage of advice for the unions in 'selling themselves' in terms of member services: credit cards, mortgages, Filofaxes and so on. However, there is nothing new about member services: the earliest unions (friendly societies) offered 'mutual' benefits such as insurance, unemployment, sickness and funeral benefits. The emphasis in the context from the 1980s was that individual membership services were to become the *rationale* for joining a trade union, especially for groups of employees who, it is assumed, would have no interest in 'militancy', or collective, solidaristic reasons for joining. The assumptions of a purely individualistic orientation, however, have not been verified, as new members surveyed have been found to have strong 'instrumental' reasons for joining a trade union, such as an expectation that unions would improve their pay and conditions through the means of collective representation (Waddington and Whitston, 1995).

In terms of dealing with employers, 'new realism' has focused on forming new relationships with management, based on mutual goals and cooperation to improving productivity and quality, a joint approach often cited as that in operation at the Rover car company and Blue Circle (Guest, 1995: 120). In some US companies such an approach has been proclaimed by Kochan as heralding a 'transformation' in industrial relations (Guest, 1995: 119) although evidence for this claim is limited to a small number of firms primarily in the automobile industry, and where unions are well entrenched. The response of 'new realism' appears to complement the rhetoric of HRM, wherein reference to power relations, the notion of opposing interests, and daily struggles over the 'wage–effort' bargain are generally unacknowledged. While trade union members and officers might not have 'bought into' such ideas, but have at times cooperated in the knowledge that a 'mutual gains' approach is the best on offer given the climate it remains to be seen whether real benefits can be delivered. This has not been the only method employed by trade unions to regain lost ground, however. The major alternative approach to business unionism has been a more 'traditional' collectivist approach, focused on the need to attract new members in the sectors that were hard to penetrate, especially women and young people. A television advertising campaign was launched by the public service union Unison during 1995 which was aimed at young people: 'Using the image of a bear which cannot be shifted by one ant alone, but is moved by an army of ants, Unison is hoping to drive home the traditional trade union message of strength in numbers' (*Guardian*, 12 December 1995: 2).

Other campaigns to increase membership in the USA, whose trade union membership was also in decline for over 30 years, have encouraged British unions in the belief that decline is not irreversible. Campaigns by the American Federation of Labor and Congress of Industrial Organizations (AFL-CIO) among the low paid and immigrant workers have produced a 3 per cent rise in membership over two years, and a more vigorous and militant approach to counter more aggressive management and the squeeze on wages (*Guardian*, 11 September 1995: 9). Such developments have not countered the decline of the unionised sectors overall, however.

Guest summarises the available strategies that trade unions could pursue (Guest, 1995: 130):

- The promotion of a high quality of working life campaign, as part of a more desirable pursuit of a high quality, high productivity environment, in comparison with the low-cost labour market policies at the centre of Conservative policy. This would capitalise on many of the features of European social policy, such as the value of pluralist, partnership structures and employee involvement.

- The 'Friendly Society' strategy, which emphasises advice, services and information for members as individuals. This could be valuable at a time of state withdrawal of benefits, and the increase in grievances over discrimination and unfair dismissal handled by bodies such as ACAS (Guest, 1995: 135).

- Pursuit of the 'HRM' strategy, which subscribes to the benefits and opportunities that members could avail themselves of at least in 'soft' HRM policies, such as good qual-ity training. Furthermore unions could push which promises 'quality', or 'excellence', by and cooperating with management in the insisting on their own agenda (such as job s

Guest suggests that these three possible strateg tion in trade unions acting as a collective voice structive' voice which management may value enterprise (1995: 136). He does, however, ackn resent their 'best chances of survival', as an alt tion promised by the 'black hole' scenario. Ho management as well as union acceptance of su general fears that managerial prerogative could tive bargaining. Perhaps more importantly, ho

the fundamental attitudes of workers themselves towards collective organisation, their work or their employers (McIlroy, 1995: 399): 'we must not confuse change in the balance of forces between employers and unions with shifts in attitudes to unions or a move towards unitary conceptions on the part of workers'.

EMPLOYER RECOGNITION AND NON-RECOGNITION OF TRADE UNIONS

Despite the major losses in union membership in the past 20 years and the decline in the coverage of collective bargaining, the significance and extent of union influence on the workplace must still not be underestimated. Those companies that do recognise trade unions tend to be large and significant employers, mostly with household names. Of the top 40 of these companies, employing some 30 000 workers in the UK, 37 of these recognise trade unions (Labour Research, September 1994: 15). Of those that do not, two are in the retail sector, which has been notoriously difficult for trade unions to penetrate.

However, there has been a growth in the decline of unionised workplaces, since the mid-1980s, from 66 per cent of workplaces having at least one recognised trade union in 1980, to 53 per cent of workplaces by 1990 (Millward et al., 1992: 70). This decline is particularly notable in sectors such as newspapers, shipping, manufacturing, private services and the public sector (Millward et al., 1992: 102). Millward et al. note that the drop in recognition is patchy within these various sectors, being particularly prevalent in smaller workplaces in the private sector, and in the public sector it is concentrated in two main groupings, explained by the loss of collective bargaining rights for nurses and teachers during the 1980s. This is a little misleading, since the withdrawal of national collective bargaining and its substitution by Pay Review Bodies arguably did not amount to derecognition (Burchill, 1997: 58), which according to their own definition means 'the complete withdrawal of trade union negotiating rights over pay at a workplace' (Millward et al., 1992: 74).

TUC research on recognition and derecognition, reported that of 44 per cent of the TUC-affiliated unions who responded in a survey, 56 per cent had secured new recognition agreements with employers in the previous six months (TUC statistics) although many included education and health, where single establishments were able to set up new agreements due to privatisation or loss of national union recognition. In total, some 18 275 workers had achieved union recognition in a variety of companies. In the same survey, 10 of the 32 unions who responded had experienced some form of derecognition but the number of workers affected was just 1 394. In spite of these new agreements, however, the failure of trade unions to gain a foothold in new establishments is apparent, and private services, hi-tech industries and new manufacturing sites are particularly difficult to penetrate.

Employers actually withdrawing recognition from trade unions in the workplace remain rare; just 1 per cent of managers in workplaces without recognised unions report recognition in the previous six years. Equally, however, cases of new recognition of unions entering agreements were rare, although there was contradictory evidence er data (Millward et al., 1992: 75).

conducted by IRS explored the reasons why some employers did not recognise IRS Employment Trends, 1995: 3). Almost two-thirds of employers in the nise at least one trade union, but of those who did not, the main reason cited by respondents was that they had never been asked to grant recognition. Other reasons cited included the existence of 'alternative' systems of employee representation, that trade unions were not company policy or that management prerogative was the preferred method. Table 5.12 sets out employer responses when asked why trade unions were not recognised at the organisation.

■ **Table 5.12 Why employers do not recognise trade unions**

Organisation	Comment
Autoglass	'There is no history of unionism within this relatively new industry.'
BP Exploration, Aberdeen	'No employee requests.'
Brightreasons Restaurants	'No formal union in place.'
Bristow Helicopters	'Have never recognised unions.'
British Pregnancy Advisory Services	'Staff have been approached by several unions but have not expressed any interest. Nursing staff do belong to the RCN.'
Camberley Auto Factors	'No reason. No known union members among employees. No previous applications for recognition – no tradition in the motor trade either, for small branch outlets.'
DuPont Pharma	'Not necessary.'
Eli Lilly & Co., Basingstoke	'Not in line with company philosophy for this site.'
Hashimoto	'Third-party intervention obstructs good communication.'
Hills Pharmacy	'All retail employees covered by JIC for retail pharmacies.'
Kent Training & Enterprise	'As far as we know, no employees are members of a trade union and no Council request has ever been made for representation of this sort.'
Kuwait Oil Co., London	'Only a services office.'
Link House Advertising Periodicals	'Derecognised with effect from 1 January 1994.'
Medelec	'Never been a requirement.'
Norton Healthcare, Harlow	'Don't perceive a need.'
Orbit Valve, Ashchurch	'Greenfield site – management prerogative.'
Pitney Bowes	'We have staff associations.'
Polaroid UK, Dumbarton	'Have own employee representative elected system with full-time chairperson.'
Private Patients Plan	'So far as I know, no trade union has ever sought recognition.'
Sea Containers Services, London	'Not approached by any trade union.'
Servowarm	'Staff consultative reps at each location covering all types of employment status.'
UCB Group	'This has never been an issue raised by employees and/or the company.'
Wiltshier	'No approaches.'

Source: IRS Employment Trends, (1995: 4).

IRS surveyed employers who did recognise trade unions, and asked about the perceived advantages and disadvantages of recognising a trade union in the organisation. Among the perceived advantages were that a stable employee relations framework and a structured method of representing employee views, was advantageous, or that unrepresentative views can be filtered out. Others suggested 'smooth industrial relations' and 'problems are raised before molehills become mountains' (IRS Employment Trends, 1995: 9) Guest (1995: 126) cites evidence that trade union recognition is more likely at new establishments where there is already a trade union presence elsewhere in the company, suggesting that 'management accepts, on the basis of experience, that unions have some value.'

Perceived disadvantages to recognising trade unions included resistance to change among trade unions, time consuming or slow decision making or lack of flexibility.

■ Non-Union Sector

What kind of employee relations exists at these union-free workplaces? How is pay determined or employees represented in cases of disciplinary action?

Two main approaches have been identified, which can be loosely classified as 'non-union' and 'anti-union'. The former is associated with the 'paternalism' of large retail corporations such as the John Lewis Partnership and Marks and Spencer, which 'pre-emptively' avoid trade unions by making it difficult or unnecessary for them to organise. Interestingly, Marks and Spencer *does* recognise trade unions in the Republic of Ireland alone, of the twenty countries in which it operates (Hourihan and Gunnigle, 1996: 272). US multinationals such as Intel, IBM and Hewlett Packard remain wedded to non-unionism also, substituting union organisation with other mechanisms for 'employee voice', sometimes paying employees more than unionised firms. In the anti-union version, usually a 'hire and fire' policy operates, amounting to an authoritarian regime in which attempts at union organisation are dealt with severely – for example, the dismissals at the Grunwick Processing Laboratory in 1977 when substantial numbers of workers were fired for seeking union recognition, including strike action in support of it, and despite a statutory procedure whereby ACAS had recommended the employer recognise a trade union. Such anti-union regimes are common among small firms, and in the fast food trade, hotels and catering, but became increasingly common in the privatised sections of catering and cleaning formerly belonging to the unionised public sector. Increasingly, what Guest has termed a 'black hole' is prevalent (Guest, 1995), in which neither industrial relations nor HRM policies is emphasised. Problems for unions to gain a foothold, in the absence of supportive state machinery have been discussed, and the failure of employers to extend recognition at new establishments makes it more difficult for trade unions to gain an influence later on. Where there is no union recognition, Guest concludes that, 'there is little evidence that management replaces it with an HRM strategy to obtain full utilisation of the workforce, by gaining its commitment to company goals and values'. Fewer procedures exist for health and safety than in unionised sectors, there are fewer channels for communication, consultation and information, and more dismissals and compulsory redundancies (Guest, 1995: 126–7).

CONCLUSIONS: FUTURE PROSPECTS

The British trade union movement has certainly faced severe constraints and suffered enormous defeats throughout the 1980s, yet in many areas, continuity is the order of the day, and non-unionism is far from being widespread in many significant sectors of the economy. Moreover, many of the challenges have been faced by continental trade unions also. Yet the political marginalisation and setbacks have left them somewhat more exposed than trade unions in France or Germany. With no legal rights to employer recognition throughout recent periods and the continuing impact of deregulation and casualisation of the workforce, this situation hardly seems likely to improve their diminishing base of collective bargaining within Britain, let alone across European frontiers.

McIlroy (1995: 341) sets out how these issues may have the effect of excluding British unions from any European-wide initiatives of this nature, which may emerge:

> The dilemma facing British unions is a frustrating one. They are seeking to overcome problems in this country by spreading their wings in Europe. But the possibility of successful international flight is undermined by their weakness on their own ground. The ability to develop transnational bargaining and exploit EU legislation is constrained by the deficiencies of the unions in Britain. Naturally, they turn to the state but legislation on basic issues such as organisation, bargaining rights and industrial action remain the preserve of Westminster, not Brussels.

Following the Labour Party's election victory in 1997, trade union members were under no illusion that 'New Labour' would restore their former powers, however exaggerated these powers may have been. Labour in opposition repeatedly stated they would not repeal the anti-union legislation introduced since 1979. In addition, the Labour leader Tony Blair took steps to distance the Labour Party even further from the trade unions which created it, and rumours have circulated that the constitutional link would soon be broken completely (Heery, 1997: 104). Yet most commentators suggested that a difference in emphasis in relation to Labour's employment policy, including employment law, would be forthcoming, which some trade unions would welcome. First, the commitment to minimum standards at work includes various legal entitlements which are not quite clear, but which include a minimum wage. Such a policy has long been an aim of unions, particularly in the public sector, even if firm commitment to an hourly rate and its coverage has been a controversial subject at TUC and Labour Party Conferences in recent years. Furthermore, in relation to collective rights, Labour expressed its intention to introduce the right for employees to be represented by a trade union if they so wish, so that employers would be obliged to recognise a trade union for bargaining purposes (Heery, 1997: 103). Certainly, within its first few weeks of office, the government repealed the ban on trade unions at GCHQ; however, other measures in relation to 'fairness at work' were shelved from the first Queen's Speech. A White Paper entitled *Fairness at Work* was published in May 1998, containing among other proposed employment rights, a statutory union recognition procedure which would apply where there is support for such recognition, among the majority of employees in firms employing more then twenty employees. The Labour government ended Britain's opt-out of the EU social legislation, thus paving the way for new employment rights for atypical workers, and in the areas of information and consultation. While Labour appears more 'Euro-friendly', in rhetoric at least, than the previous Conservative governments, the Prime Minister Tony Blair, remains hightly sceptical of excessive regulation and wedded to the notion of a 'flexible labour market'.

The second aspect of the Labour government's emphasis relates to the workplace, and also has a somewhat European tradition, namely the promotion of 'social partnership' between workers and employers, at the level of the workplace. This represents a policy of attempting to move 'beyond' adversarial collective bargaining towards a more 'cooperative' relationship between the parties, in which the emphasis is on 'mutual gains', with unions actively contributing to modernisation and other initiatives. Partnership agreements at national level, similar to those operating in other EU countries, are to be encouraged so that parental leave and other European directives may be adopted by employers, trade unions and the government (Heery, 1997: 104). Some 'model' agreements such as those at Blue Circle and Rover are among the rare examples of such an approach, although such companies are hardly representative of British industry.

Bearing in mind the setbacks of the recent past, and the somewhat tentative and partial changes being mooted, any wholesale transformation of the trade union movement seems unlikely for what remains of the century.

QUESTIONS

1 What are the essential features of a trade union and what are its key functions?

2 Outline the factors which may influence whether (i) an individual or (ii) a group of employees will join a trade union or not. What are the anticipated benefits of union membership for employees?

3 How is trade union power perceived by different parties, and how can it be measured? Give examples of how state or employer policies have affected union powers in different ways, in Britain and in other parts of the world.

4 What are the principles of democratic organisation behind the two 'models' of union democracy, the parliamentary and participatory models? How necessary is legislative reform of trade unions' internal affairs, and what have trade unions done to increase their own democratic 'credentials'?

5 How significant is trade union membership in Britain in the 1990s and what factors produce a variation in membership among different parts of the labour force? How can the decline in union membership in Britain over the past twenty years be explained?

ACTIVITY

You are a London regional trade union officer at a banking and finance union which has been concerned in recent years about fluctuating membership levels. There are currently 3500 members in your region, who are employed in the major high street banks which recognise trade unions. A further 4000 would be eligible to join the trade union, however; a small number of these belong to others but the majority are not union members even though pay and conditions negotiated on an annual basis with the employers are awarded to all employees except senior managers. Approximately 70 per cent of the employees are female and most work in lower level, relatively low paid and routine jobs; one-third work part time. In the past two years the banks have been closing smaller branches with the consequence that staff have been made redundant; other changes in banking such as new technology and telephone banking, have led to hundreds of job losses in your region.

Along with colleagues, you deal with recruitment of union members, but your responsibilities mainly involve providing information, advice and services for members and representing members who are subject to discipline or dismissal by the employers.

The Union's Annual Conference has pledged to commit the union to (i) increase membership within the region, and (ii) take more account of workplace issues particularly affecting women, and equality issues. Your task is to devise a strategy for the union's area, to attract more bank employees into membership.

Members of the group should prepare a presentation or written report for the NEC, outlining which policies you would recommend in order to meet these goals, and highlighting issues which may be of key concern to potential union members. Other members of the group can design recruitment literature aimed at persuading non-union members to join.

CASE STUDIES

If trade unions did not exist, management would have to invent them!

Bearing in mind the perceived advantages and disadvantages to employers of recognising a trade union, what key considerations would figure in the decision by a clothing manufacturer to participate in the employers' forum described in Exhibit 5.2?

■ Exhibit 5.2

Action on clothing sweatshops

Register will list manufacturers that observe agreed working conditions

The British Apparel and Textiles Confederation is to produce a register of clothing manufacturers that observe nationally agreed working conditions, as part of a drive to end the industry's use of sweated labour.

The move coincides with an agreement yesterday by the confederation, which represents clothing manufacturers, and the British Retail Consortium to take part in a national forum with the same aim. The forum was called for last week by C&A, the high street retailer. C&A said yesterday that representatives from the Department of Trade and Industry, the Health and Safety Executive and other clothing retailers, including Sears, had also agreed to participate. The moves come after the *Financial Times* published the results of a two-month investigation into pay and conditions at clothing manufacturers in Birmingham. It found that several high street retailers are using UK-based clothing suppliers that pay staff as little as £1.50 an hour to work long shifts in often squalid conditions.

Mr John Wilson, director-general of the BATC, said the clothing industry had a national agreement on terms and conditions, agreed each year between employers and unions. 'It is not that onerous, and is widely followed,' he said. Retailers could go a long way to improving working conditions for the staff that make their clothes by using the agreement that already existed, he said.

To assist in this, the confederation, which has more than 2000 member companies, has offered to produce a register of manufacturers that observe the agreement. The companies on the register would not necessarily be unionised, but they would be observing the rates of pay, holidays, hours and other conditions laid down in the agreement.

One possibility is that the register would be used to assist retailers in identifying subcontractors that conform to their codes of conduct. C&A's code of conduct states that 'wages and benefits must be fully comparable with local norms' at subcontracting companies. Great Universal Stores has set similar guidelines.

Mr Wilson has also said the confederation would be willing to talk to retailers about using the register as the basis for a label to be attached to clothing. A C&A spokesman said retailers would consider this proposal at the forum.

Source: Jenny Luesby (1996) *Financial Times*, 11 October.

Unions trade pay for jobs

Outline the main elements of the new agreement at Blue Circle described in Exhibit 5.3. How is it distinguishable from 'traditional' management–union agreements? How would the management and trade unions at the company hope to benefit? How likely is it that such deals might become widespread in British industry?

■ **Exhibit 5.3**

The future – partnership and mutual gains?

Labour presents deal cemented with Blue Circle as model for the future.

Blue Circle and two of Britain's biggest unions yesterday unveiled a continental-style deal offering employees five years of job security in return for pay restraint and flexible working practices.

The deal struck by the cement company with the GMB general union and TGWU transport union was hailed by Labour as a 'ground-breaking' agreement. It said such 'social partnership', tackling the core issue of job insecurity, should become a model for future employer–employee relations.

It mirrors long-standing arrangements in Europe, particularly in Germany's highly regulated labour market, under which firms and unions sign long-term deals covering pay, hours and working practices. Europe's biggest union, IG Metall, last year proposed a national 'alliance for jobs and growth' under which increased employment would be traded for pay moderation and greater flexi bility at the workplace.

For Labour, yesterday's deal is evidence that pay may be becoming secondary to job security. An incoming Blair government hopes to avert an explosion of pent-up pay demands, especially in the public sector, by making job security the core issue.

Allan Black, GMB national secretary, said: 'The pressure from our members is on job security, not pay. This reflects a change of emphasis over the past few years.'

The settlement initially covers only 124 distribution drivers employed by the company who are to get a 3 per cent pay rise from this month, along with a one-off £200 payment and a one-hour cut in the working week.

Next year they will face a pay freeze, with pay levels in the last three years of the five-year deal determined by a joint review body. The settlement will produce significant annual savings for Blue Circle, which has agreed there will be no more contracting out of haulage and no compulsory redundancies among drivers in the five years.

If approved by GMB delegates tomorrow, a deal covering about 2000 process workers and other staff will offer pay increases worth the official inflation rate plus 0.25 per cent for the next three years, with a commitment to continue on an annual basis.

Clocking-on will cease to exist under a shake-up of working practices that should eradicate the difference between blue- and white-collar staff conditions, while Blue Circle has agreed there will be no compulsory redundancies and extensive retraining.

In exchange, said Mr Black, Blue Circle will get guaranteed increases in productivity. The drivers' deal alone will save £1.2 million a year, according to Ross Dunn, Blue Circle personnel director.

Mr Black said the deal, which took 12 months to negotiate, had prompted other firms to consider a similar approach. 'Some companies are already experiencing skill shortages – if they want to secure their workforce for the future then they should be establishing deals to compete with Blue Circle.' Peter Hain, a Labour employment spokesman, said: 'In government Labour will encourage such agreements because we want business to think long-term and focus upon jobs, skills and flexibility as the best passport to Britain's economic success.'

He added: 'Since job insecurity is the curse of the British labour market, from the highest manager to the lowest cleaner, what we need to do to get a long-term perspective is to encourage these social-partnership deals.'

Source: David Gow (1997) *Guardian*, 7 January.

REFERENCES

ACAS (1995) *Annual Report, 1995*. London: ACAS.

Bain, G.S. (1983) *Industrial Relations in Britain*. Oxford: Blackwell.

Bain, G.S. and Elsheikh, F. (1976). *Union Growth and the Business Cycle*. Oxford: Blackwell.

Blackburn, R.M. (1967) *Union Character and Social Class*. London: Batsford.

Blyton, P. and Turnbull, P. (1994) *The Dynamics of Employee Relations*. Basingstoke: Macmillan.

Bridgford, J. and Stirling, J. (1994) *Employee Relations in Europe*. Oxford: Blackwell.

Brown, W., Deakin, S. and Ryan, P. (1997) 'The effect of British industrial relations legislation 1979–97', *National Institute Economic Review*, 161, 69–83.

Burchill, F. (1997) *Labour Relations*. London: Macmillan.

Certification Officer (1996) *Annual Report of the Certification Officer*. London: HMSO.

Clegg, H. (1972) *The System of Industrial Relations in Great Britain*. Oxford: Blackwell.

Clark, J. and Winchester, D. (1994). 'Management and trade unions' in Sisson, K. (ed.) *Personnel Management, A Comprehensive Guide to Theory and Practice in Britain*. Oxford: Blackwell.

Coates, D. (1983) 'The question of trade union power', in Coates, D. and Johnston, G. (eds) *Socialist Arguments*. Oxford: Martin Robertson, pp. 55–79.

Cockburn, C. (1991) *Brothers: Male Dominance and Technological Change*. London: Pluto Press.

Colgan, F. and Ledwith, S. (1996) 'Sisters organising – women and their trade unions', in Ledwith, S. and Colgan, F. (eds) *Women in Organisations: Challenging Gender Politics*. Basingstoke: Macmillan.

Crouch, C. (1982) *Trade Unions: The Logic of Collective Action*. Glasgow: Fontana.

Cully, M. and Woodland, S. (1996) 'Trade union membership and recognition: an analysis of data from the 1995 Labour Force Survey', *Labour Market Trends*, May.

Daly, M. (1994) 'Women and trade unions' in Nevin, D. (ed.) *Trade Union Century*. Dublin: Mercier Press.

Dickens, L. and Colling, T. (1990) 'Why equality won't appear on the bargaining agenda', *Personnel Management*, April.

Edwards, P.K. (1995) (ed.) *Industrial Relations, Theory and Practice in Britain*. Oxford: Blackwell.

Fairbrother, P. (1983) *The Politics of Union Ballots*. London: WEA.

Farnham, D. and Pimlott, J. (1995) *Understanding Industrial Relations*. London: Cassell.

Flanders, A. (1970) *Management and Unions*. London: Faber and Faber.

European Industrial Relations Observatory (1997) 'Equal opportunities and collective bargaining in the EU', comparative supplement, *EIRO Observer*, Dublin: European Foundation for the Improvement of Living and Working Conditions.

Freeman, R.B. and Pelletier, J. (1990) 'The impact of industrial relations legislation on British union density', *British Journal of Industrial Relations*, 28 (2) 141–64.

Gallie, D., Penn, R. and Rose, M. (eds) (1996) *Trade Unionism in Recession*. Oxford: Oxford University Press.

Gospel, H.F. and Palmer, G. (1993) *British Industrial Relations*. London: Routledge.

Heery, E. (1997) 'Annual review article 1996', *British Journal of Industrial Relations*, 35 (1), 87–109.

Hourihan, I. and Gunnigle, P. (1996) 'HRM and trade unions: Marks and Spencer (Ireland) Ltd', in McGoldrick, G. (ed.) *Cases in Human Resource Managment*. London: Financial Times Pitman Publishing.

Guest, D. (1995) 'Human resource management, trade unions and industrial relations,' in Storey, J. (ed.) *Human Resource Management: A Critical Text*. London: Routledge.

Hollinshead, G. and Leat, M. (1995) *Human Resource Management: An International and Comparative Perspective*. London: Financial Times Pitman Publishing.

Hyman, R. (1975) *Industrial Relations: A Marxist Introduction*. London: Macmillan.

Hyman, R. and Fryer, R.H. (1975) 'Trade unions: sociology and political economy' in McKinlay, J. (ed.) *Processing People*. New York: Holt, Rinehart & Winston.

IRS Employment Trends (1995) 'Employee representation arrangements 1: the trade unions', no. 586, June, pp 3–9.

Labour, Research, September 1994.

Ledwith, S. and Colgan, F. (eds) (1996) *Women in Organisations: Challenging Gender Politics*. Basingstoke: Macmillan.

McIlroy, J. (1995) *Trade Unions in Britain Today*. Manchester: Manchester University Press.

Metcalf, D. (1991) 'British unions: dissolution or resurgence?', *Oxford Review of Economic Policy*, 7(1), 18–32.

Millward, N., Stevens, M., Smart, D. and Hawes, W.R. (1992) *Workplace Industrial Relations in Transition*. Aldershot: Dartmouth.

Pelling, H. (1974) *A History of British Trade Unionism*. Harmondsworth: Penguin.

Phizacklea, A. and Miles, R. (1993) 'The British trade union movement and racism' in Braham, P. Rattansi, A. and Skellington, R. (eds) *Racism and Antiracism: Inequalities, Opportunities and Policies*. London: Sage/OUP.

Purcell, J. (1993) 'The end of institutional industrial relations', *Political Quarterly*, 64 (1), 6–23.

Sisson, K. and Marginson, P. (1995) 'Management: systems, structures and strategy' in Edwards, P. K. (ed.) *Industrial Relations, Theory and Practice in Britain*. Oxford: Blackwell.

Sly, F. (1995) 'Ethnic groups and the labour market: analyses from the spring 1994 Labour Force Survey', *Employment Gazette*, June.

TUC (1997) *Partners for Progress: Next Steps for the New Unionism*. London: TUC.

Waddington, J. (1992) 'Trade union membership in Britain, 1980–1987: unemployment and restructuring', *British Journal of Industrial Relations*, 30 (2), 287–324.

Waddington, J. and Whitston, C. (1995) 'Trade unions: growth, structure and policy' in Edwards, P. K. (ed.) *Industrial Relations, Theory and Practice in Britain*. Oxford: Blackwell.

Webb, S. and Webb, B. (1920) *The History of Trade Unionism*. London: Longman.

Chapter 6

THE STATE IN EMPLOYEE RELATIONS

Mike Salamon

Learning objectives

By the end of this chapter, readers should be able to:

■ identify the differences between 'state' and 'government' and the importance of the government in determining the nature of a country's employee relations system;

■ explain the extent to which the government is free or constrained in the development of policies and strategies towards employee relations and the labour market;

■ identify the differences between *laissez-faire* and corporatist political ideologies and their effect on national systems of employee relations;

■ understand government strategies relating to

   (i) managing unemployment, promoting labour flexibility and regulating wage levels,

   (ii) promoting social justice within the employment relationship and

   (iii) regulating industrial conflict.

INTRODUCTION

In the modern world, the 'state' comprises a wide range of governmental institutions. At its centre is the institution and process of 'government', operating within a political mechanism, whose authority is backed by the legal system. Government policies and strategies play a major, if not fundamental, role in shaping, directing and regulating the social structures and interactions which make up any society. Indeed, government policies (actual or potential) have played an important role in 'defining' social problems and 'setting the agenda' for national debates about employee relations (Winchester, 1983: 105). However, no government in a democratic society, not even the Thatcher government of the 1970s, is 'omnipotent and omnicompetent' (Marsh, 1992: 239). The direction and scope of government policies may be constrained within the political mechanism by other political parties and 'pressure' groups or in the wider society by the actions of individuals and groups. The potential transient nature of governments within democratic societies, together with differences in ideology between contending political parties, means that there is always a potential for change in the government's policies and strategies towards employee relations. Furthermore, there is a range of state 'agencies' (including the judicial system) that are responsible for the implementation and enforcement of the government's policies and decisions (*see* Fig. 6.1). The existence of such agencies raises two important issues:

1 The extent to which any such agency may become almost a permanent feature of the system (transcending changes in government) or is of limited duration and closely associated with a specific short-term government policy or decision.

2 the extent to which the agency is constrained to support the government or is able to act independently and place a check on exercise of governmental authority.

The importance of the government's influence on employee relations can be seen in three main areas. First, it is the 'third' actor in the employee relations system (Poole, 1986: 99) and one which, by virtue of its unique role as the law maker in society, has the power and authority to 'change the rules of the system' (Crouch, 1982: 146). Legislation provides a society-wide enforceable framework of rights and responsibilities, which reflects the government's subjective value judgements regarding such concepts as 'fairness and equity', 'power and authority' and 'individualism and collectivism' within the employment relationship. Second, governments may control, directly or indirectly, a wide variety of organisations within the 'public' sector: ranging from government departments (responsible for the provision of public services such as health, education, police, fire, prisons, etc.), through public utility corporations (communications, transport, coal, electricity, gas, water, etc.), to state-owned commercial organisations which compete with private sector organisations (aircraft and car manufacture, steel production, banking, etc.). The precise extent and mix of organisations within the 'public' sector varies from country to country, and over time, and is dependent on the ideological beliefs of the political party in power. The importance of the public sector in influencing employee relations comes not only from its size (as a proportion of the national workforce) but also from its potential to demonstrate a government-preferred 'model' of employee relations. Third, the government's policies and strategies on economic and social matters are significant influences on the general environment within which management, employees and unions (both private and public sector) have to conduct their relationships.

The diversity of national employee relations systems can be explained, at least in part, by differences in underlying political ideology and consequent variations in the nature and extent of government intervention in economic or social issues (Waarden, 1995: 110). Certainly, the economic development of most South-East Asian countries (such as Korea, Singapore and Taiwan) appears to have been based on a unitary corporatist 'political economy' approach – including government restriction or control of trade unions in order not to jeopardise the economic development process and, in particular, to secure and maintain inward foreign investment (Bean, 1994: 218). Singapore's institutionalised 'symbiotic' relationship between the ruling political party and trade unions, since the early 1960s, has made the two almost indistinguishable (Leggett, 1993: 101) and, coupled with the establishment of a National Wages Council, has eliminated collective bargaining as a 'political tool' (Beng and Chew, 1995: 83). Similarly, in Taiwan (Lee, 1995) and South Korea (Park and Lee, 1995) governments have, among other measures, prohibited unions from undertaking political activities, allowed the government to veto candidates for union elections and restricted the capacity of unions to undertake strike action. These moves have been aimed as much at ensuring that unions did not provide a focus for political challenge to the government as at achieving economic progress. In both cases, the success of economic growth itself created pressure for political and industrial relations reform (late 1980s) and, indeed, the Korean government's attempt to reintroduce union controls in 1991 was defeated by a revitalised union movement. How these governments respond to the financial collapse of 1997 remains to be seen.

The approach of these countries has been in marked contrast to the post-war post-capitalist pluralistic approach which has been more prevalent in the older industrialised countries (the UK, Europe, the USA, Canada and Australia). This approach regards both the organisation and society as being multi-structured and competitive in terms of groupings, leadership, authority and loyalty and, therefore, accepts the expression of divergent and opposing views as rational, inevitable and legitimate.

THE UK SINCE 1960: A CASE STUDY IN CHANGING GOVERNMENT PHILOSOPHY

In 1960 Kahn-Freund stated that there was 'no major country in the world in which the law has played a less significant role in the shaping of [employee relations] than in Great Britain' (1960: 44). However, this ignores the fundamental importance of early legislation – the Trade Union Act 1871, the Trade Disputes Act 1906 and the Trade Union Act 1913 – which reflected a shift in political ideology from the 'liberal individualists of 1830' to the 'democratic socialists of 1905' (Griffith, 1990). It freed trade unions from the nineteenth-century socio-economic legal doctrines of 'restraint of trade' and 'conspiracy', thereby allowing them to organise, undertake industrial action and participate in wider political activities without the constant threat of being 'outlaws'. Without such legalisation, trade unions would not have been able to develop in the UK. However, the content of the employment relationship itself (terms and conditions of employment) remained to be determined primarily through 'free voluntary collective bargaining' between management and unions (i.e. without state intervention).

The role of government in industrial relations during the 1960s and 1970s contrasts starkly with the period of Conservative government, 1979–97. The 1960s and 1970s was a period of apparent 'consensus politics' under which both Conservative and Labour governments adopted an interventionist (corporatist) approach, based on Keynesian policies aimed at managing the demand side of the economy, to support their commitment to the maintenance of full employment and the welfare state. Trade union and employer representatives were involved in discussions with government on a wide range of economic and social issues through the National Economic Development Council – established in 1962 by a Conservative government. The tripartite formula was maintained in the establishment of a number of state agencies in the 1970s concerned with implementing government strategies – first, the Manpower Services Commission (MSC) in 1973 under a Conservative government and then the Health and Safety Commission (HSC) and Advisory, Conciliation and Arbitration Service (ACAS) in 1974 under a Labour government (see Figure 6.1). The role of the MSC and HSC, together with the Equal

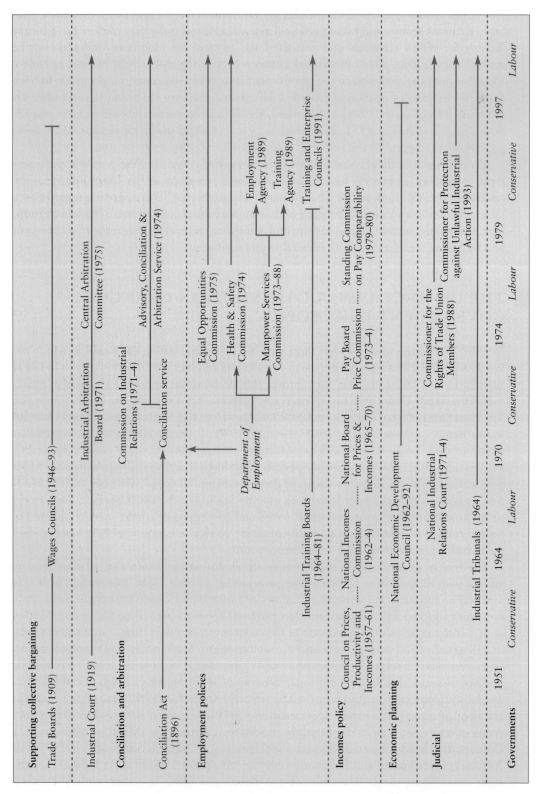

■ Fig. 6.1 State agencies in th UK

Opportunities Commission, was to promote the government's positive employment policies and complemented the work already started with the creation of Industrial Training Boards in 1964.

However, this emphasis on tripartite cooperation did not preclude the use of statutory, as well as voluntary, incomes on policies to regulate incomes, and the period saw a number of short-lived state agencies charged with implementing and regulating these policies. Nor did it prevent government concern for the impact of industrial action. In 1969, despite the Donovan Commission report (1968) advocating voluntary reform rather than legislative control, the Labour government felt it necessary to propose changes to the law that would 'help to control the destructive expression of industrial conflict' (White Paper, 1969: 5). The government did not proceed because of pressure from trade unions and the TUC's offer of a voluntary undertaking to press for moderation in trade unions' demands. Nevertheless, a change of government resulted in the Conservative's Industrial Relations Act 1971, which tried to balance some positive gains for trade unions (statutory recognition procedure, rights to disclosure of information, etc.) with bringing them under greater statutory regulation and public accountability. It also sought to establish a system of specialised labour courts and agencies by not only extending the role of Industrial Tribunals (which already existed and had a judicial role under earlier 1960s legislation) but also creating a new National Industrial Relations Court and Commission on Industrial Relations (neither of which survived the demise of the government). The legislation provoked such hostility and active resistance by trade unions and members alike that, despite the imprisonment of shop stewards, fines against trade unions and sequestration of their funds for non-payment of the fines, the legislation soon became unworkable.

The subsequent Labour government (1974–79) reconfirmed positive state support for trade unions as part of its 'social contract'. The Industrial Relations Act was repealed – apart from the provisions relating to unfair dismissal and statutory recognition procedure – and the Employment Protection Act 1975 not only provided additional individual employee protection rights (particularly in respect of maternity) but also confirmed union rights to disclosure of information, redundancy consultation, time off for trade union activities, etc. Similarly, the terms of reference set for the Bullock Committee on Industrial Democracy quite clearly stated that there was a 'need for a radical extension of industrial democracy in the control of companies by means of representation on boards of directors' and 'the essential role of trade union organisations in this process' (1977: v).

However, Marsh believes that the 1960s and 1970s were an 'exceptional' period in respect of the unions' political role and involvement with government (1992: 240). Certainly, the effect of the Conservative government's strategy based on a free market *laissez-faire* ideology, developed under Thatcher during the 1980s and continued into the 1990s, has been to remove, or at least significantly reduce, direct government economic planning and to rely on market forces, monetarism and unemployment to enhance Britain's international economic competitiveness. It has sought to create employment opportunities, increase labour flexibility and emphasise individualism through deregulating employment. The series of substantial pieces of legislation passed between 1980 and 1993 curtailed trade union power and provided management with the opportunity to re-exert its prerogative. In particular, these Acts restricted substantially the boundary of lawful industrial action, introduced stricter legal requirements for the conduct of industrial action and undermined the unions' organising abilities (most importantly, by abolishing the statutory recognition procedure). Despite the fact that, as in the early 1970s, the initial legislation was resisted by trade unions (once again including major disputes and court cases resulting in unions being fined for contempt of court and having their funds sequestrated), the continuing re-election of a Conservative government gave the unions little prospect of the legislation being changed. However, it has been argued that economic conditions (recession and international competition) coupled with employment restructuring (particularly the decline in manufacturing) provided the conditions for the government to exert its authority and ensure union compliance (Marsh, 1992).

However, the Conservative governments' strategy was not confined simply to legislation on trade unions and industrial action or confronting unions in the public sector in its role as employer (Telecom, 1983; NCB, 1984/5; GCHQ, 1984; teachers, 1987). At the same time, the role of many state agencies was changed. The government initially played down the joint approach to economic development, and then disbanded the NEDC in 1992, as well as reducing the tripartite basis of managing the activities of agencies such as the MSC and ACAS. The government no longer regarded trade unions as 'joint managers' of the industrial and economic system but rather as a major impediment to the government's strategy for economic change. As part of the process of deregulating the labour market, the focus of implementing training policies was devolved from the centralised co-ordination of the ITBs and MSC to the local business needs control of Training and Enterprise Councils. Wages Councils (the only statutory support for collective bargaining in a number of poorly organised and low-paid industries) were first restricted (in 1986) and then abolished (in 1993) as part of the government's strategy to 'price people back into jobs' and, at the same time, the duty 'to promote collective bargaining' was removed from ACAS's terms of reference. Furthermore, throughout the period, the government sought to limit the effects of EU Directives on the UK and even 'opted out' of the Social Chapter of the Maastrict Treaty. However, the government did feel it appropriate to create new state agencies to provide support and assistance to individuals seeking to take legal actions against trade unions – the Commissioner for the Rights of Trade Union Members (in 1988) and the Commissioner for Protection Against Unlawful Industrial Action (in 1993).

The experience of the UK during the 1980s demonstrates how a change in the dominant political ideology within a society can produce a substantial shift in its employee relations system. The Thatcherite policies and strategies towards employee relations in the UK were driven by an overriding objective of subordinating employee relations to economic reform and development, a strategy very similar to that of the governments of the 'tiger economies' of South-East Asia. The position has changed with the election of 'New' Labour in 1997 – but not necessarily fundamentally. The new government remains committed to increasing labour flexibility, but has introduced legislation to establish a National Minimum Wage and signed up to the Social Chapter. It has stated that it will not repeal the legislation enacted under the previous Conservative governments, but its White Paper on 'fairness at work' (1998) gives substance to its manifesto pledges to reintroduce a statutory recognition procedure and provide some further limited protection for employees dismissed for undertaking lawful industrial action. It does not seem to favour the re-establishment of a formalised mechanism for tripartite discussion of economic and social issues, but it does appear to be prepared to consult more broadly with both management and unions.

GOVERNMENT APPROACHES TO EMPLOYEE RELATIONS

Economic factors, directly or indirectly, appear to dominate government thinking, policies and strategies. In recent years, governments in the UK and Europe have become particularly concerned not only with creating the 'right' conditions for economic restructuring and growth in the face of greater international competition, but also with the increasing costs of tackling social issues (such as unemployment, retirement and the provision of education and health services). Government strategies appear to centre on three main elements of the operation of the labour market: the level of employment, the nature of the employment relationship and the distribution of economic rewards (Poole, 1986: 102). However, the extent, direction and manner of the desired control will differ depending on the political ideology of the government and the relative importance it attaches to social as well as economic objectives (that is, the type of society it wishes to create or, at least, encourage). For example:

- To what extent should the government accept responsibility and take action not only for securing economic development and creating jobs but also for mitigating the social costs of unemployment and economic change?

- What constitutes a 'fair' basis for labour competition (both between organisations and between countries) and how far should employees be protected against exploitation by legislation?

- How far should employees and trade unions be able to exert their collective power through the use of industrial action?

- To what extent should management decisions and actions within the organisation be required to be subject to the consent, or at least influence, of its employees?

- Should governments regulate wages, through a national minimum wage and incomes policy, not only to control pay levels for the benefit of economic growth but also to ensure fairness and the maintenance of a reasonable standard of living for employees?

Government Autonomy

The inextricable link between economics and politics is reflected in the use of thephrase 'industrialised capitalist democracy' to describe countries like the UK. The question that arises from this is how does a democratic government fit within the capitalist economic system? The essential nature of 'democracy' appears to rest on two elements. First, significant differences of view exist among the population regarding the nature of the desired society and/or the policies that should be pursued to create or encourage the development of that society. Second, processes exist within the society which allow for the expression of these different ideologies and sectional interests (political parties) and provide the means to implement the desired policies through the authority and power of government (obtaining popular support in elections). In the UK, this difference of ideology and sectional interest has, at least in the past, been expressed through the Conservative Party (supporting capital's interests) and the Labour Party (supporting workers' interests), while in Europe it has been expressed primarily through Christian Democratic, Social Democratic and Communist parties.

However, many people believe that the 'national interest' should prevail over sectional ideological interests once a political party becomes the government. In the employee relations area, this is reflected in an expectation that the government remains 'neutral' and favours neither management nor trade unions. The role of government is to protect individuals and the wider society from any 'abuse of power' by either interest group. However, within any democratic society, there will always be significant differences of view about the causes and solutions of most economic and social issues and, consequently, no universal consensus of what is the 'national interest'. All government strategies and policies, therefore, inevitably reflect the government's particular ideological base.

In a similar way, both Hyman (1975: 125) and Blyton and Turnbull (1994: 139) have argued that the political system, irrespective of which political party is in power, must support the maintenance of the capitalist interest. The needs of 'capitalism' for confidence in economic and social stability restrict any 'radical' initiatives in economic or labour policies: government needs capital more than capital needs government. Indeed, Hyman argues, from a Marxist perspective, that even government non-intervention is, in effect, support for capitalism by not challenging the unequal power balance between employer and employee which is inherent in the capitalist economic and legal relationships. Even if governments have not, in the past, always been 'a captive of class forces, economic forces or the capitalist mode of production' (Beaumont, 1992: 17), there is little doubt that it is now increasingly possible for the power of capitalism to constrain or negate any individual government's strategy, as a consequence of the current liberalisation of world trade and the increasing dominance of multinational global organisations (which owe no allegiance to any particular country).

While there is little doubt that the UK Conservative government's legislative strategy after 1979 was 'a key instrument facilitating labour-market restructuring' (Dickens and Hall, 1995: 256), it is more difficult to be certain whether this change in policy direction is evidence of government autonomy, the pursuit of a sectional managerial interest or the inherent demand of the capitalist system under the guise of 'national' interest. Perhaps more significantly, the Labour Party leadership has felt it necessary to move away from its traditional base as a 'worker's' party (that is, remove the perception that it represents a sectional interest) and be seen to have the support of the business community in order to make it more 'electable'. Similarly, since being elected in 1997, it has maintained a significant degree of continuity with the previous Conservative governments' approach and not sought to introduce radically different economic, fiscal and labour policies.

Nevertheless, there are differences in government strategies, which can be seen in practice both within and between countries, resulting from different priorities and approaches to the main areas of concern in the labour market (regulation, justice and conflict), and these are a reflection of differences in the underlying political ideology (*see* Fig. 6.2).

■ Political ideology and forms of employee relations

Two basic, but very different, political ideologies may be identified. First, the *laissez-faire* (free market) ideology regards 'free' competition for goods, services and labour within the economic system as the prime basis for regulating society. Not only the work rela-

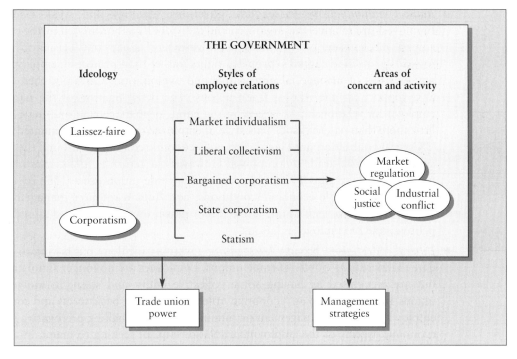

THE GOVERNMENT

Ideology · Styles of employee relations · Areas of concern and activity

Laissez-faire

Corporatism

Market individualism

Liberal collectivism

Bargained corporatism

State corporatism

Statism

Market regulation

Social justice · Industrial conflict

Trade union power

Management strategies

■ Fig. 6.2 Government and employee relations

tionship but also the acquisition and provision of 'social' services, such as education and health, are seen as primarily contractual 'economic' matters between individuals (even where, as in most cases, one of the parties to the contract is an organisation). The emphasis is on the individual being responsible for his or her own well-being, rather than being provided for by the state. The role of government is primarily one of minimising regulation and distortions in the operation of the 'marketplace'. The organisation and collective power of labour, through trade unions, is certainly regarded as a distortion of the normal market mechanism.

Second, the *corporatist* (interventionist) ideology regards economic and social aspects of life as interrelated parts of a whole and a proper matter for political influence and regulation – therefore, the different segments of society should be incorporated into the process of government (particularly 'capital' and 'labour'). It believes that government should accept responsibility, through interventionist regulation, for both protecting individuals from the social problems arising from the operation of capitalism and improving their quality of life. There is concern for ensuring not only that the operation of the economic system is constrained by the need for 'social justice' but also that the governmental process involves consent through mechanisms of social partnership.

The differences between these two basic political ideologies form the foundation of a typology of employee relations (Crouch, 1977, 1982; Strinati, 1982). Different styles of national employee relations result from differences in the governing ideology relative to the power position of trade unions.

- *Market individualism*: *laissez-faire* governing ideology and weak trade unions. Employees are relatively unorganised and individually subordinated by the competitive control mechanisms of the 'market'. Government policy and legislation is directed towards protecting capital's 'property rights' rather than protecting employees against any excesses of managerial prerogative and exploitation. Certainly, there is little, if any, support for the role of trade unions. The determination of the nature of the employment relationship is largely in the hands of management and may, at best, be little more than paternalistic. This style of employee relations predominated during the UK's industrialisation until legislation and economic conditions, around the turn of the century, increased trade union power. However, the return to a *laissez-faire* governing political ideology after 1979 and reduction in trade union power, due to a combination of unfavourable economic conditions, new human resource management strategies and restrictive legislation, resulted in a return to a more individualised and competitive style of employee relations.

- *Liberal collectivism*: broadly *laissez-faire* governing ideology but having to accommodate the increasing power of trade unions. Employees are no longer simply individuals but are recognised as having some collective entity and strength. However, trade unions are restricted to an 'economic' role in negotiating basic terms and conditions of employment, while management maintains its decision-making prerogative in the non-economic aspects of the employment relationship. In seeking to maintain a degree of a 'free market' system, the government may intervene to ensure a power balance between management and trade unions. The concepts of 'pluralism' and 'voluntarism' associated with this approach have been important elements of UK employee relations during much of the twentieth century.

- *Bargained corporatism*: corporatist governing ideology and strong independent trade unions. The employment relationship is based on the development of a bipartite 'social partnership' between management and unions at the organisation level and a tripartite relationship between the social partners and government at the national level. It becomes an integrated responsibility, determined at both organisational and society levels. The government is prepared to involve trade unions and management in determining government strategy, not only on employment issues but also on more general economic and social issues, in return for their cooperation in maintaining stability in employee relations to support the achievement of that strategy. This style of employee relations has been a characteristic of Sweden, Germany and the Netherlands (which have had long periods of Social Democratic government) and the underlying principle in the EU's approach to employee relations. This approach may be subdivided (Taylor, 1989: 97) between, at its simplest level, management and unions being consulted frequently by government and, a more advanced form, the formal institutionalisation of the relationship within a broader consensus-based framework of government policy formulation and administration. The UK adopted a partial 'bargained corporatist' style of employee relations in the late 1970s, with the 'social contract' between the Labour government and trade unions.

- *State corporatism*: corporatist governing ideology (often involving a long-term dominant or even single political party) and politically subordinated trade unions. Control over the employment relationship is exercised through the political system rather than economic free-market forces. While this style was the foundation of employee relations in the former Communist countries of Eastern Europe, it can also be seen in the government's strategy for economic development in some of the 'tiger' economies of South-East Asia. Singapore's 'symbiotic' relationship between the government, which has ruled continuously since independence in 1959, and the National Trade Union Congress includes cross-organisational leadership between trade unions and the political party, union exposition and exhortation of national economic development needs to its members and the government's use of legislation to de-register unions which challenge the NTUC or its policies.

■ *Statism*: corporatist governing ideology and industrially weak unions. In this style of employee relations, the government redresses the industrial power imbalance between employer and employee by establishing a framework of legislated terms and conditions of employment for all employees. Consequently, trade union activities become more focused on a political as opposed to an industrial role.

It has been suggested that only the extremes can produce stable employee relations – where labour is subordinated either by 'free market' forces within the economic system or by agencies supporting government strategies within the political system (Crouch, 1995: 231). Significantly, perhaps, the UK and other European countries have been largely characterised by 'liberal collectivism' or 'bargained corporatism' styles of employee relations.

THE LABOUR MARKET

There are two interrelated areas in the operation of the 'labour market'. The first relates to the price mechanism (wages). The level and relative distribution of pay is influenced by a variety of factors such as, on the employees' side, income expectations and the development of collective power to pursue these expectations, and, on the management side, labour costs and productivity. The second area is concerned with the level and structure of employment (the characteristics of the supply and demand for labour). This is affected not only by the general level of economic activity within organisations or the economy but also by shifts in the economic and industrial structures, technological development and changes in the participation rates within the working population. There have been substantial changes affecting the older industrialised countries over the past 20 years (Fevre, 1992: 2–9). These include:

■ global redistribution of economic activity and jobs away from these countries and towards Asia, Eastern Europe and other developing economies;

■ increased labour supply through greater female participation in the labour force;

■ changes in industrial and employment structures – away from manufacturing and towards service industries; away from manual to non-manual jobs;

■ technological developments generally requiring less, but more technically skilled, people;

■ continuing long-term relatively high levels of unemployment, and employment coming to be seen, by both employees and employers, as more temporary and transient.

Governments have an interest in the operation of both areas of the labour market. The primary concern of all governments is to ensure that the operation of the labour market supports, rather than hinders, economic change and development – in particular, that it promotes labour efficiency and minimises labour unit costs to underpin international competitiveness. A second potential focus of government concern is to mitigate the social and political consequences of economic change (in particular, unemployment). The manner in which a government seeks to 'regulate' the labour market, and the relative importance it attaches to the two areas of concern, will depend, to a large measure, on its underlying political ideology. While in some countries (for example, Japan, Germany, Sweden and Singapore) the government has been prepared to intervene directly in the working of labour market mechanisms, in other countries (such as the UK and the USA) the governments have encouraged management to accept responsibility for the operation of the labour market (deregulation). This is indicative of a 'basic division ... between those approaches which see the labour market as an arena of competition between individuals and those which see it as shaped and controlled by collective institutions, pressures and customs' (Claydon, 1994: 75) (*see* Exhibit 6.1).

■ Unemployment and labour flexibility

A major focus of attention since the early 1980s has been the continuing high levels of unemployment among the labour force. It is useful to identify two main groups of government labour market policies (Schmid *et al.*, 1992): *passive* policies (the provision of financial support to the individual during periods without work – unemployment benefit) and *active* policies (the provision of state funds to aid the unemployed in obtaining a new job – training, mobility allowances or job creation). The operation of these policies raises two important issues:

1 How should they be funded – indirectly by society as a whole (through government allocation of funds from general taxation) or directly by those currently in the labour market (through contributions from employers and employees)?

2 How should the two policy areas be managed – separately, with active policies being implemented through 'employment', 'trade' or 'education' agencies and passive policies being managed within a broad 'social welfare' agency, or integrated together in one agency?

Periods of recession and high unemployment heighten the potential tension between the two sets of policies. They are faced with reduced funding, whether from a decrease in the government's general 'tax-take' or less coming from direct contributions in the employed sector, at the same time as the costs of both types of policies are likely to increase. Direct contributions, by both employers and employees, are a major 'add-on' labour cost for the organisation and, therefore, any increase in the level of these contributions will increase the organisation's unit labour costs. This has the potential for making organisations more uncompetitive or reducing the number of employees, and thereby further increasing the level of unemployment. The alternative is to reduce the cost of, in particular, the passive policies by reducing the level of benefit or tightening the regulations which determine who is (or is not) entitled to receive such benefit. Certainly, the increasing and continuing high cost of maintaining an adequate level of unemployment benefit, which in most countries is a legal welfare entitlement, has become a major concern in the older industrialised countries (particularly in the UK and other EU countries).

■ **Exhibit 6.1**

ILO: Plan needed for full employment   **FT**

In its annual employment report, published today, the ILO argues a renewed commitment by national governments to the concept of full employment with a sustained annual global rate of more than 3.5 per cent could help to resolve the crisis. The report says that full employment is 'not passé' but 'still feasible and highly desirable'.

'Current levels of unemployment make no economic sense and are neither politically nor socially sustainable,' said Mr Michel Hansenne, the ILO's director-general yesterday.

'It is not just heartless but pernicious to assume nothing can be done to remedy unemployment, that so called jobless growth (when a country's gross domestic product grows with no substantial jobs growth) is the best that can be hoped for in an increasingly competitive economy or that current unemployment rates somehow constitute a natural and inevitable outcome of market forces.'

The report seeks to demolish a range of assumptions about world employment. 'It is not true globalisation is an uncontrollable supranational force that has largely usurped national policy autonomy,' it says. According to the ILO the nation state is 'still the dominant influence on economic and labour-market outcomes. Global financial markets punish unsound macro-economic policies which are, in any case, undesirable in their own right.' It adds, 'The empirical evidence suggests trade with developing countries and the relocation of industries has been only a minor explanatory factor behind the rise in unemployment and the declining wages of unskilled workers in industrialised countries.'

The report questions the popular view that the world is running out of jobs. 'Much of the "end-of-work" literature rests on unwarranted extrapolations from dramatic episodes of corporate downsizing, ignoring job creation elsewhere in the economy.' The ILO says the employment growth rate has remained 'almost unchanged over the last three-and-a-half decades and has not slowed down significantly since 1973', with the pace of job creation remaining steady in the face of the reduced economic growth rate of the 1970s and 1980s.

Nor does the ILO accept job changes are becoming more frequent and employment more unstable, saying there has been an increase not a decline in the length of job tenure. 'On average, individuals currently employed have been in their jobs for six to 12 years depending on the country and this figure has not been declining,' it says. Only in Spain have job moves become increasingly frequent, 'probably because of institutional changes'.

The report doubts whether 'labour market imperfections' are 'either the main or sole cause of the upward drift in European unemployment,' although it does not suggest they have had no effect. 'Labour market rigidities have not been increasing over the period of rising unemployment', says the ILO.

It says the main 'underlying' cause of increased unemployment is the slowdown in economic growth since 1974. It also criticises the rise in wage inequality, particularly in the US, UK and New Zealand, which it argues is partly due to the decline in trade union density and decentralisation of collective bargaining.

The report states: 'There is no convincing evidence that it is supply-side constraints, rather than a deficiency in demand that have caused the prolonged period of low growth.' It adds: 'Higher growth is possible provided a sustained period of expansionary policies is supported by credible policies to prevent a resurgence of inflationary wage increases and to overcome the skill shortages that will be generated. Without this the expansionary impulse will indeed be choked off by the reaction of the financial markets.' The ILO calls for a return to co-ordinated pay bargaining, the creation of social pacts between unions and employers, as well as the encouragement of profit-sharing or 'some form of tax-based incomes policy if there are no better alternatives'. It wants more efficient labour market policies with subsidies for low wage employment, training focused on the most disadvantaged, incentives for recruiting long-term jobless and improved benefit transfer programmes linking benefits and work more closely together.

The report says developing countries should also be committed to full employment and it argues this can be achieved by creating more open and competitive economies that benefit fully from expanding trade and investment flows in the global economy. The ILO believes, however, the 'trickle-down effects of market reforms will be weak unless they are accompanied by programmes to strengthen the productive capacity of the poor' through improvements in rural infrastructure, education and health services.

Source: Robert Taylor (1996) *Financial Times*, 26 November.

Political ideology, not surprisingly, appears to be an important factor in determining how governments have sought to respond to this situation (Hollinshead and Leat, 1995: 132). Those with a more corporatist governing ideology have been reluctant to reduce levels of unemployment benefit, which they regard as an important element of the welfare system in protecting the individual's living standards. They have tended to concentrate on supporting organisational training (in order to equip existing employees to adjust to change and, thereby, remain competitive and in employment) and developing state-funded and organised training for those not in employment (particularly the young and unemployed). It is those governments with a more *laissez-faire* (free market) ideology which have favoured strategies that reduce benefit levels or increase the restrictions on eligibility. They believe that, by reducing financial support when unemployed, the individual will be more prepared to accept those jobs that are available – even if only temporary, part-time or low-paid. In this way they aim to 'price people back into jobs'. At the same time, responsibility has been placed on management and the individual for ensuring that adequate training takes place, and for its funding.

Certainly, since the early 1980s, the UK government's strategies towards the labour market have reflected this latter approach. First, for example, claims for unemployment benefit have become subject to much closer scrutiny (particularly, requiring the individual to prove that they are 'actively' seeking work) and the long-term unemployed may be compelled to attend 'training' courses under the threat of losing their benefit if they do not. At the same time, the annual increase in the level of social security benefits generally, including unemployment benefit, has been unlinked from the annual change in average earnings so that the gap between the two has widened (increasing the pressure on an unemployed person to take any work available). The broad strategy of encouraging people 'off benefit and into work' is being continued by the new Labour government, although its changes in benefit regulations for single parents and the disabled have come in for strong criticism from with the Labour Party itself and from a variety of pressure groups.

Second, throughout its period of office, the Conservative government consistently resisted the adoption of EU Directives intended to establish employment protection rights in respect of 'atypical' workers and working time. It argued that such regulations would inhibit the competitiveness of UK organisations in the international market. Even changes in the retirement age and the abolition of legislation restricting the work of women were presented not so much as measures to support the development of equal opportunities but as measures to increase labour 'flexibility'. There has been some change in direction since the election of the new Labour government in so far as it has 'signed-up' for the Social Chapter and accepted the adoption of EU Directives. However, it appears (like its predecessor) to be arguing within the EU for the adoption of policies which will encourage greater labour flexibility.

Third, the Conservative government abolished the tripartite and national based approach of the Industrial Training Boards and Manpower Services Commission and transferred responsibility for training to employer-led Industry Training Organisations (ITOs) and locally based Training and Enterprise Councils (TECs) (Keep and Rainbird, 1995).

■ Incomes policy

While fiscal and monetary policies may allow governments to manage the macro-level impact of incomes on the economy, not all governments seek to regulate directly the pay outcomes of collective bargaining (*incomes policy*). An incomes policy may serve two functions. First, it may be used as an economic 'weapon' – restricting pay increases to reduce pressure on labour costs and prices in periods of inflation or regulating pay increases in periods of economic growth in order to avoid inflation. Second, it may act as a mechanism to promote greater 'social justice' by exerting pressure for the realignment of pay levels between different groups within society.

The use of formal incomes policies was an important feature of the UK's employee relations system throughout most of the 1960s and 1970s. After 1979, however, the Conservative government confined itself to a simple 'self-induced if invisible incomes policy' (McCarthy, 1993: 7) of cash limits on the public sector to reduce government expenditure. Although the primary role of the previous incomes policies was as an economic 'weapon' – to restrict pay increases, reduce labour costs and inflation and, thereby, maintain the UK's international competitiveness – they did result in some realignment of pay differentials (particularly, a compression of the pay differences between non-manual and manual employees and between skilled and unskilled employees within the manual group). However, attempts to address specific issues of 'social justice' were not successful. While special emotive groups (such as health service and fire service workers) were sometimes, because of their accepted low pay position, treated as exceptions and allowed to receive increases above the 'economic' norm, so too were groups (such as miners) who, because of their industrial power, represented a potential direct challenge to the overall acceptance of the incomes policy. Even the 'low pay' incomes policy in 1975, which restricted pay increases to those below £8500 per annum, resulted in only a temporary improvement in the position of the lower paid because their increase was 'absorbed' within subsequent pay negotiations.

One of the most difficult issues with any incomes policy is how to enforce its terms. Without the full and active support of both management and unions the government must rely on some form of statutory-based state agency. The problem is compounded when, as in the UK, collective bargaining is decentralised and fragmented; inevitably the attention of the regulating agency is directed towards the smaller number of major centralised private sector multi-employer agreements and, of course, negotiations under the direct or indirect control of the government itself. Pay increases above the 'norm' made at the organisational level, whether through collective bargaining or not, may easily escape notice. Furthermore, who should be penalised – the employer, the employees or both? And what form should the penalty take? Certainly, it is better to avoid breaches in the first place.

The only time the UK came close to a voluntary cooperative approach was during the Social Contract (1975–9). However, successive governments in Ireland (Prondzynski, 1992) managed to establish tripartite 'understandings' or 'programmes' on national economic and social strategies linked to incomes policies. It was perhaps most effective in regulating pay during the 1970s with centralised National Wage Agreements. Similarly, Whitfield (1988) believes that the Australian 'Accord' in the 1980s was successful not only because it linked pay issues with other economic, fiscal and social policies and was endorsed by a specially convened National Economic Summit Conference (comprising representatives of federal and state governments, employers, unions and various social welfare groups), but also because the Australian 'arbitration' system of collective bargaining provided a centralised but flexible way to implement the incomes policy. In Singapore (Beng and Chew, 1995), however, the success of the incomes policy may be attributed more to the 'incorporation' (subordination) of trade unions into the political system. The annual wage guidelines set by the tripartite National Wages Council, established in 1972, are required to reflect the performance of the economy and be consistent with maintaining employment and economic growth and are certainly intended to influence collective bargaining in line with public policy.

UK trade unions have always expressed strong reservations about the operation of a formal incomes policy. They have felt that it marginalises their role in negotiating pay increases for their members: the level of pay increase becomes determined by the incomes policy, not union negotiators, and is likely to be similar across most groups and organisations (irrespective of whether they are unionised or not). However, they do support some form of central national discussion of pay and the economy. In 1990, the TUC Congress accepted the idea (GMB/UCW, 1990) of an arrangement which would co-ordinate major pay negotiations to take place following a 'public' tripartite discussion of the government's annual Economic Review and linked to the setting of the rate for a national minimum wage. The unions do not favour any statutory pay restraint, nor do they regard this approach as an 'incomes policy'; rather it would establish a climate within which negotiations would take place freely.

SOCIAL JUSTICE

The existence and range of employment protection legislation is, perhaps, one of the clearest expressions of a government's concern, or lack of concern, for 'social justice' in the operation of the labour market. The UK developed a range of individual employment protection legislation during the 1960s and 1970s – most importantly, in the areas of discrimination (both race and sex), equal pay, health and safety, dismissal and redundancy. While some additions were made after 1979, Dickens and Hall point out that the 'free market' ideology of the Conservative government regarded such legislation 'not as essential minimum standards but as "burdens on business" (particularly in respect of small employers) which deter the employment of more people' (1995: 257). Hence, the government raised the qualifying period before being able to claim unfair dismissal from six months to two years and resisted the expansion of further employment protection rights resulting from EU Directives. Furthermore, a number of the more important developments in individual protection which did take place during the 1980s and 1990s only did so as a result of external pressures to comply with EU regulations – for example, equal pay for work of equal value; equal treatment in access to employment, vocational training and promotion; protection on transfer of the undertaking; and common qualifying periods, as between part-time and full-time employees, before qualifying for protection rights. Indeed, the government appeared to be more prepared to provide individuals with rights that might be enforced against trade unions than it did to extend enforceable rights against management.

The final establishment of the Single European Market in 1992, in the midst of increasingly competitive world markets, heightened rather than diminished the issue of social policy regulation. The objective of EU social policy is to ensure that employees share in the organisational benefits gained from the 'single market'. However, Teague (1993) suggests that it is perhaps easier to achieve 'negative' integration (centring on the abolition of regulations and barriers which might restrict the free movement of goods and capital) than it is to achieve 'positive' integration (including the development of common social strategies to ensure that labour is not exploited). A similar tension exists at the global level between the World Trade Organization (liberalising world trade) and the ILO (seeking to establish and enforce international labour standards). Certainly, two main area of 'social justice' have recently been the focus of UK attention: a national minimum wage and 'labour dumping' resulting from the business decisions of transnational organisations.

■ National minimum wage

Perhaps the most crucial foundation to ensuring 'social justice' in the labour market is the establishment and enforcement of a minimum wage below which no one will be paid. Despite any disagreement about what should be its actual level, the existence of a national minimum wage is a clear expression of the principle that employees should receive a 'living wage' which would help alleviate extreme poverty. Many countries have a statutory national minimum wage – including the USA, which is often regarded as the bastion of free market capitalism – and the UK has been singularly out of step with most other EU countries in not having one.

Until 1993, the UK did have a partial 'minimum wage' mechanism in the form of statutory Wages Councils in a limited range of industries, albeit encompassing some 2.5 million employees. These industries (principally retail, catering, clothing and agriculture) have a high level of female and part-time labour working in small organisations with low unionisation. The Councils were tripartite bodies (comprising union and employer representatives plus government-appointed independent members) and there was a separate Wages Inspectorate with responsibility for policing the application of the Wages Councils' Statutory Orders (agreements) within these industries. It can be argued that, without such government support, it would have been difficult for collective bargaining to have been established and maintained on a voluntary basis. However, their role in dealing with the problem of low pay is more debatable: despite policing by the Wages Inspectorate, many employers still paid below the Wages Council rate and these industries have remained among the lowest paid.

The Conservative government abolished Wages Councils in 1993. They argued that they 'priced people out of jobs', by maintaining artificially high wage rates and restricting the potential for employment growth, as well as creating an undue administrative burden on both the government and small employers. However, employment levels in these industries do not appear to have increased since the abolition of the Wages Councils, although wage levels have remained virtually static (i.e. decreased in real terms) (TUC, 1996). Not surprisingly, the Conservative government was also opposed to any suggestion of introducing a national minimum wage. Not only did they regard it as the antithesis of a 'free market', but they also believed that its introduction would have a 'knock-on' effect in pushing up all pay levels. However, one estimate suggested that such a 'knock-on' effect would be likely to be limited to only the lower levels of the pay structure and any resulting reduction in the employment level would be small (Bazen and Benhayoun, 1992).

One of the first moves by the new Labour government has been to initiate legislation to introduce a national minimum wage – hopefully by early 1999. The first step was to establish an independent commission to recommend a figure for the minimum wage which 'must be sensible' and 'not harm competitiveness' (Labour Party, 1997). Some unions pressed for a figure of £4.40 per hour, but the CBI believed that anything above £3.20 per hour could significantly damage organisational competitiveness. Perhaps more importantly, the commission was asked to consider whether employees undertaking recognised training and/or under the age of 26 should be exempted. Significantly, the TUC and CBI agreed that all employees over 19 years of age should be covered (unless in training) but the CBI wanted the exclusion extended to include those under 25 years of age who have been previously unemployed for more than six months and are being employed as part of the government's 'Welfare to Work' programme (*see* Exhibit 6.2). The commission finally recommended a general rate of £3.60 per hour with a lower rate of £3.20 per hour for those aged between 18 and 21.

■ Exhibit 6.2

Minimum wage offers maximum return

According to the theory of the free market, lowering wages leads to higher employment. It doesn't. Will Hutton explains why.

Fairness has a powerful grip on the popular imagination. In vain do right-wing politicians, free-market economists and the business élite plead that the rich need and deserve incentives while the only way for the poor to price themselves into work is for there to be no potential minimum to their wages. It is seen as one law for the rich and another for the poor – and so it is.

This week the British business élite's double standards were vividly on display. On Monday the Greenbury Committee reported, arguing for some minimal changes and safeguards to limit the more outrageous boardroom abuses but essentially leaving the existing structures in place. On Tuesday the Confederation of British Industry (CBI) reaffirmed its opposition to the minimum wage.

Market forces, business will claim, must do their felicitous work at each end of the income scale. If the country feels that the results leave those at the bottom too poor, then it should supplement their income with benefits for which the taxpayer foots the bill. At the top, the processes by which pay is determined should be transparent and properly taxed – but beyond that the market must rule.

In this conception the market is a somehow impersonal arbiter of economic fortunes. The great forces of power and equity that lie at the bottom of market relations, and the social and political institutions through which they are mediated, are abstracted away. It is all supposedly a matter of supply and demand. The rise in executive salaries is explained as a price signal showing that there are too few people coming forward with the ability to run British companies. So their price gets bid up.

But as Paul Ormerod argues in the *Death of Economics* the notion that the pay of directors, investment bankers and the like has anything to do with supply and demand operating in a competitive labour market is palpably absurd. Tens of thousands apply to get on the management training courses of the top 100 companies or City investment banks, but still their salaries spiral upwards rather than are bid down; meanwhile, there are chronic shortages of applicants for jobs on the railways – and still Railtrack resists paying more than 3 per cent. The one thing that you can honestly say about the labour market is that it does not operate according to the laws by which British business claims that it does.

Leading theorists in economics are now challenging the simple nostrums that inform the British debate, which amount to little more than a return to the axioms of early 19th century political economy, in which price of labour is meant to be like the price of tomatoes; lower it and more is demanded – raise it and less is sought.

▶

Late last year, David Blanchflower and Andrew Oswald published the most rigorous cross-country survey of the labour market ever undertaken – the *Wage Curve*. Over four years the two used 9000 computer hours to survey the relationship between wages and employment of 3.5 million people in 12 countries, delivering results that show that every word the CBI, the Government and the *Economist* – the British *Pravda* to the Conservative élite – utter on the labour market is balderdash.

Employment is not highest where real wages are lowest, and lowest where real wages are highest. Nowhere has lowering real wages led to higher employment. Put another way, unemployment serves to lower real wages by a predictable degree – a doubling of unemployment lowers real wages by about 10 per cent everywhere – but that lowering wages does not lead to a rise in employment.

There is no disputing the numbers; the task is to find an explanation that fits the data. The answer lies in the way wages are fixed and maintained. The dynamic component of the labour market is not the price of labour, it is the demand, and wages are fixed not in relation to what terms the unemployed might accept but an internal calculus by individual firms of the worth of their workforces. This 'efficiency wage' comprises the best combination of incentives, the cost of rehiring, the value of knowing the capacity of the existing workforce and its marginal productivity – all traded off against the value of what is produced. It is a complex mix in which the level of unemployment is at best only one element, at worst peripheral.

Unemployment therefore does not lower real wages to price the unemployed into work; it acts to discipline the wages and behaviour of those who are employed. It is only if the demand for labour rises that the unemployed will find work – which is why Blanchflower and Oswald find that high unemployment and high wages go hand in hand and that low wages and high unemployment are similarly correlated.

Top executives' pay is one proof of this theory; they are the beneficiaries of high demand for their services and the need to secure their loyalty to one firm – a kind of efficiency wage for senior directors. Their pay has nothing to do with the competitive interaction of supply and demand, as in a textbook free-labour market.

Another proof is new evidence from the US that a minimum wage for the low-paid is also an instrument for promoting efficiency in the labour market, and that as long as it is set at reasonable levels it promotes rather than reduces employment.

In *Myth and Measurement*, Professors David Card and Alan Kreuger from Princeton University show that just as in the wider labour market unemployment acts as a discipline on wage levels for those in employment rather than an active force for lowering the jobless totals, so this same process is at work at the bottom of the labour market. The difference is that here wages are so low that they create social difficulties for those earning them.

Free-market theory predicts that a minimum wage must lower employment because it raises the price of labour. In a variety of empirical tests, notably in the US fast-food industry, Card and Kreuger show the opposite is true. In a free market, firms set their wages so low that they have high turnover rates and longer periods in which they cannot find workers. Although this may appear to boost margins in the short run, the actual wage is below the efficiency wage. A minimum wage reduces turnover rates, raises skills and even increases output by having extra manpower to service customer needs. A minimum wage raises employment as long as it brings the efficiency wage and money wages into line; but if the minimum wage is set above the efficiency wage, job losses will result.

It also serves to promote social cohesion and alleviate poverty. In Britain it used to be argued that low wages are not a cause of poverty – single parenthood or bad pensions were the main reasons for low incomes. But that was before the labour market was deregulated, with the wages of the bottom 10 per cent falling in real terms since 1979. Two-fifths of the workers who would benefit from a minimum wage of £3 an hour live in the poorest 10 per cent of households.

The CBI and the Government are united in opposing a minimum wage in principle, preferring to boost the incomes of the poor through family credit. But this is no more than a contemporary version of the Speenhamland system which at the beginning of the 19th century locked the working class into appalling dependence and poverty for a generation. The idea was that the very poor were to be saved from starvation by being offered a subsis-

■ **Exhibit 6.2 continued**

tence income devised by local magistrates and funded by the ratepayer. But, just as today, the free labour market bid down wages and the ratepayers found themselves subsidising rapacious employers. Poverty exploded, the rates became insupportable and the economy began to wind down as levels of demand fell away. It was inherently absurd.

Yet that is the path Britain is now set upon. Spending on family credit has already exceeded £2.4 billion and must increase as the processes bidding down the wages of the bottom 10 per cent extend up the income hierarchy. Essentially the taxpayer is funding cheap labour.

It is the oldest story in capitalism, and during this week's special pleading for the rich and assault on the idea of a minimum wage for the poor, no one in Britain should ever forget it.

Source: Will Hutton (1995) *Guardian Weekly*, 23 July.

■ Social or labour dumping

The term 'social dumping' relates to the transfer of work, by transnational organisations, to take advantage of labour differences between countries: reducing employment in one country, while expanding in another. The problem has become highlighted as trade barriers have been reduced or removed with the creation of regional 'single' markets (like the EU, ASEAN and NAFTA) and the general liberalisation of world trade through the WTO. The 'labour' element is an important aspect of both organisational and national competitiveness, and significant national variations exist in a number of areas:

- direct labour costs (wage levels reflect differences in the cost and standard of living);
- indirect labour costs (hours of work, holidays, fringe benefits and health and safety provisions);
- social 'add-on' costs (employers' costs associated with social security contributions, dismissals and redundancy);
- use of 'vulnerable' groups (females, children, homeworkers, bonded labour, prison labour, etc.).

Within the EU, the problem of 'social dumping' was graphically illustrated by Hoover in 1993 (EIRR, 1993). The company made an agreement with the AEEU for its Cambuslang (Scotland) site which included not only significant changes in working methods to improve labour efficiency and flexibility but also, and perhaps most importantly, measures to reduce labour costs – in particular, a one-year pay freeze and the recruitment of new employees to be initially on two-year fixed contracts at 15 per cent lower wages than existing employees. Then, three days later and without prior warning, Hoover announced that its factory in Longvic (France) would be closed and its work transferred to Cambuslang. While this would create an extra 400 jobs in Scotland, 600 French employees would lose their jobs. French workers were critical of not only Hoover management but also the AEEU, which they felt had accepted an 'appalling agreement'. However, the AEEU argued that it was 'in the business of defending its members' and had got 'the best deal it could'.

There appear to be three central questions:

- What is a 'fair' basis for labour competition?

■ Can governments balance a 'social justice' objective of providing employment protection with an 'economic' objective of facilitating employment creation?

■ Should national self-interest take precedence over international cooperation?

The conflict between the UK, under a Conservative government, and its EU partners over the Social Chapter in the Maastricht Treaty has been described as a 'conflict between the proponents of "solidarity" and "subsidiarity", and between the advocates of lesser rather than greater labour market regulation' (Rhodes, 1993: 298). The dispute had not only an ideological element but also a pragmatic one – for one country to gain a competitive edge over other countries (Towers, 1992). Certainly, trade unions believe that, in the face of competition between national governments to attract or maintain investment and employment by offering lower labour costs, greater labour flexibility and a more compliant workforce, employees are virtually powerless to prevent the 'transfer of unemployment' from one country to another. The solution, in their view, lies in limiting the nature and degree of such competition through more international regulation of employment protection rights, harmonisation of social 'add-on' costs and co-ordination of national employment promotion programmes.

'Social dumping' is not confined to relations between EU countries, but has become a matter for concern on a wider global scale. The older industrialised countries, particularly in Europe and North America, are threatened by the liberalisation of world trade and the nature of employment relations that exist in many of the newer industrialised and industrialising countries. This has led to calls for 'social clauses' (minimum labour standards) to be included as part of any trade agreements between the EU and ASEAN countries and in the WTO. This approach may be seen as simply the most effective way of defining and enforcing the limits of 'fair' labour competition, especially the ability of multinational organisations to take advantage of national fragmentation and engage in 'social dumping'. However, Asian countries certainly regard it as both a form of self-protection – which will restrict their competitiveness and, in turn, their continued economic development – and an unwarranted attempt to impose on them a 'Western' style of employee relations. Like the UK government's view of EU regulation, they also see this approach as interfering with their right to determine their own approach to and standards of employee relations (*see* Exhibit 6.3).

INDUSTRIAL CONFLICT

The potential for conflict always exists within any social structure. While the dominant group in the social structure may perceive conflict as a threat to the established order which must be controlled or even suppressed, those who seek to challenge the *status quo* may regard it as a necessary part of the process of developing a new order. Within a pluralistic perspective, conflict is seen as a means of expressing different interests (which have to be resolved) and, therefore, is a necessary element in maintaining the continuity and stability of the social structure. The use of industrial action within the employee relations system is an explicit, collective expression of both concern and power. It is intended to help secure a more favourable outcome to a negotiation or to resist unacceptable management actions. Its 'power' derives from the capacity to create a situation of temporary disorder within the employment relationship and, by so doing, 'prevents even the

■ Exhibit 6.3

WTO summit: Unions warn over workers rights

Trade union leaders warned yesterday that the credibility of the World Trade Organisation would be 'on trial' at its first ministerial meeting, to be held in Singapore next month. They are demanding that ministers create a working group to examine how the WTO's rules can be adapted to link workers' rights with global trade.

The International Confederation of Free Trade Unions, a Brussels-based body representing trade unions responsible for 127m workers in 136 countries, said it wanted a 'mutually reinforcing relationship enhanced between core international labour standards and the multilateral trading system'.

Unions plan to hold a conference in Singapore to press their demands on the eve of the WTO meeting.

But it seems increasingly unlikely that the governments at the summit will accept the ICFTU's demands, despite support for them from the US and within the European Commission.

An alliance of industrialised countries – including the UK and Japan – and developing nations such as India, Malaysia and Indonesia remain opposed to any WTO link between labour standards and trade.

The ICFTU said the Singapore summit would show whether the WTO existed 'only to help a minority of the world's population make profits' or if it would 'create the opportunity for the majority to work for a decent living'.

Without universal respect for basic human rights at work, 'which enabled working men and women

to struggle for a better deal, the multilateral trading system constructed by the WTO will become unenforceable', it said.

The organisation wants countries to accept five minimum standards – freedom of association, the right to collective bargaining, a minimum age for employment, no forced labour and no discrimination in employment.

'These are enabling rights which provide an absolute minimum of humane treatment at work and which would provide workers and employers with the means to negotiate improvements as trade and development expand', said Mr Bill Jordan, the ICFTU's general secretary.

'If intellectual property rights can be strictly enforced, why should minimum standards ... be treated differently?' the ICFTU asked.

'The right to free market access confers a duty on all WTO members to observe fully the core labour standards defined by the International Labour Organization.

'A fair and transparent multilateral mechanism for dealing with the gross and persistent abuse of international labour standards is both essential to preventing the resurgence of protectionism and as a sound basis for constrictive competition in the global market.'

The ICFTU argues that intensified global competition has led to a lowering of production costs through wage cuts and worsening conditions.

Source: Robert Taylor (1996) *Financial Times*, 29 November.

most enlightened managerial regime from becoming mere paternalism' (Grunfeld, 1966: 367). However, those who support the *laissez-faire* 'free market' ideology believe such disruption to be an 'intolerable abuse of economic freedom' and 'type of warfare' which allows some groups to make gains at the expense of others (Hutt, 1973: 282–3).

■ Public interest in industrial action

The concepts of 'national interest' and 'social control' are, perhaps, nowhere more intertwined in employee relations than when considering the use of industrial action. The legislation (social control mechanism) which governments create in this area is generally projected as being 'in the public interest' and therefore if some action is stated to be 'unlawful' then, by implication, it is also morally 'wrong' and people become socialised into accepting it as such (Edwards, 1995: 447). Certainly, the UK approach of granting employees and trade unions 'immunity' from legal action when undertaking 'lawful' industrial action implies that it is a privilege – not granted to other groups in society – rather than a right, and, as such, it may be withdrawn if it is not exercised in a 'responsible' manner (that is, in a manner which is acceptable to the government as the guardian of 'national interest'). Governments determine how wide or narrow is the boundary of what is 'lawful'.

The Conservative government's measures after 1980 increased state control over the use of industrial action. They not only restricted the scope of immunity, by narrowing the boundary of lawful industrial action and tightening the procedural requirements (ballots, independent scrutiny, notifying employers, etc.), but also widened the range of 'interested parties' who can instigate legal action against trade unions to include not just management or even union members but any private citizen who feels he or she might be adversely affected by the industrial action. Furthermore, state support for such individuals provided through the creation of the Commissioner for Protection Against Unlawful Industrial Action (whose very title is emotive). However, the substantial decline in industrial action seen in the UK over the 1980s and 1990s cannot be attributed solely to this increase in legislated 'social control'. Other countries, which have not changed their legislation, have also experienced a decline. It would seem that economic factors, such as recession, unemployment and decline in manufacturing, might have been more influential than the 'social control' factor (legislation).

While trade unions, as organisations, have been the main focus of legal actions relating to their conduct of industrial action, it is the preparedness of the individual members to withdraw their labour and lose pay which really provides the collective strength of such action. Therefore, the extent to which the state supports a 'right' to strike depends, perhaps, more on whether or not the employee is protected against dismissal than on whether or not he or she may be sued for damages by management. The concept of 'immunity' may be important in protecting union funds but is largely irrelevant for the individual employee – few employers are prepared to take their own employees to court and secure compensation (damages) which are likely to bankrupt the individual. The more important legal principle, under UK legislation, is that the strike is regarded as a fundamental breach of the contract of employment that justifies management terminating the contract. The only protection for the individual is that, if the strike is 'lawful', a dismissal will be unfair if management dismisses some but not *all* employees engaged in the strike: thus, any constraint on management is an economic rather than a legal one. However, if the industrial action is 'unlawful', management has complete discretion to dismiss whomever it chooses – an employee selected in this way cannot take a claim to an Industrial Tribunal. The Labour Party (1997) has said that it does not intend either to prevent employers from dismissing strikers or to compel them to reinstate any who successfully claim unfair dismissal, but is 'merely' proposing that employees engaged in 'lawful' industrial action should be able to pursue a claim for compensation at an Industrial Tribunal even if management dismisses all of them. However, this is more than just a minor change. It will involve a significant shift in the Tribunal's role: from judging management's equality of treatment among employees, to judging between the competing interests of management and unions. They will have to determine the circumstances in which the dismissal of 'lawful' strikers becomes 'fair and reasonable'.

Another area which has been a focus of attention is whether or not the 'right to strike' should continue to exist in essential services (such as gas, electricity, water and sewerage, health services, teachers, transport, refuse collectors, etc.). The disruption caused to other employers, workers and the general public by industrial action in these services is frequently felt to be unacceptable. Furthermore, in so far as these groups are in the public sector, any industrial action inevitably appears to be 'political' – a challenge to the policy or action of the elected government. The removal of the 'right to strike' in these services is usually linked to the use of some form of automatic arbitration to resolve dispute. Without this, the employees would be powerless and open to management exploitation without any form of redress. However, one side effect of privatisation has been the removal of many of these services from 'public' responsibility. While a government may wish to constrain the social disruption resulting from strikes in these areas, the management of these private organisations is likely to see any accompanying requirement to accept a process of automatic arbitration, not required of other private sector management, as an unacceptable restriction of its freedom to manage and determine its own terms of employment. Significantly, attempts by some state governments in the USA to remove the 'right to strike' in private sector 'essential' services, in return for compulsory arbitration, were held to be contrary to the Taft–Hartley Act (1947) which applied to all non-government employees and which specifically permitted strikes. In both Canada (Beaumont, 1992: 130) and Italy (Bridgford and Stirling, 1994: 150) the governments have sought to mitigate the worst effects of strikes in pubic sector services, not by abolishing the 'right to strike', but by requiring employees to maintain a minimum essential level of service during the strike – which has often been the case in the UK, but on a voluntary basis (*see* Exhibits 6.4 and 6.5)

■ Role of the state in dispute settlement

Most governments believe that industrial action, because of its potential disruptive economic and social effects, should only be used as a 'weapon of last resort'. In order to facilitate the maintenance of industrial peace, the government may provide for conciliation and arbitration to be available to the parties at public expense – these services were initially established in the UK under the Conciliation Act 1896 and Industrial Courts Act 1919. The use of such processes is voluntary (i.e. at the discretion of the management and union involved in the dispute). However, during the 1980s, the Conservative government appeared to become less concerned about ensuring the maintenance of industrial peace (perhaps because strikes were becoming less of a threat as they declined in both numbers and working days lost) and, like management, more concerned about the effect arbitration might have on management's freedom and responsibility to manage the organisation. Both viewed arbitration as potentially inducing 'unreasonable' claims and intransigent 'non-negotiation' on the part of unions, in the expectation of obtaining a better settlement from an arbitrator than from management (which, in the public sector, was the government itself or one of its agents), and certainly resulted in decisions being made by an 'outsider' (the arbitrator) rather than management. Management was encouraged to say 'no' to union requests for arbitration and the union could do nothing, if management adopted an intransigent 'non-negotiable' approach, other than accept or resort to the use of industrial action.

■ Exhibit 6.4

Trade unions: UK government plans crackdown on strikes

The government is proposing further extensive changes to employment law, making trade unions liable to damages where strikes have a 'disproportionate or excessive' effect on other businesses or consumers.

The proposals are in the late draft of a green paper entitled Industrial Action and Trade Unions which was leaked to the Trades Union Congress last night.

They will not become law during this parliament, but ministers will attempt to use them during the election campaign to embarrass the Labour Party over the unions and industrial strife.

Mr Ian Lang, trade and industry secretary, told the Conservative party conference in September that he would take measures to tackle strikes by public sector workers following a wave of disputes on the railways, Royal Mail and London Underground.

The main proposals are:

- Unions will be open to legal action and claims for damages where a strike is held by the courts to have a 'disproportionate or excessive effect'.
- The notice period for industrial action after workers have voted in favour will be doubled from seven to 14 days.
- Rules covering pre-strike ballots will be changed to require the support of a majority of those entitled to vote, rather than a majority of those voting.
- Rights to time off for trade union duties will be abolished, as will the requirement for employers to produce information for collective bargaining.

Mr Lang said the government believed there was widespread recognition that the right to call strikes should be constrained.

The draft says that the government considered banning strikes in monopolies or near-monopolies like the public sector, but found there were problems of definition. 'The government considers that a better approach is to focus on the effects of a strike,' it says.

The document adds that judges will decide what is 'disproportionate or excessive' by building up case law. Strikes at most commercial undertakings where there are readily available alternative sources of supply will not be affected.

Mr John Monks, general secretary of the TUC, accused the government of 'plumbing new depths' and said the plans were 'far more damaging' to unions than expected. Mr Stephen Byers, shadow employment and training minister, said: 'These laws seem to be a triumph of political dogma over good industrial relations.'

Source: Andrew Bolger (1996) *Financial Times*, 2 November.

Even in the past, during periods of incomes policy, the government tried, by exhortation or even direct instruction, to regulate the decisions of arbitrators in wage disputes. Such an approach could easily compromise the independence of arbitrators and result in them being perceived as little more than administrators of government policy or 'branded as unpatriotic, irresponsible or deaf' if they took a different view of the 'national interest' (Lowry, 1990: 83). Indeed, it was doubts on the part of both management and union about the continuing impartiality of the Department of Employment's conciliation and arbitration services that led to the creation of ACAS, in 1974, as an autonomous body outside direct ministerial day-to-day control. The determination of ACAS to maintain its independence and not be simply a mechanism for implementing government policy has been borne out not only by its refusal to be an enforcement agent for incomes policy (under a Labour government) but also by its refusal to draw up codes of practice on picketing and the closed shop (during the early days of the Thatcher government) (Mortimer, 1981: 24).

■ **Exhibit 6.5**

Stability and co-operation

The key to orderly and effective industrial relations is to establish a fair and effective balance between rights and responsibilities that will promote partnership, not conflict, at the workplace.

This is the principle that will inform our whole approach to industrial relations.

The Conservatives are scaremongering when they claim a Labour government would turn the clock back, reverse trade union immunities to allow secondary industrial action, and alter the rules on picketing. There is not a word of truth in any of this. The existing laws on industrial action, picketing and ballots will all remain unchanged.

Every employee should be free to join or not join a trade union. We will not impose trade unions on employees or return to the closed shop. When they do decide to join, and where a majority of the relevant workforce votes in a ballot for the union to represent them, we believe that the union should be recognised.

Strikes in support of recognition claims today are trade disputes covered by the existing legal immunities. Our proposal offers a better way and removes any need for industrial action by a trade union in support of a claim for recognition. We believe that this is a step forward in promoting orderly industrial relations.

In government we will consult widely with both sides of industry on the best means of implementing these proposals.

It is complete nonsense to suggest that it is our policy to prevent employers dismissing those who are on strike. We have no such proposals. The law will remain as it is now.

And an employer cannot be compelled to reinstate those who successfully claim unfair dismissal. That will remain the position.

We propose merely that, whereas at present employees who are selectively dismissed when on lawful strike can claim compensation from an industrial tribunal for unfair dismissal, this should apply also to the situation where all those on lawful strike are dismissed. This reflects an entirely fair balance between the rights and responsibilities of employers and employees at the workplace.

Source: Labour Party (1997) *Labour's Business Manifesto: Equipping Britain for the Future.*

However, the ultimate power of the government to push the employee relations system in the direction it wants, through its ability to 'change the rules of the system', has been demonstrated by the removal of the duty to 'encourage collective bargaining' from ACAS's terms of reference in 1993. Despite ACAS's desire to be independent, impartial and apolitical, the government was able to ensure that its work must be brought in line with government policy. However, ACAS's role in individual conciliation has more than doubled over the past decade with the establishment of new individual legal rights relating to payment of wages and breach of employment contract. In 1995 it settled over one-third of the 91 000 Industrial Tribunal applications. The high number of applications for legal redress to individual employment disputes might indicate an increasing individualisation of the contractual relationship and a weakening in the unions' ability to protect members.

CHAPTER SUMMARY

This chapter opened by explaining the importance of the government (particularly as the law maker and controller of state agencies) in determining the nature of the national system of employee relations and how this has been demonstrated in the radical changes in UK employee relations after 1979.

It is clear that any government's approach to employee relations is determined primarily by its political ideology – either *laissez-faire* (free market) or corporatist (interventionist). It is the differences between these political ideologies, linked to the relative power of trade unions, which explains variations in national systems of employee relations and changes in national systems over time. The differences in ideology affect the way in which governments interpret their role and objectives in the management of the economy and dealing with consequent social issues.

Two areas have dominated government activity in the labour market: First, the problem of unemployment: whether this is best tackled through a positive balance of passive policies (provision of social benefits) and active policies (training) or through reduced employee protection and labour market regulation to induce greater labour flexibility. Secondly, the extent to which, if any, the government can and should seek to manage the pay side of the labour market through formal incomes policies.

Governments also have a responsibility to promote some level of social justice in employee relations. In addition to individual employment protection legislation, many governments maintain some form of minimum wage below which nobody should be paid. More recently, concern has been expressed about the extent to which deregulation of the labour market (for example, in the UK), or the absence of effective international labour standards, will result in 'social dumping' as multinational organisations seek to take advantage of national differentials in labour costs.

All governments are concerned about expressions of social conflict – not least in employee relations. While some see the expression of such conflict as unacceptably harmful (to be restricted and curtailed by legislative controls), others see it as an inevitable and necessary element of expressing and resolving differences within a dynamic social system. The government's approach to social conflict is clearly demonstrated through the legislative framework it creates (in particular, the extent to which it allows or restricts both the individual's and the unions' use of industrial action) and its approach towards the institutions and processes, particularly arbitration, intended to help in the resolution of disputes.

QUESTIONS

1 Explain the importance of the government in determining the nature of employee relations. By what means can governments influence employee relations?

2 What are the differences between the *laissez-faire* (free market) and corporatist (interventionist) ideologies? How do the changes in the UK government approach to employee relations over the past 100 years reflect these differences?

3 Consider the role of an incomes policy and compare the UK's experience with those of other countries. What appear to be the essential ingredients for a successful incomes policy?

4 To what extent, and in what ways, do you believe governments can and should promote 'social justice' in the labour market? In your answer, consider both the national and international dimensions.

5 Should governments restrict 'the right to strike'? If so, why and how; and has the UK government gone too far, far enough or should it go further?

ACTIVITY

Electronics (UK) plc is about to undertake a joint venture with Deutsch Electronics GmBH to establish a new manufacturing operation in Indonesia to serve the South-East Asia market. In order to comply with Indonesian government requirements, they will have to include a local partner – Indon Electronics Sdn Bdh. The unions in Electronics (UK) plc and the works council at Deutsch GmBH have expressed 'serious reservations' that the development of the new operation may lead to a loss of jobs in the UK and/or Germany and have asked for assurances that the workers in Indonesia will receive comparable terms and conditions of employment to those in Europe. However, Indon Electronics Sdn Bdh, which does not recognise trade unions, believes that this will restrict the successful management and competitiveness of the new operations (certainly in comparison to other local electronics firms).

1 In groups, consider the issues and arguments which might be put forward by the European management, European unions, Indonesian management and Indonesian workers.

2 As the European HR Director, prepare a report for a forthcoming meeting of the three partner companies which analyses the feasibility and desirability of common labour standards.

REFERENCES

Bazen, S. and Benhayoun, G. (1992) 'Low pay and wage regulation in the European Community', *British Journal of Industrial Relations*, 30 (4), 623–38.

Bean, R. (1994) *Comparative Industrial Relations: An Introduction to Cross National Perspectives.* 2nd edn. London: Routledge.

Beaumont, P.B. (1992) *Public Sector Industrial Relations.* London: Routledge.

Beng, C. S. and Chew, R. (1995) 'The development of industrial relations strategy in Singapore' in Verma, A., Kochan, T. A. and Lansbury, R.D. (eds) *Employment Relations in the Growing Asian Economies.* London: Routledge, pp. 62–87.

Blyton, P. and Turnbull, P. (1994) *The Dynamics of Employee Relations.* Basingstoke: Macmillan.

Bridgford, J. and Stirling, J. (1994) *Employee Relations in Europe.* Oxford: Blackwell.

Bullock Committee (1977) *Report of the Committee of Inquiry on Industrial Democracy.* London: HMSO.

Claydon, T. (1994) 'Human resource management and the labour market' in Beardwell, I. and Holden, L. (eds.) *Human Resource Management: A Contemporary Perspective.* London: Financial Times Pitman Publishing.

Crouch, C. (1977) *Class Conflict and the Industrial Relations Crisis.* London: Heinemann.

Crouch, C. (1982) *The Politics of Industrial Relations.* 2nd edn. London: Fontana.

Crouch, C. (1995) 'The state: economic management and incomes policy' in Edwards, P. (ed.) *Industrial Relations: Theory and Practice in Britain.* Oxford: Blackwell.

Dickens, L. and Hall M. (1995) 'The state: labour law and industrial relations' in Edwards, P. (ed.) *Industrial Relations: Theory and Practice in Britain,* Oxford: Blackwell.

Donovan Commission (1968) *Report of the Royal Commission on Trade Unions and Employers' Associations.* London: HMSO.

Edwards, P. (1995) 'Strikes and industrial conflict' in Edwards, P. (ed.) *Industrial Relations: Theory and Practice in Britain*. Oxford: Blackwell.

EIRR (1993) 'The Hoover affair and social dumping', *European Industrial Relations Review*, no. 230, 14–20

Fevre, R. (1992) *The Sociology of Labour Markets*. Englewood Cliffs, NJ: Prentice Hall.

GMB/UCW (1990) 'A New Agenda: bargaining for prosperity in the 1990s'.

Griffith, J. (1990) 'The collective unfairness of laissez-faire', *Guardian*, 14 June.

Grunfeld, C. (1966) *Modern Trade Union Law*. London: Sweet & Maxwell.

Hollinshead, G. and Leat, M. (1995) *Human Resource Management: An International and Comparative Perspective*. London: Financial Times Pitman Publishing.

Hutt, W. H. (1973) *The Strike Threat System*. New Rochelle, NY: Arlington House.

Hyman, R. (1975) *Industrial Relations: A Marxist Introduction*. Basingstoke: Macmillan.

Kahn-Freund, O. (1960) 'Legal framework' in Flanders, A. and Clegg, H. A. (eds) *The System of Industrial Relations in Great Britain*. Oxford: Blackwell.

Keep, E. and Rainbird, H. (1995) 'Training' in Edwards, P. (ed.) *Industrial Relations: Theory and Practice in Britain*, Oxford: Blackwell, 515–42.

Labour Party (1997) *Labour's Business Manifesto: Equipping Britain for the Future*. London: Labour Party.

Lee, J. S. (1995) 'Economic development and the evolution of industrial relations in Taiwan, 1950–1993' in Verma, A., Kochan, T. A. and Lansbury, R.D., *Employment Relations in the Growing Asian Economies*. London: Routledge, pp 88–118.

Legget, C. (1993) 'Singapore' in Deery, S. J. and Mitchell, R. J. (eds), *Labour Law and Industrial Relations in Asia*. London: Longman, pp. 96–136.

Lowry, P. (1990) *Employment Disputes and the Third Party*. Basingstoke: Macmillan.

Marsh, D. (1992) *The New Politics of British Trade Unionism*. Basingstoke: Macmillan.

McCarthy, W. (1993) 'From Donovan until now: Britain's twenty-five years of incomes policy', *Employee Relations*, 15 (6).

Mortimer, J. (1981) 'ACAS in a changing climate: a force for good IR?', *Personnel Management*, February.

Park, Y. and Lee, M. B. (1995) 'Economic development, globalization, and practices in industrial relations and human resource management in Korea' in Verma, A., Kochan, T. A. and Lansbury, R.D. (eds) *Employment Relations in the Growing Asian Economies*. London: Routledge, pp. 27–61.

Poole, M. (1986) *Industrial Relations: Origins and Patterns of National Diversity*. London: Routledge and Kegan Paul.

Prondzynski, F. von (1992) 'Ireland: between centralism and the market' in Ferner, A. and Hyman, R. (eds) *Industrial Relations in the New Europe*. Oxford: Blackwell, pp. 69–87.

Rhodes, M. (1993) 'The social dimension after Maastricht: setting a new agenda for the labour market', *International Journal of Comparative Labour Law and Industrial Relations*, Winter.

Schmid, G., Reissert, B. and Bruche, G. (1992) *Unemployment Insurance and Active Labor Market Policy*. Detroit, MI: Wayne State University Press.

Strinati, D. (1982) *Capitalism, the State and Industrial Relations*. London: Croom Helm.

Taylor, A. J. (1989) *Trade Unions and Politics*. Basingstoke: Macmillan.

Teague, P. (1993) 'Between convergence and divergence: possibilities for a European Community system of labour market regulation', *International Labour Review*, 132 (3).

Towers, B. (1992) 'Two speed ahead: social Europe and the UK after Maastricht', *Industrial Relations Journal*, 23 (2), 83–9.

TUC (1996), 'Pay falling in former wages councils sectors', *TUC Press Release*, 30 August.

Waarden, F. van (1995) 'Government intervention in industrial relations' in Ruysseveldt, J. van, Huiskamp, R. and Hoof, J. van (eds) *Comparative Industrial and Employment Relations.* London: Sage.

White Paper (1969) *In Place of Strife*. London: HMSO.

White Paper (1998) *Fairness at Work*. London: HMSO.

Whitfield, K. (1988) 'The Australian wage system and its labour market effects', *Industrial Relations*, 27 (2), 149–65.

Winchester, D. (1983) 'Industrial relations research in Britain', *British Journal of Industrial Relations*, XX, 100.

Part III

EUROPE AND
THE CHANGING
REGULATIONS

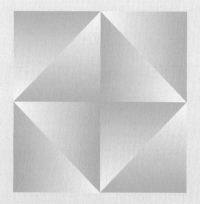

Chapter 7

THE EUROPEAN UNION

Mike Leat

Learning objectives

By the end of this chapter, readers should be able to:

- distinguish and explain the roles of the major institutions in the European Union (EU);
- understand and explain the main legislative processes;
- appreciate the significance of EU treaties and the difficulties experienced in the development of the social dimension;
- understand the initiatives that have been taken to enhance equality of pay and treatment between the sexes and assess their impact;
- explain the significance of some of the initiatives taken in the areas of employee participation and the regulation of working time;
- discuss the arguments for and against, the options and the likelihood of the development of an EU-wide system of employee relations.

The views expressed by Commissioner Flynn in Exhibit 7.1 touch upon a number of the issues addressed in this chapter and on one of the main themes of this book, the notion that the election of a Labour government in the UK in 1997 may herald the gradual implementation of an employee relations system that is based on the principles of partnership rather than on those of division that were promoted by the liberal individualist Conservative governments of the period 1979–97. This latter period was one in which government adopted a negative position with regard to trade unions; they introduced a much tighter regulatory regime, excluded trade unions from the relevant decision-making processes and forum, and re-asserted both the efficiency of the market and managerial prerogative almost irrespective of the interests and wishes of the labour force.

Commissioner Flynn seems to be suggesting an EU-wide system of industrial relations as a prerequisite to full European integration and as support to a strong social dimension. He expresses the view that monetary union and the single market are both vulnerable without such a strong social dimension and there is the implication in his views as quoted that development of the EU has so far been unbalanced in the favour of the achievement of economic, rather than social, objectives such as the single market and a single currency.

■ Exhibit 7.1

EU industrial relations call

European Union integration will not be complete without the creation of a Europe-wide industrial relations system in which trade unions and employers exercise joint power and responsibility, according to Mr Padraig Flynn, the European social affairs commissioner.

In a speech today in the Hague, Mr Flynn will argue that future social legislation should come not from governments but through dialogue between the European trade unions and employers. This does not mean creating a 'single, harmonised system of industrial relations to replace the way we do things now in different member states', he argues. But he wants unions and employers to 'make their real views known and to develop their own initiatives'. This, he says, is the way the EU should develop so that there can be 'a better balance between economic and social objectives'.

'Monetary union is knocking loudly at our door. But a Union without a strong social dimension cannot be a Union worthy of the name, and without it, the single market and the Emu [economic and monetary union] will both face an uncertain future.'

Source: Robert Taylor (1997) *Financial Times*, 29 April.

There is, however, a more radical dimension to the views reported and this lies in the suggestion that such an EU-wide system should include trade unions and employers exercising joint power and responsibility. This is a concept that is much closer to that of co-determination, common in some member states, than to any notions of partnership that may be envisaged by New Labour.

Flynn is reported as arguing that future social legislation should be the product of dialogue between the Social Partners (the unions and employers associations). Presumably the reference here is to the Social Protocol procedures, which provide for the Social Partners to reach framework agreements that may then provide the base for legislative intervention at the EU level. However, he takes pains to point out that the intention is not to impose a single harmonised system and so it would seem likely that he has in mind a set of minimum legal rights and obligations determined at the EU level which would then be given effect at the national level through voluntary agreement and implementation by the Social Partners. This would maintain consistency with the principle of subsidiarity. In the UK this would also be revolutionary since there is no tradition of the 'Social Partners' reaching and voluntarily implementing agreements at this level. Presumably the decline in influence of both social partners over the past 20 years would have to be reversed for such a system to work. Such arrangements would also pose problems of internal government for the UK peak associations (the Trades Union Congress and Confederation of British Industry) since they have never had much in the way of power or control over the activities of their members.

There are implications in these views for the power and influence at an EU level of both trade union movements and employers' associations, as well as for the other law-making institutions and processes. These views, if implemented, would presumably lead to some greater degree of convergence between the different national systems, systems that are largely still intact even after 40 years of association.

In this chapter we examine most if not all of these matters: we look at the decision-making institutions and processes, including those associated with the Social Partners, the need for and nature of a social dimension, the issues of subsidiarity and harmonisation, some of the interventions already initiated by the Commission and agreed by the Social Partners and the likelihood of convergence between the various national systems. In the context of notions of partnership we also examine matters relating to employee participation.

INTRODUCTION

The EU started life as the European Economic Community (EEC), with six members (*see* Table 7.1), later became the European Community and in 1993 became the European Union after the ratification of the treaty changes agreed at Maastricht in 1991.

Perhaps inevitably there is a tendency to see the EU as an organisation primarily concerned with economic and trading matters but these were not the only reasons for the formation of the EEC and are not the only justifications for membership and enlargement. Major motivations for the formation of the Community in 1957 also included the desire to prevent war within Europe and to halt the spread of Communism. The latter may no longer be the spectre that it was but the belief that the EU helps to maintain peace in Europe is still strong. It is argued that both peace and capitalism are enhanced if countries are joined together in a single market with reciprocal trading and economic interests and in a community which demonstrably benefits the citizens of the various nation states in membership both through the generation of wealth and the operation of a form of welfare capitalism that ensures minimum levels of social protection. Monetary union and any progress towards further political union would in theory strengthen these beliefs.

It is important to realise that in the EU the term 'social' encompasses employment and related matters and therefore when we refer to social policies in the EU we are including those relating to employment and to industrial and employee relations.

The UK's membership of the EU has already had (*see* Exhibit 7.1) an impact upon the system of employee relations in the UK. In the main this has been achieved through the acceptance of guiding principles, such as those relating to the imperative of equality of pay and treatment between the sexes, the creation of individual rights, such as the right to equal treatment, and the imposition of some constraints upon substantive outcomes, such as upon rates of pay in the context of equality between the sexes.

So far there has been relatively little intervention in or interference with the established procedures and processes of collective interaction and conflict resolution in individual member states. Employee representatives and employers have had some rights and obligations imposed upon them with regard to the provision of information and consultation requirements on a limited range of subject matter (e.g. collective redundancies, transfers of ownership and health and safety). However, it may be that the European Works Council (EWC) Directive and the comments of Commissioner Flynn quoted in Exhibit 7.1 are impose EU-wide procedural prescriptions.

Outline of the chapter

This chapter falls quite naturally into three main sections:

1 In the first we examine the main institutions and decision-making processes of the Union as they particularly impinge upon issues of employee relations.

2 In the second section we examine some of the more important articles of the founding treaties and initiatives in recent years to amend them and enhance the social dimension. In this context are included the Social Charter and associated Social Action Programme (SAP), the Social Protocol Agreement on Social Policy (SPASP) that was attached to the Maastricht Treaty and most recently the proposed revisions to the EC Treaty agreed at Amsterdam in June 1997. We also examine some of the debates surrounding the role of the EU in this area and the principles that cover EU initiatives and objectives. We then concentrate on some of the more important individual interventions and initiatives, such as the EWC Directive mentioned above, and the objectives that they are intended to achieve. As far as possible a chronological approach is adopted to these matters. As we examine each of the various initiatives we attempt to point up, where relevant, the impact, known or speculative, upon employee relations in the UK.

3 The last section is where we examine the issues of convergence, the Europeanisation of industrial relations and the prospects, as far as they can be deduced, for the future. As part of this discussion it is necessary to identify the different employee relations models within the member states and the ideologies and perspectives that underpin these various traditions, one of which is a tradition of social partnership between employers and employees represented by their trade unions or other representative associations.

MEMBERSHIP, INSTITUTIONS AND THE DECISION-MAKING PROCESSES

The EU currently has 15 member states (Table 7.1) and it is very likely that up to a dozen additional members will be admitted in the early part of the twenty-first century.

Institutions

There are four main EU institutions: the *European Commission*, hereafter referred to as the Commission, the *Council of the European Union* (often also known as the *Council of Ministers*), the *European Parliament* (EP) and the *Court of Justice of the European Communities* (ECJ). This is not the place for extensive analysis of these various institutions but it is important that the reader has an understanding of their various and respective roles, and these are briefly described below. Figure 7.1 demonstrates in simple diagramatic form the main roles of each of these four institutions and the relationships between them.

There are also a number of other institutions within the aegis of the EU that are relevant to the subject matter of this chapter. We describe below a number of these, including the *Social Partners* and the *European Foundation for the Improvement of Living and Working Conditions* (EFILWC).

The *Council of Europe* is a completely separate and larger organisation with some 40 nations in membership that has absolutely no connection with the European Union other than that the EU member states tend also to be members of the Council of Europe.

■ Table 7.1 The 15 member states of the EU

Country	Joining date
Germany	Founder member, 1957
France	Founder member, 1957
Italy	Founder member, 1957
Netherlands	Founder member, 1957
Belgium	Founder member, 1957
Luxembourg	Founder member, 1957
United Kingdom	1973
Denmark	1973
Ireland	1973
Greece	1981
Spain	1986
Portugal	1986
Austria	January 1995
Sweden	January 1995
Finland	January 1995

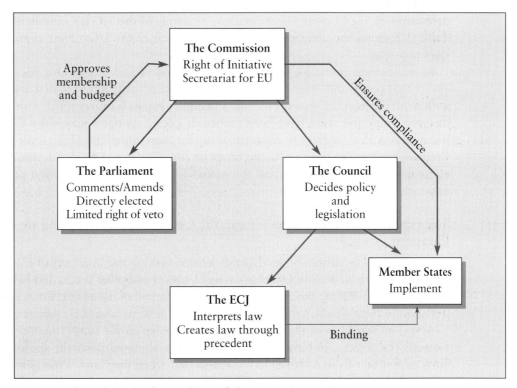

■ Fig. 7.1 The role and relationships of the major institutions

The European Commission

The Commission provides the secretariat for the EU and perhaps more importantly has the *Right of Initiative* with respect to proposals for Union level policy and legislation, although it must be realised that there are plenty of opportunities for interest groups to lobby and influence the Commission and the Commissioners and initiatives taken by the Commission are commonly the product of such lobbying. In many ways it is the institution that sets the agenda for the EU. The term Commission is used to refer both to the organisation as a whole and to the group of Commissioners who meet together as the senior internal decision-making forum. It is the latter group that agrees policy and other proposals and initiatives before they go outside to the others for the purposes of consultation and discussion. The Commissioners are nominated by individual member state governments and their appointment is subject to the approval of the European Parliament. The 'big five' member states – Germany, France, Italy, the UK and Spain – all have the right to nominate two Commissioners each and the other ten each nominate one. Commissioners are supposed to work for and represent the Commission and the EU as a whole and not their home member states.

The work of the Commission is split into various areas of subject matter or policy areas, and administrative sections. The subject matter or policy areas are each allocated to a Directorate General (DG), each of which is headed up by one of the Commissioners. Currently there are 23 DGs and 20 Commissioners and therefore some Commissioners look after more than one policy area. The DG that deals with the subject matter of employment and other areas of social policy is DG V (five) and is titled 'Employment, Industrial Relations and Social Affairs'. As Exhibit 7.1 demonstrates, the Commissioner currently in charge of this DG is Commissioner Flynn. Table 7.2 shows the areas of responsibility of each of the DGs. Note that DG XVIII does not exist.

In addition to initiating policy the Commission is also responsible for seeking to ensure that policy and other legislative decisions are actually implemented and complied with in all the member states. This role sometimes brings it into conflict with individual member states and there have been numerous occasions upon which the Commission has taken action against a member state for non-compliance. In some areas the Commission has the right to decide issues of compliance and such a decision has legal effect in such circumstances upon the parties to the dispute, competition policy being one such area.

The Council of the European Union (the Council of Ministers and the European Council)

This is the body or institution that has the decision-making role in respect of EU policy and legislation. There are various consultation requirements and other checks and balances built into the decision-making processes (*see* later) but at the end of the day the Council decides as it wishes – subject, that is, to its ability to actually come to an adequately supported decision.

Actual membership of the Council varies according to the subject matter under discussion. The object is to have present for decision-making purposes the appropriate government minister from each member state, so that when the Council meets as the Social Affairs Council each member state is represented by the member of government with responsibility at home for the subjects to be discussed. The members of the Council are supported by home country civil servants, who do much of the detailed and preparatory work and negotiation. The Council therefore is not a directly elected body and the members are not accountable to any particular constituency of electors; they are accountable to the member state government of which they are a member. The Council is commonly referred to as an inter-governmental body.

When issues can be decided by a qualified majority, each member state is afforded a number of votes linked indirectly to population, so that the unified Germany, Italy, France and the UK all have the same and largest number of votes (*see* later for the areas of subject matter to which this applies and for details of votes per country).

Twice a year the Heads of Government meet as the *European Council* and it is to this body that issues of a general and significant nature go for decision; for example, the draft Social Charter, the draft Maastricht Treaty and the draft Amsterdam Treaty were all put to this forum for decision.

■ **Table 7.2 The areas of responsibility of the 23 DGs**

DG	Area of responsibility
DG I	External Relations (there are also Ia and Ib dealing with particular regions and areas of activity)
DG II	Economic and Financial Affairs
DG III	Industry
DG IV	Competition
DG V	Employment, Industrial Relations and Social Affairs
DG VI	Agriculture
DG VII	Transport
DG VIII	Development
DG IX	Personnel and Administration
DG X	Audiovisual, Information, Communication and Culture
DG XI	Environment, Nuclear Safety and Civil Protection
DG XII	Science, Research and Development
DG XIII	Telecommunications, Information Industries and Innovation
DG XIV	Fisheries
DG XV	Internal Market and Financial Services
DG XVI	Regional Policies and Cohesion
DG XVII	Energy
DG XIX	Budgets
DG XX	Financial Control
DG XXI	Customs and Indirect Taxation
DG XXII	Education, Training and Youth
DG XXIII	Enterprise Policy, Distributive Trades, Tourism and Cooperatives
DG XXIV	Consumer Policy

The European Parliament

The Parliament has a history of little power and influence despite the fact that it is the only directly elected institution within the EU. Until recently the roles of the Parliament in the formulation of EU policy and the passage of legislation have been limited to lobbying and being one of the bodies that had to be consulted as part of the specified processes. As part of this consultation process the Parliament can put forward   amendments but without any means of ensuring that they are accepted by the Council; they can delay but they cannot stop or force change. More recently and as part of the Maastricht Treaty the Parliament acquired limited powers of veto on issues put to the Council for adoption in some specified areas of subject matter, one of which is enlargement of the Union (*see* the following discussion of the various legislative processes, the co-decision procedure being the new one). The 1997 Amsterdam Draft Treaty extends these limited powers of veto to include many social policy areas and the role and influence of the EP may be substantially increased when this Treaty is ratified and implemented.

Each of the member states has allotted to it a number of Members of the European Parliament (MEPs). The allocation is intended to be roughly proportional on population grounds, so that the unified Germany, the country with the largest population, has the greatest number of MEPs. The distribution of MEPs by member state is shown in Fig. 7.2. At the beginning of 1995 when three new member states joined the Union the total number of MEPs was increased from 567 to 626. It would seem inevitable that as the Union is further enlarged the numbers of MEPs will continue to grow. It is hard to envisage member states agreeing to a reduction in the number of MEPs that they can currently elect.

Although elected by electors in and on behalf of a particular member state, the MEPs tend to ally themselves in multinational political groupings. They are not sent to the Parliament with a brief to look after the interests of the particular member state from which they come.

The Parliament also has the right to approve the nomination of the Commission and the annual budgets and spending programmes.

The Court of Justice of the European Communities

The ECJ is the final arbiter of European Community/Union law. It is the Court of Last Resort. It tends to deal with two different categories of case:

1 Cases that are concerned with matters of EU-level significance such as a member state alleging that the Council or the Commission has acted improperly or unlawfully, or where the Commission is seeking to ensure that a member state complies with EU legislation or where one member state is in legal dispute with another. An example of this first category would be the UK government's allegation that the Directive adopted on working hours was improperly adopted as a health and safety issue. Cases of this kind could not realistically be processed in the judicial system of one of the member states. These cases are sometimes referred to as Direct actions.

2 Cases that commence within individual member states but require the ECJ's final decision on what the law means or how and when it should apply. Examples would include applications by individuals to the UK courts that the UK government had improperly

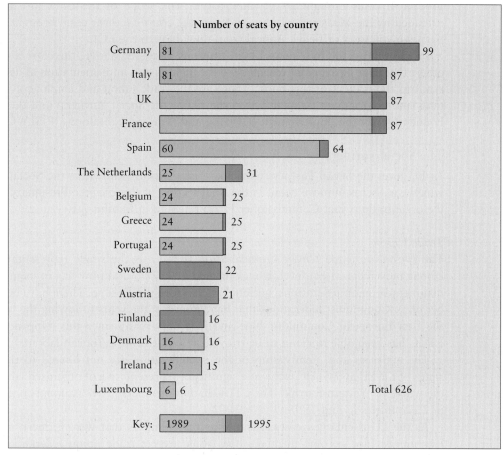

Number of seats by country

Country	1989	1995
Germany	81	99
Italy	81	87
UK		87
France		87
Spain	60	64
The Netherlands	25	31
Belgium	24	25
Greece	24	25
Portugal	24	25
Sweden		22
Austria		21
Finland		16
Denmark	16	16
Ireland	15	15
Luxembourg	6	6

Total 626

Key: 1989 1995

■ **Fig. 7.2 Number of MEPs for each country**
Source: Adapted from *Financial Times*, 14 June 1994.

applied the Directives on Collective Redundancies and Transfers of Undertakings or that the EU law on Equal Pay was not being properly applied by a particular employer, each of which start in the UK structure of Courts and eventually reach the ECJ as the final arbiter.

The ECJ is made up of 15 judges, one from each member state, and 9 Advocates-General (A-Gs) drawn from the ranks of academics, judges and lawyers in the member states. Each case that reaches the Court is allocated an A-G and he or she is expected to present the Court and the parties with an opinion on the case before it is heard by the Court itself. Very rarely are the opinions of A-Gs not followed by the Court.

The ECJ must be distinguished from the *European Court of Human Rights* (ECHR), which is nothing to do with the EU – it has more connection with the Council of Europe than with the EU. The ECHR was established under the European Convention on Human Rights. It has not been uncommon in recent years for members of the UK government and the media to confuse this.

Associated with the ECJ is the *Court of First Instance* (CFI). This was established by the Single European Act (SEA) of 1986 and was intended to help speed up the judicial process in cases brought by private parties. The scope of the CFI's jurisdiction was extended by the Maastricht Treaty and now the court can hear cases brought by private parties in all areas or fields. Appeal from the CFI is to the ECJ.

In addition to the four main EU institutions discussed above, there are a number of others that have a particular relevance to the making and implementation of decisions relevant to the content of this book. These are the trade union and employers' confederations and associations (known within the EU as the Social Partners) and the European Foundation for the Improvement of Living and Working Conditions (EFILWC).

The Social Partners

At EU level the Social Partners participate in a process known as the Social Dialogue, which we discuss in more detail in the final section of this chapter. Presumably these are the organisations that Commissioner Flynn refers to in Exhibit 7.1.

Trade Unions

The *European Trade Union Confederation* (ETUC) is the single representative of the labour movement at EU level. It was formed in 1972/3 and now has in membership all major trade union federations, national and sectoral, in Europe. There have been a number of ex-Communist federations that have joined in the years following the break-up of the East European Communist bloc and it is only really since this happened that the ETUC has been able to claim to be truly representative of European labour.

The activities and membership of the confederation are not limited to the member states of the EU and ETUC is the sole significant representative of organised labour across the whole of Western Europe. The ETUC had in membership 47 national confederations in 22 countries in mid-1995.

As the EU is enlarged eastwards and as the countries that were formerly part of the Communist bloc become members one would expect trade union federations in those countries to seek membership of the ETUC. In part, the formation in 1990 of the European Trade Union Forum, which seeks to promote cooperation between the ETUC and eastern and central European unions, can be seen as paving the way for such developments.

However, the ETUC is a massively diverse organisation and it would be wrong to give the impression that there is much cohesion within the movement. The nature and traditions of the many union confederations in membership vary considerably as also do their autonomy and authority in respect of their own membership. Visser and Ebbinghaus (1992) described the ETUC as 'united but fragmented and with little internal cohesion'.

The organisation has much to thank the EU for, and in particular the Commission, which has been a continuing source of both political and financial support. The importance that the Commission has over the years attached to the creation and maintenance of an effective labour movement with a voice and influence at the level of the EU has been considerably beneficial to the ETUC and it is doubtful that the organisation would have been as united and effective as it is (for example, in promoting the Social Dialogue, *see* later) without this support. Again, one can see this as evidence of the continuing influence of the corporatist traditions in much of the EU. This support should not be seen as a purely altruistic approach since it has long been the view of the Commission that an internal market and other dimensions of economic integration would only be possible with the support/acquiescence of European labour.

University of Newcastle
Robinson Library
CheckOut Receipt

07/04/2003
06:59 pm

Item: Trade unions in the developed economies
Item ID: 081040411
Due Date: 14-05-03   10:00pm

Item: Labor-management relations in a changing

environment
Item ID: 095115435
Due Date: 14-05-03   10:00pm

Item: Employee relations
Item ID: 098169256

Due Date: 14-05-03   10:00pm

Please keep this receipt as it has details of the date(s)
by which your item(s) should be returned.

To renew your books use the library catalogue
either via the web or in the Library

Turner (1996) takes a relatively optimistic view of the future of the ETUC despite acknowledging that in many respects the development of structures at such a transnational level seems to be at odds with the trends towards the decentralisation of decision making and collective bargaining. He suggests that the EWC Directive will assist the process of cross-national collaboration within and between labour movements and representatives; and that while this will initially be at the level of the individual multinational organisation, the structures that do now exist within the framework of the ETUC may be both used and reinforced. However, he does also point out that the development of an effective labour movement at this EU level needs, in addition to the structures, transnational rank and file protest and he thinks this most likely to occur in protest at some specific EU-level policy, although it is difficult to conceive what such a policy might be.

Below the level of the EU there are a number of international sectoral federations, many of them affiliated to the ETUC, that are active in their respective industries and that often provide the employee representative mechanism for activities at the level of the individual MNE. Examples of these sectoral federations include the: European Metalworkers Federation (EMF), the European Federation of Chemical and General Workers Unions (EFCGU) and the International Union of Food Workers (IUF).

These latter are the organisations that have been in the forefront of negotiating voluntary EWCs in those companies and groups that have them.

Employers' organisations

There are two main employers' organisations operating at the level of the EU:

■ the *Union of Industrial and Employers' Confederations of Europe* (UNICE), which represents primarily private sector employers, and

■ the *European Centre of Public Enterprises* (CEEP), representing primarily public sector employer interests.

UNICE was formed in the late 1950s and, like the ETUC, represents employers from a much wider constituency than the EU. Carley (1993) suggests that there were national federation members from 22 different countries in 1989.

At the level of the EU the organisation wants to be influential as an organisation representing a particular interest to the legislators and policy makers but, unlike the ETUC, it has not been keen to become involved with the Commission and ETUC in policy making as a Social Partner and it is even less keen to become involved in any EU-level bargaining arrangements with the ETUC. To some extent this is no doubt due to the fact that it does not have a mandate to act in this way, and it and the ETUC do not have compatible structures.

The membership of CEEP tends to be comprised of individual employers rather than federations and the geographic spread of the members of this organisation is much smaller than that of either of the other two above. As with UNICE, the direction of the organisation's activities are primarily to represent interests to the policy makers and legislators and not to participate in that process in any more direct way.

Within the UK the Social Partners at a national level are the Trades Union Congress (TUC) and the Confederation of British Industry (CBI) although they have not traditionally been referred to in these terms. In the past the TUC with its voluntarist traditions was very sceptical of the UK's membership of the EU and of the regulatory initiatives taken at an EU-level. However, in the latter part of the 1980s and early 1990s it became one of the more avid supporters of the whole European project, perceiving it as one of its best chances of obtaining and retaining employment and social protection(s) for its members in the face of successive attempts by UK governments to deregulate and minimise such protection.

The CBI also tended to support the EU concept, although for different reasons – those associated with the prospects for business to be derived from the creation of a single market and in the 1990s from monetary union. Both of these UK partners are active members of the appropriate organisations at the level of the EU.

The European Foundation for the Improvement of Living and Working Conditions

The Foundation was established in May 1975. It is based in Dublin and financed via the Commission. Its prime activity is to encourage and commission research into appropriate areas of interest and activity.

The organisation is managed by an administrative board comprised of representatives from and of the Commission, the trade unions, employers and the governments of the member states.

The last four-year programme covering the period 1993–96 identified three distinct areas of interest and activity:

1 increasing economic and social cohesion and fighting against the exclusion of disadvantaged groups;

2 improving the health and well-being of European workers and citizens;

3 maintaining the move towards a sustainable and integrated development of the social, economic and ecological aspects of living and working conditions.

■ Legislative forms and decision-making procedures

The EU can adopt a number of different legislative instruments:

- *Regulations*. These are relatively rare but once adopted they are applicable directly and generally throughout the EU; they are immediately binding on member states and individuals and do not require any action at member-state level to render them effective. In cases of EU Regulations conflicting with national law, the EU regulation takes precedence. The Council can empower the Commission to make regulations.

- *Directives*. A Directive is not immediately applicable. It requires some action at member-state level to be brought into effect, although this action need not be legislative. (Implementation can, for example, be through agreement by the Social Partners. Normally this device specifies an objective to be achieved and the date by which it should be achieved but leaves the means of achievement to the individual member states. Once the implementation date is reached, the Directive becomes the law within the EU.

■ *Decisions*. These can be made by the Council, and in some instances by the Commission, and once made they are binding on the parties that sought the decision in the first place. They do not automatically have general effect.

There are also a range of non-binding instruments that can be used, such as *Recommendations*, *Communications* and *Opinions*. These are often used when one or more of the institutions wants to exert influence but either knows that there is not sufficient support for the proposal or that the competence to act is lacking.

The consultation procedure

The tradition has in the main been that legislative intervention/action at the level of the EU requires the unanimous support of the member states, and where this is the case the decision-making procedure to be used is called the *consultation procedure*. This is the least complex of the decision-making procedures and is shown in outline form in Fig. 7.3. In the early days of the EU this was the only procedure and for many years now there has been an assumption that decisions reached using this procedure will only be reached unanimously irrespective of whether this was strictly required by the Treaty. As can be seen quite clearly from the figure, the procedure provides for consultation with a number of forums, but only once, and the Council's decision is final; it may or may not take note of the comments and amendments suggested by these various forums as part of the procedure.

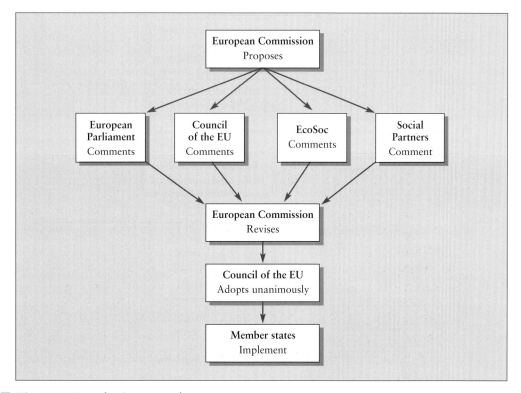

■ Fig. 7.3 Consultation procedure

The cooperation procedure

The tradition of unanimity as a prerequisite for legislative action has limited the ability of the EU to progress and change. When in the mid-1980s the Council agreed to create the Single Market by the end of 1992 it was also agreed that the principle of qualified majority voting (QMV) should apply for many of the measures necessary to the creation and effective operation of the market. As a consequence the *Single European Act* (SEA) included the creation of this new decision-making procedure.

The outline of this procedure is given in Fig. 7.4. The two main differences between it and the original consultation procedure are that it arguably extended to the Parliament a greater opportunity to influence the legislative process by giving it a second opportunity, or reading, to comment and amend and it specifically provides for the use of majority voting.

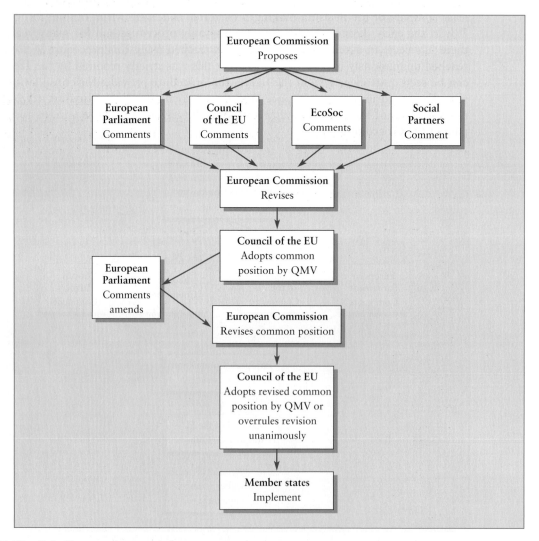

■ Fig. 7.4 Cooperation procedure

Note that where on second reading the Parliament has rejected the common position adopted by the Council at the end of the first round of consultations the Council can only overturn that rejection or proceed in accordance with its original common position on the basis of unanimity. If the Council is happy to accept the amendments made by the Parliament on second reading then it can proceed on the basis of a qualified majority. However, the final decision always rests with the Council and if the members states have a mind to they can reject the amendments and/or do nothing.

The SEA did not extend the cooperation procedure to legislative interventions concerning tax, the free movement of people and, most importantly from the viewpoint of the social dimension, the rights and interests of employees. What this meant in practice was that it was only on health and safety issues that matters of direct concern in the workplace and to the employed were covered by this procedure.

For many within the EU this was an inadequate outcome and there have been several arguments since involving member states and the Commission as to whether a particular proposal fell inside the appropriate definitions and interpretations of health and safety. The most infamous of these concerned the UK and the Directive adopted in 1994 that sought to protect employees from being forced to work long hours. The ECJ was required to adjudicate on this issue.

The system of QMV is simple enough in that each member state has a specified number of votes in Council and these are apportioned roughly in accordance with the relative populations of the countries (*see* Table 7.3). In total there are 87 votes available and 62 are required in favour of a proposal for it to be adopted via the QMV process. Sometimes reference is made to the *blocking minority*; this figure is currently 26 Council votes.

■ Table 7.3 Qualified majority voting

Member state	Votes per member state
France	10
Italy	10
Germany	10
UK	10
Spain	8
Portugal	5
Netherlands	5
Belgium	5
Greece	5
Austria	4
Sweden	4
Ireland	3
Denmark	3
Finland	3
Luxembourg	2
Total	87

Votes required for a qualified majority = 62.

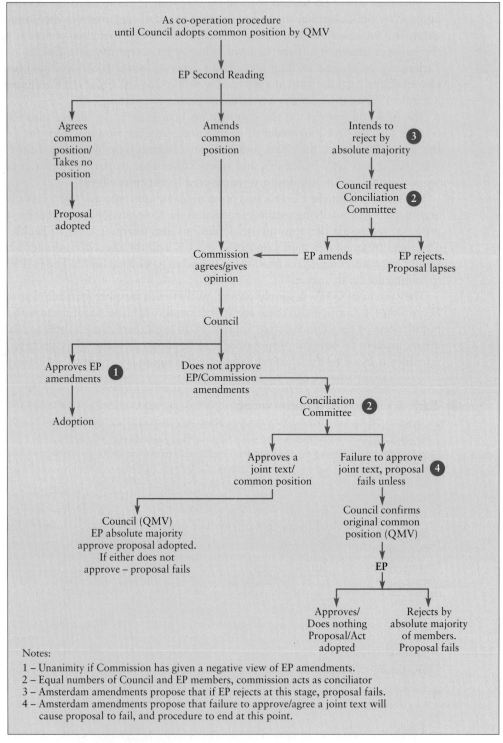

Notes:
1 – Unanimity if Commission has given a negative view of EP amendments.
2 – Equal numbers of Council and EP members, commission acts as conciliator
3 – Amsterdam amendments propose that if EP rejects at this stage, proposal fails.
4 – Amsterdam amendments propose that failure to approve/agree a joint text will
    cause proposal to fail, and procedure to end at this point.

■ Fig. 7.5 Co-decision procedure

The co-decision procedure

This is a procedure that provides for decisions to be reached and legislation adopted via the use of QMV but it is different from the cooperation procedure. The desire for the Parliament to have a more influential role in the legislative process can be seen behind this new variation on the cooperation procedure introduced via the Maastricht Treaty. This new procedure was of relatively little interest prior to the Amsterdam Treaty revisions of 1997 since it was to apply only to certain aspects of free movement of labour and vocational training.

The difference between this and the normal cooperation procedure begins after the Parliament's second reading if the Parliament intends to reject the common position already adopted by the Council or if it seeks to amend the common position and the Council then rejects these amendments. As is indicated in Fig. 7.5, in the event of both these eventualities the procedure calls for the establishment of a joint Council–Parliament Conciliation Committee with the Commission also involved as the conciliator trying to broker an agreement between the other two institutions. Where the conciliation is successful the outcome is subject to the subsequent approval of both Parliament and Council; where there is no agreed outcome or the outcome agreed by the Conciliation Committee is not acceptable to both the institutions, the proposal lapses. If the Council after the conciliation process seeks to adopt its original common position the Parliament now has the right of approval, and if the Parliament rejects the common position again, the proposal lapses. It is in the context of this new procedure that one can argue that the Parliament does now have an effective right of veto over proposals in some of those areas of subject matter applicable to the QMV process.

The Amsterdam draft Treaty revisions propose both a shortening of this process (*see* Fig. 7.5) and also in two respects a significant extension of the influence of the EP, its ability to stop Council proposals and the wider coverage of the procedure.

Under these new proposals a legislative proposal will be deemed to have failed if:

- the EP rejects it by an absolute majority of component members, or
- if there is no agreement in conciliation on a joint text.

An additional change is that there will only be recourse to conciliation in the event of the EP proposing amendments to rather than rejecting the Council's common position. It has been argued that this will put greater pressure upon the Council to reach agreement through conciliation.

As for coverage, the new (post Amsterdam) shortened version of the co-decision procedure is to apply to a wider range of social issues as detailed in the proposed new Articles 118(1) and 119(3):

- improvement in particular of the working environment to protect workers' health and safety;
- working conditions;
- the process of informing and consulting of workers;
- the integration of persons excluded from the labour market;
- equality between men and women with regard to labour market opportunities and treatment at work;

- ensuring application of the principle of equal opportunities and equal treatment of men and women in matters of employment and occupation, including the principle of equal pay for equal work or work of equal value.

The Protocol procedure

This procedure was included in the Maastricht Social Protocol Agreement on Social Policy (SPASP) and was the product of the desire by the Commission and member states other than the UK to increase the Social Dialogue between the Social Partners at EU level and to increase their role in the decision-making process. This was to include giving the Social Partners the opportunity to enter into agreements and contractual relations. The comments of Commissioner Flynn in Exhibit 7.1 are consistent with this intention.

This procedure is depicted in Fig 7.6. As can be seen, the Social Partners can be given the opportunity to reach an agreement between themselves on a proposal for action that has come out of the Commission. If the Social Partners can reach agreement on the content of the proposal they can further agree to seek to give effect to the proposal via collective agreements at national level; alternatively, having reached agreement on the content of the proposal, they can ask the Commission to process the agreement through the normal consultation or cooperation procedures, as appropriate, depending upon the subject matter.

At the time of writing this procedure has been 'completed' on three occasions. In the first instance the Social Partners were unable to agree the content of proposals that eventually became the EWC Directive; in the second they did manage to agree the pro-

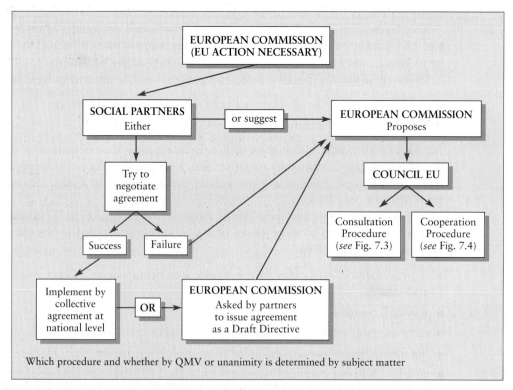

■ Fig. 7.6 Protocol decision-making procedure

posals that became the Directive on Parental Leave; the third was a framework agreement on equality between the rights of part-time and full-time workers, which was adopted as a Directive in December 1997. In each of these last two cases the Social Partners were concerned to agree only the basic principles and provisions with the detail to be determined at national level, an approach which is felt to be consistent with the principle of *subsidiarity*.

Subsidiarity

One of the debates that simmered throughout the 1980s and early 1990s concerned the question of whether and when action should be taken at the level of the EU compared with the level of the nation state (or lower). The UK governments of the time were at the centre of these debates and generally they took the view that action at the EU level should be a measure of last resort and linked the debate to the issue of national sovereignty. Other interests, with perhaps greater ambitions for the creation of EU-wide systems, and those keen on Europe becoming a Union much more like the United States of America tended to argue for more and wider and deeper action at the EU level.

The debate resulted in a restatement of the principle in Article 3b of the Treaty agreed at Maastricht:

> In areas which do not fall within its exclusive competence, the Community shall take action, in accordance with the principle of subsidiarity, only if and in so far as the objectives of the proposed action cannot be achieved by the member states and can therefore, by reason of the scale or effects of the proposed action, be better achieved by the Community. Any action by the Community shall not go beyond what is necessary to achieve the objectives of this Treaty.

The implication is clear, the Commission and the EU should seek to act only when it is clear that the objectives cannot be achieved at the level of each of the member states *and* that they can be better achieved through action at the centre.

This restatement of the principle and its enunciation is significant in that it both indicates a shift of intent away from the production through Union-level interventions and upward harmonisation of Union-wide and convergent systems, and a greater willingness to try to achieve common objectives while retaining national and diverse traditions and practices.

The meaning and application of this principle has been further developed in the Amsterdam Treaty draft. The Inter-Governmental Conference at Amsterdam agreed a new Protocol on subsidiarity.

SOCIAL POLICY INITIATIVES

In the first part of this section we examine some of the background, the debates and the relevance of the EU Treaties to the development of social policy within the EU.

In the second part we concentrate upon some of the more relevant individual initiatives that have been taken and that impinge upon employee relations in the UK.

In the context of the EU, social policy and the social dimension encompass matters that relate to the employment relationship and employee relations as well as to more general areas of social protection. As Commissioner Flynn points out in Exhibit 7.1, his, and presumably the Commission's, view is that without a strong social dimension the EU will not be worthy of the name 'union'.

Nevertheless, the development of the social dimension has been the subject of much debate and disagreement over the years with different perspectives as to the need for and desirability of action and regulation at the level of the EU.

Generally social issues and the 'need' for action and regulation have been addressed in the context of the implications of and for economic integration, the creation of the single market and more recently monetary union.

It was recognised at the outset by its architects that the market and economic integration process would inevitably create some dislocation of industry and employment and a need for restructuring – that there would be losers as well as winners.

In the main the debate has been between those who considered that intervention would be necessary in order to cushion these effects and promote restructuring and a more efficient use of labour, and those who took the view that while integration might have these effects the solution was to leave the market to cope and that to intervene would simply prevent the adjustment mechanisms of the market working effectively. Circumstances justifying intervention should be limited to those in which the intervention itself contributed to the process of market integration.

As Hall (1994) explains, the Commission and most of the member states have viewed the social dimension as:

> an important vehicle for securing the support of the European labour movement for the single market project and for enhancing the 'social acceptability' of the consequent economic restructuring ... the human face of the EC.

This is a debate that has not been resolved and the same perspectives can be seen to inform deliberations within the EU on solutions to the problems of unemployment and international competitiveness. The Commission and the European labour movements have tended to argue the case for the protection of those in employment and the regulation of the labour market to ensure social justice, with employers and other interests arguing the case that economic performance in Europe, including job creation, is actually being undermined by excessive intervention and regulation leading to labour market inflexibility.

These different perspectives can also be seen to inform and underpin the different traditions in the member states, which we describe in the last section of this chapter, the former being consistent with notions of corporatist integration and social or welfare capitalism whereas the latter is consistent with the notions of economic liberalism and liberal individualism.

■ The Treaties and social policy

Even at the outset of the creation of the Community back in the 1950s these differences of view can be seen to have contributed to the fudging of the issue of social policy. As Hall (1994) says:

> To date, the evolution of the EC's (Community) social policy role has been uneven and limited. The Treaty of Rome did not establish a clear Community competence in this sphere.

The Treaty-based system of law within the EU requires that the founding Treaties specifically provide for the relevant authorities and institutions to take the actions envisaged; if the Treaties do not do this then action cannot be initiated.

In the early years the absence of such a base does not appear to have posed major problems, partly because there were specific Treaty articles covering matters of:

- equal pay between the sexes (Article 119);
- the free movement of labour (Articles 48 and 49);
- assistance with the relocation and retraining of individuals harmed by the integration process as it caused dislocation and restructuring. Article 123 provided the basis for the creation of the European Social Fund (ESF), which has been the main mechanism for achieving improved employment opportunities and enhancing geographic and occupational mobility.

The latter two were both considered essential to the process and objective of integration since failure to take measures to facilitate these aspects might have produced, on the one hand, imperfections in the market allocating process and, on the other, opposition to and negative impressions of integration.

The absence of specific Treaty bases enabling the Commission and the member states to intervene legislatively where necessary on issues of employee rights and the development of a social policy came to the fore for the first time in the mid-1970s. It was the Council agreement to create the single market, embodied in the SEA (1986), however, that provided a significant impetus to the resolution of this inadequacy in the Treaty and therefore in the EU.

After the adoption of the SEA the Commission, the labour movements and some member state governments became increasingly concerned about the dangers of *social dumping*. In this context the term refers to the tendency for multinational companies to locate and in some instances relocate their production facilities in those parts of the EU where the labour costs of production and the degree of regulation of the labour market are lowest. The fear was particularly acute in those countries with the most developed labour standards and the correspondingly highest labour costs. Of course, other factors influence location decisions and the counter-argument from the direction of economic liberalism suggests that the market mechanism would eventually lead to adjustment and a new equilibrium somewhere between the two opening positions. Putting it bluntly, the fear was that employers would go *regime shopping* and use the variation in labour costs either to guide their location decisions and/or to beat down the labour costs and standards in those countries that were most developed.

Concerns about social dumping and the absence of an appropriate Treaty base for action on social policy led the Commission to propose the adoption by the Council of a statement of minimum social rights. These were contained in the document known as the *Social Charter*. By the time the Charter was presented to the Council at its meeting in Strasbourg in December 1989, the Commission had also developed a Social Action Programme (SAP) containing 47 proposals for EU-level action to give effect to many of the minimum rights contained within the Charter.

The Social Charter

The rights proposed and incorporated in the Charter fell into 12 main sections:

1 Freedom of movement, including the removal of obstacles arising from the non-recognition of diplomas and equivalent occupational qualifications.

2 Employment and remuneration, including the rights to fair and equitable wages thereby enabling a decent standard of living.

3 Improvement of living and working conditions, with specific reference made to working hours, weekly rest periods and annual leave, temporary, fixed-term and part-time contracts. It is clearly the intention that there should be an upward approximation/harmonisation.

4 Social protection, where the term means adequate and sufficient protection in keeping with the particular situation.

5 Freedom of association and collective bargaining. Both workers and employers should have the right to form and join, or not, associations for the defence of their economic and social interests. The associations should have the right to negotiate and conclude collective agreements and the right to take collective action including strike action. Conciliation, arbitration and mediation should be encouraged and in all cases these rights should be subject to and exercised in accordance with existing national conditions and practice. This section also refers to improvement of the dialogue between the Social Partners at European level.

6 Vocational training. All workers should have the right of access to such training and retraining throughout their working life with particular reference made to the acquisition of new skills in the light of technological developments.

7 Equal treatment for men and women should be assured, and equal opportunities should be developed. Particular mention is made of equality of access to employment, remuneration, working conditions, social protection, education, vocational training and career development. Mention was also made of measures to facilitate both men and women reconciling their work and family lives/obligations.

8 Information, consultation and participation of workers, taking into account the practices in each member state and with particular reference to organisations with establishments or companies in two or more member states. In particular, these rights should apply in cases of technological change having major implications for the workforce in terms of working conditions and/or work organisation, where restructuring or mergers also have an impact upon the employment of workers and in cases of collective redundancy procedures.

9 Health, protection and safety at the workplace. This section refers to satisfactory health and safety conditions in the workplace and harmonisation while improvements are maintained. Specific mention is also made of training, information and consultation.

10 Protection of children and adolescents. They should receive equitable remuneration, be protected from working below a certain age and particular arrangements should be made to ensure that their development, vocational training and access to employment needs are met. There should also be limits on the duration of such work and their working at night. There should also be an entitlement to initial vocational training upon leaving full-time education.

11 Elderly persons upon retirement should have an entitlement to a decent standard of living.

12 Disabled persons should be entitled to measures aimed at improving their social and professional integration and in particular to vocational training, ergonomics, accessibility and mobility.

These Social Charter proposals were acceptable to 11 of the 12 member states, the odd one out being the UK, but because the Charter could only be adopted via unanimity, the UK had an effective veto. Legally, therefore, the Charter had no status and remained only a statement of intent on the part of all member states other than the UK.

As noted earlier, a SAP was devised that was designed to give effect to some of the specified Charter rights, but not all of them. Some of the proposals were for legislative intervention in order to put particular rights in place throughout the EU but many others were either not addressed at all in the action programme or the proposals were of a non-legislative and non-binding nature.

It is neither possible nor necessary in this chapter to explain the full contents of the SAP but it is worth pointing out that there were no proposals in this programme for the legislative imposition of rights for workers in the areas of:

■ control or specification of minimum levels of pay;

■ imposing or constraining the right of freedom of association (this includes the right to join a trade union or employers' association);

■ the right to strike or impose a lock-out;

■ imposing or constraining the process and status of collective bargaining and/or co-determination.

It is also worth pointing out that considerable care was taken in both the Charter and the SAP not to impose rights in a manner that was inconsistent with the traditions, practices and laws of the various member states. In other words, there was a general concern to act in a manner consistent with the principle of subsidiarity.

However, the significance of the Social Charter is greater than might be expected given that its adoption was vetoed. It has subsequently formed the base for:

■ the draft Social Chapter of the Treaty on European Union at Maastricht in December 1991; and

■ the agreement at Amsterdam in 1997 on a new Treaty Social Chapter.

At Maastricht in 1991 the UK government refused to agree to a revised Treaty that contained the draft Social Chapter. As a consequence of this refusal or effective veto the other member states decided to reach their own agreement which was appended to the Treaty under a device known as a Protocol as the Social Protocol Agreement on Social Policy (SPASP). We have already examined the new decision-making procedures involving the Social Partners that were agreed at Maastricht and formed part of the Protocol (see p. 228).

The Protocol Agreement, as it is commonly known, specified clearly in Article 1 what the objectives of the agreement were. They include the promotion of:

■ employment

■ improved living and working conditions

- proper social protection
- dialogue between management and labour
- the development of human resources with a view to lasting high employment
- the combating of exclusion.

The SPASP set out clearly the areas of subject matter to which it applied and indicated which adoption procedure was to apply in respect of each. The outcome of this is that qualified majority voting and the cooperation procedure apply to:

- improving the working environment in order to protect worker's health and safety;
- working conditions;
- the informing and consultation of workers;
- equality between the sexes;
- the integration of those excluded from the labour market.

Unanimity is still required before measures can be adopted in respect of:

- social security and social protection of workers;
- employee protection in circumstances of termination of their employment contract;
- the representation and collective defence of both employers' and workers' interests to include the issue of co-determination;
- conditions of employment for third-country nationals resident in the EU.

It is also quite clearly stated that the provisions of the agreement are not intended to apply to pay, the right of association, the right to strike or the right to impose a lock-out, and there are no means by which the member states signatory to the agreement can, via the agreement, take action to implement rights related to these areas of subject matter. Such issues remain subject to the unanimous agreement of all members of the EU and arguably there is still no clear treaty base that gives the EU the ability to act in these areas.

Amsterdam June 1997: Treaty outcomes and amendments

At the time of writing (late 1998) there is still an amount of uncertainty surrounding the implementation of these revisions to the Treaty agreed unanimously at the Amsterdam Inter-Governmental Conference (IGC). The revisions have to be ratified at the level of the individual member state, a process that takes different forms and is likely to take a considerable time.

However, on the assumption that the draft Treaty is ratified there will now be a treaty base for the EU to pursue objectives and take action in a number of the social and employment areas that was not possible before.

The SPASP is to be repealed and Articles 117–120 of the proposed Treaty now contain in large measure the contents of the SPASP. In the main, the Protocol procedures involving the Social Partners and the separation of subject matter into categories requiring unanimity and those where it is possible to act via QMV have remained intact, as in the SPASP.

There are some differences; for example, the new shortened co-decision procedure is extended to those issues that in the SPASP were subject to the co-operation procedure, and in one or two instances the proposed Treaty articles constitute a mix of the original EC Treaty articles and those in SPASP.

There was acceptance that it would be important prior to ratification of the Treaty for the various UK interests to be allowed to participate in the discussions that would until ratification continue within the auspices of the Protocol Agreement. This was in recognition of the UK New Labour government's agreement to the accession into the Treaty of the contents of the Protocol Agreement, effectively as the new Social Chapter, and that the UK should be bound by the Directives already adopted via the Protocol procedures – for example, the EWC Directive, which will now be applicable to the UK activities of MNEs.

In addition to the new Social Chapter, and arguably one of the more potentially significant of the agreements at Amsterdam, the ability of the EU in the future to pursue objectives and take action on matters of discrimination has been greatly enhanced by a new Article 6a, which provides the Council acting *unanimously* with the power to take **'appropriate action to combat discrimination based on sex, racial or ethnic origin, religion or belief, disability, age or sexual orientation'.**

Within months of this agreement the new Labour government in the UK was expressing its determination to secure EU-wide legislation outlawing discrimination on the grounds of race and ethnic origin, although it has to be admitted that some other member states will have greater difficulty with this proposal. An example is Germany where foreign nationals and those of different ethnic origins are presented already with often insurmountable obstacles to obtaining citizenship and thereby the rights to equal treatment that are associated with citizenship. Additionally, they are denied the rights and protection provided by EU Treaties and initiatives since these accrue in the main only to citizens of one of the member states.

Amsterdam Treaty agreements

The new Article 118 is concerned to provide a legal base for the Union to take action, and in particular sets out those areas of subject matter where the appropriate procedures are to involve the opportunity for the adoption of measures by QMV and those where the principle of unanimity is to apply.

The list where it will be possible to take action by majority vote is largely the same as in Article 2 of SPASP with the exception that the procedure to be used is changed from cooperation to co-decision. The list is:

- improvement in particular of the working environment to protect workers' health and safety;
- working conditions;
- the informing and consultation of workers;
- the integration of persons excluded from the labour market;
- equality between men and women with regard to labour market opportunities and treatment at work.

Paragraph 3 of Article 118 sets out the areas in which unanimity is to apply:

- social security and social protection of workers;
- protection of workers where their contract of employment is terminated;
- representation and collective defence of the interests of workers and employers, including co-determination;

- conditions of employment for third-country nationals;
- financial contributions for the promotion of employment and job creation.

Finally, paragraph 6 of Article 118 specifies that:

> The provisions of this Article shall not apply to pay, the right of association, the right to strike or the right to impose lock-outs.

The new Article 118a is SPASP Article 3, and Article 118b is Article 4 of SPASP. These two Articles are the ones specifying the procedures whereby matters may be dealt with by the Social Partners.

The new Article 119 is specifically concerned with the issues of equality for male and female workers and is a statement of the obligation upon each member state to ensure that the principle of equal pay is applied. It encompasses much of SPASP Article 6 but is not identical, the differences being quite significant: SPASP Article 6(1) refers to equal pay but only for equal work; the new Article 119(1) refers also to equal pay for work of equal value.

Paragraph 4 of the new Article 119 is also interesting in that it can be seen as an attempt to address the issue of positive action and the difference between it and positive discrimination. This is not addressed directly but can be perceived from the changed wording compared with Article 6(3) of SPASP. The new Article 119(4) seeks to preserve the right to positive action:

> With a view to ensuring full equality in practice between men and women in working life, the principle of equal treatment shall not prevent any Member State from maintaining or adopting measures providing for specific advantages in order to make it easier for the *underrepresented sex* to pursue a vocational activity or to prevent or compensate for disadvantages in professional careers.

SPASP 6(3) said 'women' in place of the words in italic.

■ Policy initiatives – equality, participation and working time

It is impossible in a chapter of this size to examine all the individual and specific initiatives that can be argued to impinge upon and to influence employee relations in the UK. Consequently, we have decided to examine those that have arguably had the greatest impact and those that may have in the future.

In this context we examine initiatives seeking to establish minimum rights for employees:

- to equality of pay and treatment between the sexes;
- for their elected representatives to be given information and to be consulted on specific issues such as on the transfer of undertakings, collective redundancies and health and safety matters and within multinational organisations the range of subject matter detailed in the EWC Directive.

In this latter category of rights to consultation we concentrate upon the EWC Directive adopted through the Protocol procedures.

We also discuss the *Directive on Working Time,* to which the UK government raised objections on the grounds that it had been improperly adopted as a health and safety issue under Article 118a.

Equality

There are various dimensions to the issue of equality between the sexes and commonly distinctions are drawn between equality of pay, equality of access to work and equality in terms of treatment at work.

There has over the years been a great deal of debate as to what may be the major causes of this inequality and, given the causes, what might be the best means of seeking to remedy and reduce the extent of the inequality. Evidence that there is inequality is reasonably easy to obtain in areas such as pay and labour force participation but very much more difficult in areas more associated with the treatment dimension such as career development, training, promotion opportunities and sexual harassment.

Pay

When it comes to charting and discussing EU initiatives the first thing to point out is that Article 119 of the founding Treaty, the Treaty of Rome, as amended by the Maastricht Treaty on European Union, applies directly, as presumably will the new Article 119 agreed at Amsterdam and detailed in the previous section. Treaty articles take precedence over national legislation, customs and practice and they should where necessary be implemented into national legislation. The current Article 119 provides that:

> All member states should ensure and maintain the principle that men and women should receive equal pay for equal work.

Pay is defined within the Article as:

> the ordinary basic or minimum wage or salary and any other consideration, whether in cash or in kind, which the worker receives, directly or indirectly , in respect of his employment from his employer.

The Article sought to define equal pay without discrimination based on sex as meaning: This Article was given specific effect in the UK via the Equal Pay Act of 1970.

(a) that pay for the same work at piece rates shall be calculated on the basis of the same unit of measurement;

(b) that pay for work at time rates shall be the same for the same job.

Despite these efforts to define pay, many of the cases that have been determined by the ECJ have been concerned to determine more precisely the meaning of pay in the context of both Article 119 and the Directive (75/117) (*see* below).

For example, as a result of various cases it has been decided that for the purposes of this legislation pay includes:

- redundancy payments whether statutory, contractual or ex-gratia (Barber *v* Guardian Royal Exchange Assurance Group);

- payments under an occupational pension scheme (Barber);

- other ex-gratia payments made after the contract has ended (Garland *v* British Rail Engineering).

The possibilities for the further extension of the definition of pay can be seen from the interpretation given by one of the Advocates-General in the case described in Exhibit 7.2.

Without going into great detail Article 119 and the implementing legislation also failed to adequately define *equal work*, and eventually a Directive was adopted in 1975 (75/117) that sought to deal with issues of *equal work and value*, so that to all intents and purposes the requirement became that men and women should be paid *equally for work of equal value*. The Equal Value Regulations of 1984 constitute the relevant UK legislation.

However, there has been and still is considerable debate about the concept of equal value and its precise interpretation and measurement, and there have also been a number of important cases, each of which determined particular issues.

Macarthys Ltd *v* Smith established that the comparable work does not have to be undertaken at the same time; the comparison could be with the person who did the job before. However, this same case also established that the comparison could not be hypothetical; it must be possible to make 'concrete appraisals of the work actually performed by employees of different sex within the same establishment or service', although as Cox (1993) points out, the ECJ has subsequently in the Danfoss case indicated that generalised pay practices within an undertaking may be covered by the legislation even if the comparison is not with a named comparator.

The legislation does cover circumstances in which the work of the plaintiff is of greater value than that of the comparator although such a finding of greater value cannot then be used to justify the imposition of a rate of pay that is greater than that of the comparator (Murphy and others *v* An Bord Telecom Eirann).

There have been numerous cases that have determined that the legislation can be appropriately used in instances of indirect as well as direct discrimination.

> *Indirect discrimination* covers circumstances whereby an employer applies policies or practices that in practice disproportionately and adversely affect one sex and that cannot objectively be justified on grounds other than sex. Examples of such indirect discrimination have been found to include payment systems and arrangements that attached pay to the possession of longevity of continuous service, the completion of specified training and an ability to work flexible hours.

There are a number of other difficulties associated with the concept of value. First, the criterion of value to be used has to be decided, and this can itself concentrate upon either inputs or outputs. For example, the criterion could be:

- the effort, skill and responsibility put into the work;

- the content of the work;

- a measure of the value of the output;

- a mix of these.

Job evaluation and classification schemes tend to be based upon a mix of input and content rather than upon output.

■ **Exhibit 7.2**

Pay ruling gives gays equal rights in Europe

HOMOSEXUALS scored an 'historic' victory at the European Court of Justice in Luxembourg yesterday, in a test case over the denial of job perks to same-sex partners.

In a preliminary opinion, advocate general Michael Elmer held that South West Trains Ltd's denial of travel concessions to the woman partner of Lisa Grant, a ticket clerk, breached European law guaranteeing equal pay.

The case has far-reaching implications for employment rights in Britain. If the full court follows the opinion (which it does in four out of five cases), employers will have to offer same-sex partners the same perks, including pension benefits, available to unmarried partners of the opposite sex. Pay includes any benefits in cash or kind provided by an employer.

Ruth Harvey, Ms Grant's solicitor, said companies would have to look at all aspects of pay – salary, pensions, loans, mortgages and benefits – or risk claims against them.

However, the ruling could lead employers to limit perks to married partners. The advocate general held that this would not be contrary to EU law. Nor would it be unlawful under English law.

Ms Grant, aged 38, who lives in Southampton with her partner Jillian Percey, a nurse aged 30, went to an industrial tribunal after she was refused concessions worth £1000 a year for Ms Percey. Her predecessor in the job had received free and cut-price travel for his unmarried female partner.

The case was referred by the tribunal to the European Court where Ms Grant, represented by Cherie Booth QC, claimed the refusal breached article 119 of the EC treaty which guarantees equal pay. After a definitive ruling by the court, the case will go back to the tribunal for a final decision in about six months.

The advocate general said yesterday that discrimination could not be justified on the basis that an employer wanted to benefit heterosexual but not homosexual couples. He also ruled that article 119 could be directly applied by courts and tribunals in Britain; if the full court agrees, this opens the way for tribunals to decide similar cases without reference to Europe.

Ms Percy said afterwards: 'We're ecstatic. It's more than we could have hoped for. Some companies give health insurance to partners and they [same sex partners] will have that extended to them as well, as long as the opinion is upheld by the full court. We knew we were changing the law. It has been a hard campaign but well worth it.'

Angela Mason, director of Stonewall, which campaigns for equal rights for homosexuals, said: 'We are all absolutely delighted. This is an historic day for lesbian and gay rights, not just in this country but in the whole of the European Union.'

The opinion follows a ruling from the Luxembourg court extending protection from discrimination at work to transsexuals. Lawyers believe this paves the way for a similar ruling before long protecting homosexuals from any sort of discrimination at work.

Advocate general Elmer concluded: 'There is nothing in [EU law] to indicate that the rights and duties which result from the [law], including the right not to be discriminated against on the basis of gender, should not apply to homosexuals, to the handicapped, to persons of a particular ethnic origin, or to persons holding particular religious views.

'Equality before the law is a fundamental principle ... The rights and duties which result from EU law apply to all without discrimination, and therefore also to the approximately 35 million citizens of the EU who are homosexual.'

Source: Clare Dyer (1997) *Guardian*, 1 October.

Despite the fact that the Directive on Equal Pay specifies in Article 1 that job classification systems should be based on the same criteria for men and women and designed so that they exclude any discrimination on grounds of sex, there are still many unresolved dilemmas in this area. There have been many criticisms over the years that traditional and existing schemes often did demonstrate a bias in favour of the jobs that were 'male' as opposed to 'female', emphasising more or awarding more points to the characteristics associated with and forming part of the male jobs.

The Commission sought to address some of the remaining problems concerning the meaning, measurement and application of this principle of equal pay for work of equal value via a Memorandum (94/6); pursuant to that it has issued a Code of Practice on the Implementation of Equal Pay for Work of Equal Value for Women and Men COM (96) 336.

In the introduction to the Code the Commission confirms the relative lack of success achieved by the prior interventions on matters of equal pay between the sexes: '**Despite these provisions of Community law having been adopted and transposed into the legislations of the member states 20 years ago, the differences in pay between women and men remain considerable.**'

The pay differences are confirmed to be greater for non-manual as compared with manual workers and the Code suggests that the differences in men's and women's incomes are due to a number of factors.

The Commission states that in particular the Code aims to eliminate sexual discrimination whenever pay structures are based on job classification and evaluation systems, and makes two main proposals:

- that negotiators at all levels should carry out an analysis of the remuneration system and evaluate the data required to detect sexual discrimination in pay structures so that it becomes possible to devise remedies;

- that a plan for follow-up should be drawn up and implemented so that sexual discrimination is eliminated.

Interestingly, the Code states quite clearly that the prime responsibility for the avoidance of discrimination rests with the employers.

It is in the context of this principled obligation that it is sometimes argued that the burden of proof in such cases should be upon the employer; the obligation is upon them and of course they control much of the evidence that may be required.

Well-intentioned though the Code of Practice and the Commission are, it should be remembered that interventions of this kind are subject to the dangers that the greater the degree of the discrimination or wage/earnings gap, the greater may be the employment impact of the interventions directed at narrowing or eliminating that gap, and the greater the extent of occupational segregation, the smaller will be the impact of the equal value interventions.

The Commission's (1997) Annual Report on Equal Opportunities for 1996 suggests that the scale of the earnings gap between the genders has changed little over the years despite the existence of the legislation. It concludes that women on average earn some 20 per cent less than their male counterparts. Among manual workers women seem to earn between 65 and 90 per cent of male earnings, variations within this range being apparent between countries. The report suggests that while there is relatively little data it seems that the gender pay gap in the non-manual sector is actually wider still.

Treatment

The Directive on Equal Pay was followed by the *Equal Treatment Directive* in 1976 (76/207), which sought to ban discrimination on the grounds of sex in all aspects of employment. The UK implementing legislation was the 1976 Sex Discrimination Act and more recently the Employment Act of 1989.

There have been other Directives concerned specifically with equal treatment in respect of:

- State Social Security (79/7);

- Occupational Social Security (86/378); this Directive excluded occupational pensions from the scope of the requirement to make occupational benefits equal between men and women (this was overridden by the ECJ decision in the Barber case in 1990);

- the self-employed (86/613).

The ECJ has also had a role to play in this area of equal treatment interpreting the legislation and its meaning, an example being in the treatment of the sexes by occupational pension schemes. The case 152/84, Marshall *v* Southampton and South West Hampshire Area Health Authority, was concerned with the application of unequal retirement ages and also with the matter of whether there should be a ceiling on the damages to be awarded in cases of sex discrimination.

In recent times much of this judicial activity has been in connection with issues relating to part-time workers and their rights in comparison with those of full-time workers.

EU activity in this area has also been given a boost by the SPASP appended to the Maastricht Treaty since in Article 2 there is the provision that issues of equality between the sexes 'with regard to labour market opportunities and treatment at work' should no longer be subject to the requirement of unanimity. Initiatives in this area are now subject to the QMV requirements. This remains within the Amsterdam revisions with the addition that the new shortened co-decision procedure should be used.

The significance of the SPASP can be detected from the fact that of the first three matters to be dealt with using the QMV facility and the Protocol procedures, two were concerned with equal treatment. The first was concerned with the matter of parental leave and the second with extending equality to part-time workers.

The Protocol Framework Agreement between the Social Partners was adopted as a Directive on Parental Leave in June 1996 (96/34). The main provisions are:

- that both parents should be entitled to three months' unpaid leave after the birth or adoption of a child, the leave to be taken before the eighth birthday of the child;

- protection from dismissal for asking for parental leave;

- protection of the right to return to work after the leave;

- provision for additional time off in urgent family circumstances such as sickness and accident.

As noted in the first section of this chapter, the Directive quite deliberately leaves many of the details to be decided at the level of the member state, either by the member state government or by the partners operating at that level. In this case, therefore, there were no agreements at EU level on what might be an appropriate length of service qualification and the number of days leave that may be reasonable or allowable for the urgent family leave referred to in the agreement.

While this Directive seeks to create a minimum right for employees it does not seek to impose particular mechanisms or details, and options are left open on whether the agreement should be given effect at member state level through legislation or through further voluntary agreements between the Social Partners. In this way the diverse traditions and practices of each member state can be largely maintained while at the same time there is some harmonisation of minimum rights.

This Directive has not stopped arguments about the value to employees, employers and the government of the provision of paid as opposed to a right to unpaid parental leave. Some of these issues are referred to in Exhibit 7.3.

The second framework agreement between the Social Partners that was adopted as a Directive was concerned with equal rights and treatment for part-time workers in comparison with full-time. The main provisions are that those with an employment contract or relationship for less than normal hours compared with a full-time worker should be entitled to equality of treatment on a pro-rata basis. Employees should not be discriminated against solely on the grounds that they work part-time rather than full-time. In addition to enhancing the equality of treatment of part-time workers, this Directive is also concerned to facilitate the development of part-time work. Again, as with the Directive on parental leave, many of the details were deliberately left for determination at national level.

■ Exhibit 7.3

Pressure for paid parental leave 'will grow'

The government's promise to provide British parents with three months' unpaid parental leave will fuel demand for paid leave, according to Demos, the left-leaning think-tank.

A Demos report published yesterday said only 21 per cent of working people aged under 40 would be likely to take up parental leave if it was funded by themselves. Such leave is all that will be guaranteed following the government's recent decision to sign the European Union's social chapter.

Ms Helen Wilkinson, author of the report, predicted the government would come under pressure to respond to public opinion, which overwhelmingly supports paid parental leave – 74 per cent of 16–34-year-olds agree there should be a right to full parental leave on the birth of a child – and mounting concerns about the impact of long working hours and poor quality childcare on children.

Demos argues for a universal right to parental leave, funded by a small premium on national insurance, and says the costs would be lower than expected.

'The government could potentially save £600m as unemployed people come off income support and begin to pay tax,' says the report. 'British businesses could benefit from better staff retention and less absenteeism – currently costing them £12bn each year.'

Ms Wilkinson said: 'Even ignoring the tax and income support advantages to the state, the direct costs to government would be only £300m – less than one tenth of the cost of the married couples' tax allowance.'

Demos, which commissioned a Mori poll of public attitudes and surveyed 300 employers, said fewer than 3 per cent of British employers currently offered even limited parental leave.

'But 75 per cent of public sector managers believe that parental leave would help them to retain and attract senior female managers, 71 per cent say it would help them to retain skills and 60 per cent believe it would increase staff loyalty to the organisation,' it said.

Mr John Monks, general secretary of the Trades Union Congress, said he welcomed the report's approach, but said it ran contrary to current political shibboleths, which opposed raising tax, national insurance contributions or public expenditure.

Source: Andrew Bolger (1997) *Financial Times*, 22 July.

This Agreement and Directive have a long history that can be traced back to the Social Charter and subsequent Action Programme. However, the initiative was given impetus by various court decisions since early 1994, which have ruled that discrimination between part-time and full-time employees in terms of rights to redundancy payments, rights to join an occupational pension scheme and rights to claim unfair dismissal was indirect sex discrimination. The essence of the grounds upon which these matters can be argued as equality issues rests on the fact that the majority of part-time and fixed-term employees within the EU are female and therefore to discriminate against these categories of contract or employee is to discriminate indirectly on the grounds of sex.

Examples of relevant cases include Vroege ECJ (September 1994) and Warren Southampton IT (July 1994).

There are a number of other proposals under discussion. An adjustment of the burden of proof in sex discrimination cases has been under discussion since 1988 and was switched into the Protocol procedure in April 1995 although the Social Partners have failed to reach agreement.

The Draft Directive on Equal Treatment in Occupational Social Security Schemes COM (95) 186 seeks to take account of the decision in the Barber and Coloroll cases. The intention is that occupational pensions should be included in the general requirement to treat and pay men and women equally. Outside of the Protocol Agreement this proposal requires unanimity.

One of the most significant ECJ decisions in recent years was in the Kalanke case in October 1995 since the decision of the ECJ raised considerable doubts about the lawfulness of positive action in favour of one sex in employment and raised the matter of the distinction between positive action and positive discrimination.

The Land of Bremen was operating a policy of automatically giving priority to women candidates for recruitment and promotion in sectors where they were underrepresented and where a female candidate had the same qualifications as a male candidate.

The ECJ found the practice to be in contravention of Article 2 (4) of Directive 76/207/EEC (the Directive on Equal Treatment) and found that rules and procedures giving one sex *absolute* and *unconditional* priority go beyond promoting equal treatment or opportunities and overstep the provisions for positive action provided for in Article 2 (4).This allowed for action to be taken to remove obstacles to the equal treatment of the sexes as an exception from the main requirement not to discriminate. However, the ECJ found that to *guarantee* women priority went too far.

This decision appeared in the first instance to outlaw the type of *de facto* quota systems that had been the practice in the state of Bremen, and in many other places.

In addition to proposals to redraft the Directive, concerns about the impact of this ruling encouraged the Commission to issue a Communication, COM (96) 88, in which the Commission puts forward the view that the Kalanke decision only rendered unlawful measures that give absolute and unconditional rights or priority. The Commission seeks to approve positive action measures in the form of targets in terms of quotas and time limits that express preference but that do not imply automatic preference irrespective of qualification and that do allow for exception. The provision of incentives to employers and funding support for training, childcare and the reorganisation of work so as to benefit the underrepresented sex should all be considered and remain lawful.

We have not included in this section on equality between the sexes the Directive on the Protection of Pregnant Workers (92/85) since this was adopted as a Health and Safety measure.

In addition, there are some non-binding instruments relevant to issues of equality between the sexes at work and in connection with employment:

- Council Recommendation 92/241, concerned with childcare, which among other things encourages the promotion of flexible working as well as a sharing of parental responsibilities.

- Council Resolution on Balanced Participation of Men and Women in Decision-making 95/C168/02.

- A Commission document and a Code of Practice on the Dignity of Women and Men at work, which seek to address the issue of sexual harassment at work and provide policy guidance to practitioners as well as to member state governments and the Social Partners as formal participants.

As the ECJ and national courts continue to enforce the law on equal treatment and, in time, the Directive on equality for part-time workers, and to the extent that this increases the costs, both actual and relative, of the currently disadvantaged labour, there is the danger that demand for it may fall. Similar warnings have been given in respect of the impact of the EU initiatives on protecting pregnant women, maternity pay and leave.

Employee participation

There is a history stretching back to the late 1960s and early 1970s of EU initiatives of various kinds designed to provide legislatively supportable rights for employees and their representative institutions to participate more in the activities and decision-making processes of their employing organisations.

Some of these initiatives have sought to encourage participation across a range of strategic and financial/business issues, whereas others have been very much more specifically targeted. In the main, these initiatives have been concerned to promote participation of a representative and downward communication/consultative nature, although some of the earlier proposals were more ambitious and proposed to introduce schemes consistent with notions of co-management and co-decision.

Many of these proposals were not adopted by the Council. Hall (1994) explains this failure by suggesting that:

> only EC measures which require information, consultation or participation procedures in respect of certain specific social issues and which accommodate member states' existing employee representation arrangements rather than specifying particular institutional forms have gained acceptance by the Council.

More recently there have also been efforts to encourage various forms of financial participation for employees. The Commission has sought to encourage the development of both profit and equity sharing arrangements. In 1992 the Council adopted a non-binding Recommendation 92/443 on Equity Sharing and Financial Participation, which encourages member states to themselves promote such schemes via the creation of sympathetic legal and fiscal environments and regimes, and provides advice on the issues and criteria that those seeking to encourage and introduce such arrangements should consider. More recently the Commission has encouraged the Social Partners to consider an agreement on the matter. In the main, the attraction of these schemes is in the belief, supported by some evidence, that there is an association between employee financial participation and increases in productivity. Conservative governments in the UK between 1979 and 1997 supported these schemes and provided a favourable tax regime to encourage their take-up.

Many of these participation initiatives can be seen to be rooted in an ideological position that runs counter to the voluntarist tradition of the UK and is even more at odds with the neo-*laissez-faire*, liberal individualist position adopted by Conservative governments in the UK since 1979. It is not unrealistic to view the differences between the UK and the other member states on this, as with other issues, as the product/symptoms of a clash of philosophies on how best to regulate a modern capitalist market economy and the desirability and acceptability of particular outcomes.

Commission initiatives can be seen as:

- an expression of the desire for and belief in a community founded on consensus and harmony with undertones of equity and democracy, participation rights providing a counter to the otherwise unfettered rights of capital;

- an expression of the belief that providing employees with the right to participate is central to achieving enhancement of the efficiency and competitiveness of the economies of the member states, a means by which competitive advantage can be obtained through the contribution and commitment of the labour force, their knowledge, skill, problem solving capacity and innovation;

- a means by which the increasing autonomy and influence of multinational companies might be countered or at least mitigated. The initiatives discussed below have all to some degree been motivated by the perceived power of multinational capital to make decisions in one country that impact upon employees in another.

The motives of the Community/Commission are based in the belief that greater employee participation has the potential to yield benefits for employees, employers, national economies and the economy and social fabric of the EU as a whole.

In the remainder of this section we concentrate upon three particular initiatives, those seeking to ensure consultation for employees on the issues of collective redundancies and transfers of undertakings and those aimed at the encouragement of a particular form of participation within Community-scale undertakings.

The Directive on Collective Redundancies (75/129 extended by 92/56)

This Directive, which was adopted in 1975, provides that employee representatives should in the circumstances of impending redundancies have the right to be both informed and consulted.

The information requirement specifies that employers/management should give in writing all relevant information, including:

- the reasons for the redundancies;

- the numbers to be made redundant;

- the numbers usually employed;

- the time period over which the redundancies are to take effect.

The consultation should take place before the redundancies take effect and should be at the workplace, and by local management, where the redundancies are to occur even if the decision has been taken elsewhere, including in another member state.

The object of the consultation should be to *agree* on ways of avoiding or mitigating the number of redundancies and their consequences. The legislation applies only where specified minimum numbers of people are to be made redundant within a specified time scale.

The weakness of this Directive in the face of employers acting in a manner that is inconsistent with it was shown by the experience of Belgian workers when Renault decided to close one of its plants at Vilvoorde (*see* Chapter 4).

Directive on the Transfer of Undertakings (77/187)

This Directive, which is also known as the Acquired Rights Directive, is primarily concerned with the protection of employees' rights and terms and conditions of employment on the sale or transfer of a business. However, as part of the strategy for ensuring that these acquired rights are protected, the Directive also provides employees and their representatives with rights to be both informed and consulted on:

- the reasons for the transfer;
- the legal, economic and social implications of the transfer for the employees;
- measures envisaged in relation to employees.

It also specifies that they should be consulted 'in good time', on any measures that are envisaged by either the transferor or the transferee.

The obligation to consult seems to apply to employers in respect of their own employees, so that the transferee appears able to avoid consulting with employees of the transferor until after the transfer occurs. However, there is an obligation upon the transferee to inform the transferor of measures proposed, and where the transferor is aware of measures proposed by the transferee it should inform and consult its employees.

In the UK there has been considerable debate over the years concerning the way in which the original Directives on Collective Redundancies and Transfers of Undertakings had been implemented. In particular, there was concern that the implementing legislation in the UK provided for information and consultation to be with the representatives of 'recognised trade unions' rather than, as specified in the Directives, with 'employee representatives'. It is interesting that the Labour government that implemented the EU Directive limited the information and consultation requirements to recognised trade unions, at least in part, because it sought to encourage trade union membership and this recognition at a time when the unions were experiencing considerable competition from staff associations.

However, as the density of trade union membership and frequency of trade union recognition declined throughout the 1980s and 1990s the legislation became less and less relevant and binding upon employers since in the absence of recognised trade unions there was arguably no obligation to inform and consult employees at all.

As a consequence of its concern, the Commission challenged the UK government's interpretation of the original Directive and in June 1994 the ECJ ruled that the requirements of the Directives did apply to non-unionised workplaces, that the UK interpretation was incorrect and that non-unionised employees were effectively deprived by the UK implementing legislation.

As a result of this ruling the Collective Redundancy and Transfer of Undertakings (Amendment) Regulations 1995 (effective on 1 March 1996) require that UK employers:

- choose whether to consult with a recognised and independent trade union or with elected representatives of the employees that are affected by the events in question. Elected representatives are to be employees of the employer and the consultation is to be on an *ad hoc* basis; there is no requirement that permanent or standing arrangements be created in order to satisfy these new requirements;

- give elected employee representatives similar rights and protections as would be enjoyed by the representatives of an independent recognised trade union;

- consult 'in good time' and not at 'the earliest opportunity', as was the prior terminology.

However, these new regulations do not define 'elected representative' and do not appear to require employers to inform their employees that they are entitled to elect representatives for the purposes of this consultation. The trade unions in the UK have challenged these new regulations.

In September 1994 proposals were put forward by the Commission which seek to revise the 1977 Directive. The new draft is called the Draft Directive on Safeguarding Employees' Rights in the event of Transfers of Undertakings, Businesses or Parts of Businesses (COM (94) 300). The main thrust of these proposed revisions does not relate to the information and consultation procedures. However, there are some relevant proposals:

- that the minimum threshold for the requirements to apply should be 50 employees; undertakings employing fewer than 50 people should be exempt from the requirement to consult employee representatives;

- where there are no employee representatives the workforce would have a right to be informed in advance that a transfer is to take place; it is unclear whether the requirement will extend beyond notification that there is an agreement to transfer;

- clarification that the obligation to inform and consult is to apply wherever the decision is taken, even if in another state.

The European Works Council Directive 94/45/EC

As noted earlier, this was the first Directive to be adopted under the Social Protocol Agreement. Implementation was in September 1996.

This Directive can be traced directly back to the Social Charter and indirectly back to some of the earlier and unsuccessful initiatives by the Commission, in particular the Vredeling proposals. Cressey (1993) refers to this Directive as 'son of Vredeling'.

It must be remembered that the Directive is aimed only at transnational or Community-scale undertakings and should be viewed as a response to Commission, labour movement and some member state concerns about the autonomy and power of the multinational to take decisions in one member state that affect employees in one or more other member states.

The intention of the Directive is to ensure that all employees in the same Community-scale undertaking/group are both properly and equally informed and consulted about such decisions. The Directive is in part therefore a response to the increase in the number and scale of multinational activities and undertakings that accompanied and followed the creation of the single market, their ability to divert capital investment from one member state to another, and the absence of alternative employee representative arrangements and structures.

This is a Directive that is consistent with the principle of subsidiarity (see earlier) since it is only at EU level that action could effectively be taken, although whether you think such action necessary is another issue. The Directive leaves it open to the parties to form and implement arrangements consistent with national traditions and practices as long as certain minimum requirements are satisfied and/or the parties are in agreement.

For the purposes of the Directive 'Community-scale' has two labour force size dimensions. A Community-scale undertaking is one:

1 that employs at least 1000 employees in member states covered by the Directive, and

2 employs at least 150 in each of two such member states.

Both of these workforce size criteria have to be satisfied and the calculations are to be based on the average labour force over the preceding two years.

The Directive applies to companies of any nationality. There is no requirement that the company/undertaking be domiciled in one of the member states, and once covered by the Directive all of an undertaking's establishments within the member states should be covered by the one procedure. At the time the Directive was adopted and on the date of implementation the only exempt establishments and employees were those in the UK. However, UK companies were not exempted altogether. If their non-UK EU activities qualify them as Community-scale then they have to comply with the Directive in respect of all their employees and activities within the other member states, not just those in which they employ in excess of 150.

The content of the Directive

The responsibility for organising the process of implementation and/or compliance with the Directive rests with the central management of the undertaking and may be undertaken at their own initiative or at the request of employees. Employees and their representatives can initiate the process by submitting a written request on behalf of 100 employees in each of at least two member states.

The detail of the Directive provides that in such circumstances central management has the responsibility to set up a Special Negotiating Body (SNB) of employee representatives and to convene a meeting with it to 'negotiate in a spirit of co-operation with a view to reaching an agreement' (Article 6.1). The constitution of the SNB should reflect the distribution of the labour force of the undertaking within the EU.

There are a range of possible outcomes of this negotiation process, from a refusal to negotiate, to a failure to agree, to an agreement that is satisfactory to the parties and satisfies the requirements and spirit of the Directive.

If the employer refuses to negotiate within six months of an appropriate employee initiative, or in the event of the parties being unable to agree upon voluntary arrangements within three years of the original request for negotiations, the 'subsidiary requirements' included in the annexe to the Directive and which specify a particular form of information and consultation arrangement may be imposed. This is sometimes referred to as the *mandatory model*.

The mandatory model

The main points of the specified/mandatory model of an EWC are:

1 the EWC must have between 3 and 30 members;

2 the EWC should be comprised of employees of the undertaking or group elected or appointed by them and in accordance with the national legislation or practice;

3 the competence of the EWC should be limited to information and consultation on matters concerning the undertaking or group as a whole or at least establishments or undertakings in two different member states;

4 the composition of the EWC should include at least one member from each member state in which the undertaking or group has an establishment, with the remaining membership determined on proportionate grounds;

5 such an EWC is to be reviewed after four years and the parties may choose to allow it to continue or negotiate an alternative;

6 the EWC has the right to an annual meeting with central management to be informed and consulted on the basis of a written report provided by management and concerned with 'the progress of the business of the Community Scale undertaking or ... group of undertakings and its prospects'.

The subject matter of the meeting is then detailed:

■ the structure of the business;

■ the economic and financial situation;

■ the probable development of the business and of production and sales;

■ the situation and probable trend of employment;

■ investments and substantial changes concerning the organisation;

■ introduction of new working methods or production processes;

■ transfers of production;

■ mergers, cut backs or closures of undertakings, establishments or important parts thereof;

■ collective redundancies.

Impact of EWC Directive

Early estimates suggested that in excess of 1150 companies would qualify as Community-scale and would therefore be covered by the Directive and that among them were companies domiciled in 25 different countries. Germany topped the list with 274 qualifying companies, followed by the USA with 187, France with 122 and the UK with 106 (ETUI, 1995). There were also 101 companies that qualified which were based outside the European Economic Area (EEA) but had their largest European operation in the UK. It was estimated that in excess of 300 UK companies would be required to comply with the Directive if UK operations and employees were not excluded from coverage.

The Directive therefore impacts upon a number of the UK's largest companies. Another measure of the potential impact of the Directive in the UK was the estimate by the Engineering Employers' Federation (EEF) that among its members in the UK were nearly 900 companies that were subsidiaries of companies likely to be of Community scale in respect of their non-UK activities (*Financial Times*, 7 December 1995).

One of the issues raised by the UK's initial non-participation as one of the countries in which employees and activities are subject to the Directive was whether both UK and non-UK companies subject to the Directive in respect of their non-UK activities would voluntarily choose to include their UK activities and employees in the arrangements established in order to comply with the Directive. Many UK companies have indicated their intention to do so and all of the first dozen to conclude voluntary arrangements in advance of the implementation of the Directive included their UK activities – ICI, British Telecom, National Westminster Bank, Pilkingtons, United Biscuits, Coats Viyella, BP Oil, Courtaulds, GKN, Zeneca, T&N and GEC-Alsthom. The EEF research referred to above indicated that none of the 66 companies in membership covered by the Directive in respect of their EU/EEA activities intended not to include their UK operations and employees in procedures introduced in order to comply with the Directive.

Of the first 100 or so companies creating EWCs or similar other arrangements, only one took the opportunity to exclude its UK operations and employees (ING, the Dutch finance group that included the UK Barings Bank) where these were significant (*European Works Council Bulletin*, 1996) and also Exhibit 7.4.

The *Financial Times* on the day that the Directive became effective gave slightly different figures, indicating that the number of UK companies covered was 113, that another 127 would have been covered were it not for the UK opt-out and that by the implementation date some 38 of the UK companies covered had reached voluntary agreements, with 20 more in negotiations. Overall throughout the EU, as Exhibit 7.4 suggests, in excess of 200 of the 1150 companies immediately affected by the Directive had reached agreements on voluntary arrangements by this date. In many respects this represents a relatively low rate of voluntary compliance.

It is too early to estimate the number of companies that will wait for their employees to take the initiative and institute the proceedings culminating in the establishment of the SNB and how many may then choose to do no more than specified in the mandatory model EWC. There are attractions to employers in adopting this approach if they are opposed to the intent of the Directive. They can delay implementing the information and consultation for three years and there are cost advantages. Many employers may also find the arrangements in the annexe preferable as being relatively limited and probably the least that they can reasonably expect to get away with, particularly where they are confronted by a trade union actively representing its members and seeking to widen the scope of the information and consultation arrangements.

The annexe provides a ready-made set of arrangements and the employer can be certain that employees will have no grounds to appeal against the arrangements as not being adequate or satisfactory when measured against the requirements of the Directive. Against this, of course, is the argument that in choosing to allow a system to be enforced upon it the employer loses control and flexibility, and the ability to design and implement a system that fits with the requirements and structure of the organisation.

The EWC or suitable similar arrangements envisaged in the Directive are not going to provide employees and their representatives with rights and a role that imply an element of co-decision or co-determination, only rights to bilateral communication and discussion. In terms of employee participation the proposals are therefore quite limited. Nevertheless, employers are to have their unilateral 'right' to manage curtailed by the Directive.

In addition to not wanting their prerogative curtailed and being confronted by arrangements and objectives that they are not used to, UK management have tended to be critical of the proposals on the grounds that divulging certain elements of the information referred

■ **Exhibit 7.4**

Unions to press 800 EU companies to set up works councils

European trade union leaders plan to target more than 800 multinational companies and demand they set up consultative works councils for employees under the European Union law that came into force this morning in 17 EU and European Economic Area countries.

An estimated 20 per cent of the multinational companies covered by the legislation have already negotiated voluntarily with trade unions to create such an information and consultation body at the corporate level of their businesses.

From today employers will be compelled by law to create a works council if asked to do so by their workers.

Estimates by both the Warwick University Business School in the UK and the EU-funded European Foundation for the Improvement of Living and Working Conditions suggest that over 200 out of an estimated 1152 companies covered may have negotiated agreements with their employees or trade unions.

The EU legislation requires every company (including those which are US- and Japanese-owned) which employs more than 1000 workers in the 17 countries, with over 150 in at least two member states, to establish an employee consultation and information committee.

The largest number of European works councils so far negotiated have been in Germany (27 per cent of them, or more than 41) followed by France (22 per cent or over 25). But 14 per cent of agreements are with UK companies, despite the UK's opt-out from the social chapter of the Maastrict treaty which does not require those companies to create works councils to include their UK workers.

Only one agreement – the Dutch-owned banking and insurance group ING – explicitly excludes its British workers from its works council.

The European Foundation survey found a third of all works council agreements included countries outside the area covered by the law, such as Switzerland, the Czech Republic, Hungary and Poland.

As many as 35 per cent of the existing agreements (61) are in the metalworking sector, followed

by 25.4 per cent in chemicals (44) and 14.5 per cent in food, hotels and catering (25), according to the Warwick Business School report, compiled by Mr Mark Hall from its industrial relations research unit. By contrast, only one retail company has negotiated a European works council, and there is one in telecommunications.

A study of 111 voluntary European works councils published today by the European Foundation found at least one in four French companies and one in six of UK companies had signed such an agreement voluntarily.

It also said that although trade unions were not specifically mentioned in the directive they had been 'heavily involved' in their creation, with 55 per cent of agreements signed by a trade union organisation.

The survey suggests only about 15 per cent of works councils have been created without trade union influence.

The study has also found full-time trade union officials are directly taking part in half of the works councils so far created, and more will participate as so-called experts in an advisory role on the new bodies. Two thirds of all the negotiated councils provide for trade unions to nominate employee representatives in all or some of the European countries covered.

Three-quarters of the works councils are joint management-employee bodies and 80 per cent cover all the operations of the multinational, with the rest providing for divisional-level structures. Their average size is 25 on the workers' side, with size ranging between seven and 70. Around half have smaller select committees created to prepare for the council meetings which 90 per cent of companies hold once a year.

In 84 per cent of agreements, worker representatives are allowed to meet without the company management being present. Over half provide for a report back to the workforce as a whole in the operation of the works councils.

Source: Robert Taylor (1996) *Financial Times*, 23 September.

to in the Directive might be dangerous from a competitive and profitability perspective, and that the process is inevitably time consuming, expensive and damaging to performance.

However, it would appear from the research of Fernie and Metcalf (1995) that not only is there no general evidence of unfavourable relationships between formal joint consultative committees and economic and industrial relations outcomes but on two particular counts, productivity growth and industrial relations climate, such arrangements are favourably associated with performance. They cite German research, which similarly found no adverse association between works councils (stronger bodies than the UK joint consultative committees) and productivity, profit and investment. They further suggest that UK employers should throw off their blinkers and work in harmony with unions or employees to improve performance, although to do so through the mechanism of formal joint consultative committees would require a reversal of the trend identified by the 1990 Workplace Industrial Relations Survey. This latter research indicated that less than 25 per cent of establishments in private sector manufacturing had such arrangements in 1990 compared with 36 per cent in 1980 (Millward *et al.*, 1992).

Marginson and Sisson (1994) suggest that the impact of the Directive in the UK will be profound because of its nature and the degree of contrast between its requirements and the traditions of UK industrial relations. In particular, they comment upon the lack of experience that UK managers have of statutory forms of employee participation and that the Directive facilitates the introduction of participative arrangements that are not trade union based, unusual in the UK.

Trade unions and their officials have generally welcomed the Directive and it is clear from Exhibit 7.4 that unions throughout the EU are determined to put pressure upon employers to comply. However, some have expressed concerns that the mandatory model of an EWC specifies that the EWC members are to be employees of the company and that this will result in their own role and influence being diminished relative to the role of lay trade union and other employee representatives.

The Directive provides for groups or undertakings to be exempted from the detailed requirements if on the date of implementation of the Directive (22 September 1996) they had in force transnational information and consultation agreements covering the entire workforce. This provision has led to other trade union concerns, namely that some managements might try to use it to bypass the trade unions. Certainly early efforts by Marks and Spencer to establish an EWC were criticised by trades unions who felt that the company was seeking to establish arrangements that were not adequate substitutes for the arrangements specified in the Directive and which were at least in part inspired by the desire to avoid an anticipated approach from trade unions on behalf of their employees.

Rivest (1996) has studied the first 59 agreements establishing voluntary EWCs in the decade preceding September 1995. The conclusions of this research may serve to partially assuage these trade union fears. This analysis indicates that national and international trade union organisations were involved as signatories to the agreements in 47 per cent and 44 per cent, respectively, of the instances. Other findings of this analysis are that where trade union organisations have been party to the agreement it is likely that the employee representatives on the EWC will normally be nominated by the trade unions and it is more likely that trade union officials will have rights of participation or attendance. The EFILWC study referred to in Exhibit 7.4 found that of 111 voluntary EWCs only some 15 per cent had been created without trade union influence and that full-time trade union officials were actively taking part in half of those created by that time.

As noted above, one of the first UK companies to agree an arrangement with the trade unions was United Biscuits. The company and the unions agreed in November 1994 to establish an EWC covering operations in eight countries (including the UK) and comprising twenty employee representatives. A management representative stated the company's position as a belief that:

> A workforce that understands the objectives of a business and the pressures on it is better able to respond appropriately to necessary operational changes. (*Guardian*, 10 November 1994)

One of the possible developments from this Directive, a form of cascading-down effect with the EWC replicated at a national level, might have a particular importance for the UK and its traditions. The Danish multinational ISS has created a UK works council as a branch of its EWC (*Guardian*, 4 July 1995) and an early survey of eight companies already operating EWCs by January 1995 found that all were operating works councils at a national level (Coopers and Lybrand, 1995).

The achievement of the Directive is really in the level at which the consultation is to take place and in the 'strategic' nature of the subject matter: for the very first time many multinational organisations are to share information with employees at a supra-national, Euro-corporate level and there is obvious potential in these arrangements for the development of trust and further joint arrangements, which we pursue in the final section of this chapter.

New Labour

The election of a New Labour government in 1997 seemed to present an opportunity for a shift of ideological emphasis away from liberal individualism and unitarism in the direction of social partnership and greater employee participation. There was a more or less immediate commitment to reverse the previous government's position on a Social Chapter in the EC Treaty and integral to this was acceptance of the so-called Protocol procedures involving the Social Partners, which were described earlier, and the Directives that had been adopted via the SPASP. These include the EWC Directive, and at some point in the future UK activities will become subject to the requirements of the Directive.

However, it was also clear early in the new government's period of office that there was no intention to return to a form of social partnership that implied a return to corporatism – the Social Partners were likely to be involved more in consultations with government but there was no indication that the new government intended to devolve or cede decision making to them or to mechanisms of a tripartite nature. It seems unlikely that the social partners within the UK will be given the opportunity to collectively determine the details necessary for the implementation of the Directives on parental leave or equality for part-time workers. They will play a part in formulating the detailed proposals but the decisions will remain the preserve of government and implementation is more than likely to be through the traditional legislative route and not through the mechanism of collective agreement at national level.

A government that is so publicly committed to the retention of labour market flexibility is unlikely to take notions of partnership to the point where it allows the partners the ability to agree requirements and regulations that might be inconsistent with the flexibility imperative.

Partnership in this New Labour context seems to have more in common with adopting a cooperative approach and attitude than with sharing decision making or power. This notion of social partnership, where partnership is perceived as a preferable alternative to conflict, rather than as joint decision making or power sharing seems to offer employees little more than is offered by the EWC Directive, the opportunity to receive information and express a view.

We may be seeing the emergence of a new perspective on employee relations, one in which trade unions are recognised as having a limited right to recognition as representatives of employees' interests but where they are also expected to be team players – a form of unitarism that encompasses collective organisation and in which employees and their representatives are expected to subjugate their interests to those of the organisation in which they are partners.

The Directive on the Adaptation of Working Time 93/104

This Directive was adopted in November 1993, to be implemented by November 1996. The Directive was adopted as a health and safety matter under Article 118A of the EC Treaty and therefore via the co-operation procedures (QMV).

At the time the UK government was very unhappy with the nature and contents of the Directive and did manage to secure some significant changes to the original proposals as they went through the legislative process – for example, in securing exceptions for particular occupations and circumstances such as the exemption of trainee doctors, who in the UK regularly work hours considerably in excess of the limits specified in the Directive. They also managed to ensure that the limits upon working hours could be voluntarily varied given the agreement of the parties, whether this be individuals agreeing to work longer hours or the parties agreeing a variation via a collective agreement. Perhaps strangely given their unhappiness, they did not vote against the Directive in the Council; they merely abstained. *See* Exhibit 7.5.

In addition to the detailed content, the UK government unhappiness with the Directive centred upon two particular issues which are of more general relevance.

The first of these concerns the assertion that the Directive was incorrectly adopted as a health and safety issue. This challenge was ruled upon by the ECJ in November 1996 and the Court's judgment affirmed the original decision that the measure was properly introduced.

There are concerns that in forcing the issue the UK government has actually engendered a situation in which, given the relatively liberal interpretation by the ECJ, it may now be easier for the EU to adopt measures on other issues concerning employment utilising Article 118A.

The Court cited the World Health Organization's definition of health (all member states are members):

a state of complete physical, mental and social well being that does not consist only in the absence of illness of infirmity.

■ Exhibit 7.5

Poetic justice of Brussels' victory

As the European Commission celebrated its victory in Brussels yesterday, EU officials mulled over the chequered history of Britain's challenge to the 48-hour week directive.

Some were quick to point out that Britain should be blaming Baroness Thatcher, the former British prime minister, for the present impasse over social legislation. It was she who signed the Single Market Act in 1986 which contained the article at the centre of the present dispute.

The act's Article 118a states that member states 'shall pay particular attention to encouraging improvement, especially in the working environment, as regards the health and safety of workers.'

But the real row started in 1993 when EU social affairs ministers started debating the commission's proposal, based on Article 118a, on a 48-hour working week.

During heated debates, and much publicity, British ministers fought a successful campaign to weaken the legislation. 'Countless concessions were made to the British,' said one official. These included exemptions for workers in the transport sectors, junior doctors and priests. In addition, the directive was made virtually voluntary.

There was outrage, therefore, when Britain failed to back the proposal when the vote was finally taken. Instead, its minister abstained. 'They succeeded in winning a lot of flexibility on the directive. Then they abstained. We were astounded. They simply turned the thing into a political football,' the EU official said.

But the coup de grace was to come. Once the decision had been taken, the British government promptly announced it was referring the issue to the European Court of Justice.

For many in Brussels there was poetic justice in the court's judgement yesterday.

Source: Caroline Southey (1996) *Financial Times*, 13 November.

From a lay viewpoint it does seem reasonable to suggest that there are health and safety risks to working long hours with insufficient rest periods and breaks, and that night work is likely to have additional health and safety implications.

Second, as discussed elsewhere in this chapter, the regulation of working hours, rest periods and entitlement to annual leave ran counter to the ideology of the government and to the voluntarist traditions of the UK. It is understandable that a government, convinced that the key to competitiveness lies in a deregulated and flexible labour market, should object to something it sees as both unnecessary and damaging to competitiveness and therefore to the prospects for growth.

Adnett (1996: 262) points out that the proposal to limit maximum working hours to an average of 48 per week over a four-month reference period would affect only 3 per cent of the total hours worked in Britain. Given that a number of specific occupations (see below) are exempted and that employees and employers can voluntarily agree to working in excess of these limits this may be compatible with the New Earnings Survey for 1996 data, which indicates that approximately 12 per cent of employees in the UK work more than 48 hours per week and, indeed, that these employees average 57 hours per week. Eurostat data (1997) shows that average usual full-time hours per week worked in the UK in 1996 exceeded any other member state at 43.9 hours compared with an EU average of 40.3.

The main exceptions cover particular 'problematic' occupations – road, rail, sea or air transport workers as well as managers and trainee doctors – and industries where continuity of production or service is required such as health, the media, postal and telecommunications, emergency and public services, security services and public utilities.

Some will argue that by imposing a maximum upon the number of hours that can be worked by an individual there will be a job creating effect in that if the need/demand for labour is there it will be met from the employment of more individuals, although there is little evidence to confirm that this is the effect of such measures. Another argument is that measures of this kind serve to protect those in employment rather than creating employment for those that currently are not. The suggestion is that these measures, perhaps particularly those concerned with leave entitlement (see later), will increase the cost of employing labour, and this will mitigate any positive impact upon labour demand.

We have noted above the main provision of the Directive with respect to maximum working hours, that they should be limited to an average of 48 per week over a four-month reference period although this can be extended to twelve months either by member states or by the parties via collective agreement. Other provisions of the Directive are that workers should have or receive:

- a minimum of 11 hours' consecutive rest in 24 hours, implying a maximum working day of 13 hours (this can be averaged over a two-week period);
- a minimum of 35 hours' consecutive rest per week in principle to include Sunday (this can be averaged over a two-week period);
- a rest break after 6 hours' consecutive work;
- four weeks' paid annual leave (three weeks for the first three years of employment) and no payment in lieu (in other words the intention is that the leave should be taken);

The extra provisions covering night workers seek to limit the average length of a night shift to 8 hours in 24, and propose that night workers should have free and regular medical check-ups and the right to transfer to day work on medical grounds.

The main derogation provides that the parties can voluntarily by collective agreement introduce greater flexibility in implementing the Directive as long as adequate and appropriate compensatory rest is given (see above).

In practice it seems that the maximum hours element of the Directive becomes relevant only in circumstances where an employer is seeking to pressure employees into working in excess of the stipulated maxima against their will and there is the threat of penalty if they refuse.

The greatest benefit to employees may come from the provisions dealing with paid annual leave; it has been estimated by the Labour Force Survey 1996 that there are as many as 2.7 million full-time workers with less than four weeks' holiday entitlement per year, with 1.8 million entitled to less than three weeks. The Directive was given legal source in the UK in October 1998.

THE EUROPEANISATION OF INDUSTRIAL RELATIONS

For many years now there has been discussion of the extent to which and how industrial relations may be conducted at an EU or multinational level. This could be at a number of different levels:

- the level of the EU itself, usually referred to as the inter-sectoral level;
- the level of the industry or sector;

- some intermediate cross-national regional level;
- the level of the single multinational company.

In this section we are particularly interested in the first and last of these.

It has long been among the objectives of the Commission that the Social Partners participate in a dialogue at the level of the EU. This was given impetus by the SEA, resulting in the founding Treaties being amended to incorporate Article 118B, which states that the Commission should:

> endeavour to develop the dialogue between management and labour at European level which could, if the two sides consider it desirable, lead to relations based on agreement.

The intent was that dialogue between the partners would lead to the development of initiatives in the field of social policy that were based on an agreement between them, and that the dialogue would lead to a form of collective bargaining and collective agreements. It was thought that if this could be achieved the initiatives would stand much more chance of being successful and a better chance of being adopted by the Council. Exhibit 7.1 indicates that this is still the view of influential interests within the Commission.

Of the Social Partners themselves the ETUC has tended to be more favourably disposed to developments and interventions in the area of social policy and to collective bargaining at a multinational EU level than either of the two main EU-level employers' associations (UNICE and CEEP), although it should be noted that by no means is there unanimity within and between the trade union movements as to the desirability of collective bargaining at this level rather than at sectoral or national level. The traditions in the various member states differ, with some national federations used to engaging in bargaining at the national level and others never having had this role. For example, the TUC in the UK and the DGB in Germany have not normally engaged in collective bargaining at a national level, whereas the national confederations in Italy and Sweden have (Hollinshead and Leat, 1995).

The employers' associations have tended to rely upon their ability to influence governments and marshal enough opposition to social policy interventions to prevent them ever being adopted all the time that such interventions were subject to the principle of unanimity. It was only when they thought it possible that the Council, as part of the Maastricht Treaty, might adopt the proposal that a very much wider range of social policy be covered by the QMV procedures that they agreed to participate in the procedures of the Social Dialogue eventually agreed as part of the Protocol Agreement. In that context an enhancement of the Dialogue was perceived as the lesser of two evils.

This SPASP did not include all of the member states (we pointed out earlier that the UK refused to agree) and therefore its effects were bound to be limited. Nevertheless, we can detect the intent of those party to the Agreement, the mechanics of the new procedure and some of its potential from an examination of the Agreement itself and the way in which the procedure operated on the first two occasions when it was used. These were the attempts to introduce EU-wide initiatives in the areas of Works Councils in large multinational companies and minimum rights to parental leave. It is important to bear in mind that the first of these initiatives was itself an attempt to enhance dialogue and relations at the level of the multinational organisation referred to above.

Article 3 and the subsequent Article 4 give the detail of the so-called Protocol procedure described earlier and presented diagrammatically in Fig 7.6. This procedure provides that, if the Partners want, the Dialogue between them may result in the development of 'contractual relations including agreements'.

This procedure does not give the Social Partners the right to initiate dialogue on a particular issue at this level; although they can ask the Commission for the opportunity to try to reach an agreement; the right of initiative remains with the Commission. In the early days it seemed likely that the employers' organisations would remain reluctant partners in this process and that they would seek to reach an agreement with the unions at this level only when they were reasonably sure that the alternative was the Council adopting a measure via the QMV procedures.

Where the Partners do reach an agreement there are two possible options with respect to its implementation:

1 Leave it to the parties at national level, presumably through some form of implementation arrangements agreed between the Partners and perhaps also government at a national level.

2 On an issue that can be determined via the QMV procedures, the partners can jointly request that the Commission makes a proposal to the Council upon which the Council then makes a decision, the latter being legally binding. This is the procedure that has so far been used on the occasions when the Social Partners have reached agreement. In each case they have asked the Commission to propose a draft Directive to the Council.

It is also clear from SPASP that the intention was that any such agreements reached between the Social Partners should take the form of frameworks or agreements on principle, the details to be worked out at individual member state level, if at all. This is very much what has happened with the first two such agreements, parental leave and rights for part-time workers.

It is doubtful that the Partners will either want or be able to reach agreements at this level that create binding or contractual relations, and it is in fact debatable whether either of them has a mandate from their members to do so. As noted above, the partners did manage to reach agreement on the provisions for parental leave and the rights of part-time workers but they did not intend that these agreements at this EU level should create contractual relations or that they should be binding at sectoral or national level upon the federations and associations that they represented, hence the request to the Council and the subsequent Directives.

These agreements are arguably indicative of what is the much more likely outcome of the two options referred to above.

In his discussion of the prospects for what he calls a 'Europeanisation of Collective Bargaining', Schulten (1996) (even at a sectoral level) identifies a number of obstacles:

1 Neither of the Partners has the institutional or organisational structures to effectively bargain at this level, and, as noted above, they have no political mandate to negotiate or sign agreements at this level.

2 The political interests of the actors are still predominantly national in perspective; they have different national traditions and interests in that they are at different stages of economic development.

3 There are fundamental differences between the actors as to the desirability of social policy interventions at the EU level, the unions generally being in favour with the employers generally against. He makes the point that the interests of European employers tend now more than ever to be 'to minimise social restrictions and to shift social regulation even further from the state to the market'.

4 The basic character of the EU integration process militates against the development of an EU-level collective bargaining system. By this he means that there is little evidence of the development of a European state; the EU cannot impose such a system from above. The member states are to varying extents concerned to preserve their national identities and sovereignty, and the dominant notion of integration is of a form that can be achieved through market forces and not through political reforms. In this context national systems are likely to continue as the dominant focus for the majority of employers and unions, and, as we noted above, the EU Social Dialogue and accompanying outcome options contained within the Social Protocol Agreement tend also to emphasise the level of the member state and national practices and traditions when it comes to working out the details of implementation.

Hyman (1995) comments that even enthusiasts and optimists concede that the prospects for a convergence of national institutions and outcomes are minimal and that even if Maastricht does prove to have eased the process it seems clear that on the key industrial relations issues of trade union rights, the status of collective bargaining and wage regulation the EU will have little if any jurisdiction. The Social Policy Agreement specifically excludes some of these areas from its jurisdiction: pay, the right of association and the rights to strike or lock-out (Article 2(6)) and the others are covered by the requirement of unanimity (this has not been substantially altered by the agreement at Amsterdam in 1997). He does concede that the single market project, in its encouragement of the mobility of capital and labour, might prove to be a powerful force for convergence but he doubts that multinational employers will encourage such convergence given that their interests would seem to be better served by a policy of divide and rule.

Much of the debate about the convergence and Europeanisation of industrial relations has centred on this latter issue – the role and impact of the development of the multinational organisation within the EU that has been encouraged by the single market programme of economic integration and specifically the derestricting of the movement of capital. This is discussed in Chapter 4.

The implications and prospects for the future have been and still are, of course, debatable. It was clear that without a change of political climate in the UK there was no chance of the Social Dialogue acquiring the EU-wide importance that the Commission and the other member states have intended. The election of a New Labour government in 1997, of course, changes this scenario. Early signs are that the new government will accept the principles and practices embodied within the SPASP and to which they effectively and retrospectively agreed at the Amsterdam summit in the summer of 1997. We have already noted earlier that they have agreed to accept the Directives that have been adopted within the Protocol procedures and that these procedures are to be taken into the Treaty as amended and, of course, at this stage subject to ratification.

The intentions or wishes of the Commission seem also still to perceive this Dialogue as a preferred mechanism for the determination of social policy and as possibly forming the base for the development of a more common system of industrial relations, procedural rather than substantive, within and throughout the EU.

The Commission 1997 consultative Green Paper, *Partnership for a New Organisation of Work*, is also concerned with issues of employee participation and involvement. The authors of this document argue the desirability of:

■ 'a new balance of regulatory powers between the State and the Social Partners, in particular in the areas connected with the internal management of firms';

■ 'the need to review and strengthen the existing arrangements for workers involvement in their companies';

■ 'consultations with the Social Partners on the advisability and direction of Community action in the field of information and consultation of employees at national level'.

There are some indications here that while the subject matter is information and consultation and involvement rather than participation or collective bargaining, there are interests within the Commission that seem to support notions of greater procedural uniformity at all levels – the EU, national and within the firm.

■ Different traditions and systems and convergence

We alluded earlier to the differences between the member states in terms of the traditions of social philosophy and legislative intervention, the latter being significantly influenced by the former. Gold (1993) adopts Teague's (1989) distinction between the social protectionist and the deregulatory perspectives. The social protectionist perspective encompasses the Socialist, Social Democrat and Christian Democrat philosophies, all of which, though to varying degrees and with different priorities, accept the principle of intervention and the need for government to regulate the labour market, insist upon minimum employee rights and promote social justice. This perspective, shared by the majority of the political groups within the EU and also crucially by influential groups within the Commission, can be contrasted with that of the UK Conservative governments since 1979, which has been portrayed as an essentially deregulatory approach. In terms of philosophy or ideology, these UK governments can be characterised as liberal individualist, putting their faith in the market mechanism and individual choice, contract and decision making as the base for competitiveness and growth.

Hall (1994) and Gold(1993) both seek to locate the regulatory systems in the EU in one of the following three categories:

1 *The Roman–German system*. Here the state plays a crucial role in industrial relations. Gold (1993) follows Due *et al.* (1991) in pointing out that in these systems there is a core of fundamental rights and freedoms guaranteed by the constitution and it is these that constitute the base of national industrial relations. It is common in such systems for there to be quite extensive legal regulation of areas such as working time and the rights of employees to be represented and the mechanisms of that representation. Germany, France, the Netherlands, Belgium and Italy are quoted as being in this category/tradition.

2 *The Anglo-Irish system*. Here the role of the state is more limited and there is a much less extensive set of legislatively created and supported basic rights and protections. Governments in these countries have traditionally left more to the parties themselves and stepped in to regulate and protect only when necessary to defend either the national interest and/or the interests of certain vulnerable minorities, such as children. In this

context Hall (1994) refers to these systems as voluntarist. Both the UK and Ireland are in this category. In the UK it is arguable that this tradition began to be eroded from the 1960s onwards, and through much of the 1960s and 1970s there was a much greater willingness to intervene and to regulate to provide basic rights and freedoms and to encourage trade unionism and collective bargaining.

3 *The Nordic system.* Prior to the enlargement of the EU in 1995 only Denmark fell into this category, although as Gold (1993) points out the other Scandinavian countries that were part of this enlargement, Sweden and Finland, also share this tradition. The difference between this system and the Anglo-Irish group is in the degree of emphasis and reliance placed on and in the collective agreement. It is suggested that in these countries more emphasis is placed upon the basic agreement freely entered into, usually at national or sectoral level, by both employer and trade union and it is this that provides the central element of the industrial relations system. The state has intervened to regulate only at the request of the parties.

The Commission has traditionally pursued policies and taken initiatives consistent with the Roman–German tradition and there is plenty of recent evidence that this is still the inclination of the Commission Directorates with responsibility for social affairs. The debate on unemployment, which has occupied the member states, Commission and other interests substantially since the early 1990s, illustrates these preferences, with the Commission often arguing that while it may be desirable to reduce the regulation of the labour market and labour costs so as to encourage employment, this should not be achieved at the expense of social justice and the weakest and poorest members of the EU (EC White Paper on Social Policy, July 1994). However, it is also clear that there are other interests within the Commission – for example, those with responsibility for industry and competition policy – that are distancing themselves from the traditions of the Roman–German system of regulation and social protection and becoming more willing to countenance deregulation as a necessary response to the pressures of international competition and the need to enhance flexibility in terms of response to the market and labour usage.

Hall (1994) points out that the leading proponent of the view that an extensive EU social policy/dimension would damage competitiveness since it would raise employment costs and reduce labour market flexibility was the UK Conservative government. This was a consistent position after its election in 1979 and was demonstrated by its opposition to a number of individual proposals, in addition to its refusal to adopt the Social Charter and to agree to the Maastricht Treaty until the Social Chapter was removed.

The subsequent debate on unemployment, which may turn out to be the greatest problem facing the EU, served to focus even further attention upon the compatibility of international competitiveness on the one hand and a model of labour market regulation providing a floor of minimum employee and trade union rights, joint decision making and high employment costs. In this context the architects of deregulation in the UK presented it as a source of competitive advantage in the global marketplace and as a means of attracting foreign investment into the UK, much to the annoyance of other member states.

It is plausible to view the history of the UK government position since 1979 as presaging the emergence of a new model or trajectory for employee relations in the EU, a model which becomes more widespread as governments confronted with high unemployment, high employment and welfare costs, and highly regulated and inflexible labour markets are attracted to deregulation and cost cutting, which are perceived as an essential means of regaining international competitiveness.

Grahl and Teague (1991) envisaged the development of two distinct trajectories that were compatible with greater flexibility, the constructive and competitive trajectories.

The constructive trajectory depicts strategies that seek to combine greater flexibility with the traditions of social protection and cohesion and with an emphasis upon output expanding activity. The competitive trajectory depicts strategies based on the deregulated, market-orientated, low wage and employment costs, and anti-trade-union model developed in the UK during the 1980s and early 1990s.

Grahl and Teague pointed out that the majority of the member states lay somewhere between these two extremes, and were of the opinion that the institutions and structures of welfare capitalism and widespread social and political opposition both had and might continue to significantly limit the extent to which the competitive model could be given effect in many of the member states. However, as time has gone on, it would seem that more member state governments seem inclined to deregulate labour markets and diminish employee rights, protection and benefits as the solution to Europe's high unemployment, poor record of job creation and lack of competitiveness.

Many employers have responded to competitive pressures by seeking to cut costs and this has resulted in further and substantial job losses, putting further pressure upon governments to deregulate as the price of encouraging employers to employ labour.

Reductions in the membership and influence of the trade unions have also been widespread (Hollinshead and Leat, 1995: 107–10) and governments seem increasingly prepared to stand firm in support of their deregulatory and cost cutting policies in the public and welfare sectors even when the trade unions were able to mount effective opposition (examples in 1995–6 would include the public sectors in the UK and France and various sectors in Germany, the Netherlands, Greece and Italy).

If deregulation of the workplace and the employment relationship is a necessary response to international competition and a prerequisite of employment-led/intensive growth there are clear threats to the traditional Roman–German system.

Such traditions are also under threat from a different direction. The convergence criteria for the achievement of qualification for monetary union have also begun to encourage several of the governments in countries in this group to reappraise the feasibility of maintaining the welfare state, including both employment- and unemployment-related benefits, in the face of the need to control public expenditure and debt. Their determination to comply with the convergence criteria has encouraged them to begin to pursue deflationary policies and further encourages the process of reducing the scale and scope of the welfare state and social protection. In examining the effects of such policies upon jobs, the European Parliament's committee on employment estimated in a report to the Parliament in July 1995 that between 1994 and 1999 some 1.5 million jobs would be lost as a result of budgetary restrictions in pursuit of convergence.

Attempts to obtain a commitment to the pursuit of full employment in the single currency model and the inclusion of employment level among the criteria of eligibility for membership have not succeeded, although there was agreement at Amsterdam on a new Title on Employment to be included in the Treaty and to some initiatives aimed at greater co-ordination of member state policies towards the reduction of unemployment. The main thrust of EU policy towards unemployment remains deregulation and greater labour market flexibility mixed with efforts to improve the quality of the labour force, mainly via vocational education and training.

There are those who fear that the single currency project will create an EU that has locked in to it high unemployment and low growth, a combination that may encourage a downward spiralling deregulation in the vain pursuit of competitiveness, growth and employment.

In other words, the traditions of the Roman–German system of industrial relations seem to be under threat from several different directions, and the attractiveness of the competitive flexibility model (or something very similar) to employers, governments and some Commission interests would seem to have increased as the EU has perceived itself to be under greater pressure to be competitive, as unemployment has risen and as the commencement date of the single currency project comes closer.

It may be that there is less justification in the mid- to late 1990s to be as sanguine as were Grahl and Teague at the beginning of the decade and we may well be witnessing the terminal decline of the Roman–German system and its domination of the approach and policies of the EU as well as the majority of the member states. Undoubtedly this will occur at different rates and to varying extents from one member state to another depending upon the particular circumstances, traditions and, as Ferner and Hyman (1992) suggest, the strength and flexibility of the institutions themselves. The successful truck drivers' strike of November 1996 and the degree of public support for their case may well indicate that in France both the resistance to the demolition of the welfare state and the support for social justice may be greater than in other member states.

Nevertheless, it may be that we are witnessing the beginnings of a variable rate convergence of European systems of industrial relations, not on the Roman–German base, but around principles and characteristics that have much more in common with the model developed in the UK over the past two decades. This encompasses as its major features:

- rejection of the principles of social protection;
- deregulated labour markets and an emphasis upon labour flexibility and cost reduction;
- weakened trade unions, greater legal constraints upon industrial action and less employee protection;
- an emphasis upon individualism, individual contract and employee commitment to organisational goals;
- devolution and decentralisation of decision making and the dismantling of national/sectoral industrial relations institutions;
- less collective bargaining and joint decision making and enhanced managerial prerogative.

The New Labour government in the UK seems to want to pursue a kind of middle or hybrid course emphasising:

- the need for labour flexibility;
- the avoidance of onerous labour market regulation;
- a determination to impose greater barriers to the continuing receipt of unemployment and other social security and disability benefits as part of a package of measures designed to provide incentives for the unemployed to join/rejoin the working population;
- greater expenditure upon education and vocational training as a means of improving the quality of the labour force and dealing with skills shortfalls;

- an emphasis upon partnership as cooperation rather than participation;
- the replacement of the notion of a right to work with that of a duty to work, at the same time as they intend to introduce:
  - a minimum wage
  - limited rights to trade union recognition, and
  - acceptance of the new Social Chapter agreed in draft at Amsterdam.

Overall, New Labour's approach emphasises flexibility and competitiveness at the same time as a more limited concept of social justice and protection.

It is as yet too early to predict the extent to which the Labour government will be successful, as it is still too early to say with any certainty what the outcome will be throughout the rest of the EU.

CHAPTER SUMMARY

The EU is an expanding and dynamic organisation of nation states progressing gradually towards different forms of union. So far the emphasis has been upon economic and monetary integration, the creation of single markets in capital, goods and services, and labour, and the creation of a single currency. The social dimension of the EU is relatively underdeveloped in comparison.

The institutions of the EU and the member states are increasingly seeking to take decisions utilising processes that provide the opportunity for majority as opposed to unanimous decisions and involve the Social Partners in the process. Agreements at Amsterdam also seem likely to give greater weight to the views and influence of the European Parliament.

The major achievement of the Amsterdam Treaty revisions may well prove to be the extension of the treaty base for the adoption of policies and other initiatives in the social field.

So far the influence of the EU in the social and employment field has been relatively limited, with nation states successfully seeking to preserve their traditions and their autonomy except in the areas of equality between the sexes and health and safety at work. There have been few initiatives adopted in other areas, some providing rights to information and consultation on particular issues and some concerned with an enhancement of the freedom of movement of labour and labour mobility.

There are clearly interests within the EU that seek further convergence of the social (including employee relations) systems within it, although it is important that we remain aware of the distinction between procedures and substantive matters. There would appear to have been some procedural progress but enforcement remains a problem. Those efforts that there have been to regulate substantive outcomes (equal pay) have arguably had relatively little impact.

There are clearly a number of different views on both the desirability and prospects of further convergence and upon the direction that it might take. However, there are clear signs that the traditional social protection model that has been a defining characteristic of European systems is under threat and that we may be witnessing its gradual replacement with a model throughout the EU that has much more in common with the competitive flexibility trajectory.

In this latter context we may in future witness an enhancement of the tensions between the central institutions – trying to maintain the traditional social protection model and emphasising the convergence of procedural systems and the minimum rights of employees and citizens of the EU (*see* the views of Commissioner Flynn in Exhibit 7.1) – and the various member states, resisting such developments and arguing the need for a much more flexible and competitive model in which they are able to dispense with many of these procedural constraints and the rights of employees.

Notions of partnership that mean little more than employees being more cooperative with managements in their pursuit of competitive advantage fit relatively conveniently with such competitive models.

QUESTIONS

1 Examine the nature of the Social Dialogue and the role of the Social Partners. To what extent is it correct to argue that the trade unions can now make the law?

2 Why is it that there are remaining inequalities of pay between men and women and how would you remedy the situation?

3 Consider and discuss the arguments for and against a social dimension to the single market.

4 Explain why the attitudes of the Social Partners in the UK are pro-EU.

5 How may the EWC Directive provide the opportunity for an extension of collective bargaining at a multinational level?

6 Discuss the proposition that New Labour's promotion of the notion of social partnership provides genuine opportunities for enhanced employee participation.

7 How do you see the draft Social Chapter agreed at Amsterdam affecting the rights of employees and employers and the balance of power between them?

TABLE OF CASES

Barber *v* Guardian Royal Exchange Assurance Group: C–262/88 (1990).

Coloroll Pensions Trustees Ltd *v* Russell *et al.*: C–200/91 (1994).

Danfoss case (Handels og Kontorfunktionaerernes Forbund I Danmark *v* Dansk Arbejdsgiverforening (acting for Danfoss): 109/88 (1989)).

Garland *v* British Rail Engineering: 12/81 (1982).

Kalanke *v* Freie Hansestadt Bremen: C–450/93 (1995).

Macarthys Ltd *v* Smith: 129/79 (1979) apld) (1981).

Murphy and others *v* An Bord Telecom Eirann (1988).

Vroege *v* NCIV voor Volkhuisvesting BV: C–57/93 (1994).

Warren Southampton IT July 1994.

EU DIRECTIVES AND OTHER INSTRUMENTS

Code of Practice on the Implementation of Equal Pay for Work of Equal Value for Women and Men COM (96) 336.

Communication from the Commission of the European Parliament and council on the Interpretation of the Judgement of the Court of Justice in Kalanje. COM (96) 88.

Community Charter of the Fundamental Social Rights of Workers (The Social Charter).

Council Recommendation on Childcare 92/241.

Council Recommendation 92/443 on Equity Sharing and Financial Participation. PEPPER I.

Council Resolution on Balanced Participation of Men and Women in Decision-making 95/C168/02.

Directive on the Adaptation of Working Time 93/104.

Directive on Collective Redundancies 75/129 extended by 92/56.

Directive on the Establishment of a European Works Council or a Procedure in Community Scale Undertakings and Community Scale Groups of Undertakings for the Purposes of Informing and Consulting Employees 94/45.

Directive on Equal Treatment: Occupational Social Security 86/378.

Directive on Equal Treatment: Self-employed 86/613.

Directive on Equal Treatment: State Social Security 79/7.

Directive on Parental Leave (96/34). Introduced pursuant to an agreement between the Social Partners in accordance with Article 2.2 of the Social Policy Agreement.

Directive on the Protection of Pregnant Workers: The Tenth Daughter Directive 92/85.

Directive on the Transfer of Undertakings 77/187. To be amended by the Draft Directive on Safeguarding Employees' Rights in the event of Transfers of Undertakings, Businesses or Parts of Businesses COM (94) 300.

Draft Vredeling Directive. Draft Directive on Procedures for Informing and Consulting Employees in Undertakings with Complex Structures COM (80) 423 Revised by COM (83) 292.

Draft Directive on Equal Treatment in Occupational Social Security Schemes COM (95) 186.

Draft Directive on Reversal of the Burden of Proof in Sex Discrimination Cases COM (88) 269.

Equal Pay Directive 75/117.

Equal Treatment Directive 76/207.

Green (Consultative) Paper, *Partnership for a New Organisation of Work* COM(97) 128.

PEPPER II: *Promotion of Participation by Employed Persons in Profits and Enterprise Results (Including Equity Participation) in Member States* COM (96) 697.

Proposed Directive concerning the Framework Agreement on Part-Time Work concluded by UNICE, CEEP, and the ETUC COM (97) 392 (adopted December 1997).

REFERENCES

Adnett, N. (1996) *European Labour Markets: Analysis and Policy*. London: Longman.

Carley, M. (1993) 'Social dialogue' in Gold, M. (ed.) *The Social Dimension – Employment Policy in the European Community*. Basingstoke: Macmillan.

Coopers & Lybrand (1995) *European Works Councils. Consultation and Communication in European Companies – A Survey*. London: Coopers & Lybrand.

Cox, S. (1993) 'Equal opportunities' in Gold, M (ed.) *The Social Dimension – Employment Policy in the European Community*. Basingstoke: Macmillan.

Cressey, P. (1993) 'Employee participation' in Gold, M. (ed.) *The Social Dimension – Employment Policy in the European Community*. Basingstoke: Macmillan.

Due, J., Madsen, J. S. and Jensen, C. S. (1991) 'The social dimension: convergence or diversification of industrial relations in the single European market', *Industrial Relations Journal*, 22(2), 85–102.

ETUI (1995) *Les comités d'entreprises européens: inventaire des entreprises concernées*. Brussels: European Trade Union Institute.

European Commission (1994) *White Paper on Social Policy: The Way Forward for the Unions*. Brussels: European Commission.

European Commission (1997) *Annual Report on Equal Opportunities for 1996*. Brussels: European Commission.

European Works Council Bulletin (1996) no. 3, May/June.

Eurostat (1997) *Statistics in Focus, Population and Social Conditions*, 2/1997.

Ferner, A. and Hyman, R. (eds) (1992) *Introduction in Industrial Relations in the New Europe*. Oxford: Blackwell.

Fernie, S. and Metcalf, D. (1995) 'Works Councils are the Future, but there is no need to be afraid', *Guardian*, 22 May.

Gold, M. (1993) 'Overview of the social dimension' in Gold, M. (ed.) *The Social Dimension – Employment Policy in the European Community*. Basingstoke: Macmillan.

Grahl, J. and Teague, P. (1991) 'Industrial relations trajectories and European human resource management' in Brewster, C. and Tyson, S. (eds) *International Comparisons in Human Resource Management*. London: Pitman Publishing, pp. 67–91.

Hall, M. (1994) 'Industrial relations and the social dimension' in Hyman, R. and Ferner, A. (eds) *New Frontiers in European Industrial Relations*. Oxford: Blackwell.

Hollinshead, G. and Leat, M. (1995) *Human Resource Management: An International and Comparative Perspective on the Employment Relationship*. London: Financial Times Pitman Publishing.

Hyman, R. (1995) 'Industrial relations in Europe: theory and practice,' *European Journal of Industrial Relations*, 1(1), 17–46.

Marginson, P. and Sisson, K. (1994) 'The structure of transnational capital in Europe: the emerging Euro-company and its implications for industrial relations' in Hyman, R. and Ferner, A. (eds) *New Frontiers in European Industrial Relations*. Oxford: Blackwell.

Millward, N., Stevens, M., Smart, D. and Hawes, W.R. (1992) *Workplace Industrial Relations in Transition*. Aldershot: Dartmouth.

Rivest, C. (1996) 'Voluntary European Works Councils', *European Journal of Industrial Relations*, 2(2), 235–53.

Schulten, T. (1996) 'European Works Councils: prospects of a new system of European industrial relations', *European Journal of Industrial Relations*, 2(3), 303–24.

Teague, P. (1989) *The European Community: The Social Dimension*. London: Kogan Page.

Turner, L. (1996) 'The Europeanisation of labour: structure before action', *European Journal of Industrial Relations*, 2(3), 325–44.

Visser, J. and Ebbinghaus, B. (1992) 'Making the most of diversity? European integration and transnational organisation of labour' in Greenwood, J. Grote, J.R. and Ronit, K. (eds) *Organised Interests and the European Community*. London: Sage, pp. 206–37.

ADDITIONAL READING

Leat, M. (1998) *Human Resource Issues of the European Unions*. London: Financial Times Pitman Publishing.

Chapter 8

LEGAL REGULATION OF EMPLOYMENT

Richard Snape

Learning objectives

By the end of this chapter, readers should be able to:

- understand the basic nature of law in the UK, and changing emphases in the past few decades in the fields of collective and individual rights and obligations;
- comprehend the nature of the contract of employment;
- gain an insight into basic legal provisions on discrimination and equal pay;
- consider key legal provisions in the area of unfair dismissal.

INTRODUCTION: THE COLLECTIVE AND INDIVIDUAL AMBITS OF LAW

In Great Britain, the historical tradition has been for the law to play a minimal role in regulating employee relations institutional arrangements and processes. The principle of 'voluntarism' (Clegg, 1970: 344) has been consistent with state abstention from modelling the processes of interaction between the parties through collective bargaining, and agreements made between them will not normally have the force of law. In the previous Conservative era, modifications occurred in the legal framework as part of the governmental drive to deregulate the labour market. This not only involved some reduction in the scope of protection for individuals at work, but also, most notably, those underpinning the rights of trade unions. The new Labour administration has not signalled any immediate intention to reverse the tenets of its legal inheritance regarding trade unions (Edwards *et al.*, 1997). However, British statute law can, be seen to impinge on the employment relationship in three main ways.

First, the law provides a 'floor of rights' (Kahn Freund, 1965) for the individual on matters such as unfair dismissal, redundancy, equal opportunities, maternity leave, employment rights for the disabled, the confidentiality of computerised information on personal employee data, and health and safety at work. Key statutes and statutory instruments have included the Health and Safety at Work Act 1974, the Equal Pay Act 1970, the Sex Discrimination Act 1975, the Employment Protection (Consolidation) Act 1978, the Transfer of Undertakings (Protection of Undertakings) Regulations 1981, the Data Protection Act 1984, the Trade Union Reform and Employment Rights Act, (TURERA) 1993, the Disability Discrimination Act 1995 and the Employment Rights Act 1996. A number of the main statutory principles have been enacted in response to European Directives, and such employee protection exists in parallel with rights accumulated through the precedents of common law, in which the rights and duties of employer and employee have been established through judicial decisions over time (Lewis, 1990). The 'floor of rights' has been the subject of diminution through a number of quite recent modifications. So, for example, the qualifying period for protection for unfair dismissal, including dismissal on the grounds of pregnancy, was extended to two years. This has now been overtaken by the implementation of a European Directive (via the Trade Union Reform and Employment Rights Act 1993, which states that women cannot be dismissed on grounds of pregnancy from the date their employment commences. The promotion of individual, at the expense of collective, rights is manifested also in TURERA, in providing inducements to employees to switch from trade union membership and collective bargaining to individual contracts.

Second, a traditional function of law has been to provide some underlying structural support for union organisation and collective bargaining. Over the past couple of decades, however, legal mechanisms which served to legitimise the principles of collectivism and pluralism have been whittled away through a progressive series of statutes (Dickens and Hall, 1995: 275). Not only has internal union organisation been subjected to greater regulation and scrutiny, but also organisational rights have been circumscribed. The major instruments of legislation have been the Employment Acts of 1980, 1982, 1988, 1989 and 1990, the Trade Union Act of 1984 and the Trade Union Reform and Employment Rights Act of 1993. Taken together, these Acts, which are now consolidated into the Trade Union and Labour Relations (Consolidation) Act 1992, have had the following significant effects on trade unions and their members:

- The 'closed shop', or union membership agreement, has been effectively outlawed. This was a familiar aspect of union organisation procedure until the 1980s, representing an acknowledged custom and practice by which employees would be obliged to join a recognised union within a specified period of time.

- The previous ability of unions to obtain funds through automatic 'check off' from members' salaries has been restricted, written consent now being required from members every three years. Furthermore, political funding of the Labour Party is subject to a postal ballot of members.

- In the area of union–member relations, where up until the early 1980s internal union rules had prevailed, all voting members of union executive committees are now subject to election every five years by secret postal ballot. In addition, a Commissioner for the rights of trade union members has been appointed, charged with the responsibility of assisting members who want to take legal action against unions – for example, if they feel they have been unjustifiably disciplined.

Third, the law serves to restrict the scope of lawful trade union action in respect of industrial conflict. This legal tenet has been based on the 'golden formula', established by the Trade Disputes Act 1906, which protects trade unions from legal penalties providing they act 'in contemplation or furtherance of a trade dispute'. The extent of this immunity has varied during its lengthy existence, and during the 1980s its scope was narrowed considerably through the provisions of the Trade Union Act of 1984, and subsequent pieces of legislation. Thus, only direct action against the employer in question is permissible, and the right to picket has been reduced. To be lawful, industrial action must be preceded by a postal ballot of potential strikers. Moreover, the union must now give at least seven days' notice of the fact that it intends to call industrial action on a particular day and whether this action will be continuous or discontinuous. Where a strike is unlawful, there is also provision for citizens to resort to legal action if the supply of goods and services has been affected.

The Labour government elected to power in May 1997 is committed to retaining the key elements of 1980s employment legislation on ballots, picketing and industrial action. However, a more regulatory and collectivist orientation may be signalled by its proposals to introduce measures to oblige employers to recognise unions for the purpose of collective bargaining if a majority of the relevant workforce vote for this. Similarly, provisions for a statutory minimum wage signal a return to the legal principle of providing a 'safety net' for the low paid, which was dismantled over the 1980s and 1990s. The government also aims to promote employee involvement through the implementation of employee share ownership plans, and measures to prevent discrimination against older workers and the disabled. As a signatory to the Social Chapter, a range of European measures, as discussed in the previous chapter, will exert a noticeable regulatory effect on UK employment (Edwards *et al.*, 1997). At the forefront of the European agenda are measures on European (and subsequently nationally based) works councils, maximum working hours, full employment rights for part-time workers and parental leave. Furthermore, through the 1990s, the area of health and safety at work has been elevated as a policy area, demanding systematic and planned approaches to health and safety management on the part of employers, and also broadening the definition of health concerns to encompass factors such as stress, AIDS, smoking and harassment.

The centre of gravity, therefore, in the field of employment law has shifted towards individual rights and obligations over the past couple of decades, and it is with the detail of this aspect of law that the remainder of this chapter is concerned.

■ The Contract of Employment Formalities

It is important to note that every employee has a contract, i.e. a legally binding relationship, with his or her employer. There is nothing in law which requires this contract to be written although, obviously, it is always desirable that the major terms of the contract are written to avoid possible disputes as to the rights and duties of the employee in the future. Moreover, since 1963 employees have been entitled to receive written evidence of some of these major terms. The right to written particulars of the major terms of the contract was, in fact, the first modern piece of legislation designed to protect the individual employee, with the exception of health and safety and wages legislation. It marked a clear move towards increased interventionism on behalf of Parliament within the individual employment relationship. The provisions are now contained in Section 1 of the Employment Rights Act 1996, a statute which we will become accustomed to referring to over the following pages. Thus, not later than the end of the second month of employment, the employer should have provided evidence in writing of various terms, including the following:

- names of the parties;
- commencement date of employment;
- details of pay including rate and intervals between payment;
- hours of work;
- sickness rights;
- pension rights;
- any collective agreements which are incorporated into the contract;
- a rough indication of the area of employment;
- an indication of job title;
- reference to disciplinary and grievance procedures.

Large numbers of employers fail to comply with these provisions. This does not in any way derogate from the fact of a legally binding relationship between employer and employee: the contract still exists. The employee can, however, apply to an industrial tribunal, which will draw up the requisite written statement on behalf of the employer. Claims are, needless to say, very rare.

Terms of the contract of employment

Having ascertained that there is very little in the way of formalities to the contract of employment, we will go on to analyse some of the individual terms. Any contract, and not merely an employment contract, will contain numerous terms. Some of these terms will be expressly agreed between the parties, whether or not subsequently incorporated in writing. Usually, although not always, the major terms of the contract will be so expressed: matters such as pay, hours, holidays – indeed many of the terms for which evidence should be included within the Section 1 statement above. Little can be said in general about these terms. They tend to be peculiar to the individual contract of employment. Other terms will be implied on behalf of the parties, however. These terms will apply, usually in the absence of some express provision to the contrary, whether the employer or the employee appreciates their existence or not. The implied terms are more general to all employment contracts, thus it is to these that we will pay some attention. Many of the implied terms were evolved by the courts at a time before Parliament became involved in the employment relationship. Most of the terms are creations of the judiciary, some stemming back to the nineteenth century. The legislature is still reluctant to intervene within the actual terms of the contract, with notable exceptions, in relation to equal pay and minimum notice periods, as we shall see.

■ Implied terms binding the employee

Faithful service

The first, and perhaps most important, implied obligation upon the employee is to faithfully serve his or her employer, also variously described as a duty of trust and confidence. This encompasses a whole series of fidelity obligations, of which a failure to perform will constitute a breach of contract with resulting possible disciplinary action or, in relation to a gross breach, as we shall see below, dismissal.

Incorporated within the concept of faithful service would be an obligation not to commit theft, not to defraud the employer, to cooperate with the employer and not to frustrate the common venture. A work to rule, although acting strictly within the rule book, would amount to such a breach (this was the conclusion in Secretary of State for Employment *v* ASLEF (1972)). The reason for this is that a part of the employee's unwritten duties is to further the employer's objectives at all times.

Other examples of breaches of faithful service include fighting at work, drinking at work, swearing, lateness and absenteeism, accepting secret bribes and profits, misusing confidential information and working in competition where the employee has confidential information to impart.

To prevent an employee working in competition with the employer after employment has ceased is more difficult. Here, an express contractual term must be included. This term, called a restraint of trade clause or a restrictive contract, is not favoured by English law and will be declared void unless it goes no further than needed by the employer to protect legitimate interests. Legitimate interests include trade secrets and customer contacts but not, it appears, mere competition. Moreover, the clause must extend no further in terms of time and of geographical area than required by the employer to protect his interests.

Obedience

The second implied duty imposed upon the employee is that he or she should at all times obey lawful and reasonable orders incidental to employment. Again, a failure to do this may result in disciplinary action or, in extreme cases, summary dismissal.

The employee need not obey unlawful orders. Moreover, the last few years have seen the development in the courts of the concept of an overriding term which in the absence of a clear express provision will limit the liability of the employee under the contract.

Thus, where the employee's contract contained a mobility clause whereby he could be required to move from one office to another, he needed to be given more than five days' notice of a move from Leeds to Birmingham and objected, stating that he required more time to prepare. The court held that there must be an overriding term that the express term of the contract must be exercised reasonably (United Bank *v* Akhtar (1989)). More notice of the move was therefore required. In the most famous case in this area, Johnstone *v* Bloomsbury Area Health Authority (1992), it was stated that an employer could only exercise an express term requiring the employee (a junior doctor) to be 'on call' in a reasonable fashion and in accordance with health and safety considerations. Requiring an employee to be available for work for over one hundred hours per week was unreasonable.

Care

The other major implied obligation which binds the employee is one of care. The employee must not only take reasonable care of himself and others, but also of the employer's property. A failure to do this amounts to neglect and a breach of contract, which, dependent on the seriousness of the breach, may result in disciplinary proceedings or dismissal.

■ Implied terms binding the employer

Trust and confidence (respect)

Just as the employee must faithfully serve the employer, so must the employer treat the employee with mutual trust and confidence or with respect.

Examples of breaches of respect are numerous. For instance, in Isle of Wight Tourist Board *v* Coombes (1978) a secretary overheard her superior telling a fellow employee that 'she's an intolerable bitch of a Monday morning'. Following a further altercation, she walked out of her job and claimed constructive dismissal (a type of unfair dismissal, as we shall see at a later stage in the chapter). To be successful in such a claim there must be shown to be a fundamental breach of respect, so serious that it undermines the whole working relationship. This was the case here. The secretary would never be able to work for the employer again, bearing in mind how the close personal relationship between manager and secretary had been undermined.

Likewise, where a dispute arose between employees and the employer was clearly seen to side with one group against the claimant, this was clearly a breach of respect (ATS *v* Waterhouse (1978)). Failing to provide adequate support for the employee and undermining his authority when he was found to be unable to cope with a role which he had been promoted to (Wetherall *v* Lynn (1978)) and falsely accusing an employee of incompetence in front of fellow employees (Courtaulds *v* Andrew (1977)) have also been held to constitute activities giving rise to a fundamental breach of respect and a successful claim for constructive dismissal.

Further examples of serious breaches include falsely accusing of theft, a failure to listen to grievances, failing to provide an adequate work environment, failing to look at health and safety consideration, swearing at employees, arbitrary treating an employee less favourably than his or her colleagues, and playing practical jokes on the employee.

Claims for breaches of respect are potentially numerous. Employees actually bring fewer actions than might be expected, primarily because of ignorance of the law but also due to the fact that the amount of compensation available in the event of a successful claim would rarely be sufficient to justify giving up their job.

Payment of wages

If there is one term of the employment contract that is likely, above any others, to be expressly agreed it is the payment of wages. However, what is the situation where there is no work provided for an employee due to, for instance, a period of lay off or suspension? The basic principle surprises many people. If the employee is available for work he or she is entitled to full payment even though no work is provided to do (for instance Devonald *v* Rosser (1906)) but contrast Browning *v* Crumlin Valley Collieries (1926). There is no such duty where the failure to provide work is due to circumstances beyond the employer's control. Moreover, if the employee's wages are wholly or partially based on commission, there must be provision of a reasonable amount of work to do to earn the commission, or, failing this, wages in lieu based on the commission which would reasonably have been expected.

Thus, during lay off or suspension, full pay should be paid. It is always open to the employer to expressly override this term and quite frequently it is overridden to such a great extent as to become customary not to pay wages. There are provisions, in the Employment Rights Act 1996, whereby the employee is guaranteed a minimum payment during lay off but these are rather limited in their effect and need not concern us here.

The provision of work

The implied term with respect to whether or not work must be provided for the employee to do is less clear cut. It appears that, normally, if the employer is prepared to pay the employee, the latter cannot complain that no work is provided to do. However, there are some exceptions to this, most notably, as we have seen above, where the employee is commission based and entitled to be provided with work in order to produce results. The other situations where work must contractually be provided for the employee to do are limited but include highly skilled employees, who should be provided with work in order to maintain and enhance their skills.

Indemnity

There is a fourth implied term that the employer must make good any out-of-pocket losses which were directly incurred as a consequence of the employee performing his or her employment duties. An obvious example of the duty to indemnify the employee would be the payment of expenses for travel, meals and accommodation. In fact, in circumstances where expenses are likely to have to be paid, the employer will usually include express provision as to how much will be paid, and major problems seldom arise.

Care

The final implied duty automatically imposed upon the employer is to take reasonable care of his workers. This involves setting up a reasonably safe system of work including matters such as training, instruction, protective equipment and clothing, safety procedures, safe access and exits, fire drills, etc. There must also be reasonably safe plant and appliances, including vehicles, tools and machinery and reasonably safe fellow employees who do not, through foolishness or incompetence, put others at risk.

The employer's duty is not usually strict; he or she need only act reasonably and is not necessarily liable for every accident which occurs within the workplace. A failure to act reasonably which results in an accident may give rise to both a claim for damages by the injured employee and possible prosecution and a fine, or, rarely, imprisonment for a breach of the Health and Safety at Work Act 1974. This latter piece of legislation does not in itself give rise to contractual terms of which the employee may directly take the benefit. It does, however, represent the culmination of well over a century of Parliamentary intervention aimed at preventing health and safety disputes arising. The contractual claim, unfortunately, only provides a remedy after the breach has occurred.

■ Variation of the contract of employment

Finally, with respect to contracts, something will be said about variation of the contract. It may be important for the employer to be able to vary the contract to meet changes in circumstances. For instance, a promotion or a pay rise will usually involve a variation of contract. These usually involve little dispute. However, if the employer intends to reduce pay, or, for instance, increase or change hours this may result in disagreement.

The basic principle is that any variation must be mutual between both employer and employee. The employer cannot unilaterally impose new terms upon the employer. Agreement may be implied, however, where the employee works a new system for a sufficient time period without objection. The length of time required for a variation depends on the type of term being varied and whether it would be reasonable to expect the employee to object within a comparatively short period or not: usually up to two years will give rise to an implied variation. For example, in Armstrong Whitworth Rolls *v* Mustard (1971), the employee worked for 60 hours per week for seven years. Despite the fact that his original contract stated that he was employed on a 40-hour week, his working without objection for such a long term resulted in an implied variation by conduct.

DISCRIMINATION IN EMPLOYMENT

■ Introduction

There are three areas within employment where discrimination is prohibited: on the grounds of sex, race and disability. We will look at the legislation covering each of these three areas one by one. Particular emphasis is given here to a discussion of legislation against sex discrimination; the treatment of race discrimination by the law is very similar to that of sex discrimination, hence this area can be dealt with comparatively briefly. The Disability Discrimination Act 1995 is very recent, having come into force on 2 December 1996.

■ Sex discrimination

Sex discrimination is prohibited by two mutually exclusive pieces of legislation. The Sex Discrimination Act 1975 covers discrimination in, among other areas, employment but only where the discrimination occurs outside the contract of employment. Areas thus covered by the Act would include discriminatory advertisements, recruitment, job interviews, terms on which employment is offered, training, promotion, dismissal and harassment.

The Equal Pay Act 1970 deals with discrimination on the grounds of sex within the employment contract, most obviously with respect to pay but also, for example, with respect to holidays and sickness entitlements.

Any student in this area also needs to be aware of Article 119 of the Treaty of Rome, which specifies that member states must provide and subsequently maintain equal pay for equal work between the sexes. Article 119 gives individuals rights within member states which may be greater than the national legislation. If this is so, the European provision prevails. In addition there are two European Directives dealing with equal treatment and equal conditions. The Directives are secondary pieces of legislation which should subsequently be enacted within UK law. Prior to this they do not bind private individuals but only governmental bodies and emanations of government.

An individual may therefore bring an action against a governmental body for failing to comply with a Directive. Most famously, this is what happened to the Ministry of Defence when, in 1991, its policy of dismissing pregnant women was held to be a breach of the Equal Treatment Directive regardless of the fact that at the time it was excluded from the provisions of the Sex Discrimination Act 1975.

The Sex Discrimination Act 1975

As we have already seen, the Sex Discrimination Act 1975 prevents discrimination outside the contract of employment. It gives rights to both men and women and also prevents discrimination on the grounds of marital status. A moot point at the time of writing is whether homosexuals can take the benefit of the Act. The European Court of Justice surprised everyone when they held that homosexuality was outside the scope of the legislation (Grant *v* South West Trains (1998)). However, legislation to the contrary seems likely in the future.

The Act prevents three types of discrimination: direct, indirect, and victimisation. We now turn our attention to each of these.

Direct discrimination

Direct discrimination involves treating a person less favourably on the grounds of their sex. If there is another reason for the less favourable treatment, for example, the applicant for a job is under-qualified, or unreliable or not physically strong enough, then a failure to employ is, of course, perfectly permissible. However, what an employer must be sure of avoiding is making assumptions about a particular sex, such as, for example, all women being weak and therefore refusing to consider any woman for a job requiring physical strength. Applicants must be considered in accordance with their individual merits and not their sex.

Usually, direct discrimination is the most obvious type of discrimination, the only problem being met involving proving that discrimination has occurred. In less obvious circumstances, the courts have adopted a 'but for' test to determine whether or not discrimination has occurred, i.e. the question is asked whether the person would be treated in the same way 'but for' his or her sex. Thus, in a non-employment case, James *v* Eastleigh Borough Council (1991), Mr and Mrs James were both aged 62. The local swimming baths allowed those beyond state pension age to use the baths free of charge. Mrs James, being over state pension age for women, was allowed in free; Mr James, not being of state pension age for men, had to pay 75 pence. This was direct discrimination against Mr James: but for his sex he would not have had to pay. Although state pension ages are currently excluded from the legislation, benefits linked to state pension age are not. In an extremely important European Court of Justice decision, Barber *v* Guardian Royal Exchange (1990), it was further held that differential ages between men and women for qualifying for an occupational pension were discriminatory. Another area of direct discrimination which has caused problems is with respect to dismissals of women who are unable to perform their work due to pregnancy. In Webb *v* EMO Air Cargo (1994), the European Court of Justice made it clear that the dismissal of a woman on an indefinite contract connected with her being pregnant (in the present case because she was unavailable for work at a critical time) would automatically be discriminatory. Thus, in a subsequent case, Rees *v* Apollo Watch Repairs (1996), the employee took maternity leave. During her absence it was found that her replacement, also a woman, was much more efficient at carrying out the work and she was subsequently dismissed, the replacement being kept on in her place. This amounted to sex discrimination. The only reason the employer knew that the employee was incapable of doing her job was because she was taking maternity leave. The dismissal was therefore connected with her sex.

Indirect discrimination

Indirect sex discrimination is usually more insidious than direct discrimination. Frequently, employers will not realise that their actions may well constitute indirect discrimination. Management must always be aware of the possibility of their actions constituting this type of discrimination.

A claim for indirect discrimination depends on four conditions being met:

1 the employer attaches terms or conditions to a particular job;
2 the terms or conditions are such that the proportion of women who can comply with them is considerably smaller than the proportion of men;
3 the terms or conditions cannot be shown to be justified irrespective of sex;
4 there is no objective justification for the terms or conditions.

If all these four requirements are met, then the applicant will have a claim for sex discrimination.

Examples of indirect sex discrimination are numerous. In one of the earliest cases, Price *v* Civil Service Commission (1977), application for a post included an age criterion, that the applicant must be between the ages of $17\frac{1}{2}$ and 28. Price, a woman aged 36, argued that this amounted to sex discrimination (there being at present no anti-age discrimination legislation in the United Kingdom). The requirement was held to be discriminatory in the absence of a justification. Women are more likely to have career breaks to have and bring up children within these ages. Considerably fewer women can therefore comply with the condition as to age. As the applicant had herself had such a career break, she had a potential claim.

In London Underground *v* Edwards (1998), Edwards, a single mother, argued that the introduction of a shift system requiring her to start work as a train driver early in the morning was discriminatory. This was held to be potentially the case. Women are more likely to be single parents who look after young children and who are unable to find child-care facilities at anti-social hours. Edwards herself was a single parent and thus subjected to a detriment. Moreover, in the circumstances there could not be said to be any justification in requiring Edwards to work anti-social hours. There were enough train drivers who did not have child-care difficulties to cover for her. Refusing to consider job sharing for a female employee on returning to work after maternity leave has also been found on the facts to be discriminatory. See, for instance, Given *v* Scottish Power (1994). Women are more likely to be bringing up young children and thus to require job sharing or part-time work. Frequently, a refusal of job sharing will, of course, be justified on objective grounds. However, this was not the case in this particular dispute.

It has been recognised that a mobility clause, requiring the employee to move from one locality to another on being given notice, was potentially discriminatory against women, who were more likely to be secondary earners in a relationship than men and who thus could not move work unless their partner was also able to do so (R *v* Secretary of State *ex parte* Seymour-Smith and Perez (1997)). Of course, mobility clauses may always be justified: the employer will not usually include such a clause unless it is a reasonably necessary requirement of the job. Nevertheless, without such a justification, the clause may well be discriminatory.

Perhaps the greatest developments with respect to indirect sex discrimination, and among the greatest developments in relation to individual employment law of recent years, involves not an employer being faced with a potential claim, but action being brought against the government under European law claiming that various statutory requirements for obtaining individual rights were discriminatory.

Thus, until 1994, part-time workers (i.e. those who worked less than sixteen hours per week, or, if employed for five or more years, less than eight hours per week) were unable to claim statutory unfair dismissal and redundancy rights (R *v* Secretary of State *ex parte* Equal Opportunities Commission (1994)).

The Equal Opportunities Commission, the body charged with overseeing and enforcing anti-sex discrimination legislation, has successfully argued that such a limitation of part-time workers' rights was discriminatory against women. It is undoubtedly the case that considerably fewer women can comply with the requirement of full-time work as a condition of claiming statutory rights: some 85 per cent of part-timers are women. The House of Lords went on to find that there was no justification for excluding part-timers from the same rights as full-timers. As a consequence part-time workers, who have the requisite two years' continuous service, have the same employment rights as full-timers have on termination of the contracts. A subsequent European Court of Justice (in the case of R *v* Secretary of State for Employment *ex parte* Seymour-Smith and Perez (1997)) decision has, in a similar manner, extended part-time workers' rights to join any occupational pension scheme of the employer on the same basis as any full-time worker.

It has also been argued that the very existence of a two-year qualifying period before an employee has any right to claim unfair dismissal or redundancy is discriminatory against women. The argument goes that women are more likely to have career breaks to bring up children than men and are thus less able to show the requisite length of service. The implications of a finding in favour of the female applicants would be quite enormous for employers and employees alike: there would be no right to dismiss by merely giving a short contractual notice period or wages in lieu of notice prior to the two-year qualifying point. Currently, the issue is being considered by the European Court of Justice (in the case of R *v* Secretary of State for Employment *ex parte* Seymour-Smith and Perez (1997)) and a final decision can be expected in the near future. This represents yet another illustration of the inevitability of European law intervening to an increasing extent in UK employment law. Interestingly, this is occurring regardless of whether or not the Social Chapter is to be implemented.

Victimisation

The final type of recognised sex discrimination is the rarest: victimisation. This occurs where an employee, regardless of sex, is treated less favourably due to making allegations of discrimination, or giving evidence, or bringing proceedings or intending to do any of these things. Claims under this head are comparatively rare and a detailed discussion of victimisation need not concern us here.

Remedies

An action alleging sex discrimination must be brought in an industrial tribunal and the application must normally be made within three months of the relevant act of discrimination which is being complained of. If, the employee is successful, the tribunal will make a declaration as to the fact, recommendations as to the future conduct of the employer, and an order for compensation.

Compensation is meant to put the successful applicant in the same position as he or she would have been in if no discrimination had occurred. It is usually primarily based on financial loss suffered by the applicant, for instance, time out of work and lost wages due to being dismissed on the grounds of sex. This will include future loss of wages based on the likelihood of the applicant being able to find employment in the future, there being a duty to take positive steps to try to find suitable work.

Damages may also include an element to reflect injury to feelings. This part of the claim should not normally be substantial. Despite some well-publicised awards, compensation for sex discrimination claims in 1993–94 was only some £5700.

The Equal Pay Act 1970

The second piece of anti-sex discrimination legislation is the Equal Pay Act 1970. This works primarily by inserting an equality clause into the contract of employment whereby, other things being equal, men and women are entitled to the same terms and conditions, including pay.

As with the Sex Discrimination Act 1975, the Act applies equally to both men and women. Where an applicant wishes to claim equal pay or conditions he or she must first find a comparator or comparators, i.e. a person or people of the opposite sex working for the same employer at the same establishment who has more favourable terms. The comparator must also be engaged in one of three types of comparable work, that is:

1 like work; or

2 work rated as equivalent; or

3 work of equal value.

Like work

Like work is perhaps the most obvious type of work to provide a comparison. It amounts to 'work of the same or a broadly similar nature such that any differences are not of practical importance'. Little need be said about this; suffice to say that the comparable jobs need not be identical but merely broadly similar and tribunals have proved willing to take a wide view of what amounts to broadly similar work. Thus, in Capper Pass *v* Lawton (1978), female cooks providing meals for the company directors were engaged in like work to male chefs who provided food in the canteen for the staff. They were thus able to claim a pay rise to bring them into line with their male colleagues (*see* Chapter 10).

Work rated as equivalent

Work will be rated as equivalent if it has been given equal value in accordance with a properly conducted job evaluation scheme which has been carried out by the employer. Nothing more need be said about job evaluation at this point, except to say that if there is a finding of equal value under such a scheme, employees engaged in disparate types of work may be entitled to claim equal pay and conditions.

Work of equal value

The concept of work of equal value was first introduced in 1983 to meet the problem that the conducting of a job evaluation scheme is purely voluntary. If there was no such scheme in existence and no employees of the opposite sex engaged on like work with whom comparison could be made, then there could, as originally drafted, be no equal pay claim. In 1982 the European Court of Justice found that UK law, as it stood, did not fully provide for equal pay between the sexes. Reluctantly, the government had to bow to this European pronouncement and implement a new and important means of comparison. The concept of work of equal value allows the employee to present his or her own job evaluation, which may in its turn be disputed by the employer. In the event of a dispute, the industrial tribunal may appoint an independent expert who will conduct his or her own scheme from which a decision may be reached.

Genuine material differences

There is one final issue which raises itself before a decision as to whether an employee is entitled to equal pay and conditions to the comparator can be made. A large number of differences in pay, for example, between people performing even identical jobs, are nothing to do with sex. They are said to be genuine material differences other than sex. Thus, if there is such a genuine material difference which justifies different levels of pay, a potential applicant will have no claim. Examples of genuine material differences include seniority, level of qualifications, degree of responsibility and red circling – that is, where an employee's job has been downgraded, that employee may have been allowed to keep the previous, higher, pay.

In addition, market forces may act as a genuine material difference. Thus, in the case of Rainey *v* Greater Glasgow Health Authority (1987), male prosthetists were paid a higher wage than the female employee to attract them into working in the public sector. This did not constitute discrimination as there was a genuine reason for offering the higher wage. On the other hand, a local authority has failed in its argument that school dinner ladies should be paid a lower level of wages than various males it employs as this was necessary to ensure that the employer was the successful tenderer for the services. A market force argument could not be used to ensure that a traditionally female-dominated group received less pay than male-dominated groups of employees (Ratcliffe *v* North Yorkshire (North Riding) County Council (1995)).

■ Race discrimination

Race discrimination is covered by the Race Relations Act 1976. There is no corresponding European legislation and, indeed, in European law, as yet, there is no obligation to prevent race discrimination. In its scope it is very similar, and drafted in similar terms, to the Sex Discrimination Act 1975. Thus there are similar concepts of direct discrimination, indirect discrimination and victimisation, although there is one further type of discrimination: segregation. This arises where different racial groups are treated no less favourably but are separated from one another by the employer and perform distinct roles.

The Race Relations Act 1976, unlike the Sex Discrimination Act 1975, also provides for discrimination both outside the employment contract and within it – for instance, in relation to wages and holidays.

Race is defined as including 'colour, race, nationality and national or ethnic origins'. The Act is therefore wider in its scope than race *per se*. It does not, however, directly prevent religious discrimination. Contrary to much popular belief, religious discrimination is not unlawful in Great Britain (although it is in Northern Ireland, where there are separate provisions). In two situations, particular religions are seen as being synonymous with particular racial groups and so subject to discrimination on the grounds of race. These two religions are Judaism and Sikhism. On the other hand, a claim by a Rastafarian to constitute a member of a separate racial group has failed.

Much of what has already been said about sex discrimination is equally applicable to race discrimination. It will suffice here to give some examples of potentially indirect race discrimination. Seemingly innocuous acts of the employer such as attaching an English language requirement or qualification to a job application may constitute race discrimination as considerably fewer members of ethnic minorities may be able to meet the requirement where English is their second language. Of course, the requirement may always be justified and would in a large number of jobs be an objectively reasonable condition to meet. There would, therefore, be no discrimination.

Thus, where the majority of the workforce were Moslems, the employer's failure to allow them to take part of their annual leave during a Moslem festival constituted indirect race discrimination. Although Moslems do not constitute a separate racial group, Asians, who do constitute a separate race, are more likely to be Moslems than the rest of the population. As there was no justification for not adapting holidays to cater for the Moslem festival, race discrimination was proven (Hussain *v* J H Walker (1996)).

■ Disability discrimination

The final proscribed area of discrimination in Great Britain is also the most recent: disability discrimination. Again, this is a purely British piece of legislation with no European equivalent.

The employment provisions of the Disability Discrimination Act 1995 came into force on 2 December 1996. The passage of the Act through Parliament proved controversial, with the Government refusing to support an alternative Civil Rights (Disability) Bill which promised to introduce much more far-reaching obligations on employers. The Act that was eventually passed is a much watered-down piece of legislation. It does, however, introduce a major new limitation to the managerial prerogative in determining who to employ or dismiss, and the terms on which employment exists (although not as great a limitation as would have existed if the Private Members Civil Rights (Disability) Bill had been adopted). The provisions are not as far reaching as those of sex and race discrimination. One major limitation to the effectiveness of the new law is that small employers, employing fewer than twenty staff, are excluded.

A disability is defined as 'a physical or mental impairment which has a substantial long-term adverse effect on a person's ability to carry out normal day-to-day activities'. It thus includes both physical and mental illness or injury as long as the illness is sufficiently recognised by a substantial body of medical opinion. The illness must also be more than minor or trivial in its effect and be long term in that it must last for at least a year or, if the illness is terminal, for the rest of the person's life.

The definition of a disability goes on to include past disabilities, i.e. once the impairment can be shown to constitute a disability within the Act, then the applicant is protected against possible future discrimination. Progressive conditions such as multiple sclerosis, HIV and cancer are also caught by the definition in the Act even though they do not as yet have a substantial long-term adverse effect. All that is required is a likelihood that there will be, in the future, such an effect. Genetic predispositions towards a particular illness are not however covered until the condition manifests itself.

Conditions that are able to be treated by drugs or by artificial aids will still constitute disabilities. Thus, for instance, those with artificial limbs, hearing aids, or on medication which remedies the disability, such as certain types of epilepsy, will all come within the provisions of the Act. The one exception to this is the wearing of spectacles. Providing the glasses perform their function, the wearer is not categorised as being disabled. Certain types of mainly anti-social illnesses are also expressly excluded from the definition of a disability – for example, kleptomania, arson, voyeurism, sado-masochism, and, surprisingly, hay fever.

Finally, the disability must have a substantial long-term adverse effect on ability to carry out normal day-to-day activities. There is an exhaustive list of such activities, including:

- mobility;
- manual dexterity;
- speech, hearing and eyesight;
- confidence;
- physical co-ordination;
- ability to lift and carry normal objects;
- ability to concentrate, learn and understand;
- perception of the risk of danger.

Once a disability is established, the employer must ensure that there is no direct discrimination, i.e. that the disabled job applicant or employee is not treated less favourably on the grounds of his or her disability.

There is, note, no concept of indirect discrimination within the Disability Discrimination Act 1995, although victimisation is rendered unlawful. Moreover, the employer may always go on to justify direct disability discrimination by showing that the reason for the less favourable treatment was a substantial and not a trivial one. However, finally, the Act goes on to say that there can be no objective justification of discrimination by the employer if he has failed to make reasonable adjustments, either to the manner of the work or to the workplace itself, in order to accommodate the disabled person and has failed to ensure that he or she is not put at a substantial disadvantage vis-à-vis able-bodied applicants or members of staff.

Example

Suppose the employer requires someone for a particular job, part of which requires an ability to type. The applicant is partially sighted and thus within the statutory definition of being disabled.

The employer must not treat the applicant less favourably than others because of the disability, i.e. he must ignore the disability when deciding whether or not to employ. Thus, if regardless of the disability, the applicant was not the best person for the job, their being turned down will not constitute disability discrimination. Furthermore, the employer may take into account the applicant's poor eyesight if he is justified in doing so. If, for instance, a large part of the work involves reading and typing, then there may well be a clear justification of the refusal to employ. Finally, however, the employer must consider reasonable adjustments which might be made in order to accommodate the disabled applicant. These may, dependent on the circumstances, include provision of a Braille keyboard, or a reader or interpreter, or requiring another employee to perform certain tasks. The great unknown in this example is how far reasonable adjustments might be expected to go. The government anticipated, in the passage of the Disability Discrimination Bill through Parliament, an initial cost of some £200 per disabled employee. This is, to say the least, a small sum of money. Whether the tribunals and courts take such a conservative view as to the scope of the employer's liability in the future remains to be seen. Early indications from industrial tribunal decisions do not look hopeful for the disabled applicant, however.

Remedies for disability discrimination

The remedies available to a person who has been subjected to unjustified disability discrimination closely mirror those available to a claimant under the Sex Discrimination Act 1975. Thus, any application must be made to an industrial tribunal within three months of the discriminatory act complained of. If the applicant is successful, there will be a declaration, recommendations as to the future, and compensation. The compensation will be without financial limit and will reflect both financial loss suffered by the applicant and injury to feelings.

DISMISSAL FROM EMPLOYMENT

There are three potential claims that may be made where an employee is dismissed by the employer. These are:

1 wrongful dismissal;

2 unfair dismissal;

3 redundancy.

The first two claims overlap to some extent and the employee must choose the action that will provide the greatest amount of compensation. Usually this will be unfair dismissal. However, for those on long fixed-term contracts, or for those with little service with the employer, a wrongful dismissal claim will, as we shall see, be more beneficial.

Redundancy is slightly different. Here, the employer will have quite lawfully dismissed the employee. However, if the reason for dismissal was due to a lack of work then the employee will be entitled to compensation by way of a redundancy payment. This concept was introduced by the Redundancy Payments Act in 1965, the second major piece of Parliamentary intervention of the 1960s into the individual employment relationship and the rights of the employer to freely negotiate the nature of the relationship with the employee. The original 1965 Act represented part of a growing recognition by government that employers should have a status of irremoveability in their job, regardless of what might be said in their individually negotiated contract. Employees, it might be argued, do not have the bargaining capacity to enter into terms which are always favourable to themselves. The employer should be forced to accept that employees have rights in their job. If there is no work available for the employees, they should be entitled to a sum of money, determined by their length of service, which reflects the loss of a proprietary right in their job.

We now look at the three claims in some detail, dwelling on the most frequent: unfair dismissal.

◼ Wrongful dismissal

A claim for wrongful dismissal basically amounts to a claim that the employer has unlawfully breached the contract of employment by terminating it otherwise than by its terms. As the employee is claiming such a breach, the employer is always able to defend such an action by either showing that he lawfully terminated the contract or by showing that, in fact, he was merely responding to an employee breach of contract which itself brought the contract to an end and which justified dismissal by the employer.

The employer may lawfully terminate the contract of employment and avoid a claim for wrongful dismissal (although not unfair dismissal, as we shall see) by giving the employee the correct notice period. All contracts contain a notice period, which may be either express or implied. Should the employee be on a fixed-term contract, then, in the absence of any break clause allowing it to be brought to an end early, the employee must be allowed to work out the fixed term. An implied notice period will operate in the absence of any express period and will depend on the employee's length of service and degree of seniority. Highly senior and long-serving members of staff may be entitled to between six months and one year implied notice. The average employee is probably only entitled to a matter of weeks, however. In addition to the above, the Employment Rights Act 1996 is the latest in a long line of pieces of legislation which provides that all employees are entitled to a statutory minimum notice period, depending on their length of service (Table 8.1).

It should be noted that these notice periods are statutory minima. If the contract provides for a greater period, either expressly or implicity, this greater period will prevail.

The other manner in which an employer may avoid an action for wrongful dismissal is by showing that the employee is in fundamental breach of contract and that he is merely responding to this employee breach. The types of action which would give rise to a fundamental breach by the employee justifying dismissal include gross misconduct, gross neglect and gross insubordination – very much the same types of action which would give

◼ Table 8.1 Statutory minimum notice periods

Length of service	Length of notice
After four weeks	One week
Four weeks to two years	Two weeks
Two years to three years	Three weeks
Three years to four years	Four weeks
⋮	⋮
After more than twelve years	Twelve weeks

rise to a defence to an unfair dismissal action. We will therefore look at this in more detail shortly, when discussing unfair dismissal.

Should an employer wrongfully dismiss the employee, then the latter has six years in which to bring a claim for damages for breach of contract. The aim of such damages is to put the employee in the same position as he or she would have been in if the contract had been performed. Thus, the employee will be able to claim wages for the notice period which should have been given, plus any lost commission and lost fringe benefits such as a company car. However, the compensation will be reduced to reflect the fact that the wages would have attracted tax and National Insurance. Furthermore, if another job is found by the employee during the notice period, the money earned in the employment will be deducted as the employee would not have been able to earn these wages if he or she had still been in the previous employment. Moreover, the employee is under a positive duty to mitigate (minimise) his or her loss and must actively seek comparable new employment. Should the employee fail to do so, the wages will be reduced anyway. If no new work is found then any benefits received during the notice period will be deducted.

■ Unfair dismissal

Unfair dismissal is by far the commonest claim to be made in connection with termination of the employment contract. There are some 40 000 such claims made every year to employment tribunals, although somewhat less than one-third of these actually make it all the way to a full tribunal hearing.

Unfair dismissal, unlike wrongful dismissal, is a statutory claim arising through an Act of Parliament. It was originally introduced by the Industrial Relations Act 1971 although the provisions are now contained in the Employment Rights Act 1996. This original Act went one stage on from the Redundancy Payments Act 1965 and represented a further recognition of a status of irremoveability in favour of employees who could show a certain length of service. Regardless of the contract, after (currently) two years in employment with the employer, the employee has a right to his or her job which cannot merely be ended by giving a notice to quit. The law gives every employee to whom it applies a right not to be unfairly dismissed, regardless of the contractual notice period. However, not all employees may avail themselves of a claim for unfair dismissal. Certain categories are excluded. The most important exclusions are:

1 Employees who are continuously employed by the employer for less than two years. As we have already seen when discussing sex discrimination, at the time of writing this exclusion is subject to a referral to the European Court of Justice as being potentially discriminatory against women. What will happen to this, the most important exclusion, remains to be seen.

2 Employees on a fixed-term contract of more than two years who expressly exclude their rights in writing. Unbeknown to many employers and, indeed, employees, there is a right to claim unfair dismissal at the end of a fixed-term contract if this is not renewed. Employers can avoid such a claim by requiring the employee to sign an express exclusion of any rights they may have prior to the contract being entered into.

3 Employees who have passed normal retirement age. Normal retirement age is what it says it is, i.e. the age at which people would be normally expected to retire in that particular employment. If there is no normal retirement age within the establishment then the relevant age is deemed to be 65.

4 Employees who ordinarily work outside Great Britain. If an employee's base of operation is normally outside Great Britain then he or she has no right to claim unfair dismissal.

Having established that an employee is not excluded from making a claim for unfair dismissal, the next stage is to show that the employee has actually been dismissed. Usually, the fact that there has been a dismissal is quite clear from the surrounding circumstances. However, if there is a dispute, the burden is upon the employee to show that he or she has actually been dismissed.

There are three types of dismissal for unfair dismissal purposes:

1 The employer terminates the contract with or without notice. This is the most common and, indeed, the most obvious type of dismissal. The employee is told that he or she has been dismissed. Questions may arise over semantics, however, and if, by the words used, the employer intended to dismiss the employee. Here the words that the employee relies upon to show a dismissal must be construed as a reasonable person would construe them. Thus, in Futty *v* Brekkes (1974) in the course of an argument between Mr Futty, a fish filleter, and his supervisor, the employee was told 'If you don't like the job you can f*** off.' Mr Futty left employment and claimed unfair dismissal. The tribunal found for the employer. There had not in fact been a dismissal but a resignation. The employer had given Mr Futty the choice of whether to stay or to leave and he had chosen the latter alternative.

2 A fixed-term contract ends without being renewed. As we saw above, and contrary to the belief of most employers, an employee has been dismissed and is thus able to claim unfair dismissal if he or she is working on a fixed-term contract which is not renewed. Of course, the employee must have two years' overall service and the employer may always expressly exclude the right to claim in writing. Moreover, the employer can always show that the dismissal was in fact fair. Nevertheless, many employees could make use of this provision and bring an unfair dismissal action. In fact, claims under this head are rare, largely due to employee ignorance.

3 The employee terminates the contract, with or without notice, because of the employer's conduct. We have met this type of dismissal earlier when discussing the contract of employment. The claim is one of constructive dismissal, and the conduct justifying the employee in walking out must amount to a fundamental breach of contract. In Futty *v* Brekkes, above, the employee claimed a constructive dismissal in the alternative. He failed: there was no breach of respect or mutual trust and confidence in the circumstances as swearing was all too common on the fish filleting floor.

If the employee cannot show that he or she has been dismissed then, inevitably, any claim for unfair dismissal must fail. Examples of termination of the contract that do not amount to a dismissal include resignation, mutual termination where both employer and employee jointly agree to bring the relationship to an end, and frustration.

Frustration of the employment contract is rare. It occurs where an unforeseen intervening event beyond the control of the parties occurs which renders substantial performance of the contract impossible. If this happens then both employer and employee are automatically relieved of their obligations. Examples of frustrating events within the employment relationship include long-term illness of the employee with little hope of being able to perform the contract in the future, and prison.

■ The types of fair dismissal

Merely because an employee has been dismissed does not mean that he or she will succeed in a claim for unfair dismissal. It is always open to the employer to justify the reason for the dismissal and show that it was fair, although in practice any attempt to show that a constructive dismissal is fair will be fraught with difficulty.

There are five potentially fair reasons for dismissing the employee, contained in the Employment Rights Act 1996. These are:

1 incapability or lack of qualifications;

2 misconduct;

3 redundancy;

4 where continued employment is in breach of statute;

5 some other substantial reason.

If the employer can show that the dismissal was due to one or more of these reasons then the industrial tribunal which hears the claim, must then decide whether the employer has acted fairly, i.e., in the words of the statute, 'in accordance with equity and the substantial merits of the case'. If the employer has acted fairly then the dismissal will be fair; if not, or if the employer cannot show that a potentially fair reason for dismissal exists, then any dismissal will be unfair and the employee will win his or her case.

Before moving on and looking at the potentially fair reasons for dismissal individually, something should be said about procedure. An employer should, of course, have a procedure in place to deal with any dismissal. This may include a disciplinary procedure relating to cases of misconduct, or a redundancy selection procedure where there is insufficient work available for the employee.

Adherence to a fair and reasonable procedure is a very good pointer towards the fairness of any dismissal. On the other hand, a failure to follow the set procedure may result in a successful claim of unfair dismissal being made against the employer. Many a successful applicant could have been quite fairly dismissed had the employer followed the correct procedure.

Above all, an employer should always be prepared to carry out a proper investigation prior to any dismissal. This is the effect of the seminal case of Polkey v Dayton (1987), where the House of Lords made clear that an investigation would usually be an essential prerequisite for any fair dismissal regardless of the fact that, with hindsight and in full knowledge of the facts, the employer would have been quite justified in dismissing the employee.

Having said this, we now turn our attention to the potentially fair reasons for dismissal, and a discussion of how the employer must behave to act fairly when faced with such a reason.

Incapacity or lack of qualifications

This heading may be conveniently broken down into several aspects. The first is _long-term illness_. As we have already seen, if the employee is absent from work due to a long-term illness, this may have the effect of frustrating the employment contract without the need for a dismissal. Industrial tribunals are guarded against such a finding, however, as it takes out of their control any discussion of the reasonableness of the employer's behaviour.

Thus, it is much better for the employer to dismiss the employee and then try to justify his behaviour on the grounds of incapability. Whether it is reasonable to dismiss an employee who is genuinely ill depends on several factors, such as the nature of the illness, how long it has lasted and how long it is likely to last, the length of service and how long employment was likely to last, whether the employee is likely to be able to perform his or her duties on return to work, the need of the employer to find a permanent replacement, the possibility of the employer accruing further obligations, for instance with respect to an unfair dismissal claim, and whether sick pay is still being paid. Moreover, it would almost certainly be necessary to seek medical advice prior to deciding whether or not to dismiss. Above all, the employer must act reasonably and compassionately towards the employee. Use of any disciplinary procedure, for instance, is unacceptable.

Second, there may be *a series of short-term illnesses* which over a period of time result in the employee being absent from work for a substantial time period. Here, medical advice should once more be consulted. The employer may also be justified in bringing into play any disciplinary procedure and warning the employee. If the illnesses are genuine, this may have the effect of encouraging the employee to see a doctor. If the employee is not genuinely ill then he or she may think twice about taking time off in the future (see, for instance, International Sports *v* Thompson (1980)).

A third type of incapability may occur where the employee is *inherently incapable* of performing his or her job. As the employee must have two years' service to bring any claim, presumably this is likely to arise not when employment commences but when, for instance, the employee is promoted and cannot perform the new job or where new technology is introduced which the employee is unable to adapt to.

In situations such as these the employer must act reasonably by considering alternative jobs that the employee may be able to do or by offering adequate instructions, training, supervision and materials to enable the employee to do the work. If none of these will help and if no suitable alternative jobs exist then the employer will be justified in dismissal.

Fourth, the employee may *not be performing the job to the best of his or her ability* due to neglect. Here, the employee is quite able to perform the work but is not doing so to the best of his or her ability. This type of incapability is perhaps more akin to misconduct. It will therefore be appropriate for the employer to initiate disciplinary proceedings and, with respect to gross neglect, the employer may, after an adequate investigation, be justified in summary dismissal.

Finally, the employee may be dismissed for *not having the correct qualifications* to do the work. This is in fact rare. To dismiss on this ground the holding of the qualification must be a necessary part of the contract of employment as opposed to being merely convenient. Moreover, even then the employer must act reasonably when faced with an employee who fails to obtain a particular qualification, for instance by considering whether the employee is likely to obtain the qualification if given another chance.

Misconduct

Misconduct is perhaps the most obvious reason for which an employer might wish to dismiss. It is also the obvious situation in which the use of any disciplinary code is appropriate, remembering once more that a dismissal is likely to be unfair on purely procedural grounds if the employer fails to carry out an adequate investigation.

An employer may, of course, be justified in dismissing summarily for a one-off act of gross misconduct without the need to use any warning procedure. Most disciplinary codes will make clear the types of act which the employer deems to constitute gross misconduct justifying summary dismissal.

One particular act of misconduct which almost certainly justifies summary dismissal is where the employer is satisfied, after an investigation, that the employee has committed theft or fraud against him or her. In this situation it is important to remember that the employer is not acting as a criminal prosecutor and that he or she need not be satisfied that the theft has occurred on a criminal burden of proof, i.e. beyond all reasonable doubt.

Thus, in British Home Stores *v* Burchell (1978) it was stated that three requirements must be met before an employer can dismiss someone suspected of theft:

1   the employer must have carried out investigations;

2   the employer must believe the employee to be guilty;

3   both of the above must be reasonable.

It is thus quite possible for an employee who is prosecuted for theft to be found not guilty in the criminal courts but nevertheless to have been fairly dismissed.

Moreover, the employer may, where appropriate, carry out blanket dismissals of two or more employees whom he or she believes may have been guilty of theft. For example, in Whitbread PLC *v* Thomas (1988) four employees were dismissed from an off-licence where there had been a long history of theft of stock. Thorough investigations had been carried out and no culprit(s) could be identified. Nevertheless, as any of the staff could have committed the offences and as there had been reasonable investigations, all employees were fairly dismissed.

A further problem that arises with respect to misconduct is the extent to which misconduct outside employment may result in the employer being able to dismiss. In fact, the circumstances here are comparatively rare. Usually the employer should wait for a successful criminal prosecution before acting and even then the dismissal will only be fair if the misconduct has some bearing on the job. This will be so if the act complained of either calls into question the employee's trustworthiness or in some way brings the employer into disrepute.

Thus, for instance, a teacher was fairly dismissed after having been convicted of offences of indecency (Gardiner *v* Newport Borough Council (1974)) and a senior shop assistant was quite justifiably dismissed after having been found guilty of shoplifting in another shop (Moore *v* C&A Modes (1981)). In both of these situations the trustworthiness of the employees in carrying out their jobs was called into question. An activity is more likely to bring the employer into disrepute if carried out by senior management, who are more likely to be seen, in the eyes of the public, as being the alter egos of their employer. Thus, in Richardson *v* Bradford Metropolitan Borough Council (1974), the employee, a senior environmental health officer, was convicted of theft from the funds of a local rugby club of which he was treasurer. This action justified his dismissal.

Redundancy

The third potentially fair reason for dismissing an employee, redundancy, is somewhat different from the other reasons in that the employee will not lose out completely but will be entitled to a redundancy payment. Redundancy is a claim in its own right and will thus be discussed quite separately at a later stage.

However, it may suit the employee to argue that in fact there was no redundancy situation, or, if faced with a genuine redundancy, the employer has acted in an unreasonable manner. The consequence of this will be that the employee may be able to successfully claim unfair dismissal and thus obtain a greater level of compensation.

Faced with a redundancy situation, the employer must therefore act fairly. This will entail having a proper selection procedure, agreed in advance possibly with trade union participation, and, save where exceptional circumstances demand it, complying with this procedure. In the absence of any prearranged procedure, the general rule as accepted by tribunals is LIFO (Last In First Out), i.e. the last person to be employed should be the first to go.

An employer must also give as much notice as possible to the employee of any impending redundancy and during this notice period consider whether there are alternative jobs that the employee may be able to perform. Finally, the employer should be prepared to consult with trade unions or emplyee representatives as to the method of handling the redundancy.

Breach of statute

An employer is potentially justified in dismissing an employee where his or her continued employment in a particular type of work would be illegal. This, in fact, is a fairly rare reason for dismissing but examples would include lorry drivers or sales representatives who lose their driving licence. They obviously can no longer drive in the course of their employment without breaking the law.

As with all the other potentially fair reasons for dismissing, however, the employer will have to act reasonably. He may, for instance, consider alternative work that the employee may be able to carry out without the need for driving. He does not have to find non-existent work, however, and if there are no alternatives the employer may well be justified in dismissing.

Some other substantial reason

Finally, the employer may dismiss the employee for 'some other substantial reason'. At first glance this seems very nebulous and may appear to encompass various activities. However, it is not quite as vague as it might appear.

To dismiss under the heading there must be a good economic, technical or organisational reason for dismissing. Case law abounds with examples. Thus, in Storey v Allied Breweries (1977), where the employee refused to change her hours to work under a shift pattern as this would require her to work on Sundays and she objected to this on religious grounds, the employer successfully argued that her subsequent dismissal was fair on the grounds of some other substantial reason, i.e. the shift work was desirable on the grounds of a substantial commercial benefit to the employer.

Likewise, in Sycamore v Myer & Co (1976), where the employee refused to accept a variation of contract which would result in his performance-related pay being substantially reduced, when he had originally been paid more than the employer intended due to an administrative error, his subsequent dismissal was held to be fair as otherwise the employer's pay structures would be compromised.

In Farr v Hoveringham Gravels (1977), the employee was the regional transport manager and thus categorised as a valued employee. The business relocated a distance of 44 miles. The employee was quite prepared to travel the extra distance to work but the employer insisted that he also move home, closer to his new workplace, and offered relocation expenses to enable him to do this. The employee refused and was fairly dismissed on the grounds of some other substantial reason, i.e. it was necessary that an employee who may have to be called in to work on his days off and with little notice should live close to the workplace.

In passing, it may be seen that the claim of some other substantial reason is a method whereby employers may be able to unilaterally force changes to the contract of employment. If the employee objects to the change then he or she may be given contractual notice to quit, thus avoiding any claim for wrongful dismissal. This will not, however, enable the employer to defend a claim for unfair dismissal. Nevertheless, if the employer had a good commercial reason for desiring the change and has acted reasonably, for example by giving notice and by attempting to negotiate, any subsequent dismissal may be fair.

Automatically fair dismissals

In one situation, the dismissal of an employee will be automatically fair: the tribunal is instructed that it is not able to look into the background of the case. This is where the employee is dismissed for taking part in industrial action. The provision is currently contained in Section 238 of the Trade Union and Labour Relations (Consolidation) Act 1992 but has always been an integral part of unfair dismissal legislation.

Many people are surprised to hear of this fact, which is not dependent on whether or not there has been a ballot or whether there is secondary action. If the trade union has conducted a ballot, is not engaged in secondary action and has given due notice of the action, then it cannot be sued. This does not, however, affect the proposition with respect to the workforce who take part in the action. They may be dismissed. There is one proviso to this, namely, the employer (save in the case of unofficial action) cannot be selective in who to dismiss. All those taking part in the action on a particular must go. The employer may then selectively re-engage the dismissed employees, provided at least three months have elapsed from the date of the dismissal.

Finally, the provisions apply not merely to strike action but to any form of industrial action. Thus, in Power Packaging Casemakers *v* Faust (1983), where the employees withdrew voluntary overtime as part of a trade dispute, although there was no contractual requirement to work overtime, this amounted to industrial action and the employees were fairly dismissed.

Automatically unfair dismissals

There are also several grounds on which the employee cannot be dismissed. A finding that an employee has been dismissed on one of these grounds will result in an automatic finding of unfair dismissal. The employer can never justify a dismissal under these headings. Moreover, there is no need to satisfy the requirement of two years' continuous service with the employer when relying on these grounds. The grounds are, first, dismissal for being a trade union member or proposing to join or refusing to leave a trade union or for taking part in trade union activities at a time when the employee is not obliged to be in work. Likewise, dismissal for refusing to join a trade union or for proposing to leave a trade union is also now, without exception, unfair. There was previously a proviso that where there was a union membership agreement (a closed shop) in operation, dismissal of non-union members would be fair. The heyday of the closed shop was the 1970s. Such a concept was, however, anathema to the Conservative government elected in 1979 and, commencing in 1980, legislation slowly eroded the efficacy of the closed shop and introduced more and more exceptions to its validity. Finally, the closed shop was declared unlawful by the Employment Act 1990 (the provisions are now contained in the Trade Union and Labour Relations (Consolidation) Act 1992).

Second, since 1993, as a consequence of the Trade Union Reform and Employment Rights Act, it has been unlawful to dismiss someone if the reason for dismissal is that he or she is a person with health and safety duties and the dismissal is due to the exercising of these duties. Likewise any employee who is dismissed for bringing to the employer's attention by lawful means any health and safety issue, or for taking steps to prevent a potential danger to health and safety, or for leaving or proposing to leave the workplace as a consequence of a safety danger will be successful in the claim. A major impetus for this piece of 'whistleblowing' legislation was the Piper Alpha disaster of 1987 where the workforce had felt threatened with loss of their jobs had they complained about perceived safety fears.

Third, dismissal for asserting a statutory right will be automatically unfair. The various rights covered here are numerous but would include, for instance, the dismissal of someone, on being given a Section 1 statement of the major terms of employment, as would the dismissal of someone who complained about an unlawful deduction from his or her wages, or who complained of a refusal to be given time off work to perform trade union or health and safety duties. These various employee rights are contained in the Employment Rights Act 1996. Dismissal of an employee for trying to enforce such rights would be unfair. The employee must show that he or she had a *bona fide* belief in the right: the right itself need not necessarily exist.

Finally, as we saw in the introduction to this chapter and as a consequence of the European Pregnant Workers Directive, it is automatically unfair to dismiss a woman due to her pregnancy or for reasons connected with pregnancy, for having taken maternity leave, or where she is suspended on health and safety grounds during maternity or a period of breast feeding. It is also automatically unfair if she is selected for redundancy during a period of maternity leave. In this scenario there would be an alternative potential claim for sex discrimination. In fact, this latter claim will frequently result in higher levels of compensation and will consequently be the more likely claim to be pursued.

Remedies for unfair dismissal

Any claim for unfair dismissal must be lodged with the employment tribunal within three months of the effective date of termination of the contract, i.e. usually within three months of the date of dismissal or of the end of the employee's notice period, should notice be given. There is a possibility of the tribunal being prepared to extend this rather short time period if it was not reasonably practicable to bring the claim in time. However, the circumstances in which this is allowed are comparatively rare and no employee should ever rely on the possibility of an extension of the time period for a claim.

Should the employee succeed in his or her claim there are three alternative remedies: reinstatement, re-engagement and compensation. *Reinstatement* amounts to obtaining one's old job back at the same level of seniority and grading and with a sum of money by way of compensation to reflect the time spent out of work prior to the order being made. *Re-engagement* amounts to obtaining suitable alternative employment with the employer plus compensation for any time out of work. Originally, reinstatement and re-engagement were intended to be the primary remedies available to dismissed employees. However, only something around 1.5 per cent of successful claims in front of the tribunals result in either of these orders being made. The primary reason for this is that the employee does not normally want his or her old job back. Indeed, unless this is specifically requested in the employee's application to the tribunal, it will never be considered. In any case, if the employee has contributed to his or her dismissal or if the old job has disappeared, for instance in an unfair redundancy dismissal, and no alternative job exists then reinstatement or re-engagement will not be a suitable remedy.

Thus, the vast majority of successful claims give rise to an award of *compensation* for the employee for loss of the job.

The level of compensation is based on four different awards: the basic, compensatory, additional and special awards. The successful applicant is always entitled to be considered for the first two of these; the latter two awards are rather specific and may be considered in the alternative in rare situations. The level of *basic award* is reached by means of a simple calculation (Table 8.2).

■ Table 8.2 Calculation of basic award

Full years within a particular age		Basic wage per week		Number of years continuous service
(up to 21) = ½				
22–40 = 1	×	(maximum £220)	×	(maximum 20)
41–65 = 1½				

The basic award may be reduced if the employee has contributed towards his or her dismissal. In the case of a procedurally unfair dismissal where the employer, had he followed the correct procedure, might have quite fairly dismissed, this reduction may be substantial. The £220 per week basic wage is increased from time to time but seldom in line with inflation. In the case of automatically unfair dismissal on trade union grounds, the basic award will always be a minimum of £2900.

As well as a basic award the employee will also always be entitled to be considered for a *compensatory award*. This, as the name suggests, is designed to compensate the employee for any financial loss suffered. It will therefore include, most obviously, lost wages both up to the date of the tribunal hearing and for the future, this latter calculation being dependent on evidence of the likelihood of the employee obtaining work in the future. The compensatory award will also include compensation for loss of commission, loss of fringe benefits such as a company car, and also a small sum for loss of statutory employment rights in that on commencing new employment the employee will have to start amassing employment rights afresh. The above losses could potentially amount to a sizeable sum of money. However, unfortunately for the employee, there is a maximum compensatory award, currently set at £12 000. Moreover, the employee may have the compensatory award reduced if he or she contributed towards the dismissal. Zero awards, although rare, are not unheard of.

The *additional award* is only awarded when there has been an order for reinstatement or re-engagement which the employer refuses to adhere to. No tribunal has the power to force an employer to re-employ someone against his or her will. However, an extra sum of compensation may be ordered. This will usually amount to between 13 and 26 weeks' pay, subject to a maximum of £220 per week, although in cases where the original dismissal was a consequence of sex or race discrimination, the additional award will be assessed as an amount between 26 and 52 weeks' pay.

The *special award* is awarded when there has been an automatically unfair dismissal on the grounds of trade union membership or non-membership or of a health and safety official for reasons connected with the performance of duty. The level of the special award depends on whether or not reinstatement or re-engagement has been requested. If it has but is refused by the tribunal the special award will be either 104 weeks' pay (with no maximum per week) or £14 500, whichever is the greater, subject to an overall maximum of £29 000. If reinstatement or re-engagement is ordered but the employer refuses to abide by the decision of the tribunal, the special award will be either 156 weeks' pay or £21 800, whichever is the greater, and with no upper limit. The compensation, which is awarded in addition to any basic and compensatory award, may consequently be comparatively high. It must be stressed, however, that such awards are rare. In 1996 the average compensation for a successful applicant for unfair dismissal was £2499 and indeed the maximum level of compensation for unfair dismissal has far from kept pace with inflation since the introduction of the claim in 1971. It should be noted that, at the time of writing, the government has published proposals that the maximum financial limit for an unfair dismissal claim is to be abolished. It is also proposed to reduce the number of years' continuous service required to make a claim to one year.

The circumstances when a claim for wrongful dismissal would be more beneficial for an employee than an unfair dismissal action may also now be seen. Some employees, most obviously those with less than two years' qualifying employment, are only able to claim wrongful dismissal and are only likely to obtain small levels of compensation based on a few weeks' pay. On the other hand, there is a maximum amount which may be claimed for unfair dismissal. A highly paid employee who is on a long fixed-term contract or who has the benefit of a substantial notice period will be entitled to quite considerably more compensation through claiming wrongful as opposed to unfair dismissal. However, for most dismissed employees an unfair dismissal action would be the norm.

■ Redundancy

Redundancy is the third claim which an employee may have when faced with termination of the contract of employment. It is somewhat different from wrongful and unfair dismissal as it reflects no real blame on the employer, whose actions are quite lawful. However, as we have seen, since the Redundancy Payments Act 1965 it has been thought correct that an employee who is faced with loss of the job through lack of work should be entitled to be compensated for the previous service. The current provisions are once more contained in the Employment Rights Act 1996.

As with unfair dismissal, not every employee may claim a redundancy payment. There are a similar list of exclusions, most notably employees with less than two years' continuous service with the same employer, employees past normal retirement age, employees on a fixed-term contract who expressly exclude their right to claim in writing, and employees who ordinarily work outside Great Britain.

In addition, employees in a private household who are close relatives of the employer and employees who are not yet eighteen years of age, among others, are unable to claim a statutory redundancy payment.

With respect to the entitlement to redundancy, a qualifying employee must first show that he or she has been dismissed. Redundancy is a type of dismissal and without this first requirement there can be no claim. The types of dismissal for redundancy purposes are identical to those for unfair dismissal, i.e.:

1 the employer terminates the contract with or without notice;

2 a fixed-term contract ends without being renewed;

3 the employee terminates the contract with or without notice because of the employer's conduct.

In addition, there is a fourth type of dismissal peculiar to redundancy:

4 the employment terminates due to the death, dissolution or liquidation of the employer or the appointment of a receiver.

If employment ceases due to the employer's business being brought to an end, then this also constitutes a redundancy dismissal.

As to a situation which does not give rise to a dismissal and where, consequently, there is no redundancy claim, consider the case of Morton Sundour Fabrics *v* Shaw (1966), where the employer announced that there would be a need for redundancies in the near future and that the employee concerned was likely to be one of those who would have to leave. The employee pre-empted the situation and left before the actual notice of redundancy, to find another job. As there was at the time no dismissal, there could be no right to a redundancy payment. The employee had in fact resigned.

Once a dismissal has been shown, which does not usually present problems, then the presumption is that the dismissal was for reasons of redundancy. Either side may wish to rebut this presumption, however – the employer to show that there is a fair dismissal, the employee to show that the dismissal was unfair with a consequent possibility of greater compensation.

Having said this, there are three types of redundancy: (i) where there is a total cessation of business, (ii) where there is a cessation or diminution of work of the type of which the employee is employed to do, and (iii) where there is a diminution of work at the place at which the employee is employed.

A total cessation of work causes few problems; the other two types of redundancy present greater difficulties, however.

With respect to a diminution of work, the obvious question which requires an answer is what type of work is the employee employed to do? The tribunals have developed a wide approach here. What is looked at is not the work actually done but the work which the employee could have been required to do.

Thus, in Hindle *v* Percival Boats (1969), where the employee was a boat builder, skilled in making wooden boats, boat manufacture turned primarily to the use of fibre glass, a process and material which the employee was unable to adapt to. He was eventually dismissed for being 'too good and too slow' at his job. His subsequent claim for a redundancy payment failed. The job he was employed to do was to build boats, be they made of wood, fibre glass or any other substance. As there was no diminution in the requirements to build boats generally there could not be said to be a redundancy. Whether there would nowadays be an unfair dismissal is perhaps a separate issue, however.

Likewise, there was no redundancy where an unqualified teacher was replaced by one with qualifications (Wren *v* Wiltshire County Council (1969)). Where the employee is replaced there cannot be a genuine redundancy.

In Johnson *v* Nottinghamshire Combined Police Authority (1974), employees were required to work in shifts, instead of from 9.30 a.m. to 5.30 p.m. as previously. They failed in their claim for redundancy payments. There was no diminution in the requirement for that type of employee: the employer merely required the staff to do their work at different times.

With respect to a cessation or diminution of work at the place at which the employee is employed, a difficult issue, that of area of employment, arises. Every employee has a contractual employment area. This should preferably be expressed in the contract. However, failing this, it may be implied. The implied term is that the employee may be required to move within an area designated by a reasonable day's travel from his or her current place of work. If required to move outside the contractual employment area due to a lack of work within it, then there will be a genuine redundancy. If an employee refuses a reasonable request to move within the contractual employment area there may well be a fair dismissal for misconduct, as in the case of O'Brien *v* Associated Fire Alarms (1969), where the employee was required to move from Liverpool to Barrow-in-Furness, a distance of some 120 miles, due to the closing down of the Liverpool office. In the absence of an express term in the contract this amounted to a redundancy. Such a distance does not constitute a reasonable day's travel. There was consequently a dismissal due to a lack of work in the contractual employment area and the employee was entitled to a redundancy payment.

Offer of suitable alternative employment

An employer may defend a claim for a redundancy payment if he or she can show that the employee has unreasonably refused an offer of suitable alternative employment made by the employer.

Suitable alternative employment must be objectively justified having reference to such matters as levels of pay, entitlement to bonuses and fringe benefits, working conditions and travel to and from work. An employee may reasonably refuse this offer based on subjective criteria peculiar to the particular employee – for example, refusing a move which would disrupt children's education, loss of friends, etc.

Compensation

Should an employee succeed in any claim he or she will be entitled to a statutory redundancy payment. In the event of a dispute, the employee may bring an action in an industrial tribunal, the application having to be made within six months of the effective date of termination of the contract. As with unfair dismissal, there is provision for extending this time period but an applicant should never rely on the possibility of an extension.

If successful, the applicant will obtain a sum of money calculated in the same way as the basic award for unfair dismissal, and dependent therefore on the age, basic wage per week and number of years' continuous service with the employer. There can be no claim, however, for any years' in employment where the applicant was below the age of eighteen.

The level of statutory compensation for redundancy is consequently rather low. The maximum to which an applicant may be entitled is currently only £6600. Any payment above and beyond the statutory level is a purely voluntary act of the employer. It can also be seen why there may be a desire for a former employee to argue that there was an unfair dismissal due to the procedurally incorrect manner of handling the redundancy. In the event of a successful unfair dismissal action, there will be an entitlement not merely to a basic award, equivalent in value to a redundancy payment, but also to a compensatory award.

CONCLUSION

This chapter has outlined key aspects of legal regulation in the field of individual employment rights. In practice, it is clear that in the fields of security of employment and equal opportunities, the intentions of legislators are overtaken by the brutal realities of labour markets and the actions of less scrupulous employers. Thus it must be noted that in each of these areas the successful implementation of law has been limited by factors such as an unwillingness on the part of employees to take action, due to cost and the possibility of failure, and a tendency on the part of some employers to place economic expediency ahead of notions of fair employment practice. The agenda of deregulation in the 1980s and 1990s served to bolster employer power in the employment relationship, somewhat paradoxically by engaging in an unprecedented degree of intervention into trade union affairs.

While individual rights have also been whittled away, they remain a central focus of law in the late 1990s. It remains to be seen whether New Labour will succeed in implementing a programme which strengthens the hand of collective groups in employment to assist in countering the worst abuses by employers, and which establishes partnership arrangements between labour and management in the pursuit of flexibility, efficiency and fairness. One future field of development which seems inevitable, however, is the fact that Europe will become more and more involved in the regulation of both individual and collective employment law. As can be seen from the above, this process is well under way. Some areas of employment law bear little resemblance to how they looked some ten years ago. This process is an ever increasing one. In the future to understand employment law the lawyer, and to a lesser extent the layperson, will have to be versed in European law.

REFERENCES

Clegg, H. (1970) *The System of Industrial Relations in Great Britain*. Oxford: Blackwell.

Dickens, L. and Hall, M. (1995) 'The state; labour law and industrial relations' in Edwards, P. (ed.) *Industrial Relations; Theory and Practice in Britain*. Oxford: Blackwell, pp. 255–303.

Edwards, P., Gilman, M., Hall, M., Keep, E., Lloyd, C. and Sisson, K. (1997) *Hot Topics: The Industrial Relations Consequences of New Labour*. Warwick Business School.

Kahn Freund, O. (1965) 'Industrial relations and the law: retrospect and prospect', *British Journal of Industrial Relations*, 7, 301–6.

Lewis, D. (1990) *The Essentials of Employment Law*. 3rd edn. London: IPM.

Part IV
PATTERNS AND PRACTICES

Chapter 9

COLLECTIVE BARGAINING

Mike Salamon

Learning objectives

By the end of this chapter, readers should be able to:

- identify the continuing importance of the collective bargaining process;
- explain the different functions collective bargaining performs in regulating the conduct of the employment relationship and the different styles of collective bargaining relationship;
- understand recent trends and developments in the structure of collective bargaining institutions (particularly relating to decentralisation);
- appreciate the significance of recent changes in the bargaining relationship (particularly resulting from the introduction of HRM strategies).

INTRODUCTION

The Webbs (1902) used the term 'collective bargaining' as part of their categorisation of trade union activities. Trade unions can provide individual members with *mutual insurance* (monetary benefits to support the individual in the event of sickness, unemployment, industrial action, etc.), so helping them to withstand management impositions. They can, with strong membership and stable organisations, force employers to deal with labour as a collective entity, rather than as isolated individuals, and so secure better terms and conditions of employment (*collective bargaining*). Furthermore, through the politicisation and influence of the working classes within society, they can seek universal legislative regulation of the labour market and protection of the individual worker (*legal enactment*). Despite the development of individual employment protection legislation in the UK since the mid-1960s, collective bargaining has remained the dominant focus of trade union activity.

The basis of collective bargaining is that 'employees do not negotiate individually, and on their own behalf, but do so collectively through representatives' (Donovan Commission, 1968: 8), resulting in agreements which regulate the employment relationship on a group rather than individual basis. Unlike joint consultation, where management largely controls the process (determines the agenda for discussion and retains the right to decide the final outcome), collective bargaining is founded on the principle of joint regulation. It allows employees (through their representatives) to initiate discussion of issues of concern to them as well as respond to issues raised by management and, most importantly, it requires both sides (employees as well as management) to accept or agree to the outcome. Not surprisingly, management has had a historical reluctance to accept collective bargaining or, once accepted, to see its scope extended. Thus, there are two fundamental requirements for effective collective bargaining to take place:

1 Employees need to see themselves not simply as individuals but also as part of a group with similar objectives and interests in regulating the employment relationship. However, this feeling has to be given substance through some form of employee organisation (usually by individuals joining an already existing external trade union) which provides the necessary power and representational capacity to undertake joint regulation through collective bargaining with management.

2 Management must be prepared not just to accept the existence of the employees' organisation but also to acknowledge its right to represent the interests of employees (grant recognition). This involves accepting some restriction on its authority to make unilateral decisions (managerial prerogative). The extent to which organisational decisions become subject to negotiation and agreement is a reflection of preferred management style, employee/union power and any legislative intervention.

These two requirements are interlinked and both have been subject to considerable pressure in the UK since the beginning of the 1980s. In the first place, trade union membership has declined (due to an unfavourable economic environment, industrial restructuring and changes in management attitude) and this, together with more restrictive legislation, has reduced the ability of trade unions to exert pressure on management to secure favourable outcomes within the collective bargaining process. In the second place, many managements have adopted HRM-based strategies which emphasise the individual nature of the employment relationship and seek to reduce, if not remove, the influence of trade unions on its decision making. Milner's analysis (1995) of the relationship between union membership levels in the UK and the proportion of employees covered by collective bargaining shows that at its peak, in the mid-1970s when about 50 per cent of employees were members of unions, 85 per cent of employees were covered by 'collective pay-setting institutions' (of which about 8 per cent were covered by statutory Wages Councils). Thus the benefits of collective bargaining extended well beyond the limits of trade union membership. By the early 1990s, not only had trade union density declined to below 40 per cent but also the gap with the coverage of 'collective pay-setting institutions' had fallen to about 7 per cent, principally because of the decline in multi-employer national collective bargaining arrangements. However, the position can also be seen in a more positive light: collective bargaining still 'remains the main method of pay determination for almost half the workforce in Britain' (IRS, 1993: 7). The UK Workplace Industrial Relations surveys for 1980, 1984 and 1990 confirm this picture (Millward et al., 1992). Although there was a decline in the proportion of both establishments and employees where collective bar-

gaining was the 'basis of the most recent pay inc[
sector), nevertheless 70 per cent of manual em[
employees in manufacturing still had their pa[
1990. The level was, perhaps not surprisingly, [
in the private services sector about 40 per cent [
ees had their pay determined by collective bar[

Changes in the water industry

The case of the water industry demonstrate[
led to the abandonment of national multi-[
but also two quite different strategies at th[
improve organisational performance – one [
other working in partnership with unions.

Until its privatisation in 1989, the water industry (Ogden, 1993) had a formalised 'Whitley-based' multi-employer collective bargaining arrangement (National Joint Industrial Councils or Committees) with separate agreements for manual production workers, craft maintenance workers, non-manual staff and chief officers and senior staff. These provided common pay levels and terms of employment across the industry with joint consultation over other issues at the organisation level. Despite the increasing independence of the individual water organisations, between 1983 (when the statutory National Water Council was replaced by two voluntary employer bodies) and privatisation in 1989, national multi-employer bargaining continued on a voluntary basis – primarily to avoid competitive pay leap-frogging between the organisations – although issues relating to productivity improvements and incentive schemes were devolved to the organisation level. This was supported by the trade unions, whose own policy was for a continuation of uniformity across the industry. However, some Regional Water Authorities wanted to develop their own more strategic and flexible HRM approaches at the organisational level. The withdrawal from multi-employer bargaining of Thames Water in 1986 and Northumbrian Water in 1989, plus the indication of a further two or three withdrawals in 1990, made the continuation of multi-employer bargaining almost impossible – although some would have preferred to keep the uniformity and stability provided by the national framework. Since 1989, local variation has increased as organisations have been structured differently (some being bought by foreign firms) and have developed different approaches to such issues as single-table bargaining, long-term agreements, performance-related pay, the individual employee–management link (with a reduced role for the trade union) and so on.

Northumbrian Water (IRS, 1992) introduced perhaps the most radical changes in employee relations intended to personalise employee representation (rather than conducting it through a third party – the unions). Having failed to introduce a single-union agreement, management agreed to continue its recognition of the eight existing unions, but only as a joint Confederation of Northumbrian Water Trade Unions (CNWTU) and with the formation of a Northumbrian Water Ltd Employee Association (NWEA) to represent the 17 per cent of employees who were not members of these unions. It also introduced a system of 'employee councils' in each operating area and an overall Company Council to integrate the processes of communication, consultation and negotiation. The seven company councillors are expected to 'conduct themselves in such a way as to pro-

303

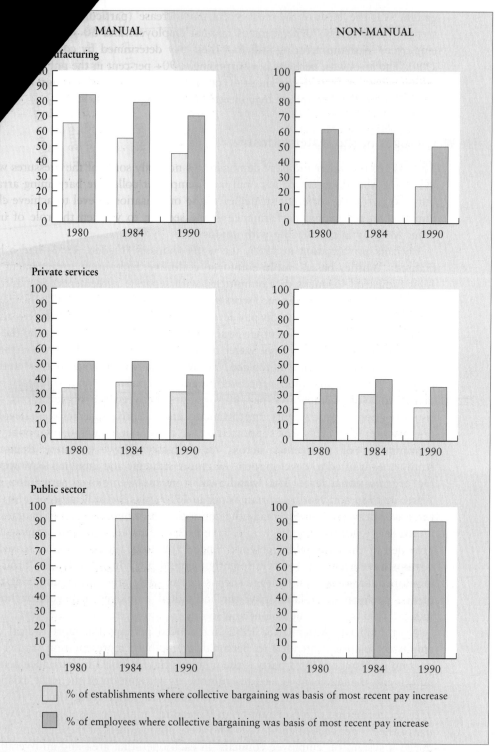

MANUAL   NON-MANUAL

Manufacturing

Private services

Public sector

☐ % of establishments where collective bargaining was basis of most recent pay increase

▨ % of employees where collective bargaining was basis of most recent pay increase

■ **Fig. 9.1 Collective bargaining basis of most recent pay increases**

Source: Millward and Stevens (1986: tables 9.1, 9.3, 9.4, 9.9, 9.10); Millward *et al.* (1992: tables 7.1–7.3, 7.5–7.8, 7.9).

mote harmony and progress of employee relations' and the two representatives of the CNWTU and NWEA are present at Council meetings only as 'advisors' (although at least one is required to be present whenever an 'agreement' is made by the Council). Significantly, its first pay negotiation (a three-year deal negotiated in 1991) resulted in endorsement of management's 'final' offer by the Council but rejection by the employees in a ballot, followed by an independent review and an increase in management's offer.

Welsh Water (IRS, 1992) adopted what it termed a 'partnership approach' to its reform of collective bargaining arrangements. In moving to single-table bargaining, it introduced a 'representative council' to combine consultation and negotiation with the employee-side representation comprising union full-time officers as well as union lay representatives. Thus the unions' position was not threatened by the change although NUPE was derecognised because of its small number of members. Its approach to pay bargaining contained two important features. First, it continued to guarantee that there would be no compulsory redundancies. Second, and perhaps more importantly, it developed a pay formula which encompassed not only organisational performance but also changes in the Retail Price Index (which determines its prices) and the results of an independent survey of pay movements in selected Welsh companies. The arrangement also contains a provision to either increase pay or reduce the next pay increase in the light of the pay survey findings. It is perhaps not surprising that Hyder (the merger of Welsh Water with South Wales Electricity) has been cited by the TUC as a case study of good practice which supports its case for union recognition (TUC, 1997).

THE PROCESS OF COLLECTIVE BARGAINING

Flanders (1968) noted that collective bargaining does not involve the actual sale or hire of labour; it is a rule-making process which determines and regulates, in varying degrees, the terms on which individuals will be employed. However, the importance of collective bargaining is not limited simply to determining pay and other substantive terms. Its real significance, perhaps, lies in management acceptance of a style of employment relationship which is based on the legitimisation of the expression of the different interests within the organisation (conflict), on joint regulation (constraining the unilateral exercise of managerial authority over employees) and on the principle of employee involvement and influence in a range of organisational decision making. Furthermore, collective bargaining 'is strictly a relationship between organisations' (Harbison, 1954: 270): the collective agreement has an existence within the organisational system independent of the individuals who, at any point in time, are its managers and employees. Any new employee is, in practice, bound by its terms although he or she was not a party to the agreement. Similarly, all managers are bound by the same set of procedural principles and processes for the conduct of the management's relationship with individual employees. It is also important to recognise that both the establishment of collective bargaining and the outcome of the bargaining process depend, to a major extent, on the relative power balance between the two parties (management and the employees collectively). Hence, Flanders (1968) described collective agreements as being 'compromise settlements of power conflicts'. The demonstration of industrial power, through strikes or other forms of industrial action, forms an integral part of collective bargaining.

■ Regulating the employment relationship

Collective bargaining is, of course, not the only method for determining and regulating terms of employment and the nature of the employment relationship. They can also be determined unilaterally by management or set by government through legislation. Arguments in favour of the use of collective bargaining generally stem from, on the one hand, a belief in the injustice of unconstrained management discretion (potential employee exploitation) and, on the other, a preference for voluntary arrangements determined by the parties themselves (which allow variability) rather than uniform statutory compulsion. As already indicated, the role of collective bargaining covers more than just negotiating pay increases; Chamberlain and Kuhn (1965) identified three quite different but interrelated functions:

Establishing economic contractual terms

The process is primarily concerned with the distribution of economic wealth through the determination of the substantive terms of the employment contract – such as pay, hours, holidays and other benefits (pension, sick pay, etc.). In the UK, these terms become incorporated into the individual's contract of employment and are, thereby, not only legally enforceable on the employer but also automatically amended whenever the terms of the collective agreement change. It also means that if management terminates the collective agreement, the individual's previous rights cease and become subject to individual negotiation or, more usually, unilateral management determination. Similarly, where so-called 'fringe' benefits become part of the terms of a collective agreement, they cease to be an 'optional' extra to be granted (or not) at the discretion of management but become an integral standard 'right' within the contract of employment.

Constraining managerial power and authority

Many collective agreements are procedural, rather than substantive, in nature. The initial 'recognition' agreement establishes the foundation for all subsequent collective bargaining: it confers legitimacy on the trade union's role and defines those issues which may be subject to joint regulation. Once the union is recognised, further procedural agreements may be negotiated. Some, most obviously the grievance and disciplinary procedures, cover the conduct of the individual employee–manager relationship, while others, such as consultation in the event of redundancy, are concerned with the organisational relationship between management and the union. Taken together, procedural agreements provide, in effect, a body of 'constitutional' rules which govern 'managerial', rather than 'economic', relations by constraining the exercise of managerial authority. Such rules seek to balance management's desire for control of labour and the employees' desire for protection against arbitrary management decisions and actions; collective bargaining provides a form of 'government by consent'.

Allowing employee influence in organisational decision making

The scope of negotiations within the organisation may extend beyond the economic and constitutional functions and allow employees, through their representatives, to influence a wide range of management policies, strategies and decisions which affect their working life. The advantage of collective bargaining, to employees, lies in its implicit assumption that the output will be a joint *agreement* (in effect requiring the employees' acceptance of management's plans before implementation). The nature of the work, the way it is carried out by employees and the way management assesses their performance have, over the years, been the subject matter of collective bargaining, first through 'productivity' agreements, then 'new technology' agreements and, more recently, 'flexibility' agreements. Employees have been able to influence the design and introduction of new working arrangements by securing agreements on such issues as labour force levels, job flexibility, time flexibility, use of contractors, etc.

Each of these functions emphasises a different concept of the collective bargaining process, but they are not mutually exclusive in that most negotiations contain all three elements. However, the extension of collective bargaining beyond the simple economic and constitutional functions and into wider, more strategic, areas of management decision making, is indicative of a more cooperative 'management by consent' style of employee relations associated with the wider concept of 'employee participation'.

■ The influence of legislation

Collective bargaining in the UK has been relatively unregulated by legislation, despite its importance in changing the character of the employment relationship. Significantly, apart from a short period under the Industrial Relations Act 1971, there has been no statutory support for trade unions seeking recognition (a prerequisite for the development of collective bargaining). Yet, during its brief existence, the statutory recognition procedure provided both a direct and indirect pressure on employers to grant union recognition and collective bargaining – particularly among non-manual employees in the private sector. The Labour Government White Paper (1998) includes proposals not only to reinstate the collective right for a union to be recognised if a majority of employees in the bargaining unit work it, but also to introduce an individual right for an employee to be reprsented in grievance and disciplinary situations. However, even if management does recognise a trade union, it is still free to retain its decision making prerogative by adopting a 'non-negotiable' (take it or leave it) stance in any discussions with a trade union. Trade unions must rely on their industrial power to constrain this freedom.

Similarly, collective agreements in the UK are, by their wording and the intention of the parties, not regarded as 'contracts in the legal sense and are not enforceable at law ... they remain in the realm of undertakings binding in honour' (Mr Justice Lane in Ford *v* AUEFW and TGWU (1969) 2QB 303), although its terms are legally enforceable through the individual's contract of employment. The Conservative government of the early 1970s tried to change this position (Industrial Relations Act 1971) – collective agreements were presumed to be legally enforceable between management and union unless they contained a clause to the contrary. Despite this change in the law, virtually all managements accepted union demands for a 'TINALEA' clause – 'This is not a legally enforceable agreement'. Since the subsequent Labour government's Trade Union and Labour Relations Act 1974, a collective agreement is legally enforceable only if it is a written agreement and contains a clause that the parties 'intend the agreement shall be a legally enforceable contract'.

The only direct statutory support in the UK for collective bargaining, introduced in 1909 but repealed in 1993, gave the government power to establish Wages Councils in low paid industries where trade unions were too weak to secure collective bargaining on a voluntary basis (primarily in retail, catering, clothing and agriculture). The awards of these Wages Councils were legally binding on organisations in the designated industries.

However, statutory support for the trade unions' role in collective bargaining has been provided in one important area – disclosure of information. Since the Employment Protection Act 1975, trade unions have had the right to request from management information without which they would be 'materially impeded' in carrying out their collective bargaining role or which would be 'in accordance with good industrial relations practice'. Clearly, access to information is one factor in determining the type of bargaining relationship and, in particular, the balance of power between the two sides. However, obtaining access to management information may not always be to the union's advantage (Hussey and Marsh, 1982), or the union may not have sufficient industrial power to take full advantage of the information it receives (Moore, 1980). More importantly, the legal requirement to disclose information is limited to the *existing* range of issues which are subject to collective bargaining; management is under no legal obligation to provide information to trade unions on those issues which are only subject to consultation (except redundancy). It is, therefore, in management's interests to limit the scope of collective bargaining, thereby restricting the information a union may demand.

Clearly, legislation in respect of collective bargaining can be either negative or positive – it can constrain or support its development. In Malaysia, for example, certain issues are defined as areas of 'managerial prerogative' and excluded from collective bargaining (including the allocation of work, dismissals and redundancy) (Ayadurai, 1993: 84), while in Singapore all collective agreements have to be approved by the Industrial Arbitration Court, which is charged with ensuring that the terms of any agreement are 'in the interests of the community and particularly the economy' (Legett, 1993: 111–12). The USA, on the other hand, has had legislation since the 1930s which not only provides a statutory union recognition procedure culminating in a 'representation election' conducted by the National Labor Relations Board (NLRB) but also places a duty on both management and unions to 'bargain in good faith'. The NLRB and courts have also influenced the range of collective bargaining by dividing issues into *mandatory* (bargaining must take place at the request of one party) and *permissive* (both parties must agree to bargaining over the issue). The mandatory group covers a wide range of issues relating to wages, benefits and work-related matters, including work schedules, job security, dismissals, rest breaks, holidays and safety (Mathias and Jackson, 1994).

For almost two decades (1979–97), the Conservative government in the UK was unsupportive of collective bargaining. It not only abolished the statutory recognition procedure (1980) and Wages Councils (1993), but also substantially reduced the trade unions' ability to exert industrial power within the bargaining process, progressively narrowing the definition of 'lawful' industrial action and increasing the rights of both management and individuals to challenge the actions of unions in the court. In 1993, it also removed the duty 'to encourage collective bargaining' from the terms of reference of the Advisory, Conciliation and Arbitration Service (ACAS). Furthermore, the government appeared to favour a change in the law to 'encourage' employers and unions to agree to legal enforceability of collective agreements (Green Paper, 1991). Unions might then have been legally liable for breach of contract when, in management's view, they did not comply, for example, with a clause to cooperate with management initiatives to improve productivity and flexibility. The government also favoured the removal of the unions' right to information from management – the only major legal underpinning for the collective bargaining process. It is perhaps ironic that it was pressure from the European Union which led the Conservative government to undermine the trade union role further, in respect of transfer of undertaking and redundancy, by widening the consultation requirement to 'employee representatives', rather than confining it to representatives of recognised independent trade unions; nevertheless, management also now has to consult 'with a view to seeking agreement to measures to be taken'. While there is no absolute requirement to reach an agreement, management must now, at least in this one area, appear to be 'bargaining in good faith'.

However, the direction of public policy appears to have shifted with the change of government in 1997. Although the new Labour government does not intend to relax any of the previous government's legislation relating to the exercise of industrial power, it has initiated legislation to introduce a National Minimum Wage by early 1999. While this can be seen as part of the process of *legal enactment* (rather than collective bargaining), it will, for the first time in the UK, provide a national base wage to underpin wage determination through collective bargaining. Certainly, the CBI has expressed concern that an annual updating of the National Minimum Wage might be seen as setting a 'going rate' or norm for all wage increases. More importantly, one of the central features of the government's White Paper (1998) is the proposal for the restoration of some form of state-supported recognition procedure. The TUC sees the requirement to recognise unions, if that is the wish of the majority of the workforce, as an integral part of building a partnership between management and employees to face competitive pressures (TUC, 1997). Significantly, the CBI believes that the government is sympathetic to its view that such recognition should be limited by, among other things, exempting small organisations, excluding training from collective bargaining and allowing individuals to 'opt out' and negotiate individual contracts even where a union gains recognition and negotiates a collective agreement. It also appears to favour the inclusion of a procedure for derecognition as well as recognition (Taylor, 1997).

CHANGES IN THE STRUCTURAL FRAMEWORK

Few countries have a single uniform set of institutional arrangements (*structure*) for collective bargaining. In order to understand the varied forms of collective bargaining structure, it is useful to separate multi-employer institutional arrangements (that is, arrangements intended to cover more than one organisation) from single-employer collective bargaining (*see* Fig. 9.2). Multi-employer collective bargaining is usually conducted at the industry or sector level (although it may also exist at a sub-industry or regional level). However, economy-wide arrangements can also be included in this category, even though such arrangements are usually tripartite rather than bipartite (involving government) and may not be collective bargaining, in the strict sense, in that they do not necessarily result in formal collective agreements. Any multi-employer bargaining arrangement, at whatever level, has the effect of providing a form of external regulation of the individual organisation, whereas single-employer collective bargaining can be seen as part of an organisation's own internal regulation. However, the two arrangements are not mutually exclusive but may be interrelated to provide a 'layered' structure (that is, the terms of a multi-employer industry agreement may be added to or topped up at the individual organisational level).

■ Multi-employer and single-employer arrangements

Economy-wide framework arrangements have been used, for short and long periods, in a variety of countries and are primarily associated with government interventionist strategies to regulate the wage element in the economy. Generally, they make recommendations or provide guidelines for improvements in wages and other terms of employment which are expected to be taken into account by management and unions in negotiations at industry and/or organisational levels. The intention is to ensure that, at the macro economy level, any improvement in employees' terms and conditions are in line with the country's economic performance. Management gains from a stabilisation of its labour costs and a reduction in competitive bidding-up of wages (whether by powerful trade unions or by organisations themselves). Trade unions gain not only from being able to influence government economic and social policy but also from the uniformity achieved by greater standardisation of improvements across different organisations and groups of employees.

One example of this type of arrangement was the UK's 'social contract' (1974–79). This was primarily an accommodation between the Labour government and trade unions (the CBI was not an active party to the arrangement) as an alternative to a government-imposed incomes policy. In Ireland, also during the 1970s, it was employers and unions who came together to establish National Wage Agreements which 'set the agreed rate of pay increase for the entire national workforce in all industries and sectors' (Prondzynski, 1992: 78) – again, as an alternative to a government-imposed incomes policy. In Singapore, on the other hand, a permanent tripartite National Wages Council was established by the government in 1972, following increased restrictions on trade unions and collective bargaining, to provide 'authoritative guidelines for annual pay settlements in

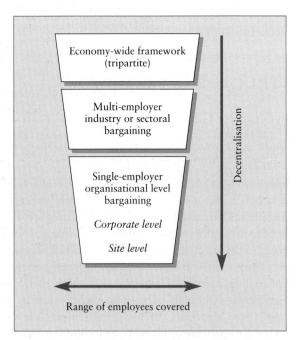

■ Fig. 9.2 The structure of collective bargaining

accordance with prevailing economic conditions' (Leggett, 1993: 100). Centralised agreements, encompassing a 'solidaristic' wage principle based on 'equal pay for equal work', played an important part within Sweden's centralised 'corporatist' approach to industrial relations until the early 1980s (Hammarström, 1993). However, these agreements were implemented and supplemented by further negotiation at the industry and/or organisational levels.

The most common form of *multi-employer collective bargaining* in most Western European countries is at the industry or sector level. Such agreements are negotiated by national officials of the trade unions and employers' association and apply to all employees, or a stated category of employees (for example, manual process employees, maintenance employees, etc.), of organisations that are members of the employers' association. In some countries (for example, Italy, Belgium, France and Germany) these collective agreements can be extended by legislation to apply to *all* organisations within the particular industry or sector (even those which are not unionised or a member of the employers' association). In the UK, even without legislative pressure, such organisations have, on a voluntary basis, often adopted the terms of the relevant industry agreement (where one existed) in order to ensure that their terms and conditions of employment are in line with other organisations in the industry.

Trade unions in the UK and the rest of Europe have favoured multi-employer industry-level collective bargaining because it promotes fraternalism and solidarity within the workforce, rather than competitive segmentation. It is the embodiment of the principles of 'common rule' and 'rate for the job'. Industry-wide agreements ensure that people doing the same work receive the same terms and conditions of employment, irrespective of differences in their individual performance, the performance of their organisation or local labour market conditions – it limits labour competition based on differential wage levels. At the same time, trade unions are able to 'equalise' their bargaining power within the industry by, in effect, using their strength in some organisations or geographical areas to support those where they are weaker. In some countries, through state support for industry-level bargaining, the level of employees covered by collective bargaining far exceeds the level of union density. For example, in France the level of union density is only 10 per cent while collective bargaining coverage is 92 per cent and in the Netherlands the figures are 26 per cent and 71 per cent (IDS, 1994).

Management has also benefited, certainly in the past, from industry-level collective bargaining. In the early days of the development of trade unions, it provided a means of employer protection against being 'played-off', one against the other, in a continuous series of 'leap-frogging' union claims based on comparisons between organisations. It also helped to prevent 'unfair' competition between organisations in the same industry: the organisation which was outside the industry agreement, and hence able to pay lower wages, was seen as a threat by both trade unions and other organisations. At the same time, industry-level collective bargaining focuses primarily on the economic or market regulation function and, therefore, may be to management's advantage in distancing trade union activity and influence from management strategies at the organisational level. Certainly, in Germany there is a clear distinction between the economic collective bargaining role of trade unions at the industry or sector level and the work regulation function of Works Councils at the organisation level (Jacobi *et al.*, 1992).

Single-employer (organisational) bargaining may either be an alternative to multi-employer industry bargaining or exist alongside it as part of a layered set of arrangements. While industry-level bargaining about economic matters, particularly pay, may allow management to limit the trade unions' role and influence over other matters at the workplace, it also has the effect of reducing management's control over wage costs within the organisation. Single-employer bargaining is, by its very nature, specific to the needs of each organisation and conducted by management and trade union representatives from within the organisation. In particular, management is able not only to integrate the regulation of economic and managerial relations, but also to do so within a comprehensive strategic HRM framework that supports business needs. However, it provides a greater opportunity for unions to pursue 'key bargaining' and/or 'leap-frogging' comparability strategies that may result in greater instability in the overall wage determination process.

Certainly, some UK industries, generally characterised by a relatively small number of large (often multinational) organisations, have relied entirely on single-employer bargaining (for example, car manufacturing and oil refining). It is also the predominant structure in some countries. It has been favoured in the USA – with its emphasis on a 'free market' capitalism philosophy and its geographically dispersed and segmented labour markets. In Japan, it has been its neo-feudal employment relationship, with its emphasis on a strong internal (organisational) labour market, which has encouraged enterprise-based unions and collective bargaining.

As early as 1968, the Donovan Commission's analysis of UK employee relations identified the existence of a 'two-tier' collective bargaining arrangement in most private manufacturing industries. The formalised system of industry-level agreements provided irreducible uniform minimum levels of pay which were often enhanced by less formalised and fragmented organisational-level bargaining where unions were strong or management was prepared to pay more (for example, because of better organisational performance, to attract better quality employees or to secure employee cooperation in introducing new working arrangements). At that time, the so-called 'wage drift' resulting from organisational-level bargaining over and above national rates was regarded as a significant inflationary factor in the economy which needed to be controlled. National pay rates, rather than being the significant factor in determining actual pay increases at the organisational level, were primarily a 'safety net' or ratchet mechanism within the pay system. As pay rates at the organisational level increased, so unions were able to safeguard the gain, at least in part, by an upward shift in the national industry minimum (Brown and Terry, 1978).

During the 1970s, reform of organisational collective bargaining focused on increased formalisation as part of management's strategy to regain control. The more recent focus, in the 1980s and 1990s, has been on shifting collective bargaining away from multi-employer arrangements (*decentralisation*) as part of a government and management strategy to create a more flexible responsive labour market. However, it is important to recognise that there are a variety of dimensions to 'decentralisation'. First, it is not always simply a process of abandoning multi-employer in favour of single-employer arrangements but, rather, changing the balance between the two levels (IRRR, 1987). The industry agreement can become less of a uniform regulation and more of a framework of common aims or principles within which organisations have freedom to determine their own rules. Second, decentralisation may also encompass shifts *within* single-employer bargaining

(Deaton and Beaumont, 1980). Organisations may devolve more authority for the determination of terms and conditions of employment to local management within lesser or greater degrees of central corporate co-ordination. Third, the degree of decentralisation is, in part, a reflection of the nature of the previous arrangements. For example, the first step in decentralisation in Sweden (or any other country which has relied on economy-wide arrangements) has been to shift the focus of collective bargaining to the industry or sector level (EIRR, 1992) – which in the UK is seen as a centralised bargaining level (*see* Exhibit 9.1).

Moves away from multi-employer bargaining

The role of multi-employer collective bargaining in the UK has declined substantially during the post-war period. Whereas in 1950 some 60 per cent of employees in the private sector had their pay determined through multi-employer agreements, it had already declined to 35 per cent by 1970 and dropped further to only 10 per cent in 1990, suggesting the abandonment of multi-employer bargaining as even the base for a 'two-tier' arrangement (Brown *et al.*, 1995: table 5. 1). Figure 9.3 shows that multi-employer bargaining is still more predominant among manual workers (affecting 19 per cent in manufacturing and 13 per cent in the service sector) than it is among non-manual employees (affecting only 6 per cent in both sectors). However, it still remains a significant feature in the public sector, applying to over 70 per cent of both manual and non-manual employees. Significantly, plant- or establishment-level collective bargaining is the dominant feature of single-employer bargaining in the manufacturing sector, while the corporate level appears to predominate in the service industries.

   Not surprisingly, a significant number of national multi-employer bargaining arrangements have, for different reasons, ceased to exist in the UK over the past decade (including the biggest – the engineering industry, covering some 900 000 employees). The withdrawal of larger organisations was certainly a major factor in the break-up of national bargaining in banking (withdrawal of National Westminster Bank), multiple food trade (withdrawal of Tesco and other major supermarket groups) and shipping (withdrawal of Sealink, Cunard and P&O). However, the abolition of multi-employer bargaining among national newspapers and independent television arose primarily from a common management objective, in a highly competitive environment, to take advantage of new computer-based technology to make substantial changes in working arrangements. However, in the engineering industry it was the union's own strategy in pursuing organisational-level agreements to secure a shorter working week, following a breakdown in national negotiations, which finally led to the EEF abandoning national multi-employer bargaining completely (Blyton, 1992). In other industries, such as the ports and water supply, it was management's desire to establish new organisational cultures, consequent on privatisation, which was the main driving force for abandoning multi-employer bargaining. Even within the remaining multi-employer bargaining in the public sector, the Conservative government encouraged fragmentation and decentralisation through the introduction of executive agencies in the Civil Service, hospital trusts in the NHS and locally managed schools (with the authority to determine their own terms and conditions of employment), as well as by supporting local authorities which wished to 'opt out' of national collective bargaining arrangements and establish their own arrangements for

■ Exhibit 9.1

The end of the line

With the collapse of the rail strike, the era of national disputes may be over (but local bargaining is not without its pitfalls).

This summer's dispute on Britain's railways had the makings of a long, bitter confrontation. In the red corner stood Britain's 12 000 rail drivers, famously loyal to their union, the Associated Society of Locomotive Engineers and Firemen (ASLEF), who had voted by 5732 to 3757 to turn down a pay offer of 3%. They had already held two one-day strikes, and planned a series of them, running into September. In the blue corner stood the board of British Rail, seconded by the government, determined to keep public-sector pay under control. 'This is a dispute we simply cannot afford to lose', said one cabinet minister.

They didn't. On July 24th, the railmen gave up. In return for a vague promise of future cuts in the working week, ASLEF suspended the action, though another ballot will be held to confirm the settlement.

More important, this third successive year of national trouble on the railways will inevitably be the last. British Rail's operations will be broken up between Railtrack, providing infrastructure, and individual train-operating companies, half of them privatised by next year. Each will negotiate separately with the unions, perhaps on different dates, certainly on different offers. A national dispute will no longer be possible.

The change is not confined to the railways. In the early 1980s there was a series of confrontations between unions and public-sector employers: in British Steel, the Post Office and, in a year-long strike, British Coal. Later there were national battles with ambulancemen and with teachers, and a dispute with nurses loomed even this year. But mounting such disputes is becoming ever harder.

Some of what were once public employers have been privatised. They face domestic and international competition. They no longer enjoy an open government cheque book and are consequently less of a push-over for the unions in negotiation.

Other public employers are breaking up. Opted-out schools enjoy some local discretion over pay and conditions. So do hospital trusts. Indeed, the railmen aside, it is increasingly hard to think of a group of public-sector employees who could plau-

sibly stage a national confrontation with their employers and have any hope of winning.

Nor is the change confined to the public sector. The unions are much weaker in the private sector too. Only one private sector employee in five is a union member.

Even where bargaining is still collective, it happens down the line. The multi-employer national agreements that used to determine private-sector wages have collapsed – in engineering, banking, cotton textiles, food retailing, cement and newspapers, for example. In every case, according to David Metcalf, professor of industrial relations at the London School of Economics, the change has been initiated by management and opposed by the unions.

In 1990, the authoritative Workplace Industrial Relations Survey, carried out by a group of academics, showed that, of every five workers on whose behalf collective bargaining still took place, only one was covered by a national deal. Four were covered by deals for each individual firm. Even company-wide bargaining is breaking down as firms settle pay and conditions at the workplace level, or for particular groups of employees within each workplace.

Taking public- and private-sector workers together, around half of British employees now have their pay and conditions affected by collective bargaining, compared with three-quarters 20 years ago. This has helped to reduce strikes. Whereas in 1978–79, when Labour was last in power, a day per employee per year was lost through strikes, last year the average came to five minutes.

More surprisingly, those who are not covered by collective agreements have done better than those who still are. Though unionised workers are still paid more, in every year since 1980, pay increases in bargaining units not covered by unions have been bigger than increases where the unions are still present.

On July 25th, the TUC launched a new policy to force a change in the law so that collective bargaining would have to take place wherever a majority of employees in a bargaining unit want it to. But even if a future government made the change, unions will struggle to get beyond the 50% threshold unless they can persuade potential recruits they have something to offer.

▶

■ Exhibit 9.1 continued

The future, then, is one in which collective bargaining, where it takes place at all, takes place between local management and local union representatives. The trick will be to reconcile the employees' desire for more money with the employers' need to contain costs. The only way to do this is by reorganising work practices, so that each employee produces more. And the greatest scope for doing this lies in doing local deals.

However, there are two caveats. First, the collapse of national bargaining will not necessarily mean an end to disputes. Some unions, indeed, may find it easier to get a particular group of workers in a smaller bargaining unit to strike than to organise a national stoppage. It would certainly cost the union less. And such disputes could still be disruptive – as a future dispute in the rail operating companies covering London commuters could yet show.

Secondly, employers will have to get their act together or risk humiliation. For example, the Royal College of Nursing has run rings round negotiators for the new hospital trusts, who had no previous negotiating experience. 'Local bargaining requires much more management,' says Mr Metcalf. If it does not get it, Britain may yet come to look back on the era of national bargaining with nostalgia.

Source: © The Economist, London, 29 July 1995.

---

determining pay and terms of employment. Finally, of course, the Conservative government abolished the Wages Councils as part of its strategy to deregulate the labour market. However, for smaller employers there may still be advantages in multi-employer bargaining – for example, new voluntary national multi-employer bargaining arrangements were set up in three industries (licensed clubs, lace finishing, and flax and hemp) even before the abolition of their Wages Councils and the smaller firms in multiple food retailing re-established a multi-employer bargaining arrangement for themselves after the withdrawal of the big supermarket groups.

The catalyst for decentralisation in the UK, and other countries, has been primarily management's desire to optimise its use of labour (achieve greater labour flexibility) to meet the increased threat of international competition. This was supported by the

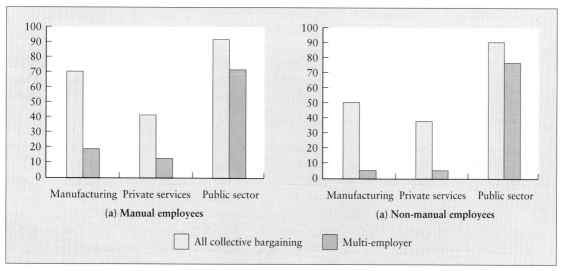

■ Fig. 9.3 Importance of multi-employer bargaining (1990) (%)

Source: Millward *et al.*, 1992: Tables 7.3, 7.6 and 7.9.

Conservative government during the 1980s and 1990s. It believed (Green Paper, 1989) that the maintenance of common pay rates through multi-employer bargaining created rigidity in the labour market which did little to reduce inflation and unemployment. Increased competitiveness could only be achieved, in its view, if pay levels and increases were more related to the profitability or performance of the organisation and local labour market conditions. It has been suggested that, for most managements, decentralisation is an integral part of developing a performance approach within the organisation's management of human resources and enhancing individualism, not simply a mechanism to lower wages or vary them according to local labour market conditions (Jackson *et al.*, 1993; Brown *et al.*, 1995). However, the two elements may not be so easily separated. For example, through creating separate business units, British Airways was able to introduce different (lower) pay and terms of employment for its European operations (centred on Gatwick) and its inter-continental operations (centred on Heathrow) (Colling, 1995). There is likely to be a further 'lowering' as BA seeks to break into the 'no-frills' air market with operations based at Stanstead.

Changes at the organisational level

The degree to which management seeks uniformity in terms and conditions of employment across the organisation results from a combination of structural factors (the nature of business development, organisation and strategy) and industrial relationship factors (management and union views of the scope and control of bargaining) (Ogden, 1982; Purcell, 1989). Corporate bargaining is more likely to be a feature of organisations which have a relatively integrated production pattern with similarity of work undertaken by employees in different parts of the organisation and central control of finance; devolved bargaining is more likely in diversified organisations with significant variations in production and working arrangements and where the different units compete for investment resources from the centre. Similarly, devolved bargaining at the unit level may allow for greater control of pay in relation to actual improvements in working methods and performance, while corporate-level determination of pay issues may allow management greater freedom at the unit level to make decisions about changes in working methods without having to agree them with trade unions. However, while corporate-level bargaining may allow management to set pay negotiations within the wider financial context of the organisation and its goals and plans, nevertheless it may also create an expectation and opportunity for union representatives to influence these strategic corporate decisions.

However, the apparent devolution of collective bargaining decision making to unit level does not mean, necessarily, that managers at these levels have complete freedom and discretion to determine pay and terms of employment in their part of the organisation. Most organisations maintain some form of corporate co-ordination and control over these issues, through formal corporate policies or guidelines, or through regular discussions among the different site management or with corporate-level management (Marginson *et al.*, 1988; Kinnie, 1990). The 1990 WIRS survey (Millward *et al.*, 1992: 234) identified that 60 per cent of managers involved in establishment-level pay negotiations for manual workers 'consulted' with higher management prior to commencing negotiations; however, it is not clear which level actually determined management's negotiating mandate.

It is perhaps surprising, given the weakened power of trade unions, that management has not used decentralisation as an opportunity for wide-ranging derecognition of unions. Indeed, successive ACAS annual reports during the 1980s and 1990s have referred to derecognition being 'rare'. However, two surveys (Claydon, 1989; Gall and McKay, 1994) identified a total of some 400 cases of derecognition up to 1994 but, because of the partial or grade-specific nature of most of the cases, the number of employees was relatively small (about 150 000). Importantly, in the context of decentralisation, Gall and McKay identified that, at least in some NHS trusts, management did not regard the non-granting of recognition for bargaining as 'derecognition' because the union(s) concerned had not previously had bargaining rights at the organisational level – only at the national 'multi-employer' level. Management's main strategy has been to rationalise and restructure bargaining arrangements at the organisational level in order to overcome the problems of multi-unionism and multiple bargaining units (more complicated negotiation process, inter-union disputes and a reinforcement of differences between groups of employees). Management's primary objective has been to introduce arrangements which facilitate greater intra-organisational consistency, labour flexibility and employee cooperation by introducing single-union agreements and single-table bargaining – which may involve derecognition of some unions in the workplace.

Under a *'single-union agreement'* (SUA) management gives one union sole and exclusive recognition rights for most or all employees within the organisation. Bassett described such agreements as a 'radical' reform of employee relations which offered 'the prospect of stable, consensual industrial relations' (1987). Certainly, many of the agreements include one or more of the following: employee involvement mechanisms (often with a new Employee Council within which negotiations are conducted with 'employee' rather than 'union' representatives); harmonisation of terms and conditions of employment across the organisation; and the inclusion of a 'no-strike' clause linked to the use of pendulum arbitration to resolve any differences. As a package, these developments support other elements of management's HRM strategies aimed at increasing labour flexibility and employee cooperation (such as team working, performance-related pay, training and development, etc.).

SUAs were a particular feature of the 1980s, although their actual number appears to have been limited. Gall (1993) found only 135 such agreements, 15 of which had existed before the 1980s (including four long-standing agreements at Tesco and Asda supermarkets and the Midland and TSB banks, which together accounted for about 75 per cent of all employees covered by SUAs) and only 14 of which had been introduced since 1990. This apparent decline in management interest in SUAs can be attributed, in a major part, to the availability of other, perhaps less radical and traumatic, approaches to reforming bargaining arrangements (in particular, single-table bargaining) and the success of other HRM strategies in achieving increased labour flexibility and employee commitment. However, it is quite likely that any statutory recognition process introduced by the new Labour government may well support a single-union approach.

The most criticised feature of some SUAs, certainly in terms of their effect on the subsequent bargaining relationship, has been management's use of a competitive, so-called 'beauty contest', approach to selecting which union should be recognised. The winning union has to satisfy management's criteria if it is to gain, and retain, recognition. Indeed, in a 'greenfield site', the SUA may be concluded before any employees are recruited. As a consequence, the union's *raison d'être* may easily become perceived as one of supporting management strategies and ensuring employee cooperation, rather than one of expressing employee interests and challenging management actions. This process of union incorporation is the complete opposite of unions being formed by and belonging to the employees themselves.

An alternative approach has been the establishment of *single-table bargaining* (STB) to overcome the long-standing segregation of manual and non-manual employees in most UK organisations (reflected in the use of differentiated terms, such as 'blue-collar' and 'white-collar' or 'works' and 'staff', and the existence of separate unions, bargaining units, collective agreements and terms and conditions of employment). The introduction of STB involves amalgamating existing organisational-level bargaining units into one, resulting in a single common collective agreement covering both manual and non-manual employees, but retaining multi-union recognition and representation. The concept builds on the past practice, in many organisations, of a Joint Union Negotiating Committee (JUNC) to bring together several unions representing different segments of manual employees.

A number of factors have led management to consider STB as a way of bridging the gap between manual and non-manual employees (Marginson and Sisson, 1990). First, at a pragmatic level, the existence of a coherent and integrated pay grading system across the organisation provides management with a *prima facie* defence against any legal claim from an employee based on 'equal pay for work of equal value'. Second, at a structural level, technological and organisational changes, and the accompanying changes in working arrangements, make it increasingly difficult to distinguish between what is manual and non-manual work. Third, at a relationship level, the continuation of differential treatment between these groups is perhaps incompatible with obtaining the involvement and commitment of *all* employees. All of these factors point towards increasing organisational integration and the need for harmonisation and common terms of employment (hours, holidays, sick pay, pensions, etc.) across all groups of employees.

Change in the structure of bargaining arrangements created by the introduction of STB has often been accompanied by changes in the bargaining relationship. Management has used the opportunity to broaden the areas of discussion, beyond pay and conditions, to encompass 'all matters affecting employees at work' (including strategic organisational change and human resource management). In doing so, the processes of informing, consulting and negotiating have become more integrated. While this may allow unions more opportunity to influence a wider range of organisational decision making, management's primary intention is to inculcate a more 'reasonable' and 'responsible' approach on the part of unions. At the same time, drawing unions together into a single negotiating body requires them to reconcile their different, and potentially conflicting, interests *prior* to any single-table negotiation, rather than management coordinating the *outcomes* of multiple negotiations to ensure intra-organisational consistency. The process of reconciliation may be complicated by the form of union representation in STB: if it is *pro rata* to the unions' membership, then the interests of the larger unions may dominate; but if it is equal representation, then the smaller unions may have undue influence. One approach adopted in Pilkington Insulation (IRS, 1990) has been to create a dual system composed of the unions' negotiating team, based on equal representation, and an 'advisory' body, based on *pro rata* representation, which determines the unions' negotiating mandate and ratifies agreements.

CHANGES IN THE BARGAINING RE

The process of collective bargaining assumes that the
relationship between management and employees
would prefer to resolve their differences, on a mutual
the relationship. However, within this general princ
or styles of collective bargaining relationship (Char
and McKersie, 1965): conjunctive or distributive ba
grative bargaining.

Conjunctive or distributive bargaining

This is generally characterised by:

- the issue being related to the relative distribution of a limited finite resource (particularly, the distribution of money in simple pay bargaining), which creates a 'win-lose' situation (one side's gain is inevitably the other side's loss);
- although the parties accept that they must achieve some agreement, there is little, if any, positive cooperation between them; the relationship is a competitive one which relies primarily on coercion and bargaining power to determine the outcome.

Cooperative or integrative bargaining

This is generally characterised by:

- the issue being perceived as a complex problem solving process (for example, the linking of changes in working arrangements to pay and job security), which has the potential, through the decisions of the two parties, to produce a varying value to the negotiation, so creating a possible 'win–win' situation (both sides achieve a gain);
- although the two parties are pursuing different interests or goals, both parties recognise the need to make concessions to secure a mutually beneficial compromise; the relationship is a cooperative one in which any gain made by one side is dependent on gains being made by the other side as well.

McCarthy and Ellis (1973) argued, at a time of relatively strong unions, that the most effective way for management to obtain employee support for organisational change to meet competitive pressures was through a strategy of *management by agreement*.

They believed that the development of a cooperative bargaining relationship, which sought to predict and plan for future needs of both management and employees, was preferable to a recriminatory relationship which dwelt on past decisions. However, this requires two fundamental changes. First, management has to accept the extension of employee influence into a wide range of managerial decision making areas. Second, unions have to accept that their role is no longer simply to oppose or challenge 'management' decisions but to be an active party in identifying and resolving organisational problems. Beaumont (1992: 120) noted that, in the public sector, the distributive bargaining relationship increasingly evident in national wage negotiations during the 1970s and 1980s had an adverse 'spill-over' effect on the more cooperative relationship associated with the joint consultative arrangements at the organisational level.

y noted, changes in the structure of collective bargaining inevitably have an
the nature of the bargaining relationship. At the same time, the collective bar-
g relationship has been affected by a number of HRM developments at the organi-
ional level which have been directed towards enhancing organisational performance,
securing employee commitment and strengthening the individual employment relationship.

Organisational performance and labour flexibility

The 'wage–work' exchange is at the heart of organisational performance and the collective bargaining process: while management is constantly seeking to improve labour efficiency, employees and unions are seeking to exercise some influence or control over the
introduction and form of new working arrangements. Management's drive, in the 1980s
and 1990s, for better performance and greater labour flexibility has produced a number
of pressures on collective bargaining.

So far as the content of collective bargaining is concerned, Brown *et al.* (1995) argue
that there has been a decrease in the range of issues subject to collective bargaining and
that they have become more closely linked to pay (concessionary bargaining) as management seeks to exert greater control over working arrangements. Dunn and Wright (1994)
present a more complex picture of the changes during the 1980s. Procedural provisions
(such as recognition, scope of bargaining and union facilities) were essentially unchanged
– if not actually expanded. They argue that the *de jure* basis of these provisions made it
more difficult for management to repudiate them even when the power balance with
unions shifted in their favour. Substantive provisions, on the other hand, have changed to
reflect greater labour flexibility. In this area, they argue, management has always maintained it has the right to determine and control production, organisational and working
arrangements, which are primarily areas of line management concern and control (rather
than the HR or personnel specialists, whose role focuses more on the procedural aspects
of the employment relationship). However, the way in which greater labour flexibility has
been reflected in the actual substantive provisions of collective agreements appears to
have been equally divided between 'general managerial prerogative clauses' and 'more
detailed, formal prescription' of the changes – the latter where management perceives a
'continuing problem of imposing the agreement'.

A significant aspect of the drive for greater labour flexibility has been the growth in the
so-called 'atypical' or 'peripheral' worker (employees working under a variety of short-
term contracts and/or part-time working). The very concepts of *'core'* and *'peripheral'*
employment are based on a separation of employees between those whose employment
relationship is relatively secure and determined by the organisation's internal labour market and those whose employment relationship is more tenuous and reflects external labour
market conditions (Atkinson, 1984; Atkinson and Meager, 1986). The 'peripheral' workers act as a buffer which allows management to increase or decrease its labour levels
quickly in response to organisational requirements. Peripheral working is not new; but in
the past collective bargaining was directed primarily towards regulating the pay and conditions of permanent full-time employees. Union interest in the organisation's use of
peripheral workers surfaced periodically, usually at times of recession, but primarily only
to limit their use in order to protect the jobs of full-time permanent employees (the bulk
of their membership). Consequently, their terms of employment were often left to management discretion or there was only limited regulation through collective bargaining.

However, the shift in the pattern of employment structures resulting from the increased use of such 'flexible' contracts – particularly, the 5.7 million part-time workers (accounting for 25 per cent of the total workforce and 44 per cent of female employment) – must inevitably affect the unions' ability to maintain regulation even within the organisation's internal labour market. The separation of the two groups of employees provides management with a greater opportunity to 'divide and rule'.

Consequently, trade unions are seeking to represent these workers in their own right, rather than collude with management in using them as a protection for full-time permanent employees, and, in so doing, to extend the bargaining agenda to encompass issues which are of direct benefit to such workers (many of whom are women and young people) – not least by securing equal rights for them. However, trade unions have not only, at a pragmatic level, to reconcile the potentially conflicting interests of permanent full-time employees and 'peripheral' employees but also, at an ideological level, to oppose the perception of labour segmentation. Management may be reluctant, however, to accept regulation of the pay and conditions of 'peripheral' workers because it will restrict the very freedom and labour flexibility it is seeking.

Even among the 'core' group of permanent full-time employees, there has been a move in some organisations (in both the private and public sectors) to weaken collectivism and enhance individualism. For some groups, particularly managerial and professional employees, this has involved the complete abandonment of the previous collective basis for determining the employment relationship, often established during the wave of white-collar recognition in the 1970s, and its replacement by *'personal' contracts*. For other employees, it may only be a partial personalisation of the contract, such as the introduction of individual performance-related pay. The development of personal contracts has been heralded, from a 'free market' perspective, as a liberation of employees which places 'ordinary workers on a par with directors and senior managers ... and the end of the "wage slave mentality"' (Mather, quoted in Pickard, 1990: 41), while others see it as liberating management, not the employee, by providing management with 'a license to arbitrarily alter pay levels and job content' (*Labour Research*, 1989: 13).

There is no doubt that individualisation of the contractual relationship is the antithesis of collective bargaining. The development of a collective basis to determining the employment relationship was intended to overcome the inherent power disparity between the individual employee and management, and, certainly, there is little evidence to suggest that this power disparity is any less in the 1990s than it was in the 1890s. At the same time, any weakening of the employees' collective power in the area of economic regulation must also weaken their ability to influence management in the areas of managerial relations and organisational decision making. Significantly, management has often been successful in adopting an incremental approach which weakens collective bargaining, perhaps as a prelude to its final abandonment, by offering the inducement of better terms to those individuals who voluntarily accept 'personal' contracts.

An important element in the performance and individualisation process has been the development of *performance-related pay* – 'unique amongst payments systems in stripping away those collective procedures and institutions which have obscured the essentially individualistic nature of the employment relationship' (Kessler and Purcell, 1992). At the very least, it introduces a personal variable element of pay, under the exclusive control of management, into an otherwise common uniform pay structure. Perhaps more importantly, the process for determining this element of pay is both decentralised and on an individual basis: it is the line manager's assessment of the individual's performance which determines his or her pay increase.

However, performance-related pay is not a form of individual 'bargaining'. The appraisal process is concerned with assessing performance, not negotiating the level of the pay increase: the individual can, at best, only seek to influence the manager's assessment of performance and without the support of a union representative. While unions have been reluctant to cooperate in the introduction of a system that reduces their role in pay determination, they cannot ignore it completely without risking isolation from any potential influence on its operation. They may still retain an important collective pay bargaining role in determining general increases in the pay grade bands or even the overall amount of money to be allocated under performance-related pay and, certainly, can seek to ensure fairness and consistency in its application through the joint determination of the procedural aspects of the appraisal process. They may also have a role, in relation to both performance-related pay and personal contracts, in supporting the individual member in their 'negotiations' with management – and for this they need information. This was supported by the Central Arbitration Committee in a decision relating to both performance-related pay in British Airways. In their judgement, although such systems 'severely restrict the role of the trade unions in [traditional] negotiations', they nevertheless required 'more sophisticated monitoring and checking' by unions to ensure fairness (IDS, 1990: 27).

Certainly, a combination of the individualisation of the contract and the development of 'responsible autonomy' forms of work organisation means that 'key areas which were subject to regulation by collective bargaining have been reintegrated into the sphere of management prerogative' (Bacon and Storey, 1993: 15). (*See* Exhibit 9.2.)

■ Developing forms of employee involvement

The focus of management attention has shifted from indirect, representative, power-centred participation through trade unions to direct task-centred employee involvement. Two elements of recent HRM strategies, aimed at increasing employee involvement and commitment, are particularly important in terms of their potential effect on collective bargaining: the delegation of work-related decision making to individuals and work groups, and the creation of employee or works councils.

During the 1970s, employee involvement generally centred on the redesign of the sociotechnical system as a means of satisfying employees' needs and improving the quality of their working life. However, since the early 1980s the emphasis has become more managerialist and focused on improving organisational performance. The characteristics of the new approach are embodied in phrases such as 'task ownership', 'empowerment' and 'responsible autonomy'. The underlying principle is that employees, on an individual or group basis, should be given delegated responsibility (and accountability) for the management and performance of their work, rather than being controlled through constant direct supervision. A significant part of the development of semi-autonomous work-groups involves not just organising task allocation and time-off among the individual members but, more importantly, determining work targets, maintaining cost and quality controls, co-ordination of activities with other parts of the organisation, etc.

All of these activities were previously classified as the essential elements of management's role. While in the 1970s managers may have resented such changes as a 'loss of

■ Exhibit 9.2

Brothers in alms

The deal struck between Ford and its workers may terrify General Motors. But it also shows how weak America's trade unions have become.

'Jobs for life'. That has been the dream of America's trade unionists for more than a decade. Intimidated by the spectre of downsizing and layoffs, and inspired by the example of countries such as Japan, they have sought to allay the insecurity under which their members constantly toil. Now America's workers appear to have neared their most cherished goal in their most beloved industry – cars.

On September 17th the United Autoworkers Union (UAW) wrapped up a new three-year agreement with Ford, which carries a promise that has been interpreted as a job guarantee for the firm's employees. The UAW now plans to carry the same blue-print into its negotiations with Chrysler and General Motors. Is the American car worker safe at last?

Each of Ford's 105 000 workers will receive a first-year 'signing bonus' of $2000, followed by 3% annual rise in the second and third years of the contract, roughly enough to match inflation. With an increase in pension benefits this should allow employees to maintain their present living standards.

All eyes are focused, however, on the contract's job-security provisions. During its negotiations, the UAW pressed hard to get Ford to stop 'outsourcing' production of parts to external, non-union suppliers. This has been the key to the industry's efforts to reduce its labour costs: the average UAW worker costs $45 an hour, compared with as little as $10 for some non-union suppliers.

The UAW succeeded in drawing the line. Although Ford has made no explicit promise to forgo further outsourcing, it has agreed to a minimum size for its internal workforce. During the next three years it will maintain at least 95% of its current number of jobs; if workers retire, quit or get sacked, the firm will have to add new jobs to replace them.

How much had Ford really given away? The company has already sent many of its parts jobs to outside suppliers. Productivity gains over the past 15 years have helped Ford reduce from five to two the number of workers it needs to make each car per day, according to Harbour and Associates, a consultancy in Detroit. The company can thus

afford to ease up for a while. Indeed, it has been steadily gaining market share for the past few years, and with domestic sales booming has been hiring new employees in recent months.

Moreover, as part of the agreement Ford has persuaded the UAW to accept a two-tier wage structure that allows it to pay new hires less than existing ones. With many of its senior workers retiring during the next few years, this provision makes it cheaper to honour its promise to replace them.

The UAW now hopes to push through similar contracts at Chrysler and GM. Chrysler will probably embrace the idea. On a percentage basis, it has been hiring even more workers than Ford, and it builds even fewer of its parts in-house. GM, however, cannot afford to give in without a fight. During the 1980s, while its competitors were busily scaling back and outsourcing, GM continued to build new factories and roll out ever more labour-intensive models. In the process, the company managed to lose 15 percentage points of precious market share: it now holds only 31% of the domestic market.

GM is trying to catch up with less-labour-intensive cars and outsourcing plans of its own. But industry insiders reckon it needs to cut another 50 000–75 000 jobs to remain competitive. Or, put another way, it would have to regain nearly 15 points of market share to justify its current hourly workforce of 220 000. If the company promises to leave its internal workforce at anywhere near current levels it could be signing its own death certificate.

The UAW may decide that the issue is so important that it will strike. That could inflict substantial damage on GM. Car makers' growing reliance on lean production, which means fewer stocks of parts lying about, makes it easier for a targeted strike to cripple an entire company. Last March, for example, workers at two GM parts factories walked out for 17 days, and quickly brought to a halt almost every one of GM's North American assembly plants. In theory, GM's weakness should put it in a strong bargaining position. In practice, it feels far more vulnerable to the UAW than Ford or Chrysler do. The same point applies to some other weak American businesses, in industries where unions will strike fear into bosses' hearts.

▶

■ **Exhibit 9.2 continued**

The airline business, in which a big carrier cannot afford to leave billions of dollars of equipment sitting idle on the runway, is one. But such businesses are the exceptions not the rule.

The union's plight has long been linked to the falling proportion of manufacturing jobs. But there has also been a marked decline in the union's power within that shrinking heartland. Last year, America's Bureau of Labour Statistics recorded just 31 strikes, the lowest number since it began counting them in 1947. The ability of America's unions to inflict damage has been diminished by two big trends.

The first is the growing anxiety – off the charts on almost every measure – felt by workers themselves. Terrified of losing their jobs, they are more willing to take whatever comes along. This growing pool of displaced and often part-time workers has made it far easier for upstart competitors to form non-union shops. Two decades ago, a strike would cost a firm's shareholders their profits. Now, in many industries, it will put the firm out of business.

There has also been a subtle shift in the labour laws. In the 1980s, the National Labour Relations Board made it far easier for companies to hire permanent replacements for striking workers. This has had a chilling effect on unions. Indeed, the UAW itself was crippled by this tactic last December, when Caterpillar, a tractor manufacturer, finally bludgeoned it into accepting defeat after a four-year contract dispute.

With their hand thus weakened, unions in most sectors are forced to accept whatever reassurances they can extract from their employers. The Ford agreement, in which the firm agreed in effect to replace retiring workers at a lower cost, is a good example. 'The agreement is a fairly effective defensive move [for the union]', says Charles Hecksecher, an expert on labour relations at Rutgers University, 'but there's no doubt that it is defensive.'

As their powers wane, America's trade unions are trying to cope in two ways. First, they are reaching out to new kinds of workers, especially 'knowledge workers'. But modern office workers are proving hard to woo. Many of them perform disparate tasks, making collective bargaining less useful. Thanks to the fashion for empowerment, many 'workers' now manage things themselves, so they are less likely to see senior management as an enemy.

Another line of attack is political – and the target is the Republicans and their anti-worker ways. Last year, when John Sweeney took over as head of the AFL–CIO union federation, he vowed to finance a $35m war chest to fight for pro-labour causes in this year's elections. New unions are also broadening their appeal by becoming more like employee co-operatives. They may not bring the boss to his knees, but they will offer you dental care, training and a union credit card.

In short, unions are lowering their expectations. As Stephen Yokich, the boss of the UAW, who negotiated the Ford deal, puts it: 'Our members did not elect us to go out on strike. They elected us to bring in an agreement'. Workers of the world, relent.

Source: © *The Economist*, London, 21 September 1996.

control, threat to their position and authority and anarchy on the shop floor' (Bailey, 1983: 106), developments in the 1980s and 1990s suggest that the process only appears to give employees greater control and, in reality, remains 'dominated and restricted by management' (Huiskamp, 1995: 166). The boundaries of the individual's or workgroup's authority, responsibility and autonomy are determined by management and are limited to areas which will increase organisational performance. Management values, interests and objectives become an integral part of each job. As a consequence, it becomes more difficult for employees to identify and justify, even to themselves, the pursuit of interests which are different to those of management. The determination of working arrangements are no longer a management initiative to be negotiated and agreed, on a collective basis, with trade union representatives prior to their implementation (during which process the two distinct interests, management and employees, can be identified and reconciled through compromise). Management is free to determine these issues directly with the individual or small groups of employees.

The development of individual identification with and commitment to management values and goals may be complemented by the creation of 'company', 'employee' or 'advisory' councils at the collective level. Such councils are intended to change the basis of traditional collective bargaining in two ways. First, all employees are generally afforded the same rights of representation, whether unionised or not, thereby reducing the importance of trade unions within the bargaining process. Second, they seek to develop a cooperative, problem-solving style which integrates the joint process of negotiation with the management controlled processes of information giving and consultation. It is perhaps significant that in establishing European Works Councils, at a time when the Conservative government had 'opted-out' of the EU Social Chapter and was resisting the European Works Councils Directive, some UK organisations (like United Biscuits) accepted union involvement in the new 'council' and a clear link to established collective bargaining arrangements. Others (like BP Oil, which also recognises trade unions for normal collective bargaining) based the council exclusively on 'employee' representation (EIRR, 1994). Thus, these European consultative bodies may be an alternative forum to traditional collective bargaining or they may lay the foundation for the possible future development of transnational collective bargaining.

In most other EU countries there is a legal requirement for the establishment of similar 'works councils', which not only have to be informed and/or consulted by management on general organisation matters (including strategic issues such as investment and rationalisation plans), but also, importantly, have to agree to changes in certain defined labour matters before management may implement the change (for example, working hours and payment systems). However, it is important to recognise that such councils have been developed within a collective bargaining structure which, in effect, contains the unions' role in the more conflictual (distributive) determination of pay and conditions of employment to multi-employer bargaining at the industry or sector level. This has left management free, at the organisational level, to develop a more cooperative problem-solving relationship with employee representatives, through the works council, which focuses on organisational needs. It is not surprising, therefore, that management find such councils generally supportive of their position and organisational needs and are prepared to persuade employees to accept management plans (Beaumont, 1995: 165). However, decentralisation of collective bargaining will inevitably bring the works councils, most of whose members are already trade unionists, n   the distributive negotiating area of regulating economic relations, with a conse   ⸱⸱⸱ relationship to management. Certainly, the 1976 Co-determination/   ⸱⸱ded union bargaining rights at the organisational level, mac
dant (Kjellberg, 1992: 121).

326

Dispute resolution

Conflict of interest is an inherent part of the emplo
putes' – management and union unable to resol
times involve the threat or use of industrial acti
an integral part of collective bargaining). Mu
nisms usually include a Disputes Procedure to
isational level. Consequently, the decline in r
also reduced the availability of such proced

ciliation or arbitration through ACAS. There is a clear preference, in the UK, for using *conciliation* (which facilitates the two sides reaching their own resolution) rather than *arbitration* (where an independent person adjudicates and makes an award). The number of collective conciliations undertaken by ACAS has been running at two or three times the number of strikes throughout the 1990s. However, it is in the area of arbitration that the most significant development has taken place.

Many UK managers have, in the past, criticised conventional or 'open' arbitration because they felt that trade unions were able to obtain a better settlement from an 'outsider', who not only has no managerial responsibility for the continuing well-being of the organisation but also has freedom to decide what is a fair and equitable settlement – often a compromise between the union's claim and management's offer. This, it was claimed, produced a potential 'chilling effect' on the conduct of negotiations by inhibiting the exploration of the full range of possible concessions and compromises during the negotiation; either or both sides may keep something in reserve to cover the possibility of an arbitrator 'splitting the difference'.

Consequently, not only has management been more reluctant to accept union requests for arbitration but it has also sought the introduction of *'pendulum' or 'straight choice' arbitration* where the arbitrator must find in favour of either the union's claim or management's offer. This approach is not new in UK employee relations (Treble, 1986); most 'disputes of right' require the arbitrator to make a choice between either the union's or management's position. Its application to 'disputes of interest' has been brought over from the USA, where it was introduced during the 1950s and 1960s to balance the legal restriction on strike action among essential workers when collective bargaining rights were extended to public sector employees. Its significance for the bargaining relationship is that the 'win–lose' situation in pendulum arbitration provides a 'cost' factor, similar to the use of industrial action, which both sides have to take into account in making their negotiating decisions (Stevens, 1966). However, the 'winner takes all' approach of pendulum arbitration is intended primarily as a deterrent (like the *threat* of industrial action) to induce the parties to bargain 'reasonably' during the negotiation and find their own mutually acceptable solution. Nevertheless, it can be seen to run counter to the principle of seeking a mutually acceptable compromise which underpins the negotiation process (Kessler, 1987).

The reality in pay negotiations is that the differences in the amounts being claimed and offered generally arise from differences in the factors being used by each side to justify their position. While management usually favours internal organisational factors (such as profitability and productivity), unions often wish to relate a pay increase to external factors (such as cost of living or comparability with the pay of other organisations). In conventional or 'open' arbitration the arbitrator is not required to choose between these different, but equally legitimate, reference points but can, in effect, provide a compromise. However, under pendulum arbitration the arbitrator, by having to decide between the two cases, appears to accept one or other set of justifications. It can be argued that, in so far as arbitrators may find it difficult to ignore management arguments ...ed on its 'ability to pay', pendulum arbitration may have the effect of legitimising ...l organisation factors as the proper basis for determining pay increases. Certainly, ...rbitration is not without its problems – particularly where the arbitrator has ...omplex, multi-issue dispute or where the positions of neither management ...easonable (Singh, 1986; Kessler, 1987).

CHAPTER SUMMARY

This chapter began by showing that collective bargaining continues to have an important role in regulating the terms of the employment relationship. However, as the example of the water industry demonstrated, there have been important changes in both the structures of collective bargaining and the relationship between management and unions.

The importance of collective bargaining lies in redressing the power imbalance between management and the individual employee. It is not just concerned with the economic process of determining pay but, equally importantly, it provides a means of constraining managerial prerogative and allowing employees to influence organisational decision making. Yet, unlike other countries, there has been little direct legislative support in the UK for collective bargaining.

Multi-employer bargaining, a traditional feature of most European countries, creates standardised terms of employment and stabilises wage competition between organisations. However, a major feature in all industrialised countries has been management desire to decentralise collective bargaining (and in some cases in the UK to rationalise its organisational bargaining arrangements through single-union agreements or single-table bargaining) as part of its HRM strategies to improve international competitiveness through greater labour flexibility. This has been supported, in the UK at least, by the past Conservative governments' strategy to deregulate the labour market.

The collective bargaining relationship should not be seen automatically as an adversarial one but may be conducted on a cooperative basis as well. HRM strategies directed toward greater use of peripheral workers and the individualisation of pay and contracts have narrowed the scope of collective bargaining. Similarly, HRM strategies aimed at increased employee opportunities to influence, if not control, their immediate working arrangements and the introduction of employee councils weaken trade union influence within the collective bargaining relationship.

Management has been attracted to the concept of pendulum arbitration because they believe it will induce unions to act more 'reasonably' in the conduct of collective bargaining.

QUESTIONS

1 Why is collective bargaining important? Explain how the different functions of collective bargaining, each in its own way, regulate part of the employment relationship,

2 In what ways do the 'conjunctive or distributive' and 'cooperative or integrative' approaches to the bargaining relationship reflect different views of the mutual interdependence of management and employees? Consider how the use of pendulum arbitration may affect the bargaining relationship.

3 What are the advantages and disadvantages of multi-employer and single-employer collective bargaining structures? Why has management been in favour of decentralisation?

4 In what ways do the different elements of an HRM strategy within the organisation impact on collective bargaining?

ACTIVITY

Forest Rural Hospitals is about to become an NHS trust next year. It employees some 2000 employees in two small hospitals (15 miles apart) and five health clinics scattered throughout other parts of the area. Until now its pay and conditions have been determined nationally through the Whitley Council system. It has had three Joint Consultative Committees (medical, administrative and ancillary staff) for some years on which a range of trade unions are represented – BMA, RCN, RCM, Unison, MSF, TGWU, GMB and AEEU.

1 In two groups (management and union) prepare for a forthcoming meeting to consider (a) whether or not the new Trust should establish its own single-employer bargaining arrangements, and (b) what form these might take.

2 As the HR manager, chairing this meeting, prepare a report for the Board explaining the advantages of single-employer bargaining (and any disadvantages) and analysing the pros and cons of the different forms this might take (including your recommended course of action).

REFERENCES

Atkinson, J. (1984) *Flexible Manning: The Way Ahead*. London: Institute of Manpower Studies.

Atkinson, J. and Meager, N. (1986) *Changing Working Patterns: How Companies Achieve Flexibility to Meet their Needs*. London: National Economic Development Office.

Ayadurai, D. (1993) 'Malaysia' in Deery, S. J. and Mitchell, R. J. (eds) *Labour Law and Industrial Relations in Asia*. London: Longman, pp. 61–95.

Bacon, N. and Storey, J. (1993) 'Individualization of the employment relationship and the implication for trade unions', *Employee Relations*, 15(1).

Bailey, J. (1983) *Job Design and Work Organisation*. Englewood Cliffs, NJ: Prentice Hall.

Bassett, P. (1987) *Strike Free: New Industrial Relations in Britain*. Basingstoke: Macmillan.

Beaumont, P. B. (1992) *Public Sector Industrial Relations*. London: Routledge.

Beaumont, P. B. (1995) *The Future of Employment Relations*. London: Sage.

Brown, W. and Terry, M. (1978) 'The changing nature of national wage agreements', *Scottish Journal of Political Economy*, 25(2), 119–34.

Brown, W., Marginson, P. and Walsh, J. (1995) 'Management: pay determination and collective bargaining' in Edwards, P. (ed.) *Industrial Relations: Theory and Practice in Britain*. Oxford: Blackwell, pp. 123–50.

Blyton, P. (1992) 'Flexible times? Recent developments in temporal flexibility', *Industrial Relations Journal*, 23(1), 26–36.

Chamberlain, N. W. and Kuhn, J. W. (1965) *Collective Bargaining*. New York: McGraw-Hill.

Claydon, T. (1989) 'Union derecognition in Britain in the 1980s', *British Journal of Industrial Relations*, 27(2), 214–24.

Colling, T. (1995) 'Experiencing turbulence: competition, strategic choice and the management of human resources in British Airways', *Human Resource Management Journal*, 5(5), 18–32.

Deaton, D. R. and Beaumont, P. B. (1980) 'The determinants of bargaining structure: some large scale survey evidence for Britain', *British Journal of Industrial Relations*, X(viii), 202–16.

Donovan Commission (1968) *Royal Commission on Trade Unions and Employers' Associations.* London: HMSO.

Dunn, S. and Wright, M. (1994) 'Maintaining the "status quo"? An analysis of the contents of British collective agreements, 1979–1990', *British Journal of Industrial Relations*, 32(1), 23–46.

EIRR (1992) 'The rise and fall of centralised bargaining', *European Industrial Relations Review*, no. 219, April, 20–22.

EIRR (1994) 'The first UK European Works Councils', *European Industrial Relations Review*, no. 251, December, 20–22.

Flanders, A. (1968) 'Collective bargaining: a theoretical analysis', *British Journal of Industrial Relations*, vi, 1–26.

Gall, G. (1993) 'What happened to single union deals? – a research note', *British Journal of Industrial Relations*, 24(1), 71–5.

Gall, G. and McKay, S. (1994) 'Trade union derecognition in Britain 1988–1994', *British Journal of Industrial Relations*, 32(3), 433–48.

Green Paper (1989) *Employment for the 1990s.* London: HMSO.

Green Paper (1991) *Industrial Relations in the 1990s.* London: HMSO.

Harbison, F. H. (1954) 'Collective bargaining and American capitalism', in Kornhauser, A. Dubin, R. and Ross, A. M. (eds) *Industrial Conflict.* New York: McGraw-Hill.

Hammarström, O. (1993) 'Industrial relations in Sweden' in Bamber, G. J. and Lansbury, R. D. (eds) *International and Comparative Industrial Relations.* 2nd edn. London: Routledge, pp. 197–219.

Huiskamp, R. (1995) 'Industrial democracy, employee participation and operational autonomy' in van Ruysseveldt, J., Huiskamp, R. and van Hoof, J. (eds) *Comparative Industrial and Employment Relations.* London: Sage, pp. 155–72.

Hussey, R. and Marsh, A. (1982) *Disclosure of Information and Employee Reporting.* Aldershot: Gower, pp. 17–33.

IDS (1990) *Incomes Data Services Report*, no. 570, June.

IDS (1994), *IDS European Report*, no. 395, November.

IRRR (1980) 'CAC disclosure of information awards', *Industrial Relation Review and Report*, January.

IRRR (1987) 'Pay bargaining: to centralise or decentralise?', *Industrial Relations Review and Report*, no. 397, August, 13.

IRS (1989) 'Developments in multi-employer bargaining: 1', *IRS Employment Trends*, no. 440, May.

IRS (1990) 'Single-table bargaining – a survey', *IRS Employment Trends*, no. 463, May, 5–11.

IRS (1992) 'Industrial relations developments in the water industry', *IRS Employment Trends*, no. 516, July, 6–15.

IRS (1993) 'Decline in multi-employer bargaining charted', *IRS Employment Trends*, no. 544, September, 7–11.

Jackson, M. P., Leopold, J. W. and Tuck, K. (1993) *Decentralization of Collective Bargaining.* Basingstoke: Macmillan.

Jacobi, O., Keller, B. and Müller-Jentsch, W. (1992) 'Germany: codetermining the future?' in Ferner, A. and Hyman, R. (eds) *Industrial Relations in the New Europe*. Oxford: Blackwell, pp. 218–69.

Kessler, I. and Purcell, J. (1992) 'Performance related pay: objectives and applications', *Human Resource Management Journal*, 2(3), 34–59.

Kessler, S. (1987) 'The swings and roundabouts of pendulum arbitration', *Personnel Management*, December, 40–42.

Kinnie, N. (1990) 'The decentralisation of industrial relations? – recent research considered', *Personnel Review*, 19(3).

Kjellberg, A. (1992) 'Sweden: can the model survive?' in Ferner, A. and Hyman, R. (eds) *Industrial Relations in the New Europe*. Oxford: Blackwell, pp. 88–142.

Labour Research (1989) 'Contract to kill collective action', December, 13–14.

Leggett, C. (1993) 'Singapore' in Deery, S. J. and Mitchell, R. J. (eds) *Labour Law and Industrial Relations in Asia*. London: Longman, pp. 96–136.

Marginson, P. and Sisson, K. (1990) 'Single table talk', *Personnel Management*, May, 46–9.

Marginson, P., Edwards, P. K., Martin, R., Purcell, J. and Sisson, K. (1988) *Beyond the Workplace: Managing Industrial Relations in the Multi-Establishment Enterprise*. Oxford: Blackwell.

Mathias, R. L. and Jackson, J. H. (1994) *Human Resource Management*. 7th edn. St Paul, MN: West, chapters 18 and 19.

McCarthy, W. E. J. and Ellis, N. D. (1973) *Management by Agreement*. London: Hutchinson.

Milner, S. (1995) 'The coverage of collective pay-setting institutions in Britain, 1985–1990', *British Journal of Industrial Relations*, 33(1), 69–91.

Millward, N. and Stevens, M. (1986) *British Workplace Industrial Relations* 1980–1984. Aldershot: Gower.

Millward, N., Stevens, M., Smart, D. and Hawes, W. R. (1992) *Workplace Industrial Relations in Transition*. Aldershot: Darmouth, pp. 217–75.

Moore, R. (1980) 'Information to unions: use or abuse?', *Personnel Management*, May, 34.

Ogden, S. (1993) 'Decline and fall: national bargaining in British Water', *Industrial Relations Journal*, 24(1), 44–58.

Ogden, S. G. (1982) 'Bargaining structure and the control of industrial relations', *British Journal of Industrial Relations*, xx(2).

Pickard, J. (1990) 'When pay gets personal', *Personnel Management*, July, 41–5.

Prondzynski, F. (1992) 'Ireland: between centralism and the market' in Ferner, A. and Hyman, R. (eds) *Industrial Relations in the New Europe*. Oxford: Blackwell, pp. 69–87.

Purcell, J. (1989) 'How to manage decentralised bargaining', *Personnel Management*, May.

Singh, R. (1986) 'Final offer arbitration in theory and practice', *Industrial Relations Journal*, winter, 329–38.

Stevens, C. (1966) 'Is compulsory arbitration compatible with bargaining?', *Industrial Relations*, 5(2), 38–52.

Taylor, R. (1997) 'UK unions: employers sense victory on recognition rights', *Financial Times*, 9 December.

Treble, J. G. (1986) 'How new is final offer arbitration?', *Industrial Relations*, 25(1).

TUC (1997), *The Business Case for a Union Voice – Take your Partners*. London: Trade Union Congress.

Walton, R. E. and McKersie, R. B. (1965) *A Behavioural Theory of Labor Negotiations*. New York: McGraw-Hill.

Webb, S. and B. (1902) *Industrial Democracy*. London: Longman.

White Paper (1998) *Fairness at Work*. London: HMSO.

Chapter 10

PAY

Jane Evans

Learning objectives

By the end of this chapter, readers should be able to:

- identify the contemporary contextual factors influencing pay in the workplace;
- examine the functions of pay within the employment relationship;
- consider the implications for pay of changing employee relations frameworks;
- examine the process of pay determination in the workplace;
- analyse the constituent elements of pay and pay systems.

INTRODUCTION

A commonly used term such as 'pay' needs little introduction as to its general meaning but its monosyllabic appeal does disguise a topic of considerable complexity. In this chapter 'pay' is used to denote the wages, salaries or fees paid by employers in return for the provision of labour. The term includes allowances, overtime and variable elements (such as bonus or performance-related pay) and benefits which have a financial value and are perceived by the employee to be linked to their pay (e.g. life assurance, leave entitlement and pension contributions).

This description of pay is reasonably neutral in that it does not anchor itself firmly within any one particular perspective of employee relations. However, in reality pay is not determined within a vacuum and does introduce questions of employer, employee and union values as well as those of society as a whole. This chapter explores the territory of pay from a number of different perspectives but does not seek to be prescriptive in terms of recommending particular approaches to address specific problems.

Pay as a topic cannot be addressed in isolation from other aspects of employee relations. For example, there are links with legislation, collective bargaining and discrimination in employment. An understanding of the different theoretical frameworks and of the trends within employee relations is necessary background.

Pay is an enduring and central feature of the relationship between employer and employee which is recognised in this book by its treatment as a separate topic. This is an exciting time to explore pay as it is currently typified by change, diversity and experimentation. This chapter addresses the reasons for change and the resultant diversity and experimentation. In particular, it examines:

- the contemporary contextual influences on pay;
- the functions of pay within the employment relationship;
- the implications for pay of changing employee relations frameworks;
- the process of pay determination;
- the constituent elements of pay.

CONTEMPORARY CONTEXTUAL FACTORS

The determination of pay in the workplace is influenced by a range of factors including government policy on employment and the economy, the legislative framework, employment trends and labour markets, technological change and societal values. Increasingly the UK's membership of the European Union and globalisation of markets introduce an international dimension.

Government policy on employment

The change in government in 1997 to a Labour administration after eighteen years of Conservatism signalled a new era in employment policy. The tone for employment reforms was set by a policy document (1996) entitled *Building Prosperity – Flexibility, Efficiency and Fairness at Work*, with the election manifesto targeting for reform the three areas of trade unions, the EU Social Chapter and the national minimum wage.

In terms of pay, trade union reform affects both the climate for pay determination and the role undertaken by the unions. The Labour government has stressed that it will not dismantle all the anti-union laws put in place by the Conservatives or favour unions, and that it seeks 'partnership not conflict between employers and employees' (election manifesto). The main reform affecting pay is that of compulsory trade union recognition if the majority of the relevant workforce vote in a ballot for union recognition. Supporting legislation is unlikely to be in place until 1999 although consultation and a White Paper are due in 1998. The adoption of the Social Chapter signalled the government's commitment to European-wide minimum standards of employment although its stated policy is to resist the extension of the Chapter to include pay matters.

The introduction of a *national minimum wage* (NMW) has major implications for pay, with some commentators arguing that this reform (among others) means that 'UK industrial relations looks set for a period of radical change' (Hotspots, 1997: 11). The NMW aims to address low pay (in particular affecting women), reduce the social benefits liability of supplementing the wages of the low paid and bring the UK in line with other industrialised countries – for example, the USA, Japan and continental Europe. It represents an interventionist approach to pay, in contrast to the free market views that the Conservative government espoused, which were put into practice with the abolition in 1993 of the Wages Councils for low pay sectors.

The independent Low Pay Commission, established in 1997 under the chairmanship of Professor Bain (Principal of the London Business School and an acknowledged specialist in employee relations), is charged with advising the government on what the NMW should be. The Commission's membership is intended to reflect the views of the business community although its opening composition has been criticised for its domination by academics and its lack of small business representatives (one member only out of nine being drawn from this sector). Two of the members are drawn from unions, with a third from the TUC.

One of the key issues in setting the NMW is its ratio to that of the average wage; the higher it is the greater the 'bite' of the minimum wage policy. International comparisons provide differing benchmarks. For example in the USA the minimum wage is approximately one-third of the average wage whereas in continental Europe it is 50–60 per cent.

From the viewpoint of government policy the 'knock-on' economic effects are critical in terms of the implications for the national wage bill and possible job losses. The higher the ratio the greater the economic consequences. TUC figures have suggested that 10.1 per cent of people are paid below £3 an hour and 17.6 per cent below £3.50 (*Sunday Times*, 1996a). The New Earnings Survey (1996) indicates a lower proportion of British Workers on less than £3 and £3.50 (*see* Fig. 10.1). Estimates suggest that NMW at one-third of average earnings would add less than 1 per cent to the national wages bill, affect up to 18 per cent of the workforce (mainly concentrated in certain sectors – for example, hairdressing, textiles, hotel and catering), and lead to few, if any, job losses (Philpott, 1996). The public sector appears unlikely to be much affected as minimum pay rates are mainly above £3.50. For example, local government workers have a £4.00 an hour minimum (*Financial Times*, 1997a).

However, estimates and projections are based on certain premises which are in themselves contentious. It is not clear whether a NMW would force employers to increase productivity to remain competitive (thereby protecting employment) or whether employers would respond by cutting jobs. Any widespread attempt on the part of employees to restore differentials might trigger spiralling wage costs (Philpott, 1996).

The national picture disguises a number of particular patterns. There are regional variations; for example in London, where pay is generally higher, the proportions affected would be less in contrast to the northeast, where pay is lower. Although low pay affects mainly female workers, there has been a marked change since the late 1960s in that males in their 30s and 40s form an increasing proportion of low paid workers (Joseph Rowntree Foundation, 1996). Small companies are particularly 'hit'. The CBI concludes that the majority of the low paid work is almost exclusively in small companies (*Financial Times*, 1997b).

The Labour government has consistently been reluctant to commit itself to a specific level for the NMW although it is urged typically by employers and the CBI to adopt a lower ratio and by trade unions and the TUC to bring the UK into line with continental Europe.

It is not just the level of the NMW which is problematic. There are important questions about what the 'wage' should include, for example in respect of bonus, benefits or tips, and therefore issues of comparability between groups of workers. An inclusive approach, i.e. one in which all elements of pay are included in the calculation of an hourly rate, would reflect more accurately total earnings. Such a system is potentially open to abuse as low paying firms could take refuge behind 'payment in kind' (e.g. company discounts). In addition, in a low paying industry (such as textiles) where shift pay-

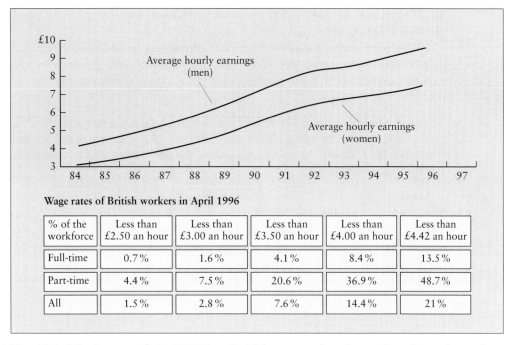

Fig. 10.1 The impact of the NMW on British average hourly earnings for males and females (1984–96)

Source: DataStream and *New Earnings Survey*, Office for National Statistics

ments and productivity bonuses are common, an inclusive approach could reduce effectiveness and make it difficult to attract or retain staff if they can earn the same on a minimum wage without incentive payments. In their submission to the Low Pay Commission, clothing, leather and retail employers in Leicester explained that 'the basic hourly contractual rate does not provide an adequate measure of employee income'. At the same time representatives of female Asian home workers described their 'bleak life ... a depressing picture of long hours and job insecurity with irregular work ... pay comes from the incentives of the piece work system' (*Financial Times*, 1997c).

Second, the issue of enforcement is key given the problems experienced during the time of the Wages Councils. In the twelve years preceding their abolition very few prosecutions took place despite some 100 000 firms allegedly paying below the Wages Council level. Effective enforcement depends upon satisfactory policing through 'inspectors' and a political willingness to deal firmly with transgressions.

Third, the mechanisms for updating the NMW are critical. An annual revision sets a 'going rate' or a norm for pay settlements generally, which the government may wish to avoid. On the other hand unions are reluctant to allow the NMW to stay unchanged for longer periods of time.

Fourth, there is the issue of exemption from the NMW in respect of youth employment and trainees. It is generally accepted that such an exemption is desirable although the age ceiling for youth employment is more contentious. Exemption for trainees becomes problematic if it is seen as a disincentive to learning. The official Downing Street line has been that the Commission must either set a different minimum for those under 26 or none at all. Companies do not appear to want a blanket exemption of all aged under 25 (*Financial Times*, 1997c).

Lastly, there is the question of regional allowances to address the regional variations in pay. Any move along this route effectively destroys the principle espoused by the Labour government that the minimum wage should be a national one:

> 'The government wants a simple system which has a universal rate' said the DTI. Officials said that regional rates would create problems over where to draw boundaries and whether staff should be treated according to where they live or where they work. (*Financial Times*, 1997c).

The issues surrounding the NMW are certainly complex. The *Financial Times*' (1997c) comment that the 'commission has an unenviable task producing a figure that reconciles fairness and efficiency and satisfies most people' aptly summarises the challenges (*see* p. 348).

■ Government policy on the economy

The Labour government is committed to a market economy which is internationally competitive and strong with flexible labour markets. There are a number of policy areas relevant to pay which have been evident in the opening period of this government.

First, the government is keen to hold down public spending and, therefore, restrain public sector pay for (at least) its first two years in office with pay settlements being funded within cash limits. The government as paymaster can directly restrain pay and so encourage productivity. For some groups of public sector workers (such as doctors and dentists, school teachers and the armed services) the government needs to take into account the recommendations of independent pay review bodies. The government is certainly mindful of the problems of bitter and long running public sector pay disputes faced by previous Labour administrations in the 1970s.

Second, the government shares with its predecessors the desire to keep inflation low. Inflation, or the fear of it, has historically driven pay settlements, with the wage–price spiral most evident in the 1960s, '70s and late '80s. Employees and unions, anticipating price increases during such periods, sought pay settlements in line with these, sometimes re-negotiating several times yearly. The annual growth of average earnings has been relatively steady since 1993 (*see* Fig. 10.2). The evidence of the mid- to late 1990s suggests that the wage–price spiral is not in operation.

The government inherits from the previous administration an economy in which wages fell to their lowest share of gross domestic product (GDP) in the forty years since records began. Such a statistic has fuelled debates about whether workers are getting a fair share of what is known as the 'national cake'. The Labour government continues to call for wage restraint. However, whether workers will heed that call is less clear. 'What sort of reward could workers expect for their virtuous self-denial?', asks the *Financial Times* (1997d). Its answer is a cautious interpretation of the Treasury view that pay restraint will help sustain higher growth, lower unemployment and contain inflation. It seems likely that the 'fair share debate' will continue although the NMW seeks to ameliorate the position of the low paid workers.

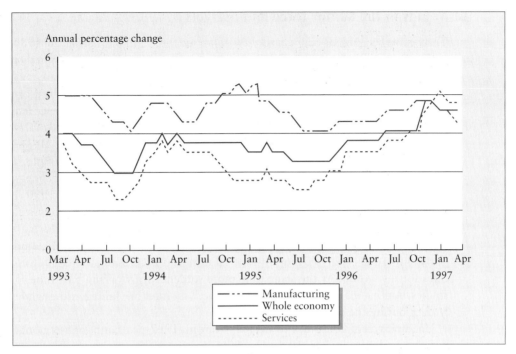

Fig. 10.2 Underlying average earnings index, Great Britain (1993–7)

Source: Labour Market Trends, July 1997: 251.

Third, taxation policies are relevant to pay determination. Direct tax has an impact upon take-home pay and indirect taxation affects household budgets. Employers are wary of changes in corporation tax that influence what they feel they can afford to pay employees. The government's declared policy has been to restrain tax increases, which has arguably contributed towards a stable climate for pay determination.

Legislative framework

Pay is regulated to some extent through legislation. In particular, the Equal Pay Act 1970 (with the Amendment Regulations 1983 and 1996) aims to ensure that men and women are not discriminated against in terms of pay on the grounds of sex. The Employment Rights Act 1996 (formerly the Wages Act 1986), regulates deductions from pay. The Trade Union Reform and Employment Rights Acts 1993 includes references to itemised pay statements and written particulars of employment. (For more detail on the relevant legislation, *see* Chapter 8).

ACAS has taken the view 'that developments in the law, including those coming out of Europe and the European Court of Justice, continued to have a substantial impact on employment relationships in 1996 and increased the number and complexity of cases in which ACAS became involved' (ACAS 1997: 19). This observation is certainly applicable to equal pay, which is addressed later in this chapter. In common with other employment legislation the Equal Pay Act 'proscribes' and renders unlawful certain behaviours whereas the Code of Practice on Equal Pay (1997) seeks to 'prescribe' desirable behaviours. (For more detail on the legal status of Codes of Practice, *see* Chapter 8.)

■ Trends in the labour force and markets

There have been major changes to the UK labour force and markets in the 1980s and '90s.

The loss of jobs from the manufacturing sector and the decline in manual employment in the early 1980s was followed a decade later by redundancies of white-collar workers in the service sector. The extent to which these changes represent a radical or permanent shake-up in the labour markets is open to dispute; for example, the average length of time staff stay with an employer has changed little over the past decade (*Social Trends*, 1996). The proportion of employees in temporary jobs remains small (*see* Fig 10.3).

However, workers' perceptions of job security have altered. For example, a 1996 survey of employee satisfaction found that the percentage of workers feeling secure with their current employer had fallen from 76 per cent to 43 per cent since 1990 (IRS, 1996).

The labour force, after declining in the first part of the 1990s, is now steadily rising (mainly due to demographic reasons) with activity rates generally increasing for women and decreasing for men. There are variations between age groups; for example, the proportion of 16–24 year olds in full-time education is increasing, thereby affecting activity rates for this group. At the same time more students are working part-time to fund their studies. Among male workers aged 55–64 activity rates are falling, although less markedly than during the early 1980s.

Unemployment continues to decline from its 1992 peak although regional variations persist, as shown in Fig. 10.4. The fall in unemployment may explain why the trend towards early retirement has become less marked in the 1990s. Among those who are economically inactive a small core remain 'discouraged', believing that work is unavailable.

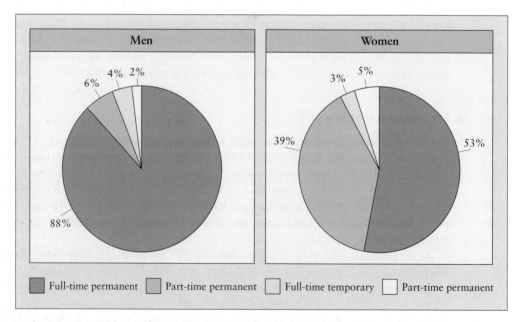

■ Fig. 10.3 Proportions of British male and female employees in temporary full- and part-time employment – Winter 1996/97

Source: Labour Market Trends, July 1997: LFS 36.

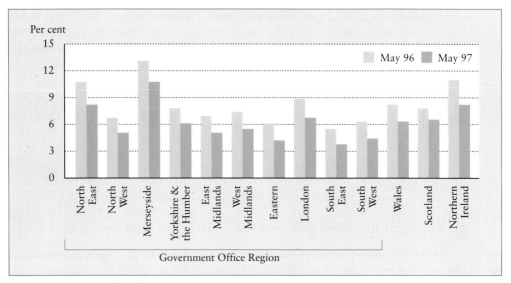

■ **Fig. 10.4 Regional claimant unemployment rates UK**
Source: Labour Market Trends, July 1997: 251.

Government social welfare policies influence patterns of participation in the labour force. For example, financial incentives aimed at the jobless or at single parents on benefits seek to encourage the economic participation of these groups.

Patterns of employment and unemployment shape the perceptions and expectations of those 'selling' and ' buying' labour, and hence the pay bargain struck between them, as well as having an impact on the total size and composition of the labour force.

■ Technological change

Technological change has had an impact on the skills profile of jobs resulting variously in deskilling, reskilling and skills upgrading. Where such changes occur they have implications for pay levels and pay hierarchies.

The print industry provides a recent example of the impact of technological change. News International introduced (secretly) in 1986 new technology at a 'greenfield' site (Wapping), including a 'direct input' system so that journalists could type copy directly into the computer. Previously this work had been done by the NGA, a craft union recognised by both management and unions as powerful, gaining good pay settlements and working conditions for its members. Journalists who were working for the corporation faced apparently the loss of their jobs and therefore generally agreed to the new system. The secretive imposition of new technology without the negotiated consent of the print unions led to a bitter and prolonged dispute. However, the skills profile of a craft group was irreversibly changed and their powerful position in respect of pay undermined.

Technological change has commonly been associated with greenfield sites and the promise of competitive advantage where there is also the chance for innovation in terms of employee relations/personnel policies and systems. The extent to which such innovation has happened on greenfield and other sites is not clear (McLoughlin and Clark, 1994: 89). New technology agreements which may be an indicator of employee relations change generally have not been widely adopted in either unionised or non-unionised organisations (Daniel and Millward, 1993). Nevertheless, it is likely that technology does bring modifications in pay and payment systems in recognition of changing skills profiles and the willingness of workers to accept new technology. These circumstances argue for payment systems that encourage flexibility and adaptability (Buchanan, 1989: 78–100).

THE FUNCTIONS OF PAY WITHIN THE EMPLOYMENT RELATIONSHIP

Pay is central to the employment relationship in a number of ways, fulfilling a number of functions.

■ The legal function: pay and the contract of employment

In the contract of employment, the employee agrees to provide a personal service for the employer in return for payment; such 'consideration' binds the parties and is therefore at the heart of the contract of employment. The level and nature of the payment is the outcome of negotiations between the parties, who in a legal sense have freely and voluntarily come to an agreement (and seek to update that as long as the contract continues). In reality the negotiations may be governed by collective agreements, restricting the capacity of the employee to reach a purely personal contract, although in theory all contracts of employment are personal. The power relationship between the two parties is unlikely to be strictly equal, so the bargain struck may lead a party to feel coerced.

Historically within the UK the basis of the contract was that of master/servant so that in consenting to the legal relationship, the employee accepts the status of subordination to the authority of the employer (such legitimate authority being known as the managerial prerogative). The ongoing negotiations between the parties to update pay has to be set, therefore, within this context. In matters of pay the employer can seek to exercise managerial prerogative, for example in the choice of payment systems.

The importance of pay to legal relationships is reflected in the statutory requirement to give written particulars of employment and an itemised pay statement for all employees working at least eight hours weekly (Trade Union Reform and Employment Rights Acts 1993).

■ Pay as a mechanism for fulfilling employer, employee and union objectives

An understanding of 'pay' depends upon examining further the possible objectives of employers, employees and unions involved in pay determination. There may be areas of common interest but there may be inherent conflict. Differing interpretations of the relationships between the parties are important. For example, a *unitarist* perspective (assuming mutuality of interest between employers and workers) suggests that there need not be conflict between them. A *pluralist* perspective (acknowledging a range of interests) indicates that conflict is possible. A *Marxist* perspective (with a clear divide between 'capital' and labour' argues that conflict is inevitable. (For more consideration of the theoretical frameworks of employee relations *see* Chapter 2.)

Employer objectives

Pay is a key mechanism by which an employer can persuade individuals to join and stay with the organisation, and make use of their labour and skills in pursuit of organisational objectives. Pay is therefore connected with the attraction, retention and deployment of workers.

Typically employers have a mix of objectives. Torrington and Hall (1995: 565–8) cite the following: (i) the prestige to be gained from being a 'good payer', (ii) the need to be competitive to ensure a sufficient supply of labour, (iii) the need for control over workers, (iv) the need to motivate and improve the performance of workers and (v) the need to control costs.

The employer's capacity to attract and retain employees at an affordable cost to the organisation is the result of a mix of variables reflecting the contextual factors discussed earlier in this chapter. It will depend partly on the employment opportunities in the marketplace that are open to potential employees and the relative perceived financial and non-financial merits of the competitors' bids for their labour. The potential employee may also make decisions about whether to enter the labour market and whether it is personally financially viable to withdraw temporarily or permanently, for example during periods of study or to take early retirement.

The employer's ability to utilise labour to the organisation's benefit through the instrument of pay raises questions of the relative strength of pay as a motivator and the quality of the relationship struck with the individual and unions. These issues are explored later in this section.

Employee and union objectives

From an employee's perspective pay fulfils economic and social objectives. It provides a certain standard of living, enables lifestyle choices to be made and is an indicator of societal status. Individuals' objectives in respect of pay change according to circumstance; for example, security of employment may be valued more highly than the level of pay at certain stages of life.

Employees, therefore, have a mix of objectives just as employers do. Torrington and Hall (1995: 563–5) identify these as (i) purchasing power, which determines the standard of living, (ii) 'felt fairness' about a 'fair rate', (iii) rights to a fair 'share' in profits or the nation's wealth, (iv) the need to maintain relativities in relation to other workers, (v) the need for recognition and (vi) the need for a suitable composition of pay.

Unions, in pursuit of members' interests, seek typically to secure continuity of employment and an optimum share of the profit in the private sector or of the 'cash allocation' within the public sector. Their objectives reflect particular circumstances. For example, the *Social Trends* report (1996) found that twice as many union members wanted their unions to pursue job security as pay.

The TUC's agenda is that of 'decent treatment and high standards at work ... We need to take the high road to high skills and high pay' (TUC Deputy General Secretary, conference speech, Employment Law and Practice, IPD/JSB 1997). The emphasis put by the TUC on the need to find common ground signals support for a social partnership model of employee relations and a less confrontational approach to pay determination.

> **Rover's three-year deal: an exercise in meeting employer and employee objectives**
>
> I'm determined and completely dedicated to making Rover a profitable, commercially successful company, which is respected as a player in car business terms world-wide. (Chief Executive, Rover, 1997; quoted in *Sunday Times*, 1997a)
>
> BMW had taken over Rover in 1994. At the start of 1997 Rover's annual loss was approximately £103 million. Sales output was the highest for eight years at 500 000 vehicles in 1996 but its UK market share was its lowest ever, at 10 per cent. The European car market (employing some 9 million people directly and indirectly, and representing about 10 per cent of the European Union's manufacturing output) was highly competitive. The car industry's Western European manufacturing capacity was 20 million and its sales only 13 million.
>
> In a period of high investment the shareholder is looking for areas of uncertainty to be minimised. Job insecurity is a major issue and this [deal] offers a significant period of stability for the workforce and real certainty on the part of the company about expectations and risks to payroll. (Personnel Director, Rover, 1997; quoted in *People Management*, 1997a)
>
> We are certainly happy to see it [the deal] recommended. (TGWU spokesperson, 1997; quoted in *People Management*, 1997a)
>
> The deal reached through negotiations between the unions and the company provides a 3.5 per cent increase for the first year from November 1997. In the following two years the increase is inflation plus 0.5 per cent or 3.5 per cent, whichever is highest. Associates (i.e. employees) with 12 months' or more service in 1997 receive an extra 1 per cent. Profit-related pay is replaced by holiday bonuses of £200 rising to £250 after three years.
>
> The agreement reached appears to satisfy the company's financial requirements, the employees' need for employment security and to keep pace with inflation and the unions' desire to be involved in collective negotiations on behalf of their members.

■ Pay as a mechanism for control and motivation

The need for management control and for employees to feel motivated are important employer and employee objectives, as indicated above. This section explores the effectiveness of pay as a mechanism for achieving such objectives by reviewing some of the many theories on motivation.

Pay as reinforcement

This approach is largely derived from the work of behavioural psychologists such as Skinner (1974). Individuals learn primarily through experience; positive and negative schedules of reinforcement can be used to shape behaviour. In terms of the workplace, pay can be crudely interpreted as positive reinforcement in that it sends clear messages about what behaviours are acceptable and desirable from a management viewpoint. Withholding pay (or pay increases) in some way will be negatively reinforcing.

Pay as satisfaction of need

'Content' theories of motivation focus on individuals as being in a constant state of need whose behaviour is directed towards equilibrium. A well-known theory emanating from this school of thought is Maslow's Hierarchy of Need (1954). In the workplace pay may be seen as a way of satisfying a particular need (e.g. paying the household bills), and to that extent it can be used to motivate. However, once the need is satisfied then it is no longer a motivator.

Herzberg's Two-Factor (1957) theory distinguishes between intrinsic factors (i.e. those linked with the job), which are motivational, and those which are extrinsic ('hygiene' factors, of which pay is one), which are not motivational in themselves, although their absence may lead to dissatisfaction. Such an approach reduces the role of pay in the control repertoire of the manager.

Pay as a factor in the process of motivation

'Process theories' of motivation focus on the cognitive processes underpinning behaviour. One of the main examples of this approach is Expectancy Theory (Vroom, 1964). Individuals make mental connections between behaviours and outcomes, assessing the probability that a given action will lead to a particular outcome (or set of outcomes) on which they place a personal value. Based on this 'calculation' individuals may be motivated to act. In the workplace pay may be seen by employers as a way of inducing particular behaviours; for example, financial incentives may lead to increased performance if an individual can make the mental connection between the effort required for increased performance and the promised financial reward. At the same time the individual must value the financial reward. Financial incentive schemes based on extrinsic rewards are only likely to be successful if the links between effort and reward, and the probability of achieving targets are clear, and if the money on offer is sufficiently attractive. Employee perceptions are therefore critical.

Criticisms are levelled against these theories of motivation – for example, on grounds of the soundness of the evidence on which they are based (Maslow's theory has not been validated by empirical research) or that they give only a partial picture of motivation (behaviourist approaches marginalising cognitive processes). However, many of these theories have an intuitive appeal that has led to an enduring set of beliefs about what motivates employees in the workplace – beliefs that have been translated into the popularity, for example, of financial incentive schemes.

A consideration of motivation theories highlights the potential managerial problems, such as expecting guaranteed or rapid success from a 'quick fix' solution (e.g. financial incentives applied to a performance problem) or assuming that a uniform approach to using pay as a motivator will work (individual differences may be crucial and a scheme that works well with one group may not necessarily do so with another). Misperceptions are not the exclusive province of management; unions with diverse constituencies may fall into similar traps of seeking uniform solutions for their pay agenda. There may be unintended consequences for unwary management even in apparently more sophisticated incentive schemes. Kinnie and Lowe (1990: 58) point to the possible manipulation by employees of piecework as one of the reasons for its decline. A similarly 'obstructive' response to a well-intentioned team-based incentive scheme is theoretically equally likely.

Pay may satisfy the financial needs of individuals and its level is likely to be, therefore, an important factor in attracting and retaining employees. However, employees will make mental links between the effort needed relative to the rewards that they can expect; in some instances they may decide that the temptation of a higher paid job is not worth the extra effort or risk of moving from their current employer. On the other hand, the offer of an intrinsically more interesting job or the prospect of career progression may tempt an employee to move for a similar or even lower level of pay, the latter 'deferring gratification'.

■ Pay as a visible manifestation of the 'psychological contract'

The notion of the psychological contract (Schein, 1965) helps explain the centrality of pay in the employment relationship in that it stresses the importance of the unwritten expectations that both parties have. Pay is a visible and tangible manifestation of the value that an employer places upon an employee and confers status. Below this surface statement is a tangled web of mutual expectations with many tensions. When employees talk of 'equity' and 'fairness' or employers of 'reasonableness' in relation to pay, both parties are alluding more to unwritten expectations than to a legally determined position. If one side believes that the other is frustrating its legitimately held expectation, then a progressive breakdown in the employment relationship will follow.

Where unions are involved there is a triangular arrangement in that the employee has a psychological contract with both the union and the employer. As a union member, the employee has unwritten expectations that the union will not, for example, 'sell out' to the employer. The union expects that its members will support it as required; for example, if it calls for strike action in support of a pay claim, it expects such support to be forthcoming.

Employees' perceptions of fairness are partly determined by their view of how much other employees are paid. The question of differentials is important, i.e. the maintenance of the 'gap' between their earnings and those of other groups in the organisational pay hierarchy. Employees also reference their pay by looking at the earnings of groups outside the organisation, making judgements about the fairness (relativity) of their own situation.

The extent of possible breakdown in mutual expectations in relation to pay is reflected within the advisory, conciliation and arbitration work undertaken by ACAS. In 1996 45 per cent of collective conciliation casework, some 21 per cent of advisory mediation work and 71 per cent of arbitration and dispute mediation were attributable to pay and grading issues (ACAS, 1997: 34, 44, 56).

THE IMPLICATIONS FOR PAY OF CHANGING EMPLOYEE RELATIONS FRAMEWORKS

■ A new pay order?

In the last couple of decades the UK employee relations landscape and climate have changed, reflecting competitive pressures and the political agendas of both Labour and Conservative governments as well as the perceptions and views of the 'actors'.

Corresponding changes have taken place in terms of pay – for example, widespread interest in pay initiatives such as performance-related pay, and the moves away from national collective bargaining. The extent to which these represent a primarily pragmatic response by the 'actors' involved in pay or the emergence of a new pay order is an important question. Both perspectives have their supporters but the lack of empirical evidence and the difficulties of defining 'old' and 'new' pay are problematic.

The concept of 'new pay', emerging in the US in the late 1980s and early '90s, is based on what is held to be a distinctive philosophy with a managerialist slant. The terms 'reward management' or 'employee reward' are more commonly used to delineate the departure from traditional pay and the arrival of a new pay order within a UK context. Armstrong (1996a: 3) in marking out the territory of 'employee reward' argues for an underlying pay philosophy based on 'the stance that people ought to be rewarded according to their contribution and competence...not just compensated because they have come to work'. The link between business and reward strategy is seen as critical to the development and success of the latter.

The new pay order appears to fit more comfortably within HRM than in traditional employee relations approaches. It is important, therefore, to place debates on pay within the broader framework of employee relations changes.

Pluralism/unitarism: collectivism/individualism

There are a number of possible dimensions on which changes in employee relations can be mapped. Attempts to construct thematic classification systems which describe end states associated with 'traditional' employee relations or HRM as a distinctive employment approach often touch on common themes. Such systems draw attention to the multidimensional aspects of change along a continuum.

Among the common themes are those of pluralism/unitarism and collectivism/individualism. Storey (1992), for example, in identifying 27 points of difference between 'industrial relations and personnel' and 'HRM' describes the nature of relations as pluralist in the former, with conflict institutionalised, and unitarist in the latter, with conflict de-emphasised. Another dimension of labour management in the same model associates collective bargaining contracts with industrial relations and personnel and individual contracts with HRM. The very use of the term 'collective bargaining' in respect of pay suggests a pluralist rather than unitarist framework. The decline in membership of trade unions and the restrictive climate they faced under the Conservative government as well as a resurgence of the managerial prerogative arguably have undermined the traditional pluralist framework for pay. In one sense collective bargaining, in that it provides the mechanisms for a failure to agree, institutionalises the scope for conflict.

The stated commitment of the Labour government to collective bargaining through compulsory trade union recognition may strengthen the pluralist foundations for pay. At the same time the government has called for a 'stakeholder economy' and a 'partnership' approach to employee relations. It has made it clear to the unions in urging modernisation that it does not want to return to the confrontational climate faced by the Labour administration in the 1970s.

The TUC's official response is broadly supportive although there is unease about this policy among some trade unionists for whom it represents an unacceptable compromise brought about by their weakened industrial position. The TUC General Secretary has reflected, 'There is no alternative to capitalism that I can see but are we to have the US model with few rights for workers, the authoritarian model of the East Asian tiger economies, or the European model of social partnership? ... For small countries like ours, I think it is the only model' (People Management, 1997b). The CBI's policy seems to be one of cautious support for partnership although it is opposed to compulsory measures for trade union participation.

The new pay order espouses the concepts of the stakeholder and employee involvement, identifying unions as one of the stakeholders (Armstrong, 1996a). Collective bargaining is accepted although minimally addressed within reward management. There is emphasis on varying pay to acknowledge individual contribution. Employee involvement is managerially driven and seeks to minimise the risk of conflict. Overall reward management (as a pay orthodoxy) is more unitarist than pluralist and more individualistic than collectivist rather than exclusively one or the other. The rhetoric of 'partnership' and 'stakeholders' is shared by those who support a pluralist framework and as such may be seen as a counterbalance to adopting more extreme positions at either end of the continuum.

Business strategy and pay

Another set of possible changes in employee relations relates to the extent to which practices are driven by business or corporate strategy and are integrated horizontally as well as vertically (Marchington and Wilkinson, 1996). Storey (1992) describes the initiatives within industrial relations and personnel as 'piecemeal' and those within HRM as 'integrated', and the corporate plan as 'marginal' to the former and 'central' to in the latter. The new pay order clearly stakes its claim to be strategically driven (by management) and stresses the integrative processes that link all aspects of pay to performance management. Such rhetoric does not feature in more traditional approaches to pay.

'Soft' and 'hard' approaches to pay

The question of strategic intervention by management raises issues of 'soft' and hard' HRM (Guest, 1989), where the former aspires to gain employee commitment and encourage resourceful behaviour, and the latter to utilise labour fully. The new pay order seeks to integrate aspects of both although there are inherent tensions. For example, paying for performance may encourage the full utilisation of labour but it can risk losing the commitment of those who contribute loyally but are average rather than high performers.

Management style, strategy and pay

In practice HRM and 'traditional' industrial relations and personnel are found in varying forms in different sectors of the economy and types of organisation. The variations may be explained in part by management style and lead to a particular employee relations strategy (a topic discussed in more detail in Chapter 3). For example, the Management Style Matrix proposed by Purcell and Ahlstrand (1994) identifies a number of possible management choices on the dimensions of individualism and collectivism. The former can vary from management viewing employees as no more than a commodity through to recognising them as a resource. The latter ranges from a unitary position through an adversarial one to cooperative collectivism. The combination of choices open to management leads to a variety of styles and strategies. The matrix recognises that styles evolve and change. Employee relations strategies clearly have implications for pay, and so the matrix is a useful analytical device in understanding the complexities of pay.

If management view employees as no more than a commodity and take a unitary stand (described in the matrix as a '*traditional style*'), then it is likely that the resulting strategy on pay will be driven solely by cost considerations, and any union recognition or involvement in pay determination will be opposed. Pay represents in such circumstances no more or less than the acceptable (market) rate for exchange. In low pay sectors (for example, hotel and catering), those managements adopting this style will be especially affected by the NMW and by proposals for compulsory union recognition.

In those situations where management recognise trade unions (but adopt an adversarial view) and do not especially see employees as a resource (described in the matrix as a '*bargained constitutional*' style), then it is likely that collective bargaining over pay will be conducted as a battleground with both guerrilla and open hostilities. In a sense this approach to employee relations fits uncomfortably with the calls for 'partnership' and is associated with the industrial unrest of the 1970s.

There are some styles, typified by recognising employees as a resource, which are closer in spirit to what might be called HRM approaches. The matrix distinguishes between those managements that take a unitary view and those that take a cooperative collective view (the former style is referred to as '*sophisticated human relations*' and the latter as '*sophisticated consultative*'). The sophisticated human relations style is likely to seek to exclude union participation but will not see cost minimisation as an appropriate way to approach pay. IBM is a good example of this type of company. It discourages unionisation but has prided itself on paying its employees well. The sophisticated consultative style implies that the involvement of unions in pay determination will be welcomed as parties to what may be seen as a problem solving exercise in 'fair' distribution of the profit. Rover, the company featured earlier in the chapter, is a typical example of the 'sophisticated consultative' style. The company is unionised and has made considerable efforts to move from an adversarial collective stance (which characterised employee relations in the car industry in the 1970s) to a more cooperative one reflected in the 1997 deal.

Such a discussion highlights variety and change as key issues in pay. A combination of factors (for example, government policy and the strategy of management and unions at national and workplace level) is triggering change and experimentation in approaches to pay, probably particularly so among organisations taking a more sophisticated view of pay. There is a degree of instability and uncertainty as organisations seek to find an effective pay formula. The emergence of reward management needs to be seen in that context of change representing a move towards either sophisticated human relations or sophisticated consultative styles. It has been argued that within HRM, reward management systems are particularly significant as symbols in that they 'send messages' about what management may value – for example, individual performance and commitment (Tyson, 1995). In such circumstances management often seek to link pay to a broader change management programme.

Empirical evidence to support the extent or precise direction of change within pay is elusive, just as it is more generally for the emergence of HRM. There is some survey evidence; for example, the CBI / Hay Management Consultants survey (1996) suggests that many organisations are making or looking to make changes to pay linked with business performance. More generally, writers such as Legge (1995) and Tyson (1995) are unconvinced that there has been the overthrow of one symbolic order (or orthodoxy) by another (i.e. personnel and industrial relations by HRM). A similar argument seems appropriate for pay. The reality may not match the rhetoric (Legge, 1995).

In practice, change is most probably taking place but the new pay order may not be so clearly delineated in practice as it is in its pure form in the literature. The Pirelli study (Clark, 1995) suggests that employee relations strategies are evolving to find a compromise position between that of traditional personnel and HRM within a UK framework.

THE PROCESS OF PAY DETERMINATION

Collective bargaining and unilateral action by management

All organisations need to develop processes and procedures, mechanisms and institutional arrangements to determine how much of the profits in private industry and the cash limits within the public sector is to be allocated to payroll, and how that allocation is to be distributed among employees. Such processes and arrangements may involve joint determination between employers and trade unions resulting in collective agreements (i.e. collective bargaining) or unilateral determination by management subject to any outside intervention – for example, via the NMW or pay review bodies. In practice collective bargaining only covers a minority of employees (Millward et al., 1992). (Collective bargaining is addressed in Chapter 9.)

The 'actors' and their network of relationships can be complex. Employers, employees and their representatives (trade unions or staff associations) all have their own expectations and objectives. Employers may be part of an employers' federation and trade unions members of the TUC or involved in multi-union bargaining. The government's role can be direct (as paymaster in the public sector) or indirect through social and economic policy and legislation. If the parties fail to agree, the help of an outside and independent body such as ACAS may be enlisted.

There have been a number of developments in the last couple of decades in collective bargaining which are particularly relevant to a study of pay in that they contribute to the climate of change and experimentation.

The decline in multi-employer, industry-wide pay bargaining

This approach to collective bargaining results in nationally set pay rates which may be enhanced through local negotiations at employer or plant level. By the late 1980s a number of companies had withdrawn from multi-employer agreements (for example, in banking) despite union resistance. The tradition of often informal and fragmented workplace bargaining on top of national pay rates within the private sector had arguably led to wage drift and escalating payroll costs.

For large and often diverse companies, management sees single employer and local pay bargaining as a way of responding flexibly to competitive pressures. Pirelli General, for example, opened a technologically advanced factory on a greenfield site in 1992 in Aberdare, South Wales. The company had withdrawn from multi-employer bargaining in 1987 as part of a break with what it saw to be traditional employee relations patterns. For the new factory collective bargaining was to be locally conducted and, after considering 'bids' from five unions to represent the workforce, it chose the GMB, with whom it concluded a single-union agreement – a typical development in greenfield unionised sites. The agreement gave local union representatives the right to bargain over pay for the workforce and included a 'no strike' clause with binding arbitration as a final stage in instances of 'non-agreement' (Clark, 1995). Such examples signal the apparent willingness on the part of some employers and trade unions to reach accommodation over pay arrangements in the light of changing economic circumstances.

Decentralisation in the public sector

In the public sector in Britain there has been a long tradition of centralised pay bargaining with complex and complementary sets of arrangements to cover diverse groups of workers. The pay of health service workers, for example, has been negotiated centrally by their various unions through the auspices of the Whitley Council, leading to national agreements for different occupations.

Under the Conservative government privatisation and other initiatives such as competitive contract tendering and the establishment of Health Trusts led to some decentralisation and fragmentation over pay negotiations. The dismantling of often long-established procedures has been destabilising. For example, in the privatised electricity industry Northern Electric plc wanted to pull out of central bargaining and negotiate pay separately for each of the eleven companies it had set up. The unions resisted the proposed changes. Agreement was only reached after conciliation through ACAS (ACAS, 1997: 41–2).

In the National Health Service, the Conservative government had wanted Trusts to set pay locally. By 1997, after six years, only 15 per cent of the workforce were on local terms and conditions. Frustrations were evident. The issue of local pay was put on hold and national awards made – for example, by the pay review body for nurses and therapists. The NHS Trust Federation (representing a managerial viewpoint) said in respect of the 1996/7 negotiations, 'Never has so much effort been expended over so little money' and Unison (representing a range of health service employees) judged the process a 'shambles' (*Financial Times*, 1997e).

Single-union deals and single-table bargaining

In both of the above cases the process is streamlined with only one union negotiating for all employees or, in the case of the latter, unions agreeing on a collective negotiating position. Single-union deals are often associated with greenfield sites and linked with 'no-strike' clauses and pendulum arbitration (the use of a third-party arbitrator) – for example, the Pirelli Aberdare plant discussed above. Unions representing workers in local authorities have agreed to single-table bargaining (this agreement is discussed later in this chapter). Again, these changes apparently signal acceptance of the willingness of employers and trade unions to seek accommodation to meet current circumstances.

Similar themes of decentralisation, fragmentation and streamlining apply to unilateral management action over pay. The forces for change in collective bargaining apply equally to non-union organisations where the capacity for independent management action is unfettered by union representation. In multi-divisional (M-form) companies, where decentralisation and divisionalisation are accompanied by a reduction in central personnel departments, then local management may find themselves without specialist expert advice.

Decentralisation, fragmentation and streamlining of collective bargaining and unilateral management action over pay may bring problems as well as gains. For example, multi-employer collective bargaining may be cumbersome and slow but it can avoid leapfrogging claims and escalating payroll costs as unions seek to play one employer off against another. Single-table bargaining can be an effective mechanism for combining unions and employer, and focusing on mutual interests but it may exclude from the agenda (and marginalise, therefore) the 'non-standard workers' less likely to be covered by union representation. Devolved decision making over pay affords faster and more flexible responses to competitive pressures. However, if such decisions are coupled with the dilution of organisational expertise (typically found in centralised specialist departments), then management action may be misguided. A review of pay processes in public and private sector organisations prompts Murlis to question the 'pay literacy' of some managers: 'We are still living with a generation of senior managers whose appreciation of the influences on pay ... is far from complete' (Murlis, 1996: 151).

Reconciling internal and external pressures on pay

Decisions about pay, whether unilaterally made by management or collectively with unions, need to take into account the requirement for internal equity and fairness as well as the external pressures of the marketplace and of the legislative framework.

Setting pay hierarchies and structures: job evaluation

In small organisations senior managers rely on a personal knowledge of the jobs, the individuals and market rates to set these into some sort of pay hierarchy. It is typically an informal approach with scope for personal negotiation. In larger organisations the informality and 'ad-hocery' are less sustainable and employers often seek a more systematic and formal approach to determining the internal relative value of different jobs/roles within the organisation on which a payment system can be based. This judgmental process is called *job evaluation*, which is a generic term covering a range of different approaches and schemes.

The introduction of job evaluation may be a management-led initiative. Trade unions also seek involvement in job evaluation at the workplace and are likely to participate in the initial grading of jobs and the subsequent appeals procedure. Job evaluation can be *a mechanism*, therefore, for supporting a pluralist or stakeholder approach to employee relations.

There are broadly two categories of job evaluation scheme: *analytical* and *non-analytical*. The difference between the two approaches is that non-analytical schemes make assessments of relative worth by comparing whole jobs whereas analytical schemes break the job into component parts (known as factors, e.g. skill and knowledge, mental and physical effort required), using these as the basis for comparison. Commonly factors are given minimum and maximum numerical values, i.e. points, and weighted to show their relative importance, so that jobs can be 'measured' against these and therefore with one another. Schemes that award a numerical score on this basis are referred to as 'points rating'.

Organisations can develop their own analytical or non-analytical evaluation schemes but many make use of 'off the peg' schemes marketed by consultants (one of the most widely used is the 'Hay Method' from Hay Management Consultants, which evaluates jobs under the framework headings of 'know-how', 'problem solving' and 'account-ability'). Some schemes are computerised although human judgement still underpins their design and operation. Organisations may need to make use of several schemes to cover diverse groups. For example, manual and white-collar jobs have traditionally been eval-uated separately within local authorities but employers and unions have agreed to move towards a scheme suitable for all employees as part of a single-status deal reached in 1997 (discussed later in this chapter).

It is difficult to establish how widespread job evaluation has become. A review of the recent survey evidence by IDS (Focus, 1996: 4–5) concluded, however, that 'not only is job evaluation widely used, its use is actually increasing'. The growth is marked in the public sector and small, fast-growing companies. The majority of organisations use ana-lytical schemes (IRS, 1993: 4), which offer protection against equal pay claims (see below). For those critics of job evaluation who had predicted its decline, the increase in its use has been a surprising trend.

The criticisms from academics and practitioners have mainly centred on the perception of job evaluation as essentially a bureaucratic system in that it reinforced the strict 'peck-ing order' and tight boundaries of jobs associated with bureaucratic structures. It put an exclusive focus on the job, so ignoring the contribution of the individual. As a process it was seen as overly elaborate and paraded itself as a science when at best it was system-atic. Lawler (1986: 20, 27–8) led the way with a strong attack on points rating schemes in what he saw as an 'admittedly "biased" article because it focuses on the downside of point-factor approach'. He concluded that the approach 'reinforced a particular value system … once installed it can be terribly captivating … but as traditional management is becoming less appropriate, so are point-factor job evaluation approaches'. Elaborate job evaluation schemes that derived their legitimacy from traditional organisations were seen as inappropriate. They seemed incompatible with functional flexibility, less rigid organi-sational structures, the breaking down of job boundaries and a non-bureaucratic style of management. Decaying job evaluation schemes are seen to lead to what is known as 'grade drift', i.e. pay increases are gained through unjustified upgradings. Such drift leads to escalating pay costs.

The supporters of job evaluation argue that its principles are sound, and so are par-ticular schemes, but that scheme design needs to reflect the changing climate. Armstrong and Baron (1995: 47) argue that 'job evaluation processes in fluid and adaptive organi-sations must therefore be designed and operated flexibly'. For example, in some of the traditional schemes the focus for job comparison was on the tasks associated with a par-ticular job; now the focus has been broadened to take more account of the overall role or part played by the individual. Some job evaluation schemes have been modified to fit with competency or skills-based approaches to pay (discussed later in this chapter). Commentators (Armstrong, and Baron, 1995: 111; Murlis and Fitt, 1991: 43) argue strongly that competency and skills-based pay do not replace the need for job evaluation and, if so used, risk cost escalation (Pritchard and Murlis, 1992: 22).

Job evaluation, therefore, despite the criticisms, does seem to satisfy a basic organisational need for internal order, control and equity on the part of employers, employees and unions. If an analytical approach is used, it can be a defence against equal pay claims. There does seem to be some evidence that organisations are introducing job evaluation in response to change. 'However flexible and fast moving an organisation … job evaluation provides the essential link between business direction and individual role value' (Murlis and Fitt, 1991: 43). It has been argued (IDS, 1996: 6) that the more devolved and flexible pay systems become, the greater the need for order.

Job evaluation in practice: No-Such Brewery

The brewery has a number of different types of jobs including those connected with the brewing and conditioning of beer, its bottling and kegging, and warehousing/despatch.

Management has agreed with the union representing the workers that it will introduce a job evaluation scheme as a basis for pay and grading after union concerns that there are pay inequities between different departments. The personnel department engages a consultant to help with the design of a tailor-made scheme in consultation with the union.

The scheme will be implemented by management using a trained member of the personnel department and a joint management–union panel to evaluate jobs and hear appeals on gradings.

The proposal is to base the scheme on the factors listed in Table 10.1.

Table 10.1 Factors for job evaluation scheme

Factor headings	Outline factor description*
Knowledge and skill	Formal training; experience; physical ability[+]
Supervisory responsibility	Responsibility for work of others
Responsibility for product	Responsibility for product or service
Decisions made	Discretion / scope for independent action
Concentration	Mental, auditory and visual attention
Physical effort	Physical / explosive effort
Stamina	Stamina / sustained physical effort
Contacts	Contact with others
Working conditions	Exposure to 'disagreeable' conditions; exposure to hazards[+]

* A plus sign (+) denotes that the factor is further divided into sub-factors.

Each factor and sub-factor is divided into a number of defined 'levels' for which a detailed description is given. For example, the sub-factor of 'experience' has three levels which identify the amount of 'on-the-job' experience required by the job holder to perform the job competently. Level 1 is defined as needing up to and including one week's experiential (on-the-job) learning to perform the job to a competent level. Any job in the brewery which falls within that category will be awarded 'level 1' on that sub-factor.

▶

A maximum number of points is set (at the discretion of the consultant) for this scheme. As the factors are seen to be of equal importance or weight, the points are distributed equally between them. A numerical value is thus allocated to each level within every factor and sub-factor.

A job will be 'scored' by deciding the appropriate level in respect of each factor or sub- factor, giving a total numerical value for the job as a whole. For example, a labouring job in the brewery scores highly on the sub-factor of 'physical effort' but less high on 'decisions'.

The scheme is 'analytical' in that it breaks jobs down into component parts, and described as 'points rating' as it uses a numerical scoring system. It sorts the jobs into a hierachy.

Setting pay hierarchies and structures: pay structures

Job evaluation, in determining the internal relative worth of jobs, sets a hierarchical framework on which basic pay structures can be pegged. That hierarchy makes explicit the common worth of certain jobs so that they can be grouped together for the purposes of pay. In organisations where there is no job evaluation such groupings are also necessary and are the result of a mix of factors, e.g. management judgement, collective bargaining, historical precedent.

Typically and traditionally employers separate white-collar and manual employees for pay purposes, recognising further groupings within these. Particular occupations may be grouped together into a job family and have their own pay structures. Murlis and Fitt (1991: 40–41) see engineers as a typically identifiable group with a career structure and a number of possible salary scales/pay grades. Within such families 'benchmark' (i.e. representative) jobs provide a reference point for job evaluation and pay.

Unskilled manual workers are traditionally separated for pay purposes from their skilled counterparts, the latter differentiated by trade or craft. The drive for functional flexibility and technological change have broken down some of the job boundaries between them and led to simplified pay structures. Armstrong (1996a: 205) cites the Prestige Group as having replaced twelve rates of pay with four day rates for production operators, operators/adjusters, setters and skilled toolroom operators.

Sometimes a 'rate for the job' (also known as a spot rate) is set by management unilaterally or through collective bargaining for all those in a particular grouping. Alternatively, a range of pay (or a number of salary scales) may be attached to a group of jobs, and rules devised to determine where individuals are placed initially within that range and their progression. Such rules will reflect organisational values and pay objectives, e.g. progression may be linked to individual demonstration of competence, skill acquisition, performance or length of service or be linked to career development. The rules also typically reflect external job market pressures, e.g. the range allows employer and employee flexibility when agreeing starting pay. Traditionally spot rates have been associated with wages and ranges of pay with salaries, reflecting and reinforcing the divide between white-collar and manual jobs. In collective bargaining the divide may also be evident, with different unions representing the interests of white-collar and blue-collar workers.

There is no set formula for determining the number of pay groupings and the type of salary structure. Armstrong (1996a: 204) argues that the structure is linked to the type of organisation and employees. However, certain contemporary trends are discernible. Delayering of organisations and functional flexibility have led to the reduction of the number of pay grades in organisations and to the consequent widening of salary bands (called 'broad banding'). Pay progression is no longer, therefore, so clearly linked with hierarchical promotion. Harmonisation has led to the removal of strictly delineated pay groupings for white-collar and manual workers. Organisational restructuring and technological innovation in the workplace have prompted employers to rationalise pay structures and compress pay grades, and unions to accept these.

Executive and senior management jobs are often addressed outside the pay hierarchies and structures of the organisation as a whole. The recent trend has been for a limited number of such jobs, regarded by organisations as key to their success, to receive increasingly high pay. This has widened the gap with average national earnings, and the pay of others within the organisation itself. In British Airways, for example, the most highly paid executive earns fifty times the average wage whereas eight years ago it was less than eleven times the average wage. Attempts to reverse the trend have not been particularly successful. For example Salomon Brothers (an international American investment bank) have had to restore substantial cuts to bonus payments to retain staff (*Sunday Times*, 1996b). The implications of what has become known as a 'winner takes all' philosophy have yet to be fully assessed. The legitimacy of such high payments has been challenged by government, reflecting public concern, most particularly in respect of privatised utilities. From an employee and trade union perspective the philosophy raises the fundamental question of internal equity. It may lead also to wage drift and wasted resources if payments are subsequently not 'earned'.

Pay grading example: nurses and midwives

The current national agreement on a clinical pay grading structure for nurses and midwives was introduced in 1988, replacing a scheme which had been largely unchanged since the introduction of the National Health Service in 1948. The original scheme had grouped them mainly according to their statutory qualifications and gave little recognition for subsequent specialist training and the variation in skills and responsibilities in different posts.

The current structure aims to:

1 identify an appropriate relationship between nurses, midwives and health visitors;
2 recognise the wide variety of tasks, flexible responses and responsibilities undertaken;
3 allow for career progression.

The structure is organised in the following way:

■ There are nine scales, grades A–I.

- Scales A and B are for 'helpers' who assist professionally qualified staff and have no statutory nursing/midwifery qualifications; grade I is the highest.

- Each grade is defined by factors recognising (i) skill, knowledge and experience, (ii) direct patient/client care, (iii) teaching responsibilities, (iv) responsibility for staff, (v) responsibility for resources, (vi) independence and initiative and (vii) physical and mental effort.

- Each job is placed within these scales by reference to these factors.

The agreement was introduced through the Nursing and Midwifery Staffs Negotiating Council, comprising the 'management side' and 'staff side' with the support of an independent academic adviser. Re-grading was carried out in 1988 covering 80 per cent of the nursing workforce (nearly half a million staff in Great Britain). In practice there was some disagreement between management and the staff side about the inter- pretation of the scheme, although the wording had been agreed jointly.

Following the introduction of the agreement, there was dissatisfaction on the part of nurses, evidenced by appeals from approximately 100 000 nurses in 1988. The appeal system itself was lengthy and time consuming and, despite streamlining the procedure, it was estimated that approximately 21 000 appeals were outstanding in 1993, and, after government intervention, just under 6000 in 1994. In 1994 the Council introduced Central Adjudication Panels under Independent Chairs nominat- ed by ACAS; the panel's decision was final.

Some groups of nurses felt especially dissatisfied; for example midwives were aggrieved that the basic midwifery grade was the same as the basic qualified nursing one. As most midwives qualify as staff nurses before taking midwifery training, they felt that they were entitled to a higher grade. For a minority it meant a drop in pay.

The following lessons should be learned:

- A pay grading exercise on such a scale is very complex and unlikely to be to the satisfaction of everyone despite well-established negotiating machinery and repre- sentation from the staff side.

- A written agreement, although necessary, does not guarantee that there will be no conflict.

- Appeal systems need to resolve differences relatively quickly.

The current system is under pressure. For example:

- changing skills profiles (such as unqualified 'helpers', sometimes known as health care assistants, relieving nurses of more basic clinical and non-clinical duties) raise questions about grade definitions;

- equal value issues in the NHS raise questions about grading throughout the NHS (see below in respect of the equal value claims of speech therapists);

- typically, grading systems (in common with pay systems) are subject to decay and require regular renewal.

Internal equity and fairness: complying with equal pay legislation

The Equal Pay Act 1970 entitles employees to claim pay equal to that of another employee of the opposite sex in the same employment if they are doing 'like work' or if the work that they do is rated as equivalent under a job evaluation scheme. The Equal Pay Amendment Regulations 1983 extend this entitlement to include 'work of equal value' and make provisions for the designation by ACAS of 'Independent Experts' to investigate and report to tribunals in respect of equal value claims. The legislation gives employers the right to claim a 'material defence' factor even if the jobs are of equal value. For example, market forces if objectively justified may constitute such a defence (for more detail of the legislation *see* Chapter 8).

The impact of the legislation is difficult to assess. IDS (1996) concludes that equal value has not been a primary driver when employers are considering job evaluation. However, once the decision has been taken, compliance with the legislation is seen as essential.

The impact measured crudely in terms of equal pay cases appears limited. ACAS (1997, unpublished statistics) cites an average of 12 claims per year (some with multiple applications) referred to Independent Experts, although in 1996 the figure was 28. There were 38 new 'like work' claims in 1996 (*Bargaining Report*, 1997).

A recent survey of equal pay claims (*Bargaining Report*, 1997) notes a 'surge' and that the total amount won by the unions over the twelve-month period 1996/7 was 'in excess of £1 million'. *Bargaining Report* (1997: 6) sounds a cautious note in its interpretation of the statistics:

> It is 27 years since the first Equal Pay Act 1970, but following an initial spurt between 1970 and 1975, when the pay gap narrowed by nine percentage points, the pace slowed, narrowing by just two percentage points in the next ten years and by less than six in the last decade. Bargaining Report calculates that at the current rate of increase it will be at least another 31 years before pay equality between men and women is achieved.

Union activity in the field of equal pay may account for the recent increase in equal pay claims. Critics of the legislation argue that the slowness and costs of the legal procedures deter applicants; for example, *Bargaining Report* (1997: 6) notes that 22 per cent of equal value cases have been in legal process for more than three years. The previous Conservative government introduced changes to the legal procedures in 1996 to try to reduce such delays. However, despite some reduction in the length of time taken in claims, the costs and delays are problematic for individuals who pursue claims without union support.

Enderby *v* Frenchay Health Authority and the Secretary of State for Health, which started in 1986, is an illustration of the potential for delay and mounting costs. Dr Enderby was a speech therapist claiming work of 'equal value' with hospital pharmacists and clinical psychologists (the comparators). Speech therapists are mainly female while pharmacy and psychology are male-dominated occupations. Enderby's claim was followed by other speech therapists. Legal process, including an initial rejection of the claim by an industrial tribunal and a ruling by the European Court of Justice (ECJ) in 1993, resulted in the Enderby case (and a selection of other cases) being referred to Independent Experts in 1996. A government statement put the cost of the equal pay claims at £1 million (EOR, 1997). The applicants have had union and EOC support. Enderby's case was settled in her favour in 1997, outside the tribunal. The first three cases to be heard in the tribunal went in favour of the speech therapists and a settlement of outstanding cases subsequently made.

Such set pieces receive most publicity among equal pay claims, demonstrating the importance of union and financial support for applicants. However, the majority of the cases referred to Independent Experts in 1996 involved single applicants and up to three comparators and proceeded without such publicity. Up to 50 per cent of cases are settled. For example, in 1990 Sainsbury settled a claim in respect of female checkout operators and male warehouse workers who were paid more. A new job evaluation scheme addressed the problem of pay inequity (IDS, 1996: 9)

As indicated above, the impact of the legislation on the gender gap in wages is modest. Average gross hourly earnings in 1996 for women were 79.9 per cent of men's (*Bargaining Report*, 1997: 7) although it has been estimated that women who work part-time receive only 58 per cent of the hourly rate paid to full-time male workers (EOC, 1997). An occupational example of a pay gap roughly in line with the former is that of female solicitors. A Law Society survey (1996) found an unexplained difference of £1700 between male and female associate/assistant solicitors.

It appears, therefore, that discrimination in terms of women's pay persists. Armstrong (1996a: 143) concludes that women's work has been undervalued 'across the pay market, and because of inherent gender bias in job evaluation'. Segregation in labour markets is apparent. (For more detail on discrimination in employment, *see* Chapter 2.)

It has been argued that collective bargaining models need to change. A case study of equal pay claims in the electricity supply industry (Gilbert and Secker, 1995: 191–207) concludes that trade union organisation is not sufficient. The necessary conditions appear to be 'real bargaining strength ... single table centralised pay determination ... that trade-unions recognise inequality ... members have influence over the pay agenda' (205). The Enderby case also focuses attention on collective bargaining models. The speech therapists' pay was subject to a separate bargaining process. The ECJ ruling (1993) was that separate pay bargaining processes could not be used to circumvent the principle of equal pay. Employers and trade unions therefore need to ensure comparisons across bargaining groups.

■ **Exhibit 10.1**

Gender bias in job evaluation: some examples of sex bias

Scheme design:

- An education factor/sub-factor that relies heavily on qualifications may unfairly discriminate against women (some women's jobs may have had less emphasis on formal qualifications).
- A physical effort factor/sub-factor dealing with lifting and ignoring stamina may disadvantage women (the former is characteristic of some types of male work).

Scheme implementation:

- Gender of job holder revealed in job descriptions.
- Evaluation carried out by management only.

Source: Wainwright Trust (1993).

The question of gender bias within analytical and non-analytical job evaluation schemes has to be addressed. The latter are not legally sufficient to act as a defence in equal pay claims. Bias can occur in terms of the design of schemes (for example, in the choice and weighting of factors) and their implementation. Such schemes can simply reinforce the status quo with its possible inherent inequalities of pay (*see* Exhibit 10.1).

The most recent initiative to support the Equal Pay legislation and encourage best practice in the workplace is the Equal Pay Code (EOC, 1997). It requires employers to draw up a policy, review pay and tackle inequality. Importantly, it encourages not just a review of grading (and job evaluation schemes) but a wider scrutiny of the different components of pay, including performance- and competence-based pay. Such scrutiny has been supported by trade unions. Pay structures may bring inequity. A trade union research paper (Hastings, 1994) suggests that broad banding allows most individuals to be assimilated in new pay structures at current salaries. Women are more likely to be assimilated in the lower ranges so that 'historical discrepancies are perpetuated in a new guise' (Hastings, 1994: 4).

The newness of the Code makes it difficult to evaluate its impact. In the meanwhile it appears that the legislation has made slow progress towards addressing gender issues in respect of internal pay equity.

External labour market forces: aligning pay with market values

The preceding sections on equity have examined the processes by which the relative internal worth of jobs is established. All employees, therefore, are located within an internal labour market but they make judgements about the fairness of their pay based on their view of differentials and relativities. Perceptions of external labour markets and prevailing rates of pay shape their expectations.

Changes in labour markets (outlined earlier in the chapter) mean that referencing pay externally is problematic for employers, employees and unions. The sense of job insecurity felt by many workers (and their apparent desire to put security above pay) is likely to hold down their pay demands, at least in the short term.

Young people in further/ higher education have sought the part-time and casual work found in core–peripheral models of employment. Such models offer work for other groups prepared to take less than 'standard' (i.e. 'permanent, nine to five' type) employment. Women, increasingly economically active, are more likely than men to be in part-time and temporary jobs. In sectors such as hotels and catering where core–periphery models are common and union representation of peripheral workers is not widespread, pay has been held at a low level. The NMW aims to address low pay to a certain extent in such sectors but is unlikely to radically change the workers' expectations of pay and conditions given fears about job security and a history of low pay. Hendry (1995: 392–405) argues that the *ad hoc* pursuit of core–periphery models has been mostly in those sectors that already had a casualised workforce. The result is that 'such approaches become permanent and institutionalise the disadvantages which accompany part-time and temporary employment. The impact falls especially on women.'

The core–periphery models of employment are not necessarily associated with low pay. 'High-tech' industries in which the business is project- or contract-based are more likely to rely upon temporary or fixed-term employees who provide the requisite skills to supplement a core workforce. Such employees are highly skilled, with the expectation that their pay is correspondingly enhanced to offset advantages accruing from more permanent employment (e.g. employer pension scheme, support for training).

Job markets are characterised by diversity and change. There are many different job markets operating at the regional, national and international levels, covering a range of occupational groupings. The transferability of skills between occupations and industries is problematic. Skill shortages co-exist with unemployment in line with the decline of certain industries, such as ship-building, and the rise of others, such as advanced electronics. Torrington and Hall (1995: 582) distinguish between those occupations where skills are readily transferable and those which are organisation-specific. Hendry et al. (1995: 108–37) note the complexity of labour markets relevant to small and medium sized companies, concluding that 'small firms may be more vulnerable to the evolution of forces in the external labour market' (1995: 137).

Such diversity and change make it difficult for employers, employees and unions to establish a market rate in practice. The decline in national and multi-employer collective bargaining means that the notion of a 'going rate' set typically annually in the 'wage (bargaining) rounds' is less clear than a decade ago. Armstrong (1996a: 161–2) concludes that 'the concept of a market rate is elusive', compounded by the problems of 'matching jobs' across organisations and gaining up-to-date data. Market intelligence will yield, therefore, a range of possible rates within which employers, employees and unions seek a consensus. The sources of market pay data include nationally or locally published surveys covering occupations, sectors and particular industries. Management consultants and recruitment specialists also develop databases. Employers (and unions) carry out their own surveys or group together with others to pool intelligence on pay (referred to as 'pay clubs').

In parts of the public sector external referencing of pay is delegated by government to pay review bodies, which take an independent view of pay for groups such as doctors and dentists, school teachers and the armed forces. Identifying occupational groups for comparison in these instances is problematic. However, the occupational groups (and their unions) often seem in little doubt that they are 'falling behind' in terms of pay relative to peers and that their living standards are being eroded. In a joint submission to the School Teachers Review Body (1997) three of the main teaching unions have demanded a substantial increase above that required by inflation and average earnings in order to deal with what they see as a recruitment crisis. The National Association of Head Teachers has pointed to skill shortages as the tangible outcome of what they perceive to be inadequate pay – for example, the number of unfilled head teacher posts in the 1997/8 academic year. Their demand was for 10 per cent. The Labour government has taken a cautious line, with the Secretary of State for Education calling for the pay review body to exercise restraint (*Independent*, 1997).

External labour market forces: aligning pay with international markets

For a limited number of job markets pay is referenced internationally – for example, corporate financiers (*Sunday Times*, 1997b). International salary surveys raise issues about the relative purchasing power of personal income, and the taxation and social security charges in different countries. Tokyo, for example, is rated as one of the most expensive cities in which to live, with the cost of living 60 per cent higher than in London, whereas that of Bombay is less than half that of London (Black Horse Relocation Services, 1997). Cost of living is reflected in pay levels, although enhanced payments for expatriate workers may not be sufficient to offset a desire for a particular lifestyle or concern for personal safety.

Taxation and social security deductions vary from country to country, making international comparisons over payroll costs and the take-home value of pay problematic. France, for example, has one of the highest social charges in the EU. Concerns about unemployment levels have prompted government measures to reduce charges and provide incentives to employers to take on new employees. Grants and employment incentives similarly operate in a number of EU countries. Such schemes typically focus on problems particularly pertinent to that country – for example, cushioning unification in Germany. Some problems are common across the EU – for example, youth unemployment (IDS/IPD, 1997).

There are international variations in the composition of pay which make comparisons problematic. For example, the 'welfarism' of Japanese companies means that employee benefits are wide-ranging and hence an important feature. The recent economic difficulties in Japan and the collapse of the 'tiger' economies have meant reductions in company 'welfarism'.

THE CONSTITUENT ELEMENTS OF PAY AND PAY SYSTEMS

Introduction

Pay comprises a number of different elements, some 'fixed' and contractual (for example, a weekly wage negotiated as part of the contract of employment) and some 'variable' and at management's discretion (for example, pay linked to individual performance). Total pay consists of basic pay (wages, salaries), additional elements (such as performance pay) and benefits (such as private health care). This section considers those elements.

The composition of pay has been changing as the new pay orthodoxy challenges the more traditional approaches. Such changes are likely to be reflected in the composition of pay, with the emphasis on the individual rather than the collective. Basic pay which applies collectively is enhanced by those payment systems that seek to differentiate between individuals in some way. Management, keen to control costs and gain financial flexibility, strive for payment systems that are discretionary and variable. The stakeholder philosophy argues for an approach to pay that recognises different interest groups, preferably in a cooperative rather than conflictual way. In general the composition of pay and payment systems is characterised by change and diversity.

Basic pay: wages, salaries and harmonised pay

Basic pay is time-based payment and is essentially a standardised rate for the job. Wages, salaries and harmonised pay are the terms used to describe that part of pay which the employer contractually agrees to give the employee at regular intervals in return for the provision of a specified number of hours of labour over a given period. These are therefore 'fixed' and contractual.

The terms 'wages' and 'salaries' are significant in that, until the last couple of decades, these delineated clear boundaries between two different approaches to basic pay. In the workplace there used to be a relatively clear understanding and agreement about the differential use of the terms. Wages were paid weekly, frequently in cash, to manual workers, and salaries monthly through cheque or credit transfer to white-collar workers. There was an implicit understanding that 'salaried employees' had a degree of job security and access to other benefits (e.g. pension) whereas 'wage earners' did not enjoy such advantages. These approaches were reflected in explicit and formal agreements. Salaried staff were quoted an annual amount and typically placed on salary scales which guaranteed largely regular progression year on year up that scale to a fixed point. Wage earners were more typically paid an hourly rate. It was an inherently class-based system with both explicit and implicit expectations on both sides of the employment and psychological contracts.

Union agreements reinforced the divide. In local authorities, for example, unions representing manual and white-collar workers negotiated different agreements. The move towards harmonising pay and conditions, agreed in 1997, was welcomed by unions and seen by the employers as ending 'second-class treatment' of manual workers (Local Government Management Board, 1997).

The differential use of the terms has become less easy to sustain over the last couple of decades for a variety of reasons. The Wages Act 1986 repealed the Truck Acts, generally held to be anachronistic statutes from the nineteenth century which had guaranteed payment in the 'coin of the realm', i.e. cash. Employers found themselves therefore no longer statutorily obliged to pay in cash, which was administratively expensive and cumbersome, with evident security risks. Employees were still able to claim payments in cash if that was in their contract of employment. The desire on the part of employers to move away from the weekly ritual of cash payments led in many instances to a collective renegotiation of the employment contract often with financial incentives offered in return for giving up the residual contractual obligation to be paid in cash weekly. The willingness of employees to be paid by cheque or credit transfer depended on domestic and social habits, e.g. the traditional weekly distribution of the wage packet within the home. At the same time the substitution of those cash payments by cheque or credit transfer assumed a banking facility on the part of employees. Wage payments have been therefore closely linked with class values.

The implicit connection of 'salary' with job security has also broken down. Most commentators note the persistent sense of job insecurity that appears endemic now in the UK labour force; for example, the *Financial Times* (1996) labelled this the 'age of the worried worker'. The recession at the start of the 1990s reinforced the view among white-collar workers that job security was now largely illusory. UK government statistics show that redundancies peaked in 1991 in this recessionary round and that unemployment has continued to fall from its 1992 high. Such statistics have not been translated into any sense of job security.

Harmonisation of pay between white- and blue-collar workers and moves towards single status (the same treatment for both groups) have signalled a blurring of the traditional divide between wages and salaries as employers have given wage earners access to benefits in line with salaried employees, and introduced unified pay systems. Harmonisation fits comfortably within a new pay orthodoxy. It ignores the arbitrary allocation of reward on collective status differences (for example, white collar or blue collar) in favour of encouraging more of a stakeholder philosophy.

Single status does not appear to be a widespread initiative. Hendry (1995: 354) notes research by Wood (1993, cited in Hendry, 1995) that such evidence can be found in British manufacturing. There may be more pragmatic explanations for harmonisation and single status. The introduction of new technology and the flexible deployment of labour often prompt the employer to simplify and integrate pay systems to replace elaborate but cumbersome pay arrangements built up over the years. Pirelli's (Clark, 1995) new Aberdare plant is a good example. Legislation may also have triggered changes. The 'Single Status Agreement' negotiated for local government workers (1997) was partly attributable to the need to avoid equal pay (equal value) claims.

Finally, the divide between blue- and white-collar work is no longer clear for a variety of reasons. Technology and automation have altered the content of jobs, downgrading some white-collar jobs and upgrading some blue-collar ones, and requiring common skills of many, especially in pursuit of flexibility. The labels of wage and salary are no longer such a clearly recognisable shorthand.

Some writers, for example Torrington and Hall (1995: 571), maintain that the employer still treats wage earners and salaried staff differently. Salaried employees still identify more closely with management and 'wage earners see themselves as doing the work that management would never do and which is independent of management apart from the labour-hiring element'. From this perspective class distinctions and different psychological contracts for the two groups have endured despite changes in the workplace.

Single status in local government

During the 1980s and '90s there were calls for the reform of pay bargaining in local authorities, where manual and white-collar workers were covered by a multiplicity of agreements negotiated by their respective unions. In 1997 unions and employers reached a 'Single Status Agreement'.

The agreement is:

- a commitment on the part of employers and unions to move towards single status;
- ending the different treatment of white and blue collar staff' (Local Government Management Board, 1997);
- a national scheme of pay and conditions for local application throughout the UK (Unison, 1997);
- a single-table bargaining arrangement, through the merger of the two National Joint Councils representing white- and blue-collar workers.

The agreement provides:

- 'support for the principles of high quality services delivered by a well trained, motivated workforce with security of employment, equal opportunities in employment, a flexible approach to providing services to the community, stable industrial relations' (National Joint Council, 1997);
- 'an end to low pay' (Jack Dromey, 1997);
- 'two main advantages. First if single status had not been agreed the unions would have escalated their cases at industrial tribunals ... that would have cost the Council dear, and second more scope for Councils to negotiate locally to get the kind of flexibility they need. 'Single Status is simply the right thing to do' (Local Government Management Board, 1997);

  'Throughout the negotiating process there have been three streams of ideas: equality/ harmonisation; delegation/subsidiarity; and simplicity/rationalisation. A better balance between national and local decision making and about stripping out the unnecessary layers of detail that have accumulated in the national Agreement over ... 50 years' (Nolda, 1997).

■ Additions to basic pay

There are a number of additional payments over and above basic pay which focus on the individual who carries out the job or the work group or the organisation as a whole. Such payments may be variable and discretionary or fixed and contractual. The emergence of the new pay orthodoxy suggests that there will be a growth in variable and discretionary elements linked especially to performance (at the individual, group or organisation level).

The following is a consideration of some of the commonly found additional payments but is not exhaustive. Some of these are currently attracting particular interest from practitioners and academics, and the discussion is developed here accordingly. In certain circumstances some payments may be consolidated into basic pay.

Allowances

Sometimes referred to as 'premia' or 'plussages', these are used by the employer to acknowledge a variety of circumstances, e.g. an allowance for the inconvenience of shift working, or adding extra money for being based in a high cost area, e.g. the London weighting allowance. The requirement for employees to be on 'call-out' is likely to attract an additional payment, or the employer may want to recognise particular responsibility, e.g. first aiders.

Management may make these allowances contractual and fixed, e.g. London weighting, or discretionary and variable, e.g. payment for accepting one-off individual additional responsibilities, depending upon such circumstances as the perceived relative permanence or frequency of the particular arrangement.

Over time, such allowances can become cumbersome and expensive to administer. In these circumstances management may seek to rationalise and simplify the system, consolidating into the basic wage/salary those that are relatively permanent and frequent.

Such proposed changes are likely to form a substantive issue in collective bargaining. An example of this was the pay deal reached in 1996 between ASLEF and South West Trains in respect of drivers. The previous basic rate was reportedly £11 950 per annum. The consolidation of allowances, e.g. unsociable hours, and overtime (which is discussed more generally below) together with a productivity deal, e.g. driver-only trains, was consolidated into a salary of £25 000–26 000 per annum. The ASLEF General Secretary commented that 'It is another step towards improving the living standards of drivers and rewarding them for the exacting job that they have to undertake' (*Independent*, 1996).

Overtime

Overtime, with its diverse arrangements, has been an enduring feature of UK payment systems. It is time-based payment linked to basic pay and employment status.

Wage earners have traditionally been been paid overtime at an enhanced basic rate. Salaried employees, at least at managerial level, have been expected to undertake unpaid overtime (at best with time off in lieu), reflecting different psychological contracts for the two groups. In the UK working long hours appears to be an endemic feature, with full-time British workers shown as having the longest working week of any of the EU states (*Social Trends*, 1996). Job insecurity appears to reinforce what has become a 'long hours' culture in the UK.

Overtime has been used historically and typically by employers as a way of achieving flexibility in working hours. However, it can contribute to rising costs and inefficiency if poorly managed; employees can gain clear advantage by manipulating output or work patterns so that overtime is necessary. Where overtime is a relatively fixed feature of the working week, then the employee perceives 'take-home' pay inclusive of overtime as the average weekly wage. The example discussed above of ASLEF demonstrates how management and union may seek to consolidate regular overtime into basic pay.

Bonuses, incentives and commission

These payments are based on output rather than input (i.e. hours worked). They are variable payments that seek to increase output by offering financial incentives to employees. A number of such payment systems were in existence before the move towards the new pay orthodoxy and represent an enduring concern about productivity.

The terms 'bonus' and 'incentive' are somewhat loosely used in the workplace although the former typically refers to a lump sum payment and is normally at management's discretion and will vary from year to year. Incentive payments are normally offered to employees in return for meeting specified and quantified targets; they are typically contractual and fixed in that the targets and the accompanying payments are agreed in advance by management and employees or their representatives.

The *bonus payments* have no standard shape or size. An interesting version of a bonus scheme is reported to have been introduced into Levi Strauss. It is called the 'global success sharing plan' and promises a bonus worth one year's salary in 2001 to each employee who has worked for the company for at least three years, provided that financial targets have been met. The GMB union has welcomed the plan (*People Management*, 1996a).

Bonus schemes which have attracted considerable attention are those paid to City specialists. Companies have been using the promise of bonus payments to retain high performing staff (*Sunday Times*, 1997b). During a recent bank merger of two Swiss banks, employees were even threatened with the removal of bonus for 'negative behaviour' i.e. succumbing to poaching from other companies (*Financial Times*, 1997f). Barclays Bank reportedly offered a fixed bonus of £1.25 million for 1996 and £900 000 for 1997 to the man it wanted as Chief Executive of BZW. City regulators have expressed disapproval of such payouts, arguing that they encourage risky or unethical behaviour (*Sunday Times*, 1997b).

Incentive payments have a long and chequered history in employee relations. At shopfloor level various schemes have been introduced as an addition to basic pay, such as (i) piecework where payment is directly output based, (ii) work-measured schemes where payment is linked to a standard output rate for an experienced operator set by work measurement techniques and (iii) linking pay to performance achieved over and above the standard rate set by management. By the start of the 1990s piecerate schemes were still widespread, more so in the public than the private sector. Such schemes were in decline but still represented a sizeable part of take-home pay for manual workers. The main reasons for the decline have been that such schemes may put speed before quality, discourage initiative, run contrary to flexibility requirements and may have adverse health and safety implications e.g. Repetitive Strain Injuries caused by sustained operation of particular production processes; (IPM/NEDO Survey, 1991 cited in Cannell and Long, 1991). Given that quality, initiative and flexibility have been seen as important for achieving competitive advantage, it is not surprising that concern about the efficacy of piecerate schemes has continued throughout the 1990s. At the same time the new pay order has rejected piece rates as representing too narrow a conception of worker effort (Geary, 1992).

Commission payments are typically associated with sales staff and tied to sales turnover. Armstrong (1996a: 375–6) concludes that these are more commonly additions to basic pay and on average represent approximately one-third of earnings. Salespeople may also be paid a bonus or a mix of commission and bonus where the latter takes into account broader aspects of performance rather than just sales targets. Commission, if poorly managed, can lead to what is described as 'churning' where a sales person will seek to gain financial advantage by inducing the customer to buy unnecessarily or inappropriately.

Profit sharing and share options

Profit sharing and share options are additions to basic pay that are linked with the performance of the company as a whole. Such payments arguably seek to demonstrate a commonality of interest between individual employees and the company as a whole and provide an incentive for the employee to work harder and remain committed to the company. In practice, the perceived link between individual effort and company performance may be weak, so it is not clear how powerful profit sharing is as an incentive (IPD/NEDO, 1991 cited in Cannell and Long, 1991). These payments are likely to be variable in line with annual profits and discretionary, typically based upon a predetermined formula setting minimum levels. The Finance Act 1978 allows employees to be paid the profit-related bonus in shares, subject to various regulations.

■ **Exhibit 10.1**

Commission on Pay reaches a low point: Piecework and home labour make setting a minimum wage fraught with difficulty

George Bain, chairman of the independent Low Pay Commission, and his colleagues are shocked and perplexed by what they have found on their travels around the UK. They were hearing from employers, employees, trade unions and other bodies on what the national minimum wage should be.

The more they listen, the more they recognise the enormous difficulties of the low pay issue. 'It sounds simple as a sound-bite to announce a national minimum wage figure. But it has turned out to be much harder than even we first appreciated,' said one commission member.

They have been dismayed by the despair and inertia on working class estates where paid work of any kind is hard to find, and by the low pay rates being earned by the unskilled and the young.

In Leicester on Tuesday the commissioners came face to face with the tangled questions of home working and piecework pay.

The self-employed are not covered by the minimum wage legislation. Nobody talking to the commission had any idea how a minimum wage could be imposed and monitored for home workers.

Employers in clothing, leather and retail sectors in Leicester were also perplexed by the piecework problem. The minimum wage will cover all workers whether they produce a recognised and measured volume of output. So what incentive would there be for workers to work effectively? Some negotiated industry-wide agreements indicate pay rates depend on employees working with 'due diligence'.

Source: Financial Times, 18 December 1997.

Profit-related pay and share options fit comfortably within the new pay orthodoxy although the payments treat all employees alike. Given that reward management frameworks stress the importance of recognising individual contribution, there is a tension between the even treatment of profit sharing and share options and the discerning treatment of performance-related pay (Geary, 1992).

Previous Conservative governments supported profit sharing and share option schemes on ideological grounds. During the 1980s there was an increase in the introduction of profit sharing schemes, reflecting government encouragement (IPD/NEDO, 1991 cited in Cannell and Long, 1991). Employees were broadly seen as 'shareholders'. The Labour government, with its support for the stakeholder philosophy, arguably does not oppose the principle of such payments although it may seek to revise certain aspects – for example, share option plans.

Profit-related pay is a example of the ideological principles advocated by the previous Conservative government. It is a particular term used to describe a formally recognised scheme under Inland Revenue rules that allows a portion of pay to move up (or down) with profit where any increase is tax-exempt. In the 1996 budget the Chancellor announced that the tax relief will be progressively phased out until it is fully removed by the year 2000, apparently recognising that the scheme has lost government revenue without achieving its aim of motivating employees. The Chancellor's budget speech explained the withdrawal of profit-related pay thus: 'Good managers do not need tax relief any more to know that pay should be linked to a firm's performance'.

It is estimated that 3.7 million employees have been affected by the previous Chancellor's decision and that companies which funded pay rises through tax benefits will now have to find alternatives (*Sunday Times,* 1996c: 4). The Deputy Chairman of the John Lewis Partnership, a company that has been paying profit-related pay for 60 years and reflects stakeholder principles, expressed dismay. He claimed that 'a number of recently introduced PRP schemes have been cynically devised ... the Treasury should be able to discriminate between genuine PRP and artificial schemes'. On the other hand, the TUC welcomes the phasing out of profit-related pay but will seek to make up the shortfall in take-home pay (*People Management,* 1996b: 15)

Some companies have used share options as a way of adding to basic pay and encouraging employee commitment. There are various versions, of which savings-related share option schemes are an example. Employees have the option to buy company shares in the future (3 or 5 years ahead) at a discounted and fixed amount through a savings scheme immediately operational. At the end of the period, a tax-free sum is added and the option to purchase shares can be exercised or the savings redeemed. Sainsbury is an example of a company offering such a scheme.

Share options have received hostile media coverage recently in the context of executive pay (especially in the privatised utilities) in instances where it has been felt that executives were able to exercise their share options to their personal financial advantage unconnected with their individual performance. The trend within companies recently have been to peg share option entitlement to a formula of performance criteria, making the link between pay and performance more transparent than previously (Kling, 1995).

The increase in the value of share options in respect of executive pay appears to be closely linked with stock market performance. It has been estimated that the average chief executive's annual salary and benefits for 1996 was around £400 000 (up from approximately £389 500 in the previous year) but the variable pay element – largely share options – rose from around £114 000 to £486 800 in the same period (*Sunday Times,* 1996d: 4).

Performance-related pay

Performance-related pay seeks to reward employees for individual performance and recognise the individual contribution to organisational success by linking pay increases and /or progression within pay scales to meeting performance targets, both quantitative or qualitative. It is, therefore, a broader conception of 'effort' than that found in traditional incentive schemes (Geary, 1992). Payments are discretionary and variable, affording management financial flexibility. This type of payment system fits comfortably within the new pay orthodoxy. From a union perspective, performance-related pay undermines collective intervention in that it focuses on the individual aspects of the employment relationship.

Performance-related pay became popular in the 1980s as schemes were increasingly introduced in the workplace (mainly for white-collar workers) by organisations seeking more sophisticated forms of payment. Support for performance-related pay was strong among managers and a number of employees, even allowing for perceived disadvantages. Torrington and Hall (1995: 606) conclude that performance-related pay 'appears to accord with widely supported concepts of distributive justice'. Its appeal was based on the notion of individual fairness. The previous Conservative government seemed convinced of the intrinsic value of performance-related pay and pushed organisations in the public sector in that direction.

By the 1990s a note of caution had set in firmly among both practitioners and academics. Kessler and Purcell (1992) carried out a systematic review of the state of performance-related pay initiatives. They found that performance-related pay was seen by managers as a way of attracting potential employees (i.e. it had a market value), that it contributed to retention by sending 'messages' about which employees were valued, and that it motivated by direct reference to performance. The particular systems and procedures adopted led to operational difficulties, largely in respect of the selection and use of performance criteria, the subjectivity of the assessment and the financial constraints under which managers operated. Their conclusion was that 'the link between pay and performance remains as obscure as ever'.

Kessler and Purcell were not alone in raising doubts about the efficacy of performance-related pay. The Institute of Manpower Studies research (Thompson, 1992) had echoed similar doubts. In the workplace where the principle of performance-related pay had been taken largely on trust by management, the operational difficulties of such schemes became apparent in the 1990s as the costs seemed to outweigh the benefits. Some organisations have started to experiment with alternatives such as competence-based pay and others have sought to simplify or restrict existing schemes. Currently it is estimated that only one quarter of firms directly link pay and performance (Industrial Society, 1997).

Skills- and competency-based pay

Skills-based pay

Skills-based pay makes an explicit link between skill acquisition and additional payment. In such systems employers pay additional specified amounts for demonstrable skill acquisition and /or may link that with pay progression. Skills-based initiatives have been management-led broadly in response to competitive pressures and to demands for quality and functional flexibility. They offer financial flexibility. Such payment systems encourage employees to increase the depth and breadth of their skills. The introduction of National

Vocational Qualifications has provided an enabling framework in that it is a convenient peg for skills-based pay. From the collective stance of unions, a national qualification standard reduces the scope for management to exercise their discretion in an arbitrary format. Such systems can, and do, form part of collective agreements. Skills-based pay is, therefore, an example of experimentation but does not neatly fall into the new pay orthodoxy. It is, however, a relatively cooperative approach to pay and appears to recognise that skill acquisition is of mutual benefit to employer and employee. As such it fits within a stakeholder framework.

It is not surprising that skills-based pay initiatives are found in greenfield sites, such as that of Nissan, or linked with the introduction of new technology, for example in Pirelli. Initiatives are not restricted to manufacturing, however, and are evident in other sectors, e.g. retailing and local authorities.

Skills-based pay is still relatively new, probably explaining why the literature on the subject is often anecdotal. Clark (1995: 233), in his study of the Pirelli plant at Aberdare, notes that the skills-based pay scheme introduced with union agreement had to be overhauled. There was a conflict between employees seeking to gain skills quickly and become fully functionally flexible in pursuit of financial incentives, and the organisational need for skills training to be thorough. Hendry (1995: 214–5) argues that there are inherent problems with the concept of skill itself in the workplace in that managers tend to rely on indirect indicators of skill, e.g. reference to formal qualifications, and emphasise personal qualities when describing skills. It is possible that a failure to resolve such problems may weaken the effectiveness of skills-based pay. Armstrong (1996a: 287) concludes that there is evidence to suggest that schemes are more expensive to introduce and maintain than organisations have assumed, and that the benefits are not easily quantified.

Competency-based pay

Competency-based pay differs crudely from skills-based pay in that it seeks to link pay not just to skills, which can be seen as an 'input' factor in performance, but more broadly to job behaviours and their outcomes. Such a pay system is discretionary and variable, offering the organisation financial flexibility. The emphasis on the individual, the strategic importance of such a pay approach and the link between individual competencies and organisational objectives place it within the new pay orthodoxy. It is an increasingly popular pay initiative, so it is important to examine it in more detail.

The term 'competency' has become widespread among academics and practitioners although there have been many debates about its meaning. Competency definitions include reference to both the characteristics of the individual and the behaviours associated with the job or occupation, although different models will vary the emphasis on one or the other of these elements. The job (or occupation) behaviours may be linked, therefore, to performance levels specified by management in the workplace. Armstrong (1996a: 290) offers the following definition of competence: 'For practical purposes it can be regarded simply as the ability to meet performance expectations in a role and deliver the required results. Competence refers to applied knowledge and skills, performance delivery and the behaviours required to get things done well'.

Sparrow (1996: 22) expresses considerable unease about the 'competency' vocabulary that has become widespread in managerial circles in pursuit of the desire for a link between the performance of individuals and strategic management. From an academic perspective the concept applied in the workplace to HR systems of appraisal and pay is inherently a weak one in that it is not clear what exactly is being measured in competency approaches – inputs, processes or outcomes.

Competency-based pay schemes are typically linked to a competency framework, which may well have been introduced already within an organisation as a basis for appraisal or recruitment and selection. Such frameworks vary; some may focus on 'core' competencies, i.e. those judged by management to be common and central to a given cluster of jobs (e.g. 'forward thinking' for managers), others may focus on a combination of skill areas (e.g. 'customer focus' for sales support staff) and common behaviours ('teamwork'). Other frameworks may include additionally specific objectives or targets. Such frameworks need to be derived from a sound and systematic understanding of the jobs in question, i.e. from what is called job analysis, and have to be capable of defining and distinguishing sensitively between levels of job performance from 'satisfactory' to 'outstanding'. Armstrong (1996a: 298) accepts that successful competence-based pay schemes need to meet demanding criteria, including the requirement for 'well researched and analysed competence frameworks'.

The literature has much anecdotal evidence about competency-based pay drawn from both the public and private sectors. There are examples of local authorities that have moved from performance-related pay schemes to competence-based pay for their managers in the hope that the latter will prove more effective in motivating employees. The opportunity itself to experiment with pay systems has been seen largely as a result of the move to local pay bargaining within local government in the context of central government initiatives such as compulsory competitive tendering and review and reorganisation. Commenting on the introduction of competence-based pay schemes in the local government context, Murlis argues that 'good competence based schemes need to be mixed in with PRP; I do not see the two as separate' (quoted in Thatcher, 1993: 20).

Similar experimentation is reported in the private sector. Sparrow (1996: 27) gives the example of the AA. The current Group Personnel Director has dismantled the reward system which linked competencies, performance and labour market considerations in favour of a simpler system. Competencies are used for development purposes for its top managers and professionals but pay is linked to labour market information and performance outputs. 'When you talk to managers about competencies, their eyes glaze over ... competencies ... are a shorthand way of thinking of people in their roles and looking at key requirements ... when it comes to performance, there are external environmental factors and political factors and so forth. Competencies are only part of a multi-faceted picture' (Stemp cited in Sparrow, 1996: 27).

The relative newness of the competency-based approaches to pay suggests that it is too early to validate these. Sparrow (1996) urges caution in respect of claims about competency-based pay. He argues that there are four main reasons for concern. First, the performance criteria used to measure competency are often invalidated, based for example on appraisal results or the subjective views of senior managers about what constitutes effective performance. Second, there is the question of whether all competencies should be equally rewarded under a payment scheme regardless of variables such as the length of time required to develop individual competencies or how important they are to the organisation or in labour market terms. Third, there is the problem of identifying relevant competencies during periods of organisational change. Lastly, managers may be biased.

The extent to which Sparrow's note of caution will be heeded is unclear. Armstrong expresses the view that competence-based pay 'is seen by many practitioners as the way ahead'. From a collectivist stance there is likely to be the same kind of unease about competence-based pay as there has been about performance-related pay.

Team-based pay

The individual focus of performance-related pay has been much criticised in that it runs counter to the team spirit widely heralded as important in many work organisations, and institutionalised in new labels attached to their structures, e.g. 'team leader'. Perhaps it was inevitable that such organisations would seek to link pay to the team ethos. Work group norms that govern the behaviour of individuals are developed in such circumstances. Such a payment system is discretionary and variable. Although the focus is not on the individual, team-based pay is seen as an initiative more within the spirit of the new pay orthodoxy than traditional approaches.

Typically in team-based pay a bonus pool is allocated to a working group as an incentive, and as a reward in recognition of reaching performance or output targets, or making operational savings; that bonus is then distributed to the group using an agreed formula. An IPD study (Armstrong, 1996a) indicates that team pay for white-collar workers is commonly linked to performance and shopfloor schemes to output or cost savings, a finding that he claims is supported by studies by Industrial Relations Services (1995) and the Institute of Employment Studies (Thompson, 1995). Armstrong (1996b: 27) concludes that 'organisations using team pay in the IPD Study are convinced that it works for them and, no doubt, there are many other organisations where the culture and importance of teamwork will make team pay an attractive proposition'. There is little published validation to date of team-based pay and the evidence is mainly anecdotal as its development has been within this decade. However, given that team-based pay makes use of financial incentives and links reward to the notion of 'performance' or output or savings, then it seems most probable that research studies on performance-related pay (e.g. Kessler and Purcell, 1992) or on incentives more generally will have some applicability. It may still be problematic to prove a direct link between pay and enhanced performance. There may still be tensions around individual and collective interests. The introduction of team-based pay is probably more linked with cultural and structural issues, and symbolism within an HRM framework (i.e. reinforcing unitarist perspectives, marking out and strengthening work units, and sending messages about the importance of contribution). From a collectivist stance the same concerns about performance-related pay are applicable to team-based pay.

■ Benefits

The term 'benefits' is used to describe that part of the pay package which can be broadly categorised as either payments in kind (e.g. subsidised meals, social functions) whose 'consumption' is essentially optional, or social welfare provision (e.g. contribution to pension, sick pay above minimum state entitlement, life insurance) which may be deferred until retirement, etc. or contingent upon a particular set of circumstances (e.g. ill health). Additionally, paid holidays are an element of the benefit package although typically not recognised as such by employees. Historically, benefits (sometimes described as fringe benefits or perks) have been seen as tax efficient and a 'cat and mouse game' is played out between the company's tax advisers and the Inland Revenue to find ways in which benefits could legitimately escape the tax net. (Most benefits are technically classified as part of income by the Inland Revenue and subject to tax.) Benefits are typically contractual and fixed.

The broad categorisation used above disguises the multiplicity of individual benefits which employees may receive. Torrington and Hall (1995: 613) suggest that the benefit element of the pay package has grown distinctively within the UK, more so than in other Western countries, and is a particular feature of executive pay. They do not quantify the average value of benefits within the pay package but this conclusion suggests that benefits are likely to be a significant part of the total remuneration costs for an employer. It is interesting, therefore, that more attention has not been addressed by researchers or even practitioners as to the effectiveness of benefits packages. Employers may offer benefits generally in line with competitors to attract staff but their motivational value in terms of encouraging particular behaviours receives scant consideration. Performance-related pay, in contrast, represents a far more minor element of take-home pay (Armstrong (1996a: 240) cites figures of 5 per cent addition to basic pay on average in periods of low inflation) and yet this has attracted widespread interest.

There is some anecdotal evidence that benefits packages as a whole are being more critically considered by employers as opposed to scrutiny being directed on a more *ad hoc* basis to individual benefits, e.g. the concern expressed by many employers about the rising cost of private health care schemes (Curry, 1994: 40). The changing nature of the workforce and patterns of employment may explain this change of heart. For example, Hoechst Roussel's merger prompted a review of their benefits (around one-third of their remuneration costs); the reasons cited for change were linked with structural changes in their workforce – more women, more part-timers, less likelihood of long-term employment within the company, less value placed on 'deferred gratification' of longer term benefits and limited take-up of others, etc. The solution was a move towards flexible benefits (sometimes called cafeteria benefits) in which employees were allowed to choose from a menu to suit individual needs (Crabb, 1995: 40–41). In the UK the move towards flexible benefits has been cautious despite the hype attached to individual examples, the most recent of which is Price Waterhouse, which launched its scheme in 1997 (*People Management*, 1996c: 15). Early schemes have experienced some operational difficulties. However a recent survey found that one in two employers allowed flexibility in their packages although the examples given do not confirm any high degree of flexibility (*People Management*, 1997c).

Benefits packages as a whole have also come under scrutiny due to harmonisation. One of the traditional features of benefits is that they have been status driven, not just in terms of the divide between wage earners and salaried staff but within categories of white-collar worker. A survey by the Manufacturing Science and Finance Union found that there is still a strong 'upstairs/ downstairs' culture permeating benefits in the UK (1997). The company car has been one of the most graphic illustrations of this principle of status divide – a sliding scale of makes and models reflected the employee's position in the hierarchy. This particular benefit is also a good example of how individual benefits have been scrutinised in terms of tax effectiveness and policy application (the operation of the policy on company cars is often a source of friction in the work place). The Price Waterhouse scheme (see above) rejects this notion of highly differentiated status, only putting a cash ceiling on benefits of 20 per cent of total pay.

The treatment of benefits packages in the literature is typically prescriptive and not particularly closely allied with any one school of thought. Historically, benefits were associated with paternalistic employers concerned for the welfare of their employees but there is little discussion of the development of benefit packages in respect of other management styles. Unions historically saw themselves as providers of benefits; it will be interesting to see whether they will return to this role. If they do, then this may place employee benefits higher on the pay agenda for both employees and employers.

CONCLUSIONS

Change, diversity and experimentation have been dominant themes in pay in the last couple of decades.

Change has been driven in particular by political, economic and technological factors. Both the Labour government and the former Conservative administration have rejected many aspects of the employee relations climate and frameworks of the 1960s and '70s, although from different ideological perspectives. The need for flexible labour markets and international competitiveness is their commonly held position. There are, however, differences in the ways that they believe these objectives should be met.

The economic winds of change have blown across both the public and private sectors. Despite economic revival in the mid- to late 1990s, the 'chill' factor of remembered recessions in the early '90s (and in the last couple of decades) has lingered. Technological change, in particular that of information technology, has altered radically the nature of work and skills. It seems improbable that approaches to pay can return to those of the pre-1979 era.

Diversity is the legacy of change. Individualism and unitarism enjoyed a revival under the ideology of the Conservative administrations of the 1980s and '90s. Collectivism and pluralism retreated but did not disappear. The social partnership approach of New Labour has led to a renewal of collectivism and pluralism. However, the desire to reform or 'modernise' collective arrangements seems set to continue.

Experimentation is the necessary outcome of change. Pay initiatives have been introduced although enthusiasm among management and some workers has been tempered by operational realities as well as some doubts about their efficacy. Trade unions have been prepared to break with some of the traditions of collective bargaining and support new pay arrangements.

There remain, of course, the enduring challenges for all those involved in pay determination. The perennial questions of the nature of the respective roles of government, employers, employees and unions persist. In the workplace the balancing act between external pressures on pay determination and the need for internal equity is as perilous as ever. Experimentation has not provided neat solutions but it has signalled a climate for pay that is more about renewal than decay.

CHAPTER SUMMARY

- Pay is the relatively neutral term used to denote wages, salaries and fees paid to employees in return for labour.
- It is subject to a range of influences, including government policy on the economy and employment, legislation, employment trends and markets, technological change and societal values.

- The Labour government's employment policies include the National Minimum Wage to address the problems of low pay, and flexible and internationally competitive labour markets.

- Legislation (in particular the Equal Pay Act) has had an impact upon pay in the last couple of decades.

- Patterns in employment and unemployment and in the labour markets affect the perceptions and expectations of those 'buying' and 'selling' labour.

- Technological change has impacted upon skills profiles of jobs and hence pay levels and hierarchies.

- Pay has a number of functions in the employment relationship, which include a legal function, a mechanism for fulfilling employer, employee and union objectives, a mechanism for control and motivation and a visible manifestation of the psychological contract.

- A new pay order has emerged in the last decade characterised by a move towards a stakeholder model, a greater emphasis upon unitarist perspectives, individualism and a strategic approach. Changing management styles and employee relations strategies have been reflected in new approaches to pay. The 'new order of pay' is less clearly delineated in practice than in its pure form in the literature.

- Pay can be determined through collective bargaining (covering a minority of employees) or through unilateral management action. Pay determination has become more fragmented, decentralised and streamlined over the last couple of decades. Decisions about pay need to take into account internal equity and external pressures, and job evaluation is one of the ways in which internal equity and fairness can be achieved.

- Pay hierarchies separate groups of workers into pay bands, which are typically being reduced in number and covering a broader range of pay.

- Equal Pay legislation has triggered interest in job evaluation and internal equity issues.

- Pay has to be aligned with external market rates to attract and retain workers.

- International pay comparisons need to take into account the relative purchasing power of personal income, taxation and social security charges in different countries.

- Pay consists of basic wages or salaries or harmonised pay, additions and benefits. The current trend is for employers to increase the discretionary and variable elements of pay and seek to focus pay on individual effort. The last couple of decades have been characterised by employers experimenting with payment systems to achieve flexibility and competitiveness. Benefits are an important feature of pay.

- Change, diversity and experimentation have been dominant themes over the last two decades.

EXERCISES AND QUESTIONS

1 You are the employee relations manager for a nationwide chain of four- and five-star hotels. You have been asked to prepare a briefing document for the board outlining the implications for the company of a National Minimum Wage. What will be your main points, and why?

2 Should a nurse be paid more than a police constable? What factors are likely to govern pay levels for the two occupational groups?

3 How important is pay in attracting graduates to join an organisation, and what kind of pay package are they most likely to want?

4 You are preparing a pay claim on behalf of a union representing craft workers in the building industry. What information will you need and how will you obtain it?

5 High flyers in banking, technology or management now expect the sort of rewards that those in entertainment or sport have received. What are the implications of the 'winner takes all' pay philosophy?

FURTHER STUDY

Traditionally, pay has been addressed in the employee relations literature as part of such topics as collective bargaining, state intervention or public sector pay or in respect of particular areas of interest such as low pay or performance-related pay.

In addition to the texts and journal articles referred to in this chapter, readers can pursue specialist interests through a range of sources, examples of which are given here.

■ Government publications such as *Labour Market Trends*. This provides a regular source of national statistics and discussion as well as a phone-based information service.

■ Statutory bodies sponsor and publish research and information. The Equal Opportunities Commission and the Commission for Racial Equality publish research papers in the field of equal opportunities. ACAS publishes an annual report and individual papers in which pay features in the context of workplace employee relations.

■ Publications by professional bodies. The Institute of Personnel and Development sponsors and publishes research on a range of pay issues.

■ Publications by trade unions and the TUC include survey data and studies as well as discussion documents.

■ Publications by commercial institutions – for example, Income Data Services – publishes regular surveys and studies.

REFERENCES

ACAS (1997) *Annual Report 1996*. London: HMSO.

Armstrong, M. (1996a) *Employee Reward*. London: IPD.

Armstrong M. (1996b) 'How group efforts can pay dividends', *People Management, 25 January*, 22–6.

Armstrong, M. and Baron, A. (1995) *The Job Evaluation Handbook*. London: IPD.

Bargaining Report (1997) 'Survey, equal value', *Bargaining Report*, 174, July.

Black Horse Relocation Services (1997) *International Best Cities for Business Report*. London: BHRS.

Buchanan, D. (1989) 'Principles and practice in work design: current trends; future prospects' in Sisson, K. (ed.) *Personnel Management in Britain*. Oxford: Blackwell.

Cannell, M. and Long, P. (1991) 'What's changed about incentive pay?', *Personnel Management*, October.

Cannell, M. and Wood, S. (1992) *Incentive Pay*. London: IPD/NEDO.

Chamberlain, N.W. and Kuhn, J.W. (1965) *Collective Bargaining*. New York: McGraw-Hill.

Clark, J. (1995) *Managing Innovation and Change*. London: Sage.

Crabb, S. (1995) 'Adding value with better benefits'. *Personnel Management*, July, 13.

Curry, L. (1994) 'Insuring the best policy on healthcare', *Personnel Management*, February.

CBI / Hay Management Consultants (1996) *Trends in Pay and Benefits Systems*. London: CBI.

Daniel, W. and Millward, N. (1993) 'Findings from the Workplace Industrial Relations Surveys' in Clark, J. (ed.) *Human Resource Management and Change*. London: Sage.

Doney, J. (1997) 'An end to low pay', *Financial Times*, 29 May.

EOC (1997) *Code of Practice on Equal Pay*. London: Equal Opportunities Commission.

EOR (1997) '£1 million speech therapists' defence bill', *EOR*, no. 74, July/August, 3.

Financial Times (1996) 'The age of the worried worker (comment and analysis)', 13 September.

Financial Times (1997a) 'Commission on Low Pay reaches a low point', 18 December.

Financial Times (1997b) 'Maximum worry on minimum wage', 29 April.

Financial Times (1997c) 'Call for data on local impact of minimum wage', 16 December.

Financial Times (1997d) 'Remote reward of pay restraint', 9 December.

Financial Times (1997e) 'Pay scheme on the critical list', 12 February.

Financial Times (1997f) 'UBS staff face bonus cuts for negative behaviour', 16 December.

Financial Times (1997) 'Unison accepts pay and single status deal', 29 May.

Financial Times (1997) 'Wage rise sought for 1.5m', 18 December.

Financial Times (1997) 'Pay cuts could save mining jobs', 18 December.

Geary, J. (1992) 'Pay, control and commitment: linking appraisal and reward', *Human Resource Management Journal*, 2(4).

Guest, D. (1989) 'Personnel and HRM – can you tell the difference?', *Personnel Management*, January.

Gilbert, K. and Secker, J. (1995) 'Generating equality? Equal pay, decentralisation and the electricity supply industry', *British Journal of Industrial Relations*, 33(2), 191–207.

Hastings, S. (1994) *Identifying Priority Areas in Equal Pay Work*, The Trade Union Research Unit, discussion paper no 45, Ruskin College.

Hay Management Consulting/*Sunday Times* (1995) *Employment Conditions Abroad, Epic International and Income Data Services*. London: *Sunday Times*/Hay Management Consulting.

Hendry, C. (1995) *Human Resource Management A Strategic Approach to Employment*. Oxford: Butterworth-Heinemann.

Hendry, C., Arthur, M. and Jones, A. (1995) *Strategy through People. Adaption and Learning in the Small – Medium Enterprise*. London: Routledge.

Herzberg, F., Mausner, B. and Snyderman, B. (1957) *The Motivation to Work*. New York: Wiley.

Hotspots (1997) *Special Web Edition. Hot Topics Index*. Warwick Business School, 11.

IDS (1996) 'Job evaluation', *IDS Focus*, 78, March, 4–16.

IDS and IPD (1997) *European Management Guides; Recruitment, Training and Development*. London: IPD.

Independent (1996) '£25,000 pay deal for train drivers', 12 October.

Independent (1996) 'Maximum wage will end poverty trap', 12 October, 8.

Independent (1997) 'Teachers set for clash with ministers over inflation busting claim', 20 September.

Industrial Society (1997) 'Survey on prp', *People Management*, 25 September, 9.

IPD (1996) *The IPD Policy Guide to Team Reward*. London: Institute of Personnel and Development.

IPD/JSB (1997) *Employment Law and Practice*, annual conference, London, 25 November.

IRS (1993) *IRS Employment Trends*, 546, October, 4–13.

IRS (1996) *Transition and Transformation: Employee Satisfaction in the 1990s*. London: IRS.

Joseph Rowntree Foundation (1996) *Changing Face of Low Pay*. Bath University.

Kessler, I. and Purcell, J. (1992) 'Performance related pay: objectives and application', *Human Resource Management Journal*, 2(3).

Kinnie, N. and Lowe, D. (1990) 'Performance related pay on the shopfloor', *Personnel Management*, November.

Kling, S. (1995) 'Are share options a real share in success?', *People Management*, 23 February.

Labour Market Trends (1997) *Labour Market Update*. London: Office for National Statistics, July.

Law Society (1996) Survey of solicitors' incomes by Coopers and Lybrand and Scantel, reported in the *Independent*, 12 October.

Lawler, E. (1986) 'What's wrong with point factor evaluation?', *Compensation and Benefit Review* March /April, 20–28.

Legge, K. (1995) *Human Resource Management Rhetoric and Realities*. London: Macmillan.

Local Government Management Board (1997) *Single Status: What's it all about?*, Background Briefing paper. London: LGMB.

Marchington, N. and Wilkinson, A. (1996) *Core Personnel and Development*. London: IPD.

Manufacturing, Science and Finance Union (1997) *Study on Status, Perks and Modes of Address*. London: MSFU.

Maslow, A. (1954) *Motivation and Personality*. New York: Harper & Row.

McLoughlin, I. and Clark, J. (1994) *Technological Change at Work*. 2nd edn. Milton Keynes: Open University Press.

Millward, N., Stevens, M., Smart, D. and Hawes, W. (1992) *Workplace Industrial Relations in Transition*. Aldershot: Gower.

Murlis, H. (1996) *Pay at the Crossroads*. London: IPD.

Murlis, H. and Fitt, D. (1991) 'Job evaluation in a changing world', *Personnel Management*, May, 40–3.

National Joint Council and Unison (1997) *Single status in local government: A national agreement for the future*, 6.

Nolda, C. (1997) 'A single achievement', *Municipal Journal*, 7 February, 14–15.

People Management (1996a) 'Pay and benefits: news and analysis', 7 June.

People Management (1996b) 'Pay and benefits: news and analysis', 5 December, 15.

People Management (1996c) *News and Analysis*, November, 15.

People Management (1997a) *News and Analysis*, 24 July, 15.

People Management (1997b) 'Harmonic motions (Overell, S.)', 11 September, 29.

People Management (1997c) *News and Analysis*, 9 January.

Philpott, J. (1996) *Issues in People Management*. London: IPD.

Pritchard, D. and Murlis, H. (1992) *Jobs, Roles and People: The New World of Job Evaluation*. London: Nicholas Brealey.

Purcell, J. and Ahlstrand, B. (1994) *Human Resource Management*. Oxford: OUP.

Schein, E. (1965) *Organizational Psychology*. Englewood Cliffs, NJ: Prentice Hall.

Skinner, B. F. (1974) *About Behaviourism*. New York: Knopf.

Sparrow, P. (1996) 'Too good to be true', *People Management*, 5 December.

Social Trends (1996) London: HMSO.

Storey, J. (1992) *Developments in the Management of Human Resources*. Oxford: OUP.

Sunday Times (1996a) 'Minimum Wage to be below £3.50', 17 November.

Sunday Times (1996b) 'Winner takes all', *Business Focus*, 20 October, 3.

Sunday Times (1996c) 'Employees lose their reward', 1 December, Money 4.

Sunday Times (1996d) 'Which of our bosses give the best value?', *Business Focus*, 10 November, 4–5.

Sunday Times (1997a) 'Turning Rover round', *Business Focus*, 5 January.

Sunday Times (1997b) 'City bonuses head for record', 9 November.

Thatcher, M. (1993) 'Rewarding managers for competence', *Personnel Management Plus*, March.

Thompson, M. (1992) *Pay and performance: The Employee Experience*, IMS report no. 218. Brighton: Institute of Manpower Studies.

Thompson, M. (1995) *Team Working and Pay*. Brighton: Institute for Employment Studies.

Torrington, D. and Hall, L. (1995) *Personnel Management: HRM in Action*. 3rd edn. Hemel Hempstead: Prentice Hall.

Tyson, S. (1995) *Human Resource Management, Towards a General Theory*. London: Financial Times Pitman Publishing.

Unison (1997) *Single Status in Local Government: A National Agreement for the future*, circular. London: Unison.

Vroom, V. (1964) *Work and Motivation*. New York: Wiley.

Wainwright Trust (1993) *Equal Value Training Manual*. London: Wainwright Trust.

Chapter 11

EMPLOYEE PARTICIPATION AND INVOLVEMENT

Mike Richardson

Learning objectives

This chapter offers a definition of employee participation and involvement (EPI), outlines some theoretical views, considers empirical research, contemplates rationales for EPI and provides some case studies of real situations for students to work on. While space restricts the treatment of all aspects of the topic area in depth, this chapter is designed to ensure that learning outcomes are maximised.

The overall objectives are to provide readers with a meaningful introduction to the subject, a guide, by way of a bibliography and further reading, and the opportunity, by means of case study material, to examine EPI practice within organisations.

More specifically, though, the chief concerns of this chapter are to enable readers to:

- distinguish and discern varying interpretations of what employee participation and involvement (EPI) is;
- attain familiarity with key concepts associated with EPI;
- gain a historical insight into the subject area;
- grasp an understanding of competing and complementary theoretical perspectives;
- identify the most popular forms of EPI and assess the character, level, scale and scope of these forms;
- be mindful of and understand the rationales behind EPI;
- express an informed opinion on the subject utilising case studies to illustrate and illuminate the main theoretical and empirical issues;
- evaluate the strategical approaches of employers and trade unions to EPI.

INTRODUCTION

Since 1979, as trade union influence has declined and new employment strategies associated with human resource management (HRM) have emerged, uncertainties about the future direction of employee relations have brought about a widening interest in employee participation and involvement (EPI), not least in government circles. In 1989, Norman Fowler, then Secretary of State for Employment, wrote a foreword to the government publication *People and Companies: Employee Involvement in Britain* designed to promote new EPI initiatives by way of a number of exemplary illustrations. One of these illustrations is given in Exhibit 11.1 for use as an introductory case study. The example selected is Coloroll, which in the 1980s was the largest home fashion group in the UK, producing wallpaper, textiles, carpets and all types of tableware. The version is unabridged and should be read critically, keeping in mind that the information comes from a government source with the objective of encouraging more employers to adopt EPI.

According to Blyton and Turnbull (1994) EPI has traditionally been the Cinderella of employee relations. But just as Cinderella habitually returns every pantomime season to beguile a new generation of children with fresh interpretations of an old theme, EPI also repeatedly manages to attract a new audience. The form, range, scale and scope of EPI may vary from one generation to the next. But the idea that it can, from the employer's perspective, fulfil a fundamental role in fostering good employee relations as well as improving productivity and profitability has remained. Moreover, the position adopted in the mid-1970s by the Trades Union Congress (TUC), though not without internal dissent, that EPI is progressive for workers in the sense that it advances industrial democracy, is also enjoying something of a renaissance. The TUC now seeks to bolster its influence through 'a new "social partnership" approach to industrial relations' (Fernie and Metcalf, 1995: 379) backed by legislation.

Whether or not the employers' and the TUC's view of EPI coincide, it is pertinent to explore why it has continued to attract advocates from representatives of both capital and labour. Certainly, as we approach the millennium it does seem appropriate to question why it is that the political system in Britain (and other mature capitalist societies) has managed to accommodate participation by the people, whereas in the workplace this liberal democratic practice has yet to be established. By the end of this chapter readers should be able to formulate their own views on this question.

This chapter is arranged to convey to the reader substantive ideas and perspectives of EPI in combination with detailed and illuminating empirical studies. The first four sections serve to acquaint the reader with some of the most significant definitional and theoretical issues necessary to clarify the subject area and provide some explanations that will act as a guide towards understanding important developments in EPI practice. The object is to penetrate the surface appearance of EPI to gain access to more revealing and comprehensive knowledge. Sectional headings are provided to make it easier for the reader to follow.

The first section deals with the theoretical origins of EPI in Britain tracing them from the beginnings of capitalist development when democratic ideas associated with the modern state first began to emerge. The second section undertakes to clarify the meaning of EPI. Definition is important, for to define something one has to explain it and to explain requires clear information about the subject matter. The focus of study then shifts to the theoretical frames of reference commonly used to explain the fundamental nature of the employment relationship. The various theoretical approaches offered provide the current stage on which EPI operates and the basis for its rationale, form and character. Next, the specific theories associated with EPI are investigated that cover shifts in power relations between capital and labour, cyclical patterns of EPI and contingent factors to explain the EPI phenomenon. We then turn to explore empirical information covering four important areas of EPI that in combination with the case studies gives the reader the chance to make the interconnections between theory and practice. A concluding view is then offered and finally a historical case study is given where many of the issues and theories raised in this chapter feature in their empirical form. To increase their understanding of EPI, readers are encouraged to interpret this case study and the others featured at various pertinent points in this chapter.

■ Exhibit 11.1

Coloroll

Team briefing Coloroll has a very active employee involvement programme, the first step of which is Coloroll's excellent two-way communication system. Every month 10 000 employees stop work for 30 minutes and meet in teams of 8 to 15 to receive the team brief. The purpose of the team brief is to disseminate only relevant information to every employee in the Group. There is input from employees' supervisors and managers at every level up to, and including, the group managing director.

The success of the system is the result of the open and honest attitude of the management team and the willingness to answer questions, however difficult or challenging these may be. This is made possible by a unique system which ensures that an answer is obtained from the most suitable person (often the managing director), and automatically returned to the originator within a week. The team brief is supported by a lively newspaper.

At team briefs people begin to ask 'How are we doing?' Coloroll takes this opportunity to involve them more by providing 'How are we doing?' boards. These are designed by employees and give up-to-date information on production, sales and quality.

Ideas Scheme The ultimate aim at Coloroll is for employees to gain greater job satisfaction by involvement in the day-to-day running of the company. To help them, an extremely successful ideas scheme has been set up with an award system paying the originator 20 per cent of the first year's savings. In the first 12 months ideas were received from 50 per cent of employees and 17 per cent of these were adopted.

QUIPS (Quality Improvement Programmes) By taking much of the mystic out of quality improvement, Coloroll has succeeded in setting up effective quality improvement programmes offering an even greater degree of participation.

Family atmosphere However, Coloroll's employee involvement programme goes further than this. In an endeavour to bring a family atmosphere to the group, Coloroll has set up a children's educational trust, with an annual budget of £100 000 to benefit employees' children. Furthermore, to enhance the lively atmosphere the walls everywhere display large bright posters which wholeheartedly encourage people to take advantage of the involvement programme.

Source: Employment Department (1989), Crown copyright, reproduced with the permission of the Controller of Her Majesty's Stationery Office.

Question

How effective do you think the EPI programme would be in securing the commitment and motivation of Coloroll's staff? Consideration of this rather one-sided example of EPI acquaints the student with the subject matter in its prejudiced form. We now move on to explore EPI more critically.

THEORETICAL ORIGINS OF EPI IN BRITAIN

To fully comprehend EPI in its contemporary forms one must be aware of its theoretical roots, as historical and contemporary experiences are closely linked. Hence, it is of value to briefly trace developments associated with EPI from the seventeenth century up to the end of the nineteenth century, when large-scale firms and organisations, the forerunners of today's monopoly companies, began to emerge.

In correlation with the rise of capitalism in the seventeenth century, rationalist thinkers increasingly challenged the assumption that the existing arrangements concerning the organisation and government of society were 'natural' and immutable. This contributed significantly to the transformation not only in the way Britain was governed but also to the everyday experiences of the population. Philosophers at particular times have made important contributions to political, economic and social reform that have had crucial implications concerning the development of democracy, the employment relationship and EPI practice. Shortage of space constricts this section to barely touch on this development, but despite its brevity it still serves as a useful introduction to the subject area and provides a basis to further an understanding of contemporary developments in EPI.

Since the seventeenth century, as capitalism began to emerge from the womb of feudalism, differences over the meaning of democracy and who had the 'right' to participate in a democratic process were apparent. The Levellers'[1] demand for increased political democracy did not extend to the lower orders (servants, wage labourers or those on charity) for fear that private property rights might be threatened. The Diggers,[2] on the other hand, did not regard private property as sacrosanct and called for the abolition of wage labour and support for a Communist programme (Hill, 1980). But this was only the beginning of the development of liberalism. The conditions of upheaval at this time that gave life to radical movements proved to be only temporary.

Not until the process of industrialisation created a mass working class, and the fusion of economic interests between the new capitalist class and the old aristocracy, did a new wave of radical liberalism come to the fore. John Stuart Mill, nineteenth-century philosopher, economist and Member of Parliament, was convinced that by giving democratic rights to the working class they would have a stake in the system and therefore would be less likely to rise up against it. Mill was concerned that increasingly workers viewed their interests as opposite to and in conflict with those of their employers. He analysed movements and ideas that promoted participation and matters of common interest between employers and workers (Mill, 1909). While, like the Levellers, he defended the principle of private property and stressed the advantages of competition, he argued that this mode of production could only be sustained and enhanced if forms of EPI were adopted. One of the nineteenth century radical experiments in which he took particular interest was *cooperative production* based on the principles espoused by Robert Owen, mill owner, philanthropist and utopian socialist. Commonly-owned self-managed factories, Mill argued, had one economic and moral advantage over the private capitalist – 'the common interest of all the workers in their work' (Mill, 1909: 790). He was convinced that private capitalists could capture some of this advantage by introducing profit-sharing, thereby ostensibly tying the efforts of the individual with the fortunes of the firm while contributing to social justice. From an anti-capitalist perspective, Karl Marx (1973: 288) attacked these profit-sharing schemes as a way of obfuscating the antagonistic relationship between capital and labour.

This initial discussion concerning democracy and the workplace and the merits or otherwise of profit-sharing already implies variance over the question 'what is EPI?'. EPI can generate enthusiasm or hostility among participants and arguments between academics concerning its rationale. These reactions often depend on the definition placed on EPI and its linkage with theoretical differences concerning the analysis of industrial relations. Thus, differing definitions of EPI adopted by commentators, whether constrained by set parameters or based on analytical and theoretical disagreements, need to be considered. These definitions can then be associated with particular theoretical approaches to industrial relations to study and see how these inform and account for the interest in and controversy over EPI.

WHAT IS EPI?

A useful starting point is to make a distinction between the terms *participation* and *involvement*.

Participation

Hyman and Mason (1995: 21) classify participation as:

> state initiatives which promote the collective rights of employees to be represented in organisational decision-making, or to the consequence of the efforts of employees themselves to establish collective representation in corporate decisions, possibly in the face of employer resistance.

Collective bargaining, despite its decline in the 1990s, is most commonly associated with this form of participation (*see* Chapter 9). Other topical participatory schemes such as works councils and worker directors are likely to become increasingly important if, as seems likely, Britain becomes more integrated with Europe (*see* Chapter 7). These schemes were viewed by Conservative governments as forms of collective bargaining through the back door. There are participatory measures, however, that are outside the ambit of collective bargaining, although these are more generally referred to as forms of industrial democracy.

Workers' cooperatives, where workers themselves own the enterprise and have the right to elect the management team, fall into this category. Also the Guild Socialists, despite campaigning vigorously on a workers' control ticket, particularly between the years 1911 and 1921, supported the joint management of industry by the state and the trade unions with ownership in public hands. Weaker versions of Guild Socialism continued to have some influence in the Labour movement in the 1970s and '80s (Kelly, 1988). The idea that, despite the negative experiences of post-war nationalisation in this respect (Coates and Topham, 1975), state ownership of key industries and services can provide workers with greater opportunities for participation in major strategic decisions, forms an important part of the industrial policy of the Socialist Labour Party. Even during the 1984–5 miners' strike, the National Union of Mineworkers (NUM) proposed a settlement based on the *Plan for Coal*, a strategy agreed between the National Coal Board, the NUM and the government in 1974, and reaffirmed in 1981, for this state-owned industry, reflecting continuing support for this form of participation (*Labour Research*, 1984; Freeman, 1986).

However, the push for joint control in state run enterprises was a feature more associated with the 1970s. Labour's programme for fighting the 1974 General Election stated:

> We intend to socialise existing nationalised industries. In consultation with the unions, we shall take steps to make the management of existing nationalised industries more responsible to the workers in the industry and more responsive to their consumers' needs. (cited in Craig, 1990: 192)

Therefore, this concept of industrial democracy is often associated with the 'them and us' industrial relations environment of the 1970s. While this is still relevant (Kelly, 1988; Kelly and Kelly, 1991), it no longer fits well with either the employers' concept of empowering workers within the new industrial relations order that emerged during the 1980s (Bassett, 1987; Wickins, 1987) or the TUC's idea of 'social partnership' in the 1990s.

What is also absent today, at least in a strongly organised form, is any significant movement advocating workers' control. Although it still has its adherents (in the Basque region of Spain for instance) syndicalism is currently at a low ebb. It is important, however, to know what the syndicalist concept of workers' control is. Syndicalists reject joint control or indeed state ownership of the means of production, arguing that the revolutionary overthrow of the capitalist system can only be achieved by the struggle for workers' control based on direct action through industrially organised unions.

Since 1979, a significant shift from a participatory to an individually-based involvement agenda has taken place. Employers have taken the initiative to introduce new or rediscovered schemes that are 'task rather than organisation based' (Hyman and Mason, 1995: 18) as part of a strategy of securing workers' loyalty and commitment to the organisation as well as increasing productivity. This approach is commonly labelled as employee involvement (Guest, 1992: Marchington *et al.*, 1992).

■ Involvement

Changes, in the last twenty years, to the national economic, political and legal context in which the employment relationship has operated, as well as the intensification of international competition and the restructuring of the world economy, have been instrumental to employers seeking new or revived ways to achieve a competitive edge. During this period changes in organisational and job design to increase the effective use of human resources emerged, the implementation of which is associated with more sophisticated techniques of motivation and control of the workforce. Emphasis in many of the organisations that looked to improve labour productivity began to be redirected towards a management strategy promoting the consent and cooperation of the workforce through task centred and individually focused employee involvement schemes. It should be noted, however, that there is a debate as to whether this strategy has been more concerned with eliminating organised workers' resistance than with the benefits of organisational change (Geary, 1995).

In broad terms, therefore, there is clear division between involvement and participation, although it would be wrong to say that there is no overlap or link between them. It is not unusual to find participation and involvement operating in the same organisation. More often than not this occurrence results from the pragmatic introduction of the HRM strategy, which fosters involvement schemes as a method of securing employee loyalty and commitment but recognises the organisational reality that existing industrial relations practice cannot always be abolished overnight, if indeed at all (Blyton and Turnbull, 1992).

In short, the meaning and function of participation is that those employees who have previously been excluded from the organisational decision making process are actively engaged on a collective basis. Involvement relates to management-initiated policies and practice where empowerment is constrained to operational tasks, rather than organisational decision making, targeting the individual. This still leaves the level, scale, range and form of participation and involvement to be considered but these questions will be dealt with later, outside the remit of definition.

Table 11.1 provides a typology and examples of different types of EPI, although it should be regarded with due caution. Implementation of schemes may vary between organisations. Moreover, often there are fine dividing lines between communication, consultation, involvement and participation, as well as differences in interpretation. Readers should take these factors into account and not use the table in a deterministic fashion. The same applies to Table 11.2, where some basic definitions are provided for guidance as well as the likely directional flow of communication and involvement.

■ **Table 11.1 Classification and types of EPI**

Classification	Type
Workers' control	Worker self-managed cooperatives
Representative participation	Collective bargaining
	Worker directors
Representative consultation	Joint industrial councils
	Joint consultative committees
	Works councils
Financial participation	Profit sharing
	Employee share ownership
	Unit wide bonus schemes
Task-based involvement	Quality circles
	Teamworking
	Total quality management
	Suggestion schemes
	Customer care programmes
Non-representative consultation	Attitude surveys
Communicative involvement	Team briefing
	Company journal/newspaper
	Employee reports
	Videos

Source: Adapted from Marchington *et al.* (1992) and Ramsay (1992).

Exhibit 11.2 provides an example of a large public sector organisation attempting to change the 'them and us' relationship that prevailed between management and employees in a situation where interpretations of industrial democracy, participation and involvement play an important part in shaping the attitudes and actions of the prime participants.

THEORETICAL APPROACHES TO INDUSTRIAL RELATIONS

Interpretations of the manner in which participants define, initiate and respond to EPI vary to a large extent, depending upon the theoretical approaches used, although this point should not be exaggerated because participants' views or practice can often be located in more than one approach. The distinctions between the theoretical frames of reference concerning industrial relations have been outlined elsewhere in this book (*see* Chapter 2). Suffice it here to identify and associate some of the main features from the unitarist, pluralist and radical perspectives informing and shaping the thoughts and actions of the actors in EPI.

■ **Table 11.2 Employee involvement: some definitions**

Downward involvement	
House journal/newspaper	A publication produced on a regular and continuing basis by the company for distribution free to staff and other interested parties, which contains information about the organisation and its employees.
Team briefing	A regular, structured system to enable top management to cascade throughout the organisation news and developments which are thought to be relevant to particular groups of employees.
Upward involvement	
Attitude survey	A questionnaire survey of employees on a one-off or regular basis, which is designed to discover their views about a variety of factors connected with work. It is generally distributed to a sample of employees.
Customer care programme	An initiative designed to involve employees in improving relations at the interface between staff and the customer, and to encourage staff to treat customers in a positive way.
Quality circle	A small group of employees who meet voluntarily on a regular basis to identify, analyse and solve quality or other operational problems relevant to the organisation.
Suggestion scheme	A formal procedure which enables employees to put forward ideas to management for improvements at work, and which provides for a system to reward acceptable suggestions which save money.
Total quality management	A systematic process of management in which all employees are expected to see others, both internal and external to the organisation, as customers for their services.

Source: Marchington *et al.* (1992).

■ Exhibit 11.2

The Royal Mail

The Royal Mail is a state-run industry and has been throughout its existence. It employs about 120 000 postmen and women, 18 000 of whom are higher grade employees known as PHGs. The Union of Communication Workers (UCW) is the main trade union representing these workers and union density is high. Since 1992 Royal Mail has operated as nine separate regional divisions. It has been extremely successful, measured in terms of both profitability and service.

Issues/Experience related to participation and involvement over the last twenty years

The Post Office was one of a few organisations that experimented with workers' directors following the proposals of the Bullock Committee in 1977. The scheme was dropped soon after the election of a Conservative government in 1979. While the scheme was ineffectual (Batstone *et al.*, 1983) it did reveal significant differences between management and the union on the interpretation of and desire for industrial democracy. In particular, worker directors were marginalised in the area of key organisational decision making.

Collective bargaining, however, remained central to the conduct of industrial relations throughout the 1980s but despite a moderate union leadership conflictual relations were a feature of this period. A militant if rather parochial UCW membership had an uneasy alliance with its leadership and a strained relationship with Royal Mail managers (Gall, 1995).

Spurred on, after the 1987 General Election, by government policy designed to make the public sector more sensitive to consumer needs, the Royal Mail management, in 1988, launched a total quality management (TQM) programme. Unable to get union agreement, the introduction of teamworking was delayed (Jenkins *et al.*, 1995), although other aspects of the TQM programme proceeded.

In an effort to overcome opposition to teamworking and employee involvement, Royal Mail sought and obtained an agreement with UCW in 1992 that set the parameters to a new industrial relations approach. Partnership was the buzz word, where the union was to be privy to more company information. Moreover, the agreement implied that the union would be involved in strategic matters (Bacon and Storey, 1996), although exactly what this means is unclear. Attempts at privatisation of

Royal Mail were successfully defeated through a campaign led by the UCW based on lobbying Conservative MPs rather than mobilising its membership through mass demonstrations and threatened strikes (Gall, 1995).

Frustrated by its inability to gain consent for the introduction of team working, Royal Mail management in 1996 put forward a package of changes to pay and conditions, known as the Employee Agenda. A key feature of this agenda was the introduction of team working and the abolition of PHGs (IDS, 1996: no. 714). A UCW membership ballot conducted in May 1996, after talks on the Employee Agenda had collapsed, resulted in favour of industrial action, a decision which, after a summer of disrupted postal services, was reconfirmed in October 1996. Rejection of team working carried much weight in the decision to continue the dispute (IDS, 1996: no. 725). Settlement of the dispute was only reached when Royal Mail agreed to separate talks on team working from the Employment Agenda package (IDS, 1996: no. 726).

However, in 1997, Post Office workers seemed set on another series of stoppages unless Royal Mail droped its plans to introduce team working. The new Labour government is considering ways of avoiding this situation occurring. One proposal, favoured by Royal Mail management, being examined is an employee share ownership scheme that would give Post Office workers a 49 per cent financial stake in the business. Government spokesperson Ian McCartney said he hoped that this would create a climate where Royal Mail employees and managers 'come together with a common approach and a common objective' (*The Times*, 18 August 1997). To date, fears of further conflict alluded to above have not materialised.

Questions

1 Compare and contrast the 'partnership' approach to employee involvement in Royal Mail with the 'workers' directors' participation experiment.
2 To what degree has EPI in Royal Mail been defined and shaped by the fact that it is a state-run industry?
3 How mindful was Royal Mail of introducing team working into an environment characterised by traditional industrial relations?

■ Unitarism

Since the emergence in the 1980s of HRM as a serious challenger to the more conventional style of personnel management, unitarism, which during the 1960s and early 1970s seemed to be only of peripheral significance, has regained its status as an important frame of reference. This predominantly managerial orientated perspective, with its essentially individualistic as opposed to collectivist values, now informs HRM thinking on contemporary involvement schemes (Guest, 1989), although the extent of this influence is open to debate. It is worth looking back a couple of decades, however, to see how the basic principles of unitarism, despite the apparent dominance of pluralism at the time, still seemed 'natural' to some employers, and indeed employees, in order to stress the continuity of the unitarist perspective as well as identifying some of its key features in practice that are relevant today.

The well-known memorandum of Sir Halford Reddish, the chairman and managing director of the Rugby Portland Cement Co. Ltd, expressing by implication (Farnham and Pimlott, 1995) the principles and values of unitarism, in evidence submitted to the Donovan Commission in 1966 (Reddish, 1975) is revealing. The ideology and practice of Reddish and his company in the 1960s mirrors that of some HRM-orientated organisations of the 1980s and 1990s closely associated with involvement schemes. The term industrial relations was deplored by Reddish, who preferred to operate in the human relations tradition, which was strongly influenced by unitarism (Fox, 1975). This approach was based on a hierarchical order with authority being rooted in a strong leadership. The company did not belong to the pluralist-inclined institution the Joint Industrial Council (JIC) for the cement industry, and notable by its absence in the Reddish memorandum is any mention of trade unions or conflict.

Nevertheless, this company, like other unitarist organisations, recognised the need to furnish its employees with a package concerned with the means to enhance their effectiveness and sustain motivation. Preferably this was to be achieved without trade union involvement, although in some cases this was impracticable (Fox, 1975). Recognition of trade unions does not fit well with the unitarist premise that the interests of all members of the organisation, managers and employees, are locked together in a common purpose. This thinking determined the Rugby Portland Cement Company's behaviour in regard to its employees and is often cited as the mainstay of HRM strategy in organisations such as Hewlett Packard, Marks and Spencer and IBM in the 1990s (Blyton and Turnbull, 1994). The key features identified by Reddish in his memorandum to buttress this approach were chiefly based on effective communication. For instance, important notifications were conveyed to staff via noticeboards before general release; employees were issued with a copy of the Directors' Report and Accounts at the same time as shareholders; each individual plant had a works committee that met monthly; and profit-sharing and employee shareholding schemes were in operation (Reddish, 1975).

While contemporary involvement schemes have much in common with the unitarist-driven practice of Rugby Portland Cement, other factors derived from HRM, such as the strategic connection of involvement schemes with overall business objectives, have added coherence and purpose (Storey, 1992). Critically, however, this has come about as a result of the changed environment of the 1980s and '90s, a period that has seen the intensification of international competitiveness, an end to the social democratic consensus of the 1960 and '70s, consistently high levels of unemployment, and diminishing power, influence and membership of trade unions. These elements have brought unitarist thinking back into play. While HRM and many of the accompanying involvement schemes were imported into Britain from Japan via America when the political and economic conditions were ripe in the 1980s, the theoretical support for what is in essence a unitarist approach had long been in place.

Pluralism

This does not mean that the unitary approach has by any means displaced pluralism as the dominant industrial relations perspective. The situation is more complex, although a full discussion is outside the remit of this chapter. Suffice it to say that pluralism, where conflict is accepted but regulated by collective bargaining (*see* Chapter 9), has proved fairly resilient. More accurately, derivatives of pluralism have been very adept at keeping alive the regulatory role in organisations active in taking up HRM initiatives (Storey, 1992). It is doubtful, though, whether they match up to the generalised description of pluralism outlined by Fox (1975). He defined pluralism as an approach where oppositional interests, recognised as both legitimate and desirable, are kept in check and balance through negotiation based on compromise and underpinned by the principle that neither side seeks to destroy the other.

The management styles identified by Purcell and Sisson (1983) are perhaps more useful in portraying the thoughts and actions of managers concerning industrial relations, particularly in the 1980s and '90s. Purcell (1987) explains that the unitarist and pluralist frames of reference are rather narrow, restrictive and, most importantly, 'mutually exclusive'. He focuses on the interconnections between individualism and collectivism, arguing that the wide variations found in unitary and pluralist practice often overlap. This may explain why managerially initiated HRM unitarist-influenced employee involvement schemes such as team working and TQM have in a number of cases been introduced on the basis of agreement through negotiation in situations where trade unions have maintained collective bargaining rights (Monks, 1994). To what extent this 'social partnership' approach has or will affect the pace and direction of managerial practice from collectivised to individualised work relations, and the consequent implications for trade unions, is still not clear (Bacon and Storey, 1993: Taylor, 1997).

Radicalism

Radical critiques of EPI influenced by Marxist thinking do vary, although there is little disagreement that EPI must be considered in the context of society as a whole. Workplace relations is only one part of Marx's analysis of the organisation of society. Marxist theory purports that a society's economic base, or mode of production, wields the most power in shaping social, political and religious institutions as well as conditioning ideology to reflect the interests of the dominant class (Hyman, 1975). The dynamic in Marx's analysis is embodied in the relations of production, by which he meant the class structure of society: 'The history of all hitherto existing society is the history of class struggles' (Marx and Engels, 1952: 40). Marx refers to the transition of Western civilisation from the stages of primitive communism, slavery and feudalism to capitalism to illustrate his approach to historical change. Marxist theoretical works have subsequently been drawn on as a guide to action: 'The philosophers have only *interpreted* the world, in various ways; the point, however, is to *change* it' (Marx, 1946: 65, italics in original).

Interpretation is the point of departure among those contemporaries influenced by Marxist thought concerning EPI. Their approaches to EPI range from total hostility to enthusiastic support. The argument put forward by those of radical persuasion opposed to EPI schemes of any description is that they only serve to obfuscate the antagonistic relationship between capital and labour and act as a barrier to the development of class consciousness (Kelly, 1988). The gist of this analysis is that EPI schemes legitimise the relationship between capital and labour and 'will bring about the more effective integration of workers into existing economic and social relations rather than produce any alteration in the capitalist system' (Clarke, 1977: 375). By staying aloof from these schemes and adopting an independent defence of their interests workers, however, can begin to establish the link between conflict at work with the working of the capitalist system in its totality, thus shifting the struggle from the economic to the political sphere.

In contrast, those supporters of radical persuasion for 'encroaching control', popularised by the Guild Socialists (Cole, 1975), believe that EPI schemes should be welcomed provided that inroads into managerial decision making, whether at task or organisational level, can be demonstrated, the logic being that the workers' position is strengthened *vis-à-vis* the capitalist class. Moreover, under certain conditions workers may be encouraged to intrude further into areas formerly controlled by management, until the time is reached where the strength of the working class is seen as incompatible with the interests of the capitalist class, giving rise to a revolutionary situation.

The problem with this approach is that capital is hardly likely to concede any form of control that threatens its very existence (Kelly, 1988) unless, literally speaking, a gun is held to its head. Conversely, workers are unlikely to reject EPI for what they might see as some distant utopian goals if they see immediate benefits for themselves. Expediency and realism, strongly influenced by the power imbalance between capital and labour in both the particular and general situation, more so than obligation, are the most likely explanations of workers' behaviour (Fox, 1977). This adds weight to the findings of Kelly and Kelly (1991), who found little evidence to support the diminution of 'them and us' attitudes in firms adopting involvement schemes.

Having considered the part played by the main industrial relations perspectives in providing the rationale for and against EPI, we now move on to look at more concrete theoretical explanations of EPI practice that take into account differences in power relationships, cyclical patterns and contingent factors.

THEORIES OF EPI

The impact of power relations and values on the realities of participation

Michael Poole's (1986) study of workers' participation, first published in 1975 when the participation debate in the political and industrial arena was at its height, recognised the importance of advancing a theoretical perspective in revealing the sources that drive developments in the practice of industrial democracy. Poole draws on the theories of Marx, Dahrendorf, Parsons and Weber to assist with building an explanatory framework for the subsequent discussions on management, worker, trade union and state initiatives in relation to industrial democracy.

Poole's central argument is that the form, extent, scope and range of participation in industrial life reflect the basic power processes in society. Thus the advancement of industrial democracy is determined to a large degree by shifts in power relations within society at the national or indeed the international level.

> Participation is viewed as very much the offspring of deeper, *latent* power processes which operate in society and the values about participation which obtain at any given point in time in particular societies and organisations. (Poole, 1986: 14, italics in original)

Poole emphasises that changes in the practice of industrial democracy are more strongly influenced by changes in 'latent power' than the role of values, although both are interrelated in a complex web of cause-and-effect relationships.

The latent power factor of Poole's theoretical perspective rests particularly though not exclusively on the Marxist view, expressed here in simple terms; the changes in the social relationships of each class of humans to the means of production (plant, machinery, tools, technology, skills, knowledge and raw materials) are the result of class struggle between those who own or control the means of production and those divorced from ownership and control. The latter, with only their labour power to sell to secure means of subsistence, are thus open to subordination. But this labour power is a vital resource giving rise to the notion of interdependence between capital and labour (Poole, 1986). Unsurprisingly, therefore, the terms conflict, cooperation, compromise and compliance, have all been used to describe continuity and change in social relations, revealing on the one hand the dynamics of latent power and on the other the difficulty of measuring its impact.

The real foundations on which latent power rests, according to Poole, are economic and technological factors along with government action. Economic factors that affect the power relationships between the main participants concerned, workers and management, and shape the character of employee relations are market power, the rate of profit, sales, growth, the degree of industrial concentration and competitive pressures. Small firms in a competitive market are more likely to look to the short-term, prioritise profits and adopt an authoritarian approach to employee relations with little room for EPI. In contrast, large-scale firms or monopolies have long-term objectives and may prioritise growth or sales rather than profits. These firms have much more leeway in the conduct of employee relations (Friedman, 1977) and thus are more likely to recognise unions and favour or even foster participation schemes (Poole, 1986).

Poole, in his theoretical approach, however, was not espousing economic determinism. In his model, values and ideologies of the participant parties concerned also influence the practice of participation, though only within the confines of the framework of latent power discussed above and the existing levels of participation. Moreover, the existing pattern of EPI must also be explained through tracing the historical development of participation. It is through such an examination that EPI has been associated with cyclical trends. Periodic interest in EPI in this theoretical model, according to Poole, is closely linked with heightened industrial unrest. The view that management are more inclined to be attracted to formal participation schemes when their authority seems to be under particular threat, however, has been developed most fully by Ramsay (1977). Thus we now turn to look at his perspective on the cyclical pattern of worker participation in Britain.

■ Cycles of participation

Ramsay's contribution looks at phenomena shaping participation chiefly from the macro rather than the micro level. His theoretical rationale is that only through an understanding of the contradictory development of all factors influencing the actions of participants in relation to EPI policy, rather than at the micro level of appearance only, is it possible to advance useful insights into the nature of EPI.

Ramsay purports that by tracing the history of formal participation schemes over a century or more, a distinctive pattern emerges. In times of heightened class tension, when the challenge to managerial authority from workers and their organisations intensifies, evidence suggests that the amount, scope and extent of formal participation schemes expand. A distinct cyclical pattern can be discerned associating fluctuations in the popularity of managerial initiated participation schemes with the ebb and flow of workers' resistance to managerial authority. From this perspective 'participation is thus best understood as a means of attempting to secure labour's compliance' (Ramsay 1977: 481). But this gives rise to a contradiction. Ramsay, applying a Marxist analysis, reasons that participation is built on the unitary of interests but the relationship between capital and labour is fundamentally antagonistic. Thus, unsurprisingly, the expected outcome of participation schemes from this perspective should be relative failure. Ramsay argues that this analysis can only be seriously called into question if participation schemes prove dominant and enduring. The evidence he draws on in his original article reveals that participation schemes can be expected to have only a transient existence. There are three main examples:

1 'Triviality' schemes where only non-controversial issues find their way on to the agenda. These schemes deteriorate quickly, handling only 'petty affairs (the "tea, towels and toilets" syndrome)' (Ramsay, 1977: 482). This pattern of events is just as likely an outcome whether the organisation in question is unionised or not. In establishments that recognise unions and employ collective bargaining procedures other forms of participation have less influence and tend to wither away. In non-union establishments workers are too weak to make an impact on any matters of substance.

2 The case of 'instability'. When serious issues of conflict arise management attempts to resolve them through participation schemes other than collective bargaining and the union recognition this entails. In short, management tries 'to impose a unitary frame of reference' (Ramsay, 1977: 482) on a conflictual situation with the likely outcome of deepening the divisions between management and employees.

3 The 'change of committee status', where management integrates collective bargaining with other forms of participation. When participation schemes are introduced to complement collective bargaining they are more likely to last. However, these schemes tend to be peripheral rather than central, hence their influence is minimal.

Ramsay offers a ready explanation for the phenomenon that participation schemes have been and still are attractive to some workers. Both capital and labour see participation in a different light. Management usually introduces participation schemes to facilitate an increase in productivity but often in conditions where its authority is under threat. In so doing it attempts to infuse its employees with a dose of unitary medicine. In this situation, however, employee representatives are more likely to see this as an opening to exert greater influence and advance industrial democracy. Thus, temporarily, participation is compelling to both sides as the contradictory situation between them is not always immediately apparent.

The resurgence of EPI schemes in the 1980 and '90s has prompted a questioning of Ramsay's theory. Out of an empirical investigation into the motivation and character of these schemes Ramsay's theoretical perspective on EPI has come under attack. Ackers *et al.* (1992) and Marchington *et al.* (1993) have argued that the 'cycles of control' theory does little to explain the reasons for management's adoption of EPI in the 1990s. Pressure from below since 1979 has evaporated as trade union authority and influences have waned. Ramsay's theoretical model, they argue, puts too much weight on the relations between capital and labour. This has resulted in the relative neglect of examining contingency factors at the micro-level – that is, within the company or organisation. It is at this micro-level, with a co-ordinated challenge from below noticeable by its absence, that Ackers *et al.* (1992) locate the main source of new EPI initiatives.

▪ Contingency factors

Thus, according to Ackers *et al.* (1992), it is in response to a multiplicity of contingency factors that EPI in the last twenty years has evolved or been transformed. Responses will vary depending on factors such as the particular stage of development reached in the business life cycle, the extent of market pressure, the strategy and structure of organisations, the presence or otherwise of active trade unionism, inter-managerial relations and ideologically driven polices of the state or even employers. As a result, a diversity of experience at company level has emerged, which the detailed, wide-ranging micro-study conducted by the Department of Employment reveals (Marchington *et al.*, 1992).

Marchington *et al.* make use of the wave metaphor to capture these new and disparate developments in EPI. Rather than give support to the idea that EPI schemes follow a recurring historical cyclical pattern driven by the state of play in the power relationships between capital and labour, the 'wave' concept according to Marchington *et al.* is more adaptable and analytically useful. The basic argument emerging from this perspective is that:

> the shape of EI in organisations varies significantly over time, and can be characterised in terms of wave patterns. These are subject to a range of forces, one of the most important (and frequently overlooked) of which is the career aspirations and mobility of managers, and conflicts between different functions and levels in the organisational hierarchy. (Marchington, 1993: 555)

Thus, a fluid, empirically driven enquiry is offered in preference to the rather deterministic theoretical approach adopted by Ramsay.

To conclude this section, it should be noted that Ramsay (1993: 79) has responded to the critique of his theory by emphasising the importance of considering an empirical micro-analysis in relation to an overarching theoretical standpoint:

Industrial relations like any other discipline needs theories and facts, debates on method as well as a determination not to draw explanation from the armchair field of vision. Or to put it another way, waves are no substitute for cycles (or vice versa).

The evidence arising out of recent empirical investigations, however, has deepened our understanding of EPI, as Ramsay (1993) has acknowledged, placing the debate concerning theories and motives for EPI centre stage.

EPI IN PRACTICE

This section focuses on four areas of EPI – communicative involvement, non-representative consultation, task-centred involvement and financial participation – examining some of its most popular forms. It is intended to introduce to readers the practical experiences and consequences of developments in these areas, considering change and continuity, the degree and extent of certain forms of EPI influence, weaknesses in their application and the provisions required for success.

Communicative involvement

House journals

As a downward form of communication the company magazine or newspaper ranks as one of the most popular (Marchington *et al.*, 1992; IRS, 1996). Company magazines have a long history. Lever UK[3], for instance, first introduced a company journal in 1898 as a means of buttressing its paternalist[4] approach to employee relations. During the twentieth century, to varying degrees, Lever UK has transmitted the culture of paternalism through its company magazine. Moreover, this internal medium has been used as a vehicle to advocate acceptance of work measurement schemes in 1950 and a job evaluation scheme in 1953. More recently, in the early 1990s, the magazine has used its pages to promote flexible working and the harmonisation of working conditions central to the company's Horizon 2000 strategy (Griffiths, 1995).

Clearly, as the Lever UK experience demonstrates, the house journal can be used to reinforce company culture or convey in a favourable light changes required in working practices. However, a continual one-way flow of information may well prove to be counterproductive. Employees can become very cynical if management-initiated information is constantly drip fed through the medium of its house journal. The question of worker representatives and column space for employees to air their views without undue editorial interference, both considered by Lever UK (Griffiths, 1995), would no doubt give more credence to company magazines by actually involving employees. Some companies encourage this form of involvement but this seems to be the exception rather than the rule.

The most recent trend is for companies to publish the state of their finances in a company report, for internal consumption, with the view that 'opening the books' will improve employee commitment to the organisation (IRS, 1996). This trend, which focuses on industrial economics, implies that the success of the organisation and the well-being of its employees depend on profitability and growth. The idea behind it is that the revealing of financial information to employees is an expression of trust and partnership, fostering the view that it is in the best interests of management and the workforce to pull together in one direction to bring financial and commercial success to the organisation. The problem is that, when a company is doing badly, employees are more likely to think that management is practising 'creative accounting'. When a company is performing well, however, employees might demand a greater share of that prosperity.

Team briefing

Team briefings, according to a survey by the Industrial Society in 1995, are increasing in popularity (IRS, 1996). In its contemporary form, this system of communication involves line managers disseminating information, approved by top management, to the workforce on a regular basis. This system was promoted by the Industrial Society in the 1980s with a set of objectives in mind: to advance employee commitment, improve efficiency, control the information airways, gain acceptance of change and give more weight to the line manager's role, thus furthering middle management commitment (Marchington, 1989; Ramsay, 1992). The 'team brief' emphasises local issues where middle management and employees can identify their input and, therefore, should be more responsive to change or indeed initiate improvements in work practices themselves.

The weakness associated with team briefings, even when they are informative, well-structured and held on a regular basis, is that management assumes that the interests and concerns of employees concur with those of management. Given this unitary perspective and the buttressing of the middle management role, unsurprisingly, the atmosphere where employees can have an effective say is rather stifling. However, most organisations in the IRS survey (1996) claimed that team briefings allowed communication to flow in both directions. Moreover, this survey shows that team briefings, along with company journals, are the most prevalent form of communication used in organisations in the 1990s. This is not proof of their effectiveness, however, as this survey also reveals that organisations were divided over whether team briefings matched expectations.

■ Non-representative communication

Attitude surveys

An increasing number of organisations are adopting attitude surveys as part of the EPI package, although it should be noted that this practice is not new. Attitude surveys have been in use in Britain since the 1930s when the National Institute of Industrial Psychology first applied them to industry (Townley, 1994). IBM has regularly used opinion surveys to test employees' views on a wide range of issues including job satisfaction, job specifications and the organisation and management of the company (Bassett, 1987). In the Marchington *et al.* (1992) study these attitude surveys were conducted in 20 per cent of the 25 organisations that cooperated in their research. In a more recent study (IRS, 1996), however, of 26 organisations 54 per cent used attitude surveys.

Evidence from this study and a recent Gallop poll suggest that a significant minority of companies has made major changes based on the findings of these surveys. This point should not be exaggerated, however, as the experience of a single survey in one large organisation, Granada, led it to abandon the project (IRS, 1996). This highlights the problem that, once surveys have been conducted, they become the property of management and the communication process ceases. Action based on attitude surveys is the prerogative of management. The danger in not responding to surveys, however, is that the situations revealed as problematic are likely to be exacerbated by inaction.

None the less, some positive results have been forthcoming. Cussons (UK), the soap manufacturers, for instance, introduced an equal opportunities policy and an awareness training programme targeted at tackling problems of harassment in response to the feelings expressed by the staff in their survey (IRS, 1996). Thus opinions or problems uncovered by surveys can provide an important source of information in the formulation of policy, a point highlighted by Brown (1954) over forty years ago. He realised that the disclosure of grievances and tensions in the workforce, which often have a negative impact on performance, helped to avoid misunderstandings but unless followed by positive action was of little value. In short, employees need to see that their views can actually influence decision making.

The next case study (Exhibit 11.3) is mainly based on information taken from two Co-operative Bank plc publications: *Strength in Numbers*, a first report (1997) and *In Touch*, a special edition of the Co-operative Bank customer newsletter (1997). It provides the opportunity to think about EPI in practice using as an example an organisation that claims to still strongly value the co-operative principles on which it was built.

■ Exhibit 11.3

The Co-operative Bank

Employing over 3900 staff and profit performance in 1996 achieving record levels for the third year running, the Co-operative Bank's position as one of the leading high street banks looks secure. This success, according to the Bank, is the result of the redefining of traditional cooperative values and adapting them to the business environment of the 1990s as introduced in its Mission Statement of 1988.

What is particularly interesting is that the partnership approach emphasised in the Mission Statement seems to be in keeping with the TUC's 'social partnership' approach to industrial relations and the new Labour government's 'stakeholding' policy. The seven distinct Partner groups are: customers, staff and their families, shareholders, suppliers, local communities, society at large and past and future generations. The partnership approach stresses the importance of the interdependence of the Partner groups in creating a dynamic environment healthy for long-term prosperity. According to *Strength in Numbers*, however, the Bank places more weight on the contribution of its employees to the attainment of this end:

It's fair to say that, in terms of ensuring continued success, we depend on nobody more heavily than our staff. (*Strength in Numbers*, 1997: 14)

Terry Thomas, the managing director of the Co-operative Bank, places great store in the benevolent and paternalist ideas espoused by the nineteenth century mill owner, Robert Owen. Like Owen, though, Thomas maintains that the building of a partnership approach was not done out of altruism but was a prerequisite to the achievement of a profitable and successful business:

Many commentators have said that stakeholding is a threat to enhancing shareholder value. They then get lost in a dogmatic argument as to what stakeholding actually is or is not. My life-long experience as a banker tells me that a combination of the Anglo-Saxon capitalist model with Robert Owen's inclusive approach to a company's key partners, provides this. (*In Touch*, 1997: 2)

Owen's scientific approach to managing the workforce rather than his socialism is the predominant factor reflected in the Co-operative Bank's employee

■ Exhibit 11.3 continued

relations strategy in the 1990s. The Bank's mission statement stresses the importance of involving the partnership as a whole to forge an organisational conscience strong on ethics and with shared values, a common purpose and commitment to success. As part of this strategy the Bank has pledged to conduct employee attitude surveys on all aspects of the business:

> We [Co-operative Bank] are committed to carrying out this type of survey on a regular basis to ensure that we remain in touch with the views of our staff in everything we do. (*Strength in Numbers*, 1997: 12)

The Bank expresses the desire to explore all avenues to help staff to secure job satisfaction. A pilot scheme has been established to provide in-house facilities to study for National Vocational Qualifications as part of a programme to increase the 'employability' of its staff. Schemes such as 'homeworking' where staff are supplied with the necessary equipment to work from home are given as an example of balancing the interests of the organisation and its staff.

To conclude, a few relevant facts taken from an alternative source (Storey, 1995) should be of assistance in tackling the questions accompanying this case below. Union membership at the Co-operative Bank is high at about 90 per cent density. The Banking, Insurance and Finance Union (BIFU) rep-

resenting most of the Co-operative Bank's employees has become increasingly concerned about the introduction of personal contracts and the decline in collective bargaining. Moreover, a staff council was established which BIFU has boycotted because it allowed for the representation of non-union as well as union staff. Team briefings have been brought into operation at times of crisis to channel information to staff over the heads of union representatives. For instance, the Chief Executive of the Bank warned of the dire consequences if staff voted to take strike action in a ballot organised by BIFU in response to the announcement of a pay freeze in 1991. BIFU did not get a mandate to call for industrial action on that occasion. This additional information provides a little more insight and background to the relaunching of the Co-operative Bank's partnership approach in 1988.

Questions

1 From the evidence given here, to what extent, if any, do you think the Co-operative Bank is committed to an EPI strategy?

2 Is 'stakeholding' or the 'partnership approach' compatible with EPI?

3 What would you recommend as a way forward for expanding or improving EPI techniques at the Co-operative Bank?

■ Task-centred involvement

Total quality management

While the quest for improved product quality and customer service, to sustain a competitive edge, is not new, globalisation, liberalisation of markets, the pace of change in product markets and technology have all shifted up a gear, demanding a fresh managerial approach (Wilkinson, 1996). Total quality management (TQM) with its customer (internal and external) driven agenda is regarded by some as being able to give companies the edge in this new competitive environment (Juran, 1988, 1991). Moreover, in contrast to many other forms of EPI, TQM's design lends itself to be of a permanent and enduring fixture. If indeed this proves to be the case and TQM can be shown to empower workers, then Ramsay's 'cycles of control' theory may indeed require reconsideration (Hill, 1991).

The survey conducted by Marchington *et al.* (1992) revealed that TQM and customer care programmes[5] were indeed popular in that they were operative in 76 per cent of the organisations surveyed. Other surveys published in the same year also point to the expansion of TQM initiatives (Cruise O'Brien and Voss, 1992; Economic Intelligence Unit, 1992). The IRS research (1996), on the other hand, hints at a fall in the popularity of

TQM.[6] Only 56 per cent of the respondents in this more recent survey acknowledge the use of TQM and customer care initiatives. Of these, however, we do not know whether TQM has been introduced in full or only in part.

On their own, therefore, these statistics do not suffice. Just what TQM comprises is still unclear. Hill and Wilkinson (1995) in particular, however, have contributed much to clarifying the situation by bringing together the common attributes of TQM across various academic disciplines to provide a generic definition. Thus, it has been made easier to differentiate those organisations consciously moving towards full TQM practice and those mistakenly claiming to be implementing TQM. Investigations have found that some organisations have only selected parts of the TQM package and/or operate TQM at certain levels of the business (IDS, 1990; Cruise O'Brien and Voss, 1992). Moreover, TQM has been found in some cases to be little more than a compilation of old schemes, such as job redesign and quality circles, bolted together (Wilkinson, 1996).

To be successful, TQM has to integrate individual and organisational goals into one unitary objective. To achieve this requires a flatter management structure and commitment from all employees to forge a new quality culture based on continuous improvement (Snape *et al.*, 1995). The problem is, however, that to work successfully TQM has to be driven from the top of the organisation down and it will take several years to become fully established (Hill and Wilkinson 1995). This does not seem to bode well for employee involvement extending beyond operational task levels or holding employee interest and commitment, given that managers' powers are enhanced first before empowerment trickles downwards.

Snape *et al.* (1995) investigated the difficulty of achieving this aim. The proponents of TQM assume the presence of a unitarist employee relations culture. However, despite fundamental changes in key areas of employee relations, and an increase in managerial authority, over the last 25 years, it is a common error to think that traditional employee relationships no longer have an influential role (Hyman and Mason, 1995). Some evidence of resistance to TQM at the shopfloor level, therefore, should not be surprising (the Royal Mail case study in Exhibit 11.2 is one example). This is in keeping with Ramsay's (1977) and Hyman's (1975) view that capitalist social relations of production are fundamentally antagonistic.

Hill suggests, however, that at the operational level employees 'have become more involved in issues that were previously the prerogative of management' (Hill, 1991: 565). As he implies later (Hill and Wilkinson, 1995), however, the debate over 'empowerment' and what that means in terms of EPI is yet to be resolved. Contingency factors as much as anything else may explain contrasting views in this debate. No real evidence has surfaced to suggest that TQM will extend employee involvement to the level of organisational decision making.

As many commentators argue, the role of EPI in TQM programmes is focused on empowering workers at the point of production, and remains detached from the idea of extending EPI into the realms of decision making in policy areas such as restructuring, investment, acquisitions and so forth (Snape *et al.*, 1995). Proponents of TQM are concerned with motivating 'employees to convert tacit knowledge of the work process into continuous process improvement and innovation' (Cruise O'Brien, 1995: 115). It is easy to see that TQM could end up as redundant in the same way and for similar reasons as quality circles. Snape *et al.* (1995) imply that this might well be the case unless EPI is increased and management style and work organisation are not radically altered and integrated to attract rather than advocate employee commitment. Cruise O'Brien (1995) echoes this. She argues that a climate of trust is more important to the success of TQM than any problem with design faults. Trust can only be achieved, however, if TQM arrangements do not increase managerial control or incur job losses (Jones, 1997). In today's competitive environment this might not be possible.

◼ Financial participation

Employee financial participation has been the subject of much attention by writers concerned with EPI (Baddon *et al.*, 1989; Bell and Hanson, 1987; Fernie and Metcalf, 1995; Hyman and Mason, 1995; Knudsen, 1995; Pendleton *et al.* 1995; Poole, 1986, 1989; Poole and Jenkins, 1990; McLean, 1994; Matthews, 1989). Such was the optimism of the Industrial Participation Association (IPA) in 1984 that it concluded an attitude survey on profit sharing and employee shareholding with the prediction that:

> It is not farfetched to think that employee ownership may become as significant a part of employee relations by the turn of the century as unions have been throughout the century. (Bell and Hanson, 1984: 252)

However, the growth of employee share ownership, in which workers have a financial stake in the organisation that employees them, according to Smith (1993), has been due largely to tax incentives and the privatisation programme (where most employee share ownership plans (ESOPs) are to be found) pursued by Conservative governments in the 1980s and '90s.

It is the distribution of workers' shares that often grabs the headlines. Employee shareholders in Medway Ports, for example, saw the value of their shares increase dramatically after being taken over eighteen months after privatisation (*Financial Times*, 23 September 1993, cited in McLean, 1994). Examples such as this, however, are rare. More common, perhaps, are cases such as the flotation of Topps Tiles in June 1997, which made its owners millionaires. In contrast, the 300 employees of Topps stood to gain relatively little. Topps' owners proposed to give their 300 employees 'workers shares equal on average to 7 per cent of basic salary from their own holdings' (*Financial Times*, 28 May 1997). By October 1997 Topp Tiles' share price had increased from the flotation price of 100p to 199½p (*Financial Times*, 1 October 1997).

However, a full assessment of the stimulus for and impact of financial participation schemes can only be made by looking at past experience. The main reasons put forward for the introduction of such schemes are (i) to secure employee compliance (Baddon *et al.*, 1989; Matthews, 1989), (ii) philanthropic or reward for loyalty (Baddon *et al.*, 1989; Matthews, 1989), (iii) to weaken the trade union presence and influence and reduce or eliminate the need for collective bargaining, thereby increasing control over workers (Matthews, 1989) and (iv) to counteract periods of heightened industrial unrest (Ramsay, 1977). At the macro-level financial participation schemes have been used as part of the overall drive to bring about a shareholding democracy (Copeman *et al.*, 1984).

Historical perspective

Matthews (1989) provides the most comprehensive analysis of profit-sharing in Britain over a long time period. Reaching back to the mid-nineteenth century, he considers the motives for and the effectiveness of profit sharing up to the late 1980s. He concludes that 'profit-sharing seems to have been consistent with profit-maximizing behaviour by the firm and can be seen largely as a strategy of labour management' (Matthews, 1989: 440). Evidence of political and philanthropic motives was much less convincing. The effectiveness of profit sharing in Britain over the last century or so, according to Matthews (1989), is weak, though this is based more on a qualitative rather a quantitative analysis due to the difficulty of measurement. This could well explain the paradox that profit sharing is still valued by some employers. The experience of the John Lewis Partnership, with its particular brand of financial participation, deserves to be mentioned here as one of the few examples of employee involvement that has seemingly stood the test of time (*see* Bradley and Taylor, 1992, for a full account). However, while profit sharing and share ownership schemes have generated considerable interest, they have never become widespread.

Although largely invigorated by tax incentives, the resurgence of interest in financial participation schemes since 1978 has also been associated with other EPI schemes as part of a package aimed at improving the financial performance of organisations (McNabb and Whitfield, 1995) and improving employee attitudinal behaviour (Bell and Hanson, 1984). Moreover, employee share ownership schemes have been examined to see whether evidence of a shift towards increased participation or even industrial democracy exists (Pendleton *et al.*, 1995). With these points in mind we now turn to consider some of the more recent developments concerning financial participation.

Types of financial participation

The shortage of space prohibits the exploration of the full range of individual and collective financial participation schemes. But below brief consideration is given to profit sharing and employee share ownership plans (ESOPs).

Profit sharing

Profit sharing can be used as a form of monetary discipline on employees, if it makes up part of their wage, and is meant as an incentive to work harder. There are some problems with this view, however. Evidence linking individual effort and profit is difficult to determine (Baddon *et al.*, 1989). It can be differentiated from share ownership in that clearly there is no property ownership link, thus commitment to the firm is based on the cash nexus. The end result might be the same, however.

For the employer profit sharing offers the advantage of wage flexibility. Labour costs automatically adjust to the firm's economic standing. This means that it is less necessary to lay off labour in times of recession. Consequently, when the economic situation picks up, the workforce and the necessary skills are in place to take immediate advantage of the improved climate (Baddon *et al.*, 1989; McLean, 1994).

At the macro level, according to the Weitzman theory, if profit sharing is widespread then unemployment would fall without generating inflation (Baddon *et al.*, 1989; McLean, 1994). The hiring of additional workers is relatively cheap in companies operating profit sharing schemes as the cost is in part shared by other workers, who will in effect take a cut in wages as the profit-based part of their income has to be apportioned to an increased number of workers. The problem is how do you universalise this sort of arrangement to run concurrently (Badden *et al.*; 1989). How low wages will fall in times of depression must also be considered. The other side of the coin, however, is that employees may feel that their jobs are more secure, and in more prosperous times profit sharing could well be economically advantageous (McLean, 1994).

This form of economic democracy, however, is likely to have a negative impact on EPI, for if workers are involved in the hiring or firing of labour clearly it will be in their economic interests to reduce rather than increase employment levels, making the whole scheme impracticable (Nuti, 1986).

Employee share ownership plans

The ESOP is an American import. It works like this. An ESOP trust is set up to facilitate the execution of all aspects of employee share ownership. It is designed to make loan-capital available to employees, expressly to invest in company shares. The appeal to employees is that the future financial benefits, expected to be engendered from the ownership of these shares, should enable them to repay their original loan and accumulate a tidy surplus. The trust acquires loan-capital from external sources, for example the Unity Trust Bank, to purchase company shares, using company assets as collateral. Settlement of loans is achieved through employer donations and contractual repayments from shareholding employees (Cornford, 1990). Of course these arrangements can vary considerably but the difference between ESOPs and earlier share option schemes, such as approved deferred trust (ADST) and save as you earn schemes (SAYE), is that they can deliver a comparatively high level of employee share ownership, a possibility that may well have tracted some employers from adopting ESOPs (Baddon *et al.*, 1989; Hyman and Mason, 1995; Pendleton *et al.*, 1995).

The Labour government of 1978 initiated the recent revival in financial participation in its Finance Act by making tax concessions available to firms that made shares (ADSTs) obtainable to all of its employees. The Conservative Finance Act of 1980 encouraged full-time employees, subject to service qualifications, to participate in SAYE share option schemes. The 1984 Finance Act offered tax inducements to selected individuals opting to participate in discretionary or executive share schemes. Favoured members of staff were invited to purchase shares at generous rates. In 1989 this principle was extended to cover the whole workforce but has not proved so popular with companies (Hyman and Mason, 1995). For an update on profit sharing and employee share ownership options see IDS (1998).

There is evidence to suggest that ESOPs and profit sharing have resulted in an attitudinal change by employees from conflictual to more cooperative relationships with employers, although mainly in conjunction with other EPI initiatives (Poole and Jenkins, 1990). The Kelly and Kelly (1991: 32) survey, however, concludes that profit sharing and share ownership have made no real 'difference to underlying "them and us" attitudes among participants'. Moreover, ESOP experience in the UK provides little encouragement to those advocating that this form of financial participation will be instrumental in extending employee participation into the realms of industrial democracy (Pendleton *et al.*, 1995).

Of course this debate might now be academic given the changes announced in the November 1996 budget phasing out tax incentives for financial participation schemes. If tax incentives have been the main impetus for increased economic democracy in the 1980s and '90s, then Bell and Hanson's (1984) prediction quoted above will most certainly be wide of the mark.

CONCLUSION

While clearly there is not a consensual view of EPI, research findings do reveal that different forms of EPI become prominent at different times for different reasons. In the 1980s and '90s EPI was reconstructed by management, to restrengthen the competitive power of British companies in a global market, to engender employee commitment by extending workers' influence in task-centred matters (Guest, 1992). Doubts, however, have been expressed as to how successful British management has been in changing workers' attitudes (Kelly and Kelly, 1991; Geary, 1994, 1995).

Most forms of EPI in the 1980s and '90s have empowered workers only at the point of production with respect to work tasks in order to improve productivity and profitability. However, the attraction of task-centred EPI and financial participation is that seemingly direct managerial control techniques could be jettisoned in favour of responsible autonomy (Friedman, 1977), where workers are given more authority and responsibility over operational tasks. Research data from International Survey Research published at the end of 1995 reveals, however, that UK workers are dissatisfied and distrustful of management: 'Motivation and commitment to the company were lower even than in the strife-torn days of the mid-1970s' (*Financial Times*, 12 July 1997). Kelly's (1997) findings also support this view. Furthermore, he also identified research that found employees were becoming increasingly dissatisfied with EPI and thought that the level of involvement in decisions affecting their work was diminishing. This evidence underpins Geary's (1995: 370) view that 'management are more concerned to root out shopfloor challenges to their right to manage than to transform the manner in which work is organised.'

However, despite this increasing scepticism and evidence of workers' resistance to EPI, as illustrated in the Royal Mail case study (Exhibit 11.2), it seems likely that it will continue to be an important part of labour management strategy for the foreseeable future. This view is strengthened by the fact that the TUC and the Labour government are seemingly committed to a stakeholding economy. Moreover, the probability is that British workers will soon have the right to be represented on EWCs (*see* Chapter 7). Whether this will be enough to win workers' trust and commitment remains to be seen, but unless democracy is extended to the workplace traditional forms of managerial control, and all the associated problems, are likely to continue.

The final case study (Exhibit 11.4) provides the opportunity to examine EPI experience in one company since its foundation over a century and a half ago. This will facilitate the testing of theoretical perspectives and provide food for thought as to why Mill's (1909) view that workers should have a stake in the system has not yet materialised. A word of warning, however – findings cannot be universalised on the basis of one example.

■ Exhibit 11.4

DRG FP/Rexam[7]

The difficulty of relating the experience of a company over a long time period is to take account of the changes brought about by takeovers, acquisitions and mergers. This case is no exception. Hence, to trace the history of EPI in DRG FP/Rexam, the firms of ES & A Robinson Ltd (ES & AR) and John Dickinson and Co. Ltd (JD), which merged to form the Dickinson, Robinson Group (DRG) in 1966, are examined. More recent ownership changes have led to a break-up of the DRG Group. The Pembridge Group acquired DRG in 1989 and quickly put into action a restructuring programme that included the dispersal of what were once seen as core sections of the business. Thus, DRG was effectively broken up, destroying most of its character and heritage. Rexam, perhaps, still carries, albeit rather tenuously, the DRG connection. Therefore, aspects of employee relations in Rexam's Bristol operation are transcribed to see if there is evidence of continuity in respect to EPI. The point here is to trace EPI experience in one organisation over a long period and consider it in the light of contemporary theory and research findings.

ES & AR first began trading as a family firm in Bristol in 1844. It expanded rapidly and by 1885 was employing 600 people. In 1893 ES & AR registered as a limited stock company. Workers' shares, for those over 21 and with more than two years' service, were made available at this time. A profit sharing scheme was introduced in 1912.

By 1918, ES & AR had started a programme of expansion based on acquisitions where ES & AR acted as the parent holding company. Employees in its Bristol factories numbered about 2000 after the First World War and were well-represented by trade unions at the collective bargaining table. After 1918 ES & AR actively participated in its appropriate employer organisation, which dealt with regional and national negotiations concerning wages and conditions, and was also well-represented on the printing industry's JIC. In 1929 the firm created the new post of a personnel manager to deal with an ever-increasing workforce.

By 1935, the Bristol workforce numbered over 5000, the majority being young women. Notably, in this year nine members of the Robinson family held almost one-third of the ordinary share capital, thus the shift towards the separation of ownership from

control in ES & AR proceeded very slowly. Its employees held by this time about £75 000 in workers' shares. This sum, however, represented only 4 per cent of the £1 848 000 share capital. Moreover, workers' shares did not carry any voting rights.

In 1919 a new bonus scheme based on 25 per cent of net profits was introduced. In an attempt to break the impact of a national strike in 1922, ES & AR declared that skilled printers belonging to the Typographical Association would lose their profit bonus if they did not return to work, which may well have contributed to the speedy resolution of the strike locally.

For the first time, after the 1926 General Strike, ES & AR introduced a contributory pension scheme for men over 21 and under 52 years, which the firm administered and supported by tendering an annual contribution. This scheme was made a condition of employment and involved the appointment of a trustee from the workforce.

Works committees, as recommended by the Whitley Council, were operational in ES & AR throughout the inter-war years, although the craft unions refused to participate. A house journal, first published in 1914, was a regular feature of communication right through to the 1980s. After the merger in 1966, most individual plants also published their own magazines.

In the post Second World War social, economic and political climate collective bargaining flourished. Low levels of unemployment, increased demand and the reversal of the 1927 Trades Dispute Act assisted in the enhancement of trade union authority. This state of affairs was apparent in ES & AR. JICs still functioned but were hardly ever called upon to resolve problems as up to 1959 disputes were rare. But in the national stoppage called by the print unions in 1959 the JIC machinery failed. By 1967, the use of JICs in the printing industry was abandoned. After the 1959 dispute ES & AR increasingly looked to settling industrial relations problems 'in house'.

JD established a stationery business in Hertfordshire in 1804 and by 1838 had diversified into papermaking. It was the stationery sector that flourished, however, and by 1914 JD employed over 2500 workers, many of whom were women. In 1886 the firm became a joint stock limited

▶

■ Exhibit 11.4 continued

liability company. The pace in the shift from ownership to managerial control, however, is not clear, although there were no family members on the board of directors after 1928.

JD never really warmed to trade unions. Craft workers in the firm joined trade unions at the beginning of the twentieth century but there is no evidence to suggest that they gained recognition rights. During the First World War, however, recognition rights were conceded to craft and non-craft workers. Moreover, JD welcomed the formation of a JIC in the paper industry in 1920. However, fraternisation with this form of industrial relations was short-lived. After the 1926 General Strike, employees were banned from belonging to a trade union. It became a condition of employment for employees to join the Union of the House of Dickinsons, a company union. JD also severed all connections with employer organisations. Communication was channelled through a house magazine.

In 1920, £50 000 was diverted from company profits to initiate a contributory pension scheme. That same year employees were also given the opportunity to buy company shares and by 1933 the number of employee shareholders exceeded 1400, about 20 per cent of the workforce. After 1926 and the formation of a company union JD sponsored a new pension scheme to the tune of £100 000. The scheme was contributory, workers paying a levy of 2.5 per cent of their wages topped up by a contribution from the company based on profit levels.

The Union of the House of Dickinson was sustained through the war and continued to influence heavily the relationship between management and employees until the merger with ES & AR in 1966. In 1946, however, a works committee was set up in one of JD's paper mills to suggest ways of improving efficiency in production areas, and employees were no longer forbidden from joining a trade union.

Following the formation of DRG in 1966, moves were made towards combining the various pension schemes. It was agreed that pensions management should include the consultation and participation of its members. It was not until 1978 that one common pension was achieved. A system was set up to elect employee representatives and trustees who have the power to make decisions on behalf of their members.

By 1981, 70 per cent of the 14 000 people employed by DRG in the UK belonged to a trade union. Collective bargaining was now the dominant feature of industrial relations. Increasingly, however, despite national agreements, interpretation had become a matter for in-house negotiation, particularly on matters such as payment for machine extras.

In the 1980s works councils were introduced in many of DRG's plants. They were not always supported by the trade unions. Other EPI schemes apart from collective bargaining included job evaluation, although only for white-collar workers. In one such scheme the evaluation panel consisted of two employee and two management representatives. Some of the house magazines were under employee rather than management editorship. Suggestion schemes were in operation, which included payment for ideas that were successfully adopted.

By the 1990s the employment relationship had changed considerably. The DRG group no longer existed, its constituent parts having been divided among a number of new owners, and trade union representatives were forced into adopting a much more submissive role. Rexam Medical Packaging, which acquired an important segment of the DRG business, identified in 1994 that one of its goals was to achieve 'a total quality approach'. By 1996 it believed it had achieved this. According to the company, training and motivating staff provided the key to this success. New working practices, a flatter management structure and the involvement of staff in resolving work task problems were adopted when a new plant opened in 1992.[8] However, in January 1997, the *Financial Times* reported that the Rexam packaging group planned to dispose of many of its subsidiaries by 1998, thus putting the credibility of EPI from the perspective of its employees in jeopardy.

Questions

1 To what extent do you think the DRG/Rexam experience validates either Ramsay's cyclical theory or the contingency model put forward by Ackers *et al.*?

2 Is it evident that managerial attraction to EPI was a means to weaken trade unionism, substitute trades unionism or provided as an added dimension to participation?

3 To what extent do you think acquisitions, mergers and job losses weaken EPI objectives?

NOTES

1 The Levellers, reflecting the interests of the middle orders, small property holders, artisans, hus-bandmen and yeomen, agitated for the extension of the suffrage to male householders.

2 The Diggers, a radical religious poltical grouping, believed that private property robbed people of their common rights. God created earth and its life sustaining treasures for all to share equal-ly and not to be exploited by the few to dominate the many.

3 Lever UK started out life as Lever Brothers Ltd, Port Sunlight.

4 Paternalism is a relationship existing between a powerful employer and a weak workforce; a paternalist relationship requires employers' commitment to a clear set of economic and social obligations designed to secure workers' deference.

5 In the survey conducted by Marchington *et al.* (1992) TQM and customer care programmes are classified together.

6 In the IRS (1996) survey TQM and customer care initiatives are classified separately.

7 Unless otherwise indicated, the sources of information for this case study are Richardson (1991, 1995).

8 This information taken from an interview with Tony Commons, Human Resource Director of Rexam Medical Packaging, conducted by Peter Nichols, School of Human Resource Management, University of the West of England (Nichols, 1996).

REFERENCES

Ackers, P., Marchington, M., Wilkinson, A. and Goodman, J. (1992) 'The use of cycles? explain-ing employee involvement in the 1990s', *Industrial Relations Journal,* 23(4), 268–83.

Bacon, N. and Storey, J. (1993), 'Individualization of the employment relationship and the impli-cations for trade unions', *Employee Relations,* 15(1), 5–17.

Bacon, N. and Storey, J. (1996) 'Royal Mail: a new industrial relations framework' in Storey, J. (ed.) *Blackwell Cases in Human Resource and Change Management.* Oxford: Blackwell.

Baddon, L., Hunter, L., Hyman, J., Leopold, J. and Ramsay, H. (1989) *People's Capitalism?* London: Routledge.

Bassett, P. (1987) *Strike Free.* London: Macmillan.

Batstone, E., Ferner, A. and Terry, M. (1983) *Unions on the Board.* Oxford: Blackwell.

Bell, D. W. and Hanson, C. G. (1984) *Profit Sharing and Employee Share-holding Attitude Survey.* London: Industrial Participation Association.

Bell, D. W. and Hanson, C. G. (1987) *Profit Sharing and Profitability.* London: Kogan Page.

Blyton, P. and Turnbull, P. (1992) 'Afterword' in Blyton, P. and Turnbull, P. (eds) *Reassessing Human Resource Management.* London: Sage.

Blyton, P. and Turnbull, P. (1994) *The Dynamics of Employee Relations.* London: Macmillan.

Bradley, K. and Taylor, S. (1992) *Business Performance in the Retail Sector: The Experience of the John Lewis Partnership.* Oxford: Clarendon Press.

Brown, J. A. C. (1954) *The Social Psychology of Industry.* Harmondsworth: Penguin.

Clarke, T. (1977) 'Industrial democracy: the institutionalized suppression of industrial conflict?' in Clarke, T. and Clements, L. (eds) *Trade Unions under Capitalism.* London: Fontana.

Coates, K. and Topham, A. (eds) (1975) *Industrial Democracy and Nationalization.* Nottingham: Spokesman.

Cole, G. D. H. (1975) 'State ownership and control' in Coates, K. and Topham, A. (eds) *Industrial Democracy and Nationalization.* Nottingham: Spokesman.

Copeman, G., Moore, P. and Arrowsmith, C. (1984) *Share Ownership.* Aldershot: Gower.

Cornford, J. (1990) *A Stake in the Company*. London: Institute for Public Policy Research, Economic Study, no. 3.

Craig, F. W. S. (1990) *British General Election Manifestos 1959–1987*. Aldershot: Parliamentary Research Services.

Cruise O'Brien, R. (1995) 'Employee involvement in performance improvement: a consideration of tacit knowledge, commitment and trust', *Employee Relations*, 17(3), 1110–20.

Cruise O'Brien, R. and Voss, C. (1992) 'In search of quality', London Business School Working Paper, London.

Economist Intelligence Unit (1992) *Making Quality Work: Lessons from Europe's Leading Companies*. London: EIU.

Employment Department (1989) *People and Companies: Employee Involvement in Britain*. London: HMSO.

Farnham, D. and Pimlott, J. (1995) *Understanding Industrial Relations*. 5th edn. New York: Cassell.

Fernie, S. and Metcalf, D. (1995) 'Participation, contingent pay, representation and workplace performance: evidence from Great Britain, *British Journal of Industrial Relations*, 33(3), 379–415.

Fox, A. (1975) 'Industrial relations: a social critique of pluralist ideology' in Barrett, B., Rhodes, E. and Beishon, J. (eds) *Industrial Relations and the Wider Society*. London: Macmillan.

Fox, A. (1977) 'The myths of pluralism and a radical alternative' in Clarke, T. and Clements, L. (eds) *Trade Unions under Capitalism*. London: Fontana.

Freeman, M. (1986) 'The road to power', *Confrontation*, no. 1.

Friedman, A.L. (1977) *Industry and Labour*. London: Macmillan.

Gall, G. (1995) 'Return to sender: a commentary on Darlington's analysis of workplace unionism in the Royal Mail in Britain', *Employee Relations*, 17(2), 54–63.

Geary, J. F. (1994) 'Task participation: employees' participation enabled or constrained?' in Sisson, K. (ed.) *Personnel Management*. 2nd edn. Oxford: Blackwell.

Geary, J.F. (1995) 'Work practices: the structure of work' in P. Edwards (ed.), *Industrial Relations*. Oxford: Blackwell.

Griffiths, J. (1995) '"Give my regards to Uncle Billy ...": the rites and rituals of company life at Lever Brothers, c.1900–c.1990', *Business History*, 37(4), 25–45.

Guest, D.E. (1989) 'Human resource management: its implications for industrial relations and trade unions', in Storey, J. (ed.) *New Perspectives on Human Resource Management*. London: Routledge.

Guest, D.E. (1992) 'Employee commitment and control' in Hartley, J. F. and Stephenson, G. M. (eds) *Employment Relations*. Oxford: Blackwell.

Hill, C. (1980) *The Century of Revolution*. Surrey: Nelson.

Hill, S. (1991) 'Why quality circles failed but total quality management might succeed', *British Journal of Industrial Relations*, 29, 541–68.

Hill, S. and Wilkinson, A. (1995) 'In search of TQM', *Employee Relations*, 17(3), 8–25.

Hyman, J. and Mason, B. (1995) *Managing Employee Involvement and Participation*. London: Sage.

Hyman, R. (1975) *Industrial Relations*. London: Macmillan.

IDS (1990) *Report* no. 457. London: Income Data Services.

IDS (1996) various reports. London: Income Data Services.

IDS (1998) *Report* no. 641. London: Income Data Services.

IRS (1996) 'Assessing employee involvement strategies', *Employment Review*, no. 614, 4–12.

Jenkins, S., Noon, M. and Lucio, M. (1995) 'Negotiating quality: the case of TQM in Royal Mail', *Employee Relations*, 17(3), 87–98.

Jones, O. (1997) 'Changing the balance? Taylorism, TQM and work organisation', *New Technology, Work and Employment*, 12(1), 13–23.

Juran, J. M. (1988) *Juran on Planning for Quality*. New York: Free Press.

Juran, J. M. (1991) 'Strategies for world class quality', *Quality Progress*, March, 81.

Kelly, J. (1988) *Trade Unions and Socialist Politics*. London: Verso.

Kelly, J. (1997) 'The future of trade unionism: injustice, identity and attribution', *Employee Relations*, 19(5), 400–14.

Kelly, J. and Kelly, C. (1991) 'Them and us: social psychology and the new industrial relations', *British Journal of Industrial Relations*, 29(1), 25–48.

Knudsen, H. (1995) *Employee Participation in Europe*. London: Sage.

Labour Research (1984) *The Miners' Case*. London: LRD publications.

McLean, H. (1994) *Fair Shares – The Future of Employee Financial Participation in the UK*. London: The Institute of Employment Rights.

McNabb, R. and Whitfield, K. (1995) 'Financial participation, employee involvement and financial performance at the workplace', Cardiff Business School Paper, Cardiff.

Matthews, D. (1989) 'The British experience of profit-sharing', *Economic History Review*, 2nd ser., XLII(4), 439–64.

Marchington, M. (1989) 'Employee participation' in Towers, B. (ed.), *A Handbook of Industrial Relations Practice*. London: Kogan Page.

Marchington, M. (1996) 'Superco' in Storey, J. (ed.) *Blackwell Cases in Human Resource and Change Management*. Oxford: Blackwell.

Marchington, M., Goodman, J., Wilkinson, A. and Ackers, P. (1992) *New Developments in Employee Involvement*, Research Series No. 2. Sheffield: Employment Department.

Marchington, M., Wilkinson, A., Ackers, P. and Goodman, J. (1993) 'The influence of managerial relations on waves of employee involvement', *British Journal of Industrial Relations*, 31(4), 553–76.

Marx, K. (1946) 'Theses on Feurbach' in Engels, F. *Ludwig Feurbach and the End of Classical German Philosophy*. Moscow: Progress Publishers.

Marx, K. (1973) *Grundrisse*. New York: Vintage.

Marx, K. and Engels, F. (1952) *Manifesto of the Communist Party*. Moscow: Progress Publishers, reprint of the 1888 translation.

Mill, J. S. (1909) 'On the probable futurity of the labouring classes' in Mill, J. S. *Principles of Political Economy*. New Jersey: Kelley, reprinted 1976.

Monks, J. (1994) 'The union response to HRM: fraud or opportunity', *Personnel Management*, September.

Nichols, P. (1996) *Work and Employment*. Bristol: University of the West of England.

Nuti, D. M. (1986) *Profit Sharing and Employment: Claims and Overclaims*. European University Institute.

Pendleton, A., McDonald, J., Robinson, A. and Wilson, N. (1995) 'The impact of employee share ownership plans on employee participation and industrial democracy', *Human Resource Management Journal*, 5(4), 44–60.

Poole, M. (1986) *Towards a New Industrial Democracy*. London: Routledge.

Poole, M. (1989) *The origins of Economic Democracy: Profit-sharing and Employee-shareholding Schemes*. London: Routledge.

Poole, M. and Jenkins, G. (1990) *The Impact of Economic Democracy: Profit-sharing and Employee-shareholding Schemes*. London: Routledge.

Purcell, J. (1987) 'Mapping management styles in employee relations', *Journal of Management Studies*, 24(5), 533–48.

Purcell, J. and Sisson, K. (1983) 'Strategies and practice in the management of industrial relations' in Bain, G. S. (ed.) *Industrial Relations in Britain*. Oxford: Blackwell.

Ramsay, H. (1977) 'Cycles of control: worker participation in sociological and historical perspective', *Sociology*, 11(3), 481–506.

Ramsay, H. (1992) 'Commitment and involvement' in Towers, B. (ed.) *The Handbook of HRM*. Oxford: Blackwell.

Ramsay, H. (1993) 'Recycled waste? debating the analysis of worker participation: a response to Ackers *et al.*', *Industrial Relations Journal*, 24(1), 77–80.

Reddish, H. (1975) 'Written memorandum of evidence to the Royal Commission on trades unions and employers' associations' in Barrett, B., Rhodes, E. and Beishon, J. (eds) *Industrial Relations and the Wider Society*. London: Macmillan.

Richardson, M. (1991) 'An examination of industrial relations in the Bristol printing and packaging industry covering the period from the end of the first world war to 1991', unpublished dissertation, University of the West of England.

Richardson, M. (1995) 'Industrial relations in the British printing industry between the wars', unpublished PhD thesis, University of the West of England.

Smith, G. (1993) 'Employee share schemes in Britain', *Employment Gazette*, April.

Snape, E., Wilkinson, A., Marchington, M. and Redman, T. (1995) 'Managing human resources for TQM: possibilities and pitfalls', *Employee Relations*, 17(3), 42–51.

Storey, J. (1992) 'HRM in action: the truth is out at last', *Personnel Management*, April.

Storey, J. (1995) 'Employment policies and practices in UK clearing banks: an overview', *Human Resource Management Journal*, 5(4), 24–43.

Taylor, R. (1997) 'New Labour, new unionism', *Financial Times*, 5 September.

Townley, B. (1994) 'Communicating with employees' in Sisson, K. (ed.) *Personnel Management*. 2nd edn. Oxford: Blackwell.

Wickens, P. (1987) *The Road to Nissan*. London: Macmillan.

Wilkinson, A. (1996) 'Three roads to quality' in Storey, J. (ed.) *Blackwell Cases in Human Resource and Change Management*. Oxford: Blackwell.

FURTHER READING

Hyman, R. (1997) 'The future of employee representation', *British Journal of Industrial Relations*, 35(3), 309–36.

Kelly, J. (1997) 'Industrial relations: looking to the future', *British Journal of Industrial Relations*, 35(3), 393–8.

Lewchuk, W. and Robertson, D. (1997) 'Production without empowerment: work reorganisation from the perspective of motor vehicle workers', *Capital and Class*, no. 63, 37–64.

McKinlay, A. and Taylor, P. (1996) 'Power, surveillance and resistance: inside the "factory of the future"' in Ackers, P., Smith, C. and Smith, P. (eds) *The New Workplace and Trade Unionism*. London: Routledge.

Waddington, J. and Whitston, C. (1996) 'Empowerment versus intensification: union perspectives of change at the workplace' in Ackers, P., Smith, C. and Smith, P. (eds) *The New Workplace and Trade Unionism*. London: Routledge.

Chapter 12

DISCRIMINATION*

Sally Howe

Learning objectives

By the end of this chapter, readers should be able to:

- define discrimination and give a picture of the effects of discrimination on employment in the 1990s;
- explain why discrimination occurs and consider the psychological, sociological, historical, structural and ethical perspectives;
- outline the role of legislation and state regulatory bodies in the management of discrimination and equal opportunities;
- understand the more radical approaches to equality management including quotas and affirmative action programmes;
- discuss the managing diversity movement and its impact on discrimination in employment;
- describe the roles and initiative taken by management, trade unions and individuals in promoting equal opportunities in the workplace.

INTRODUCTION

The two articles reproduced in Exhibits 12.1 and 12.2 illustrate well some of the complexities and dilemmas of managing discrimination and providing equality of opportunity. On the face of it, the House of Commons as a workplace provides no particular restrictive barriers to women, both sexes are free to stand for election, yet of the total number of MPs only a small percentage are women. The Labour Party decided to address this problem by taking positive action to increase the number of women candidates at the last General Election by creating all-women shortlists. The policy was interventionist and, as Exhibit 12.1 shows, was challenged by some aspiring male Labour candidates. The situation demonstrates well the difficulties inherent in affirmative action, or positive discrimination. Supporters of the policy would point to Exhibit 12.2 and say 'well, it works! A record number of women MPs was elected in 1997, changing the gender balance in the House of Commons significantly'. The detractors may reply, 'they have yet to prove their worth'.

---

*The source of the statistics utilised in the figures and table and other statistical data in the text is *Labour Market and Skill Trends 1997/8*, Department for Education and Employment. Crown copyright.

■ Exhibit 12.1

Labour's women-only shortlists ruled illegal

Labour's policy of positive discrimination to enable more women to stand for parliament was ruled unlawful by an industrial tribunal yesterday. The verdict, upholding a complaint by two male candidates frozen out by the process, threatens to scupper the policy of women-only shortlists introduced in 1993 by the late Labour leader John Smith.

Party officials expressed surprise and dismay at the court's ruling. They said it applied only to the two cases concerned and would not affect the 34 seats where candidates had already been selected on the basis of women-only shortlists.

Another nine constituencies in the middle of the selection process have been told by the party to hold off until the tribunal delivers its written judgment within the next two weeks. Labour will then consider an appeal. A further five seats were due to begin choosing from women.

Despite Labour's attempt to give a narrow legal definition to the ruling, it is likely to leave the door open to men to mount challenges in any of the 34 seats affected so far. The idea of the shortlists was to more than double the number of Labour women MPs, currently 38, in the next parliament by assigning at least half of the safe and marginal seats where the incumbent was standing down to women-only lists.

Mr Tony Blair, Mr Smith's successor, has expressed reservations about a scheme that encountered considerable local resistance and appeared destined to be scrapped after the next general election. Mr Blair has said the process of imposing shortlists on constituencies had 'not been ideal' although it may have been a necessary one-off step.

The case was brought by Mr Peter Jepson and Mr Roger Dyas-Elliott, who were turned down by constituencies in London and Yorkshire.

Mr John Prophet, the tribunal chairman, said their exclusion had violated the Sex Discrimination Act. Mr Prophet said the principle of increasing the number of women MPs might be regarded 'as a laudable motive but that has no relevance to the issue'. Mr Jepson said the decision 'sounds the death knell for all-women shortlists'.

Mr Tom Sawyer, Labour's general secretary, said the party had undertaken the policy after extensive consultation with legal experts. 'We do not believe [the ruling] to be correct and we have proceeded throughout in the belief we have been acting in accordance with the law'.

Mr Michael Trend, the Conservative deputy chairman, said: 'This decision throws Labour's entire selection process into disarray. They should now reopen the selection in all those constituencies where all-women shortlists have been imposed.'

Source: John Kampfner, *Financial Times*, 9 January 1996.

■ Exhibit 12.2

Women start to beat back pinstripe hordes

The face of the House of Commons will be transformed next week, not just by the influx of new Labour MPs but by the arrival of about 120 women members – more than twice the number elected in 1992.

They will arrive at an institution which notoriously has a rifle range but no crèche, and where ladies' lavatories are hidden away down fusty corridors.

The influx is testimony partly to Labour's attempt to ensure women were picked to fight winnable seats, using the controversial all-women shortlist policy.

Labour will have 101 women MPs on its benches, and since female members tend not to wear pinstriped suits, they stand out.

These impressions count. Conservatives are acutely aware that their image as a party of middle-class, middle-aged men sends the wrong message to women voters.

Labour's efforts to bring more women into the Commons puts the other two parties to shame. The

■ **Exhibit 12.2 continued**

Conservatives will have just 12 women MPs after the election carnage, fewer than in 1992.

Mr John Major pleaded with local associations to pick more women, but was ignored. Women on selection committees were, paradoxically, less likely to pick a female candidate than their male counterparts.

The Liberal Democrats have an equally dismal record. Their record postwar tally of 45 seats revealed the extent to which women candidates had been overlooked: the party will have just three women MPs.

The Fawcett Society, the equal opportunities campaign group, believes the presence of women in the Commons will temper the bear-pit atmosphere of the chamber, and lead to debates which are more attuned to the concerns of ordinary people.

Source: George Parker, *Financial Times Weekend*, 3/4 May 1997.

In this chapter the factors that contribute to employment profiles such as that found in the House of Commons are examined. The various explanations and perspectives on discrimination are discussed and the strategies adopted to adjust imbalances evaluated.

The management of discrimination and equal opportunities in the employment relationship is an extremely important subject for organisations and for society in general. Organisations are increasingly being asked to examine their business strategies to ensure that their aims are not simply focused on profitability but also include important issues around managing the expectations of employees and society. Most employees will spend considerable periods of their waking life in the work environment and are entitled to expect fairness of treatment, some consideration of their need for personal fulfilment, and the provision of a non-threatening work environment.

Increasingly organisations are also recognising that managing equal opportunities is part of a package of measures that can be used to create effective, committed, high performance teams of workers. The payback can be measured in both financial and non-financial terms. The ability to manage diversity and utilise all members of the working population is an essential part of creating business advantage.

For the UK the management of equal opportunities is also an important issue. It is one of the most essential elements of a free society which respects basic human rights. It is also necessary in order to prevent the growth of disaffected sections of the community who see no prospect of permanent employment. Politically, opinions on the best way to create this ideal are varied; we examine the free market and social justice approaches in this chapter.

WHAT IS DISCRIMINATION?

The dictionary definition of discrimination is 'to make a distinction'. This is an essential skill in employee relations as all organisations need to be able to make distinctions in areas such as selection, appraisal and reward management. Such distinctions must be based on objective, job-related criteria, however, to be regarded as fair discrimination. Distinctions based on characteristics that are not relevant to the job such as sex, sexuality, marital status, colour, nationality, disability or age are considered as unfair forms of discrimination which affect the basic human rights of individuals. The term discrimination will be used to denote unfair methods of creating distinctions in this chapter.

Discrimination can take a variety of forms in any organisation:

- *individual*, where a member or members of the organisation demonstrate prejudice against another individual often as a result of stereotypical thinking. Examples include: 'women with children are less reliable', 'black people are dirty', or 'older people are slow on the uptake'.

- *structural*, where the requirements for appointments or promotion have the effect of excluding certain groups or individuals. This may be deliberate or accidental and often results from an over-reliance on levels of experience and qualifications when defining entry into a job.

- *organisational*, reflecting common assumptions about the type of job certain groups of people are capable of performing. Examples include: 'women are best at secretarial work', 'men are most suited to transport and haulage'.

The consequences of unfair discrimination are many but the most significant include:

- the failure to select/promote the best individual for the job because of restrictions placed on applicants as a result of discriminatory practices;

- the failure to create a balanced workforce containing individuals with a diversity of experience whose creativity and ideas can be utilised by the employer;

- the creation of resentment and poor morale, which undermine team spirit and cooperation.

Discrimination can be examined from a number of perspectives, each contributing some insights into the patterns of labour found in employment today. The main perspectives include:

1 a *psychological/sociological perspective*, which examines discrimination as a product of how individuals learn appropriate behaviours for the society in which they live, and how social relationships evolve, particularly between the dominant majority group and minorities;

2 a *historical perspective*, which looks at changes in the pattern of discrimination over time and the factors that have contributed to it;

3 a *structural/economic perspective*, looking at labour patterns in terms of supply and demand and linking discrimination to the possession of particular attributes;

4 a *political/ethical perspective*, looking at discrimination as a basic human right and a fundamental part of a socially responsible nation or workplace.

Each of these perspectives is reviewed briefly to illustrate its contribution to a broader understanding of the nature of discrimination.

THE PSYCHOLOGICAL/SOCIOLOGICAL BASIS OF DISCRIMINATION

Studies have attempted to evaluate the degree to which discrimination is a learned behaviour or a behaviour that results from certain innate personality traits. Research into child development suggests that many aspects of behaviour are modelled through observation of others and through the process of socialisation. Giddens (1993) defines socialisation as 'The process whereby the helpless infant gradually becomes a self-aware, knowledgeable person, skilled in the ways of the culture into which she or he is born'.

Debates over the degree to which nature (genetic inheritance) or nurture (the way an individual is brought up) is most important in shaping behaviour have tended to conclude that each is important, but that social learning is an integral part of all human experience. The young child will adopt behaviours as a result of identification with the adults around him or her and will imitate observed behaviours. Important agencies of socialisation include the family, the peer group, the educational experiences and attitudes conveyed by the media. There is a tendency in all human beings to generalise from experiences and create stereotypes. Stereotypes are not necessarily formed from malice or ill-will; in many cases they result from a lack of knowledge or concrete experience on which to draw. Stereotyping can, however, lead to prejudice against individuals – holding negative attitudes towards them on the basis of their group membership, rather than on their own merits. The word prejudice comes from the notion of prejudging people as either good or bad before knowing them individually. It is this behaviour that can lead to discrimination.

Other studies have attempted to link prejudice with particular types of personality trait. Hillgard *et al.* (1979) report on investigations into Adolf Hitler's anti-Semitic prejudice in the Second World War and suggest that it can be associated with *authoritarian* styles of personality. In authoritarian personalities prejudice may reflect the individual's own insecurities. Highly prejudiced individuals may not be able to face their own weaknesses and may project undesirable traits onto minority groups. This *displacement* activity involves directing feelings of hostility or anger against individuals or groups who are not the real origin of those anxieties. This leads to *scapegoating* or blaming other individuals for the source of your own troubles. Scapegoating also frequently involves *projection*, the unconscious attributing to others of one's own desires or characteristics.

Explanations such as the one above do not fully explain widespread prejudice against particular groups in society, however. Other theories develop the idea of *social norms* – a community's implicit rules specifying the beliefs, attitudes and behaviours appropriate for its members. From particular views of social norms *ethnocentrism* may occur – a suspicion of outsiders, combined with a tendency to evaluate the norms of other cultures in terms of one's own culture. Ethnocentrism may also lead to *group closure*, whereby groups maintain boundaries separating themselves from others. The boundaries are developed and sustained by means of *exclusion devices*, which sharpen the divisions between one ethnic group and another. Such devices include the limiting or prohibition of intermarriage between the groups, restrictions on social contact and the physical separation of groups from one another in ghettos. In some cases the relationship between groups is of equal power, but in many cases the dominant group uses closure devices to maintain its privileged position.

HISTORICAL TRENDS IN ATTITUDES TO DISCRIMINATION

The previous section shows how attitudes to those around us are determined by psychological and sociological behaviours. Social norms are not static, however; they evolve over time and as society changes so do the behaviours considered acceptable or unacceptable.

In the late twentieth century, displaying notices saying 'No Blacks or Irish' would be considered unacceptable, yet in the 1950s such signs were openly seen on boarding houses. Similarly, to expect a woman to resign from her job if she married would be unthinkable in the UK today, but this still occurred in the civil service in the 1960s.

The factors causing such alterations in social attitudes are complex, but by tracing the historical trends some light can be thrown on the continuing process of change today. We start by examining the development of attitudes towards the roles of men and women in society.

■ Gender issues

Figure 12.1 shows the distribution of labour in the UK workforce based on gender and type of employment (full-time or part-time). In 1996 women made up 49.6 per cent of the total labour force, but many of these jobs were part-time. Women's share of employment also varies considerably between industrial sectors. Table 12.1 shows the distribution of female employment in 1996, and future projections to the year 2006. Female employees currently outnumber male employees in the sectors 'Mainly public services' and 'Distribution, hotels and catering'. They also form almost exactly half of employees in 'Financial and business services'. However, they represent less than a third of employees in the 'Manufacturing', 'Primary and utilities' and 'Transport and communications' sectors and only 17 per cent in 'Construction'. Women are under-represented in the higher level occupations, are more likely to work part-time, and earn significantly less on average than men.

Do these patterns reflect basic biological and physical sex differences between men and women, or are they the result of gender learning and cultural programming? Some researchers have tried to link biological factors with behavioural characteristics, for example studying the link between males and aggressive behaviour and females and passive behaviour. The evidence for particular types of behaviour being linked to sex is inconclusive; many variations occur. What is evident, however, is that despite the consid-

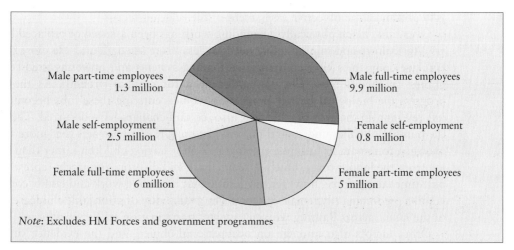

Note: Excludes HM Forces and government programmes

■ Fig. 12.1 Workforce in employment, June 1996 (United Kingdom, seasonally adjusted)
Source: Labour Market Trends.

■ Table 12.1 Female workers as share of all employees, 1996 and 2006 (projected)

Sector	1996 (%)	2006 (%)
Primary and utilities	23.4	24.4
Manufacturing	29.5	29.9
Construction	16.7	18.9
Distribution, hotels and catering	54.1	55.1
Transport and communication	27.8	28.2
Financial and business services	49.5	48.4
Mainly public services	68.4	68.8
Whole economy	49.6	51.5

Source: Business Strategies Ltd, 1996.

erable differences found in the respective roles of women and men in different cultures, there is no known instance of a society in which women are more powerful than men. Women are everywhere primarily concerned with childbearing and the maintenance of the home, while political and military activities tend to be resoundingly male. This male dominance is usually referred to as *patriarchy*. The explanation for this consistency is linked to the biological fact that women give birth to and nurse children.

Looking at the effects of biological and physical sex differences on employment, have attitudes and practices changed over time? Jobs requiring physical strength such as mining, agriculture, haulage and building have traditionally been the preserve of men. Jobs requiring manual dexterity such as assembly have been occupied by women. Are these occupational stereotypes biological in origin? Generally, men's body size and weight are greater than women's, making them stronger, but less sensitive to fine movements. This fact has led to many of the occupational stereotypes still seen today. However, although there may be general trends, there are also exceptions, and excluding all women from jobs requiring strength or all men from jobs requiring dexterity is discriminatory. What is important is the objective assessment of the relevant factor.

Over time, much physically demanding work has been assisted or replaced by machinery. Agriculture and mining today need far less brute strength and use more technology. Haulage companies have computerised loading systems and power-assisted steering and brakes on their lorries, eliminating the need for manual strength. As these changes progress the biological barrier preventing women entering these jobs becomes less and less relevant. In the area of childcare, also, certain changes have occurred. The growth in the number of childminders and nurseries in the UK demonstrates that more women are choosing to remain in full-time employment after having children rather than withdrawing from the labour force. Overall, women are still disproportionately represented in the part-time labour force, however, suggesting that balancing work and family commitments is still a predominantly female concern. The availability of affordable childcare is also one of the main factors limiting women's greater participation in the workforce.

Other factors also impinge on occupational choice, and the evidence suggests that gender learning is a particularly significant factor. Men and women learn what are the socially acceptable jobs to aspire to. Tracing these attitudes back to pre-industrial times, it is interesting to note that there was no clear distinction between the roles of men and women in feudal societies. Family units lived and worked together and roles were adapted to the tasks needed at the time. Even in the early industrial period, craft skills such as spinning and weaving were undertaken by all members of the family. It was only with the arrival of the factory system that it became normal for men to go away from home to work, and women to stay behind and look after the family. The separation of paid factory work from unpaid housework was the most influential factor in determining gender roles from then on. Although there has always been a significant percentage of women in paid employment, in general these jobs were concentrated in assembly work and textile manufacturing, and in domestic service, education and health. Even as late as 1910 more than one-third of all women employed were maids or house servants. The female workforce was also made up predominantly of single women, who would stop work when they married. The phrase 'a woman's place is in the home' typified attitudes of the time, and to have a working wife was a poor reflection on a man's ability to provide for his family.

What factors came together to change this situation? One significant change was the arrival of *reliable birth control methods*, which released women from the constant demands of child bearing and rearing. For the first time a woman could choose the size of her family and be free to pursue other activities outside the home. Another influential factor in changing attitudes was the adaptations caused by the *employment shortages during the First and Second World Wars*. During the First World War women carried out many jobs previously regarded as only suitable for men. Welding and other apprentice-trained skills were undertaken by women, as were many aspects of agriculture by land-girls. Women realised that they were capable of undertaking these jobs, and many enjoyed the social contacts and different lifestyles provided by the work environment. Rates of pay for women were invariably set at less than that of men, reflecting the assumption that the work was of lesser value. After the First World War women were prohibited from carrying on with these roles, and both the government (through the Restoration of Pre-War Practices Act 1919) and trade unions made it clear that they should withdraw their labour in favour of the returning men.

The Second World War saw a repeat of these processes. In 1941 all women aged between 16 and 49 were required to register for work and could be compulsorily directed to full-time civilian labour. By December women without children could be conscripted into the armed forces. At the end of the Second World War women were again expected to withdraw their labour but were much less ready to relinquish their jobs than before. The previous assumptions about women's capabilities had been broken, and the realisation that child rearing could be successfully managed with a job took hold.

As well as the practical consequences of the wars, another influential change factor was the *feminist movement*. Feminism has many forms but its objectives are to enhance the role of women in society, placing them on an equal footing with men. The early feminists campaigned for political rights. The most well-known group were the suffragists, who achieved the right for women to vote on an equal basis to men in the UK in 1928. After this major achievement, feminism became less evident until the end of the 1960s. The 'swinging sixties' saw many challenges to traditional thought, among which was the rising challenge by women of the male-dominated status quo. In many spheres – legal, economic and social – women questioned why systems were the way they were. Why should women take all the responsibility for child rearing? Why should women be represented in advertisements as either sex objects or slaves? Why should women be paid less than men for the same work? As these issues were debated the inequities became more apparent to both women and men.

During the 1970s, legal regulation of sex discrimination also helped to establish the principle of equal opportunities for both men and women.

The change in attitudes, as often happens, was not straightforward, however. During the 1980s feminism faced a counter revolution from those who believed that women should return to traditional values of marriage and the family. The rises in divorce, single-parent families and juvenile crime have all been blamed on the changes to traditional families. The Conservative Party in the late 1980s and '90s was particularly fond of expounding 'return to family values' policies.

Faludi (1992) examined the reactions to feminism and in particular the male backlash this has provoked. Feminist ideas have been ridiculed and trivialised and the backlash can be seen to represent a rejection by men of the gains women have made. The 'burn your bra' campaign was seized on by some as a typical example of extremist behaviour by 'women's libbers'.

The 'gender war' mentality of the 1980s has moderated over time into a less confrontational development of the rights of both women and men. Increasingly, in the 1990s it is men who are reassessing the goals set them during gender learning. In the so-called *masculinity debate* new man reflects on the social expectations of society. Many men are now rejecting the career-focused lifestyle in favour of a more hands-on approach to parenting, and a balance between work and home life. Male redundancy, early retirements and a decline in full-time manual employment have contributed to a society where many more men are outside traditional employment and the 'going out to work' philosophy. Some have found a greater quality of life as a result.

■ Race and ethnicity

Attitudes towards those of different racial or ethnic origins have also changed over time. Today, legislation prohibits any discrimination in employment on the grounds of race or ethnic origin. Nevertheless, a glance at the employment and unemployment statistics makes it clear that some groups in the UK population have a much higher incidence of unemployment than others. The unemployment rate for ethnic minorities in spring 1996 was more than double that of the white population (17.6 per cent against 7.7 per cent). Ethnic minorities are also more likely to work in certain occupations such as plant and machinery operatives, and are under-represented in craft and related occupations, clerical and secretarial occupations and management posts.

This section looks at the history of immigration and the employment of ethnic minorities to attempt to explain the background to these statistics.

A study of attitudes to race and ethnicity can start from the same basis as that of gender. Are there innate, biological differences that distinguish races and their capabilities, or are they shaped by cultural learning or ethnicity?

Attempts to separate human beings into biologically different races have always been fraught with difficulties. For every categorisation produced, exceptions have been found which make them of limited value. Genetically, a scientist could not tell by examining a cell whether it had come from a black or white body. The concept of race is therefore based almost entirely on external physical appearances.

Historically, the UK has always been made up of a variety of ethnic groups. The Royal family itself has many non-British forebears, and the population in general has French, Scots, Welsh, Irish and Dutch origins. The Irish in the mid-nineteenth century were the largest immigrant group. The Jewish community was established in the seventeenth century and increased substantially as repression drove Jews out of other countries. Dutch immigrants arrived during the Industrial Revolution, as did Chinese immigrants at a later period.

Events at the beginning of the twentieth century were profoundly affected by the First World War. Many men from the colonies fought for the British forces during the war. After it ended, however, discrimination continued, with black troops being excluded from the peace march through London in 1919. Black unemployment in Britain reached record proportions as companies gave first priority to white servicemen. The situation was somewhat different after the Second World War. Britain's colonial wealth and industrial dominance had receded considerably between the wars, and after the Second World War the government decided to build wealth at home rather than looking for it abroad. Gaps in the labour force were filled by encouraging citizens of the colonies to emigrate to the UK.

In the first two decades after the end of the Second World War, Western Europe took in some 11 million workers from abroad (about 5 per cent of the total workforce). Black workers were often faced with hostile colleagues and overt racism in accommodation and employment. Criticisms of the black workers were based on two contradictory opinions, one that blacks disliked work and were here to scrounge on the dole, and the other that blacks were so keen to work, even for low pay, that they took jobs away from British workers and undercut pay rates.

Immigrants tended to gather in the low-cost areas of housing, mostly in the inner cities and establish their own communities to support each other. This in turn led to accusations of insularity and creating ghettos from the white population.

When the employment market changed again in the 1960s and recession resulted from increased competition from the rebuilt economies, government policy altered to limit immigration from the Commonwealth. Enoch Powell headed a movement during this period dedicated to returning black workers 'back home'. The National Front, an openly racist party, was founded in 1966 to further these aims.

During the 1970s, legislation was passed to protect the rights of minority groups in the UK, while at the same time further Immigration Acts tightened up the laws on blacks coming into the country. The recession of the 1970s exacerbated the problems of ethnic minority workers. Rising unemployment hit young blacks hardest of all and during the 1980s a series of riots took place in many inner cities.

As well as these economic factors, attitudes towards racial discrimination were also affected by Civil Rights campaigners both in the USA and UK. Martin Luther King in the USA in the 1950s led a series of campaigns of active but non-violent resistance to discrimination. King's famous speech stated:

> I have a dream that one day this nation will rise up and live out the true meaning of its creed: 'We hold these truths to be self-evident; that all men are created equal'. I have a dream that one day on the red hills of Georgia the sons of former slaves and the sons of former slave-owners will be able to sit down together at the table of brotherhood. I have a dream that my four little children will one day live in a nation where they will not be judged by the colour of their skin but by the content of their character.

The 'dream' was violently opposed by some whites and King was assassinated in 1968. The Civil Rights Act 1964, which King was instrumental in promoting, established the principle of equality of opportunity for all in the USA. During this same period some black activists formed more militant and violent groups such as the Black Panther movement, in reaction to white hostility. The violence of this group eventually caused its collapse towards the end of the 1970s as blacks re-focused on more legitimate ways to change society.

Other individuals such as Malcolm X, the son of a white mother and black father, also used their lives to publicise the prejudices faced by minorities. The X was a reference to the practice of slave owners who did not allow black slaves to use a surname.

Collectively, the activities of such individuals raised the profile of black issues and helped to raise public awareness of attitudes to discrimination.

Since that period many other changes have occurred which break down the prejudice between black and white. In South Africa, the system of apartheid was finally removed in 1994, again signalling the right of every individual to be free and self-governing. These changes have been significant, but it will take many more years before ingrained attitudes disappear completely.

■ Age

Historically, attitudes to the effects of age on employment have not been as clearly researched as those of gender and ethnicity. Some factors affecting attitudes to working age can be identified, however, again reflecting social trends. In feudal times children as young as 4 or 5 would have small jobs to perform to assist their family, and in the industrial period children worked extensively in mines, factories and as chimney sweeps, etc. It was not uncommon for children to work 12–14 hour days, and this was not thought inappropriate at the time. Attitudes to child labour changed primarily as a result of increased access to education. Education was not available to all until relatively recently in the late nineteenth century. Compulsory education for all was established in 1870, and the school leaving age then rose progressively from 10 to 14. Most schools were run by private or church authorities and there was little state regulation.

The world wars, particularly the Second World War, revised attitudes to education. Secondary school education was provided for all by the 1944 Education Act, allowing more pupils to stay on after 14. Selective education based on the 11+ system was found to result in only 12 per cent of pupils continuing in education until 17. The comprehensive system, introduced in the late 1960s, removed the selection procedures in most areas of the country. Since then, the proportion of young people staying on in further education has risen. The minimum school leaving age is now 16 but the 1996/97 *Labour Market and Skill Trends* report states (Dfee, 1997):

> The proportion of young people continuing their studies to higher education level has risen rapidly over recent years, following a long period of limited growth. Student numbers have doubled since 1979, and the proportion of young people entering higher education has risen from one in eight in 1979 to almost one in three in 1994/95.

In terms of discrimination, young people are often disproportionately represented in the unemployment statistics. Achieving work experience is one of the most difficult problems with students trapped in a Catch 22 situation where they are not considered for jobs because of a lack of experience, but are unable to gain experience without a job. Various government initiatives such as Youth Training Schemes and Modern Apprenticeships and currently the Labour Party's 'New Deal' have attempted to help this situation.

At the other end of the age range, demographic changes have affected the numbers of older people in the UK. Historically, older people were perceived as having wisdom, prestige and status in society. More recently, attitudes have changed in favour of the younger age groups, particularly the 25–35 age category. Older workers may now be stereotyped as slow, reluctant to change and less well adapted to the pace of modern life.

Attitudes to retirement have also changed. In the late 1920s more than half the men over 65 were in paid employment. Retirement was related more to ill-health or physical incapability. Nowadays many individuals wish to retire before the state retirement age, allowing more time for leisure pursuits, or they may wish to move from full-time work to part-time. This trend reflects the improvements in company pension provisions for employees in the UK. Until 1992 the state retirement age was 60 for women and 65 for men. This practice has now been challenged, resulting in a retirement age of 65 being set for all, with the option of retirement at 60 if so wished. The tendency towards early retirement was also hastened by the recession of the 1980s and '90s which led many employers to encourage their older staff to take early retirement by providing enhancements to their pension arrangements. This has led to a reduction in the overall age profile in many organisations.

The baby boom generation of the 1960s, together with increased life expectancy, also means that many more people are in the older age ranges in the population and fewer are in the younger bands (*see* Fig. 12.2).

Campaigns are increasingly focusing attention on age discrimination as a negative feature of employee relations.

■ Disability

Attitudes to disability have also changed over time. In the Victorian era, both physical and mental disabilities could result in individuals being removed from society and confined in residential homes. The attitude was one of 'out of sight, out of mind' and the idea of integrating the disabled in the community was not considered. The development of more enlightened attitudes in the 1970s saw a reversal of the institutionalisation trend, and a progressive move towards more care in the community. In employment, Leach (1996) notes that:

> The 'social model' and policies of the disabled people's movement have replaced the discredited 'medical model' of disability. Until recently disabled people had been largely politically invisible. They were socially visible only as patients, clients or welfare/charity cases – under the control of medical and other disability-related professionals. The disabled people's movement began fighting for political influence and the right to control both their own lives and their own organisations.

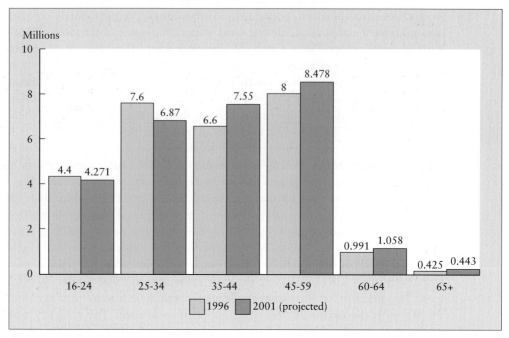

■ **Fig. 12.2 Distribution of the labour force by age (1996–2001)**
Source: Office for National Statistics.

Employment statistics show the difficulties disabled people or those with a long-term illness face in gaining employment. Out of the 1.6 million economically active people described as disabled in winter 1995/96, 21.2 per cent of them were unemployed, compared to only 7.6 per cent of the non-disabled. In addition, the proportion of the unemployed who are long-term unemployed is higher for disabled people than non-disabled; 52.7 per cent against 37.8 per cent.

The lack of awareness shown by town planners and architects to the needs of the partially sighted, wheelchair users, etc. has also been exposed.

Health care in the 1990s means that more and more people are being treated and life expectancy is increasing. Modern life brings with it many stress factors, however, and organisations are having to deal with increasing numbers of employees who are suffering from stress exhaustion. Other modern health issues revolve around the ergonomic design of offices and workstations and the effects of VDU work. Disability has to be defined quite broadly to encompass these factors as well as the more obvious areas such as blindness, deafness and physical incapacity.

Today, all of the areas outlined above have become important in the campaign to provide equality of opportunity for all. Other minority groups such as gay workers and lesbians are also affected by discrimination and organisations are having to develop policies in all these areas.

STRUCTURAL/ECONOMIC FACTORS AFFECTING DISCRIMINATION

In addition to the perspectives already considered, discrimination patterns can also be analysed by examining the economic factors affecting the UK labour force and the employment structures that result. This section looks at the position of various groups in the UK economy and examines some of the economic explanations for these patterns.

Economic explanations for discrimination include:

- human capital theory
- segmented labour market theory
- reserve army of labour theory.

Human capital theory

This economic explanation assumes that labour markets operate in a non-discriminatory fashion, rewarding workers for their productivity. Therefore, if women, ethnic minorities, the disabled or any other group are disadvantaged this is because they are less productive workers. This assumption cannot be tested easily, because measuring productivity is impossible for many jobs. Researchers therefore examine characteristics that they assume increase productivity such as the skills, experience and commitment that workers bring to their jobs. Workers' skills and experience, according to economists, constitutes their *human capital*. Through education, training and experience, workers invest in their human capital, and these investments make some workers more productive than others. Human capital theorists assume that women's orientation to their families inhibits their investment in themselves and so makes them less productive than men. Equally, the education levels and training possessed by some ethnic minority groups may also disadvantage them in comparison with other groups.

When looking at academic achievements statistics do suggest that women continue to have fewer qualifications than men. In winter 1995/96, 76.2 per cent of women of working age held a qualification, compared to 82.9 per cent of men. This gap has narrowed, however. In spring 1985 only 56.9 per cent of women held qualifications, compared with 63.8 per cent of men.

Until recently, however, educational opportunities were different for males and females. Certain subjects on the curriculum such as domestic science and needlework were available only for girls; boys were directed to metalwork and woodwork. Nowadays, such stereotyping has been addressed by the National Curriculum (1989), which provides equal access to all subjects for both gender groups. The evidence from recent studies on equality in education (Equal Opportunities Commission, 1996) suggests:

> The last two decades have seen tremendous progress in closing the gap between boys and girls in education. Girls have caught up and are doing as well as boys in mathematics and science – which used to be thought of as 'boys' subjects'. Yet it takes a long time to change attitudes about what girls or boys can study at school and beyond. For example, girls still

choose secretarial courses, while boys choose to train in areas like engineering and construction. However, women have made major inroads into the professions. Increasing numbers of women study medicine (one third of all doctors are women, as compared with one sixth in 1975), law (1 in 16 solicitors were women in 1975, as compared with nearly half now), architecture and accountancy. Men are also increasingly entering the traditional 'women's' professions of nursing and secretarial work.

As educational changes feed through the system, therefore, human capital gender differences should reduce. Other statistics also indicate that more women are continuing into further and higher education than men.

Ethnic minority groups are, as a whole, less qualified (*see* Fig. 12.3). Whereas 19.7 per cent of the white group have no qualifications, the figure for the ethnic minorities is 23.4 per cent. The overall figures mask differences between the individual groups. Fewer black people are unqualified than white people, whereas the Pakistani/Bangladeshi group has significantly more people without qualifications. Different age structures may make the difference in relative qualification rates even higher.

However, if only higher qualifications are looked at the imbalance between all the groups is very small. Indications are that this situation is going to change (*see* Fig. 12.4). Only 41.4 per cent of the white 16–24 age group are in full- or part-time education, compared to 56.9 per cent of ethnic minorities. People of mixed or other origins have the highest proportion, 64 per cent, and the black group the lowest with 53.5 per cent. This suggests that in the future the qualifications imbalance may decline, and that ethnic minority groups will be an increasingly important source of skills for employers.

Qualification levels for older workers also show distinct trends. Overall older age groups are less qualified than younger groups, due partly to changes in the education and

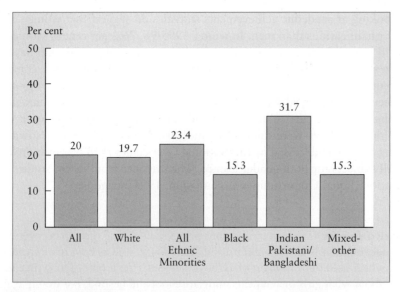

■ **Fig. 12.3 Population of working age with no qualifications**
Source: Labour Force Survey, Winter 1995/6.

training system over time. Some 67 per cent of people in the 45 to retirement age group hold qualifications, and 19 per cent hold higher qualifications, compared to 87 per cent and 24 per cent, respectively, in the 25–34 age group. The provision of further and higher education has expanded over the last fifty years. Therefore, younger people are more likely to hold more qualifications than older people. In addition, some of the qualifications held by older workers may be regarded as outdated. The lack of qualifications affects their employment opportunities. Many employers see the lack of skills among older people as the main barrier to employing them.

However, older age groups also generally receive less training. In spring 1996, only 7.7 per cent of the 50 to retirement age group had received any training in the previous four weeks, compared to 14.9 per cent of all employees of working age.

For younger workers the human capital investment in training and education is increasing. In recent years the number of 16-year-olds staying in education in England increased from 55 per cent to 72 per cent; the number of 17-year-olds increases from 39 per cent to 59 per cent.

■ Segmented labour market theory

This set of economic explanations about the different experiences of work in the UK uses the concept of segmentation in the labour market to explain discrimination. Piore (Dex, 1975) divided labour markets into two segments: the *primary sector*, which offers jobs with relatively high wages, good working conditions, chances of advancement, and employment stability, and the *secondary sector*, which tends to be low paying with poor working conditions, little chance of advancement and instability and high labour turnover. Barron and Norris (1976), looking specifically at the role of women in employment, also identified a dual labour market pattern with women concentrated in the lower paid, less skilled and more easily disposable sector of the market.

The recent trends in employment towards core and periphery workers (Atkinson, 1984) have built on this model with an emphasis on the development of a core of highly

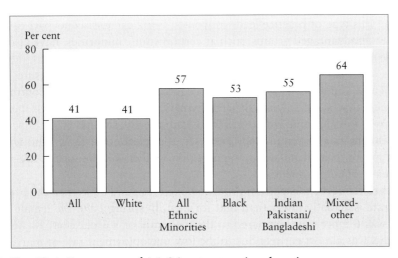

■ **Fig. 12.4 Percentage of 16–24 age group in education**
Source: Labour Force Survey, Spring 1996.

trained and developed permanent staff supported by peripheral workers and outworkers or contractors. Conditions of employment are often much better for the core group, with peripheral workers considered as more expendable and less worthy of investment. Following through this model, the explanation for disadvantage is that women and members of ethnic minority groups are more likely to be found in the flexible categories of the model rather than the core.

Some evidence for this proposition can be found in the Institute for Employment Research projections, which suggest that although employment will grow by approximately 0.8 per cent until the end of the century the increase will not happen evenly across all sectors. Male employment is projected to rise slightly (around 3 per cent) while female employment will increase more rapidly (an extra 11 per cent). Part-time employment is projected to increase by 22 per cent at the same time as full-time employment decreases by 1 per cent. Self-employment will also increase considerably, by 13 per cent. Married women in particular show a very low unemployment rate, only 4.6 per cent compared to 11.4 per cent for unmarried women.

These statistics tend to reinforce the idea that labour markets are changing, with more jobs being created in the periphery while core employment is actually reducing. Terms and conditions of employment still favour the reduced number of, predominantly male, core employees at the expense of other categories. The flexible firm model has been criticised, however, as being ill-defined (what exactly is core and what is periphery?) and lacking in actual evidence of its use. The Workplace Industrial Relations surveys carried out in 1980, 1984 and 1990 showed little evidence of any large-scale increase in the flexible forms of working they examined (part-time, fixed-term contract, freelance and homeworkers).

■ Reserve army of labour theory

This theory comes from the writings of Marx, who saw the reserve army as being labour which is only partially employed, sometimes attracted into the labour market but also repelled from it. Reserve army status affects seasonal workers and others whose job security is limited and who can be hired and fired at will. The historical section showed how women were attracted into the labour market during the world wars and then dispensed with again. This type of practice leads to women being categorised as part of the reserve army. Other disadvantaged groups, such as certain ethnic minorities, have also been used in the same way.

At times of labour shortage employers may be forced to provide measures to encourage women and minorities into the workforce (crèches, term-time-only contracts, targeted recruitment drives, etc.). When the employment situation changes these measures may be withdrawn, forcing some employees to give up their positions.

During downsizing or redundancy exercises, the selection of those who will be made redundant may also indicate an assumption that women and minorities are a more disposable source of employment.

Statistics to reinforce this pattern produce mixed results. For women the overall unemployment rate is actually lower than that for men. In spring 1996 the female unemployment rate was 6.3 per cent compared to the male rate of 9.6 per cent. As noted before, however, this was almost entirely due to the low unemployment rate of married women. Ethnic minority groups experience much higher levels of unemployment than the white population, however. The unemployment rate for ethnic minorities in spring 1996 was

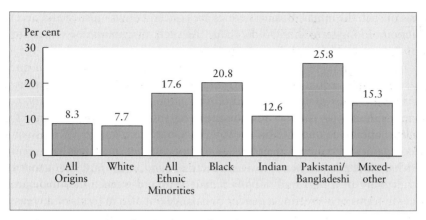

■ **Fig. 12.5 ILO unemployment rate by ethnic origin**
Source: Labour Force Survey, Spring 1996.

more than double that of the white population (17.6 per cent against 7.7 per cent). Figure 12.5 illustrates the situation for groups of different ethnic origin.

Combined together, these economic theories provide some explanations for the patterns of discrimination found in employment today.

POLITICAL/ETHICAL ISSUES AFFECTING DISCRIMINATION

The final perspective on discrimination to be examined is the political and ethical one. Discrimination in the workplace is very much affected by the values and attitudes of the society in which the organisation is located. It would be impossible to detach attitudes to employees at work from the wider social context within which the organisation that employs them exists. As a result the values and norms held in society generally need to be appreciated so that their impact on the workplace can be evaluated. Values and norms are difficult to identify, however, as no one set of beliefs dominates all members of the society. As a result what is considered ethical may be very different depending on the groups or cultures you are examining.

The relationship between social responsibility and business responsibility is also hotly debated. Elizabeth Vallance in the introduction to her book *Business Ethics at Work* states:

> business is about making profits and ethics is about being good and, realistically, never the twain shall meet. Being a tough-minded manager implies there's no room for the ethical niceties ... the currently fashionable talk about the 'social responsibility' of business has been seen by some managers as an attempt to force business to take on the role of government; to protect the environment; to regenerate the inner cities; to deal with everything that is wrong with society, from educational deprivation to racism.

She argues, however, that business ethics are about specific and identifiable moral dilemmas which emerge in the course of business activity and the framework for the logical analysis of such dilemmas. Business ethics are concerned with justice and decency and the production of long-term shareholder value. As such, discrimination issues are very much part of the moral dilemmas that need to be recognised and planned for.

For many employers there is an implied link between ethical standards and long-term business success. In equal opportunities terms organisations with a reputation for fair and responsible methods of relating to employees should have greater loyalty, commitment and success than those that do not espouse these values. Evidence to support this view is difficult to obtain, as quantifiable measures are hard to identify. There is some evidence from companies who have attempted equal opportunities initiatives that greater business success has resulted. For example, Rank Xerox found in the late 1980s that their efforts to recruit more men into traditionally female jobs and women into male areas paid off not only in terms of correcting a gender imbalance but also in terms of increased response rates and the positive attitudes expressed by applicants about the company (Paddison, 1990).

The other way of evaluating the impact is to consider the cost to the organisation of negative publicity about its business practices. A damaging racism story could well reduce the organisation's ability to attract employees and also affect the response of customers to its products.

Difficulties arise, however, when considering equality of opportunity between different stakeholder groups. Even when considering employees alone, should the organisation provide equal terms and conditions for all or is it acceptable (ethical) to provide enhanced benefits for core workers not enjoyed by those on part-time or temporary contracts? These employees may receive far fewer training and development opportunities than their full-time colleagues, and may also be denied the range of employee benefits, including pension entitlements, of others. These considerations have led to a move towards equal treatment for all workers, with legislation being enacted to underpin these rights.

The difficulties of balancing business profitability and success with acceptable and consistent standards of behaviour is, therefore, one of the key challenges of employee relations for the twenty-first century. As globalisation increases and the variety of cultural and ethnic groups in the marketplace expands, the establishment of fundamental rights and the ability to maintain equality of opportunities for all become more and more essential. Some companies like Levi Strauss have established Global Sourcing and Operating Guidelines. These specify that workers should not be younger than 14 years old (in line with the convention drawn up by the International Labour Organization), that people should not work more than 60 hours a week, and that workers should be free to join a trade union. Equality of treatment conditions may also form part of this basic package in the near future.

Having now examined various perspectives on discrimination, we now look at the different approaches that have been adopted at both state and organisational level to address the problems. The history of each approach can be traced back in many cases to assumptions deriving from the perspectives already covered. The main approaches reviewed here are:

1 the use of legislation to set and enforce appropriate standards of behaviour;

2 national initiatives and educational programmes;

3 more radical approaches such as affirmative action (positive discrimination) programmes;

4 the managing diversity approach.

THE LEGISLATIVE APPROACH TO DISCRIMINATION AND EQUAL OPPORTUNITIES

When considering a legislative approach to the management of discrimination and employment rights there are various models that the state can adopt. Morris and Willey (1996) suggest the following:

- the free collective bargaining model
- the free labour market model
- the employee protection or social justice model.

The *free collective bargaining model* is based on voluntarism and is characterised by limited state intervention, and a lack of emphasis on legal regulation. The model is based on the establishment of rights through bargaining and negotiation rather than the imposition of rights through legislation. Legislation, where it does exist, provides the basic framework for rights rather than specifying the detail. This model provided the traditional pattern in the UK from the First World War to the end of the 1970s.

The *free labour market model* characterised the UK from 1979 onwards. Morris and Willey (1996) suggest that the principles underlying this model emphasise the following:

- deregulation of the labour market, removing certain protective measures for employees, which were seen as a burden on business;
- the primary importance of individualism in the employment relationship (and the consequential marginalisation of collective interests);
- the curbing of trade union power;
- the advocacy of policies promoting cost-effectiveness, competitiveness and flexibility in the use of labour;
- the limiting of external constraints.

The *social justice model* provides the basis for most of the European Union's approach to legislation. Morris and Willey (1996) describe the principles of this model as:

- the protection of employees throughout the employment relationship by creating a regulatory framework;
- the recognition that employees have both individual and collective interests and that these have to be accommodated in a framework of employment law;
- the harmonisation of conditions of employment across member states;
- the acceptance of the principle of subsidiarity – that is, that some issues are more appropriately regulated at the level of the member state rather than at the level of the EU;
- some acceptance of the economic issues of cost-effectiveness, competitiveness and flexibility.

The UK's own framework for equal opportunities legislation was influenced by legislation enacted in the USA in the 1960s and by membership of the EEC (as it then was) in 1973. The Treaty of Rome established the constitution of the EEC and Articles 117 and 119 set out broad social policy provisions. Article 117 had the general objective of improving and harmonising workers' living and working conditions and Article 119 set out the principle of equal pay for equal work.

During the 1970s the UK enacted major pieces of legislation, including the Equal Pay Act 1970, the Sex Discrimination Act 1975, the Race Relations Act 1976. This legislation provided for equality of treatment on the grounds of sex, marital status, race, colour nationality and ethnic origin. The Acts established two forms of discrimination:

■ *direct discrimination*, where a person is treated less favourably than another person is (or would be) treated;

■ *indirect discrimination*, where a requirement or condition of work is (or would be) applied equally to all but has a disproportionately detrimental effect on one group.

The Acts also established two regulatory bodies to oversee the legislation and promote equality of opportunity. The Equal Opportunities Commission (EOC) works in the area of sex discrimination and the Commission for Racial Equality (CRE) works to promote equality for all ethnic and racial groups. As well as overseeing the legislation these organisations also produce Codes of Practice which help employers translate equality objectives into operational procedures.

The UK throughout the 1980s and '90s faced an ongoing problem in reconciling the Conservative government's free labour market approach with the EU's social justice model. The UK, while conforming to the general principles of the EU's treaties, resisted EU attempts to extend social provisions further. The European Charter of Fundamental Social Rights of Workers was adopted by all member states except the UK in 1989. Again, at Maastricht in 1991, the UK resisted attempts to include social policy issues in the Treaty on European Union. Eventually a separate Social Policy Protocol (Social Chapter) was drafted, which allowed the UK to opt out of these provisions, while signing up to the economic, monetary and political union terms. John Major presented the UK's opt-out as a victory which allowed Britain to compete in the Single Market without the 'dead-weight' of Social Chapter, employment legislation. In reality, however, the UK is still bound by employment directives based on Treaty articles and has already been obliged to implement EU Directives in the area of maternity leave and maternity rights. The 1993 Working Time Directive, which sets a maximum 48-hour working week, provides for minimum rest periods and regulates aspects of night and shift work, may also have to be adopted by the UK because it is enacted as a health and safety measure. The UK challenged the legality of this interpretation before the EJC in March 1996, but the case was dismissed. However, following the election of the Labour government in 1997 with a mandate to sign up to the Social Chapter, the relationship between the UK government and the rest of the EU is changing. The Labour Party proposes a charter of employee rights which will be much more in line with EU policies and principles. Progress on this can be seen already by the introduction of a consultation document containing Regulations on the implementation of the Working Time directive published in April 1998.

In the areas of both sex discrimination and race discrimination, criticisms have been voiced about the overall effectiveness of the legislative approach. The difficulties and costs involved in bringing cases to an industrial tribunal and the delays in hearing cases prevent many victims of discrimination from pursuing their struggles.

Industrial tribunals, which were originally designed to be less formal and more accessible to individuals, have become increasingly burdened with bureaucracy and case law complications. As indicated previously, the supremacy of EU law also makes the validity of industrial tribunal judgements open to question, further delaying the outcomes. Investigations needed to pursue an equal pay claim are costly and difficult to enact, despite some notable successes.

An analysis of the outcomes of industrial tribunals indicates that discrimination cases represent only a small proportion of the case load each year. The CRE reports that in 1990–91 only 15 per cent of the racial discrimination cases heard by industrial tribunals succeeded, commenting:

> In our view, given the level of racial discrimination revealed by research, it is highly improbable that the mere 47 cases which succeeded before the industrial tribunals in 1990–91 were a true reflection of the merits of the whole case-load heard by those tribunals.

The CRE recommends that those involved in adjudication should receive training and be knowledgeable in the complexities of the experiences involved. Many industrial tribunals at present seem to lack training, understanding and experience of dealing with race cases. The CRE recommends the setting up of a specialist discrimination division which would be given jurisdiction over all discrimination cases.

The legislative approach to managing discrimination, despite its limitations, has been utilised again in the Disability Discrimination Act, which came into effect in December 1996. The new Act abolishes the concept of a 3 per cent disabled quota system introduced by previous legislation and found to be unworkable. It does not use the concepts of direct and indirect discrimination found in sex and race legislation and it allows an employer to justify discrimination if the disability provides a *material* and *substantial* limitation on the ability of the individual to perform the job. The definition of disability in the Act is wide-ranging; a disabled person is 'one who has a physical or mental impairment which has a substantial and long-term adverse effect on his or her ability to carry out normal day-to-day activities'. The definition includes individuals with AIDS and symptomatic HIV as well as other chronic and progressive disorders. The Act requires employers of over 20 people to make 'reasonable adjustments' to accommodate disabled people.

The Disability Discrimination Act provides for the setting up of a National Disability Council but this has been criticised for not having the same powers as the EOC and the CRE in relation to enforcement and legal assistance with individual claims.

Legislation covering age discrimination is still not on the statute books in the UK. Richard Worsley (*People Management*, January 1996) comments:

> Three of the four major causes of discrimination (sex, race and disability) are now regulated by law. The fourth, discrimination on grounds of age, remains the odd one out, with no legislation and no commission responsible for addressing it. Those affected by ageism find that it is no less unfair than other forms of discrimination, and the frustration and resentment are just as severe. Yet there is not the same widespread acceptance that ageism needs to be eradicated. It is ironic that the one type of discrimination that could affect every one of us is the one that is given the lowest priority by legislators and employers.

He notes that eliminating ageism is not just a moral issue but an economic one. There are business benefits in gaining access to the widest pool of talent. The Conservative government's attitude was to attempt to persuade employers of the folly of ageism rather than compelling them to abandon age-related criteria through legislation. Labour MP David Winnick introduced a Private Member's Bill in February 1996, which sought to make the use of age limits in advertising unlawful. The bill was unsuccessful, but it raised the profile of the issue, and was supported for the first time by the CBI. Labour made a commitment to making age discrimination illegal as part of their election manifesto.

This section has highlighted some of the major achievements of the legislative approach, but also some of its limitations. Legislation provides a clear indicator of desired behaviour, but convictions are rare and, until recently, compensation payments were low. The Acts are based on the concept of equal treatment for all and the Codes of Practice outline procedural ways to meet these objectives. Despite the legislation, discrimination still remains evident in employment today, leading to frustration and a desire to move attitudes forward more effectively.

Those who favour the legislative approach tend to recommend better enforcement and *policing* of the existing legislation. Also required is a more committed approach to policy implementation by organisations. Ollerearnshaw and Waldeck (1995), commenting on a 1994 CRE survey on large companies and racial equality, stated that:

> The most striking finding of the investigation was the gap between promise and practice ... If commitment to a policy is a first step, it is only that. The contradiction between such resounding support for the principle of racial equality and the number of companies actually backing their convictions with planned action comes as no surprise. The CRE has commented with increasing frequency and urgency on the pronounced gap between words and deeds, and the need to bridge it.

The findings included the fact that 88 per cent of the companies surveyed had a commitment to racial equality, but only 45 per cent had implemented or were implementing an action plan or programme.

NATIONAL INITIATIVES AND EDUCATIONAL PROGRAMMES

As reported earlier, the Conservative governments in the 1980s and '90s had a strong preference for educating and influencing organisations by persuasion rather than by legislation. As well as enforcement, one of the other key roles assigned to the EOC and CRE is the promotion of best practice and the development of education and training initiatives.

Liff (1995) suggests that the Codes of Practice, procedural approach to managing equal opportunities is based on an attempt to control managerial behaviour by tightly specifying how they should carry out certain tasks and monitoring, whether they do it or not. Many studies have indicated that managers are very good at evading controls if they wish to. She also comments that such approaches are flawed because they attempt to change behaviour without tackling the underlying prejudicial attitudes that cause it. Discriminatory judgements are often discussed as if they were deliberate actions, yet much research suggests that they are embedded in more deep-seated and subtle processes.

Awareness training may help individuals recognise their own prejudices and the ways in which these affect their judgement. An understanding of these processes might also reduce people's resistance to EU approaches which might otherwise be seen simply as bureaucratic encumbrances. The development of approaches that move further than simply complying with the law are illustrated in Exhibit 12.3.

■ **Exhibit 12.3**

Operating equal opportunities in the health service

The health service typifies many of the discrimination issues in British society as a whole. In post-war Britain immigrants from the new Commonwealth were encouraged to come to fill the less desirable jobs, many of which were in the NHS's low-paid ancillary service. Many were steered towards harder staff specialities such as geriatrics and mental illness, and into unqualified nursing auxiliary posts. The employment pattern was established, with black and other ethnic minority staff concentrated in the lower-level, poorly paid jobs.

During the 1970s and 1980s a growing number of tribunal cases showed discriminatory practices embedded in health service procedures. Few health authorities had obtained data on their staff's ethnic origins. In the employment of women, there were also concerns. Women form 75 per cent of the health services employees, but they too are concentrated in lower-graded, frequently part-time jobs and are seriously underrepresented at senior levels. The introduction of general manager jobs into the NHS has not improved the situation. Only 4 per cent of women hold general manager jobs at district (authority) level and 17 per cent at unit level. Valerie Amos, the EOC's Chief Executive in 1990, stated that:

> The NHS expects a lifetime of full-time work, but women's lives are often quite different from that. The NHS still expects the majority of its workforce to conform to the working patterns of the minority of its employees.

Changing demographic patterns and the poor performance of the NHS in retaining and attracting returners back into the profession led to the need for some serious management thinking on equal opportunities.

The following are the key measures introduced by the West Midlands region to improve the equality of opportunity for all:

- the production of concise 'how-to-do-it' guides for managers with resource references and case studies based on best practices;
- the publication of *Vacancies Ahead*, a management guide that clearly spelled out the need for a radical change in approach, with staff being valued as an investment rather than a cost to the organisation, and with employment practices that are family friendly and promote real equality of opportunity, such as flexible working hours, child care and support for careers, career-break and back-to-work schemes and more flexible approaches to career development generally;
- awareness training for line managers, organised in two stages – firstly, a one-day workshop to gain commitment, then supporting practical sessions that would help them put plans into practice;
- management development and training courses to improve the skills levels of existing staff, particularly those who are underrepresented at higher levels.

Source: Parkyn (1991).

In evaluating the success of the equal opportunities programme in the health service outlined in Exhibit 12.3, the awareness training was seen as essential to the gaining of commitment to the changes. The systems and procedures were important, but without commitment they would have been left on the shelf, and not implemented further.

National campaigns

Another approach to discrimination involves mobilising support for equality through national campaigns led by a variety of organisations. In the area of sex discrimination the EOC and the Women's National Commission have jointly produced a National Agenda for Action which provides a basis for UK implementation of the Global Platform for Action agreed at the United Nations Fourth World Conference on Women. The Agenda highlights the essential issues that must be addressed by government and by decision makers in other organisations, including local government, political parties, business and the voluntary sector. These areas included political, social, health, economic and monitoring issues. The Agenda aims to raise awareness of the issues and mobilise individuals to lobby MPs and support the equality aims in their working lives.

Another national approach, Opportunity 2000, emphasises the business advantages that can be gained by organisations with effective management strategies. Opportunity 2000 aims to convince employers to commit to equality on the basis of the business advantages that result. The emphasis is less on moral justification and more on the likely business outcomes. Employer-led initiatives are thought to be more widely respected and influential than those promoted by the government.

Opportunity 2000 was launched in October 1991 by Business in the Community. It asks employers to make a public statement of their ambitions and goals for improving women's representation at all levels in the workplace and demonstrate clearly how they are going to achieve them. Employers also monitor progress towards their goals each year. Opportunity 2000 also carries out an independent annual progress review within its membership. The campaign is growing steadily, with over 25 per cent of the UK workforce represented at present across a wide range of large and small private and public sector organisations.

MORE RADICAL APPROACHES: AFFIRMATIVE ACTION (POSITIVE DISCRIMINATION) PROGRAMMES

Jewson and Mason (1986) suggest that there are two approaches to the management of equal opportunity: the legislative/codes of practice approach, which they describe as *liberal*, based around equal *treatment*, and the *radical* approach, which is more concerned with equal *outcomes*. The management of equal outcomes involves a commitment to achieving fair distributions, or quotas, of underrepresented groups in the workforce.

Under existing legislation the establishment of fixed quotas in employment in the UK is not lawful. A previous section mentioned the use of a 3 per cent quota for disabled people in the workforce, and it is this kind of approach which is suggested. The lack of success of the quota approach in disability discrimination was partly because of the lack of enforcement. For a quota system to be effective, the penalties for non-compliance need to be clear.

The USA has the longest experience of quota setting, through the Federal Contract Compliance Requirements, which require organisations to complete statistical returns and targets showing workforce profiles. Where candidates are of equal calibre, the organisation must select an individual from an underrepresented group if the targets set have not been fulfilled. For any company employed as a Federal contractor or subcontractor an affirmative action plan is required which includes goals and timetables. The company is required to give details of the ethnic and gender composition of the workforce. Where there is an underrepresentation of a particular group, targets are set for the number or proportion of women and/or black people employed. The Office of Federal Contract Compliance Programs (OFCPP) monitors these affirmative action programmes, and a company may be debarred from the Federal contractors' list if it does not have a good reason for non-compliance. The system has been endorsed by successive Presidents for over 30 years and has received support from both society at large and the business community.

Studies indicated that the compliance programme had made a difference to improving the employment available to women and minorities. Both groups were found to have greater job opportunities in both quantitative and qualitative terms (IPM/IDS, 1987).

Despite this finding, the UK government considers that contract compliance represents special treatment which cannot be justified. The IPM/IDS investigation suggested that there were two main reasons why contract compliance was opposed:

1 *Deregulation*: the burden on business imposed on firms represents an unnecessary constraint on the free operation of the market. Contract compliance entails large workloads on personnel staff for little return in benefits to the firm's personnel practice.Contract compliance procedures are too complex and not related to the contractors' business interests. Irrelevant clauses in contracts give an unfair competitive advantage.

2 *Value for money*: freedom to contract ensures fair competition and value for money for the purchasers. Non-commercial clauses have, by definition, nothing to do with value for money and are, therefore, immoral.

Christopher Chope (1987), wrote:

> I do not believe that local authorities should set themselves up as extra statutory enforcement agencies by withholding contracts from those who do not meet what they perceive as minimum requirements for satisfying national legislation – which, after all, properly includes its own provision for regulation and enforcement.

Although UK legislation does not allow a quota approach, it does allow positive discrimination (affirmative action) to address an imbalance in the workforce. Positive discrimination measures include:

- statements in recruitment adverts actively encouraging certain individuals to apply;
- the guarantee of an interview to all applicants of a disadvantaged group;
- targeted recruitment, utilising publications addressed to minority groups (e.g. radio for the blind, black publications in ethnic minority areas, etc.);
- providing special training for women or ethnic minority groups.

MANAGING DIVERSITY

As a consequence of the difficulties discussed above, another approach to managing discrimination has gained ground, particularly in the USA. The managing diversity approach takes as its start point the fact that all individuals are different, and that the potential of all members of the working population should be harnessed – no one is excluded, not even white, middle-class males. The differences between an equal opportunities approach and a managing diversity approach are summarised in Table 12.2.

Table 12.2 Managing diversity and equal opportunities compared

Managing diversity	Equal opportunities
Aims to be 'inclusive' focusing on the needs of all individuals in employment	Is focused on the needs of the members of particular groups and so excludes other individuals (women, ethnic minorities, the disabled, etc.)
Recognises that each and every individual is *unique* in his/her needs and experiences	Treats members of a particular group as if they all shared the same characteristics and experiences
Does not utilise positive action campaigns	Uses special iniatives to focus attention on the issues affecting particular groups
More business focused	
More acceptable to line managers	Emphasises the moral, ethical and social issues
	Led predominantly by HRM practitioners

Diversity takes individuals, not groups, as the primary focus of concern. The approach criticises targets and quotas because they emphasise difference. Heilman (1994) concluded that affirmative action helped neither organisations nor individuals. Those people who were perceived to have gained some form of advantage through affirmative action were more likely to have negative evaluations made of them by others, the reason for this being that if someone is good enough to begin with, then they would not need extra assistance. Heilman calls this 'the stigma of incompetence'. She states:

> Our research suggests that, as currently construed, affirmative action policies can thwart rather than promote workplace equality. The stigma associated with affirmative action can fuel rather than debunk stereotypical thinking and prejudiced attitudes.

Other problems with targets include the charge of tokenism, paying lip-service to equality without any real commitment.

Managing diversity is more about challenging the traditional attitude of 'this is the way we do things around here', and ensuring that the organisation is positioned to take commercial advantage of social and demographic changes. SmithKline Beecham expresses its approach to diversity as:

> Creating an environment where the potential of the skills and expertise of all our employees is realised through individual people differences being recognised and valued. (Ford, 1996)

Ford argues that the more individualistic diversity approach and the group-orientated, equal opportunities approach can coexist happily as two strategies to achieve the same end – namely, removal of discrimination. A diversity approach alone may lead to complacency of the 'I already do this' type, but the more positive image created may help disperse the hostility that some equal opportunities programmes have engendered. She quotes the case of Rank Xerox, which has combined both approaches in its organisation. The managing director, Bernard Fournier, is quoted as saying:

> Equality and diversity are about creating an environment where everyone is treated equally, whatever their race, religion, sex, colour or any other type of difference. I see differences as a source of enrichment. To be successful we have to be creative and apply diverse perspectives to business problems. Everyone should be able to contribute and should progress in the company in relation to his or her ability.
>
> Today our organisation does not reflect the diversity that exists within the community. This is not a matter of bad will, but rather one of old habits. From an ethics point of view it is clearly the right thing to do. But additionally, to prepare for our future, we need all the best talents, whoever they are.

Rank Xerox believes that a diverse workforce will only add value if it is underpinned by equal treatment. This has prompted positive action initiatives, such as recruitment advertising to encourage applications from groups that are underrepresented, support for equal opportunities legislation and an emphasis on the value of the individual. Rank Xerox's own description of itself stresses its work 'valuing equality, promoting diversity'.

Reviewing the outcomes of all the measures discussed above, the management of discrimination has been shown in this chapter to be a multi-level and multi-approach aspect of employee relations. At the level of the organisation, legal requirements and procedural guidelines help establish systems to minimise discrimination and ensure equal treatment. These systems need to be backed up with a proactive management approach, however, to avoid merely paying lip-service to the ideal. As the CRE survey indicated, it is not sufficient simply to have a policy; it must be actively put into practice and examples of good practice must be set.

When investigating the reasons why organisations with a stated commitment to equal opportunities did not act more vigorously to implement it, Liff suggests three possible explanations:

1 the relationship between line managers and personnel/HRM specialists;

2 the conflicts between equal opportunities and other priorities facing managers;

3 resistance from employees.

The relationship between line managers and personnel/HRM specialists tends to mean that responsibility for equal opportunities rests with the latter rather than the former. The personnel/HRM department often has primary responsibility for monitoring and implementing equality initiatives, but in many organisations this function is perceived as advisory only, and not necessarily tuned in to business necessity. The status of the function may well affect the importance attached to any initiative of this sort. Personnel has been associated with bureaucratic and inflexible employment systems and procedures; line managers may resist more attempts to burden them with paperwork on monitoring, etc. They may also resent the imposition of recruitment and selection systems designed to positively target underrepresented groups. As discussed in the section on quotas and affirmative action, these approaches may sometimes reinforce prejudicial thinking and stereotyping rather than helping.

For this reason, the managing diversity approach may be considered much more valid and acceptable in the eyes of traditional managers. This still begs the question about how the existing inequalities will be addressed. Some campaigners see the approach as a watering-down of the ideals and accuse organisations such as the Equal Opportunities Commission of selling-out on their commitment to women and promoting the business case more than the moral issues. Kamlesh Bahl (1996), the EOC's chairwoman, states:

> Discrimination is not only one-sided. The question is: how do you create roles where men and women are equal? ... I have never said that the business case is above the human rights case. I have a very deep understanding of what makes business adopt equal opportunities practices. Equality is central to business success.

Campaigns such as Opportunity 2000 also use the business advantages of equality to promote their approach and engage the commitment of line managers.

The changing role of specialist and line functions, with more responsibilities being devolved to the line, may either challenge or enhance the focus on eliminating discrimination. If line managers adopt the concepts more effectively it will improve the situation; if the downsizing of personnel/HRM functions leads to a reduced ability to monitor and implement equal opportunities, then the situation may worsen.

Liff's second point is that line managers have multiple priorities and conflicts may arise from the clash of the ideal situation with practical necessity. She uses recruitment and selection as an example of a situation where ideally all sources will be explored and all candidates examined against predetermined objective criteria. The cost and the time-consuming nature of these processes may seem quite unacceptable to a line manager who is losing production because he or she is short-staffed, however. A policy of always recruiting externally may be very irritating to a manager who believes that a suitable internal candidate already exists. This can lead to a sham exercise where all concerned are unsatisfied with the outcome. As a result of such pressures, line managers may show an ambiguous reaction to equal opportunities, welcoming it in theory but resenting it in practice.

Employees themselves may also be a factor in resisting equal opportunities initiatives. Those already within the organisation may be hostile to measures that appear to favour other groups. There may even be competition between different sub-groups in the organisation, with those from ethnic minority backgrounds approving of external recruitment, and women (who tend to be concentrated at the lower levels in the organisation) preferring a focus on internal development.

Work groups may also be more comfortable with a membership formed around like individuals because this gives them a common social structure. Older workers may reject youngsters whom they perceive as different from themselves; women may tease or harass men who join their group. The cultures and traditions of some ethnic minority workers may set them apart from their colleagues. All of these social influences play their part in making complete equality difficult to achieve.

In the wider framework organisational approaches to equal opportunities have to be set in the context of national and international influences. As discussed before, the UK's ideological differences with other EU countries have led to some difficulties in this area. When comparing the employment rights in the UK with those of the Netherlands or Belgium, very different management practices emerge. The constitutional underpinning of worker rights and the government machinery put in place to enforce it provide a different mechanism for equal opportunity development in these countries. The imposition of a minimum wage and other pay and benefits rights have a cost impact, and the realities of managing high levels of social provision at the same time as encouraging economic growth are causing concern in these countries.

The increasing concentration of business into conglomerates and multinationals operating across national boundaries has also focused thinking on how to manage diversity at the same time as trying to ensure parity. The degree of central control over such issues varies between multinationals, with some having a more ethnocentric focus which imposes the values of the parent country, while others have a more polycentric focus, adapting policies to local circumstances. The general points about ethics and social responsibility debated at the beginning of the chapter remain important, however, when considering the relationship between profit and practice.

Looking to the future, it seems that the social trend toward greater tolerance that has already been identified should continue. The greater range of cultures experienced by travel and through the media have removed some of the insularity that characterised particular communities. Education, particularly higher education, also exposes more young people to individuals from other cultures. The interrelationships between nation states mean that it is less easy to turn a blind eye to abuses of human rights, including employment rights. Consumer power is sufficiently well developed and substitute products are nearly always available, so organisations are increasingly aware of the practical consequences of bad publicity.

Nevertheless, discrimination still remains, and concern is expressed in some quarters about whether the underlying attitudes have simply been pushed beneath the surface by the current measures. Racial intolerance is still a feature of society, and all sociological studies show that group membership and insiders and outsiders are characteristics that have existed for as long as human societies. It is important that all the parties to the employment relationship keep the issues very much to the forefront and constantly reassess the impacts of particular measures.

The chapter concludes with a look at the role of management, trade unions and individuals in the promotion of equal opportunities.

MANAGEMENT

Within the workplace, managers have the primary responsibility to ensure that working systems provide equality of opportunity for all. As outlined before, Codes of Practice exist to promote good management practices, but these need to be implemented and enforced. What, then, are the operational realities of managing equal opportunities? In this section we look at the processes of managing in the following areas:

- recruitment and selection
- induction
- training and development

■ Exhibit 12.4

Faces that don't fit

FT

Some employers are still seeking Mr Average clones.

Fat, gay or non-BBC English-speaking – few companies would openly admit to being biased against employees who fall into these groups. But evidence from the Institute for Personnel and Development, which represents personnel staff and provides training, suggests that employers do continue to discriminate for reasons that are often irrelevant to the job.

Discussions with 30 recruitment consultants who are in a good position to gauge employers' true preferences, produced some frank admissions. Individual interviews conducted by the institute – including the three below – were also revealing.

Accent appears to be of enduring significance. A consultant remarks: 'Accent is important. It communicates background, education and birthplace, and frankly, some backgrounds are more desirable and marketable than others. Off the record, I would advise anyone with a redbrick or industrial accent to upgrade.'

Another says: 'Let's face it – people with Scouse accents sound whiny, and people with Brummie accents sound stupid.'

On weight, one consultant said: 'To put it bluntly, fat people are bad for an organisation's image. We wouldn't put an overgrown tree in the foyer, and we wouldn't let an overgrown person deal with our clients.' Said another: 'I don't think somebody would be rejected solely on that basis, but I would say it creates a bad impression.

Being overweight is equated, to some degree, with sloth.'

Geoff Armstrong, the institute's director-general, says the law in certain areas 'can play a significant role in tackling discrimination, but it is not sufficient on its own to change attitudes'. Real change depends on organisations 'taking action voluntarily because they are convinced that managing diversity makes good business sense. Those employers who succeed in recruiting and retaining people from diverse backgrounds will flourish because they can access the innovation and skills to the widest possible pool of talent.'

The institute advises employers to:

- Focus on essential and objective job-related criteria when making decisions about people.
- Introduce mechanisms to deal with harassment, bullying and intimidating behaviour.
- Actively check for and remove unfair biases in systems, procedures and their applications.

Dianah Worman, policy adviser on equal opportunities, says too many judgments are still made on the basis of outdated stereotypes. 'That is bad for the individual concerned, bad for their employer and bad for society.'

Many people never get the chance to fulfil their true potential, she concludes. 'Decisions about people's suitability ... should only ever be based on merit and ability, not petty prejudice.'

Source: Andrew Bolger (1996) *Financial Times*, 18 December.

- promotion and appraisal
- pay and terms and conditions of employment
- harassment and the handling of grievances
- discipline, dismissal and redundancy

Recruitment and selection

It is essential that any organisation with a commitment to equality of opportunity thoroughly examines its approach to recruitment and selection. Selection criteria must be based on a detailed analysis of the job to be performed. The development of a person specification is crucial to ensure that all candidates are compared against objective criteria rather than each other. There are a number of established systems of compiling person specifications such as Rodger's seven-point plan and Munro Fraser's five-point plan. Marchington and Wilkinson (1996) have pointed out, however, that:

> Both these sets of personnel specifications are somewhat dated, relating not only to a working environment which was much more stable but also to a social and legal framework where it was considered acceptable to ask questions about an individual's domestic circumstances or private life. Although the broad framework may still be valid, it is now unethical, inappropriate and potentially discriminatory to probe too deeply into some of these areas of the person specification. Moreover, it may not make much business sense either to restrict applications to people with specific educational qualifications or a certain length of experience in an industry or occupation.

When choosing sources of recruitment the organisation should check to ensure that all sections of the community will be reached by the methods. Recruitment by word of mouth has been criticised as potentially discriminatory, particularly if the workforce already has an imbalance which is likely to be perpetuated. Positive action could involve targeting particular groups by placing advertisements in journals that are read by minority groups, or using multimedia including radio to access blind applicants.

The design and content of recruitment advertisements is most important. The content should not indicate any intention to discriminate against particular groups. Many organisations choose to include a statement of commitment to equal opportunities in the advertisement. Visual images should create the right impression. Some advertisements contain photographs of white male employees only – this could send an indirect message that these are the only type of recruit sought.

When collecting information about candidates an application form provides a consistent set of data on all candidates. Curricula vitae are less reliable because of individual variations in style and content. Questions asked on an application form should be examined to make sure they do not contain discriminatory assumptions. Educational qualifications should not be structured only on the UK's system, but should allow equivalent qualifications to be recorded from other countries. The requirement to provide employment references may discriminate against those returning to the workforce. The application form should allow the candidate to state non-work experience as well as employment history. Questions about marital status, age or domestic circumstances should be avoided as they are irrelevant to the candidates ability to perform the job tasks.

Monitoring data should be collected from all applicants. Data should be provided on sex, marital status, disability, age and ethnic origin. This data provides information to show which individuals are applying for the jobs, and whether the progress through interview and final selection is affected by discrimination or not. Without the data, organisations may be entirely unaware that they are discriminating against particular groups. The categories of ethnic origin for monitoring purposes should use at least the four basic groupings: White, Afro-Caribbean, Asian and Other. The CRE recommends the use of the nine categories used in the 1991 census: White, Black–African, Black–Caribbean, Black–Other (please specify), Indian, Pakistani, Bangladeshi, Chinese, Other (please specify). Where relevant the organisation may also wish to divide the White category in order to monitor, for example, discrimination against Irish or Greek people. Confusion may arise over nationality and ethnic origin. Over 68 per cent of the ethnic minority population are British, so nationality questions should not be included.

Ideally, the monitoring information should be included on a separate sheet or tear-off section of the application form, and should not be used as part of the selection process at all. It should be reviewed regularly to ensure that bias is not occurring.

When shortlisting, the candidates should be assessed against objective criteria, and the results should be formally recorded to show the reasons why candidates were either accepted or rejected. Staff involved at any stage of the selection process should be well briefed and trained to recognise and minimise bias.

At interview, the interviewers should also have received training in how to conduct a structured selection interview. Questions asked should not be intrusive or impertinent. The interviewer should be seeking factual evidence of ability, not impressions of personality, which can be very unreliable. The EOC provides the following guidance:

> No questions should be based upon assumptions regarding women's roles in the home and the family. There was, perhaps, a time when all such responsibilities were met by women, with men being the sole breadwinners and doing nothing domestically. That situation is no longer true and questions should not be based upon any such assumption.
>
> Questions regarding intentions about marriage and having children are, rightly, regarded as impertinent, are resented and should never be asked.
>
> Any questions, which are asked to find out whether the individual can meet the needs of the job in hours, overtime, mobility, etc, should be asked equally of men and women. (However, it is not necessarily true that asking the same question of both sexes ensures non-discrimination. The use to which the answers are put may still be discriminatory).

Other selection methods, such as tests, should also be carefully chosen to ensure they do not discriminate unfairly. Tests should be obtained from reputable test agencies or consultancy organisations. Advice should be sought on the suitability of the test for the job under consideration, using a thorough job description as the basis. The tests should be validated, preferably separately for men and women, and for ethnic minority groups. The average scores for each group should be compared to see if there are any marked differences. Where differences are statistically valid, an investigation should be conducted to see if this is due to unfair bias.

Final selection should also compare the candidates against objective criteria. The results of the process should be documented for future reference.

Induction

When preparing for the induction of new employees it is essential that all materials are checked to ensure they are free from bias and do not stereotype employees. All new staff should be welcomed into the workplace and helped to socialise with others. Induction training should be structured to allow for individual variations in pace and learning.

Training and development

Access should be provided to training for all employees, and restrictions, such as the need to stay away from home extensively, should be minimised to ensure that access to training is available to all. Training and development materials should be free of bias and use a full cross-section of ages, sexes and races in examples and exercises. All training courses should contain a specific commitment to equal opportunities and evaluation of training should include equal opportunities criteria.

Promotion and appraisal

Building equal opportunities into promotion requires much the same discipline as for recruitment and selection. Many organisations seem to have a 'glass ceiling' which prevents women and ethnic minority workers from achieving the top positions in the organisation. Access to promotion should not be based on stereotypical assumptions or prejudice that excludes non-typical applicants.

Some organisations have set specific targets for the numbers of women or other underrepresented groups in senior management. Action plans can then be formulated to help bring this about.

In appraisal schemes, the criteria adopted should be carefully structured to ensure that the categories used are as far as possible quantifiable and objective. Impressionistic systems that allow greater subjectivity are much more prone to bias.

Pay and terms and conditions of employment

This is an important area for discrimination so a variety of systems are needed to ensure fairness in pay and related benefits. The pay system should be based on objective job evaluation methods and the criteria used to value jobs should be examined to ensure that they are not based on discriminatory assumptions. Women's earnings are consistently less than those of men so the basis on which value is calculated should be carefully assessed.

Membership of pension schemes and other related employee benefits should also contain the same conditions for both men and women. Part-time staff should enjoy the same pay and benefits (pro rata) as their full-time colleagues. Holiday entitlement and rest periods should also be built into the contracts of all staff.

The contract of employment itself should contain all the legal requirements, and employers should not issue consecutive fixed-term contracts to avoid the qualifying periods for statutory employment rights. The increasing use of flexible contracts should be examined to see if they disproportionately affect particular groups in the workforce, such as women, young or older workers.

■ Harassment and the handling of grievances

It is important that the organisation states its commitment to the elimination of harassment and indicates that it treats all grievances of this sort seriously. Harassment can be defined as conduct that is unwanted by the recipient or affects the dignity of any individual or group at work. Examples of harassment may include:

- physical contact ranging from unnecessary touching to assault or rape;
- comments, jokes, banter, insults and language related to age, creed, disability, nationality, race, religion, sex, sexual orientation or any other personal characteristic which are offensive to an individual or group;
- offensive or unwanted comments about dress or physical appearance;
- intrusive questions about a person's social or sexual life;
- suggestive remarks or gestures, innuendoes or uninvited propositions for sex;
- racially, sexually or religiously based graffiti or graffiti that is offensive to a group or individual;
- display of pornographic pictures, pin-ups, flags or emblems likely to give offence.

Racial or sexual harassment can be dismissed at times as 'a bit of fun', or 'just a joke'. To the victim, however, the effects of harassment are at best unpleasant and at worst can totally destroy the capacity of the individual to perform the job. Rubenstein (1991) argues:

> A decade ago the consequences of sexual harassment for its recipients were not fully appreciated. Now it is understood that harassment is no joke and that it commonly induces stress, damaging the health of victims. At that time, employers were not aware of the costs to the organisation in failing to prevent sexual harassment. Now there is growing appreciation that the price paid in terms of loss of efficiency, poor morale, absence and labour turnover far outweighs the cost of installing an effective policy to deal with sexual harassment. Back in the early 1980s, employers tended to regard sexual harassment as a personal dispute between employees, of peripheral concern to the organisation. Now it is recognised that sexual harassment damages the working environment and that the responsibility for creating and maintaining a healthy working environment rests on the employer. Not long ago also, for most trade unions, sexual harassment was mainly seen in terms of defending their members accused of a disciplinary offence. Now virtually every major trade union has a clear policy condemning sexual harassment and offers active assistance to its members who have been subjected to it.

Since the Strathclyde Regional Council *v* Porcelli case in 1987 where the judge stated, 'Sexual harassment is a particularly degrading and unacceptable form of treatment which it must be taken to have been the intention of Parliament to restrain', harassment cases can be brought under the race and sex discrimination legislation. Inciting others to racial hatred is also a totally unacceptable form of behaviour which any employer must eliminate in the most strenuous way. An extension of harassment can also be found in any form of bullying where the perpetrator seeks to gain power over his or her victim. Aggressive management styles which abuse the power of the individual should also be found unacceptable.

In order to eliminate harassment or bullying the organisation should have a clear policy on such matters. This policy should be in writing and expressly state that all employees have a right to be treated with dignity, and that harassment or bullying at work will not be permitted or condoned. The policy should also state that employees have a right to complain about it should it occur.

In the first instance employees should be encouraged to resolve the problem informally. In circumstances where it is too difficult or embarrassing for individuals to do this on their own behalf, they should seek support and ask for an initial approach to be made by a sympathetic friend or confidential counsellor. If an employee wishes to complain formally the organisation's grievance procedure should be used. Violations of the organisation's policy should be considered a disciplinary offence and the rules should make it clear what will be regarded as inappropriate behaviour at work. The penalties that the offender will be liable to should also be clearly stated.

Discipline, dismissal and redundancy

The organisation's rules on discipline must be carried out uniformly regardless of the sex or race of the individual concerned. As discussed above, discrimination offences should be clearly stated as a disciplinary matter and the individuals concerned should be disciplined according to the policy and procedures of the organisation. Forms of discrimination may also be a gross misconduct offence carrying the penalty of summary or instant dismissal. Racially motivated attacks and severe examples of sexual harassment may be examples of such offences.

In selection for redundancy, the organisation should also consider whether the criteria used unfairly discriminates against a particular section of the workforce. Selecting all part-time staff for redundancy may unfairly discriminate against women, who make up a much larger percentage of such workers. Using age criteria may also unfairly disadvantage older workers. The 'last in, first out' criterion may penalise younger workers.

TRADE UNIONS

Unions have a dual responsibility in terms of equal opportunities, first to promote equality in workplace negotiations with employers and second to ensure that within their own organisations, they adopt equal opportunities and anti-racist policies which allow for a fair representation of all workers in union structures.

The historical record of trade unions in equal opportunities has not always been a good one. In many early cases it was clear that unions engaged in activities that were either explicitly racist or showed a complete neglect of race or gender issues. Bygott (1992) reports that the TUC in 1930 passed the following resolution:

> That this congress views with alarm the continued employment of alien and undesirable coloured labour on British ships to the detriment of British seamen and calls upon the government to use all their powers to provide remedial action.

Post-war attempts were made by white trade unionists to restrict black workers to a quota of (generally) 5 per cent of the labour force. It was also understood that the principle of 'last in, first out' at a time of redundancy would not apply if this meant white workers would lose their jobs before blacks.

In the area of sex discrimination unions also have a mixed record. Unions have been found to discriminate against women (notably at local levels) and condone employer discrimination. Part of the explanation for this lies in the historical development of trade unions, which were dominated by men, particularly skilled men. Developments in the 1980s attempted to address women's issues and promote women in unions. The move for this has also been fuelled by concerns caused by declining union membership. Unions have actively sought to develop and advocate policies and negotiation strategies that are likely to attract unorganised or weakly organised workers.

Dickens *et al.* (1988) note that:

> The extent to which union negotiators will experience internal membership pressure for the removal of discrimination/promotion of equal opportunities will depend on the composition of the membership; the identity and priorities of those who are most active within the union and those who hold positions of power within its organisation; and the way in which the negotiating agenda, bargaining objectives and priorities are set.

The Colling and Dickens (1989) study into equality bargaining also looked at the degree to which equality bargaining formed part of the management/union agenda. Three areas were identified for investigation:

1 the inclusion of benefits of particular interest/benefit to women, facilitating their full participation in the workforce;
2 the equality-aware handling of commonplace bargaining agenda items, such as pay and opportunities;
3 an equality dimension to negotiation of change, such as reforming a grading structure or introducing an appraisal scheme.

The findings of their research note in crude general terms that little evidence was found of an extension of the bargaining agenda as indicated in point 1, little if any sensitivity on the part of most negotiators to equality implications in the handling of commonplace agenda items and only very exceptionally any equality dimension to change. They conclude, 'In short, women, directly or indirectly, were rarely on (or indeed at) the bargaining table'.

When investigating the reasons for the lack of importance attached to equality, the study identified problems with the nature of collective bargaining itself in many organisations. Collective bargaining tended to focus on a narrow bargaining agenda which was stable and unquestioned by the parties involved. This made it difficult to introduce 'new' issues on to the agenda. Collective bargaining was also found to focus almost entirely on increases to pay within existing structures, in other words on rates of pay. Rarely were more fundamental issues raised about the nature of the pay structures themselves, or the gender disparities that could be found within them. The study notes:

> We found among negotiators generally an unquestioning acceptance of the existing distribution of jobs and rewards. In particular, the job segregation which underpins a lot of the disadvantage of women was perceived generally by negotiators interviewed as 'natural' or objectively justifiable in terms of workers' preferences, differential skills or the nature of the work involved although, in fact, much of the rationale reflected sexual stereotypes and discriminatory assumptions.

One of the difficulties faced by trade unions in the area of equal opportunities is the degree to which unions should promote the issues of particular sections of their membership, rather than the interests of the membership as a whole. Wrench and Virdee (1996) note that unions debated the question as to whether they should concern themselves only with issues common to white and minority ethnic members or should operate special policies relating to the specific interests of minorities. Should they provide equal or special treatment?

Until the end of the 1960s the standard trade union position was exemplified by the TUC view that to institute any special policies would be to discriminate against the white membership. Wrench and Virdee (1996) report Vic Feather, TUC General Secretary in 1970, as saying, 'The trade union movement is concerned with a man or woman as a worker. The colour of a man's skin has no relevance whatever to his work'.

Around 1974 changes were detectable at the official trade union level with a recognition that there was a need to move away from a *laissez-faire* attitude towards a more positive role. By 1981 the TUC had produced *Black Workers: A TUC Charter for Equality of Opportunity* and unions were urged to examine their own structures and practices in order to find ways to remove the barriers that prevented black members from reaching union office and decision making bodies. Seven years later the TUC reissued the Charter, and also worked with the CRE in the production of a Code of Practice. In recent years the TUC has also lobbied the European Trade Union Confederation to take on board issues of migrants' rights and racial equality.

On gender discrimination, trade unions are also responding and helping to shape attitudes. John Edmonds initiated the 'Winning a Fair Deal' policy at the GMB union in 1986, which confronts issues of discrimination against women in areas covered by GMB collective agreements. A survey by Mason (1994) of 21 unions found that 10 had a national-level committee dealing with race equality issues and nearly two-thirds had taken positive steps such as targeting workplaces, organising conferences for black members and producing recruitment literature in languages other than English. Many unions have also appointed national officers to take responsibility for issues affecting ethnic groups or for women's issues.

Mirza (1995) also reports that the TUC has pledged itself to consulting unions on how improvements can be made, and is urging unions to nominate more black trade unionists to TUC bodies, the Women's Conference and Congress. The TUC has also produced a checklist which suggests strategies that unions are encouraged to pursue at branch, regional and national level.

The difficulties that the union movement has faced in recent years in terms of loss of membership and diminished resources does put in some doubt their ability to pursue equality measures further. Mirza (1995) comments:

> The initial steps that some unions have taken in recent years should be put into perspective against the inaction by a great many more. Any progress that has been made will also quickly recede if unions fail to commit themselves to maintaining, and significantly increasing, the momentum that has been initiated in this area.

INDIVIDUALS

The employment context of the 1990s puts a high emphasis on the individual in employment as well as organisational groupings. Trade unions and management can promote best practice, but ultimately it is the interpersonal relationships between individuals that determine whether discrimination takes place. Individuals need to be reminded of their own unconscious prejudices and encouraged to 'put themselves in another's shoes'. McEnrue (1993) describes the qualities needed for effective cross-cultural communications as:

- the capacity to accept the relativity of one's own knowledge and perceptions;
- the capacity to be non-judgmental;
- a tolerance for ambiguity;
- the capacity to appreciate and communicate respect for other people's ways, backgrounds, values and beliefs;
- the capacity to demonstrate empathy;
- the capacity to be flexible;
- a willingness to acquire new patterns of behaviour and belief;
- the humility to acknowledge what one does not know.

Kandola and Fullerton (1994) suggest that on a more individual level, there are things that can be done, including:

- examining your own behaviour styles, attitudes and beliefs;
- considering your own feelings and reactions to people;
- being curious and getting to know others;
- trying to see things from other people's perspectives;
- being honest with others;
- examining your own communication style;
- looking at how flexibly you treat others;

- when leading teams, taking care that all people feel part of the team;
- developing others;
- challenging accepted practices;
- acting as a role model.

Organisations that provide training to help their employees recognise the impact they have on others, and whose culture encourages the qualities listed above, may find that discriminatory tendencies are greatly reduced as a consequence. As Kandola and Fullerton (1994) note in the conclusion to their survey on managing diversity:

> Upon examination it was discovered that the skills necessary to manage diversity are essentially a restatement of an old theme, namely good interpersonal or communication skills. It is these skills that need to be emphasised in training managers in the diversity-oriented organisation. Good managers of diversity are essentially just that – good managers, and good managers are those who deal with employees as individuals rather than expect everyone to be equally motivated and to work in the same way.

CONCLUSIONS

The focus of this chapter has been the exploration of the manifestations and causes of discrimination in the employment relationship. Through the various perspectives explored, it is evident that the attitudes that cause discrimination and the practices that accompany it are deep-rooted. The instinct to judge others by the degree to which they are 'like us' provides a powerful impetus to group closure and ethnocentrism. The role a wider society plays in shaping norms of behaviour has also been seen to exert an enormous influence on workplace attitudes. Historically, the jobs available to immigrant groups, particularly post-war, has profoundly affected the employment opportunities and the position of these individuals in the occupational structure of the UK. Traditionally, work patterns, status and pay have been based on a norm of full-time employment. This has had the effect of dividing the labour market up along gender lines, to the disadvantage of female employees.

Increasingly, however, since the 1970s, public perceptions of inequality and disadvantage and the government's role in legislation has focused attention on these issues. The UK was deeply shocked by the inner-city riots of the 1970s and early '80s, which revealed a degree of anger and desperation in young unemployed and disadvantaged individuals from the inner cities. At the same time more women, particularly married women, were joining the labour force, and the UK was worried about potential labour shortages caused by the 'demographic time bomb'. Recession moderated the most alarmist predictions and employment shortages were in no way as severe as predicted, but employers and the government began to take a far more active role in examining all sources of labour supply in the market.

Changes to education in the form of a common national curriculum for all, and the setting of performance targets and indicators, have revealed shortcomings in the education provision for some groups. This has been addressed in some cases by the sending in of 'hit squads' to overhaul systems and procedures. The media have also been urged to portray a wider variety of families and work roles to prevent stereotyping and provide effective role models. Positive action programmes have also been run to attract more women into engineering or more men into nursing, for example.

Some change is evident in the types and variety of jobs taken up by women and the increased numbers of women returning immediately to full-time work after childbirth. Likewise, the second and third generations of post-war immigrants may find less resistance to their presence and better job opportunities as the UK adjusts to a multi-racial society. A number of high-profile retail recruitment campaigns, such as that at B&Q, have focused attention on the very positive attributes of older workers, and younger workers are increasingly encouraged to continue in education or training, thereby enhancing their 'human capital'.

Nevertheless, despite these positive indicators, there is little to be complacent about. Disabled individuals still experience major difficulties in finding meaningful occupation. Too many members of minority ethnic groups still feel marginalised and only really comfortable with self-employed status.

The issues around integration still occur regularly, with Norman Tebbit's recent views on ethnic minority groups and their need to embrace 'British culture' being one manifestation of this.

Instilling a respect for difference as well as similarity will take more time to filter through to all members of society. The managing diversity movement has attempted to address some of the problems caused by a backlash against positive action programmes. Although in many areas there is still a need to take some form of targeted action to address imbalances, if these measures can be seen to be inclusive, available to all depending on need, rather than exclusive, available to minorities only, they are more likely to be accepted.

Managers and trade unionists still have a very crucial role in taking anti-discrimination measures forward. It is too easy to have written policies to which 'lip-service' is paid rather than wholeheartedly embracing the intentions behind these policies. Involving as diverse a range of individuals as possible in equal opportunities initiatives will also help to ensure that real progress is made.

CHAPTER SUMMARY

This chapter has looked at a particular aspect of the employment relationship – the management of discrimination – and its impact on employee relations practice.

Discrimination is defined as 'making a distinction' but the distinction should be based on fair, not unfair, characteristics. Unfair discrimination may be individual, structural or organisational and be based on many characteristics, including sex, race, disability and age. The consequences of unfair discrimination include poor utilisation of employees and the creation of a resentful and unmotivated workforce.

There are a number of perspectives that can be examined to understand the causes of discrimination. The psychological/sociological perspective examines discrimination as a product of how individuals learn behaviours appropriate to the society in which they live. Socialisation through the influence of the family, peer group, educational experiences and the role models provided by the media help reinforce impressions that can lead to discrimination. Stereotyping is a common way of making judgments about those around you, but it holds dangers if ethnocentrism leads the individual to dismiss those who are not 'like me'. This is thought to be particularly problematic if the individual also has a personality tendency to authoritarianism, which may lead to displacement or scapegoating.

The influence of social norms can also be examined by taking a historical perspective and tracing attitudes to discrimination as they change over time. Gender patterns have altered in this way, with an increasing acceptance of women's role in employment, particularly since the Second World War. The influence of feminism in redefining the status and role of women and the moderating effects of increased technology on jobs which previously had a high need for manual strength have also challenged gender stereotypes. The role expectations of men in society and at work has also been re-evaluated as part of an ongoing debate on masculinity. Historical changes in attitudes to race and ethnicity also show greater attention being paid to these issues. The position of immigrants in the UK, particularly post-war, indicates that occupational stereotyping has occurred, forcing immigrants into low paid, manual labour. The pressures caused by inner-city unemployment led to a series of riots in the UK in the late 1970s and again contributed to a re-evaluation of the position of these groups. The Civil Rights movement in the USA, the abandonment of apartheid in South Africa and campaigns by other activists have also contributed to attitude change today.

Age discrimination affects both older and younger workers. The average age of entry into the labour market has been increasing progressively over time. This is linked to the provision of greater educational opportunities post-16 and changes to the demographic makeup of the labour force, with fewer young people. Youth unemployment still remains a key issue and successive government policies have attempted to address it. At the other end of the age range, early retirement and redundancy have reduced the overall age of the working population in recent years. Those wishing to remain economically active are seen to face many difficulties, with employers regularly using criteria in selection that restrict entrants to the 25–35 age category.

Attitudes to disability, particularly the removal of the 'medical model' of disability, have enhanced the profile of this section of the workforce. The ongoing existence of discrimination and limited employment prospects for those with physical or mental disabilities is still a reality, however. Organisations are also having to broaden their definition of disability to include employees who suffer difficulties while in employment from a range of medical or psychological conditions, including stress.

Patterns of discrimination can also be examined from an economic and structural perspective. Human capital theory, together with the segmented labour market theory and reserve army of labour theory, provides alternative explanations for the position of particular groups in the occupational structure. When reviewing human capital theory, levels of investment in education and training do show some correlation with the lower employment status of various groups. However, changes are detectable which may moderate these influences over time. The practical difficulties of classifying labour into primary and secondary sectors mean that segmented labour market theory is difficult to evaluate, although an examination of part-time and full-time employment status clearly does indicate that disadvantage is experienced by the former. The reality of the reserve army of labour theory can be examined by looking at the unemployment statistics to see if disadvantaged groups are disproportionately represented. The position of women appears to demonstrate less evidence of reserve army status than that of ethnic minorities, older workers or the disabled.

The final perspective examined is the political/ethical one, which looks at equality of opportunity as a basic human right. The role of employers in providing a working environment which meets the needs of their employees is seen as socially desirable and also 'good for business' in terms of return on investment.

Various measures have been taken to address equality issues in recent years and their success is evaluated. The legislative approach depends on the model of state intervention adopted. Since the late 1970s the UK has operated a free labour market model approach under the Conservative governments. Following the election in 1997, a period of adjustment will occur as the new Labour government moves towards a more social justice approach. The principles established by the Acts on sex and race discrimination in the 1970s, particularly on direct and indirect discrimination, are now widely recognised. The EOC and the CRE have also played a key role in enforcing and educating about gender, marital status and race issues. The latest piece of legislation, the Disability Discrimination Act 1996, attempts to address the disadvantage affecting this group in the labour force. The Act has been criticised as ineffective and lacking force, particularly as the body set up to promote it has advisory powers only. The industrial tribunal method of bringing a case against an employer as a result of discrimination is also criticised as long-winded and ineffective in the main.

Educational programmes and national initiatives are other measures taken to address discrimination. The use of awareness training in revealing prejudice and helping to recognise the points of view of others has been found to be a powerful tool in changing behaviour. National campaigns such as Opportunity 2000 have also helped to raise the profile of initiatives to improve the role of women in employment.

More radical approaches such as affirmative action and quota-setting programmes have also been adopted to force change into the system. The experience of the USA, where federal contract compliance clauses have been used to ensure ethnic mix, is ambivalent. On the one hand, the statistics do indicate that more minority applicants are getting jobs. However, the resulting backlash from those excluded has also been a major problem. The UK has not embraced similar practices, feeling that they provide a burden on business and that special treatment cannot be justified. Other forms of positive action such as statements in recruitment adverts encouraging applications from particular groups and targeted recruitment, which utilises publications addressed to minority groups, have been used, however.

The final model of managing equality examined is the more recent 'managing diversity' approach. These programmes aim to be inclusive, not exclusive, and provide measures that could benefit all sections of the workforce. The argument is that employers need a diverse workforce, not a workforce of clones, in order to maintain competitive advantage. Learning how to maximise the potential of all employees is proposed as a significant challenge for the 1990s.

When evaluating the impact of all the approaches detailed above, the rate of progress and extent of change is still limited. Factors restricting progress include the difficulties experienced between line managers and HRM specialists. Equality issues are often left to specialists rather than embraced by everybody in the workforce. The conflict between business priorities and equal opportunities priorities is also part of the difficulty, with the recession forcing managers to adopt a primarily finance-driven model of employment. Finally, the resistance provided by ordinary individuals to such policies can also contribute to the problem.

The chapter ends with an evaluation of the role of managers, trade unions and individuals in the continuing development of fair practices. The role of management in leading the way and ensuring that organisations adopt clear practices and procedures is vital. Policies and procedures need to be effected in the areas of recruitment and selection; induction; training and development; promotion and appraisal; pay and terms and conditions of employment; harassment and the handling of grievances; and discipline, dismissal and redundancy.

The role of trade unions in providing examples of best practice and pressing for equality issues to be included in collective bargaining is also vital. Historically, trade unions were dominated by white, male, full-time employees. The legacy of this traditional membership still causes difficulties when dealing with a more diverse workforce. Union attempts to respond and initiate equal opportunities measures both internally and in the wider sphere of employment need to be developed and continually moved forward.

Each and every employee also has a role to play in minimising prejudice. The qualities needed to be responsive to the needs of others are those of an effective communicator; these should be developed and form part of the overall culture of all organisations.

QUESTIONS

1 How effective has the legislation covering sex and race discrimination been in reducing unfair employment practices in the UK?

2 Outline the likely effects on discrimination in the UK if a quota system, like that operated in the USA, was set up for all public sector contracts.

3 The objectives of ethical business management and profit maximisation are incompatible. Discuss this statement in the context of equal opportunities.

4 Outline the main areas an organisation should examine to ensure that equal opportunities issues have been built in to all systems and procedures.

5 Managing diversity is just another renaming exercise to enhance the image of existing equal opportunity programmes. Do you agree with this assessment of the managing diversity approach?

6 Recent research suggests that men also face significant amounts of sexual harassment but rarely, if ever, report it. Why do you think this happens and what should be done to address the problem when it occurs?

EXERCISES

1 Investigate the equal opportunities measures taken in your organisation or university/college. What is the stated position on equal opportunities? Do you feel it is effective in practice? How do the systems compare with the Codes of Practice available from the EOC or CRE?

2 In the role of an equal opportunities consultant, outline the content and delivery methods to be used on a discrimination awareness training programme for first-line managers.

3 Contact a range of trade unions and ask them for any materials they have available on equal opportunities or discrimination. Review the content and approach taken and compare it with the approach taken by line managers.

4 Interview members of ethnic minority groups and/or women in traditionally male occupations or men in traditionally female occupations. Investigate the difficulties they have faced and how they have overcome them.

5 Review recruitment advertisements from a wide variety of sources to see if they have a commitment to equal opportunities or whether they discriminate or stereotype the applicant either directly or indirectly.

6 Look out for discrimination cases reported at industrial tribunals and try to evaluate the issues that led to them being brought.

CASE STUDY 1

Read the article on family-friendly policies in Exhibit 12.5.

1 To what extent do you believe that employers should adopt 'family-friendly' policies as part of their responsibility to the wider society in which they exist?

2 How effective do you think the cost–benefit argument is in encouraging employers to make 'family-friendly' provisions?

3 What should a 'family-friendly' policy include?

■ Exhibit 12.5

Keep mum at work

The economic argument for family-friendly policies is hard to prove.

Are working mothers an expensive luxury in the workplace or do the benefits of employing them outweigh the costs? It is a controversial issue, not least for the Equal Opportunities Commission, which organised a conference last week on the matter, and which has traditionally fought equality issues on the basis of their being a basic human right.

For some years it has been generally agreed that equality of opportunity at work between men and women is a 'good thing' on ethical grounds.

Taking the argument into the realms of cost benefits to the individual company begs the question of why, if it is such a good idea, more employers do not introduce 'family-friendly' policies.

Employer organisations, including the Confederation of British Industry and the Institute of Directors, try not to get embroiled in debating the matter publicly – preferring to promote employment on merit.

Recently the EOC, along with several other organisations promoting the employment of working mothers, has set out to promote the business case.

For, as Joan Smyth, chairwoman and chief executive of the Equal Opportunities Commission in Northern Ireland, said at the conference: 'Every time I address a group of business people about equality of opportunity – and they tend to be men – they go on about the costs of employing women, such as maternity provision and child care costs.'

▶

■ **Exhibit 12.5 continued**

But, she added: 'They never mention the benefits. I believe it does make good business sense to provide equality of opportunity. However, it is very difficult to define the cost and benefits precisely.'

Nobody at the conference was able to offer a simple formula to defend the case that family-friendly policies, such as career breaks and flexible working hours, have a positive effect on the bottom line when set against costs.

Speaker after speaker spoke of their perceptions of the positive impact of progressive employment practices. Family-friendly policies, they argued, led to:

- Higher levels of corporate loyalty with employees working with greater commitment and goodwill for organisations that they respect and trust to treat them well.

- Lower rates of absenteeism and reductions in staff turnover, thus reducing expenditure on recruitment.

- A better return on investment in training.

- Improved corporate image and the potential to attract high calibre recruits.

But how does an organisation measure and value the gain from having a corporate image that suggests it values women? Does it improve the quality of its recruits, with the most able women attracted to companies that facilitate their desire to have a career and a family? How does the same employer quantify the benefit of not having to replace an employee, in terms of recruitment and training costs as well as the time it takes for the replacement to reach full efficiency? Much depends on the job.

Some quantifiable evidence has been shed on these questions in a book, briefly mentioned at the conference, called *The Economics Of Equal Opportunity*, published by the EOC. One essay, by Sally Holtermann, examines the private costs and benefits to employers.

Holtermann, who says that more good-quality comprehensive empirical work is needed, argues that some practices that have become widespread, such as flexitime, job sharing and part-time working, provided benefits to employers that have outweighed costs.

But other types of family-friendly arrangements – such as leave entitlement and childcare assistance were much less common and pressure for them was meeting resistance from employers and government alike.

'This is perhaps an indication that the balance of benefits and costs for employers is less favourable,' says Holtermann.

She argues, however, that few employers have conducted full audits of the advantages and disadvantages of policy changes. She draws on the few studies available, such as work by Sheffield Hallam University for Bradford City Council. This looked only at the cost of replacing employees who were using a council-funded nursery and who said they would have to leave work if it closed.

The study concluded that the costs of replacing staff were higher than the annual subsidy which the council paid towards the running costs of the nursery. The study, however, was partial in that it did not look at other costs, including maternity leave and flexible working.

Holtermann warns of the potential pit-falls of pursuing the business argument and concentrating on cost-benefit ratios for employers.

There is a danger, she says, 'of a shift in attitude towards the position where equality of opportunity is no longer seen primarily as a matter of social justice, desirable in its own right, but merely as something that can be pursued if, and only if, it coincides with the employing organisation's own self-interest.'

This is the tight-rope that the EOC is now walking, with a possibility that its own agenda for promoting equal opportunities will be increasingly set by the business community.

It is here that the role of the government is most critical: it is the government's responsibility, not the individual employee's, to look at the wider social costs and benefits of offering equality of opportunity.

Sex discrimination, it was said at the conference, is rather like poor health and safety or environmental provision. It is bad for society as a whole.

Source: Lisa Wood (1995) *Financial Times*, 13 December.

CASE STUDY 2

Prepare a summary of the position of ethnic minority groups in employment in the 1990s based on the content of this chapter and the details provided in Exhibit 12.6.

■ **Exhibit 12.6**

How to isolate the racist employer

FT

Simplistic economic theory gives false hope to Britain's ethnic minorities.

Ethnic minorities form a small but growing proportion of Britain's 58m population. From 4 per cent in the late 1970s, their share rose to 5 per cent in the late 1980s and it should stabilise eventually at almost double that level.

As these relatively young communities come to be integrated more fully into the labour market, it has often been assumed that the economic disadvantage they suffer relative to the majority white population should gradually erode. But recent trends suggest not.

According to the annual General Household Survey, the labour market position of blacks deteriorated relative to that of whites between the 1970s and the 1980s. The difference between black and white wage levels rose from 7.3 to 12.1 per cent, while the difference between their unemployment rates rose from 2.6 to 10.9 percentage points.

And things may have got worse in the last few years. During the 1980s and early 1990s the unemployment rates of the ethnic minorities behaved 'supercyclically', which is to say that they did worse than the rest of the population when the economy was doing badly but better when it was doing well.

Unemployment among whites fell by 42 per cent between 1984 and 1990 and then rose by 57 per cent during the recession; among ethnic minorities over the same periods the fall was 50 per cent and the increase 109 per cent. This pattern has broken down in the present recovery, however. Since its peak, unemployment has fallen by 22 per cent among whites but only 17 per cent among the minorities.

The net result is that by the autumn of 1995 the unemployment rate for ethnic minorities was almost two-and-a-half times as high as that for whites; in 1984 it was not even twice as high.

According to Swansea University's David Blackaby, and his colleagues, it is the changing trends in unemployment rather than earnings which are central.*

This is because the blacks who lost their jobs in the 1980s had better earnings prospects than the whites who lost theirs: 'It was the declining employment prospects of blacks that exacerbated the ethnic wage gap, rather than anything else'.

Identifying the source of ethnic differences in labour market performance is no easy task. A typical approach is to look at the difference between black and white earnings levels and to work out to what extent they can be explained by differences in such factors as age, education, work experience, job description and type of employer. Any residual wage gap is assumed to be the result of 'discrimination'.

Nobel prizewinner Kenneth Arrow defined discrimination in this sense as 'the valuation in the marketplace of personal characteristics of the worker that are unrelated to productivity'. The major flaw with this approach – aside from the inevitable measurement difficulties – is that discrimination may also play an important part in determining people's productivity: perhaps by affecting their access to educational opportunities.

The analysis is further confused by the fact that differences between the circumstances of the various minority communities can be bigger than the difference between the ethnic minorities as a whole and the white population. Nonetheless, it is clear from everyday experience that discrimination remains a pervasive influence. So what could or should be done?

Imagine that a racist employer would not take on ethnic minority workers because he believed them lazier, less intelligent or less dependable than their white counterparts. In the looking-glass world of simplistic economic theory, these attitudes would receive their just deserts. Enlightened employers would attract the best ethnic minority candidates, boosting their productivity and allowing them to undercut racist employers and drive them out of the market.

Howard Davies, the deputy governor of the Bank of England, therefore concluded in a recent

▶

■ **Exhibit 12.6 continued**

speech to the Equal Opportunities Commission that one policy response should be to take a tougher attitude to monopolies, thereby edging the economy closer to the perfectly competitive theoretical ideal.

But while there are many good reasons to promote competition, this may not be one of them. The reason is that employers may be engaging in 'statistical discrimination'. Predicting a would-be employee's potential productivity is expensive, time-consuming and inherently uncertain. If an employer discerns that the productivity of whites is on average higher than that for blacks – say because of educational differences – then he or she may use race as a low-cost screening method.

This is clearly undesirable ex post if a high-quality black candidate is passed over in favour of a low-quality white. But in a world of incomplete information it may be an entirely rational way ex ante for an employer to maximise his profits. If that were the case, then tougher competition might actually encourage this discrimination.

This same uncertainty about individual productivity also makes it problematic simply to legislate against discrimination, because it is difficult to prove when it is taking place. From a libertarian perspective, one might also argue that – however distasteful it is to right-thinking people that

employers, co-workers and customers should discriminate against ethnic minorities – that is not sufficient reason to legislate against it if it falls short of an incitement to racial hatred.

The best way to tackle racial disadvantage in the labour market may therefore be to concentrate on areas like education. Studies in the US have traditionally concluded that between 30 and 50 per cent of the black-white wage gap there is the result of discrimination. But Derek Neal of Chicago University and William Johnson of Virginia University argued last year that most of this residual in fact reflects a skill gap which can in turn be traced, at least in part, to observable differences in the family backgrounds and school environments of black and white children.**

In Britain the proportion of 16–24-year-olds from ethnic minorities in full-time education is already more than half as high again as the proportion of whites. Pressing home this advantage would probably be a more effective policy response than relying on competitive pressures or legalistic regulation.

*The Changing Distribution of Black and White Earnings and the Ethnic Wage Gap: Evidence for Britain, by D. Blackaby *et al.*, University of Wales, Swansea.
**The Role of Pre-market Factors in Black-White Wage Differences, by D. Neal and W. Johnson, NBER working paper 5124.

Source: Robert Chote (1996) *Financial Times*, 17 June.

REFERENCES

Atkinson, J. (1984) 'Manpower strategies for flexible organisations', *Personnel Management*, August.

Bahl, K. (1996) 'Equality enters the mainstream', *People Management*, 22 February.

Barron, R. D. and Norris, G. M. (1976) 'Sexual divisions and the dual labour market' in Barker, D. L. and Allen, S. (eds) *Dependence and Exploitation in Work and Marriage*. London: Longman.

Bygott, D.W. (1992) *Black in Britain*. Oxford: Oxford University Press.

Chope, C. (1987) in *Contract Compliance: The UK Experience*. London: IPM/IDS.

Colling, T. and Dickens, L. (1989) *Equality Bargaining – Why Not?* London: Equal Opportunities Commission.

DfEE (1997) *Labour Market and Skill Trends 1996/7*. London: Department for Education and Employment.

Dickens, L. Townley, B. and Winchester, D. (1988) *Tackling Sex Discrimination through Collective Bargaining*. London: Equal Opportunities Commission.

EOC (1986) *Fair and Efficient Selection*. London: Equal Opportunities Commission.

EOC (1996) *Changing Inequalities Between Women and Men: Twenty years of progress (1976–96)*. London: Equal Opportunities Commission.

Faludi, S. (1992) *Backlash: The Undeclared War Against Women*. London: Chatto.

Ford, V. (1996) 'Partnership is the secret of progress', *People Management*, 8 February.

Giddens, A. (1993) *Sociology*. 2nd edn. London: Polity Press.

Heilman, M. E. (1994) 'Affirmative action: some unintended consequences for working women', *Research in Organisational Behaviour*, 16.

Hillgard, E., Atkinson, R.L. and Atkinson, R. (1979) *Introduction to Psychology*. 7th edn. London: Harcourt Brace Jovanovich.

IPM/IDS (1987) *Contract Compliance: The UK Experience*. London: IPM/IDS.

Jewson, N. and Mason, D. (1986) 'The theory and practice of equal opportunities policies: liberal and radical approaches,' *Sociological Review*, 34(2), 307–34.

Kandola, R. and Fullerton, J. (1994) 'Diversity: more than just an empty slogan', *Personnel Management*, November 1994.

Leach, B. (1996) 'Disabled people and the equal opportunities movement' in Hales, G. (ed.) *Beyond Disability*. London: Sage.

Liff, S. (1995) 'Equal opportunities: continuing discrimination in a context of formal equality' in Edwards, P. K. (ed.) *Industrial Relations Theory and Practice in Britain*. Oxford: Blackwell.

Marchington, M. and Wilkinson, A. (1996) *Core Personnel and Development*. London: IPD.

Mason, D. (1994) 'Employment and the Labour Market', *New Community* 20, 2 January.

McEnrue, M. P. (1993) 'Managing diversity: Los Angeles before and after the riots', *Organisational Dynamics*, 21(3), 18–29.

Mirza, Q. (1995) *Race Relations in the Workplace*. Institute of Employment Rights pamphlet.

Morris, H. and Willey, B. (1996) *The Corporate Environment: A Guide for Human Resource Managers*. London: Financial Times Pitman Publishing.

Ollerearnshaw, S. and Waldeck, R. (1995) 'Taking action to promote equality', *People Management*, 23 February.

Paddison, L. (1990) 'The targeted approach to recruitment', *Personnel Management*, November.

Parkyn, A. (1991) 'Operating equal opportunities in the health service', *Personnel Management*, August.

Piore, M. J. (1975) 'Notes for a theory of labour market stratification', in Edwards, R., Reich, M. and Gordon, D. (eds) (1975) *Labour Market Segmentation*. Lexington, Mass.: DC Heath.

Rubenstein, M. (1991) 'Devising a sexual harassment policy', *Personnel Management*, February.

Vallance, E. (1995) *Business Ethics at Work*. Cambridge: Cambridge University Press.

Wrench, J. and Virdie, S. (1996) 'Organising the unorganised, 'Race', poor work and trade unions' in Ackers, P., Smith, C. and Smith, P. (eds) *The New Workplace and Trade Unionism*, London: Routledge.

Chapter 13

FLEXIBLE LABOUR MARKETS, FIRMS AND WORKERS

Stephanie Tailby

Learning objectives

By the end of this chapter, readers should be able to:

- understand the concept of labour flexibility and the meanings that have been attached to it;
- locate labour flexibility in the economic and political context of the 1980s and '90s;
- understand different dimensions of the 'flexibility debate' including the theory of 'flexible specialisation' and the model of the 'flexible firm';
- examine the forms of labour flexibility sought and achieved by employers in Britain and abroad;
- assess the outcomes of government and employer initiatives and the extent to which these have secured greater flexibility in the labour market and in the work process.

INTRODUCTION

In Britain, as in other Western industrialised countries in the 1980s and '90s, politicians, business leaders, trade union representatives, academics and journalists have been joined in a debate about the meaning and extent of labour flexibility. The concept defies exact definition; indeed, its application to a broad range of issues in the organisation and control of work and in the functioning of labour markets is demonstration of its considerable elasticity of meaning. Flexibility has been discussed in relation to the adaptability of wages; the versatility of workers within the production process; the ease of engaging and dismissing employees; working-time patterns; labour's mobility between firms, industries and geographical regions; employees' career paths and expectations; and many other issues.

The concept broadly denotes the quality of responsiveness to changing conditions, although dictionary definitions of flexible also suggest 'capable of being bent' and 'compliant' as synonyms. Flexibility is often interpreted in relation to its opposite – that is, as the absence of rigidity and constraint. As applied to the world of work and employment, however, this obviously raises the issue of whose interests are at stake. Practices deemed to be rigid by management, for example, may be the source of stability and security for employees. Consequently, job protection rights and the employer's freedom to hire and fire may be a source of conflict between the parties (*see* Exhibit 13.1).

The current 'flexibility debate' has developed in the context of the more turbulent economic conditions which have prevailed in the Western industrialised economies since the 1970s, and has ranged across different levels of analysis. At the macroeconomic level, attention has focused on the causes of the long-term rise in unemployment, in Western Europe in particular, and the adjustments required to bolster economic growth and enhance industry competitiveness and the rate of new job creation. Different analyses and prescriptions have been offered. While each places an emphasis on labour's adaptability as the route to economic recovery the different perspectives have attached different meanings to the notion of labour flexibility.

The neo-liberal perspective urges a need for greater labour market flexibility defined and measured in terms of the speed of short-term price and quantity adjustment in a changing economic environment – for example, the speed at which wage levels fall in response to a rise in the level of unemployment. This perspective prescribes government intervention to weaken or remove legal and institutional constraints to the disciplining force of the 'free market'. Within Europe, it has been championed most vigorously by the Conservative government in office in Britain until May 1997.

Alternative accounts have focused on labour's adaptability in the work process, and have construed flexibility in terms of versatility, creativity and inventiveness. The 'flexi-

■ Exhibit 13.1

Labour urged to extend worker rights

The government was yesterday challenged to grant workers protection against unfair dismissal from day one of their employment – a move that has already been ruled out by ministers.

The call came in a combative speech from John Edmonds, general secretary of the GMB general union, who was applauded when he said 'day one' rights had been promised by the previous Labour leader, John Smith – 'one politician who got this right'.

The previous Conservative government increased the amount of time employees must work for an organisation before qualifying for rights from six months to two years.

Mr Edmonds welcomed the government's commitment last week to publish a white paper on employment but noted that it had promised to maintain a flexible labour market.

'When I hear the Labour government using Tory phrases, I shiver a little', he said. 'Politicians who tell us that flexibility must be encouraged at all costs should not defend a law that makes working people who change jobs wait for two long years to achieve even the most modest protection against unfairness at work'.

Mr Edmonds also dismissed talk of possible compromises, which would reduce the qualifying period to one year or six months: 'Nowadays some employers are so bloody-minded that if people get employment rights after one year, we would see the introduction of 11-month contracts'.

Source: Andrew Bolger and Robert Taylor (1997) *Financial Times* 9 September.

ble specialisation' thesis, for example, asserts that across the advanced industrialised world mass production is giving way as the engine of growth. Commercial success is said to be dependent on the firm's ability to innovate and satisfy consumer demand for high quality, customised goods. The contribution of a technically multi-skilled and behaviourally cooperative workforce is regarded as central. In this perspective government intervention is encouraged to promote a new regulatory framework which tempers competition with cooperation between firms, their supplier companies and their employees.

The 'flexible firm' model, which was influential in Britain in the 1980s, prescribes a set of practices through which an organisation can achieve numerical, functional and financial flexibility – that is, the ability to adjust the numbers employed, the skills deployed and labour costs. In these ways, the model suggests, firms can become more responsive to rapid changes in markets and technology.

This chapter explores the various meanings that have been attached to the concept of flexibility, the theories and models that have identified greater flexibility as a key objective of employers, and the forms of flexibility actually sought and achieved by employing organisations. It is organised in four sections. The first considers different dimensions of the flexibility debate. The following three sections examine the empirical evidence on the development of functional, working-time and numerical flexibility. The discussion in these sections focuses on the British experience but where relevant draws comparisons with developments in other advanced industrial economies. The concluding section returns to issues of public policy and assesses the extent to which government policies in Britain have achieved their aim of rendering the labour market more competitive, flexible and efficient.

THE FLEXIBILITY DEBATES

Origins of the debates

Employers' interest in labour flexibility is certainly not new or specific to the past two decades. In Britain in the 1960s, for example, major manufacturing employers engaged in 'productivity bargaining', tying pay increases to changes in working practices and, in particular, greater interchange in craft and maintenance areas. A number varied their use of part-time and temporary workers in order to meet fluctuating product market demands. The labels of 'functional' and 'numerical flexibility' were not applied at the time, although clearly these employer initiatives would now be described in these terms. Indeed, since the late 1970s, 'flexibility' has been appended to such an enormously varied set of employer interventions that it would appear to be employers' overriding objective.

The explosion of interest in labour flexibility in Britain as in other advanced economies, in the 1980s and 90s, needs to be interpreted against changing economic and political conditions. For the first 25 years of the post-war period, most Western industrialised countries enjoyed an unprecedented phase of sustained economic growth, rising prosperity and high levels of employment. Economic growth decelerated in the 1970s, however, and has subsequently remained uncertain; periods of growth have intervened between the deep recessions of the early 1980s and early '90s. Unemployment increased in the 1970s and in many Western European countries increased further in the 1980s and 1990s (*see* Table 13.1).

■ Table 13.1 Standardised rates of unemployment in selected OECD countries, 1976–95 (%)

	1976	1980	1983	1986	1990	1993	1995
United States	7.6	7.0	9.5	6.9	5.6	6.9	5.5
Japan	2.0	2.0	2.6	2.8	2.1	2.5	3.1
Germany*	3.7	2.9	7.7	6.4	4.8	7.9	8.2
France	4.4	6.2	8.3	10.4	8.9	11.7	11.6
Italy	6.6	7.5	8.8	10.5	10.3	10.2	12.2
Spain	4.5	11.1	17.0	20.8	15.9	22.4	22.7
Sweden	1.6	2.0	3.9	2.8	1.8	9.5	9.2
United Kingdom	5.6	6.4	12.4	11.2	6.9	10.9	8.7
Total OECD	5.4	5.8	8.6	7.7	6.1	8.0	7.5
OECD EU †	5.0	6.4	10.0	10.5	8.1	10.9	11.0

Source: OECD Economic Outlook (1996).
* Up to and including 1992, data concern West Germany.
† Includes Germany, France, Italy, UK, Belgium, Finland, Ireland, Netherlands, Portugal, Spain and Sweden.

Competition has intensified in many industries and sectors. This reflects a variety of developments and notably the 'globalisation' of markets, which has been driven forward by the expansion of multinational activity. In some sectors there has been an accelerated pace of technological innovation, and in some product markets the established producer nations have been challenged by the industrialising countries of the Pacific Rim (South Korea, Singapore, Taiwan). Japan prefigured the success of these economies. From the 1970s its major corporations encroached on Western markets for automobiles and electronics and turned from the export of goods to the export of capital. The success of Japanese 'transplants' in Europe and the United States increased the pressure on Western competitors to adjust their production techniques and labour management practices. The impact of this challenge is likely to survive the disturbance caused by the financial turmoil in South-East Asia in the late 1990s.

■ Labour market deregulation

At the level of public policy, the neo-liberal prescription of labour market deregulation has dominated the agenda in recent years. Supporters of this position argue that where markets are highly competitive (in the sense of being fragmented and largely unregulated), prices and quantities adjust rapidly to changing economic conditions to ensure the optimal allocation of resources. Obversely, they identify legal and institutional interventions in the functioning of markets as sources of rigidity and inefficiency.

In support of these propositions, unfavourable comparisons have been drawn between the structure and functioning of labour markets in the United States and in the European Union (EU) countries. In the former, unemployment has fallen fairly rapidly after each of the recessions of the early 1980s and early '90s. In many of the EU countries, in contrast, the 'recovery' of employment has been much slower and far less dramatic. Rates of new job creation have been superior in the United States since the 1970s (Chote, 1997). The differential between USA and European performance on these measures, the argument runs, is due to the more weakly regulated and 'flexible' labour markets developed in the former. Employment growth in Europe is said to have been stymied by a set of 'institutional rigidities' in labour markets which have impeded adjustments to the more turbulent economic conditions.

State intervention and trade union bargaining power in European economies, it is asserted, have resulted in:

■ wages that are too rigid and that have priced workers out of jobs;

■ legally based employment protection systems which, by limiting employers' freedom to dismiss employees, have impeded the reallocation of labour from declining to expanding industries and deterred employers from creating new jobs;

■ social security systems that add to employers' costs and dampen the incentives for the unemployed to seek work.

The analysis is summed up in the notion of 'Eurosclerosis'. The prescription which flows from it is for governments in Europe to intervene to weaken the 'rigidities' and bring Europe's labour markets to resemble more closely the deregulated, 'flexible' labour markets of the US.

Most European governments intervened in the 1980s and '90s to refashion structures of labour market regulation. Few, however, pursued labour market deregulation as ardently as the Conservative government in office in Britain between 1979 and 1997. In this period, government ministers sought to reform comprehensively established labour market institutions, and to decentralise and individualise employee relations (*see* Chapter 6). Their interventions centred on the following areas:

■ *Trade union activity*: a complex set of legislative reforms, enacted on a 'step-by-step' basis, was aimed at reducing the power of the unions and giving managements greater freedom in the conduct of industrial relations.

■ *Employment rights*: statutory employment protection was reduced, principally by extending the qualifying periods of service required to claim unfair dismissal.

■ *Minimum wage protection*: this has traditionally been limited in the UK and was virtually eliminated with the abolition in 1993 of the wages council system, which had set legally enforceable minimum terms and conditions for workers in some industries.

■ *Social security*: the level and coverage of welfare benefits was steadily reduced with the aim of lessening the disincentives to labour force participation.

The Conservative government also resisted strenuously the extension of EU social and employment legislation, which it viewed as antithetical to the aim of creating a 'competitive, efficient and flexible labour market' (Employment Department, 1994, cited in Beatson, 1995a: 1) (*see also* Chapter 6).

But the Eurosclerosis analysis and its prescription of labour market deregulation have been criticised on a number of counts (e.g. Nolan, 1994). At an empirical level, the unfavourable comparison of EU with USA labour market performance is said to be misleading. Relatively weak regulation of USA labour markets in the 1970s did not result in lower unemployment, and while employment growth has been strong in the 1980s and '90s, the quality of the new jobs generated has been questioned. Moreover, there is fairly broad agreement that the growth of non-unionism and the social welfare reforms of the 1980s have done little to promote greater social cohesion in that country.

Labour market deregulation, with its emphasis on the downward flexibility of wages and erosion of employment rights, is said to be tantamount to a 'cheap labour' policy. Critics argue that it is short-termist and can do little to advance the competitive position of Western economies *vis-à-vis* lower-waged producers in Asia. Their alternative scenario is for the advanced economies to 'restructure upmarket'. At the level of the individual enterprise this involves the pursuit of competitive advantage through the upgrading of products, processes and labour skills. Exacting labour standards, it is argued, are required to close-off 'easy' routes to profitability (competition on the basis of low-waged, disposable labour) and to encourage the reconstruction of industry on the basis of a high quality, high skill, high technology and high productivity 'production model'. Within Europe these arguments have been presented in support of the extension of EU social and employment legislation.

The agenda of Britain's New Labour government, elected to power in May 1997, has been presented as a 'third way' between US-style market liberalisation and the European commitment to social rights and employment protection. Labour flexibility remains a central pillar of government policy, and Prime Minister Tony Blair has signalled his intention of extending the campaign for flexibility into Europe. 'Fairness at work', however, has been elevated as a public policy goal, in the interests of economic efficiency and social justice. Much of the industrial relations legislation of the 1980s is to remain. However, enhanced rights for individual employees and new collective rights for trade unions have been proposed in order to deter exploitation in the labour market and to encourage a new culture of 'partnership at work'.

The new Labour government has pledged to introduce a statutory national minimum wage and, in the 'Fairness at Work' White Paper published in May 1998, has proposed:

- the right of a union to be recognised by an employer where 40 per cent of the workforce ballot in favour of recognition, or where over 50 per cent of the workforce are union members;

- a reduction from two years to one in the qualifying period of service required by an employee to claim unfair dismissal, and the abolition of the maximum limit on industrial tribunal awards for unfair dismissal cases.

Measures to promote 'family-friendly' employment practices are also included in the White Paper, and follow partly from the new government's decision to reverse the UK's 'opt out' from the Social Chapter of the EU Maastricht Treaty.

It is too early to assess the impact of the proposed measures; many have as yet to be translated into legislation, let alone tested. On paper the 'Fairness at Work' proposals amount to 'the biggest extension of rights and trade union opportunities in a quarter of a century' (*Financial Times*, 21 May 1998). As Tony Blair emphasised, however, in his introduction to the White Paper, and partly to deflect criticism from business leaders, they will still leave the UK with one of the least regulated labour markets among the leading economies of the world.

■ Flexibility in work

The theme of 'upmarket restructuring', emphasised by many opponents of labour market deregulation, has been pursued by academics interested in the ways in which new production technologies are being deployed in the restructuring of work and employment relations. Some writers have made bold claims that there is currently underway a revolution in the organisation of production and work. An earlier regime of Fordist mass production is said to be giving way to a new era of competition based on the use of more flexible technologies and forms of work organisation. It is this rupture between production regimes, rather than rigidities in product and labour markets, that is seen as the cause of the economic turbulence experienced in the Western industrialised countries since the 1970s. There are different accounts, presenting both optimistic and pessimistic visions of the future of work (*see* Amin, 1994, for an overview). Of these, the best known in Britain (and most optimistic) is the theory of 'flexible specialisation' developed originally by Piore and Sabel (Sabel, 1982; Piore and Sabel, 1984).

Flexible specialisation

This theory asserts that changing market and technological conditions have undermined the success of a formerly dominant regime of mass production. It suggests that these conditions have also created the opportunity for a renewal of economic growth on the basis of a new regime of flexible specialisation.

Epitomised by the moving assembly-line techniques pioneered by Henry Ford at his car plants in the US in the 1920s and '30s, mass production technology involved the use of dedicated (single-purpose) machinery and Taylorist forms of work organisation in the manufacture of standardised goods for distribution to large, undifferentiated markets. Economic competition was dominated by the logic of economies of scale. Firms pursued volume growth, organised production into long runs of identical parts, and laid out factories to achieve a lineal flow of work between functionally specialised departments (machining, sub-assembly, final assembly, paint and inspection). The social organisation of production resonated with the rigidities of the technical system. The extreme horizontal division of labour deskilled production workers, who were paced by the speed of 'the line'.

Flexible specialisation theory suggests that while this system formerly afforded the basis for steadily increasing levels of productivity, its viability since the 1960s has been undermined by the saturation and subsequent disintegration of mass markets. Consumers are said to have asserted a preference for quality and style and for goods customised to their individual tastes.

The coincidence of these changes in demand with the development of microelectronics production equipment, it is argued, is encouraging the re-emergence of a revitalised form of nineteenth century craft production – that is, *flexible specialisation*, which involves the use of general purpose machinery and skilled, adaptable workers in the manufacture of a wide and changing range of semi-customised goods for specialised niche markets.

The idea broadly is that because the new production technologies can be reprogrammed more swiftly to operate to different specifications, they reduce the size of the economic batch. Consequently, firms are able to reap economies of scope – the ability to shift cost-efficiently from the production of one good to another (Tomaney, 1994: 161) – and with this exploit the potential of the new market openings for quality, customised goods. As this potential is realised, it is suggested, economies of scale become less significant as the basis of inter-firm competition and small firms are placed on a more equitable footing with large corporations.

The new product-market strategy is said to facilitate and to demand far-reaching changes in workforce skills and methods of labour management, amounting to a reversal of the Taylorist and Fordist traditions of the past. Reskilling rather than deskilling is now

463

the theme. Flexible specialisation demands broadly skilled, adaptable workers who are able to use the new production technologies to engineer a variety of models and semi-customised goods and to switch flexibly between a variety of functions. Mental and manual work are thus recomposed and tasks are reconstituted into more complete job roles.

In short, flexible specialisation is presented as a progressive regime which confers benefits on firms and workers alike. Jobs are enriched and employment security is enhanced. This is because managements are increasingly dependent on the skills of their employees and since these skills cannot be replaced easily by recruiting from the external labour market, firms are obliged to seek ways and means of limiting labour turnover. Labour has now to be treated as an asset rather than a variable cost, and in order to motivate employees and secure their commitment to enterprise goals managements are obliged to modify hierarchical control in favour of a partnership approach in employee relations.

Flexible specialisation theory has aroused a great deal of academic interest. Most commentators agree that it captures some of the features of current developments in manufacturing methods. However, its analysis of these developments and the broader theory of industrial change in which it is embedded have been questioned (Williams *et al.*, 1987; Hyman, 1988). Critics contend that the analysis of economic change focuses too narrowly on manufacturing technologies and market structures, and that the mass production–flexible specialisation dichotomy is too rigid to capture past and current developments in production systems. The more specific charges are that the theory:

■ overstates the dominance of Fordist mass production in the twentieth century;·

■ exaggerates the rigidities of mass production; Henry Ford was exceptional in insisting his customers could have any colour car provided it was black;

■ relies on mainly impressionistic evidence of the break-up of mass markets;

■ overstates the flexibility of the new production technologies;

■ understates the continuing importance of scale economies.

In addition, critics have questioned whether the benefits of flexible specialisation for labour are as great as the theory suggests. Hyman (1988), for example, draws attention to the ways in which the new production and information technologies can be used by managements to direct and monitor more closely employee performance – that is, to reproduce and reinforce hierarchical management control.

■ 'Japanisation'

The idea that high-volume assembly-line production is inherently rigid – in the sense of confining firms to a narrow product range and workers to a narrow task – is apparently challenged by the innovations in manufacturing methods pioneered by Toyota and other large industrial corporations in Japan. Denoted variously as Japanese 'just-in-time' production and Japanese 'lean production', these innovations have aroused a great deal of interest among academics and managers in the West. Whether or not they can be regarded as *the* basis of Japan's post-war economic success is debatable. Nevertheless, they have come to be seen as one element of the Japanese economic system that might be emulated in other national contexts.

Various interpretations have been placed on these manufacturing techniques and the labour management practices associated with them. Womack *et al.* (1990) regard lean production as a further stage of development beyond mass production. In contrast, Peter Wickens (1993: 85), formerly senior personnel manager at Nissan's UK plant in the north-east, suggests that the system should be viewed as a set of innovations which overcome the limitations of conventional mass production without departing from its basic principles.

A popular view is that Western approaches to mass production have traded-off volume and quality in ways that have generated wasted output and production time (for example, the production of faulty parts and goods, excess stocks and work-in-progress inventories). In contrast, the Japanese approach sets the elimination of waste (in terms of underutilised or inefficiently employed human and material resources) as a guiding philosophy. Wickens argues that the system 'uses less of everything' (1993: 77). But it is perhaps more accurate to say that it uses everything more intensively so that, in comparison with a conventional mass production plant operating with the same number of employees, and type and amount of capital investment, a higher level of output is achieved.

A key goal is low-inventory/minimum 'buffer' stock production. This is pursued through a set of interrelated practices:

- quick machine set-up times, which offset the economies of long production runs and high levels of inventories, and also facilitate mixed-batch production;

- a cellular, as opposed to a sequential, production sequence; the regrouping of machinery into manufacturing cells reduces the physical distance between workstations and inhibits the build-up of stocks;

- 'just-in-time' production scheduling; parts and sub-assemblies are produced and delivered just in time for the next stage in production, thereby creating more of a flow-line at pre-assembly stages. The just-in-time principle is extended backwards to the company's suppliers and subcontractors.

Low-inventory production necessitates minimal disruptions. Since there are no 'buffers', ostensibly minor problems (for example, malfunctioning equipment or faulty parts) have a magnified impact and can bring production to a halt. Hence, the concern is to build quality control into the system and to rectify problems at source.

These objectives require a functionally flexible workforce. Supporting the system of cellular manufacturing, workers are grouped into teams and assigned problem solving and quality control responsibilities in addition to their other production tasks. There are few 'indirect' employees and direct production workers are kept fully employed because they are expected 'to do "on the spot" whatever is required to solve problems and keep subsequent processes from being starved of parts' (Schonberger, 1983).

The system therefore requires a specific configuration of labour skills. Workers must be technically proficient in a range of tasks and motivated to act on their own initiative and do whatever is required to maintain the continuity of defect-free output. They must be adaptable, cooperative and self-disciplined (Sayer, 1986).

Interpretations of Japanese work and employment practices differ quite markedly (*see* Dohse *et al.*, 1985; IPD, 1996, for useful summaries). One view is that these practices depart in significant respects from the principles of Taylorism and amount to a 'responsibility' as opposed to a 'control model'. The idea is that Japanese management methods are effective because they unleash, rather than confine, labour's creativity and innovation potential. Shopfloor employees are highly motivated because managements have entrusted to them greater autonomy and influence and have created for them jobs which are meaningful, challenging and involving. Moreover, they are willing to contribute their knowledge and skills to the 'continuous improvement' of the production system because managements have reciprocated with the guarantee of job security.

There is, however, a less favourable interpretation which emphasises the similarity with Taylorism. Continuous improvement involves the constant rationalisation of the production system, especially the elimination of wasteful movements, and the standardisation of tasks. Productivity increases are achieved through the intensification of work – that is, through the enlargement (as opposed to enrichment) of jobs and perfection of the flow line. Employees are expected to contribute to the continual improvement of the production system, leading to the claim that:

> 'Toyotism' is ... not an alternative to Taylorism but rather a solution to its classic problem of the resistance of workers to placing their knowledge of production in the service of rationalisation. (Dohse *et al.*, 1985: 128)

Worker resistance is lowered because 'management prerogatives are largely unlimited' (Dohse *et al.*, 1985: 141).

Within the enterprise there is no independent union 'voice'. Company unions in Japan are dependent upon the market success of the individual enterprise and consequently have to be broadly supportive of company policies and goals. The job security enjoyed – at least until recently – by core workers in large firms has encouraged conformity because such workers have limited labour market mobility. With company-specific skills, and lifetime employment which is non-transferable between firms, such workers cannot quit in the expectation of securing comparable terms and conditions with another employer. They are obliged to be compliant because their chances of advancement are confined to the internal labour market and dependent upon their manager's assessment of their individual contribution.

Core terms and conditions have been enjoyed by only a minority of Japanese workers (Thompson and McHugh, 1995: 86). The system of lifetime employment has been supported by strong economic growth – in the period to 1990 at least – and by the 'dualistic nature of the Japanese production system and labour market' (Tomaney, 1994: 168). 'Peripheral' employees in small firms and organisations subcontracted to the large corporations have not had job security and their wages in many instances have been relatively low. Large corporations have been able to provide core workers with job security because they have been able to use temporary workers and their networks of subcontracted suppliers to provide 'buffers' against market fluctuations (Dohse *et al.*, 1985).

■ The 'flexible firm'

The theory of flexible specialisation tries to explain the broad dynamic of industrial change and the origins of 'global' economic instability since the 1970s. The literature on Japanisation is concerned more narrowly with the sources of one country's relative economic success in a specific historical period, although many accounts present the Japanese production system as a new 'organisational paradigm' which is transforming the nature of global competition in leading industrial sectors. The model of the 'flexible firm' developed by John Atkinson (1984, 1985) and his colleagues is more parochial in its concerns (Procter *et al.*, 1994: 226).

Rooted in the British context, the model delineates an organisational response to product market and technological uncertainty that is centred on the reorganisation of the internal labour market. Its proposals nevertheless resonate with some of those emerging from other dimensions of the flexibility debate. Thus, as Wood (1989: 2) suggests, the flexible firm has some similarities with Japan's large, primary sector companies.

The flexible firm segments its workforce into core and peripheral groups in order to achieve functional, numerical and financial flexibility.

Core workers are those who possess key, company-specific skills which cannot be secured readily through the external labour market. Employed on a full-time basis, they are trained and rewarded to supply *functional flexibility*; they are expected to have polyvalent skills and to acquire new competencies as changes in technology or markets demand. To protect its investment in these skills, and to encourage employee commitment to enterprise goals, the firm offers core workers job security and access to other 'primary labour market' conditions, including relatively good pay and the prospects of career advancement.

Peripheral workers are less central to the core business and, since their skills can be secured more easily in the external labour market, they are less protected from its competitive pressures. It is the ease of their disposability which is key. Insecurely, irregularly or indirectly employed, they supply the *numerical flexibility* which enables the firm to adjust rapidly the level of labour inputs to meet fluctuations in demand and to protect employment security for the core. The peripheral group comprises three categories of employees:

- full-time workers who perform relatively routinised tasks which offer few career prospects and which are vulnerable to market or technological change;

- workers employed on 'non-standard' contracts such as part-timers, temporary workers and public subsidy trainees;

- distance workers who are not employed directly by the firm and who supply their labour under contracts for services (as opposed to contracts of service) – for example, subcontractors, self-employed workers and agency temporary staff.

The advantages of the flexible firm model for employers are said to include:

- higher productivity from the core workforce;

- lower wage and non-wage costs from the use of peripheral groups;

- the ability to tailor employment levels to demand conditions and, with this, to reduce the costs of carrying 'excess' staff (Claydon, 1997: 108).

The flexible firm model has attracted a significant amount of interest from managers, academics and journalists in Britain, yet it has also been heavily criticised, in part for a lack of conceptual clarity.

One criticism that recurs in the literature is that the model is difficult to interpret and to evaluate because its status and purpose are ambiguous (e.g. *see* Pollert, 1987). Its proponents insist that it is 'only an analytical tool to help us understand what is going on' (Atkinson and Gregory, 1986: 14). They also suggest, however, that firms are adopting the model and predict that 'this new division of labour will be a permanent feature of the labour market for years to come' (p. 13). In other words, they present the flexible firm as an analytical device and also as an explanation of what is actually taking place (Claydon, 1997).

A second criticism is that the model's key concepts are imprecisely defined and therefore difficult to operationalise. This complicates its use as an analytical tool and attempts to 'test' it against available empirical evidence. The model suggests various ways in which 'core' and 'peripheral' groups might be identified – on the basis of employment security, employment status (full-time, part-time, temporary, etc.), skills, tasks, and so on. Each of these, and all combinations, give rise to difficulties:

> ... the identification of the core ... can easily become circular; core workers have secure employment, and the fact of such employment is used as evidence for the presence of a core. If the core is more clearly defined by both its employment status (and especially its security and legal rights) and its tasks, there is a problem because some groups may have relatively secure employment but not be treated as part of the core of the business; whilst such 'peripheral' workers as part-time women workers in retailing may be central to the functioning and profitability of the business. (Wood, 1989: 5)

It is worth emphasising that any attempt to evaluate which skills are core is complicated by the fact that:

> 'skill' is socially constructed and also gendered. Thus, skills which are essential to an organisation, but are performed by women, may be socially constructed as semi- or un-skilled, and may not be rewarded by the advantages of an internal labour market (by pay, promotion prospects and other non-wage benefits). (Pollert, 1987: 17)

There is therefore the danger of confusing new divisions with an existing, gender-based segmentation of the workforce.

Given these conceptual difficulties, it is perhaps not surprising that the debate on the model's 'fit' with available empirical evidence has been heated.

FUNCTIONAL FLEXIBILITY

Functional (or task) flexibility, as suggested, refers to a firm's ability to allocate and real-locate employees among a wide range of tasks. It is a broad label and has been applied to a variety of types of change in working practices. These range from some relaxation and reorganisation of job boundaries – as, for example, where production employees are required to take on routine inspection or maintenance tasks – through to multiskilling and the introduction of teamworking.

These latter terms are often also used loosely. Multiskilling 'proper' involves the acquisition of additional skills, as, for example, where maintenance craftsmen become proficient in electrical as well as mechanical trades (or vice versa). And teamworking, in its 'most developed or purest sense', refers to:

the granting of autonomy to workers by management to design and prepare work schedules, to monitor and control their own work tasks and methods, to be more or less self–managing. There may also be considerable flexibility between different skill categories, such that skilled employees do unskilled tasks when required and formerly unskilled employees would receive additional training to permit them to assume responsibility for more skilled tasks. (Geary, 1994: 641–2)

It is these latter types of change which are emphasised in the more enthusiastic accounts of functional flexibility.

Each of the perspectives considered in the preceding section – flexible specialisation theory, the literature on 'Japanisation' and the flexible firm model – identifies greater functional flexibility as a means of enhancing productivity, quality and enterprise competitiveness. Each suggests that benefits accrue to core employees as well as to company owners and managers. Employees are said to gain more interesting, involving and 'enriched' jobs; greater employment security; and the benefits of a more participative managerial regime. Critics contend that these are overly optimistic accounts which confuse job enlargement with job enrichment, and which neglect the work-intensifying character of lean production regimes (dubbed as 'mean production' by some writers and as 'management by stress', *see* Parker and Slaughter, 1988).

These debates have raised questions about the extent of functional flexibility, the character of the changes, and the forms of employment and labour market regulation required to support the emergence of the new work regimes. Thus, while some commentators have viewed the tough anti-union stance of the former Conservative government in Britain and its programme of labour market deregulation as supportive of an 'employers' flexibility offensive' (e.g. Atkinson and Gregory, 1986: 13), others have argued that these measures have reinforced existing constraints to innovation (e.g. Nolan, 1989). Able to respond to immediate competitive pressures through labour-shedding and other cost-cutting changes in production, firms may have been deflected from the investments required to 'restructure upmarket' and enhance long-run competitiveness.

This section considers the empirical evidence. It looks first at the survey data and case studies on the extent and character of changes in functional flexibility in Britain, then turns briefly to consider some international comparisons.

■ Changes in functional flexibility in Britain

The debates on functional flexibility have centred largely on developments in manufacturing, and much of the empirical research relates to this sector. This is not to suggest that employers outside manufacturing have been disinterested. Studies have documented initiatives to secure greater flexibility in the work process in branches of the private services, in particular the financial services (e.g. O'Reilly, 1992) and in some areas of public sector services. As Vickery and Wurzburg (1996) note, however, the pressures to restructure activities on the basis of new, flexible work regimes have been most acute in industries most exposed to international competition. Consequently, attention has focused largely on developments in manufacturing and the following discussion has a similar bias.

Evidence relating to functional flexibility has come from workplace surveys (e.g. NEDO, 1986; Daniel, 1987; ACAS, 1988; Cross, 1988; Millward *et al.*, 1992), surveys of collective agreements (Marsden and Thompson, 1990; Ingram, 1991; Dunn and Wright, 1994) and a number of company case studies. The surveys relate largely to the 1980s and, as Elger (1991: 50) has pointed out, several of these are non-representative in the strict sense of the term. Problems of interpretation are compounded by the varied sectors and time periods covered. The case studies by design focus on the particular and, quite often, the exceptional, but do provide rich insights into the dynamics of change.

Focusing explicitly on manufacturing, Elger has reviewed the 1980s' survey evidence and case study data relating primarily to the motor industry. His analysis, Beatson's (1995a) briefer commentary on the survey data and Legge's (1995) interpretation of more recent case study evidence converge towards a number of broad conclusions.

■ Widespread but modest change

There is ample evidence to suggest that, in manufacturing at least, there have been fairly widespread moves towards greater functional flexibility. The changes have been real and significant. By and large, however, they have been more modest than those highlighted in the more celebratory accounts of functional flexibility and, according to Beatson (1995a: 53) have delivered a degree of flexibility which is modest by international standards.

Thus, the 1980s' survey data are consistent in reporting an uneven and generally limited movement towards multiskilling. Cross's (1988) study of 238 manufacturing sites, which was biased towards sites making change, is illustrative. He found that while at approximately 50 per cent of the sites there had been concerted efforts to revise existing practices, few had made significant changes to either production operator or engineering craft jobs in the period 1981–8, and that by 1988 only 18 per cent of the sites had developed substantial inter-craft or craft–operator overlap. A 1990 Income Data Services (IDS) 'survey' report concluded similarly that 'change for the most part is very gradual and concentrated in quite narrow sectors' and that the 'major demarcations between different groups of craftsmen and between craft and production workers continue'. Most studies found some relaxation of job boundaries and increased mobility between production operator grades, and some involvement of operators in inspection and routine maintenance. There was less evidence of teamworking; only 12 per cent of the 584 establishments in the ACAS (1988) survey reported this, more sophisticated, form of flexible working in operative areas.

Of course these survey findings are dated. Thus while they present a picture of 'usually modest and incremental change' (Elger, 1991: 53), the cumulative effect might be anticipated as more advanced forms of flexibility by the late 1990s. Certainly some of the case studies suggest that earlier flexibility initiatives had gained a 'head of steam' (e.g. *see* the Rover case study p. 476). Others, however, provide evidence of a dampening of an earlier zeal.

Even in the 1980s there were examples of more 'radical and strategic initiatives' as, for example, the efforts of major car manufacturers to 'Japanise' their operations in response to the initiatives of inward investors such as Nissan (Elger, 1991: 60–1). A 1995 Industrial Relations Services (IRS) study reports the knock-on effects of these changes for the automotive components sector. The introduction of working practices typically associated with the Japanese – including cellular manufacturing and teamworking – had 'significantly accelerated since 1990' (IRS, 1995a: 9), partly because vehicle manufacturers were placing heavier demands on their supplier companies. Yet 'teamworking' in this sector embraced a variety of practices, some rather less innovative than others. Moreover, while the companies surveyed appeared to be emulating Japanese working practices, few were making concerted efforts to recast their employee relations strategies along the same lines. In other words, the pace of change had accelerated but the breadth and depth of change remained in doubt.

■ Limits to full flexibility

Many of the more recent case studies reinforce this impression that in Britain employers' objectives have been relatively modest, falling some way short of the 'radical change' projected in the theoretical literature on flexible working. Elger concluded from his review of the 1980s' data that multiskilling has rarely been a priority for employers (1991: 55):

> Rather, the dominant rationale in reorganising both craft and non-craft work has been to reduce the 'porosity' and increase the intensity of labour, as much by cutting down pauses and waiting time as by increasing effort more directly.

Similarly, the 1994 IDS study of multiskilling notes that in general the aim has not been to create an 'all-round craftsman' but rather to equip maintenance craftsmen with 'the skills necessary to progress specific tasks more quickly, by avoiding the need to call on other craftsmen' (IDS, 1994a: 1).

Even where companies have espoused the goal of 'full flexibility', their objectives have often been more modest or have been tempered by pragmatic considerations. For example, a 1992 IRS report looked at how the flexibility deals negotiated among four companies and their unions in the 1980s had operated in practice. At two of these companies (Mobil Coryton and Toshiba Consumer Products) the agreements had 'represented part of a "big bang" for labour flexibility by establishing the principle of a total end to demarcation'. At Toshiba Consumer Products, as at CWS Deeside, the new working practices introduced in the 1980s had formed part of a 'greenfield' site agreement. And at Babcock Energy, as well as Mobil Coryton, the deals had been effected at a 'crisis time' of financial difficulty.

All four organisations reported that the agreements had played a key role in enterprise survival and/or success. Yet at each, by the early 1990s, there were signs that 'the limits of the usefulness of agreements to introduce flexible working practices have been, or are close to being, reached'. Managers had secured a considerable degree of control over labour deployment and did not face demarcation ('who does what') disputes. Yet they had come to question the extent to which the total interchangeability of labour 'is desirable or viable in practical terms'. Those interviewed argued that 'some specialisation by employees has proved essential, especially in the technologically sophisticated environment of the oil refinery' (IRS, 1992a: 9). The companies had concluded that the costs of total interchangeability (in particular, training costs) outweighed the potential benefits, given that in practice many of the 'complex skills' were used only by a small number of employees.

Greenfield sites are often regarded as the most likely location for innovative work and employee relations practices. Clark's (1995) study of change management at Pirelli General's new, fully-automated plant, opened near Aberdare in South Wales in 1988, conveys the innovating zeal of plant managers and also their pragmatism. At an older plant, located near the new and closed down in favour of the latter's development, agreement had been reached with the unions in 1983 that there would be 'full flexibility of personnel' across and within traditional demarcations. This agreement had been modified subsequently. With the opening of the new plant, management concluded a new, single-union agreement which contained the provision that all non-management staff could be deployed totally flexibly between tasks and different areas of the factory (within the constraints of their level of training). This became a contractual requirement for employees. Part of the novelty of the agreement was the expectation that employees would acquire skills from other occupational areas; in other words, that demarcation would be relaxed across the production, maintenance and clerical areas. Under conditions apparently favourable to 'full flexibility', however, it had become obvious by 1990 that this had 'neither been required nor used' (Clark, 1995: 153). There had been no flexibility of staff between the three main occupational areas, and the degree of flexibility achieved within these areas varied widely. In 1990, a formal retreat from full flexibility was signalled by an agreement 'capping' the number of skill modules which an individual employee could take and prescribing the 'primary' and 'secondary' areas of responsibility. Clark (1995: 152–3) identifies six reasons for this retreat:

- *The 'horses for courses' principle*: recognition that some employees are by temperament, interests and abilities more suited to certain areas of work than others.
- *Specialist knowledge*: managers had recognised the benefits (as, for example, in terms of contribution to quality control) of staff knowing their own job intimately.
- *Ownership of particular work areas*: management's recognition that regular allocation to one main work area encouraged commitment to that area, attention to quality, rectification and so on.
- *Training*: acceptance that 'good trainers' are those well-versed in their area of specialism.
- *Skill retention*: the idea that skills can be retained only through regular practice.
- *Tight staffing levels*: in some areas (notably administration) the specificity of individual jobs combined with tight staffing levels to limit the scope for staff to be released for training in other tasks.

Consequently, 'full flexibility' had neither been sought nor achieved. Yet as Clark suggests, the significance of the changes actually pursued should not be underplayed. He argues that a 'quiet revolution' had taken place between the working practices of the old plant and those of the new. Plant managers had achieved in practice what they had set out to achieve, 'namely full flexibility to do what they wanted'. The tangible expression of this was 'a major task and job enlargement, with most producers covering up to five or six machine processes where they had previously only covered one' (1995: 153).

■ Employee gains and losses

The movement towards greater functional flexibility in manufacturing in Britain, therefore, has embraced a variety of initiatives. For the most part these 'change efforts' have been relatively modest. Even the more radical initiatives amount to rather less than the 'paradigmatic shift' in production and work regimes suggested in the more celebratory accounts of functional flexibility. It is reasonable to assume that the benefits accruing to employees have also been less substantial.

Much of the empirical research confirms this and points to the job-enlarging, work-intensifying character of the changes pursued. Case studies of ostensibly more radical work reorganisation initiatives, in particular the moves to establish lean production techniques, tend to reinforce the broad picture rather than providing evidence of a transformation in the direction of polyvalent, high trust teamworking (Elger, 1991: 61). Thus, while teamworking within cellular manufacturing systems may be organised to allow employees greater discretion over the scheduling of work and job assignments, the introduction of new, computerised production control systems have simultaneously afforded managements tighter (if less obtrusive) control over employee performance (Bratton, 1991, cited in Geary, 1994: 648). And, in many instances – including the exemplar company, Nissan – more traditional forms of managerial supervision have been retained, indicating that 'conventional forms of authority relations persist' (Geary, 1994: 648–9). The elimination of 'buffers' – excess stocks and indirect quality inspection personnel – under just-in-time systems is intended to accelerate the rate of throughput and several studies have reported the employee's experience as one of an intensified and more stressful pace of work (Delbridge and Turnbull, 1992; Garrahan and Stewart, 1992).

Nevertheless, much of the case study based literature suggests that it is inaccurate to view the new work regimes as having either a uniformly negative or uniformly positive impact on employees. Referring explicitly to lean production systems, Rees *et al.,* (1996: 76) argue that:

> the reality of employees' experiences will tend to be a mixture of benefits and costs. Working within lean systems may be more varied and rewarding; at the same time, the nature of work may become more intense, stressful and hazardous. Or again, whilst teams can undoubtedly be sources of group support and assistance, they can simultaneously provide the vehicle for coercive pressure.

Elger, who veers towards a more pessimistic view of the employees' experience, also accepts that the evidence of work intensification should not 'conceal real sources of satisfaction even in modest forms of job enlargement and flexibility on the shop floor' (1991: 56).

Experiments with 'genuine empowerment' have been comparatively rare (Edwards and Wright, 1996), but studies suggest that such arrangements can provoke positive employee responses, even where effort levels are increased. Two studies are illustrative and also suggest the ways in which the organisational and economic context can mediate employees' experience of the new work systems.

At Pirelli General's new automated plant, employee self-supervision was a management objective from the outset. Clark notes that while many staff were initially sceptical, attitudes had changed by 1990. The majority of the producers interviewed reported that:

> the responsibility and freedom they exercised in their work – which resulted from the combination of flexible working, multi-skilling and self-supervision – had led to a much greater sense of job satisfaction compared with their previous jobs, even though this often involved intensified work effort over a shift. (1995: 154–5)

These responses need to be interpreted against the specific features of the plant (a new site, representing a significant capital investment – and therefore enhanced job security prospects – in an area depleted of 'core' production jobs) and its carefully recruited workforce. The personality of job applicants and their attitudes to teamworking were scrutinised at the selection stage (Clark, 1995: 139–40).

Edwards and Wright (1996) investigated the development of a 'high involvement work system' at Alcan's aluminium smelter at Lynemouth. The new work arrangements at this brownfield site included teamworking in its 'purest' sense. Edwards and Wright report a positive employee response. Workers interviewed cited an increase in stress and pressure but also increased job satisfaction, a greater ability to take decisions and better work relations with their colleagues.

Three interrelated sets of factors are seen as supporting the success of the new work arrangements:

- the trauma of a recent and major redundancy programme;
- the continuous process technology and pre-existing division of labour which emphasised group work;
- management–union support for the introduction of teamworking.

The plant is virtually 100 per cent unionised, and union involvement in the introduction of change satisfied employees that their interests had been represented.

High involvement work systems are intended to deliver high performance, high commitment and high involvement. The success of the arrangements at Lynemouth was reflected in workers' increased job satisfaction (high involvement), improvements in productivity and decreases in overtime, absenteeism and accident rates (high performance). There were also signs of high commitment but expressed largely in terms of employees' greater diligence in the execution of job tasks. Evidence of greater employee identification with the company and its values, or the emergence of 'high trust' worker–management relations, was thin. Edwards and Wright relate this in part to continuing uncertainty over the future of the plant in the context of volatile product market conditions.

■ Role of the trade unions

The widespread moves in the direction of greater functional flexibility in British manufacturing have been pursued in an economic, political and legal context hostile to trade unionism. Manufacturing industry, traditionally a union 'stronghold', was hard hit in the recessions of the early 1980s and early '90s, and the long-term decline in manufacturing employment accelerated sharply. Between 1979 and 1996, the number of employees fell by over 40 per cent, from just over 7 million to approximately 4 million, and manufacturing's share of all employees in employment in Britain declined from just under a third to just under a fifth. Union density dropped, affected in particular by the closure of large manufacturing sites. The Conservative government's programme of restrictive trade union legislation was implemented over this period.

This context has afforded managements a greater leeway in deciding whether to involve, or to marginalise, the trade unions in the implementation of change. The evidence is somewhat mixed. Cross's study (1988) suggests that managements have been prepared to introduce change unilaterally. Geary (1994), however, identifies the reasons why managers in many instances have been anxious to bring the unions 'on board'. Union support has often been viewed as crucial to the success of the new working practices and a means of legitimating change. Hence even where managements have asserted forcefully their 'right to manage' they have generally sought to maintain the relationship, albeit with a body of stewards perceived as more moderate.

The unions have been aware of their diminishing power resources and have generally resigned themselves to accepting change, in the interests of saving jobs and ensuring the survival of the enterprise (Geary, 1994: 645). Thus, as Dunn and Wright's (1994) study of 100 collective agreements drawn from 50 bargaining units in both 1979 and 1990 suggests, many managers have used established collective bargaining procedures to negotiate change because they have been able to secure significant reforms of the substantive provisions of these agreements:

> Substantive provisions record a considerable shift towards more flexible working practices, as demonstrated in job descriptions, grading structures and flexibility agreements. (Dunn and Wright, 1994: 38)

The paradox of these trade union agreements is, as Geary observes, that 'they often contain clauses which prohibit further negotiations over subsequent changes in working practices' (1994: 646). Dunn and Wright cite the example of the Ford 1990 agreement, in which the elimination of specific (union) job controls was agreed in detail 'while subsequent practices were left for management to define' (1994: 37–8).

The reassertion of managerial prerogative in the workplace was an objective of   the Conservative government's restrictive trade union legislation. The impact of this legislation on economic performance, however, remains a major area of controversy. Commentators such as Crafts (1991) and Metcalf (1989) have argued that by facilitating changes in work organisation and working practices, the government's industrial relations reforms made a major contribution to the upsurge in manufacturing productivity in the 1980s. Nolan (1996), in contrast, finds little evidence of a 'structural transformation' of the supply side of the economy. Highlighting the 'legacy of under-investment – in new technology, plant, and people', he suggests that the productivity gains of the 1980s were rooted in three interlinked factors:

> ... labour shedding; incremental changes in production organisation; and what some ana-
> lysts have referred to as the 'fear' factor, the central idea being that the threefold increase
> in unemployment in the early 1980s made employees more likely to acquiesce to new and
> more intensive (but not necessarily more efficient) work routines. (1996: 116–7)

This assessment suggests that the sources of change offer an insubstantial basis on which
to build new 'high-trust' production and work regimes.

While job insecurity remains pervasive in Britain in the 1990s, it seems that in some
instances managements have taken steps to cushion their 'core' employees from the
vagaries of market forces. Scarborough and Terry's (1996) study of the Rover Group's
'New Deal' is interesting in this respect.

Rover's 'New Deal'

The Rover Group and its predecessors (Austin Rover, British Leyland) in the 1970s and
early '80s had exhibited in the extreme the difficulties of the car industry in Britain.
Output was falling while in other European countries producers were raising production
levels. Exports declined and employment contracted massively. Like other Western car
producers, the company experienced the pressure of Japanese 'lean production' methods
in the 1980s as the major Japanese car manufacturers were rapidly expanding production
from their UK-based plants.

The company's response and its efforts to emulate the methods of its Japanese competitors developed over a number of years and in a number of phases. In the 1980s, under
the leadership of Michael Edwardes, company managers had asserted their 'right to manage' over trade union opposition, shed jobs and imposed a new and tighter regime over
the control of work.

By the early 1990s, however, managers had come to the view that the limits of change
and 'improvement' through job losses had been reached (Scarborough and Terry, 1996:
9). Moreover, the set-backs and advances recorded in the efforts to establish Japanese-
style work practices – including teamworking and a total quality programme from
1986/7 – had demonstrated that managerial control alone was insufficient to achieve the
productivity and quality goals of lean production.

> By 1992 Rover management had come to realise the self–limiting implications of pro-
> duction systems founded on strict management control. (Rees et al., 1996: 103)

Thus the 'New Deal' package, agreed with the unions in 1992, can be seen 'as the culmination of the group's attempts to change its industrial relations and working practices
to enable lean production to take place' (IRS, 1992b: 12).

The principal features of the New Deal included:

- single-status terms and conditions;
- a greater emphasis on teamworking and continuous improvement;
- full flexibility;

- job security;
- an integrated manual/staff grade structure;
- streamlined trade union arrangements and an updated procedure agreement.

The promise of job security to the workforce in return for flexibility was considered by management to be the key to securing employees' commitment to continuous improvement. Workers could not be expected to participate in efficiency improvements if they perceived that their jobs would be lost as a result. Scarborough and Terry suggest, however, that perhaps the most important element of the New Deal was the way in which it was struck.

> For it effectively signalled the advent of a greater spirit of co–operation between management and trade unions, recasting employee relations as the pursuit of common goals rather than a site of conflict. (Rees *et al.*, 1996: 103)

They argue that the New Deal has helped to establish the 'institutional and psychological conditions' for leaner ways of working. But they caution that the productivity gains achieved since 1992 cannot be attributed solely to the advent of teamworking and other lean techniques. These initiatives are still patchy in their implementation at shopfloor level, and other changes – in product design and production facilities – have been introduced in parallel with the new ways of working. Investment has been ploughed in by BMW, the company's new owners since 1994.

The Rover example is important and serves to emphasise that incremental changes can evolve into fairly radical work and employee relations restructuring initiatives at brownfield sites. However, the New Deal has attracted much attention precisely because the changes amount to something more exceptional than the average. Thus while there have been efforts at other brownfield sites – in the automotive and other sectors – to adopt Japanese working practices, these initiatives often remain *ad hoc* and incremental and largely divorced from attempts to refashion personnel policies. For example, while the 1995 IRS study of the automotive components sector found evidence of an accelerated adoption of 'Japanese' working practices, it concluded that:

> employee relations strategies among our surveyed companies suggest that measures to involve employees more in company affairs – which are typical of Japanese suppliers – are not being introduced with the same amount of urgency. (IRS, 1995b: 16)

Moreover, fierce competition and volatile business conditions have generally deterred companies from extending to their employees the guarantees of job security which at Rover have been considered the key to workforce participation in continuous improvement.

◼ International comparisons

A systematic review of the extent and character of changes in functional flexibility across the advanced industrial economies is no easy task and will not be attempted here. As Beatson suggests (1995a: 52) there is a paucity of internationally comparable data for the OECD countries as a whole, although a growing number of two- or three-country cross-national comparative studies offer valuable insights.

A number of these studies point towards the broad conclusion that functional flexibility remains relatively under-developed in Britain. Within Europe, the contrast is drawn most starkly with the reorganisation of manufacturing in (former West) Germany.

Writing in the late 1980s, Lane argued that the development of functional flexibility in Germany had been 'technologically-led and inspired' (1989: 193). Firms had developed new work systems in order to exploit the flexible capacities of the new production equipment in the manufacture of high quality, high value added and/or semi-customised goods for new markets. In Britain, in contrast, the impetus for greater functional flexibility had come from the liberalisation of the labour market. Firms had taken advantage of labour's weakness to end existing job demarcations but had tended to see this as an end in itself. Where new technologies had been adopted, they had been incorporated into established work systems, orientated towards established market openings, rather than integrated as part of 'upmarket restructuring'.

Streeck (1985, 1991) identifies the impetus to upmarket restructuring in German manufacturing as the existence of powerful 'institutional constraints' on managerial freedoms. He argues that the presence of strong trade unions, able to foreclose easy (quick-fix) routes to profitability (e.g. low wages and price cutting), legal restrictions on employers' freedom to hire and fire, and the statutory co-determination rights of works councils (*see* Chapter 7), have forced firms to innovate and to seek a competitive advantage by upgrading their products, production processes and labour force skills. His analysis, as Nolan (1996: 111) observes, offers a powerful challenge to the 'free market' philosophy which characterises 'institutional rigidities' in the labour market as a barrier to economic efficiency.

Vickery and Wurzburg's (1996) analysis of developments across the OECD countries also suggests that the 'relations-based approach', as they term it, in Germany and, to varying degrees, the Nordic countries and other states in continental Europe, has been conducive to the development of functional flexibility. They argue that the approach, 'based heavily on negotiation to reach consensus among a wide range of "stakeholders", including employees, suppliers, customers and often the wider community', has 'helped create a virtuous circle of skill formation, labour re-allocation, productivity growth and employment security' (p. 19). In contrast, the 'market-driven' approach of North America, Australia and New Zealand, in addition to the UK, has supported more the development of numerical and external flexibility.

As these authors advise, however, global competition is producing strains and change in both of the contrasting approaches. Multinationals have displayed their capacity to pick and choose between contrasting 'regimes' and in Europe this has provoked increasing controversy over the direction of EU employment legislation and social policy.

WORKING-TIME FLEXIBILITY

The concept of numerical flexibility denotes the ways in which employers match staffing to workload fluctuations. Atkinson and Meager (1986: 14) suggest that this can be achieved through two principal routes:

- by adjusting the numbers employed;
- by adjusting the number and timing of hours worked.

In other words, they identify working-time (or temporal) flexibility as a particular form of numerical flexibility, and other writers have often adopted a similar approach (e.g. Watson, 1994).

In the flexible firm model, numerical flexibility is achieved through the periphery of insecurely or irregularly employed workers. These include workers on 'non-standard' labour contracts – those which depart from the traditional (twentieth-century, male) standard of a full-time employment contract of no specified time duration – and others exposed to a 'hire and fire' regime. The firm increases its use of part-time and temporary workers, agency staff and self-employed subcontractors of services in order to meet workload fluctuations without jeopardising the employment security of the 'core'. It also secures financial flexibility – the ability to vary the wage bill or achieve an overall reduction in labour costs.

The model's broad definition of numerical flexibility, subsuming working time flexibility, however, can be criticised as confusing and potentially misleading, not least if it is taken as the basis for assessing the extent of the insecurely employed peripheral workforce (*see* IDS, 1994b; O'Reilly, 1992). For permanent employees working overtime, flexitime or, indeed, part-time can also contribute working-time flexibility.

Some writers have adopted an alternative approach and treat working time and numerical flexibility as distinct categories. Beatson (1995a: 1), following Hart (1987), for example, refers to flexibility on the *extensive* and on the *intensive* margin. The former equates with flexibility of numbers – the ability to adjust the headcount. It conveys the idea of bringing in additional workers and returning them to the external labour market when work levels fall and their services are no longer required. Flexibility on the intensive margin, in contrast, is achieved without changes in employment levels – either through changes in the number and timing of working hours (working-time flexibility) or through changes in the range of tasks employees perform (functional flexibility).

This section looks at the ways in which employers have attempted to develop working-time flexibility. The next turns to the issues raised by the flexible firm model and, in particular, the idea that employers are increasing their use of non-standard labour contracts as part of a deliberate strategy to create a numerically flexible, peripheral workforce. In both sections the discussion focuses on the British context but, where relevant, draws comparisons with other advanced economies.

Pressures for the reorganisation of working time

Working-time flexibility, as suggested, relates to 'changes in the number and timing of hours worked from week to week or day to day' (Watson, 1994: 240). A variety of arrangements may serve towards this end. Attempts to classify these – for example, as traditional (overtime, shiftworking, the scheduling of part-time hours) or new (flexitime, annual hours, compressed working weeks) – serve to emphasise that employers' interest in working-time flexibility is not of recent origin or specific to the 1980s or '90s.

In many service industries, where output is for immediate sale (or perhaps synonymous with the sale), employers have traditionally organised work patterns around peak sales times. The deregulation of opening hours in banking and in retail distribution in recent years has added impetus to the search for working-time flexibility, and financial flexibility in so far as an aim has been to control or reduce labour costs. In manufacturing, firms may organise working hours to ensure that expensive equipment is operated around the clock, or their interest in flexible working hours may arise from recurrent bottlenecks and difficulties in production scheduling.

Watson (1994: 241) reminds us that working-time flexibility has become an important element in the debate over 'family-friendly' working practices. Thus, employee preferences and the conditions of labour supply have also to be taken into account in examining employers' practices and policies. Various forms of flexible working – part-time employment, job-sharing, flexitime – have been championed by personnel managers and trade union negotiators as supportive of equal opportunities objectives. The labour market shortages of the late 1980s encouraged further policy initiatives. Yet the continuing (and in some instances, accelerated) expansion of part-time work in the recession of the early 1990s in some sectors appeared to be driven largely by 'business needs'.

Trade unions have pressed for reductions in the length of the working day or week; the engineering unions, for example, campaigned largely successfully for a shift to a 37-hour basic week in the late 1980s (*see* Pickard, 1990). In some instances this has prompted employers to effect other changes in order to secure maximum utilisation of contractual working time. Yet the legal framework in Britain is unusually liberal and continues to provide employers with the flexibility to draw on high levels of overtime working.

Time at work

Within the EU the UK has had fewer constraints on employers' freedom to structure working time than any other country (Beatson, 1995a: 48–9). Most other member states have regulations, either laid down by law and/or reinforced by collective agreements, which place limits on the hours that employees can work. Typically these extend from the overall duration of the working week to incorporate minimum rest periods, maximum periods of overtime and so on. Britain, in contrast, historically has had no general legislation covering the overall duration or arrangement of working time. For the most part, where these issues have been regulated, regulation has come from collective bargaining, which has never been complete in its coverage of the workforce and in the 1980s and '90s has become significantly less so.

Moreover, the legal framework was made more permissive in Britain in the 1980s. Some EU member states legislated in this period to reduce the maximum working week and/or to restrict overtime (e.g. France and Belgium). The Conservative government in Britain, in contrast, deregulated to remove the residual restrictions governing working time. EU legislation prompted the removal of restrictions on women's night work via the Sex Discrimination Act of 1986, and the alacrity of UK compliance here contrasts markedly with UK government responses to other elements of EU social and employment legislation, notably the Working Time Directive (discussed below).

Eurostat figures suggest that employers in Britain have exercised their relative freedom over working hours. In 1994, the average British working week (including overtime) for full-timers was 43.3 hours, the longest in the EU (*see* Table 13.2). Average weekly hours fell in most other member states over the period 1983–94, but in Britain increased by almost an hour (Mulgan and Wilkinson, 1995: 7). British men working full-time in 1994 clocked up an average of 45.4 hours per week, compared with 38.8 hours in Belgium, and by this date British women working full-time had reached the top of the EU's female working week stakes with an average of 40.4 hours. Britain also had the highest proportions of male and female full-time employees working in excess of 48 hours. In 1994, the average for the EU as a whole was 10.5 per cent for men and 4.4 per cent for women. In Britain it was 27.8 and 9.7 respectively (IDS, 1995: 16).

Britain also has a wide dispersion of working hours when full-time and part-time workers are considered together (*see* Table 13.2). Beatson (1995a: 47) notes that a relatively high proportion of people work long hours (over 48 hours per week) and a relatively high proportion work short hours (under 16) in comparison with other EU member states, and that the British dispersion of working hours has grown wider over the 1980s and 1990s.

■ **Table 13.2 Average hours usually worked per week: Britain within the EU, 1995**

	Males			Females		
	Full-time	*Part-time*	*All*	*Full-time*	*Part-time*	*All*
United Kingdom	45.4	16.0	43.5	40.4	17.9	30.6
Portugal	42.7	26.3	42.4	39.3	20.2	37.9
Greece	41.4	25.6	41.0	39.0	21.5	38.0
Irish Republic	41.6	21.2	40.6	37.8	18.0	33.9
Spain	41.0	19.6	40.6	39.5	17.5	36.3
Luxembourg	40.6	26.7	40.5	37.9	19.7	34.3
France	40.6	22.5	39.8	38.8	22.4	34.2
Italy	39.7	30.1	39.5	36.3	23.0	34.7
Germany	39.9	18.9	39.3	39.2	20.2	33.0
Belgium	38.8	21.1	38.3	36.9	20.9	31.9
Denmark	39.8	14.2	37.1	38.0	21.2	32.0
Netherlands	39.6	18.6	36.3	39.1	17.9	25.2
EU average	41.1	19.5	40.2	38.9	19.7	32.8

Source: Eurostat (1996) in *Social Trends*, 26, 89.

■ Overtime working

The relatively high average working week for male and female full-timers in Britain is in part a function of the exceptionally high levels of overtime working. Thus, while in Britain:

> contractual hours are not very different from those worked elsewhere in the EU, long hours including overtime are endemic, for example, in some parts of manufacturing, on the railways, in the health service, transport and distribution, often linked to low levels of basic pay. (IDS, 1995: 16)

Overtime may be a contractual requirement, or non-contractual, and may be paid or unpaid. Traditionally in Britain paid overtime has been worked primarily by manual employees in manufacturing and other production industries. The level of overtime working has tended to fluctuate with the economic cycle, rising in upturns and falling in downturns. Nevertheless, overtime working has remained a 'persistent and prominent aspect of working time in Britain, even when labour markets are comparatively weak' (Blyton, 1994: 503). And unpaid overtime, which data from the Labour Force Survey suggest may account for over 40 per cent of overtime hours worked, may have increased in Britain over the 1980s and '90s, in particular among white-collar and professional staff, including school teachers and nurses.

Overtime working provides employers with:

- a means of extending the normal working day without the expense of recruiting and training additional employees;
- the ability to operate shift patterns which do not conform with agreed weekly hours;
- a means of increasing employees' earnings without conceding a general pay increase (Blyton, 1994: 504).

For many employees it constitutes an important component of weekly earnings (*see* Osborne, 1996: 227). Thus while employers have condemned high overtime working as costly (often paid overtime commands premium rates), and trade union representatives have argued that it depresses basic pay rates and inhibits job creation, it remains an important feature of working-time patterns.

Elsewhere within the EU, some states have made an effort to restrict overtime working:

> Permitted overtime in Belgium must be compensated by time-off; in France too, rights to time-off were strengthened by 1994 legislation. Premium rates for overtime were abolished in Spain (in 1994) ... and negotiators invited to agree time off in lieu ... (IDS, 1995: 13)

Such measures have been enacted often with the broad objective of 'work sharing' – that is, of spreading available employment among a wider proportion of the workforce.

Limiting the scope for employers to compress long work hours into longer shifts and to rely on high levels of overtime working has also been an objective of the EU's Working Time Directive. This gives employees, except those in defined categories, the right to refuse to work more than an average 48-hour week, the right to three weeks' annual holiday (rising to four weeks in 1999), and lays down the length of rest periods and rules for night working (IDS, 1997b: 6).

The former Conservative government in the UK was hostile to the Directive, but its legal challenge was dismissed by the European Court of Justice in November 1996. Given the high levels of overtime working in this country, the measure could well have a significant impact. Some commentators suggest it may be the catalyst required to foster a major overhaul of working patterns and to promote more efficient, flexible ways of working. The most immediate impact, however, is likely to be on annual holidays. British Labour Force Survey data suggest that 11 per cent of the workforce currently have no right to paid holiday and a further 14 per cent have less than three weeks.

Shift working

Like overtime, shift working represents a traditional means of achieving flexibility over the timing of hours worked. IDS suggest that its use, together with night and weekend working, is on the increase across the EU 'as it allows for shorter individual hours but longer operating times' (1997a: 27). Indeed, restrictions on the duration of working hours may prompt firms to introduce or reorganise shift patterns in ways that achieve longer operating times (but with attendant implications for family and personal life).

International comparisons are hazardous; definitions are often different or imprecise. Bosworth (1994, cited in Beatson, 1995a: 43) suggests that the incidence of shiftworking in Britain increased steadily over the post-war period before peaking in the early 1980s, with a diminishing proportion of employees covered by the arrangement since then. IDS notes that two- and three-shift working is significantly less common in production industries in Britain (especially among smaller firms) than elsewhere in the EU (1997a: 3). Yet the picture looks rather different if shiftworking is considered together with evening and night work; a relatively high proportion of employees in Britain are covered by these latter arrangements (IDS, 1995: 17).

Blyton (1994: 510) notes some recent developments within the traditional working time category of shiftwork. These include a growing use of part-timers on 'twilight' (i.e. evening) shifts. In banking, this has been related to the extension of opening hours in the branches, and the concentration of 'back office' processing work in highly automated regional centres where twilight shifts are used to maximise machine use and minimise wage costs (*see* Cressey and Scott, 1992).

Annual hours

Annualised hours is a system 'of averaging working time across a year. Employees are contracted to work a given number of hours over 12 months, rather than a specified number of hours per week. ... hours of work can be varied – from week to week or even from season to season – in accordance with business requirements' (IDS, 1993a: 1). Such arrangements are often seen as a modern form of flexible working, but the concept of annualised hours is not entirely new. The first scheme in the UK was introduced in the 1950s (IRS, 1996b: 4). Employers' interest in the arrangement, in particular as a means of reducing overtime, increased in this country in the 1980s and in other EU member states where legislative reforms and negotiated reductions in working hours have been a stimulus (IDS, 1995: 17).

The principal benefits of annual hours systems for employers have been identified as:

- increased flexibility, in the ability to match employee hours more closely with production or service requirements;
- lower labour costs, through reduced overtime payments and less use of temporaries;
- increased productivity from more effective labour utilisation.

But there are some drawbacks, including the complexity of scheduling shift rotas and holidays (IRS, 1996b). Employees may gain greater predictability of earnings, but they may lose some flexibility – for example, in planning leisure time or making childcare arrangements if they are 'on call' and asked to work 'reserve hours' at short notice.

Various surveys have suggested an accelerated take-up of annual hours arrangements in Britain since 1990 and a diffusion of these arrangements from manufacturing to private and public services. However, the proportion of employees covered is still quite low with only 3.9 per cent of full-time employees and 3.1 per cent of part-time employees affected in 1996 (*Social Trends*, 1997, 27: 80). Blyton (1994: 517) suggests that the reluctance of employees and employers to forgo overtime, and the flexibility already enjoyed by employers from informal or voluntary arrangements (including unpaid overtime) has limited the use of annual hours working in Britain.

Yet it would appear that elsewhere in Europe the spread of annual hours systems has not been as rapid as might have been anticipated. And while the proportion of employees covered by annual hours in Britain is not among the highest in the EU, some surveys suggest that the rate of increase of organisational usage has been above average in the early 1990s (Cranfield Network for European HRM, 1996).

■ Flexible working time

Flexible working time – or 'flexitime', as it is often known – is an arrangement whereby:

> employees may vary their daily start and finish times so long as they work the total hours agreed for an accounting period – usually a week or month. (Watson, 1994: 242)

The system was originally developed in Germany in the 1960s and spread to Britain in the 1970s. A major stimulus to its adoption in this period was the relatively strong labour market and employers' desire to attract and retain staff by offering improved conditions (Blyton, 1994: 513). Flexitime also offers employers the ability to extend staff cover outside normal working hours (for example, to manage variable work flows), and to press forward their commitments to equal employment opportunities. Employees secure greater flexibility to manage, or balance, their work and personal commitments, and the system seems to be well received by staff (IRS, 1996a).

Flexitime is the most common of the new flexible working time arrangements, but its take-up since the 1970s has not been enormously rapid. An IRS survey in 1996 found that half of the 34 schemes examined had been introduced before 1980 (IRS, 1996a). Labour Force Survey data show that 11.3 per cent of full-time employees and 8.5 per cent of part-timers were covered by flexitime arrangements in 1995 (cited in *Social Trends*, 1996, 26: 90). Women are more likely than men to work flexitime; the system is more common in services than in manufacturing, and in the public than the private sector. And since the arrangement is generally associated with white-collar working in large offices (Watson, 1994) it is not surprising that its highest incidence is in 'banking, financial and business services' and in 'other services', especially public administration.

Summary

There has been an increased usage of certain new forms of working-time flexibility in Britain and, in particular, an accelerated take-up of annual hours arrangements since 1990. Yet the percentages of the workforce affected remain fairly low and in some instances (job sharing, the nine-day-fortnight and four-and-a-half-day week) tiny. Blyton and Beatson concur that traditional forms of working time flexibility continue to predominate. And within the EU Britain remains the highest user of overtime, which, as commentators have noted, is 'the most cost-ineffective variant' of flexible working (Cranfield Network for European HRM, 1996: 23).

NON-STANDARD LABOUR CONTRACTS: AN EMPLOYER'S STRATEGY OF NUMERICAL FLEXIBILITY?

The flexible firm model proposed that employers in Britain were increasing their use of non-standard labour contracts in order to achieve numerical flexibility. The model's 'fit' with empirical evidence has been keenly debated. Without doubt, the incidence of certain forms of 'non-standard' working has increased over the 1980s and '90s. At issue, however, has been the extent to which this reflects a new and purposeful 'core–periphery' employers' strategy. In reviewing the evidence, this section explores the factors contributing to the growth in part-time work, temporary work and self-employment in Britain in the 1980s and '90s and develops some European comparisons.

Part-time work

In Britain, for government statistical purposes, a part-time job is defined as one involving 30 hours or less work each week. On this basis, it is evident that part-time employment has increased in Britain in the 1980s and '90s, in absolute and relative terms. Labour Force Survey data show that the number of employees working part-time in their main job rose from 4.4 to 5.5 million between the spring of 1984 and 1996, and from 21 to 25 per cent of all employees in employment. This growth, however, continues a longer-term trend, predating the 1980s.

Employment Department data show that the number of part-time jobs held by employees increased from 3.3 million to 6.2 million, and from 15 to 28.5 per cent of all employees' jobs, in the 25 years between 1971 and 1996. Beatson's (1995a: 7) analysis suggests that the rate of growth was actually higher in the period 1971–81 (averaging 3 per cent per annum) than in the period 1981–94 (2.6 per cent per annum).

The growth in part-time employment (especially in the later period) arises to a large extent from changes in the industrial composition of employment. Manufacturing employment has declined, at an accelerated pace since 1979, and employment growth has been concentrated increasingly in the services, especially the private services since 1979. Full-time employment was the norm for the (largely male) manual manufacturing work-force, while many service industries traditionally have been heavy users of female part-time labour.

Male part-time employment has increased over the 1980s and 1990s. Labour Force Survey data show that the number of male employees working part-time more than doubled between 1984 and 1996, from 416 000 to 873 000. Yet part-time working remains far more common among women than among men: 44 per cent of female employees worked part-time in their main job in 1996 compared with 7.5 per cent of male employees. And the part-time workforce remains overwhelmingly female: 84 per cent of the 5.5 million employees working part-time in their main job in spring 1996 were women. Clearly employers have been able to draw on a supply of women available and willing to work on part-time terms and conditions, and here the domestic division of labour and also the lack of public childcare provision are among the influences.

The spring 1995 Labour Force Survey showed that 88 per cent of all part-time workers (including self-employed part-timers) were located in the service sector. Only 7 per cent were in manufacturing. Part-timers were concentrated, in particular, in distribution, hotels and restaurants (32 per cent of the total), and in public education and health services (33 per cent). In terms of occupational distribution, a majority (58 per cent) were in non-manual jobs. Part-timers were concentrated in particular in clerical occupations (18 per cent of the total), personal and protective services (18 per cent), 'other occupations' (18 per cent) and selling (17 per cent). Only 6 per cent were managers and administrators and only 7 per cent were in professional occupations.

The industrial and occupational distribution of part-timers provides a partial explanation for their relatively low average hourly earnings. New Earnings Survey (NES) data indicate that the average hourly earnings (excluding overtime) of part-time employees in April 1995 were two-thirds of full-time earnings (Osborne, 1996). The hourly earnings gap is widest between female part-timers and male full-timers (overall, the former earned 59.6 per cent of the gross hourly earnings of the latter) (EOR, 1996).

In general, part-timers receive the same basic hourly rate as full-timers doing the same job within the same organisation (IRS, 1994). In some instances they achieve higher hourly earnings than full-timers in comparable occupations; this is notably the case for part-timers in professional occupations (Osborne, 1996: 227). But part-time workers are concentrated in lower paying industries and many are in occupations requiring only the knowledge and experience necessary to perform simple routine jobs. An IRS report notes that many female part-timers are over-qualified for their job roles (IRS, 1994: 7).

Moreover, many part-timers have been disadvantaged in comparison with full-timers in terms of their access to elements of the remuneration package other than basic hourly rates (e.g. access to incentive payment schemes, occupational pensions schemes, and to overtime and shift premium rates). The situation has been changing, however, in large part due to the development of EU social and employment legislation.

British employment protection legislation formerly discriminated against part-time workers. Employees working betweem 8 and 16 hours a week had to accrue a longer period of continuous service with an employer in order to qualify for the right to claim unfair dismissal and the right to redundancy payments; 5 years as opposed to 2 for employees working 16 hours a week or more. Employees working fewer than 8 hours a week were excluded altogether. But a House of Lords judgement (R *v* Secretary of State for Employment *ex parte* EOC, 3 March 1994) deemed that the UK legislation discriminated indirectly against women and hence contravened EU equality legislation. The hours thresholds have now been abolished.

In June 1997, European trade unions and employers reached an agreement which, if approved by EU member governments, will become a legally binding Directive establishing the principle of non-discrimination for part-timers. The measure will give part-timers equal access to pay, bonus, shift and other additional payments as comparable full-time employees, and ensure that they are provided with equal contractual terms in occupational sick leave schemes and paid holiday leave (*Financial Times*, 6 June 1997). It will apply to the UK, following the Labour government's 'opt into' the Social Chapter, and may have a particular impact in this country.

Employer responses to the changing legal framework are likely to be conditioned by their circumstances and reasons for using part-time labour. The British Employer Labour Use Strategy (ELUS) survey, sponsored by the former Employment Department in the late 1980s, found that 'traditional' and 'supply-side' rationales for using part-timers were cited far more frequently by employers than 'new' flexibility rationales (e.g. relative wage costs and freedom to hire and fire). In most instances, working-time flexibility seemed to be a key objective, with employers reporting that part-timers were used to undertake tasks requiring a limited time, and to match staffing to levels of demand (Hunter *et al.*, 1993: 392). Of course, cost considerations (the minimisation of the overall wage bill) may traditionally have underpinned these 'traditional' rationales.

New flexibility rationales were cited as the main reason for employing part-timers by only a tiny proportion (3 per cent) of the 522 establishments surveyed. The proportions were significantly higher among employers in distribution, however, and among those increasing their use of part-time labour. A quarter of the latter reported that this increased usage was a matter of deliberate policy.

Among the large high-street retailers, there have been some dramatic examples of firms apparently pursuing such a deliberate policy in the period since the ELUS was conducted. The extension of trading hours and Sunday opening, coupled with the introduction of new technology which facilitates the precision planning of peak customer flows, appear to have been a stimulus.

The Burton Group, for example, announced in 1993 that it was replacing 1000 full-time jobs in its branches by 3000 'key time' or part-time positions. Existing staff were obliged to sign new contracts, and new staff schedules were drawn up for each store, based on customer flows as derived from electronic point-of-sale data. 'Key-timers' were to be scheduled to work during peak trading hours, and under the new contract full-timers were to work five days out of a possible continuous seven-day working week. The changes eliminated the automatic payment of overtime premium rates for weekend working (IRS, 1993).

Aligned with these developments has been some increased use of 'zero hours' and 'term-time' only contracts, and of 'twilight' part-time shifts. Under the first of these, staff are assigned neither regular nor guaranteed hours but rather are called in at short notice to provide cover. Although such contracts are not new, there is some evidence that they are now being used more widely and are estimated to cover some 200 000 people (IRS, 1997; *Financial Times*, 22 May 1998). However, the new Labour government may legislate to restrict their use as part of its programme to promote 'fairness at work'.

In retailing, therefore, where the workforce traditionally has comprised a high proportion of female part-timers, recent developments suggest that larger employers may be seeking to create new patterns of differentiation. Pay and benefits have been improved for some part-timers, as has job security, indicating that such staff are increasingly recognised if not as 'core' then at least as key to sales and quality customer service initiatives.

However, as Neathey and Hurstfield (1995: 206) observe, these workers have become 'the focus for efforts to achieve maximum flexibility of labour supply'. Employers have demanded from them greater flexibility in working time and possibly increased hours while developing also a sub-group or periphery of workers on very short and/or irregular ('zero') hours (*see* Exhibit 13.2).

■ **Exhibit 13.2**

Flexible friends

The increasing emphasis on part-time and temporary work has changed the job market beyond recognition. But while this trend has improved the productivity and flexibility of many businesses, it has raised difficult issues for managers.

How do companies find high-calibre staff prepared to work unconventional hours, often for relatively low pay? And how do they combat the widespread perception that these workers, who often have an important role in dealing with customers, are poorly trained and undervalued?

Recent research by the Roffey Park Management Institute in Sussex concluded that businesses that are successful at managing part-time and temporary employees have put more effort into meeting their needs.

Burton Group, which replaced 1000 full-time staff with 3000 part-time jobs in 1993, has responded to recruitment problems by allowing store managers to write contracts to suit individual employees. At one Topshop outlet a job is shared by a student who works in the vacation and a woman who works during the school term.

Asda, the retail group where 80 per cent of the workforce work part-time, has also felt the need to be more flexible towards part-time workers. Consultations showed that one reason for staff turnover reaching 30 per cent a year was that many wanted a longer working week.

'Employees who work very short hours, below the National Insurance threshold, are very cheap employees', says David Smith, employee relations manager at Asda. 'But we found people were leaving. So we are going against the trend and offering longer hours'. With the help of longer contracts and other measures, such as improved maternity leave, career breaks and the ability to swap shifts, staff turnover fell by 2 percentage points.

▶

■ **Exhibit 13.2 continued**

The issues concerning flexible workers are nothing new for Oxfordshire County Council, where more than two-thirds of the 16 000-strong workforce work part-time. That partly reflects the need to cover round-the-clock services, such as in residential homes and fire fighting, but offering flexible working is also a way to attract professional employees, such as legal staff, who might be paid more in the private sector. Valued staff may want time off for childcare, further education and other part-time jobs or may want to continue part-time after taking early retirement.

But much of the debate about flexible working concerns the other end of the spectrum, the poorly paid and lowly valued employees who do not qualify for National Insurance, for employment protection or for statutory benefits. Attention has particularly focused on zero-hour contracts, introduced by companies such as Burger King, in which individuals are only paid when dealing with customers. More than half the part-timers interviewed in a 1995 TUC study said employers regarded them as 'second-class staff'.

The tendency to treat flexible workers as poor relations is creating a dilemma for employers, according to Christina Evans, a research associate at Roffey Park Management Institute. 'In many organisations, it is those who work "flexibly" who have the most responsibility for customer service, at peak trading periods. In other words it is the "flexible" employees who are the ones who have the most impact on sales', she says.

... Her research uncovered many positive aspects of flexible working. Companies often commented that part-time workers were more disciplined in their time management and so more productive.

Nonetheless, the research highlighted a number of barriers to making the best use of flexible employees. Managers are often unenthusiastic about supervising them since it complicates scheduling and rota arrangements.

The assumption that part-time employees are less career-minded can be self-fulfiling. Unless companies examine their promotion policies, there may be unintended barriers to the promotion of part-time workers. For example, at First Direct, the telephone banking service, the Roffey Park study noted an assumption that an employee could not be rated 'very good' unless they worked a full shift and were exposed to all the trading activities.

Training is a particularly vexed issue for flexible workers. Most companies would agree that part-time staff need at least as much training as full-time staff, yet few provide that ...

The widespread practice of offering flexible workers worse pay, training and conditions than the full-time workforce could backfire, says the Institute of Management. It warns that the current attitude towards flexible workers could 'lead to the development of two-tier workforces – with all of the difficulties inherent in managing them'.

More effort is needed to integrate flexible employees into the company's core workforce: 'What is needed is a new approach to managing flexible workers, which acknowledges the needs of this group of employees to be valued, included and invested in', she says.

Source: Vanessa Houlder, *Financial Times*, 29 January 1997.

Questions

1 What types of flexibility have employers in the retail sector in Britain sought to achieve through the use of part-time contracts?

2 In what ways has their approach to the use of part-time labour complemented, and come in conflict with, their broader business objectives?

3 How might retail employers construct part-time contracts to meet their requirements for flexibility and quality customer service?

International comparisons are complicated by the fact that different countries use different definitions of part-time work. Moreover, the different national frameworks of employment regulation (legal and via collective bargaining) mean that like is not necessarily being compared with like. Most EU member states already accept the principle that part-timers are entitled to the same pro-rata rights and benefits as full-timers, and most have removed qualifying (earnings or length or service) thresholds for eligibility. Some countries operate incentive schemes for part-time working, usually in the form of employer subsidies or reductions in employer social security contribution rates (e.g. Italy, Spain, Belgium) (IDS, 1993b: 17).

Differences in national systems of employment regulation would appear to have had limited impact, at least on the expansion of part-time work. Part-time employment increased in a majority of EU countries over the period 1983–91. The proportion of part-time to total employment rose by 4.2 per cent in the UK, but the increases were greater in Belgium, Ireland and, in particular, the Netherlands. The UK and the Netherlands had the third highest and highest proportions of part-time to total employment, respectively, among the twelve EU member states in 1983 and again in 1991. Over the period, however, part-time employment increased by 12 per cent in the Netherlands, from 20.4 to 32.4 per cent of total employment (De Grip *et al.*, 1997). In the Netherlands, in contrast with the UK in this period, part-timers were entitled to pro-rata full-time employee rights.

The increase in the rate of part-time employment in the EU has continued, with only Denmark recording a decrease in the 1990s. As Table 13.3 suggests, the increase in the period 1990–4 was slightly greater in France (3 per cent) and Ireland (2.7 per cent), and significantly greater in the Netherlands (4.7 per cent) than in the UK (2.5 per cent).

■ Table 13.3 Part-time employment as a percentage of total employment, EU member states, 1990–4

	1990	1994	% change 1990–4
Belgium	10.9	12.8	1.9
Denmark	23.3	21.2	–2.1
Germany*	14.1	15.8	1.7
Greece	4.1	4.8	0.7
Spain	4.9	6.9	2.0
France	11.9	14.9	3.0
Ireland	8.1	10.8	2.7
Italy	4.9	6.2	1.3
Luxembourg	6.9	7.9	1.0
Netherlands	31.7	36.4	4.7
Austria[†]	8.4	8.7	0.3
Portugal	6.0	8.0	2.0
Finland[†]	6.7	8.4	1.7
Sweden	23.5	24.9	1.4
United Kingdom	21.3	23.8	2.5

* Figures for 1991–4.
[†] Figures for 1990–3.
Source: European Commission (1996) *Employment in Europe*.

Differences in employment regulation, however, would seem to have some impact on the nature of the part-time jobs created. In Britain, average hours for part-timers (men and women alike) are relatively low – the lowest within the EU. And, as has been noted, within the EU Britain has the highest proportion of people working very short hours.

■ Temporary work

Temporary work is a broad category and includes casual and seasonal employment, and the use of fixed-term contracts and agency temporary staff. Taken together, temporary workers form a small proportion of all employees in Britain. Labour Force Survey data indicate that this remained fairly constant, at around 5 per cent, over the period 1984–90. After 1990, however, there appeared to be a fairly significant increase, with the number of temporary employees in the economy as a whole rising by 30.2 per cent to 1.5 million, and to 7 per cent of the total number of employees, by 1995.

Figures compiled for the *Financial Times* by the Central Statistical Office showed that the increase was especially strong in manufacturing (81 000, or 67.5 per cent), a rise which was 'all the more noticeable given that total manufacturing employment fell 11.5 per cent over the five years' (*Financial Times*, 1 February 1996). Whether the increase is part of a longer-term upward trend, however, remains unclear. The use of temporary workers has tended to fluctuate with the business cycle, and the context of the early 1990s was one of severe economic recession. Much of the recent growth in temporary employment has come from a more widespread use of fixed-term contracts (Beatson, 1995a: 8).

Most surveys suggest that, with the exception of agency staff, temporaries are usually paid the same basic hourly rate as comparable grades of permanent staff (agency temporaries often received a higher hourly rate). However, temporaries generally have less access than permanent staff to company sick pay, holiday and pensions arrangements and temporary part-timers are most likely to be ineligible (Grant, 1991, cited in IRS, 1994). Their access to employment protection rights has also been relatively restricted. In the UK in the 1980s and early '90s, all employees – temporary and permanent – required two years' continuous service with an employer to accrue unfair dismissal and redundancy payment rights.

Overall, employers in Britain face less rigorous legal and institutional constraints on their freedom to reduce their 'permanent' workforce than their counterparts in most other EU member states (Beatson, 1995a: 37). This permissive framework of employment regulation may have reduced the incentive for employers to create or make use of special contractual forms – i.e. temporaries – to secure their (numerical) flexibility requirements. Certainly the incidence of temporary working in the UK economy is below the average for the EU as a whole (*see* Table 13.4).

The Employment Department's ELUS survey in the late 1980s found that employers in Britain cited traditional reasons for their use of temporary staff more frequently than new, flexibility rationales. Temporaries were used, for example:

- to give short-term cover for absent staff;
- to match staffing to peaks in demand.

New flexibility rationales were cited most frequently by employers in the public sector. Budget constraints and uncertainty regarding future funding, it would appear, have increased the perceived advantages of using temporaries (in particular, fixed-term contract staff) for public sector employers.

■ Table 13.4 Fixed-term contracts as a percentage of total employment, EU member states, 1990 and 1994

	1990	1994
Belgium	5.3	5.1
Denmark	10.8	11.9
Germany	10.4	10.2
Greece	16.6	10.1
Spain	29.8	33.6
France	10.4	10.9
Ireland	8.5	9.4
Italy	5.2	7.3
Luxembourg	3.4	2.7
Netherlands	7.6	10.9
Austria	n/a	n/a
Portugal	18.6	9.3
Finland *	11.5	12.9
Sweden	10.0	11.5
United Kingdom	5.2	6.3

* Figures for 1990–3.
Source: European Commission (1996) *Employment in Europe*.

There is some evidence, however, that in the context of the early 1990s, employers in a wider spread of industries have been making use of, or increasing the use of, temporaries:

■ to reduce overheads;

■ to offset the risks of uncertain demand; and/or

■ as a means of managing fluctuations in demand while reducing the size of their 'core' workforces.

The *Financial Times* study related the increased use of temporaries by manufacturing employers partly to the extension of lean production and just-in-time systems. This would suggest that work intensification for a depleted 'core' is being accompanied by the development of a 'periphery' of temporary staff used as 'buffer personnel'. A separate, although partly related, development would appear to be the use of temporary status as a screening device in recruitment and selection; Heather *et al.*, (1996: 405) found a fifth of employers in their survey sample were using temporary contracts as a 'trial for a permanent job'.

These developments, as suggested, may be specific to the economic context of the early 1990s. Certainly employers identify costs as well as benefits in using temporary workers. Many consider temporaries to be less reliable than permanent staff, and an expense in the sense that they may have to be trained! In his study of US-owned electronics plants in Ireland, Geary (1992) found that local managers were often keen to limit their use of temporary employees. Heavy use of temporaries was seen to result in reduced commitment from permanent staff, and conflicts between permanent and temporary staff which inhibited the development of good working relationships (*see* Exhibit 13.3).

■ Exhibit 13.3

Why work is just a temporary thing

From shampoo to bicycles and from chocolates to computers, Britain's manufacturers are turning increasingly to temporary workers as part of their moves to more flexible working methods.

The number of temporary manufacturing workers has almost doubled in the past five years in proportion to the whole manufacturing workforce.

This switch has been much more marked in manufacturing than in other sectors. Across the entire economy, temporary employees increased by 350 000, or 30.2 per cent, between 1990 and 1995, according to the Central Statistical Office.

Manpower, the US-owned employment services agency which specialises in hiring workers and contracting them out for industrial work, said it employed about 9000 short-term workers doing industrial jobs in its client companies – more than four times the figure in the late 1980s.

Temporary workers are often paid less than full-time staff and the employer usually does not contribute to pensions. The workers earn only when at work – which can reduce company overheads.

Many companies warn, however, that output is likely to suffer if pay rates and training are cut too much.

... About 10 per cent of the 1000-odd workers at Procter & Gamble's consumer products factory in Manchester are on temporary contracts, mainly of between one month and a year's duration.

The flexibility helps the company to compete with overseas suppliers, according to Mr Trevor Barber, the plant manager. 'Having people on temporary contracts means we can respond to increased demand from around Europe much more quickly than in the past', he said. By hiring people on short-term contracts, production can be accelerated within a month, compared with three times as long for a comparable factory staffed completely by full-time workers. Overall, employment at the plant has increased by 50 per cent so far in the 1990s.

... One of the biggest users of short-term workers in UK manufacturing is Xyratex, a maker of computer disc drives, based in Havant, Hampshire. The company employs about 2000 people – with about half on contracts of between two months and a year.

Xyratex juggles employment numbers to match demand from its customers – mainly computer makers and other disc drive companies – which commonly require a 48 hour delivery time. 'We would be unable to compete if we kept all our people on full-time contracts', said Mr Steve Barber, the manufacturing director.

At the Black & Decker factory in Spennymoor, County Durham, the company has about 1600 core workers producing power tools and garden products. The numbers are supplemented by 400 temporary staff early in the year, when demand for the company's lawn mowers peaks.

A big ice cream factory at Gloucester, run by Birds Eye Walls, part of Unilever, takes on seasonal workers depending on fluctuations in temperatures – which can trigger sudden demand changes. The company increased its short-term workers to 150 last summer, up from a peak of about 100 in previous years.

Another reason for companies taking on temporary staff is economic uncertainty. At a fibreglass factory in Wigan, Lancashire, run by PPG, a big US industrial company, total employment is at 650, compared with 400 at the depth of the recession in 1992.

But PPG has greatly increased its use of temporary workers, which now number about 60. 'There is a lot of uncertainty and we don't want to take on full-time workers only to make them redundant later', said Mr Steve McKeown, the human resources manager at the factory.

Source: Peter Marsh (1996) *Financial Times*, 1 February.

■ **Exhibit 13.3 continued**

Questions

1 What types of flexibility do employers in Britain gain through the use of temporary contracts?

2 Do the Bendicks, Xyratex, Black & Decker and Birds Eye case examples provide evidence to suggest that manufacturing employers have changed significantly their approach to the use of temporary workers in recent years?

3 How might the use of temporary workers contribute to, and constrain, improvements in manufacturers' output and productivity?

■ Self-employment

Self-employment, like subcontracting and the use of temporary agency staff, is identified in the flexible firm model as a form of 'distancing'; the firm evades the obligations of an employer by substituting a 'contract of service' for a contract of employment.

Self-employment in Britain was in long-term decline up until the late 1960s. Thereafter, it began to increase in a number of industries and the rate of increase accelerated markedly in the 1980s, to a peak of 3.4 million in 1990 (13 per cent of all in employment). But the numbers fell back in the recession of the early 1990s, and while there has been an increase subsequently, the peak level of 1990 had not quite been recovered by 1996.

The self-employed are distributed across a range of industries, although Curtis and Spence (1994) found a concentration in construction, and in distribution, hotels and catering, and repairs. The ELUS establishment case studies found that 'freelancers' were concentrated in certain skilled professional and technical occupations, including design engineers and computing specialists. The researchers also found that, in contrast with most other non-standard groups, the self-employed were likely to have a higher rate of pay than employees doing comparable jobs. Self-employment is not a homogeneous category, however, and other surveys suggest that those 'working for themselves' (e.g. as taxi-drivers, retailers or as contractors to catering firms) are among the groups most likely to work long hours (*Social Trends*, 1997).

The rate of growth of male self-employment in Britain in the 1980s was one of the fastest in Europe. The proportion of self-employment to all men in employment remained well below that in Italy and Greece at the end of the decade, but the UK's ratio had advanced to a level more comparable with that of Spain or Portugal (Dex and McCulloch, 1995: 123).

The reasons for the large proportionate increase in the UK in this period are unclear. A variety of influences may have been at work, with self-employment representing:

■ a response to unemployment;

■ a response to government tax incentives and schemes to relieve unemployment (e.g. the enterprise allowance scheme in the 1980s);

- a desire of those well-positioned in the labour market (e.g. with scarce skills) to be more independent.

The ELUS survey found that by far the most common employer rationale for using 'free-lancers' was 'to provide specialist skills'. Other rationales cited fairly frequently were the desire of workers to be self-employed (i.e. a supply-side reason) and the objective of matching staffing levels to peaks in demand, which arguably could represent a search for numerical flexibility. New flexibility rationales were given less frequently but were cited in particular by employers in construction and also in manufacturing.

In manufacturing, the contracting-out of firms' 'non-core' activities (catering, cleaning and so on) may have offered more opportunities to external contractors, including the self-employed. But the most significant developments in subcontracting in Britain have been in the public sector. Conservative government legislation compelled local authorities, health authorities and trusts to put services formerly performed 'in house' out to tender.

Again, there are potential drawbacks for the employer. A recent survey, conducted by researchers at Birkbeck College, London and reported in the *Financial Times* (8 January 1998), found that expected cost savings did not always materialise. Some employers reported that the introduction of contract work had increased employee turnover and recruitment and training costs. Furthermore, companies which had encouraged ex-employees to become freelancers 'were finding that the best of them were becoming increasingly expensive'. The trend towards flexible and fixed-term working had back-fired on some companies, creating 'contract chaos' for 'managers struggling to keep track of pay and work arrangements'.

A 'core–periphery' strategy?

In summary, certain forms of non-standard work have become more significant in Britain over the past twenty years, in particular part-time and self-employment. The growth in temporary work has been a more recent phenomenon. The growth in part-time work, however, pre-dates the 1980s and is associated partly with the sectoral recomposition of employment. The extent of the shift towards part-time work within individual industries, therefore, 'may not be as substantial as the overall growth in the number of part-time jobs suggests' (Beatson, 1995a: 7).

The Employment Department's ELUS survey, conducted in the 1980s, suggested that while non-standard working was becoming more important at establishment level, in quantitative terms the changes were not that dramatic. The survey found that employer rationales for using non-standard labour were almost always traditional ones, and also that employers had fairly traditional attitudes about the characteristics of different types of worker. For example, full-timers were often regarded as easier to manage and more flexible to deploy. Employers tended also to impose their ideas about the types of work suitable for men and women on the way they constructed tasks into full- or part-time jobs.

Finally, the survey found that explicit 'manpower' strategies were rare. Only a third of the establishments surveyed claimed to be pursuing a coherent employment strategy, of which only a third felt that 'core–periphery' described their particular approach (Hunter *et al.*, 1993). The researchers concluded that it was business strategy at a corporate level that was setting the lead for labour utilisation practices at the operating level, with business strategy in turn governed by the competitive forces at work in the 1980s. Local managements were obliged to meet exacting cost or profit objectives, and if this meant searching for labour cost savings by increasing the use of non-standard labour contracts they would proceed accordingly. Careful costing of the alternatives, however, was rare.

The second Warwick Company Level survey in 1992 suggested a similar conclusion. Coherent policies for seeking labour flexibility were relatively rare. Rather, firms tended to 'respond to particular contingencies and/or to rely on specific opportunities as they arise' (Marginson *et al.*, 1993: 49).

Of course, *ad hoc* adjustments may, over time, amount to sharper patterns of workforce differentiation. Certainly Neathey and Hurstfield's (1995) study of practices in retailing and financial services suggest that patterns of differentiation have been accentuated, although within the *part-time* workforce, as between, for example, permanent and casualised part-time staff. The particular conditions of competition in retailing, liberalisation of trading hours and permissive framework of British employment legislation have been influences. It is among the large retailers that there have been some of the most dramatic examples of employers' attempts to extend 'numerical flexibility' (as, for example, at the Burton Group).

The flexible firm model was developed originally as a model of change among large manufacturing employers. It is in manufacturing, perhaps, that moves to develop a peripheral workforce have been slowest. The *Financial Times* report cited above (1 February 1996) suggests that the situation may be changing, with some employers extending their use of temporary contracts in particular. The analysis is speculative, however, and the changes may relate to the specific circumstances of the early 1990s. As Legge (1995: 161) suggests, the one sector that offers the clearest evidence of a deliberate attempt to enact the core–periphery model is the public services. Use of subcontracting, via competitive tendering and market testing, was compelled by Conservative government public service reforms designed to elevate 'free market' over political and administrative regulation.

CONCLUSION

The more volatile economic conditions prevailing in the advanced industrialised countries since the 1970s have kept labour flexibility at the centre of public policy debate. Different meanings have been attached to the concept and different routes prescribed for achieving greater flexibility in the work process and in the labour market. The neo-liberal analysis ascribes sluggish economic growth and the persistence of large-scale unemployment in Europe to 'institutional rigidities' in product and, more especially, labour markets, and advocates a government policy of deregulation. Opponents of this view urge that more stringent, pan-European labour standards are required to stimulate the reconstruction of industry on a high pay, high skill, high productivity basis.

Adhering to the neo-liberal analysis, the former Conservative government in Britain pursued a comprehensive series of reforms of labour market institutions. Government ministers rolled out a legislative programme designed to curtail trade union power and to give employers greater freedom in the conduct of industrial relations. Employment protection legislation, which historically had been relatively weak in comparison with most other European countries, was eroded further. Employers were encouraged to decentralise pay-fixing arrangements and to introduce payment systems which related employee reward to individual performance or to that of the enterprise. Public sector reforms set the scene for a shift away from industry-level structures of collective bargaining. The impact of these labour market reforms has been hotly contested.

In his study, completed for the Employment Department in 1995, Beatson concluded that the British labour market had become more flexible since the late 1970s. At the macroeconomic level, the early fall in unemployment in the recovery from the 1990–2 recession suggested that employment had become more responsive to changes in output. Moreover, average earnings growth in the early 1990s remained low, despite the upturn in the labour market. For Beatson, however, evidence of greater flexibility was most apparent at the micro-level. Due to government reforms, and other factors, firms had secured greater external (or numerical). The diminished coverage of unfair dismissal legislation, coupled with the decline in trade union influence, had given employers greater freedom in the areas of engagements and dismissals. The growth in part-time and temporary work and self-employment in the economy as a whole suggested that employers had been constructing labour contracts to secure external/numerical flexibility. The decentralisation of collective bargaining and increased use of individualised payment systems was indicative of greater wage (or financial) flexibility. And the increased diversity of working time patterns, coupled with survey data suggesting that barriers to 'functional flexibility' in the workplace had been reduced, amounted to evidence of increased internal flexibility.

Yet Beatson acknowledged that the gains had been primarily in the area of external/numerical flexibility. 'Full-blown' functional flexibility, in the sense of autonomous workgroups and multi-skilled teamworking, still appeared to be 'something of a rarity in Britain', possibly because 'from the employer's perspective, functional flexibility involves costs (in terms of training and development) as well as benefits (in terms of higher productivity)' (1995a: 59). And other commentators have suggested that the very weakness of the legal and institutional 'constraints' on employers' use of labour in Britain have deterred the process of 'upmarket restructuring'. Able to draw on a supply of relatively cheap and disposable labour, firms have been dissuaded from investing in the upgrading of products, processes and labour skills (Nolan, 1996).

Unemployment has fallen throughout the mid-1990s, but remains high in comparison with the 1960s and '70s. The general sense of job insecurity has been widely reported. Thus it may well be, as a Trades Union Congress report suggests, that 'more people are "flexible" in that they are scared of losing their job' (1995: 11). Detailed analyses suggest that while employment growth in Britain in the 1990s was strong in comparison with the record of the 1980s, it was unexceptional by international standards (Morgan, 1996) and unimpressive by the standards of Britain's post-war past (TUC, 1995). Moreover, it remains far from clear that deregulatory policies in the 1980s and early 1990s stimulated the creation of new, more 'flexible' patterns of employment, or new approaches to working-time flexibility.

The evidence reviewed in this chapter suggests that working time patterns have become more diverse. One aspect has been the wider dispersion of working hours, with more people working very long and more working very short hours. Employers have experimented with new approaches to working-time flexibility, but the proportion of employees covered by annualised hours, job-sharing, compressed-working-week, etc. arrangements remains low. The spread of these arrangements in Britain has been no greater than in other EU countries. Traditional approaches to working-time flexibility continue to predominate in most countries. Britain remains distinctive, however, in the extent to which employers continue to depend on long hours and overtime working.

Part-time employment has grown, but this continues a long-term trend, pre-dating the 1980s, and is associated with the sectoral recomposition of employment; the decline in manufacturing and concentration of employment growth on the service sector. Part-time employment has increased in most European countries over the 1980s and '90s, and in some countries (notably the Netherlands) the rate of growth achieved has been significantly higher than in the UK. In other words, differences in the framework of employment regulation do not appear to have had an impact on the overall growth of part-time work, although there may have been differences in the quality of the part-time jobs created. While most part-timers in Britain are 'permanent' employees, there is some evidence of increased use of casualised part-time work in some industries. The growth in self-employment in Britain, which has been above the European average, is partly explained as a response to male unemployment. Temporary work has risen in the recovery of the 1990s, but its incidence remains below the European average. The relative insecurity of 'permanent' staff in Britain appears to have inhibited employers from using on any scale this most obvious form of 'numerically flexible' non-standard labour contract.

Surveys have detected a deliberate 'core–periphery' strategy among only a minority of employers, and have found relatively few employers who are willing to extend guarantees of job security to their 'core' or regular workers. Whether the result of conscious policy or of *ad hoc* adjustments, the increased use of temporary and casualised part-time jobs in the 1990s could be indicative of deepening rigidities in the labour market. Such workers are the least likely to receive training in the upgrading of labour skills. In relation to this, one of the clearest signs of labour market bifurcation in the 1980s and early '90s was the growing dispersion of pay and earnings.

It remains to be seen whether the policies proposed by Britain's New Labour Government, electected in May 1997, prompt a significant and sustained shift in employers' labour use and labour management practices. New Labour's analysis of labour markets does not differ radically from that of the Conservative Government it has displaced. Extensive regulation has been rejected as inimical to industry competitiveness and employment growth. Nevertheless, New Labour have accepted the need for certain minimum labour standards, to promote economic efficiency and social justice, and have reversed the UK's opt out of the EU Social Chapter. Among the measures proposed are a national minimum wage, intended to remove the worst excesses of low pay and to encourage employers to compete on quality rather than labour costs alone, and rights to union representation and recognition. These latter proposals have been presented by government ministers as supportive of the development of voluntary 'partnerships' in which unions and employers exchange collaboration with flexibility initiatives for enhanced employment security.

It is too early to assess the impact of the proposed measures; at the time of writing most had not reached the statute book. On paper, and viewed again the trajectory of British employment legislation over the past twenty years, they amount to a significant extension of individual and collective employment rights. But many employers remain sceptical, in particular of the union recognition proposals. And as Prime Minister Tony Blair has emphasised, New Labour's proposed 'fairness at work' legislation will still leave Britain with the least regulated labour market among the world's leading economies.

QUESTIONS

1 What factors have sustained the widespread interest in labour flexibility, in Britain and abroad, for the past twenty years?

2 What types of labour flexibility are emphasised by (a) advocates of labour market deregulation and (b) proponents of the 'flexible specialisation' thesis?

3 What is 'lean production' and in what ways does it differ from conventional mass production?

4 From the employee's perspective, what are the positive and negative aspects of lean production work regimes?

5 Why are the provisions on job security in the 'New Deal' agreement negotiated by the Rover car company considered to be conducive to flexible working under lean production?

6 Does the growth in non-standard employment in Britain in the 1980s and 1990s provide evidence that employers are reorganising their workforces in the ways identified in the 'flexible firm' model?

7 What are the provisions of the EU Working Time Directive and how might these encourage an overhaul of working time patterns and practices in Britain?

8 Why is it that Britain has one of the lowest proportions of temporary employees within the EU?

ACTIVITY

Imagine you are the personnel manager of an ice-cream factory. Your plant has relied traditionally on overtime working and the use of temporary staff to meet seasonal fluctuations in demand. Employees in the past have always been willing to work overtime; they value the additional income. The plant's location, near a university town, has meant that seasonal temporary workers have always been easy to recruit. But circumstances are changing. The Working Time Directive is to come into force, and competitor companies have made substantial productivity gains in recent years. Your managing director has asked you to brief her about viable alternatives to the work practices currently in force. What changes, if any, would you recommend?

REFERENCES

ACAS (1988) *Labour Flexibility in Britain: the 1987 ACAS Survey*, occasional paper, no. 41. London: ACAS.

Amin, A. (1994) 'Post-Fordism: models, fantasies and phantoms of transition' in Amin, A. (ed.) *Post-Fordism, A Reader*. Oxford: Blackwell, 1–39.

Atkinson, J. (1984) 'Manpower strategies for flexible organisations', *Personnel Management*, August, 28–31.

Atkinson, J. (1985) 'Flexibility: planning for the uncertain future', *Manpower Policy and Practice*, 1, 26–9.

Atkinson, J. and Gregory, D. (1986) 'A flexible future: Britain's dual labour market', *Marxism Today*, 30 (4), 12–17.

Atkinson, J. and Meager, N. (1986) *New Forms of Work Organisation*, IMS report, no. 121. Brighton: Institute of Manpower Studies.

Beatson, M. (1995a) *Labour Market Flexibility*. Employment Department Research Series no. 48. London: Department of Employment.

Beatson, M. (1995b) 'Progress towards a flexible labour market', *Employment Gazette*, February, 55–66.

Blyton, P. (1994) 'Working hours' in Sisson, K. (ed.) *Personnel Management: A Comprehensive Guide to Theory and Practice in Britain*. Oxford: Blackwell, 495–526.

Chote, R. (1997) 'The job creation barrier', *Financial Times*, 13 October.

Clark, J. (1995) *Managing Innovation and Change: People, Technology and Strategy*. London: Sage.

Claydon, T. (1997) 'Human resource management and the labour market', in Beardwell, I. and Holden, L. (eds) *Human Resource Management, A Contemporary Perspective*. London: Financial Times Pitman Publishing, 73–117.

Crafts, N. (1991) 'Reversing relative economic decline? The 1980s in historical perspective', *Oxford Review of Economic Policy*, 7 (3), pp. 81–98.

Cranfield Network for European HRM (1996) *Working Time and Contract Flexibility in the EU* Bedfordshire: Cranfield University School of Management.

Cressey, P. and Scott, P. (1992) 'Employment, technology and industrial relations in the UK clearing banks: is the honeymoon over?', *New Technology, Work and Employment*, 7 (2), 83–106.

Cross, M. (1988) 'Changes in working practices in UK manufacturing 1981–88', *Industrial Relations Review and Report*, 415, May, 2–10.

Curtis, S. and Spence, A. (1994) 'Revised estimates of the workforce in employment in Great Britain', *Employment Gazette*, May, 161–70.

Daniel, W.W. (1987) *Workplace Industrial Relations and Technical Change*. London: Frances Pinter.

De Grip, A., Hoevenberg, J. and Willems, E. (1997) 'Atypical employment in the European Union', *International Labour Review*, 136 (1), 49–71.

Delbridge, R. and Turnbull, P. (1992) 'Human resource maximisation: the management of labour under just-in-time manufacturing systems', in Blyton, P. and Turnbull, P. (eds) *Reassessing Human Resource Management*. London: Sage, 56–73.

Dex, S. and McCulloch, A. (1995) *Flexible Employment in Britain: A Statistical Analysis*. Equal Opportunities Commission Research Discussion Series no.15. Manchester: Equal Opportunities Commission.

Dohse, K., Jurgens, U. and Malsch, T. (1985) 'From "Fordism" to "Toyotism"? The social organization of the labor process in the Japanese automobile industry', *Politics and Society*, 14 (2), 115–46.

Dunn, S. and Wright, M. (1994) 'Maintaining the "Status Quo"? An analysis of the contents of British collective agreements, 1979–1990', *British Journal of Industrial Relations*, 32 (1), 23–41.

Edwards, P. and Wright, M. (1996) 'Does teamworking work and if so, why?', paper presented at ESRC seminar, the Manchester Series, Human Resource Management in Crisis? Manchester Metropolitan University, 27 September.

Elger, T. (1991) 'Task flexibility and the intensification of labour in UK manufacturing in the 1980s' in Pollert, A. (ed.) *Farewell to Flexibility?* Oxford: Blackwell, 46–66.

EOR (1996) 'Women part-timers' earnings', *EOR*, no. 66, March/April, p. 30.

Garrahan, P. and Stewart, P. (1992) *The Nissan Enigma – Flexibility at Work in a Local Economy*. London: Mansell.

Geary, J. (1992) 'Employment flexibility and human resource management: the case of three American electronics plants', *Work, Employment and Society*, 6(2), 251–270.

Geary, J. (1994) 'Task participation: employees' participation enabled or constrained?' in Sisson, K. (ed.) *Personnel Management: A Comprehensive Guide to Theory and Practice in Britain*. Oxford: Blackwell, pp. 634–61.

Hart, R. (1987) *Working Time and Employment*. London: Allen and Unwin.

Heather, P., Rick, J., Atkinson, J. and Morris, S. (1996) 'Employers' use of temporary workers', *Labour Market Trends*, September, 403–11.

Hunter, L., McGregor, A., MacInnes, J. and Sproull, A. (1993) 'The 'flexible firm': strategy and segmentation', *British Journal of Industrial Relations*, 31(3), 383–407.

Hyman, R. (1988) 'Flexible specialisation: miracle or myth?' in Hyman, R. and Streeck, W. (eds) *New Technology and Industrial Relations*. Oxford: Basil Blackwell.

IDS (1990) 'Flexibility in the 1990s', *IDS Study*, 454, March.

IDS (1993a) 'Annual hours', *IDS Study*, 554, December.

IDS (1993b) 'Atypical working patterns across the EC', *IDS European Report*, 382, October, 17–20.

IDS (1994a) 'Multi-skilling', *IDS Study*, 558, July.

IDS (1994b) 'The flexible workforce: myth and reality', *IDS Report* 669, July, 1.

IDS (1995) 'The shifting sands of working time', *IDS Employment Europe* 407, November, 11–19.

IDS (1996) 'UK to toe the line on working time limits?', *IDS Employment Europe* 413, May, 26–8.

IDS (1997a) 'Working time', *IDS Focus*, 81, March.

IDS (1997b) 'The new agenda', *IDS Focus*, special issue, May.

IRS (1989) 'Part-timers: "hours to suit" and benefits to match?', *IRS Employment Trends*, 449, October, 6–10.

IRS (1992a) 'Labour flexibility – reaching the limit?', *IRS Employment Trends*, 512, May, 8–15.

IRS (1992b) 'Lean production – and Rover's "New Deal"', *IRS Employment Trends*, 514, June, 12–15.

IRS (1993) 'Burton introduces concept of "key-time" employment', *IRS Employment Trends*, 533, April, 2–3.

IRS (1994) 'Non-standard working under review', *IRS Employment Trends*, 565, August, 5–14.

IRS (1995a) 'Lean suppliers to lean producers 1: changes in working practices', *IRS Employment Trends*, 583, May, 3–9.

IRS (1995b) 'Lean suppliers to lean producers 2: employee relations strategies', *IRS Employment Trends*, 584, May, 11–16.

IRS (1996a) 'Still a flexible friend? A survey of flexitime arrangements', *IRS Employment Trends*, 603, March, 5–16.

IRS (1996b) 'Flexible working hours – a survey of practice', *IRS Employment Trends*, 608, May, 4–10.

IRS (1997) 'The changing nature of the employment contract', *IRS Employment Trends*, 635, July, 6–11.

Ingram, P. (1991) 'Changes in working practices in British manufacturing industry in the 1980s: a study of employee concessions made during wage negotiations', *British Journal of Industrial Relations*, 29(1), 1–13.

Institute of Personnel and Development (1996) 'The people management implications of leaner ways of working', *Issues in People Management,* no. 15.

Lane, C. (1989) *Management and Labour in Europe.* Aldershot: Edward Elgar.

Legge, K. (1995) *Human Resource Management: Rhetorics and Realities.* Basingstoke: Macmillan.

Marginson, P., Armstrong, P., Edwards, P. and Purcell, J. with Hubbard, N. (1993) 'The control of industrial relations in large companies: an initial analysis of the second company level industrial relations survey', Warwick Papers in Industrial Relations no. 45, IRRU, School of Industrial and Business Studies, University of Warwick, December.

Marsden, D. and Thompson, M. (1990) 'Flexibility agreements and their significance in the increase in productivity in British manufacturing since 1980', *Work, Employment and Society,* 4(1), 83–104.

Metcalf, D. (1989) 'Water notes dry up: the impact of the Donovan proposals and Thatcherism at work on labour productivity in British manufacturing industry', *British Journal of Industrial Relations,* 27(1), 1–31.

Millward, N., Stevens, M., Smart, D. and Hawes, W.R. (1992) *Workplace Industrial Relations in Transition*, the ED/ESRC/PSI/ACAS Surveys. Aldershot: Dartmouth.

Milne, S. (1995) 'British work longest hours in EU', *Guardian*, 26 January, 3.

Morgan, J. (1996) 'Labour market recoveries in the UK and other OECD countries', *Labour Market Trends,* December, 529–39.

Mulgan, G. and Wilkinson, H. (1995) 'Well-being and time', *Demos*, quarterly issue 5, 2–11.

NEDO (1986) *Changing Working Patterns: How Companies Achieve Flexibility to Meet New Needs.* London: NEDO.

Neathey, F. and Hurstfield, J. (1995) *Flexibility in Practice: Women's Employment and Pay in Retail and Finance*, Equal Opportunities Research Discussion Series no. 16. London: Industrial Relations Services.

Nolan, P. (1989) 'Walking on water? performance and industrial relations under Thatcher', *Industrial Relations Journal*, 28(2), 81–92.

Nolan, P. (1994) 'Labour market institutions, industrial restructuring and unemployment in Europe', in Michie, J. and Grieve Smith, J. (eds) *Unemployment in Europe.* London: Academic Press, pp. 61–71.

Nolan, P. (1996) 'Industrial relations and performance since 1945', in Beardwell, I. (ed.) *Contemporary Industrial Relations, A Critical Analysis.* Oxford: Oxford University Press, pp. 99–120.

O'Reilly, J. (1992) 'Banking on flexibility: a comparison of the use of flexible employment strategies in the retail banking sector in Britain and France', *International Journal of Human Resource Management*, 3(1), 35–58.

Osborne, K. (1996) 'Earnings of part-time workers: data from the 1995 New Earnings Survey', *Labour Market Trends,* May, 227–35.

Parker, M. and Slaughter, J. (1988) 'Management by stress', *Technology Review,* October, 37–44.

Pickard, J. (1990) 'Engineering tools up for local bargaining', *Personnel Management,* March.

Piore, M. and Sabel, C. (1984) *The Second Industrial Divide: Possibilities for Prosperity.* New York: Basic Books.

Pollert, A. (1987) 'The "flexible firm": a model in search of reality (or a policy in search of a practice)?', Warwick Papers in Industrial Relations, no.19, IRRU, School of Industrial and Business Studies, University of Warwick.

Procter, S.J., Rowlinson, M., McArdle, L., Hassard, J. and Forrester, P. (1994) 'Flexibility, politics and strategy: in defence of the model of the flexible firm', *Work, Employment and Society,* 8(2), pp. 221–42.

Prowse, P. (1990) 'Assessing the flexible firm', *Personnal Review,* 19(6).

Rees, C., Scarborough, H. and Terry, M. (1996) 'Report by the Industrial Relations Research Unit, Warwick Business School, University of Warwick', in *IPD Issues in People Management,* no. 15, 'The people management implications of leaner ways of working'.

Sabel, C. (1982) *Work and Politics.* Cambridge: Cambridge University Press.

Sayer, A. (1986) 'New developments in manufacturing: the just in time system', *Capital and Class,* no. 30, 43–72.

Scarborough, H. and Terry, M. (1996) 'Industrial relations and the reorganisation of production in the UK motor vehicle industry: a study of the Rover Group', Warwick Papers in Industrial Relations, no. 58, February.

Schonberger, R.J. (1983) 'Japanese manufacturing techniques: nine hidden lessons in simplicity', *Operations Management Review,* spring.

Streeck, W. (1985) 'Industrial relations and industrial change in the motor industry, an international view', public lecture, University of Warwick, 23 October.

Streeck, W. (1991) 'On the institutional conditions of diversified quality production', in Matzner, E. and Streeck, W. (eds) *Beyond Keynesianism: The Socio-Economics of Production and Full Employment.* Aldershot: Edward Elgar.

Teague, P. (1994) 'Labour market governance in the new Europe', *Employee Relations,* 16(6).

Thompson, P. and McHugh, D. (1995) *Work Organisations: A Critical Introduction,* 2nd edn. Basingstoke: Macmillan.

Tomaney, J. (1994) 'A new paradigm of work organisation and technology?', in Amin, A. (ed.) *Post-Fordism, A Reader.* Oxford: Blackwell, pp. 157–94.

Trades Union Congress (1995) 'Has deregulation delivered more jobs?', TUC evidence to ILO Committee of Experts on Employment Policy, January.

Vickery, G. and Wurzburg, G. (1996) 'Flexible firms, skills and employment', *The OECD Observer,* no. 202, October/November, 17–21.

Watson, G. (1994) 'The flexible workforce and patterns of working hours in the UK', *Employment Gazette,* July, 239–47.

Wickens, P. (1993) 'Lean production and beyond: the system, its critics and the future', *Human Resource Management Journal*, 3(4), 75–90.

Williams, K., Cutler, T., Williams, J. and Haslam, C. (1987) 'The end of mass production?', *Economy and Society*, 21(3), 321–54.

Womack, J., Jones, D. and Roos, D. (1990) *The Machine that Changed the World*. New York: Rawson Associates.

Wood, S. (1989) 'The transformation of work?', in Wood, S. (ed.) *The Transformation of Work? Skill, Flexibility and the Labour Process*. London: Routledge, pp. 1–43.

Chapter 14

PUBLIC SECTOR EMPLOYMENT

John Black and Martin Upchurch

Learning objectives

By the end of this chapter, readers should be able to:

- discuss the origins and current composition of public sector employment;
- consider the special features of public sector employee relations and, in relation to this, discuss the concept of 'model employer';
- examine recent developments and contemporary issues in public sector employee relations, in particular the attempted transition from an industrial relations to a human resource management context.

INTRODUCTION

Employee relations in the public sector have experienced a major transformation in the past two decades. The reasons for this change are located in a reversal of the state's approach to the public sector, both in terms of the scope and scale of its activity and the relationship it has with the public as a 'provider' of public services. Ideological commitment to market forces combined with a concentration on supply-side economic forces has meant that public spending is no longer seen by governments as a panacea for economic ills during downward swings of the business cycle. The role of the public sector as a vehicle for boosting demand has been replaced by notions that 'excessive' public spending is harmful to the national economy. Indeed the Conservative government in the 1980s and into the 1990s was not alone among advanced industrial countries in being openly distrustful of the public sector, and often sought to 'scapegoat' public spending as the cause of economic demise (Ferner, 1994). The consequences for employee relations have been severe, involving restrictions on the growth of the wage bill, a cutback in levels of staffing in the drive for efficiency, and the introduction of new management initiatives designed to reflect financial accountability within a marketised environment. Two results of this 'wind of change' have been a thorough overhaul of much of the organisational culture and structure of the public services and a sharp increase in industrial disputes, both in absolute terms and in relation to the traditionally more strike-prone private manufacturing sector.

While the size of the public sector as an employer has been reduced with privatisation and contracting-out, it nevertheless still employs a fifth of the UK workforce in total, and so an understanding of developments remains important in its own right. The total employed by either central government, local government, grant-funded bodies (such as universities) or the surviving nationalised industries (such as the Post Office) numbered just over 5 million in 1997. Those directly employed by the state, as Crown Civil Servants, equalled some 600 000 in 1997. The NHS has more than a million employees, and local government is the largest sector with approximately 2.5 million employees, mainly concentrated in education, social services, and the police and fire services. The remaining nationalised industries or public corporations such as the Post Office and Bank of England have less direct control from central government but nevertheless are subject to Parliamentary accountability and restrictions on trading. Total employment in this sector is just over half a million.

This chapter begins, however, with an historical overview of the development of the public sector prior to the onset of change in the mid- to late 1970s. The structure of employment within the sector is then described before analysing in more depth why change has occurred in the 1980s and 1990s. New management initiatives will then be outlined as well as the mechanisms for establishing the difficult question of public service pay. A profile of public sector trade unionism is then given together with some analysis of disputes and strikes. Finally, the chapter seeks to address the approach of the new Labour government and the agendas for further change into the next century.

FROM 'MODEL EMPLOYER' TO 'WINTER OF DISCONTENT'

From the end of the First World War in 1918 through the development of the post-1945 welfare state, successive governments adopted a 'model employer' approach to the public service (Fredman and Morris, 1989). In practice this meant that the government, as employer, should set some example to the private sector in terms of fair treatment of employees and recognition of representation rights in collective bargaining. Fair treatment meant not only the benefits of pay and conditions but also high levels of job security, good (non-contributory and index-linked) pensions and generous sick pay schemes. 'Fair' pay was achieved by the establishment of an elaborate set of 'comparability' mechanisms that sought to assess the skills of public servants with the nearest equivalents in the private sector and to set the resultant pay level in the 'average-to-good' range of the private comparators. The role of trade unions as bargaining partners was also thoroughly institutionalised by the establishment of Pay Review Bodies and Councils such as the National Whitley Council for the Civil Service or the Burnham Committee for teachers, which allowed for formal consultation and negotiation on pay and conditions. Such a recognition of the role of trade unions came as a result of the perceived need to contain and control the growing trade union movement in the immediate aftermath of war. J.H Whitley, Deputy Speaker of the House of Commons, had produced his Committee

Report in March 1917, which recommended the establishment of joint councils between employers and employees 'to give opportunities for satisfying the growing demands made by trade unions for a share in industrial control' (quoted in Wigham, 1980). Most public sector unions were naturally quick to campaign for the introduction of the 'Whitley Councils' into the public service. Rules and procedures were also subject to joint consultation and implemented through Code Books, which allowed for national standards to be maintained (for example, the Pay and Conditions of Service Code for the Civil Service included over 11 500 paragraphs of regulations from major pay scales down to the comparative obscurity of 'daily pedal cycle allowances'). In cases of dispute an elaborate procedure of appeals and arbitration was constructed that allowed full trade union representation and staged involvement during the appeal process.

Other reasons for the establishment of this 'model employer' approach were as follows.

First, there was recognition in the inter-war period that a modern industrialised society was becoming more complex and complicated to administer and hence a professional civil and public service was needed as a result. To recruit and retain good staff it was therefore necessary to ensure that pay levels and other conditions of service were 'fair' and comparable with the private sector.

Second, the achievement of this comparability and the associated development of an effective internal labour market for professionals within the public service were in themselves difficult to accomplish. Sophisticated machinery (the Pay Review Bodies) were therefore needed to overcome this problem.

Third, it was important to 'legitimise' the process of the establishment of fairness and comparability by the involvement of trade unions within the institutional structures as representatives of staff. Thus, the formalised involvement of trade unions, including the positive official encouragement to all staff to join the appropriate and recognised union, helped the top management of the public service in the task of maintaining a sense of fairness as well as easing the considerable administrative burden of assessing hundreds of separate pay scales over a huge range of crafts and occupations. To help ease the burden further, the process of 'comparability' was best served by the establishment of strict incremental progress through the pay scales, which recognised seniority of service and could be applied easily if the employee moved jobs within the service or moved to another part of the country.

The concept and practice of 'model employer' thus created a bureaucratic and centralised machinery in which employee relations were conducted, and which gave some concession and advantage to public sector unions and their members. The associated rules and regulations governing the employment relationship consolidated the growing hierarchical organisation structure of large ministries and government agencies bound by statute in their tasks and functions.

■ Keynesianism and the welfare state

The concept of the 'model employer' continued through and after the Second World War. The public sector became more important in the atmosphere of post-war reconciliation and reconstruction for two reasons.

First, the fear of a return to the depression years of the 1920s and 1930s had created political space for the adoption of J. M. Keynes' theories of demand management of the economy. In 1944 the government had published a White Paper arguing the necessity for policies likely to produce 'high and stable levels of employment' in the post-war period, and by the end of the war Keynesian economics had been accepted as orthodoxy by the Treasury. From the 1950s through to the mid-1970s both Conservative and Labour governments then sought to maintain full employment by a variety of fiscal and monetary measures that ensured a key role for the public sector in boosting domestic demand to avoid recession.

Second, the value of public spending as a counter to recession was boosted by the perceived political need to both reconstruct British industry and society and head off social discontent with the creation of a post-war 'welfare state'. The wartime coalition government had produced the Beveridge Plan in 1942, which emerged as a 'new declaration of human rights brought up to date for an industrial society and dealing in plain and vigorous language with some of the most controversial issues in British politics'. After this post-war 'political settlement' the 1945–50 Labour government then proceeded to bring in the enabling legislation creating the pillars of the welfare state, together with legislation to nationalise key industries in an effort to rationalise and modernise. The central aspects of legislation and their practical outcomes can be summarised as follows.

The National Insurance Act 1946 and the National Health Service Act 1946 laid down the principles of 'universality', which gave equal right of access to a developing range of social benefits and free medical treatment. Such 'rights' as sickness and unemployment benefit were made available to those who had paid their share of National Insurance contributions and were available for a limited period only. The NHS legislation would of course mean the building of new hospitals as well as the expansion of General Practitioners' workload. The Housing Acts, 1946 and 1949, released local authorities from the obligation that they should only build accommodation for the 'working class' but in reality allowed councils to raise money and begin a process of building housing for the masses, first as post-war pre-fabricated bungalows to house the homeless and later as mass council estates on compulsorily purchased land. The 1944 Education Act formed a fourth pillar of the welfare state and granted free secondary education for all up to the age of 15. Together the combined effect of the legislation was to massively boost the role and scope of the public sector within the economy, leading to the creation of hundreds of thousands of jobs which included, in particular, new and expanding opportunities for female employment in the so-called 'caring' occupations such as nursing and teaching. Another important consequence of this post-war expansion was the creation of large numbers of new jobs in lower paid areas that serviced the public functions of the welfare state (cleaners, porters, junior clerks, etc.). An expanding economy meant that labour shortages were a problem, and so it was necessary to draw not only more women into employment, either as full- or part-time workers but also, in the 1950s and 1960s, to recruit immigrant labour from the Caribbean and Indian sub-continent. Special recruitment drives took place in the West Indies, for example, to fill new and vacant posts in areas such as public transport and nursing. By 1980, 2.3 million people were employed by central government and just over 3 million by local authorities.

The profile of those employed within the public sector also changed dramatically as a result of the post-war programme of nationalisation. The first organisation to be nationalised was actually the Bank of England, on 1 March 1946, but this was followed by the nationalisation of civil aviation (1946), coal, cable and wireless (1947), transport and electricity (1948), gas (1949) and iron and steel (1951). By 1961 the nationalised industries and public corporations employed 2.2 million and throughout the next two decades, until the era of privatisation, the total employed stabilised around two million. All in all, by the end of the 1970s, almost 30 per cent of all employment in the UK was in the public sector.

Employee relations during the period of 'model employer'

Employees in the public sector, especially in the post-war period, enjoyed some distinctly superior terms and conditions as a result of the 'model employer' approach to their private sector counterparts. First, their pay was generally set, under the terms of 'fair comparison', with the 'average-to-good' range of those equivalent jobs in the private sector. While inflation was relatively low (as it was through the 1950s and 1960s) any period of 'catching-up' in terms of waiting for the results of comparability exercises was not an insurmountable problem. In addition to pay, most 'white-collar' civil and public servants also enjoyed the benefits of a good non-contributory pension scheme (the contributions being offset against pay levels) and job security for the more senior grades in return for contractual obligation to accept transfer anywhere within the relevant branch of the public service (enhanced with generous relocation packages). Benefits for junior 'white-collar' grades and industrial grades were less good. Pay was generally low but other conditions of service schemes (pensions, sick pay, etc.) were superior to those found in most of the private sector. However, public sector employee relations in this period was not without its problems. One particular concern, the role and status of women in the public service, had dogged industrial relations since the 1920s over the two issues of equal pay and the 'marriage bar' (which denied employment to those, such as women teachers, who married). Campaigns were launched by the unions in favour of equal pay in the 1930s but were unsuccessful. Some of the public sector unions restored the campaign after the war but were not supported by the TUC until 1950. It was not until 1955 that the government agreed to gradually introduce equal pay into the public services in stages until full operation in 1961. This, of course, predates the 1970 Equal Pay Act, for which women in the private sector had to wait before justice was done. The campaign to end the marriage bar on married women's employment actually split the trade unions in the immediate post-war period. The Union of Post Office Workers, together with some of the senior grade civil service unions, wanted to keep the bar based on arguments that men were family 'breadwinners'. Others, such as the Civil Service Clerical Association, wanted to abolish it. Similarly, in teaching, the National Association of Schoolmasters (NAS) was in favour of retention while the National Union of Teachers (NUT) and Union of Women Teachers (UWT) favoured abolition. However, the experience of women working in the war and their increased absorption into the labour force clearly made the 'bar' anomalous, leading to eventual abolition by the government in phases during the lifetime of the 1945–50 Labour administration.

Public sector employees have also been restricted in some of the 'rights' to participate in political affairs such as standing for local councillor or parliamentary positions as members of a political party. The rules disallowing open political sympathy, or campaigning or standing in elections, have generally been applied to the more senior grades or those in 'politically sensitive' posts. Political vetting of candidates for some posts (with questions geared at political sympathy or parents' nationality) have also been designed to preserve the alleged 'neutrality' of civil appointments in the public service. The trade unions were also affected by the provisions of the 1927 Trades Disputes Act which, in the aftermath of the defeated General Strike (1926), removed the 'right' of civil service and some other public sector unions to affiliate to either the TUC or the Labour Party. These particular restrictions were repealed after the war. As the immediate post-war period receded, many of the unions also became increasingly aggressive towards government restrictions on pay, particularly as it affected the public sector. Government incomes policy aimed at restricting wage increases was always enforced more rigorously in the public sector (with the government as employer) than it was in the private sector. This, combined with increasing fears of inflation, problems of low pay, and some dissatisfaction with the machinery of pay comparison and its ability to provide compensatory increases, led to the first pay strikes throughout the public sector in the 1970s. Local authority unions conducted their first coordinated national strike over pay in the autumn of 1970 and they were followed by the Union of Post Office Workers, which led its first national strike in 1971 (ending in defeat). In 1973 the Civil Service also experienced its first national pay strike. Meanwhile in 1972 and again in 1974 the National Union of Miners went on all-out strike to re-establish their pay position in the 'earnings league' – a reference to their perceived worsening pay in comparison to other manual groups in the private sector. The miners were victorious in both their strikes and caused an election in 1974 after the Conservative Prime Minister, Edward Heath, threw down the election gauntlet in the aftermath of his attempt to control coal stocks by ordering a 'three-day working week' for all industrial and domestic coal consumers. The resultant victory for the Labour Party did not prevent public sector industrial strife. In 1977 firefighters in the Fire Brigades Union secured a new pay comparison formula after a short all-out strike in which the government utilised army-based 'Green Goddess' fire engines in an attempt to overcome the effects of the strike. Finally, after two years of wage restraint in the public sector under the 1974–79 Labour government, the pay dam finally burst in the 1978/79 'winter of discontent' as NHS and local authority workers conducted a series of all-out and selective strikes designed to restore public sector pay levels to private sector equivalents. A new pay comparability body (the Clegg Commission) was created as part of the settlement of the strikes.

The arrival of militancy in the public sector in the 1970s was also accompanied by internal factional strife in some of the white-collar unions as left-wing 'opposition' groups began to challenge the trade union leaderships' more moderate influence. In unions such as the NUT, the Civil and Public Services Association (Civil Service clerks), and the local authority white-collar union NALGO, these groups were backed by organisations such as Militant and the Socialist Workers' Party. They were often separate from the more established Communist Party led 'broad lefts' within the unions and grew to have some influence as militancy increased generally in the 1970s (see Kelly, 1988; Seifert, 1987).

In summary, with the government as direct or indirect employer and the continuation of the 'model employer' policy, many policy issues covering social affairs, such as equal pay, took place in the public sector in advance of the private sector. The experience of public sector employee relations in the 1970s and the increased tensions over pay meant that the period was very much of a 'coming of age' of the unions and their relationship with the government after the more genteel approach of the 1950s and 1960s. It is now necessary to examine the 'wind of change' that swept through the public sector in the aftermath of Margaret Thatcher's Conservative Party election victory in 1979.

MONETARISM, THATCHERISM AND PUBLIC SPENDING CUTS

The crisis of public sector funding can be traced to the onset of economic recession following the oil 'shock' of 1973/74 and the consequent hike in inflation. The new phenomenon of *stagflation* – rising prices combined with rising unemployment – threw the Labour government (1974–79) into crisis and meant the death knell of Keynesian economic management. Inflation in 1975 reached 24 per cent and, as the economy slowed and unemployment rose, public spending as a proportion of gross domestic product (GDP) soared to average 43.7 per cent in the period from 1974 to 1985 (compared to 37.7 per cent in 1970–73). Part of this increase was related to expanded social security payments to cover increased unemployment but part was also the result of the increased wage bill for public sector employees as comparability awards raced to keep up with inflation. In 1976, faced with a balance of payments crisis and increasing national debt, the Labour government was forced to seek a loan from the International Monetary Fund (IMF), which was granted on condition that the Chancellor (Denis Healey) introduced a *monetarist* economic programme aimed at capping public spending and reducing the public sector borrowing requirement (PSBR). The consequent programme of 'cash limits' for the public sector was designed to control public spending plans of individual departments and ushered in recruitment freezes and a variety of other cost-cutting measures throughout the sector.

The Thatcher government and the public sector

While the 1974–79 Labour government had set in train the reversal of policy towards public sector spending, the incoming Thatcher administration stepped up the attack with extra ideological vigour. The new government's attitude to the public sector was one of hostility as a result not only of monetarist orthodoxy but also because of a perceived need to liberate market forces in an effort to boost Britain's competitive position in the world economy. It was argued that the public sector was a *burden* to the economy in that it did not create wealth and 'crowded out' investment opportunity that could otherwise be allocated to the profit-making private sector (Bacon and Eltis, 1978). In addition, the public sector unions, and their increasingly powerful influence and militancy, were seen as obstacles to the restructuring of the British state and the introduction of *laissez-faire* market forces. As a consequence the Thatcher administration embarked on a programme of policy measures designed both to reduce the size of the public sector and confront the public sector unions and the ever-increasing wage bill. The various policy initiatives are listed below.

Privatisation and contracting-out

The privatisation programme was launched by the government in the 1980s in line with the 1979 Conservative Manifesto commitment. This was to be achieved primarily with the public offer of shares and involved a total of 43 companies by the end of 1996. The share sales had the added advantage of raising revenue for the government and temporarily reducing public sector debt. In 1983–84, for example, over £1 billion was raised and in 1984–85 over £2 billion. The peak years were 1988–89 (£7.1 billion: BP, gas and steel) and 1992–93 (£8.2 billion: BT and electricity). Programmes of the contracting-out of services to the private sector (involving a tendering process) were confined to a range of services in local authorities, the NHS and the Civil Service, such as cleaning, rubbish collection and catering. In terms of employee relations most of the privatisations and contracting-out were bitterly opposed by the unions concerned, involving one-day strikes by BT unions against job losses and fears of reduced services (such as the potential loss of rural telephone kiosks), and selective strikes against the loss of jobs and introduction of inferior conditions of service for those areas of work threatened by contracting out. Both privatisation and contracting-out also fragmented the collective bargaining framework and reduced the power and influence of public sector unions, particularly in local authorities where workers in key areas of 'industrial muscle', such as rubbish collectors, now found themselves working (if they were taken on) in un-unionised and anti-union companies.

Confrontations with the unions

The system of 'cash limits' on departmental spending engendered a series of confrontations with the unions forced to make a 'choice' between increased pay and job loss (given the restrictive limit on budgets). The increased tensions resulted in an upsurge of industrial disputes in the public sector throughout the 1980s including the Civil Service (1981 and 1987), hospital and railway workers (1982), social workers (1983), teachers (1985, 1986 and 1987), local authority white-collar staff (1989) and ambulance workers (1989). Apart from the two disputes in 1989 in every case the unions were defeated in their key objectives of either winning pay demands or opposing programmes of public spending cuts. Industrial action against specific programmes of spending cuts was particularly difficult to sustain. The NHS, for example, saw some key flashpoints when staff occupied wards (e.g. St Benedicts Hospital in South London) that were threatened with closure programmes (Seifert, 1992: ch.7). The general pattern of defeats for the unions meant that a period of relative demoralisation set into the ranks of the public sector unions as a result. The government offensive against the unions also included attacks on the 'fair comparison' principle of pay determination. In the Civil Service the pay comparability machinery for all but top civil servants was withdrawn and teachers lost their rights to negotiate on pay. These defeats for the unions opened the door for a further erosion of relative pay and enabled the government to achieve more easily some of its objectives in cutting the public sector pay bill. The institutional status of trade unions was also downgraded by employer action to redefine Facilities Agreements in the Civil Service, and many local authorities reduced the 'time-off' allocated to trade union local representatives to conduct their trade union business. The 'check-off' arrangement, whereby trade union subscriptions were deducted from wage packets automatically by employers, was also withdrawn in many areas of the public service. Finally, the provision that new staff were 'recommended' in the Civil Service to join the appropriate trade union was dropped by the new government.

In the nationalised industries confrontation was just as sharp. British Steel management defeated the unions in an all-out national strike in 1980, and decentralised collective bargaining to business divisions and rationalised jobs throughout the industry in the process (see Blyton and Turnbull, 1994: ch. 7). Most important of all was the defeat of the year-long strike conducted by the National Union of Mineworkers in 1984–85 over the withdrawal of coal price subsidies and the introduction of a pit closure programme. The defeat of the miners, and the consequent authority it placed in the hands of the government, had clear ramifications for trade union 'solidarity' in Britain, and led to some soul searching within the trade union movement. One other point of interest concerning government attacks on the public sector trade unions was the banning in 1984 of trade union membership for 8000 employees at the Government Central Headquarters (GCHQ) in Cheltenham. For forty years previously GCHQ collated signals intelligence worldwide. The ban was imposed by Ministerial Decree (i.e. without the necessity of a Parliamentary vote) by the Foreign Secretary, Sir Geoffrey Howe, on the presumption that intelligence gathering and trade union membership were incompatible. The banning followed the case of 'spying' for the Soviet Union by an (undeclared) homosexual employee at Cheltenham. Civil Service unions opposed the ban and alleged that it was instigated by President Reagan in the USA as a condition for continuing US financial support for the Centre (the US government also proposed the introduction of the polygraph – lie detector – as a test for all new recruits). Fears that the ban might spread to other civil servants in politically sensitive areas were allayed after the General Secretary of the TUC, Len Murray, went on television to call a one-day General Strike in protest at the ban. With only a few days' notice more than a million people went on strike in response to the TUC's call. One of the first tasks of the incoming Labour government in May 1997 was to reinstate trade union recognition at GCHQ.

It can therefore be seen from the above that the concept of 'model employer' no longer applied under the Conservative governments in the 1980s. The attacks on trade union power and influence, combined with their 'de-institutionalisation' and redefining of the value of pay comparison, changed the framework of public sector industrial relations. Spending cuts, privatisation and contracting-out also reduced the size of the public sector. The net effect of the cuts in the size of the sector are apparent in the fall in the number of those employed. More than 1.9 million jobs were cut between 1981 and 1994 as a result of either privatisation and contracting-out (a transfer to the private sector) or spending cuts in remaining public services. Totals employed in the Civil Service, for example, fell by 20 per cent between 1981 and 1994. The public sector share of employment in the economy has fallen from a high of 30 per cent to just over 20 per cent as a result.

While the institutional role of trade unions had changed and cuts in spending had taken place the government and public sector employers also attempted to alter management style and techniques. It is to this issue that we now turn (*see* Exhibit 14.1).

'MARKETISATION' AND NEW PUBLIC MANAGEMENT

The Conservative government was also concerned to introduce the ethos of 'marketisation' into the public sector as a way of injecting some 'discipline' into decision making and offering market choice to potential consumers of services. This process of marketisation, typified by the breakdown of units and divisions into cost and/or budget centres, has been accompanied with new levels of financial and administrative accountability for managers and new forms of management practice designed to incentivise the workforce in the absence of profit-related market discipline.

Local managers, whether heads of schools, chief nursing officers, governors of penal establishments or commanders of units within the armed forces, are now responsible for offsetting pay increases against productivity and efficiency savings. Headteachers, for example, can now choose between separate items of budget expenditure, such as staff requirements, books and equipment, or administrative items (Menter *et al.*, 1997). The

■ Exhibit 14.1

UK public sector strikes and the search for private finance

For those of a nervous disposition, last week's strikes by the UK Post Office and the London Underground might suggest a return to the bad days of the late 1970s. Taken with the likely return of a Labour government, the spectre is all too familiar: chaos in the capital, unburied corpses and rubbish in the streets. Calmer reflection suggests nothing of the kind. Transport and postal strikes catch the nation's attention; but across the economy as a whole, the reality is that strike figures are still the lowest on record. Critics might pose a different question. Recent strike threats in the private sector, such as that by British Airways pilots, have been quietly averted. Why do public sector managers seem so much less adroit in handling disputes?

The answer comes in two parts. First, today's public sector managers often come from the private sector. The Post Office chairman is an ex-director of personnel at Unilever. The head of London Underground was formerly with British Airways. His boss, the chairman of London Transport, comes from Harvard Business School, McKinsey and P&O. The second part of the answer goes to the heart of what the two disputes are about. In both cases, management is trying to change the organisation's culture: to make it less rigid and more capable of change. The ultimate goal, in both cases, is to make the workers think and act more like their private sector counterparts.

Thus, the Post Office is trying to move away from its old hierarchical culture towards a system of teamwork. London Underground is trying to reform structure in which, for instance, holiday rotas are still organised by the workforce rather than the management.

The ultimate driving force in both cases is the same: the need to attract private sector finance. At the extreme, this means privatisation: explicitly advocated by Post Office management and unlikely to be opposed by London Transport. It might seem an odd time for managers to be thinking in those terms. Even in the unlikely event of a Tory election victory, privatising the Post Office, while still a Tory objective, would prove difficult and contentious.

As for London Underground, privatisation has apparently been dropped from the Tory manifesto as being too politically sensitive. For a Labour government, of course, privatisation – under that title, at any rate – would be anathema. But the main issue would remain. The Post Office and London Underground need to invest heavily if they are to carry on doing their jobs. The more they can present themselves in private sector guise, the easier it will be to attract private finance.

In the Post Office's case, this might seem perverse. Investment is certainly needed to keep pace with the rapid development of electronic media and digital information. But in a private sector context, the Post Office would have no trouble at all in raising the money. Its management, after all, would have a good story to tell: a consistent record of profit, strong cash flow and a remarkable level of customer satisfaction. At present, the Post Office is not allowed to borrow, since that would count as government debt. But as a private company, its balance sheet would allow it to borrow well over £1bn without strain.

The case of London Underground is less clear cut. If its accounts were drawn up in private sector fashion, its operating loss might be relatively small. But by comparison with the Post Office, it is hugely capital intensive. This year, it will swallow close to £1bn of taxpayers' money, of which more than half will be spent on the new extension to the Jubilee Line.

Attempts to help out with private finance have so far proved tough going. The £2bn-plus London CrossRail project, providing an underground link between the capital's railway termini, is supposed to contain an element of private funding. But the main burden will fall upon the taxpayer. Unsurprisingly, therefore, the project has been postponed to the next century.

The government's Private Finance Initiative is supposed to help here, but the results so far are not encouraging. The Northern Line of the Underground is being supplied with some £800m worth of new trains through a leasing arrangement with the suppliers, GEC Alsthom. But even that was opposed by the Treasury as being in breach of its rules, as was a plan to lease out some of the automatic barriers at Underground stations. It would be perhaps unfair to single out the Treasury

■ Exhibit 14.1 continued

as the culprit. The history of nationalised industries in the UK has left its scars. In their heyday, investments by nationalised companies too often proved disastrous. An important reason was that since spending was ultimately backed by government, managers lacked the guidance of the market on the balance between risk and opportunity.

Given the context, today's public sector managers might well feel occasionally helpless. Their ownership structure is unsuited to the job they have to do. Their workers, meanwhile, have no incentive to speed the transition to a private sector model, since they have every evidence that it means upheaval and insecurity.

There is a central irony to all this. The City and the financial markets are criticised for being short-termist. In the closing years of the century, the reality is just the other way round. Governments – not only in the UK – are increasingly weighed down by the fiscal burden of pensions and unemployment. Long-term capital projects are no longer to be thought of, especially by governments which know that proposing taxes to pay for them would spell doom at the polls. The world is therefore reverting to a 19th century model, whereby long-term private savings are channelled by the financial institutions into long-term investments. The problem is not one of a shortage of funds. The question is rather how public sector managers, squeezed between hostile owners and resentful employees, can gain access to the money.

Source: Tony Jackson (1996) *Financial Times*, 12 August.

principle of 'consumer choice' must again be seen as an attempt to introduce market discipline. Prime Minister John Major's (1991–97) initiative on the Citizen's Charter (*see* Glossary) sought to empower consumers of public services if targets for service provision failed. Parental choice in schooling or penalty clauses for service operators of contracted-out services such as refuse collection or road sweeping are other examples.

A summary of some of the key changes follows:

■ Reorganisation of the *Civil Service* into executive agency status and further decentralisation into non-departmental public bodies (NDPB). Staff remained civil servants in status but the overall head of the agency, the Chief Executive, could be appointed either from the public or private sector. Links were maintained with the appropriate government department through a contractual 'framework document'. Pay, conditions of employment and gradings from April 1996 were decentralised to each agency and NDPB. These changes follow the '*Next Steps*' policy introduced into the Civil Service in 1988 designed to break up the Civil Service into more discrete accounting units. A study of such changes in the Prison Service is given in Black (1995) (*see* also Exhibit 14.3).

■ Simulation of competition through the purchaser–provider division (commonly called the *internal market*). Introduced in 1981, this is now apparent in the NHS, NHS Trusts and local authorities. NHS Trusts, for example, now have powers to appoint staff, establish their own conditions of service, and shape their own industrial relations procedures. Within the NHS the market measures have led to competition between hospitals and their departments for internal 'contracts'. Labour savings have clearly been identified as an aid to competitiveness, and fears over job security have arisen as a result. Employers have often responded to their new powers by challenging working practices, and tightening up on discipline and sickness procedures. The conflict between 'cost cutting' and quality service provision has also been apparent, and this in particular has led the new Labour government to re-think the logic of these market reforms within the NHS environment.

■ Within *local authorities* the ability to raise revenue through local taxation has been curtailed by the 'rate capping' procedure enacted by central government, meaning some spending cuts and service withdrawal as a result. Decentralised and devolved managerial accountability also means that many sections of local government now operate within their own budgets and staffing arrangements. Similar arrangements also exist in the school sector through the local management of schools initiative (LMS). This substitutes local authority planning in the schools sector in favour of more direct headteacher responsibility combined with parental choice for state school places. The ability of local secondary schools to opt-out of local authority financial control and raise additional monies reinforces this process of consumer 'choice', especially when combined with the publication of school 'league tables' giving results of examination performance. Both the programme of school 'opt-outs' and league tables were initially opposed by the NUT leading to dispute. The failure of the campaign to prevent the measures led to the NUT withdrawing its opposition.

Management style and technique in the public sector have been much influenced by the emphasis on performance, objectives and targets. This reflects the primary change of devolving financial accountability but also mirrors parallel changes in management techniques much associated with HRM or 'Japanisation' in the private sector. The forms of 'New Public Management' that have evolved have sought to break down the traditional bureaucratic and hierarchical organisation structures that were previously dominant. In addition, this renewed emphasis on rational managerial accountability has acted to allay some of the blame for service cuts from government policy and transfer them to the individual decisions of managers (Winchester and Bach, 1995). In many instances the change has resulted in a downgrading of the traditional importance of negotiated procedures as unions have become de-institutionalised, work has intensified, and collective bargaining has fragmented. Many of the old 'Conditions of Service Handbooks', which formerly laid down rules and regulations of conduct, working procedures and conditions of service, have been downgraded in importance or abandoned. In some cases new local agreements have been negotiated with local trade unions but in other cases, such as in Further Education Colleges, attempts have been made to completely redefine contract terms and impose new ones. Large-scale, long-running disputes with the unions concerned have resulted.

As an alternative management approach, personnel practices have concentrated much more on appraisal systems, the use of direct communication with employees (rather than through trade unions) and quality initiatives such as total quality programmes or quality circles. Teamworking (particularly in the NHS) has also been emphasised. Such changes have posed considerable problems, either because of trade union opposition or because of the difficulties of assessing 'performance' in the public service when no 'value added' contribution can be identified. What measures of performance, for example, could you apply to nurses when the fate of the sick is dependent on so many other factors than simply the care given by an individual nurse? Similarly, how do you assess the performance of a social worker or teacher when caseloads or class size are possibly more important variables in performance outcome?

However, it is in the field of pay determination that the major and most important changes have taken place, and it is this area which is now examined.

PAY DETERMINATION IN THE 1980s AND 1990s

We have already seen how the government, in abandoning the 'model employer' approach, has sought to shift the emphasis away from pay being determined by 'fair comparison' to that of 'affordability'. This shift of emphasis has also corresponded to devolved managerial authority and the perceived need to encourage individual performance and flexibility by using pay as the incentive. Despite these trends, nearly three-quarters of public sector employees still have their pay determined by collective bargaining (Millward *et al.*, 1992), with the remainder still attached to some form of indexation or review by third party. To a large extent this reflects the difficulties of assessing performance of the public servant (as already discussed) as well as the entrenched opposition of trade unions to the break up of more collectively beneficial systems. A summary of the major sectoral differences is given below.

The Civil Service

The pay comparability machinery associated with 'Whitleyism' and the 'model employer' was abandoned by the government in 1981 (despite trade union opposition involving a 20-week dispute of selective strikes in key areas). In the aftermath of the dispute the government established an inquiry into Civil Service pay (the Megaw Report) which concluded with recommendations that maintained 'informed' collective bargaining and which geared pay awards to the priorities of 'recruitment, retention and motivation'. Performance-related pay was introduced shortly afterwards for senior grade staff and the system of 'automatic' yearly incremental progression up long scales was altered to allow for performance only related 'merit' increases to be reserved at the higher end of the scales for most white-collar grades. The extra flexibility in the system satisfied some management criteria but the unions were successful in retaining automatic incremental progression for at least some part of the pay scale. The agreement was achieved on the basis that the outside pay comparisons would be at the lower end of the 'league table' rather than in the average (median) to good range. However, the introduction of agency status into the Civil Service in the 1980s and 1990s led to a fragmentation of paymasters and a devolution of collective bargaining to more discrete areas of work within the service. As a consequence the determination of the pay scales and the mix of automatic and merit increments have now become much more diverse. Pay 'bands' are now commonplace, linked to job-evaluated regrading of skills, tasks and responsibilities. The Treasury, as overall paymaster, still retains some control over pay within agencies and has the power to reverse decisions. On the other hand, some Civil Service departments are likely still to be fully privatised (Amersham International – a scientific establishment formerly part of the Civil Service – was in fact the first government privatisation) and would consequently be completely outside the scope of public sector pay determination.

The National Health Service

The NHS contains a multitude of occupational grades covered by numerous bargaining units and trade unions. Ten separate Whitley Councils have traditionally acted as forums for negotiations based within the fair comparison remit. In addition, doctors and dentists have been catered for by a review body that after consultation with all interested parties has made recommendations on pay and conditions to the government. This highly centralised system has been altered rather than fundamentally challenged in the 1980s and 1990s. Following a lengthy dispute over pay in 1982 the government created two new pay review bodies for nurses and midwives, and employers and government have since sought to influence the outcomes of these reviews by incorporating greater elements of affordability at the expense of comparability. This has resulted in continuing skirmishes between the various unions representing nurses and midwives and the government as ultimate paymaster. In particular, there has been a determined effort to relate nurses' pay to local, rather than national, labour market conditions with proposals for basic increases that could be 'topped-up' (or not) by the need to recruit and retain within the local labour market. Despite this, it has been possible to enhance nurses' pay relative to others within the NHS, either by better than average pay awards or by re-assessing the grading criteria on which individual nurses' pay is assessed. The difficulties of localising nurses' pay have been caused not just by opposition from unions but also by the problems of defining a local labour market for nurses, many of whom relate to a *national* occupational labour market and have highly individual personal profiles relating to skills, grade and contractual status. It is for these reasons that 90 per cent of NHS Trusts have reverted back to national, as opposed to local, pay rates for nurses ('NHS Trusts abandon local pay bargaining', *People Management*, 25 September 1997). One other issue which has clearly upset union negotiators has been the tendency of governments to 'stage' awards of the pay review body and save money by delaying full implementation of any award. This pattern has been repeated by the new Labour government in its decision to stage the 1998 award for nurses.

Elsewhere within the NHS the system of collective bargaining through Whitley Councils continues. The government has been more than willing, however, to utilise its policy of 'cash limits' to suppress pay rises and in 1989 this policy caused confrontation with ambulance workers, who staged a 'work-to-rule' in order to secure a pay review index similar to that enjoyed by the 'emergency services' of the police and fire service. While securing a higher pay settlement than previously offered the ambulance workers failed in their attempt to establish indexation. National agreements for Whitley-related grades have nevertheless shown signs of fragmentation as more discrete elements of local pay linked to 'recruitment and retention' have emerged and managers have begun to exercise power in seeking more flexibility in pay with links to new working arrangements.

■ Local government

Similar patterns of change are recorded in local authorities, with moves by the individual employers to establish local rates outside of the national collective agreement. The employers (i.e. the management of individual local authorities) are members of separate institutions (representing Scotland or the metropolitan or county councils), which for bargaining purposes has led to some discrepancy of position in key disputes. This was highlighted in 1989 during a dispute with the union representing white-collar staff (NALGO) when the employers failed in their efforts to dismantle and break the national collective agreement and impose more locally based agreements in its place. However, within local authorities there remains much scope for variation in pay that can be engineered through grading agreements struck at local level. Thus, it is perfectly possible for differences in remuneration for skills and occupations to arise between authorities as different interpretations of grading formula are imposed or negotiated. The evaluation of jobs and skills by formal (and sometimes informal) means has thus been a key issue in local authority employee relations, sometimes with important equal opportunity implications when it can be demonstrated that particular jobs are gender specific (e.g. canteen assistants compared with 'binmen').

More significant changes have taken place within education (*see* Exhibit 14.2). Further education colleges and the former polytechnics were removed from local authority financial control in the early 1990s, resulting in attempts by the college management and employers' forums to break with the traditional national collective agreements. This led to two national one-day strikes in the former polytechnics in order to preserve national conditions of service. The end settlement led to a revision of contractual obligations for lecturers and the establishment of local agreements within a national 'framework agreement'. National bargaining on pay was preserved, but since the transformation of the former polytechnics into 'new' universities with similar funding arrangements (but dissimilar conditions of work) to the 'old' universities there has been division of opinion between the union representing 'new' staff (NATFHE) and 'old' (Association of University Teachers) as to whether or not lecturers would be better served with national bargaining or a pay review body. The introduction of new contractual arrangements into the further education sector proved much more contentious, leading to a series of national and college-based disputes as lecturers' teaching hours were lengthened and holidays reduced. The bitterness of many of these disputes was compounded by the ability of college principals to award themselves (with governing body approval) sometimes excessive salary increases. To date there remains no agreed outcome to this dispute and in fact, in 1995 and 1996 at least, the sector has recorded in official statistics a significant proportion of 'working days lost' through strikes (*see* later section). In secondary and primary education there has been a long history of disagreement between the unions and employers as to the outputs of the Burnham Committee negotiating forum. A series of disputes led eventually to the government deciding to abolish the system of national collective bargaining in 1987 and through the 1987 Teachers' Pay and Conditions Act to enable the Secretary of State to impose pay rates on the teaching service. In 1991 a pay review body was established for teachers with a part remit to establish performance-related pay within schools. However, the introduction of performance systems within schools has been very limited. Schools rely on trust and teamwork between teachers, and few heads are likely to be willing to threaten this by the introduction of potentially divisive merit-based pay. Opposition from the teaching unions would also mean a difficult path would lie ahead in its introduction.

■ Indexation

Both the police and fire service (representing 200 000 employees) have their pay determined by indexed attachment to outside movements in earnings. The police are the one sector of civilian public employment denied by law a 'right' to strike, having lost this right in the aftermath of their strike defeat in 1919. Their indexation formula was established after a campaign organised by the Police Federation (the police union) in 1979, and initially linked annual increases to the increase in the whole economy average earnings. Since 1994 their pay increases have been linked to the median increase in private sector non-manual settlements. Other issues affecting police pay have been the baseline level

■ **Exhibit 14.2**

Plan to boost pay for top teachers

FT

The government yesterday called for a new salary structure to reward a class of advanced skills teacher it wants to introduce. In advice to the schoolteachers' review body, Mr David Blunkett, education and employment secretary, said he wanted a 'distinct new role' for particular teachers in raising standards by 'supporting and mentoring' trainee and newly qualified teachers.

Mr Blunkett has expressed concern that the only avenue for career advancement for good teachers is to go into administration. He acknowledges that under the present system there is no financial incentive for them to remain in the classroom. In his letter to Mr Tony Vineall, the review body chairman, Mr Blunkett made clear he wanted a tight pay settlement to ensure most of the extra £1bn announced for education in the Budget went to improving standards.

Mr Blunkett is having to reconcile a financial squeeze on education with the government's crusade to raise standards – to be the centrepiece of a 200-clause education bill in the next parliamentary session. However, he indicated he was amenable to funnelling more money to the new grade of teacher and asked the review body to consider how best to achieve that. 'Skilled and experienced teachers are

the key asset of our schools and we need to retain them in the profession,' Mr Blunkett said.

Teachers' unions condemned the proposal. Mr Doug McAvoy, general secretary of the National Union of Teachers, called for 'a significant increase' for all teachers. Mr Phil Willis, Liberal Democrat education spokesman, said: 'Increased salaries for advanced skills teachers can help improve schools, but they will only affect a very small proportion of teachers. The government must not allow this to become a case of robbing Peter to pay Paul.'

The review body will make its recommendations on pay for all 400 000 teachers in England and Wales in time for the government to announce the 1998–99 pay round in February. 'We need to ensure those who are in the service for 20–30 years have a career structure,' Mr Blunkett said. Plans for the new 'super-teachers', as Mr Blunkett dubs them, were outlined in a government white paper last month. Mr Blunkett also asked the review body to consider reinforcing headteachers' management role by requiring them to report to governors each year to ensure individual performance did not fall below recognised standards.

Source: John Kampfner (1997), *Financial Times*, 7 August.

(again subject to dispute in 1979) and the possibility of the introduction of performance-related pay. The latter issue again raises questions of the efficacy of linking pay to performance in a public 'service' occupation. Firefighters won an indexation system in the aftermath of their dispute with the Labour government in 1977. Their pay is linked to the top quartile of male manual earnings. As mentioned in the previous section, ambulance workers failed in 1989 to secure an indexation system; their case at the time rested on the proposition that they should be considered an equivalent 'emergency' service to the police and fire service. During the life of the 1979–97 Conservative governments it was mooted within government circles that a strike ban should be introduced in the emergency services. However, legislation, although often expected, failed to materialise before the election defeat of May 1997.

ASSESSMENT: EMPLOYEE RELATIONS OR INDUSTRIAL RELATIONS?

No assessment of the public sector is complete without recognition of the fact that the sector stands apart from the private sector in that there has been a continuing relative resilience of trade union membership and density and a higher propensity in recent years for industrial dispute. In 1996 average union density in public administration was 61 per cent; in postal services 64 per cent; in hospitals 54 per cent; in schools 59 per cent and in higher education 47 per cent. This compares with a density rate of 31 per cent for all employees in Great Britain (Labour Force Survey). In terms of industrial disputes the public sector has consistently provided the most significant proportion of 'working days lost' in every year except 1990 for the past decade as the following summary indicates (*Labour Market Trends*, June 1996, p. 273 and June 1997).

- 1988 – postal workers' strike accounted for 1.0 million (28 per cent) of the 3.7 million days lost.
- 1989 – strike by council workers accounted for 2.0 million (49 per cent) of the 4.1million days lost.
- 1990 – strike days lost were dominated this year by the engineering unions' dispute over working hours.
- 1991 – a strike by council workers over redundancy matters accounted for 102 000 working days lost (13 per cent of the annual total).
- 1992 – a similar strike by council workers accounted for 81 000 working days lost (15 per cent of the 0.5 million total).
- 1993 – a strike by civil servants over market testing, privatisation and cuts in service accounted for 162 000 working days lost (25 per cent) out of 0.6 million days total. The workers involved in this one-day strike accounted for 42 per cent of all workers on strike in 1993.
- 1994 and 1995 – a strike by college lecturers over the introduction of new contracts of employment accounted for 63 000 (22 per cent) of the 0.28 million days lost in 1994 and 39 000 (9 per cent) of the 0.41 million days lost in 1995.
- 1996 – a strike by university staff (all grades) over pay accounted for 111 700 (9 per cent) of the 1.3 million days lost; 68 per cent of all days lost in this year came as a result of productivity disputes in the London Underground and Royal Mail.

Part of the increasing prominence of the public sector in strike statistics is the result of the decline of *individual* propensity to strike in the private sector (Dickerson and Stewart, 1993). However, the continued propensity of public sector workers, both to remain relatively well unionised and to strike, does need some explanation. In addition, the relative resilience of collective bargaining as a form of pay determination and the continued legitimacy of the trade union role in the face of new management techniques need some analysis. In many respects traditional forms of adverserial bargaining have kept pace in the public sector with employer- and government-driven attempts to inject employee relations techniques designed to 'individualise' and 'de-collectivise' the employment relationship. Some reasons for this lingering 'industrial' rather than 'employee' relations framework are now suggested.

■ Trade union attachment

Membership of the public sector based trade unions grew dramatically in the post-war period alongside the growth of the public sector. However, the growth in density outstripped the growth in membership potential in most areas. For example, union membership in national and local government, education and health increased from 1.46 million in 1948 to 2.25 million in 1968 and 5.76 million in 1979, while density rates increased from nearly 60 per cent to nearly 80 per cent over the same period (Waddington, 1992). Job cuts and privatisation from 1979 on took its toll on membership in these sectors and totals fell to 3.8 million in 1987. Density, however, remained stable at just under 79 per cent before some slippage occurred in the 1990s. The pattern of membership in some of the larger unions can be seen from Table 14.1.

There exists a mixture of occupational, craft and industrial unions within the sector. For example, in the NHS, manual grades are represented by Unison (the result of a 1993 merger between NALGO, NUPE and COHSE) or GMB, whereas nurses might join the professionally orientated and non-TUC affiliated Royal College of Nursing (RCN) or Unison. Staff technicians are generally represented by MSF (Manufacturing, Science and Finance) and maintenance grades by AEEU (engineering and electrical union). In the Civil Service, unions have historically been split by occupation and grade for white-collar staff, with clerical and secretarial grades covered by CPSA and other grades in separate unions. However,

■ Table 14.1 Membership of selected public sector trade unions

Union	1960	1979	1996
GMB (LA manual grade workers)	796 000	967 000	740 319
National and Local Government Officers Association (NALGO)	274 000	753 000	na
National Union of Public Employees (NUPE)	200 000	692 000	na
Confederation of Health Service Employees (COHSE)	na	213 000	na
Unison (1993 merger of above three unions)	na	na	1 355 313
Civil and Public Services Association (CPSA) – Civil Service clerks	140 000	224 000	121 749
National Union of Teachers (NUT)	245 000	290 740	175 127
National Association of Schoolmasters/Union of Women Teachers	na	152 222	157 146

Source: Certification Office and TUC Annual Reports.

a series of mergers have created one 'conglomerate' union (PCS) for many other grades, including administrative and executive officers, security officers and inland revenue staff. Technical staff can join the IPMS (Institute of Professional Managers and Specialists) while the Association of First Division Civil Servants (FDA) recruits the senior 'mandarin' grades. In primary and secondary education the major unions are the NUT and the NAS/UWT (and the EIS in Scotland). The NUT has the majority membership in primary schools while the NAS/UWT shares membership in the secondary sector. Head teachers can join the National Association of Head Teachers (NAHT). Further education college lecturers and those in the 'new' universities are generally represented by NATFHE (National Association of Teachers in Further and Higher Education) while those in the 'old' universities are represented by the Association of University Teachers. Talks on a confederation or merger between these unions is ongoing. Administrative staffs in local authorities, education and the NHS are usually represented by Unison and sometimes MSF.

The growth in membership of the public sector unions has given them more weight and influence within the TUC and the trade union movement in general. In the 1970s the public sector unions gained more seats on the TUC General Council at the expense of some declining private sector and manually based unions. Since its creation by amalgamation in 1993, Unison is now Britain's largest union with over 1.3 million members against the Transport and General Workers' (TGWU) 800 000. The merger of the CPSA and PTC will also create effectively one single union for the majority of non-manual grades in the Civil Service (PCS) although this merger has been held up in previous years by fears from the junior grade union (CPSA) of being in the same union as their executive grade 'bosses' in the PTC. It is also worth noting that many of these 'public' sector unions now also have substantial membership bases in the private sector following privatisation or 'hiving-off' of government departments and nationalised industries.

The relatively high density of membership for many of these unions is partly a legacy of the 'model employer' years when trade unions established strong membership bases aided and abetted by the legitimacy given to them by their institutionalisation in the process of collective bargaining and working procedures.

The fact that managerial grades have also been traditional union members throughout much of the public sector may also have helped to make union membership socially acceptable within the workplace without a 'fear' of victimisation for joining.

The sustained growth of membership throughout the 1960s and 1970s is more complex to explain. White-collar staff in general were drawn into unions during this period at a greater rate than average in all sectors, leading to some debate as to the cause of this new 'white-collar' unionism. Instrumental reasons, linked to the perceived ability of unions to deliver wage increases within a framework of collective bargaining, were undoubtedly important. Further debate surrounds the contention that white-collar staff were becoming more collectivised and identifying themselves as working class within an increasingly large, bureaucratic and 'taylorised' public sector work environment increasingly typified by automated routine work procedures and the emergence of 'clerical factories' (*see* Prandy *et al.*, 1982, for a contemporary review of the debates). Public sector unions have exhibited more 'unionateness' in recent years, with the decision of some of the unions to newly affiliate to the TUC or to establish political funds for campaign purposes (although falling short of affiliation to the Labour Party).

In the 1980s and 1990s individual workloads have increased as a result of recruitment freezes, cutbacks and 'cash limits'. The need to monitor service outputs and record information for budgeting purposes has also created extra administrative burdens. More government interference and suppression of wage and salary increases have also occurred. The potential role of trade unions as defenders of terms and conditions has become much more important as a result, and where an attempt has been made to fulfil this role the resultant increase in levels of activism within the unions at local level is likely to have enhanced participation and encouraged membership recruitment and retention (Fairbrother, 1996). Pressures on individual managers to meet financial targets and to provide a public service within strict cash limits have also led to a tightening of discipline over such issues as sickness and unauthorised absence as well as the adoption of a more aggressive management style (Edwards and Whitson, 1991). Workers, in other words, are working harder within the public sector and if so then a sense of injustice is likely to arise if there is no corresponding revision of the effort-bargain. This again, within the workplace, is likely to increase feelings of 'them and us' and create opportunities for active unions to polarise feelings and cement loyalties towards the trade union case.

Many of the trade unions in the sector have also played a dual role as trade union defenders of terms and conditions and representatives of the 'professional' interests of their members. This has enabled them in many instances to offer a service to their members on training provision and career advice that enhances their appeal. In fact many of these 'professional associations', which are not affiliated to the TUC, have seen significant growth of membership in the last decade against the general trend (Farnham and Giles, 1995). The Royal College of Nursing, for example, has grown from 134 689 in 1979 to over 300 000 in 1996. Other growing associations include the Secondary Heads Association, the British Association of Occupational Therapists, and the Association of Teachers and Lecturers. In some cases the professionally orientated approach of such associations has meant that they have adopted a 'no-strike' policy (e.g. the RCN and Professional Association of Teachers) but in some cases (e.g. the RCN and RC Midwives) this policy has seen some relaxation in the 1990s, reflecting a heightening of industrial relations tension within the public sector.

The final explanatory factor for trade union attachment in the sector has been the common cause established by the unions between the defence of jobs and the defence of service provision. The deleterious effects on service provision caused by spending cuts (hospital ward or library closures, for example) have meant that unions have gained extra legitimacy for their cause in defending boths jobs *and* services. The likelihood of some success, however minimal, in resisting closure plans or cutbacks has improved as a result, particularly where it is clearly possible to reverse spending cuts within the local process of political accountability. This added political and social dimension to the role of public sector unions, if effectively deployed, gives the unions an enhanced identity which may well have acted as a spur to membership recruitment and retention.

The choice dilemmas within the sector, i.e between service provision, cost and efficiency, have also set limits to the degree of flexibility that could be expected in terms of employers' strategies to change working practices. It is to these dilemmas that we now turn.

■ Service provision versus cost cutting: a management dilemma

The pressures on managers to continue to provide a public service against the background of public spending cuts have meant that efforts to introduce many aspects of performance incentives and HRM techniques have been dampened. The difficulties of setting targets and performance objectives for individual staff in public services have already been discussed. In particular the problems of isolating 'value added' in monetary terms are apparent where no test of increased profits or market share can be made. In some cases it will be possible to determine 'outputs' if these relate, for example, to identifiable performance indicators such as increased student numbers in education or decreased empty bed space in hospitals. However, such targets, if pursued uncautiously, may well have deleterious effects on 'quality' of service or level of provision that may have contradictory effects on other performance 'indicators' that are quality related or which relate to customer/client/public satisfaction. Such policy dilemmas are also likely to create some cynicism among employees unless the performance criteria are transparent and seen to have accommodated some of the more difficult policy contradictions. These problems, combined as they are with an increasingly low-trust working environment inspired by pay restrictions and job cuts, have meant that some newer personnel practices such as appraisal, merit pay or 'quality' programmes have often met with resistance from staff and their unions. Thus, proposals for a teachers' performance appraisal system have created disputes in schools, and in further and higher education continual union resistance meant that new systems in many instances were effectively imposed by college employers (and their developmental value reduced as a result). Similarly, proposals for 'quality circles' in departments of the Civil Service in the 1980s were withdrawn after union boycotts amid fears that any emerging proposals would inspire non-negotiable service or job cuts. The risks attached to the development of lower trust relationships between management and staff as a result of cutbacks will also reflect on attempts to reorganise work. Efforts to introduce elements of employee participation and involvement might often be perceived by staff as attempts to intensify work. Data collected by the University of Warwick's 'Trade Unions into the 1990s' Project, for example, indicates that there is a lesser incidence of the introduction of quality circles and teamworking into the public sector but a higher incidence of team briefing, suggesting difficulties in establishing more radical change (Waddington and Whitson, 1996). Similarly the survey reports a higher incidence of grievances over workload and staffing levels in the public sector. The long-running series of disputes in the Royal Mail since 1988, often initiated by rank-and-file union members against the wishes of the leadership, over the introduction of Total Quality Management (TQM) and team working is a case in point. Management proposals to introduce these more HRM-based techniques have followed a programme of 'delayering' of management strata and a staff redundancy programme. Industrial relations tensions were therefore heightened in the process such that 'the re-organisation of Royal Mail left the personnel function in a somewhat ambiguous situation within an increasingly complex and politically charged industrial relations environment' (Martinez Lucio and Noon, 1994).

All of these factors have imposed some limitation on the degree to which new management techniques have been able to be introduced within the public sector. The continued relative resilience of public sector unions, despite them being placed on the defensive, has meant that employers have been forced to negotiate change whereas otherwise they might have sought to bypass or marginalise unions. Often such change has had to involve re-examining grading structures and re-aligning pay through job evaluation studies (Waddington and Whitson, 1996). De-recognition of unions in the public sector, or partial de-recognition involving managerial grades, has been much rarer than in the private sector, and has been generally confined to those instances where services have been contracted out or privatised (e.g. managerial staff in BT following privatisation). As a result, the climate of adverserial 'industrial' relations, established in particular in the 1970s, has lingered on and processes designed to individualise the employment relationship have proved more difficult to establish.

THE FUTURE?

The election of a New Labour government in May 1997 does not seem to have altered fundamentally the government stance towards public sector pay and spending. The cash limits imposed by the outgoing Conservative government were to be kept in place by the new government for at least two years and public sector pay agreements would be constrained as a result. The outcome of the Commission into Low Pay and the setting of the National Minimum Wage (NMW) are likely to affect the bargaining process within the sector, simply because so many public sector workers are likely to be affected. Potential problems of 'differential' pay comparisons may arise if the NMW is set at a high enough level to embrace more rather than less of the low paid in the sector. The possibility of further pay disputes and clashes over cutbacks in spending looks set to continue for the foreseeable future.

CASE STUDY

The Home Office Prison Service

This case study involves the Home Office Prison Service. This area has been chosen because it was one of the most controversial areas of public sector employee relations during the 1980s. However, it did not make national and international headlines until the spring of 1990 when the regime at Strangeways Prison, Manchester suddenly collapsed into disorder and inmates were sitting on the roof of an otherwise gutted and wrecked shell of a nineteenth century prison.

Changes in public sector control and management in recent years have also affected the Home Office Prison Service. These changes include market testing through compulsory competitive tendering (CCT) of certain services, including penal education and external custody escort services, the auxiliarisation of certain traditional prison officer roles, and total franchisation of parts of the Prison Service operating to Crown property prisons with private sector organisations.

The first four prisons to be totally constructed through private finance have now been approved in the Treasury's Public Expenditure Settlement (PES) for 1997. These will be located at Bridgend, Glamorgan, Fazakerley near Liverpool and Lowdham Grange near Nottingham (the site of the first open Borstal in the 1930s). The fourth establishment has been approved for 1999; its exact location has not been given. Parc Prison, Bridgend opened in the autumn of 1997. It was financed through a consortium known as Bridgend Custodial Services and is now operated by the Securicor Group. The scheme of the private sector being involved in the public sector is known as the Private Finance Initiative (PFI).

The South-West Region contains a number of prisons, ranging from the oldest in England at Shepton Mallet in Somerset, to perhaps the most infamous, Dartmoor. Others include modern structures at Channings Wood in Devon and Leyhill in Gloucestershire – the first open prison – and three city prisons, Exeter, Gloucester and Horfield Prison at Bristol. The original detention centre at Eastwood Park, Falfield, Gloucestershire became operational in 1996 as a women's Category C prison (medium security). Bristol's Horfield Prison was constructed between 1882 and 1884: it superseded three previous private and local authority prisons in the city. The Home Office took control of all penal establishments in England and Wales from 1877. The Prison Department was first controlled at arm's length from the Home Office by the Prison Commission. This was abolished in 1963, to be administered directly by the Home Office Prison Department. In 1988 it became the Home Office Prison Service (HOPS) as part of the Fresh Start initiatives which restructured the Prison Service and restricted the use of paid overtime for prison officers.

From 1991 the first franchised penal establishment to be run by the private sector was opened, the first since the mid-nineteenth century: this was Wolds Remand Centre, Humberside, currently being run by Group 4 Security.

In April 1993 both the HOPS and Scottish Prison Service gained executive agency status, due to the recommendations of the Lygo Report (1991), *The Review of the Management of the Prison Service*. Agency status currently involves over 300 000 civil servants in numerous agencies, ranging from the Benefits Agency to the Teacher Pensions Agency. Agency status is part of the original 'next steps' objectives for the Civil Service, established by the Prime Minister's office in 1988.

Under the Prison Service Agency, the Chief Executive (who is still officially known by the nineteenth-century title of Director-General) has overall day-to-day running of the Service. The Home Secretary and the Junior Prisons Minister are responsible, in theory at least, for policy. The model, in theory, is similar in structure to the original 'arm's length' control of the nationalised industries, the difference being that the employees within the executive agencies remain civil servants although Chief Executives may be recruited from the private sector. (The first Director-General of the Prison Service as an executive agency was recruited from the media industry in April 1993.)

However, this distinction became confused at the time of the Parkhurst Prison escape in January 1995 when the Home Secretary 'rode roughshod' over the Director-General and removed the governor from office. The repercussions of this action are still being felt as it is assumed by many that the governor was a scapegoat for an overall confusion of policy and role by the Home Office.

Industrial relations within the UK Prison Service have been acrimonious over the past 25 years. Serious disturbances at Hull Prison in 1976 led to changes in the system, particularly with the original control over inmates through governors' adjudications against which, until 1978, there was no appeal.

Throughout the 1970s and 1980s there was a series of long-running protracted local disputes within British penal establishments. The causes of these disputes were symptomatic of a wider penal crisis, including overcrowding and impoverished regimes for both staff and inmates alike. Most penal establishments managed to run a basic regime without recourse to serious disorder, mainly due to three factors:

1 the relentless overtime worked by prison officers;
2 the excellent cooperation from the inmate population, despite
3 an almost 23-hour day lock-down in many establishments.

Obviously this 'steam pressure system' had to escape at some point. There were serious prison disorders in 1972, 1976, 1986 and 1990; most occurred at weekends or bank holidays when staffing was severely limited.

In 1988 the working conditions for all prison staff were radically altered for the first time since 1877 under the Fresh Start initiatives. Attempts to buy out the overtime culture were introduced, whereby, within four years, all prison officers were only required to work a 39-hour week. Certain senior prison officer grades were abolished and others incorporated into governor grades (Black, 1996).

Despite Fresh Start and the subsequent changes, the penal system remains a volatile area with respect to regimes, management and industrial relations. Serious prison disorder, beginning at Manchester (Strangeways) Prison in April 1990, quickly escalated. Most West-Country penal establishments were also seriously affected by disturbances, including Dartmoor and Bristol prisons and Pucklechurch Remand Centre near Bristol.

Other changes introduced since the 1990 Criminal Justice Act include agency status, franchising, privatisation and market testing through CCT. A business culture was also introduced into the Prison Service. A particular example was the appointment of Derek Lewis from the private sector as the new Director-General. However, Mr Lewis was effectively sacked in October 1995 due to the findings of the Learmont Report, which investigated the serious breach of security at two maximum-security prisons, Whitemoor (October 1994) and Parkhurst (January 1995).

It was assumed by many that Mr Lewis was also the scapegoat for Home Office failures. Later, Mr Lewis won an out-of-court settlement in the High Court for wrongful dismissal. Attempts by external consultants (commonly referred to as head-hunters) to recruit a new Director-General from the private sector proved futile and eventually the Deputy Director-General, a senior governor grade, was appointed to the post at almost half the salary of his predecessor. It is possible that the experience of Mr Lewis as Director-General may well prove to be the one and only time that a candidate from the private sector is appointed as the Chief Executive of the Prison Service. Indeed, the curbs on expenditure have resulted in the Prison Service appointing a career civil servant rather than a candidate from the private sector as the next Director of Finance. The appointment of Mr Robert Fulton, a former Director of prison industries and farms, was met with some reservation by some members of the Prison Board (*The Times*, 9 September 1996).

The confused lines of accountability between the Minister and the Director-General of the Prison Service continued after Mr Lewis's demise in August 1996; confusion arose over release dates of inmates sentenced under consecutive prison sentences. The Director-General ordered the early release of inmates without informing the Home Secretary. The Home Secretary immediately countermanded the order and allowed the decision concerning the early release of prisoners to be taken in the High Court, who found in the Home Secretary's favour.

Most of the radical changes within the Prison Service have not been successful, however; in fact the appointment of Derek Lewis may have been an 'own goal' for the Home Office. All prison governors and prison officers have the employment status of Crown servants, therefore they do not have contracts of employment. Until the appointment of Mr Lewis as Director-General, all previous Director-Generals were appointed internally from senior governor level. Mr Lewis had a contract of employment: his dismissal reflected a breach of common law principles under wrongful dismissal. Prison custody officers employed by the private sector have contracts of employment.

Despite numerous Royal Commissions, reports and conflicting legislation since the Mountbatten Report in 1966, the Prison Service has had no clear objectivity of purpose, lines of accountability and communication, nor positive leadership.

The Woolfe Report, in the aftermath of the Manchester (Strangeways) prison riots of 1990, recommended changes to penal regimes which began to be implemented. These changes ceased abruptly after the Whitemoor (1994) and the Parkhurst (1995) fiascos. The increase in the prison population has caused many regimes to become impoverished and the 'pressure cooker' culture is now a daily occurrence in most prisons. The morale of prison staff is currently at an all-time low, yet there is no clear mandate for leadership or lines of accountability except a scapegoat culture from political leadership. The pressure for a toughening up of criminal justice and sentencing policies is popular with the public; it would seem that the prison population is set to rise dramatically within the next decade.

There is also disquiet about the running of franchise prisons. The first, the Wolds Remand Centre, opened in 1991 in East York and was criticised for its poor regime by HM Prisons Inspector. Buckley Hall Prison in Lancashire, run by the same company, has had a series of escapes and attempted escapes which have alarmed the local community around the Rochdale area, causing the local MP to call for a public inquiry.

Most legislation affecting penal reform, including the role of prison officers, has failed to replace or radically amend the 'treadmill' of the Prison Service. The original Prisons Act of 1952 is still the current legislation; it does not define the roles and duties of prison staff but delegates this function into a plethora of prison rules, Home Office circulars and instructions, and governors' orders. No generic job description is contained either in the Prisons Act or in the rules, instructions, circulars or orders, that describes the functions and responsibilities of a prison officer. What Section 8 of the Prisons Act confirms is that 'every prison officer while acting as such has the power, authority, protection and privileges of a constable'.

Yet, unlike the police, prison officers have a trade union, the Prison Officers Association (POA) for England, Wales and Northern Ireland and the Scottish Prison Officers Association (Scot POA), an independent trade union.

Most reforms in the Prison Service have come about through the independent HM Inspector of Prisons, a post enacted by statute in 1984. Judge Stephen Tumin's eight-year tenure is too well known to reiterate here. His successor, General Sir David Ramsbotham, appears to be no pushover either. Recently, Sir David and his team condemned the conditions and regime at Holloway Prison, London. This had led to the 'administrative' removal of the Governor, Ms Janet King. Currently there is disquiet about the chaining of pregnant women prisoners in NHS hospitals; again the Prisons Minister was misinformed about this situation, which led to an unreserved apology in the Commons.

Sir David was especially critical concerning the lack of educational provision. Other commentators have suggested that market testing through CCT impairs the quality of penal education when the contracts are awarded on the basis of cost alone. For a number of penal establishments, education provision is far less now than prior to CCT in 1993.

The market testing of penal education has in fact precipitated changes to the legal interpretation of the Transfer of Undertakings Regulations (TURE) 1981 and their application to the public sector (Kenny *v* South Manchester College, 1993). Legal challenges were mounted successfully with regard to the employment of part-time tutors who were dismissed at random through CCT procedures. Most penal education departments were staffed by part-time lecturers.

Areas of performance-related pay and public expenditure settlements cannot be achieved without Treasury approval. The public expenditure settlements for the Prison Service from 1996 will mean a 50 per cent reduction in capital funds and a 13 per cent reduction in baseline running costs over three years. The running cost reductions must affect the payroll cost, which accounts for some 85 per cent of the budget, yet these reductions are not being met by a contracting prison population. It is anticipated that the prison population will be in excess of 65 000 by the year 2000. It is expected currently that the Prison Service will face 3000 redundancies: these are assumed to be necessary by the Home Office as now most of the court escort duties have been privatised and are not now undertaken by prison officers. Yet there have been instances of alleged inhumane treatment of prisoners being escorted by the privatised sector.

The Director-General informed the Prison Service in June 1996 about staff anxieties and concerns. The plans for coping with the current crisis include proposals to:

- provide 1000 places through selective overcrowding at local prisons and some training prisons;
- recommission prison wings with integral sanitation, which are currently mothballed;
- provide around 2000 places in additional houseblocks;
- build up to five new private (DCMF) prisons from 2000 onwards;
- build up to seven new state prisons to open with the expected surge in the prison population.

Despite the proposed redundancies under the Voluntary Early Retirement Exit (VERSE) scheme and early retirement proposals, however, the Office for Public Service had placed a ceiling on the amount of central government funding for this scheme. Initial redundancy and early retirement packages have been withdrawn. This has also caused confusion, anxiety and contributed to a lowering of morale within the Prison Service, where this is already low.

Pressure by the POA has successfully negotiated a policy of no compulsory redundancies and has reached an agreement on defining minimum staffing levels. This point has been an area of contention for many years but had become a major cause of concern since the Fresh Start initiatives of 1988.

In this analysis of the Prison Service it is evident that the policies of the government to impose a business culture have not been too successful. Indeed, it may reflect that the criminal justice system is not an area where the market ethos should prevail. Overall, it should be the responsibility of the state, which provides the administrative support for the criminal justice system. The franchising of prisons, CCT and the shock of competition have not resolved the archaic system of penal administration. Evidence to date suggests it may actually have exacerbated the problem.

The Labour Party, when in opposition, pledged to return all privatised prisons to the public sector and to halt the prison privatisation programme. In office, the Labour government has continued the prison privatisation programme by ordering two new DCMF prisons to be built through PFI and run by private companies. The site of the original Youth Custody Centre at Pucklechurch near Bristol is to be refurbished under PFI and in November 1997 the operating contract was awarded to Premier Prisons Ltd, the UK subsidiary of a large American private prisons contractor.

Points to consider

Although a totally different public sector institution from a school, a penal establishment employs many staff of differing grades and skills.

1 What are the similarities between Exhibits 14.1 and 14.2, and this case study in terms of employee relations?

2 In appointing a Director-General of the Prison Service in 1993 from the private sector, it was assumed by the then Home Secretary that management was a generic skill which could be applied to all situations whether in the public or private sector. Is this a realistic opinion? Discuss. (Could your tutor manage the employee relations portfolio of your institution? Could the same criteria be used to manage the employee relations portfolio of your regional post office or your local prison?) Where are the similarities? Where are the differences?

3 Would your answer be different if the employee relations portfolio was your local brewery? Where are the similarities here between a public and private sector institution? Where are the differences?

4 Why do you think, in terms of employee relations, successive Conservative and Labour governments are committed to franchise and privatise prisons?

SOME FURTHER QUESTIONS

1 What advantages to employers were there of the 'model employer' approach to public sector employee relations?

2 Looking at Exhibit 14.1, why have successive governments had difficulty in injecting private sector values into public sector culture?

3 Why did the demise of Keynesian economic management cause industrial relations problems in the public sector?

4 From Exhibit 14.2, why should public sector unions oppose performance appraisal systems?

5 How do you explain the greater incidence of disputes in the public sector in the 1990s when compared to the private sector?

GLOSSARY

Citizen's Charter Initiative
This was proposed by the government in 1991 through the Citizen's Charter White Paper which emphasised four themes: quality, choice, standards and value in the provision of public services. The objectives are to improve service provision and to instil in providers a more customer-orientated culture. Service providers are required to establish and monitor performance targets along prescribed dimensions and performance is subject to independent validation. Charters for particular services have been introduced and a central unit established to oversee their development.

Comparability
The principle that the pay of particular groups of public sector employees is to be determined through comparison with comparable private sector occupations. As a principle, if not a practice, this has been superseded since 1979 by the concept of 'affordability', the idea that pay should be related to the financial circumstances of the employing organisation.

Compulsory competitive tendering (CCT)
Public sector service organisations are legally obligated to allow private contractors to bid for the right to carry out specified services. In the NHS, CCT was introduced initially for cleaning, catering and laundry services in 1983. In local government, the initiative started in direct labour organisations (e.g. in building work) and extended into cleaning, refuse collection and maintenance functions by the Local Government Act 1988. The tendering exercise has required local authorities to separate the 'client' and 'contractor' roles and hence has resulted in a radical restructuring of internal management and organisation in local government. 'Market testing' is closely associated with CCT and in recent years has been extended to white-collar central government and local authority services.

Internal market

The aim of the internal market has been to stimulate greater competition between providers of public services and in this way to improve performance. In the NHS from 1991, the main purchasers of health care (health authorities) have been separated from providers of the services (hospitals and community units). The 'internal market' has been supported by devolved budgets and financial management. General practitioners can acquire 'fundholder' status and 'purchase' hospital provision. The provision is currently under review by the Labour government.

Opting out

Since 1991 the vast majority of hospitals have opted out of district health authority control to become NHS Trusts. Trusts have greater potential autonomy to manage their own affairs, employ staff directly, set their own terms and conditions and design new employment structures. Their revenue is dependent on the ability to compete effectively for contracts from a range of purchasers who renew contracts on an annual basis. With salaries and wages representing three quarters of revenue expenditure, managers have identified labour savings as a principal means to enhance competitiveness (Winchester and Bach, 1997).

In education, the term applies to around 20 per cent of secondary schools that, after a ballot, became grant-maintained schools, no longer subject to local education authority control. All schools are covered by the Local Management of Schools (LMS) structure of devolved financial management. The policy of 'opting out' of schools has been put on hold by the Labour government.

Next Steps: civil service executive agencies

Improving Management in Government: The Next Steps was a report by Sir Robin Ibbs, head of the government's Efficiency Unit, published in 1988 and critical of the impact of the government's management reforms on the Civil Service. It suggested that the Civil Service was 'too big and too diverse to be managed as a single unit' and advocated the reorganisation of the executive activities of government (as distinct from policy advice) into separate agencies with specific responsibilities and targets. Headed by Chief Executives, often recruited from outside the Civil Service, these agencies were granted greater flexibility in financial and personnel matters. Variations between agencies (in terms of size, activities, financial regimes) in part explain the uneven pace of decentralisation of pay and conditions.

Nevertheless, this has been given further impetus by subsequent central government initiatives and devolution is currently increasing quite rapidly. By the end of 1994, 21 executive agencies and 3 government departments organised on 'next step' lines were determining staff pay and conditions and quite a few have been developing new pay structures.

Non-departmental public body

A quasi-autonomous body linked to a government department. The head of a NDPB is a Chief Executive whose powers are devolved downwards from the Minister of State. The aim is for NDPBs to take day to day control and responsibility of their respective agencies.

Pay review bodies

Standing bodies, appointed by government and able to take an independent view on medium-term developments in pay for the public service occupations covered. Currently there are pay review bodies for nurses and midwives, doctors and dentists, other health service professionals, school teachers, the armed forces and 'top salaried' senior military officials, civil servants and judges. A total of 1.5 million employees are covered. While this is rather less than a quarter of the public sector workforce, pay review body awards have influenced pay settlements for other groups within the public sector. Pay review bodies take evidence each year from relevant sources and make recommendations to government. The presumption is that, unless there are compelling reasons to do otherwise, the government will accept the recommendations.

Transfer of undertakings regulations

To comply with the EC's 1977 Acquired Rights Directive, safeguarding employee terms and conditions in the event of a business takeover, the UK government introduced the Transfer of Undertakings (Protection of Employment) (Amendment) Regulations 1981. Initially, these excluded from their provisions those undertakings that were not commercial ventures, leaving public sector employees unprotected. Following European Court of Justice (ECJ) rulings, however, the exclusion of non-commercial undertakings was removed in the 1993 Trade Union Reform and Employment Rights Act.

Further amendments have been prompted by ECJ rulings of June 1994. The Acquired Rights Directive and the 1975 Directive on collective redundancies (amended in 1992) provide for obligatory information and consultation of workers' representatives. UK legislation provided for such information and consultation only where the employer recognised a trade union for collective bargaining purposes. To bring the UK into line, the Conservative government issued the Collective Redundancies and Transfer of Undertakings (Protection of Employment) (Amendment) Regulations 1995. In the event of collective redundancies and transfer of undertakings, employers will now be obliged to inform and/or consult representatives of the employees concerned, whether a trade union is recognised or not. Where a union is recognised, the employer can decide to inform/consult representatives of the union or, alternatively, to inform/consult 'employee representatives' (*European Industrial Relations Review*, 264, January 1996).

REFERENCES

Bacon, R. and Eltis, W. (1978) *Britain's Economic Problem: Too Few Producers*, 2nd edn. London: Macmillan.

Black, J. (1996) 'An anatomy of an industrial dispute: HM Prison Wandsworth', *Warwick Papers on Industrial Relations*, no. 37.

Black, J. (1995) 'Industrial relations in the UK Prison Service: the "Jurassic Park" of public sector industrial relations', *Employee Relations*, 17(2).

Blyton, P. and Turnbull, P. (1998) *The Dynamics of Employee Relations*. London: Macmillan.

Dickerson, A. and Stewart, M. (1993) 'Is the public sector more strike prone ?', *Oxford Bulletin of Economics and Statistics*, 55(3), 253–84.

Edwards, P. K. and Whitson, C. (1991) 'Workers are working harder: effort and shop floor relations in the 1980s', *British Journal of Industrial Relations*, 29(4), 593–600.

Fairbrother, P. (1996) 'Workplace trade unionism in the state sector' in Ackers, P., Smith, C. and Smith, P. (eds) *The New Workplace and Trade Unionism*. London: Routledge.

Farnham, D. and Giles, L. (1995) 'Trade Unions in the UK: trends and counter-trends since 1979', *Employee Relations*, 17(2).

Ferner, A. 'The State as employer' in Hyman, R. and Ferner, A. (eds) *New Frontiers in European Industrial Relations*. London: Blackwell.

Fredman, S. and Morris, G. (1989) *The State as Employer: Labour Law in the Public Services*. London: Mansell.

Kelly, J. (1988) *Trade Unions and Socialist Politics*. London: Verso.

Martinez Lucio, M. and Noon, M. (1994) 'Organisational change and the tensions of decentralisation: the case of Royal Mail', *Human Resource Management Journal*, 5(2).

Menter, I., Muschamp, Y., Nicholls, P., Ozgal, J. and Pollard, A. (1997) *Work and Identity in the Primary School*. Milton Keynes: Open University Press.

Millward, N., Stevens, M., Smart, D. and Hawes, W. R. (1992) *Workplace Industrial Relations in Transition*. Aldershot: Dartmouth.

Prandy, K., Stewart, A. and Blackburn, R. M. (1982) *White Collar Work*. London: Macmillan.

Seifert, R. (1987) *Teacher Militancy: A History of Teacher Strikes, 1896–1987*. Brighton: Falmer Press.

Seifert, R. (1992) *Industrial Relations in the NHS*. London: Chapman & Hall.

Waddington, J. (1992) 'Trade Union Membership in Britain 1980–87: Unemployment and restructuring', *British Journal of Industrial Relations*, 30(2): 287–324.

Waddington, J. and Whitson, C. (1996) 'Empowerment versus intensification – union perspectives of change at the workplace' in Ackers, P., Smith, C. and Smith, P. (eds) *The New Workplace and Trade Unionism*. London: Routledge.

Wigham, E. (1980) *From Humble Petition to Militant Action: A History of the Civil and Public Services Association 1903–1978*. London: CPSA.

Winchester, D. and Bach, S. (1997) 'The public sector' in Edwards, P. (ed.) *Industrial Relations Theory and Practice*, 3rd edn. London: Prentice Hall.

SUGGESTED FURTHER READING

Beaumont, P.B. (1992) *Public Sector Industrial Relations*. London: Routledge.

Farnham, P. and Horton, S. (1993) *The Political Economy of Public Sector Change*. London: Macmillan.

Millward, N. (1993) *The New Industrial Relations*, London: PSI.

Rajan, A. and Pearson, R. (1986) *UK Occupation and Employment Trends to 1990*. London: Butterworths.

Salamon, M. (1997) *Industrial Relations*, 3rd edn. London: Prentice Hall.

Chapter 15

VALUES AND THEIR IMPACT ON THE CHANGING EMPLOYMENT RELATIONSHIP

Philip Cox and Ann Parkinson

Learning objectives

By the end of this chapter, readers should be able to:

- understand the influence of social, economic and political factors which contextualise current employee relations;
- understand the impact and implications that values have had and will continue to have in shaping the employment relationship.

In writing about people's beliefs and values, all writers draw upon their own interpretations to inform their arguments. In this chapter we are presenting a particular view of the impact of differing values on employee relations for you to use as a framework and we ask you to challenge it in developing your views of what employee relations is and may become in the context of the new Labour government's policies.

Exhibit 15.1 is based on probably the largest single 'downsizing' scheme ever undertaken in British industry. It was seen by many professional managers, the industry and the City as an example of better practice in managing the downsizing process, particularly in its capacity to harmonise competing vested interests. It is used to illustrate many of the issues and dimensions that form the subject of this chapter.

■ **Exhibit 15.1**

Release '92

In April 1992, British Telecom announced that it would be looking for 20 000 volunteers for redundancy as a result of the joint impact on the business of competition, recession, investment in new technology and price regulation. The 'Release'92' scheme was marketed heavily to all 240 000 employees at every level of the organisation, with almost all individuals being asked by their managers whether they would be interested in leaving the company. The financial package offered was very generous with several add-ons such as outplacement counselling, a training grant and temporary work or consultancy back into the company for a set period depending on the level of the employee. Much of the consultancy work was undertaken for charities in support of BT's pledge to donate half a per cent of its profits to charity.

In devising the terms of the severance payment, one key factor was the third of the stated values, 'we respect each other', and the belief that the company owed its success to the very people it would be encouraging to leave. Personnel had to defend the generous terms vigorously against shareholders and some of the newer board members. There was also the recognition that in the midst of a recession there was a potential detrimental impact on society by adding to high levels of unemployment.

In planning the Release scheme, the Director of Employee Relations recognised the need to work closely with the leader of the National Communications Union, building on the collaborative rather than confrontational relationship they had been developing over the previous years. The focus for the package design was the needs of the individual, and the union response recognised the need for downsizing and what its members as individuals would accept. There was no industrial action over the loss of some 30 000 jobs.

For many employees, this was the first time they had ever considered that they may not be leaving the company on their retirement. Many felt angry and 'let down' by a company that they thought they shared the same values with and that had now reneged on the promise of a 'job for life'. Others recognised that the Release package gave them the option to do something different that they had previously not considered or had the financial backing for. The majority of those leaving had joined the company before privatisation and placed a high value on 'public service', and although they had made the transition to dealing with customers within a private sector framework, a substantial number still felt uncomfortable with the focus on shareholders and profit. By the end of the financial year in March 1993 some 30 000 people had taken advantage of the Release package.

Subsequent schemes attracted a furthur 65 000 people over the following four years. The basic financial package stayed broadly the same although it was never open to all employees again and by 1994 there was the threat of being forced to accept less favourable terms for some groups if they were not prepared to leave voluntarily. In less than seven years BT had shrunk its workforce by over 40 per cent.

Questions

1 What were the factors that drove Release '92?

2 What factors might influence people in opting into the scheme?

3 Why should BT invest so heavily in options such as outplacement and training?

4 Why do you think there was no industrial action?

5 What are the wider implications for the relationship between individuals and their employing organisations?

INTRODUCTION

In this chapter we seek to understand some of the significant factors that are influencing changes in employee relations. The focusing of our vision is facilitated by looking through the lens of values which often attend any significant shift in relationships at work. By looking at changes in values we hope to plot shifts in thought, motives and behaviours of the significant actors in an emerging drama.

We begin by looking at the nature of values in practice through a case study, and continue with their influence on behaviour. This is followed by broadly examining changing work values through recent epochs, from the post-war revival in industry underpinned by the work ethic, to the emergent 'get a life' values of the 18–29 age group, popularly described as 'Generation X ' by Coupland (in Cannon, 1996), which challenges traditional parental work values, preferring an approach based on individualism, learning and self-development and a balanced lifestyle.

The next section looks at the interplay between the major stakeholders in the drama, with some reflection on the values and behaviours of the trade unions in transition, at a time when they seek to find a role that might be perceived as more relevant. It also looks at organisations and management and the ethical challenges and dilemmas faced in sustaining a capitalist value system in a highly competitive marketplace; and finally this section considers the influence of the state with its focus on the enterprise culture and its social consequences at work.

The end of the chapter explores the shift from collectivism to the resurgence of individualism, from exploitation and coercion to trust and empowerment, and the role of the psychological contract in understanding the changing nature of employee relations.

SCENARIO

The past few years have witnessed significant changes in the context of labour relations, in the UK. Shifts in the labour market, almost as profound as those which heralded the movement of labour from the countryside to the towns during the Industrial Revolution have begun to significantly transform the way in which employers and employees relate (Monks, 1996). The days of large-scale industrial conflicts and confrontation seem to be fewer and the literature contains more discussion of the concepts of trust, commitment, empowerment, shared goals and social partnership between employers and employees. An extraterrestial of the 1970s learning the rhetoric and behaviour of confrontation might be mystified by employees' more acquiescent behaviour of the '90s. It might stare equally incredulously at the sight of some organisations seeking to behave more ethically, sometimes at the expense of profit. Substantial changes have taken place in which pragmatic hostiles have been driven to consider collaboration and partnership. Many factors have influenced such attitude shifts. Individually each one might be considered significant enough, but their concurrency has created powerful impact.

The way work is done has undergone a major shift. The increased application of flexible working practices has changed for many the format of working life. The loss of full-time jobs, the increase in part-time temporary work, the increasing use of female labour, subcontracting, outsourcing and the rise of short-term fixed contracts have reduced the 'certainties' which once were attached to the old predictable style of working life. Pearson (1996) states that white male workers under 45 years only constitute 22 per cent of the work force. Hutton (1996) states that only 40 per cent of the 28 million workers are employed full-time, while 30 per cent make up the insecure self-employed, part-time or casual worker, with 30 per cent unemployed or working for poverty wages (Hutton, 1996). Many of these issues are explored in Chapter 13.

The impact of technology has allowed employees to be globally based. The 'virtual' organisation creates the potential for workers in India, Hong Kong and Taiwan to 'sit' alongside their European colleagues working on projects as efficiently as if they were in the same room. Teleworking has come of age. Many more organisations, such as IBM and Transco, are encouraging employees to be home-based, using computer technology and the Internet, through which they conduct their work (Barter, 1997). Organisations such as Digital have recognised the environmental value and enormous cost savings of employees working from home rather than organisational habitation. It has made savings of several million pounds simply by not having expensive office space and employee support mechanisms to facilitate its activities. In a survey conducted by the Institute for Employment Studies it was estimated that almost 10 per cent of employees (2.5 million) work from home, and the numbers are rising. These trends raise the question of the nature of the relationship between employers and 'employees'.

Organisations themselves have felt change. Intense competition has forced downsizing and restructuring, leaving many organisations acceptable to the City but anorexic in terms of their knowledge and skills base, as well as violating the long-time relationship with employees (Handy, 1996). The demise through privatisation of the large manufacturing and heavy engineering industries – coal, shipbuilding, motor vehicles, construction, steel making, gas and electricity, has left a hole in the full-time employment opportunities arena which has been slow to fill from the introduction of other industries. Full-time jobs have often been replaced by low-paid, part-time ones. The continuing rise of the service and financial sectors, with their reliance on part-time working and use of technology, has not filled the vacuum. Young, emergent non-unionised computer and high tech industries have sprung up with local, individual-based employment approaches.

Yet fundamental to most of these changes of significance has been the impact of economic change, such as the challenge of global competition and the rise of the free market economy with attendant changes to industrial law and the burgeoning progress of technology. In some areas these changes have wrought havoc to employment practices, processes and expectations.

With structural and economic change has come attitude change. Some employers no longer see their responsibility to the employee as anything more than contractual and a distant one at that (Cannon, 1996). The rise of the mentality that individuals are responsible for the attractiveness of their own employability has left many bemused, worried and incapable of an effective response. The Institute for Personnel and Development survey of 1996 suggests there is growing evidence of employees expressing lower levels of loyalty, commitment and trust towards their employers and uncertainty of their future role and value in their organisations (Guest et al., 1996).

Underpinning many of the changes has been a quiet social revolution. Attitudes to work are changing. The protestant work ethic has less potency. Particularly for young workers a new ethic has emerged (Cannon, 1996) in which the individual recognises the importance of the present and not the submission of the individual will to the collective for the future. Individuals want value from their lives now, not just dutifully working 'until you pass out' for the benefit of the corporation, as quoted by Hecht of McKinsey consultants (Hecht, 1997). They are interested in creating a life in which work success does not cost so much and is balanced by quality time for family, non-work interests and leisure (*Independent on Sunday*, 20 July 1997).

Middle-aged professionals are following their blue-collar colleagues in downshifting their careers. The stresses and pressures associated with retaining a career are not necessarily so attractive to all. Family life, personal development and alternative 'careers' are seen as more rewarding and valuable. Downshifting is as evident in the dedicated vocations as it is in other professions. GPs, consultants and ministers of religion seek to work balanced, often part-time, mixed-roles lives as much as their non-vocational and professional counterparts (Cox, 1986; Shaw, 1997).

As significant are the changing values of the young towards work. Collin (1995) and Coupland (in Cannon, 1996) suggest the emergence of a younger generation which society has failed to engage in the world of work and which is become alienated from the traditional values associated with their parents: 'this has a disastrous effect on young people, robbing them of the traditional socialising influences of employment, with its workplace role, values and intergenerational contact' (Collin, 1995). Coupland's characters illustrate the changing expectations the young have of their world. The idea of a career and its purpose is questioned if not perceived as alien to many young people in the 18–30 age group. The attitudes of Generation X question the traditional concepts of work and its role in the life of the individual. Their values differ from those of their parents. Having grown up in a world of one-parent families, unclear gender roles, unemployed middleclass professional fathers and job uncertainty, they do not envy working parents their 'presenteeism' (i.e. being first in and last out of an evening, thinking that this will demonstrate organisational commitment and so help them to keep their jobs), neither do they aspire to be top managers who work excessively long hours, lead out-of-control lives and die young (Cannon, 1996). Their values are based more on seeking interesting work, the learning opportunities it needs to provide, and individual rewards-based contribution, not collective bargaining (Hecht, 1997). They seek to work in organisations in which integrity and honesty are 'behaviours' and not rhetoric which passes with every change of CEO.

■ The nature of values and their role in understanding changes in employee relations

In analysing the changing nature of relations at work we look through a particular lens; the lens is the values that prevail in different parties and how they colour their perceptions of the employee relations context. We take this perspective because of the view that values are the foundation upon which attitudes, motivation and behaviour are based and are at the core of what constitutes a person, or a work group. Hence, understanding them can help to explain the nature of the attitudes, actions and codes which shape behaviour. Because they contain interpretations of what is right or wrong, they imply that some behaviours are acceptable while others are not. Consequently, it is inevitable that values held by individuals or groups influence perceptions and often cloud how objective and rational they can be over issues, particularly in times of confrontation and industrial dispute.

In employee relations different actors and different contexts may have different values. The dynamics that occur between them are often driven by the significant differences in the value systems of each perspective. Describing and understanding these different value systems and their (in)compatibilities and recognising their situational consequences are, in part, what employee relations is all about.

■ Describing values

Values can be seen as those underlying convictions that are held by individuals or groups. It is a broad, encompassing concept containing a moral flavour of what is right or desirable. Values usually relate to an ideal or standard which guides our conduct and a reference point against which we judge ourselves and which we use to judge others.

Rokeach (in Robbins, 1989) defines values as:

> Basic convictions that a specific mode of conduct or end state of existence is personally or socially preferable to an opposite or converse conduct or end state.

■ Value systems

Individuals or groups have a variety of values. Some are seen as more important and powerful in determining a position than others. This gives rise to a value system or the ranking of individual values according to their perceived importance to the individual or group. Different individuals or groups inevitably have different values and value systems. It is understanding these differences between the parties involved in employee relations and developing behaviours that facilitate their compatibility that is the challenge of employee relations.

By definition, these strongly held convictions are deep rooted. Values are relatively stable entities. Established and reinforced through the early years of a person's life, they are significantly influenced by parents, social upbringing and wider social and cultural experience. A similar pattern emerges with groups or organisations such as owner-manager businesses or trade unions. Strongly held values that are continually reinforced define their value systems and become part of the code of behaviour by which they operate. This often gives rise to rituals and procedures which reflect tradition. Hence, traditions tend to reinforce values and values reinforce traditions.

■ Changing values

Values tend to be stable and enduring entities, and so they tend to change very slowly. Hence individuals or groups might find it difficult to adjust to demands from or changes to their environment which may require significant adjustment and/or challenge to their core values. We return to this aspect later when we consider the impact political, legal and economic change has had upon trade unions and corporations and their difficulties in responding adequately.

■ Values dominant in the work environment

If we take an epoch perspective it may be possible to plot the changes in the work values of each generation. It is reasonable to assume that the values formed in earlier life through socialisation will demonstrate themselves in expressed values in the work situation in later years. Hence it may be possible to anticipate the dominant values of individuals according to their age and the era in which they grew up. It suggests that the values of the young employee are likely to be those dominant and reflected by that person when he or she reaches leadership positions later in life. Hence the work ethic values of the young growing up in the 1950s and early '60s would be expected to be reflected in part by leaders of the '80s (Thatcherism). Similarly the existentialist values of the '70s may be reflected in part by the values of leaders of the late '90s (New Labour). It would be interesting to conjecture what values will dominate when the current generation of young workers reach positions of leadership.

Robbins (1989) draws on several studies of values starting with the work of Allport *et al.*, (1951) to suggest that there are a number of different value systems which define the behaviours of different age groups in the working population. These form the core of Table 15.1.

Group 1 would be the oldest in the work population, whose values reflect dependency on the organisation for security and career opportunity, the importance of honest application and overriding commitment to the organisation, influenced by traditions and moral responsibility, and respectful of power and authority. Very much compliant

■ Table 15.1 Dominant values in the post-war workforce

Category	Entered workforce	Approximate age	Individual work values	Organisational work values
Protestant work ethic	1945–50s	55–65	Hard work, conservative loyalty to organisation	Command, control, efficiency, compliance, dehumanisation
Existentialism	1960s–70s	40–55	Quality of life, non-conforming, seeks autonomy, loyalty to self	Teamwork, quality, respect for individual, involvement
Pragmatism	1980s	30–40	Success, achievement, ambition, hard work, loyalty to career	Efficiency, cost reduction
Generation X	1990s	under 30	Lifestyle, loyalty to peers	Empowerment, organisational learning, self-development

Source: Robbins (1989).

and prone to coercion, these are the individuals who would have difficulty with redundancy and unemployment, feeling betrayed by the system which was supposed to look after them for all their hard effort, loyalty, conformity and compliance.

Group 2 would be more interested in the quality of their lives and would see self-expression, choice and personal freedom as the most important thing. Their values would reflect a dislike of material things, manipulation and control, coercion and compliance. They would be interested in challenging authority, organisational goals and values and less interested in materialism, manipulation and conformity. Enhancing individual freedom and the best interests of all would be their values.

Group 3 would reflect materialistic goals, putting individual interest first, self-achievement, manipulation and commercial exploitation of others and situations. These values thrive upon the promotion of the free market economy and reflect the self-interest values of 'Thatcher's children'. To this group the ends would justify the means, and their ethical stance would be very utilitarian. They are likely to reflect the values of the enterprise economy and free market economic and political values.

In addition to Robbins' descriptions, we could add a fourth group, Generation X, reflecting the values of the young joining organisations in the late 1990s. What we see with this generation is a significantly changing set of attitudes and values which young people are bringing to work. They question collectivist values and adherence to normative behaviour, with the requirement to transfer individual rights, freedoms, choices and responsibilities to a third party, and take control of their own destinies. They see the 'job for life' concept, so central to the ethos of the work ethic generation, with its emphasis on organisation career development, as outdated and inappropriate.

For this generation career means the development of a knowledge and skills portfolio which allows employability. They have many of the values of the existentialists of the 1970s, such as the importance of lifestyle, freedom, meaningful experience, growth and individualism. They too challenge the traditional work ethic by seeking to find meaning and value in life beyond the materialistic. Over-educated and under-stimulated, their interest is in 'getting a life' which contains a greater balance between work and non-work activity. Many of these young people want a holistic lifestyle, which does not mean working all hours and putting organisational interests above all else. They are not interested in the 'top job', with its living to work mentality (Hecht, 1997). The costs are perceived to be too great. They often appear disillusioned with a world of work which sends their middle-aged fathers home exhausted and queuing for a coronary, and their mothers frantic to balance the demands of a career with domestic management. They have more interest in personal growth and development (*see* Jay's Story). A survey by Coopers and Lybrand (quoted by Hecht, 1997) found that only 16 per cent of graduates aspired to climb the corporate managerial ladder or wanted a job (power) which involved organising, influencing and motivating other people. Money and status, while important, are secondary to working with talented people, on enjoyable, interesting and varied projects, seeking spiritual meaning and fulfilment in work (*see* Olivia's Story).

A further factor of significance is the desire of the talented young to work in organisations which are ethical and which reflect their own personal values. When making choices about organisations to work in, they consider the congruence of their own values with those espoused by potential employers. Choice in recruitment and selection based on values and ethics may appear novel, but talent may not gravitate to those organisations that cannot provide young people with a variety of learning experiences which are perceived as relevant and which help to improve their package of skills and experience.

Example 1 – Jay's Story

Jay, a soft-spoken 25-year-old young graduate photographer, denies his generation is arrogant. 'Older photographers tell me how sad it is that we missed out on the eighties – when four-hour lunches and being paid £2,000 a day were the norm – and how much we must be struggling.'

From a young age, Jay heard his father saying that he wished he could do something he enjoyed. 'You need to find a job you will like,' Jay was told. His father who used to work in the rag trade, died four years ago at the age of 51 of a heart attack. 'Stress at work killed him,' Jay believes.

Jay works long hours because he enjoys it. 'I'm not worried about money as long as I have got enough to stay out of trouble. Recognition from peers is more important than cash.'

(Hecht, 1997)

Example 2 – Olivia's Story

The case of Olivia, a 30-year-old solicitor for one of the larger City firms in London. Over the past 6 months she hasn't been home before 10 pm – which gives her just enough time to slob in front of the TV, knock back a bootle of Chardonnay and commiserate with the characters in her favourite soap *This Life*. It's the nearest she gets to a weekly social life. Olivia isn't happy. 'What's the point of earning pots when you haven't got time to spend it?' she says with a sigh.

Stuff the Ferrari, the business lunches at Quags and the weekends in Paris – quality time with friends and family is what upwardly mobile professionals now crave. For Olivia, the comfort £50 000 a year plus 'perks': company car, pension, etc. is, she feels, scant reward for the gruelling routine she endures. Five years ago, she would have been content with a pay rise that matched her commitment. Now, though, she is looking for precisely the opposite – less money in exchange for less responsibility. 'If someone offered me a job for £10 000 or even £15 000 less along with fewer hours I'd take it'.

(*Independent*, 1997)

Questions

1 How would you describe Jay's and Olivia's work values?

2 What might be the implications of such values for (a) Their career choices and opportunities? (b) Their employers?

3 To what extent would you see this as the pattern and trend for the future?

The think tank Demos (Cannon, 1996) suggests that organisations need to build a new contract with the young in which they provide a varied, reframed work environment, perhaps project-based, where young people can feel that they are doing meaningful, relevant and varied work which enriches their experience rather than the traditional 'apprenticeship time serving' early experience of photocopying, faxing, answering telephones and coffee making.

The past decade has reduced significantly the pool of talent available. Organisations need to rethink their position and ask the question of how they make themselves relevant to young people and how they can provide more meaningful, exciting and challenging work experiences for the young. By making work more attractive they are building a relationship with their young talent that leads to commercial competitive advantage.

SETTING THE CONTEXT: THE SHIFT FROM INDUSTRIAL RELATIONS TO EMPLOYEE RELATIONS

In this section we deal with the perspectives and values of the central parties involved in the emergence of employee relations. These are the trade unions, employing organisations and the individual employee.

But first we look at some of the major influencing contextual factors that have impacted on employee relations during the past decade. While the major elements have been largely legal and economic, Fig. 15.1 illustrates the wider contextual issues that inform the current perspective.

■ The impact of the state on employee relations since 1980

The Labour years during the 1960s and '70s saw the rise of trade union power, with its increasing use in the political arena. This was far removed from the original roots of trade unions' purpose as friendly societies, there to help individuals in a welfare capacity (Field, 1996). At this time trade union power reached its height in terms of membership and density, and influenced the 1974–9 Labour government towards employee protection legislation, industrial democracy and the 'social contract' incomes policy.

Characteristic of the Thatcher years in the 1980s was the ideological shift towards the creation of a free market, free enterprise economy in which a rugged entrepreneurial individualism reflected the values of individual innovation and creativity and the potential high rewards associated with it. The major values reflected were those of individualism, defined by Purcell and Gray (Legge, 1995) as 'policies based on belief in the value of the individual and his or her right to advancement and fulfilment at work', individual initiative, energy and drive, self-reliance, acceptance of responsibility, and preparedness to take risks and to own the benefits of the outcomes. In the process individuals would need to take responsibility for developing their knowledge and skills to deliver the promises of creativity.

The creation of privately owned, commercial enterprises with a Darwinian ethos of success or failure according to how they adapted to the commercial environment was the preferred model of the Conservative government. Its values did not reflect the notion and importance of full employment opportunity for all. Instead, they reflected the ethos in which, as Legge (1995) says, 'Firms' survival and growth depends on the "leanness" and "fitness" in dealing with the rigours of the marketplace', without the support of government intervention and restrictions which prevented fair competition and protected the inefficient. This was economic Darwinism at its height, potentially leaving the vulnerable both ill-prepared and poorly equipped to cope with the change.

This shift in values heralded the growth of privatisation of state-owned industries and public utilities, and the introduction of enterprise values into the National Health Service, local government, in the form of compulsory competitive tendering, and many other areas.

To the Conservative government of the 1980s trade unions were seen as the protagonists of the enterprise culture they were seeking to establish. It saw them as 'an institutional impediment to the operation of free markets (not to mention that of disguising from workers their own best interests)' and therefore harmful or at least unnecessary. Through the use of closed-shop agreements, restrictive practices and legal immunities,

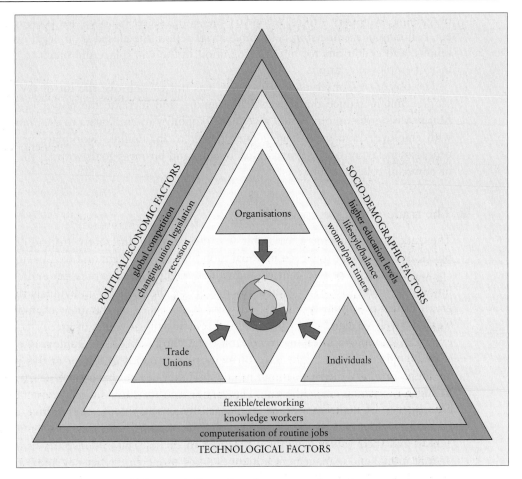

■ **Fig. 15.1 Contextual factors influencing the nature of employee relations**

they were seen to have the mechanisms for inhibiting the development of the free market central to their values. Furthermore, unions were perceived to fetter the free will of the individual and, through the collective bargaining process, to control the way in which views and actions could be expressed and presented (Legge, 1995).

This period saw the start of the shift in workplace values from collectivism to individualism which has left the trade unions in some disarray. Collectivism was seen as one of the major inhibitors of the creation of an enterprise economy. National agreements with their national pay rates were seen to distort the economy and restricted the capacity of local employers to price their products at competitive rates. A worker in Newcastle would be paid the same as a worker in London for the same job, even though the cost of living and the costs of production in the two centres were significantly different.

The Conservative government's response to the challenge of trade union resistance to its free market philosophy was to use its legislative powers. The series of labour laws passed during the 1980s dramatically changed the face of labour relations in Britain. The governments of the 1970s ignored unions at their peril. They were perceived to wield a disproportionate amount of power in industrial relations. Through the 1980s and early '90s a series of Acts relating to employment protection and unfair dismissal, collective bargaining, sympathy strikes, secondary picketing, secret balloting for trade union leaders, balloting of membership before industrial action, the closed shop, legal immunity of unions, and conditions for union recognition in the workplace did much to change the face of employee relations.

The object of Conservative legislation was not to improve the lot of the individual worker, but to reduce the power of the unions and increase the power of employers. Marginalising the unions would give more flexibility to employers to deal more directly with employees and give them greater power to manipulate workplace practices and processes in favour of their own value systems and business goals without the hindrance of powerful collective interests.

■ The trade union perspective

The trade union movement inevitably saw the situation differently. Instead of being the political monster that inhibited national economic development and well-being for workers and the 'cager' of the 'captive' individual's right to free expression and dissent, the union movement saw itself as actually protecting the rights of individuals through the great virtues of solidarity and collectivism. It saw itself as the great champion of the weak, actively engaged in confronting and resisting the attempts of greedy, coercive and exploitative employers seeking to maximise shareholder profit at employees' expense.

Although employers might have thrown up their hands in horror at this perspective and descriptions of their values and behaviours, they did not have much of a track record to suggest anything very different. The very reason for trade unions' existence was the consequence of maltreatment of employees by unscrupulous, exploitative employers. Capitalist values and ethics determined that individuals were just another resource to exploit and their values gave them the right to do so. The evidence lies in the various organisational and management initiatives taken to increase efficiency and productivity.

The Industrial Revolution saw exploitation on a massive scale. The lack of will to change matters was evident in the values underpinning the *laissez-faire* policies of consecutive governments. The enlightened tried to improve the social, housing, health and educational conditions of the workers, but in the face of those social Darwinists who saw the poor as lazy, dirty, amoral low life. To the employer the buyer of labour had all the rights while the seller of labour had none.

At the turn of the twentieth century, the emergence of Taylorism and the principles of scientific management, to improve efficiency, and Fordism, which valued 'man' as an extension of a machine, simply reinforced the views of trade unions that they were there to protect workers from the excesses of exploitation and coercion.

Even the advent of the human relations school, which emphasised the importance of social factors in the workplace, did little to dissuade organisations from their exploitative and coercive behaviours. The advent of McGregor's Theory Y, in which he espoused the virtues of people at work, and Maslow's attempt to dignify the values of employees had marginal effect on the endemic values of organisations which still approached employees in an instrumental manner. Using the twin planks of solidarity and collective action, the trade union movement sought to win a fairer share of profits for its members and to improve their welfare in the workplace.

■ Historical trade union values

But what values do trade unions represent? Historically, their need to confront the worst abuses of employer exploitation has forced them to be confrontational and to see conflict as a necessary requirement for improving the lot of their members. The diametrically opposed values of capital and labour make conflict inevitable. In fact, it is the clash of opposite value systems which creates the focus for employee relations as a process for managing the tensions and facilitating truce and compromise. For Marxists the position is so categoric that there is no need for employee relations at all, with its attempt to come to compromise (Blyton and Turnbull, 1996). There is nothing to negotiate about. Collective bargaining and participation should not be entered into since the differences between the two value systems are so profound as to make negotiation puerile.

However, it may not be perceived as all bad news. Legge describes this traditional view as 'liberal collectivism', which sees 'group conflict as inevitable and potentially beneficial, if institutionalised through collective bargaining. Management would have a co-ordinating role representing the employer's interests with the trade unions fulfilling the same role for the workforce' (Legge, 1995).

Unions see themselves as protectors of workers who cannot easily help themselves. They are there to provide pay determination through collective bargaining, care and welfare, and national campaigns to influence and lobby on social issues. Their role has been to confront organisational values and strategies which enforce passive compliance through fear of unemployment and to challenge the practices of management which alienate employees by creaming off the fruits of their labours. Their values are enshrined in the rules which govern the codes of behaviour of members. They promote and maintain the values of solidarity through group normative behaviour and have expectations of members that they do not defy the agreed codes of conduct and 'rules' of membership. They discourage the miscreant and aberrant behaviours of those who are perceived to threaten the solidarity and security of the whole. In return for providing 'safety' and protection they require the subsuming of individual will to collective responsibility and action.

Generally the historical core values of trade unionism have been confrontation through collective action and solidarity through the use of creative tension and protectionism for union members' jobs for the purpose of keeping wages up and providing better working conditions. These values have been defined and shaped by the traditional values of the coal, docks and steel industries and sustained by their group norms and codes of behaviour. The demise of these industries with their large union memberships, together with downsizing, changing working practices and a loss of 5 million members since 1979, has fragmented the trade union strategy of collectivism and solidarity.

The last decade has threatened even more the traditional positions and approaches adopted by trade unions, however, David Blunkett (1996) states that the attitudes and the actions of trade unions have to change in the light of the changes that have happened in the relationship between capital and labour. The impact of the global economy and the shift towards social partnership require the unions to change from their confrontational and conflictual stance to one of collaboration and partnership with employers and individual employees. Unions may find difficulty in making this transition since by definition their values are deep rooted and enshrined in their social history and tradition.

The economic and legal upheavals of the 1980s' legislation and the recession have combined to transform pay determination. The growth of individualism has shifted the emphasis from collective bargaining, a major plank of trade unionism, to individual determination. In 1975, 90 per cent of pay was determined by collective bargaining, with only 10 per cent determined by the employer. Now the reverse is true, with over 60 per cent determined by the employer, who, based on individual agreement, fixes the rate and invites employees to take it or leave it. Where collective bargaining does happen the trend is for it to take place at local workplace level rather than nationally.

Now we are in an era when employers expect to get more from their employees for 'paying' less, which the outdated values and strategies of trade unions can do little about.

Just as fundamental a threat to trade unions and their collective values is the trend to marginalise them in the employment setting and to make them less relevant. Many employers see unions as marginal and some see them as irrelevant in the employment context. The rise of management strategies and approaches which build on the new philosophies of human resource management with the emphasis on individual commitment and employee empowerment shifts the emphasis for responsibility directly onto the employee's shoulders. It does not necessitate the intervention of a vicarious intermediary on the part of the individual. The belief that the growth of management education and development over the past decade has encouraged managers to see individuals as people rather than units of production has further fuelled the trend towards dealing directly with the individual rather than through unions. It gives credence to the view that all good managers should want to deal with their people in a fair and equitable way and now have the training and understanding to do it: laudable values – if only it were the case. For further discussion, *see* Chapter 5.

THE ORGANISATIONAL PERSPECTIVE

This section examines the impact of values on the employment relationship within the organisational setting. It discusses how the values of the most influential group have shaped organisations, how values have been used to confer competitive advantage and what impact this has had on how organisations have related to the people within them.

■ Background to thinking in organisations

These shifts in values have also reflected how organisations view themselves as well as how organisational theory has developed, which has in turn influenced the development of employee relations practice. Organisations have traditionally taken a functional view of themselves, underpinned by a structure reflecting these, aptly named, divisions such as operations, finance and marketing. Each division often had its own culture and set of values encouraging the internal focus. The business schools also encouraged functionalism and 'scientific management' by taking a rational/economic approach in the subjects taught to developing managers, rarely taking a holistic view of organisations or teaching people skills. The role of the manager was seen firmly as that of managing the task, rather than managing the people who performed the task.

For over two hundred years classical management theory has likened organisations to machines, starting from Adam Smith's division of labour, to Fayol and Urwick's view of the task of managers in organisations as planning, organising, command and control. Organisations were designed as if they were machines with a network of interdependent parts, the functional departments further specified by precisely defined jobs. Through hierarchical patterns of authority and command they sought to make organisations into rational systems operating efficiently, seeing people as cogs rather than human beings. The key values of this era were efficiency and control.

Taylor's model of scientific management took this a step further by analysing and standardising tasks from an engineer's viewpoint, simplifying work so that workers would be 'cheap, easy to train, easy to supervise, easy to replace' (Morgan, 1997). Taylorism can still be seen in organisations a hundred years after he presented his first paper on management. As Morgan points out, scientific management worked where there were straightforward tasks to perform in exactly the same way, in a stable environment where people operating the process were compliant and willing to be 'dehumanised'. It worked in a society whose values around work came from the 'protestant work ethic' tradition, where expectations were no more than the straight exchange of 'a fair day's work for a fair day's pay'. It also worked for a generation who had grown up in a culture and were steeped in the values of the military bureaucracy that came with two World Wars and national service, used to following commands without question.

Like Taylor, organisations regarded people as a collective entity, part of a machine, numbers on the balance sheet, 'the workforce', to be treated the same way and negotiated with through representatives, not as individuals with their own aspirations, hopes and opinions. This view was also reflected in the way research into organisations and developing organisational theory was carried out using 'scientific' methods that reduced people to objects through statistics and numbers. To control and efficiency, scientific management added the values of standardisation, compliance, routinisation of tasks and dehumanisation.

The 1960s onwards saw many changes in thinking, including the emergence of a new approach to motivation theory, with McGregor, McClelland, Herzberg and Argyris all demonstrating that motivation was more than just the straight exchange of money for labour. This period also saw the emergence of a new paradigm for thinking about society and therefore organisations, based on the philosophy of Kant and the German Idealists, in 'attempting to understand and explain the social world primarily from the point of view of the actors directly involved in the social process' (Burrell and Morgan, 1979). From this time there was a shift in thinking in the social sciences that started looking at people as individual human beings and thinking of organisations primarily as the people that make them up.

The importance of values in organisations and in the theory surrounding them is in the way the values of influential individuals within shape the organisation. Mangham and Pye suggest that people in organisations draw up their organisation charts to reflect their beliefs and values at the time in how they think the world is and how it should be organised to deal with it. They report from their research that 'indeed the sharpest image that remains with us … is that of a small group of senior managers seeking to shape events and activities, improvising the music and leading the dance for others to follow' (Mangham and Pye, 1991). The senior managers they researched reinforced that their actions were informed by what they valued and influenced how they managed. For instance those with strong materialistic values were likely to support monetary incentive schemes, whether or not experience revealed greater effort and commitment, demonstrating that they see what they want to see, looking for evidence to support their beliefs, discounting that which questions them. If senior management believed that the workforce were just 'hands' to be controlled, separated from their brains, should it have been a surprise that their employees felt detached, or alienated, often putting considerably more energy into activities outside their work?

Changing organisational values: from control to commitment

It was not until the 1980s that a change of management style and values began to emerge visibly in organisations, based on the changes of thinking of the 1960s. The post-war years until the 1970s had been characterised by relative stability, a growing economy and full employment. It was in this decade that organisations began to change their view of their workforce from the rational–economic 'factors of production', recognising the workforce as being made up of individuals who had needs beyond pure financial incentives. Organisations found that having the right machinery and technology was no longer enough to be successful. They had to have a motivated, committed workforce to operate them, rather than an interchangeable pool of labour, which was all that was required by the values of scientific management.

The impact of emerging competition and the focus on marketing

The first of three factors that influenced organisations in recognising the need to change their traditional ways of thinking in managing their workforce was emerging competition. Western companies had begun to experience the threat of global competition, especially from the Pacific Rim and Japan, and had started to examine the Japanese style of management to understand their success factors. Much evidence was drawn from Japanese industry where high quality and productivity per employee plus successful product/process improvement were seen to be underpinned by employee commitment to company goals and willingness to participate in quality improvement. As one of the members of a study mission as part of the UK National Quality Campaign in 1984 wrote:

> The Japanese has one outstanding characteristic: total commitment. Work comes before any other activity. The company comes before any other organisation. Japanese-made goods monopolise his shopping list. Tradition, culture, religion, education, social history – all combine to urge the Japanese to be conscientious, loyal, single-minded and hard-working. (National Quality Campaign, 1984)

Western companies also began to recognise that the other success factor of Japanese companies was their focus on customers. The 1980s saw the development of the concept of total quality in many organisations and the parallel development of the marketing function to drive corporate strategy from customer requirements, rather than from what production was prepared to offer. Inherent in the total quality approach was the understanding of 'internal customers' within the organisation, the recognition of the part people played in achieving corporate objectives, and the need to involve the whole workforce to gain competitive advantage. For those companies engaged in total quality there was an increasing recognition of the need for a change in the values prevalent in the workplace to those of customer service, empowerment, involvement and teamwork.

Valuing excellence

Allied to this, the second influence on values and the need for commitment came out of the 'excellence' literature of the period. Ouchi's *Theory Z*, Peters and Waterman's *In Search of Excellence*, Pascale and Athos' *The Art of Japanese Management*, and Deal and

Kennedy's *Corporate Cultures*, all published in 1981 and 1982, set the agenda for commitment. They became standard reading for many managers, and were, as Campbell *et al.* (1990) put it, the start of a tidal wave of writing on the importance of culture and values. They put the 'soft' factors, which had previously been the domain of the psychologists and OD departments, on the corporate agenda and made them discussible.

This period was also accompanied by companies experimenting with different workforce strategies and apparently demonstrating how great and productive the contribution of a committed workforce can be. Examples included the Quality of Work Life joint venture between AT&T and Communication Workers of America and the Employee Involvement programmes at Ford and Cummins Engine. As Ouchi points out, however, long-term relationships, stress on participation, teamwork and consensus decision making that often characterise the Japanese style were against the conventional values and management practices in the West (Ouchi, 1981). Peters and Waterman, Deal and Kennedy, and Ouchi also found that their 'excellent' companies had a strong code of conduct and values underpinning how they conducted their business.

Creating and changing culture and values in organisations for competitive advantage

As managers and directors became formally educated in business through MBA and other qualifications, and management development came to be seen as important as training in technical skills for the workforce, in the boardroom directors began to develop a values-driven framework for their competitive strategy. Writers from Mintzberg and Quinn to Schein have emphasised the role that organisational leaders have in ensuring the organisation has a 'source of identity and core mission', which Schein would argue come from understanding and managing the culture, and articulating the organisation's values (Schein, 1985). This understanding of the 'soft' side of managing organisations was also recognised by the strategic writers such as Quinn *et al.* (1988), who suggest that the key tasks of the leaders of institutions include: the definition of institutional mission and role; the institutional embodiment of purpose; the defence of institutional integrity; and the ordering of internal conflict.

In the study that inspired their book, Deal and Kennedy found that of the 80 companies they surveyed:

- about one-third (25) had clearly articulated beliefs;
- of that third, two-thirds had qualitative beliefs, or values; the remaining third had widely understood financially orientated goals;
- all of the 18 companies with qualitative beliefs or strong cultures were outstanding performers and included those cited by Peters and Waterman, and Ouchi.

Organisational culture has been variously described as: 'the way we do things around here' (Deal and Kennedy, 1982); 'patterns of belief or shared meaning, fragmented or integrated, and supported by various operating norms and rituals ... [exerting] a decisive influence on the overall ability of the organisation to deal with the challenges it faces' (Morgan, 1997) and 'one of the most powerful and stable forces operating in organisations' (Schein, 1996).

Organisational values are core underpinnings which 'serve the normative or moral function of guiding members of the group in how to deal with certain key situations' (Schein, 1985). When the values are internalised by the organisation they become beliefs and assumptions and gradually become automatic and habitual; however, if the values are not based on actual beliefs, they are 'espoused' values only. Espoused values will predict what people will say in a certain situation but not how they will react. For instance, a company that says that it values teamwork but promotes those who achieve individual objectives at the expense of their colleagues should not be surprised when teamworking breaks down. If an organisation articulates its values it must be consistent, ensuring congruency with strategy and policy to 'resonate with and re-inforce the organisation's strategy' (Campbell *et al.*, 1990). One of the dangers that they recognised of not making values explicit was that a company's values were often built on those of the founder members, such as (Bill) Hewlett and (Dave) Packard, or the senior management team at the time, especially when an organisation was founded. When that group retire and leave the organisation to professional managers, the fit between the new senior management and the values may be broken.

In their writings Deal and Kennedy (1982) and Morgan (1997, 1986) cited well-known examples of values such as:

'IBM means service'
'Excellence in underwriting' (Chubb Insurance)
'Never kill a new product idea' (3M)

Organisations with these strong founding values found it more appropriate to manage their relationship with their employees directly rather than through a third party, hence trade unions failed to be recognised as relevant in these organisations. As the alignment between organisational and employee values became more congruent the need for trade union representation was perceived as unnecessary. Organisations wishing to move away from the traditional adversarial industrial relations of the past saw these exemplars as desirable models around which to formulate new practices of values-based employee relations.

A common characteristic of many of these values-based organisations was that they were new start-ups, often in new technology settings where they were not handicapped by the trappings of historical tradition. Organisations with a longer history, coming from an older technology base, would be bound to a greater or lesser extent by the values and beliefs of the past, not always common throughout a large organisation. During this period many of these organisations, engaged in trying to change their culture, formally articulated and published statements of what they thought their values should be – for example, in conjunction with implementing initiatives such as total quality, and BICC in its 'Business Excellence' programme (Fig. 15.2).

Following the insights of the 'excellence' literature, in the 1980s organisations became aware of the significance and symbolic consequences of organisational values, with writers such as Morgan reporting that 'many organisations have started to explore the pattern of culture and subculture that shapes day-to-day action' (Morgan, 1986). He saw this as a positive step towards the recognition of the human nature of organisations and the need to build them around people. Some ten years later he reported that the total quality and customer service movements of the time that sought to change managerial and organisational cultures had been largely successful in 'revolutionising and reinventing themselves' through these values. However, for some 70 per cent of organisations these movements became just programmes, failing to shift the dominant culture and mindset and the prevailing political patterns. These would suggest that for this group the new values had not been internalised and remained as 'espoused' and the organisations reverted to their old traditional values.

Schein (1996) has proposed an explanation for the failure of changing culture and values programmes to take hold, by the notion that there are at least three cultures operating within an organisation: the 'operators', who are the line management and workers who make and deliver the products and services of the organisation; the 'engineers', who design and monitor whatever is the core technology of the organisation; and the 'executives', who are the senior managers at the top of the organisation. The executive culture, because of the closeness to the shareholder, only sees the organisation in terms of the 'bottom line'; the 'engineers' are focused on improving the technology, seeing people as the factor that operates it and usually abuses it; whereas it is in the 'operating' culture that most of the 'culture and values' change programmes take hold. 'The research findings about the importance of teamwork, collaboration, commitment, and involvement fall on deaf executive ears, because in the executive culture, those are not the important variables to consider' (Schein, 1996).

Culture and values are a key part of defining the company philosophy, which provides the organisation with a framework against which it can assess the extent to which business decisions fit with the company philosophy and provides a mechanism for the defence of its integrity. Peters and Waterman found that their excellent companies all had philosophies that focused on the contribution of people and the need to manage them as adults, with the need to manage them through a third party. The opposite situation is reflected by the thoughts of Argyris (1960), who observed that many organisations took a negative view of human nature, treating people as infants despite motivation theories and recruiting mature, skilled people. Morgan (1997) points out that where the culture is strong 'a distinctive ethos pervades the whole organization: employees exude the characteristics that define the mission or ethos of the whole – e.g. outstanding commitment to service'.

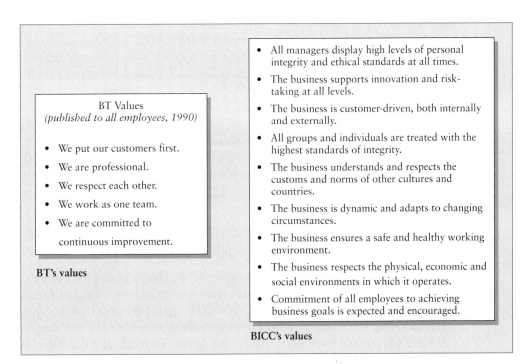

BT Values
(published to all employees, 1990)

- We put our customers first.
- We are professional.
- We respect each other.
- We work as one team.
- We are committed to continuous improvement.

BT's values

- All managers display high levels of personal integrity and ethical standards at all times.
- The business supports innovation and risk-taking at all levels.
- The business is customer-driven, both internally and externally.
- All groups and individuals are treated with the highest standards of integrity.
- The business understands and respects the customs and norms of other cultures and countries.
- The business is dynamic and adapts to changing circumstances.
- The business ensures a safe and healthy working environment.
- The business respects the physical, economic and social environments in which it operates.
- Commitment of all employees to achieving business goals is expected and encouraged.

BICC's values

■ Fig. 15.2 Organisations' value statements

However, most organisations are not made up of a single culture; organisations evolve over time and even with a strong culture from a visionary founder, as in Mintzberg's (1984) 'missionary' organisation, in time other views will develop. As he points out, the only way to keep an ideology protected from contamination is to become isolated; isolation would threaten the survival of the organisation. Both Morgan (1997) and Schein (1985) refer to the establishment of the *counterculture* as different views emerge as the result of changes in the environment the organisation operates in. They also recognise that other 'cultures' prevalent in society will impact on the organisation, formed from competing value systems such as those caused by nationality, gender, religion and professional groupings.

Trade unions have also been seen as a 'counterculture' in organisations, with a different value system to that of the organisation. Morgan (1997) suggests that they owe their existence to the traditional lack of common interests between the organisation and its employees and have their own separate cultural histories which are unique to each union grouping and industry. There is also the view that for a healthy government there should also be some form of opposition to keep them in check. However, the evolution of a stakeholder approach recognised a need to balance the wants and values of customers, shareholders, organisation, management, employees, suppliers and government to provide a more strategic view than the traditional confrontation style would allow.

Throughout the focus on quality, customers and 'excellence' during the 1980s, trade unions were increasingly marginalised as organisations experimented with 'soft' HR practices, such as employee involvement and participation, as advocated by the leading writers and consultants and learned from the 'excellent' organisations. This was seen to be supported by the external changes that were happening to the trade union movement.

As trade unions lost their traditional influence over the UK workforce, many organisations were realising that they could also achieve more through the development of a more effective relationship with their workforce rather than the more confrontational style of the past. They sought to provide a better service to the workforce in the areas where trade unions had traditionally been strong such as in communication and providing benefits to employees. Articles such as Walton's 'From control to commitment in the workplace' (Walton, 1985) introduced the concept of commitment to the wider management audience, as the outcome of implementing the strategies advocated by the 'excellence' literature. Commitment was promoted as a means of motivating and controlling employees. Morgan (1997) warns that whereas many organisations attempt to create shared meaning and involve people in the vision and values required to build a unified whole, working for the same ends and mutual benefit, it is also possible to use them manipulatively.

■ The shift from collectivism to individualism: developing a direct relationship with employees through commitment

The third factor that contributed to the interest in values and commitment was the emergence of the Human Resources school from the redefinition of motivation from the perspective of differing individual needs. The previous model of control, based in Taylorism, was beginning to suffer growing disillusionment due to the changing expectations and educational levels of the workforce on the one hand, and intensified competition on the other. These would seem to have made the scientific management model obsolete, with organisational success now deemed to depend on superior level of performance in the marketplace, which in turn required the commitment of the workforce. One of the factors common to human resource management, the success of Japanese companies, and the 'excellence' literature appeared to be the idea of gaining employee commitment through emphasis on mutuality of employer/employee objectives. The Harvard Business School developed a new core course, used not only on the MBA programme, but also on the Senior Executive programmes, which was based on the model shown Fig. 15.3, reflecting the changing understanding of the role of personnel or human resource policies in an organisation.

The role of the traditional personnel function had been changing during this period, which reflected the gradual evolution of approaches to management during the twentieth century, based on contemporary understanding of motivation as it moved away from the scientific management model, where workers were viewed as lazy, aimless and mercenary, and willing therefore to tolerate the routinised, specialised jobs of the factory for a price. The 1930s onwards saw the development of the human relations model after the Hawthorne studies led to the realisation that it is necessary to consider the 'whole person' at work. Lack of job satisfaction would lead workers to seek satisfaction elsewhere; therefore it is necessary to make workers feel wanted. This approach developed, particularly with further research into motivation in the 1960s, into the human resources model, giving rise to a new approach to personnel management. With many departments renaming themselves Human Resources, they took a more strategic role as a support function that enables business strategy rather than the more reactive and detached function that had grown out of employee welfare services.

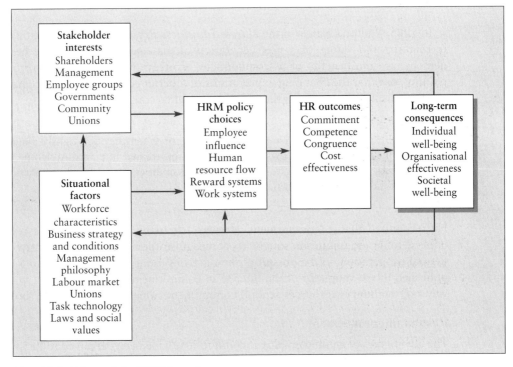

■ **Fig. 15.3 Map of the HRM territory**
Source: Beer *et al.* (1984)

The 'soft' school of HRM

The human resources school recognised that people are motivated by a complex set of factors that are interrelated, including money, need for affiliation or achievement, and the desire for meaningful work. Employees should therefore be looked on as reservoirs of potential talent and it is management's responsibility to learn how best to tap such resources. The assumptions that come from the research of this period reflect much of what is seen in the West as the Japanese management style: people want to contribute; the more they become involved, the more meaningful work can become; work does not have to be distasteful – hence job enrichment and job design; employees are quite capable of making significant and rational decisions affecting their work; increased control and direction on the job and completion of meaningful tasks can determine the level of job satisfaction. This philosophy implies a greater degree of participation in decision making and increased autonomy over task accomplishment.

The 'hard' school of HRM

As organisations were beginning to recognise the value of this philosophy, many senior managers brought up on Taylorism still felt the dilemma of capital's need to control labour while seeking its commitment and cooperation. Until the early 1980s what was taught in business schools was based on the 'hard' skills of management concentrating on strategy, structure and systems with its emphasis on the analytical and technical aspects of work. In many organisations with these values, HRM was taken literally, with people being seen as a resource to be spent like any other, and decisions were still based on people as numbers on a balance sheet and therefore people were still viewed as a collective to be managed on a collective basis.

In 1985, Walton's article in the *Harvard Business Review* was symptomatic of the shift in thinking and values of a new generation of managers. In this article he set out to demonstrate the benefits of a 'commitment' strategy over that of a 'control' strategy, pointing out that the changing expectations of a better educated workforce have led to a growing disillusionment with the old style model of control:

> workers respond best – and most creatively – not when they are tightly controlled by management, placed in narrowly defined jobs, and treated like an unwelcome necessity, but instead, when they are given broader responsibilities, encouraged to contribute, and helped to take satisfaction in their work.

He recognised that a 'commitment' strategy left many questions for the role of trade unions; some organisations sought to derecognise them, while others actively pursued mutual cooperation, in the pursuit of their active support in change. Walton's article was published in the vanguard of the interest in commitment in organisations, where, in the views of the human resources school, commitment came to be seen as the 'holy grail'.

Results of commitment

The advantages of gaining employee commitment have been perceived to be lower labour turnover, better product quality, greater capacity to innovate and employee flexibility, leading to the enhanced capability of the firm to achieve competitive advantage. In this, the work group is seen as the critical unit (Walton, 1985).

Definition of commitment

The definition of organisational commitment that is most frequently used and which forms the basis for discussion in this section is:

> the relative strength of an individual's identification with and involvement in a particular organisation. Conceptually, it can be characterised by at least three factors:
> (1) a strong belief in, and acceptance of the organisation's goals and values,
> (2) a willingness to exert considerable effort on behalf of the organisation, and
> (3) a strong desire to maintain membership in the organisation. (Porter *et al.*, 1974)

Organisations in the 1980s focused on the first two elements of the commitment definition, working on recruiting those who believed in the same goals and values as the organisation, or on organisation change programmes to engender commitment among existing employees, hoping to exchange this for willingness to 'go the extra mile'. The employee relations department often played a key role at a strategic level in working with the Board to understand and define the culture and values that were appropriate to the organisation. At an operational level they would develop and implement such programmes as employee involvement and effective internal communications to engender the common belief in organisation goals and values. These programmes also retrieved internal communications as the organisation's prerogative, from the trade unions, who had often taken on this role in the light of poor management capability and skills in this area previously.

The 1990s: a new decade dawns

Where initially global competition in the 1970s and '80s had encouraged organisations to invest in their employees through such programmes as management development, customer care and total quality management, the intensification of competition and other factors led to recession and mass unemployment at the end of the decade, often for the same group who had had their expectations raised during this period. The other factors contributing to recession included new technology, privatisation, shareholders demanding greater returns, and the changing societal values enabled by government policy taking away employment protection measures, emasculating the trade unions and reducing unemployment benefits in the UK.

The commitment equation can be seen as what the organisation wanted from the employee, with the exchange from the individual's point of view being in those intangible areas that come from involvement, such as job satisfaction. The recession of the 1990s impacted on many of the 'change programmes' underway in organisations, as many of those with long traditions and corporate memories stretching back into older work values reverted to their old type as the new values that they had been working on had not yet become 'the way we do things around here'.

As many companies downsized and restructured, any exchange had become uneven with organisations no longer wanting people to be committed to remain with the organisation apart from a few scarce skills, but still wanting the willingness to exert extra effort on its behalf. Employees, on the other hand, faced with being expected to put in more effort, partly to compensate for departed colleagues, without the traditional job security, potentially felt that the organisation's side of the exchange and their commitment to their workforce was missing. Many felt exploited. Organisations in many cases had reverted to their old style of managing but expected their employees to stay with the changes they had started to put in place.

THE INDIVIDUAL PERSPECTIVE

In order to understand the individual's perspective of the employment relationship, we consider it from two perspectives: (i) the employee–organisation relationship and (ii) the employee–union relationship. To inform the former, we view it from the perspective of the changing nature of the psychological contract existing between them. Whereas commitment reflects the organisational aspect of the employment relationship, the wider 'psychological contract' reflects the balance between organisational and employee expectations. To inform the latter, we view it from the changing needs of the employee in the context of the changing nature of work and employees' expectations of their trade union.

The employee–organisation relationship

The concept of the psychological contract

The formal contract that employees have with their organisation traditionally covered the tangible aspects of work such as hours to be worked in exchange for pay and benefits, and working conditions, which was also the area that traditionally was negotiated with the trade union. The psychological contract goes beyond the tangible contract to consider the relationship which exists directly between employees and their organisations. It can be described in two different ways: one by the perceived contents and terms of the contract and the other in how it is formed – the process of contracting. All types of contract, from the formal employment contract to this more psychological one, can be seen to have their roots in exchange theory, where individuals invest or make contributions in return for a particular reward or outcome. Like the concept of organisational commitment (Lydka, 1992), the psychological contract is also influenced by equity theory, especially where the contract has broken down.

At the centre of the relationship between organisations and their employees is the creation of the conditions that will allow employees to meet their needs and expectations while providing a high level of performance for the organisation. The term 'psychological contract' implies that there is always an unwritten set of expectations operating between the actors of an organisation:

> the actual terms remain implicit; they are not written down anywhere. But the mutual expectations formed between the employee and the employer function like a contract in that if either party fails to meet the expectations, serious consequences will follow – demotivation, turnover, lack of advancement, or termination. (Schein, 1978: 112)

The ways that the organisation demonstrates acceptance of the contract include salary increase, positive performance appraisal, new job assignments, sharing of organisation-

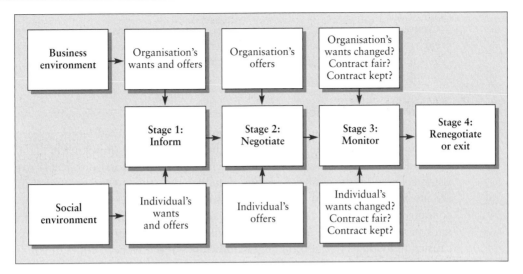

Fig. 15.4 The four stages of psychological contracting
Source: Herriot (1995).

al secrets and promotion. This is in exchange for deciding to remain, a high level of commitment and willingness to accept various kinds of constraints on the part of the employee (Schein, 1978).

Many of these expectations go further than the explicit areas of pay, training and development, and involve the person's sense of dignity and worth, wanting work that is fulfilling and opportunities to develop and grow. Schein suggests that much labour unrest and employee turnover comes from violations of these aspects of the 'psychological contract' dressed up as the explicit, and more acceptable, issues of pay, working hours and conditions which traditionally form the legitimate negotiating agenda.

Herriot's (1995) view of the psychological contract draws on the thoughts of Schein and is focused on the social process of contracting (Fig. 15.4). He suggests that it is this aspect that has the most theoretical and practical value as it is only the process that may be similar wherever contracts are made: all of the other aspects are likely to differ as they are made up of the perceptions of individuals. His model builds on Schein's conditions for success.

Rousseau, one of the main researchers into the content of psychological contracts, starts from the premise that contracts 'are a product of free societies' and that they are underpinned by choice; they arise when people believe themselves to have choice in their dealings with others. She makes the point that having a choice can engender commitment to carry out promises and takes the line of developing a behavioural theory of contracts. Her definition of the psychological contract is 'individual beliefs, shaped by the organisation, regarding terms of an exchange agreement between individuals and their organisation' (Rousseau, 1995: 9).

She emphasises that the individual voluntarily assents to make and accept certain promises as he or she understands them as a key feature of a psychological contract, which involves giving up some measure of freedom. This is similar to Schein's signal of acceptance of the contract through 'willingness to accept various kinds of constraints, delays or undesirable work', although she warns that:

> Contracts are made when we surrender some of our freedom from restrictions in exchange for a similar surrender by another. But by giving up something voluntarily, each gets much more than might be possible otherwise.

Violation of the psychological contract

The recession, starting in the late 1980s in the US, has focused recent research on what happens when the psychological contract has been violated (Brockner *et al.*, 1992; Parks and Kidder, 1994; Robinson and Rousseau, 1994). As Morrison (1994) explains, 'the issues covered by the contract are emotionally laden, thus, when psychological contracts are not working smoothly, strong feelings are provoked.' As the psychological contract contains many unconscious expectations, of which many are at the heart of an individual's perception of self, any violation strikes at more than disappointed expectations, causing individuals to question beliefs and values about respect, codes of conduct and the integrity of the organisation. The repercussions from broken promises are significant, producing anger and eroding trust between the parties to the employment relationship (Schein, 1978; Robinson and Rousseau, 1994).

The recent focus on downsizing and restructuring has meant that contracts have been changed. A formal written contract has to have consent, but with the more intangible 'psychological contract', conditions, not of their choosing, have been imposed on some employees. This has led to the situation described by Brockner *et al.* (1992) where layoffs are made and the perception of the fairness in deciding who was to leave and the reasons for leaving affected the commitment of those employees remaining. They found those who had been most committed were the most negatively affected. Their perception of the equity and fairness of decisions on who was to leave had caused them to reassess what they thought of their psychological contract.

The other area that has impacted on the structure of organisations has been the advent of flexible working and issues such as short-term contracts. The extent to which the flexible workforce have had a voice in the change of their contracts will also be informed by where they are on Rousseau's (1995) continuum between the transactional contract of a 'fair day's work for a fair day's pay', which can now mean short-term, temporary employment, and the relational contract characterised by open-ended relationships and investment from both sides. The transactional contract is closest to the traditional economic exchange, where the terms are tangible, such as money, hours and specific tasks, usually within a specified time scale. The relational contract, on the other hand, is more abstract and concerned with the relationship between the individual and the employing organisation, but has the traditional element of 'a job for life'.

Impact of the psychological contract on traditional employee relations practices

The key activities where trade unions have traditionally been involved in organisations have been collective bargaining over pay and conditions and communication. It is in these areas that many employee relations departments have expanded from their former industrial relations role during the 1990s.

The recession of the early 1990s, coupled with a 'cost cutting' focus, has seen many organisations seeking to implement a form of 'pay for performance' scheme focusing on individual performance, rather than a series of increments depending on length of time in a job up to a point where there would be just the payment to keep up with inflation. Many employees had their formal contracts of employment changed either through being 'transferred' to another company following outsourcing, or being offered an individual contract to take them out of collective bargaining. Few of those affected had much choice, and in Herriott and Pemberton's (1995) terms had little chance to renegotiate their 'psychological contracts'.

The other key area that employee relations department have retrieved from trade unions has been that of internal communications. Guzzo and Noonan (1994) would see communication between the organisation and its employees as at the heart of determining how the contract is viewed.

The employee–union relationship

The impact of changing work patterns

The world of work has been changing quite significantly during the past decade. This has produced substantial changes in the way employee relations has developed, as discussed earlier in Chapter 9. The traditional mutual employer–employee relationship has been in demise, driven there by the adoption of flexible working practices, market forces and changes in values. The psychological contract literature confirms this.

The individual relationship with the employer has not been the only relationship to change. The way in which individuals relate to their industrial trade unions has also undergone significant shifts. Much of this shift has come from the need of individuals to adopt different working practices because of the reduction in full-time permanent opportunities, the increase in short-term fixed contracts and part-time working. Much of work has become fragmented and workers transient. Individuals need to be more mobile and will not stay with the same employer for long periods of time, let alone a lifetime. Hence, the everyday interactions of individuals with their colleagues, which maintain an environment that continually reinforces the values of collectivism and solidarity, loyalties and commitment of individuals to each other, has largely passed. Flexible working practices and their concomitants have encouraged the rise of individualism. No longer do employees identify in the same way with the core values of their industries; no longer do they interact in the same way on a day-to-day basis, sharing common goals or threats so necessary to reinforce group norms, and keep behaviours and shared values current.

The large numbers of workers in the dockyards or collieries to provide the mystique, muscle and impact of solidarity are no longer there. The number of organisations employing more than 10 000 workers in the south of England can be counted on one hand (Monks, 1996). Furthermore, industrial trade unions are seen as less relevant and not providing the services individuals need in the current work forum. Hence, members have voted with their feet. Since 1979 trade union membership has fallen by five million, with the once mighty Transport and General Workers' Union losing over half its membership.

The shift away from collective pay determination to individually based pay determination has been dramatic in the past decade. Collective bargaining, the mainstay of trade union activity in the past, is not seen by the bulk of employees as so relevant in the late 1990s. In 1975, 90 per cent of public sector workers had their pay determined by collective bargaining with only 10 per cent determined by the employer. In the 1990s only about 35 per cent of public sector workers have their pay determined by collective bargaining with 60 per cent by their employers. In the private sector there are hardly any national employer agreements, with less than 25 per cent having their pay determined collectively.

Today employees are looking for more provision of services which meet their needs. While the traditional role is there for some, most no longer require the traditional range of services that unions have provided in the past. As individuals have been forced to change their work style and focus, so their needs have shifted. Support based on the best interests of the collective is no longer what the bulk of employees are looking for. Tailor-made support for individual needs is. Yet this is what the trade unions have found difficult to provide. It requires a significant culture change on their part with significant shift in values to provide services that are seen as relevant and valued.

Part of the difficulty in managing such a change lies in the difficulty in letting go of those traditional values and beliefs that have underpinned the trade union movement since the Industrial Revolution.

Professional services are needed, such as training and career development, legal support, health and welfare provision, insurance, pensions advice, and health and safety. The new individualism in employment will see employees requiring employment services from trade unions over their working life to help them remain employable and increase their employability.

CONCLUSION

Using values as our lens, we have sought to plot the changing nature of employee relations through and beyond the unionised workplace. We have explored the dramatic and dynamic changes in the context within which employee relations are acted out. The impact of 'radical' political will and the ideology of the recent Conservative governments, with resultant legislation, have done much to reduce trade union power to the point where unions are forced to reassess their relevance and their function and role. The 1990s saw a shift in power away from the unions, deregulation of the labour market and the promotion of the influence of managerialism with its emphasis on direct (and directing?) negotiations with employees rather than through third-party collective bargaining.

It remains to be seen what approach the new Labour government will adopt now that it is in power, and whether the end of the twentieth century will see another radical shift in employee relations (Tailby, 1997). Certainly New Labour's espoused values expressed through its election manifesto show differences from those of its Conservative predecessors. Emphasis has been placed on fairness at work through the creation of minimum employment standards, and its commitment to the European Social Chapter. Yet some argue that New Labour employment proposals are 'minimalist' (Tailby, 1997). Although there are proposals for a statutory union recognition procedure for the purpose of collective bargaining, there does seem to be some desire to keep unions at a distance. The retention of a flexible labour market approach, not dissimilar from its predecessors, is likely to continue. Where it does seem to differ is in terms of its commitment to employee involvement and consultation in major organisation decisions and the creation of a 'partnership' approach to relations at work. Its policies on unemployment through 'Welfare to Work' are intended to ease the plight of the young and long-term unemployed people, while its emphasis on education and training is intended to help equip individuals with relevant knowledge and skills to make them employable.

Organisations themselves are in transition. Fierce global competition has forced them to develop different forms of flexible work practices, variations in organisational structure, and the increasing use of information technology. It has also forced organisations to reconsider the human factor, with an emerging attitude shift away from seeing employees as a cost to one of valuing individuals for their potential. Through the strategic use of human resource management some organisations recognise that competitive advantage can come from empowering employees rather than controlling them. As Wooldridge (1996) says, managers are building relationships with employees on an adult-to-adult basis rather than the more traditional form of parent to child.

While economic, political and technological factors have had profound impacts on the changing nature of employee relations, it is in the area of social change and individual expectations where future significance lies. The changing values of young people towards work which emphasise individualism, a demand for interest and variation, self-development and learning, and balanced lifestyle are likely to substantially influence how employee relations are enacted. If the view holds, that the emergent values of the current young generation will inform and shape future organisational attitudes, behaviours and forms of relationships, are we likely to see an even more significant individualising and humanising of the employment relationship?

QUESTIONS

1 What are the economic, sociodemographic and technological forces that will impact on the differing value sets in organisations?

2 If you were a consultant to an organisation, what would you advise might be the consequences for its employee relations of the change in values that a Labour government might bring?

3 Does collectivism have a future? What are the factors that determine its relevance?

4 What are the consequences of the shift from 'job for life' to 'get a life' for emergent employee relations practice in organisations?

5 What values do you think the successful trade union of the future may need to reflect in relation to serving its membership?

EXERCISE

Using the 'values list' as a guide, think about what the things are about work that are most important to you. What do you value?

Achievement	Advancement	Authority
Challenge	Creativity	Change
Cooperation	Competence	Competition
Developing self	Developing others	Detail
Effectiveness	Ethical practice	Excellence
Excitement	Expertise	Family time
Friendship	Growth	Helping others
High earnings	Honesty	Independence
Influencing others	Intellectual work	Involvement

Job tranquillity	Knowledge	Leading
Learning	Location	Loyalty
Making decisions	Managing	Meaningful work
Merit	Money	Openness
Order	Peaceful environment	Power
Precision work	Promotion	Recognition
Reputation	Responsibility	Quality of what you do
Security	Self-respect	Stability
Status	Time freedom	Time at home
Time to do a good job	Team work	Travel
Variety	Working on leading edge	Working alone
Working with others	Working under pressure	

Use the space below to write down your top ten values and then spend some time thinking about their relative importance. If you had to give up one, which would it be? What if you had to give up another?

Value	*Ranking*	*Value*	*Ranking*
_____	▢	_____	▢
_____	▢	_____	▢
_____	▢	_____	▢
_____	▢	_____	▢
_____	▢	_____	▢

Which value stands out as being the most important to you?

Using whatever approach you like, rank your chosen values from 1 to 10 with 1 being what you value most about work.

REFERENCES

Allport, G.W., Vernon, P. E. and Lindzey, G. (1951) *Study of Values*. Boston, MA: Houghton Mifflin.

Argyris, C. (1960) *Understanding Organizational Behaviour*. London: Tavistock.

Barter, (1998) *An Examination into the Impact of Teleworking within BGI Transco*, MBA dissertation, University of the West of England.

Beer, M., Spector, B., Lawrence, P. R., Quinn Mills, D. and Walton, R. E. (1984) *Managing Human Assets*. New York: Free Press.

Blunkett, D. (1996) *Analysis*, BBC Radio 4, 15 December.

Blyton, P. and Turnbull, P. (1998), *The Dynamics of Employee Relations*. 2nd edn. Basingstoke: Macmillan.

Brockner, J., Tyler, T. and Cooper-Schneider, R. (1992) 'The influence of prior commitment to an institution on reactions to perceived unfairness: the higher they are, the harder they fall', *Administrative Science Quarterly*, 37, 241–61.

Burrell, G. and Morgan, G. (1979) *Sociological Paradigms and Organisational Analysis*. London: Heinemann.

Campbell, A., Devine, M. and Young, D. (1990) *A Sense of Mission*. London: Economist Books.

Collin, A. (1995) '"New" individuals for the "New Deal"', *The New Deal in Employment Conference*, City University Business School, London.

Cox, P. S. (1986) 'Occupational survival', PhD thesis, University of Bath.

Cannon, D. (1996) 'Generation X and the new work ethic', *Proceedings of Future Work Forum*, Henley Management College, June 1996.

Deal, T. E. and Kennedy, A. A. (1982) *Corporate Cultures: The Rites and Rituals of Corporate Life*. Wokingham: Addison-Wesley.

Field, F. (1996) *Analysis*, BBC Radio 4, 15 December.

Guest, D. E., Conway, N. Briner, R. and Dickman, M. (1996) *The State of Psychological Contract in Employment*, Institute of Personnel and Development.

Guzzo, R. A. and Noonan, K. A. (1994) 'Human resources practices as communications and the psychological contract', *Human Resource Management*, Fall, 447–62.

Handy, C. (1996) *The Empty Raincoat*. London: Arrow.

Hecht, F. (1997) 'A job with life ... not a job for life', *The Director*, June.

Herriot, P. (1995) 'New dealing', *The New Deal in Employment Conference*, City University Business School, London.

Herriot, P. and Pemberton, C. (1995) *New Deals: The Revolution in Managerial Careers*. Chichester: Wiley.

Hutton, W. (1996) *Analysis*, BBC Radio 4, 15 December.

Legge, K. (1995) *Human Resource Management, Rhetoric and Realities*. Basingstoke: Macmillan.

Legge, K. (1996) 'Morality bound', *People Management*, 19 December.

Lydka, H. (1992) 'Organisational Commitment: a longitudinal study of UK graduates', PhD thesis, Henley Management College.

Mangham, I. and Pye, A. (1991) *The Doing of Managing*. Oxford: Basil Blackwell.

Mintzberg, H. (1984) 'Power and organization life cycles', *Academy of Management Review*, 9(2), 207–24.

Monks, J. (1996) *Analysis*, BBC Radio 4, 15 December.

Morgan, G. (1986) *Images of Organization*. London: Sage.

Morgan, G. (1997) *Images of Organization*. 2nd edn. London: Sage.

Morrison, D.E. (1994) 'Psychological contracts and change', *Human Resource Management*, Fall.

National Quality Campaign (1984) '*You Won't Do it: Report of the Pacific Basin Study Mission*'. London: DTI.

Ouchi, W.G. (1981) *Theory Z: How American Business Can Meet the Japanese Challenge*. Reading, MA: Addison-Wesley.

Parks, J. M. and Kidder, D.L. (1994) '"Till death us do part ...": changing work relationships in the 1990s', *Trends in Organizational Behaviour*, 1.

Pearson, R. (1996) 'The changing labour market and new patterns of work', *Proceedings of Future Work Forum*, Henley Management College, April.

Peters, T. J. and Waterman, R. H. (1982) *In Search of Excellence: Lessons from America's Best-Run Companies*. New York: Harper & Row.

Porter, L.W., Steers, R. M., Mowday, R. T. and Boulian, P. V. (1974) 'Organizational commitment, job satisfaction and turnover among psychiatric technicians', *Journal of Applied Psychology*, 59, 603–9.

Quinn, J. B., Mintzberg, H. and James, R. M. (1988) *The Strategy Process: Concepts, Contexts, and Cases*. Englewood Cliffs, NJ: Prentice-Hall.

Robbins, S. P. (1989) *Organizational Behaviour: Concepts, Controversies and Applications*. Englewood Cliffs, NJ: Prentice-Hall.

Robinson, S. L. and Rousseau, D. M. (1994) 'Violating the psychological contract: not the exception but the norm', *Journal of Organizational Behaviour*, 15, 245–59.

Rousseau, D. M. (1995) *Psychological Contracts in Organisations: Understanding Written and Unwritten Agreement*. New York: Sage.

Schein, E. H. (1978) *Career Dynamics: Matching Individual and Organisational Needs*. Reading, MA: Addison-Wesley.

Schein, E. H. (1985) *Organisational Culture and Leadership: A Dynamic View*. Jossey-Bass.

Schein, E. H. (1996) 'Culture: the missing concept in organization studies', *Administrative Science Quarterly*, 41, 229–40.

Shaw, M. (1997) *The Role of Women Methodist Ministers*, PhD thesis, University of West of England.

Tailby, S. (1997) 'New Labour, new IR', *Work and Employment*, Bristol Business School, no. 5.

Walton, R. E. (1985) 'From control to commitment in the workplace', *Harvard Business Review*, March/April, 77–84.

Wooldridge, E. (1996) 'The new psychological contract', *Proceedings of Future Work Forum*, Henley Management College, June.

FURTHER READING

Guest, D. (1994) 'Important players in a different game', *People Management*, December.

Handy, C. (1997) *The Hungry Spirit*. London: Hutchinson.

Journal of Business Ethics

Legge, K. (1996) 'Morality bound', *People Management*, 19 December.

Morgan, G. (1997) *Images of Organization*. 2nd edn. London: Sage.

Walton, R. E., (1985) 'From control to commitment in the workplace', *Harvard Business Review*, March/April, 77–84.

Winstanley, D., Woodall, J. and Heery, E. (eds) (1996) 'Business ethics and human resource management', *Personnel Review*, 25(6).

AFTERWORD

This book has presented a contemporary picture of employee relations. In organising our approach around the major themes of parties, the regulatory framework, and patterns and processes, the more familiar features of the employee relations landscape have been reviewed, while scope has existed to explore new influences on the employment relationship in Britain. Although the primary focus of our analysis has been domestic, it is recognised that international factors increasingly influence the working lives of British managers and workers. Not only is the substance of the employment relationship subject to European-wide legal measures and to the corporate deliberations of multinationals, but also interactions between management and labour are played out within increasingly globalised markets for products and labour.

As mentioned in the Preface, this field of study is one in which various perspectives and versions of events are permissible. So, for example, a strike will inevitably be viewed in contradictory terms by strikers themselves, their families, affected management, the police, the media, the public and so on. In order to make some sense of the range of views which impinge upon the subject area, broad theoretical strands of thought have been exposed which assist in the interpretation of unravelling events and apparently irreconcilable opinions. What emerges from such consideration is that there is no single version of 'truth' or 'reality' in this domain, but that a range of legitimate perceptions and interpretations of employment matters are permissible. Against this backcloth, the pivotal significance of the major interest groups of management, trade unions and the state has been reinforced.

Despite the implication of much contemporary literature in the field of personnel or human resource management that management is virtually the sole progenitor of policy in the field of employment, we would return to notion that arrangements established with the actual or implicit consent of the representatives of both labour and capital continue to exert a potent influence on workplace behaviour. Moreover, the inclusion of the representatives of labour, and of government, in the employee relations arena serves to confirm our premise that work itself cannot be viewed as conflict free, and that it is imperative to air a non-managerial version of the experience of work. Nevertheless, in our coverage of the key participants, the ascendancy of management over the past few decades has been acknowledged through charting a proactive managerial role in restructuring facets of the employment relationship, apparently breaking previous traditions of tripartitism and replacing them with more unilateral forms of employment regulation. Yet the manifestations of managerialism remain somewhat contradictory and multifaceted. Non-union employment has been highlighted; it remains, to a great extent, a sector in which conditions of employment are impoverished and insecure. Alongside these 'Dickensian' regimes, however, exist the influential multinational enterprises, whose experimentation with HRM-influenced initiatives have been regarded as exemplary for those claiming sophistication in the field of employee relations management.

Much of the agenda for change which has been charted in this volume has been attributed to the need for organisations to reconstruct previously familiar, and collectively orientated, facets of industrial relations structure to respond with fluidity and flexibility to market pressures. In the private sector, the ethos of consumerism has apparently been at the expense of employee security and status in many instances, and analogous changes have occurred in the public sector. Here, the process of privatisation which has occurred since the onset of the Thatcher era has unlocked many 'articles of faith' concerning model employment, exposing what were often highly collectivised, hierarchical and stable employment conditions not only to market forces, but also to the discretion of entrepreneurially minded executives.

Change has not only been apparent in employee relations structures, but also in the detail of the employment relationship, and policy formulation. Thus, while collective bargaining is still 'alive and well', the processes of pay determination have mutated in recent years to incorporate more strands of compliancy on the part of trade unions. In many instances, mechanisms to involve employee representatives in corporate decision making and to induce commitment of staff to management goals are operating in parallel with or supplanting more conventional and adversarial collectivist approaches. The inception of concepts and practices associated with human resource management in the 1980s implied not only greater organisational sensitivity to the performance of the individual or small group, but also a greater managerial determination to monitor and control such performance more stringently. Observable shifts towards individualism in employment occurred alongside a revamping of the legal system which whittled away much of the latitude for collective action at work, and more intangible cultural and ethical shifts in the wider society concerning the promotion of self-interest.

As we enter the new millennium, Britain has a new government which, at least at a rhetorical level, is re-emphasising more collectivist and caring values, and an intention has been declared to subscribe to the European Social Agenda, which will result in greater regulation of minimum standards in employment and the establishment of compulsory systems for consultation of employee representatives. A theme which has been apparent in this book is that the field of employee relations has evolved through various epochs, and that each epoch may be characterised by waxing and waning power relationships between the parties in employee relations, and varying degrees of intimacy between them. Taking a historical view of the discipline, such configurations and reconfigurations appear somewhat cyclical in nature. Yet behind the current political and organisational aspiration towards the establishment of partnership between management and unions, a perennial anxiety still hovers, which is the extent to which such arrangements will permit employees to gain any real control over their working lives and how the fruits of their labour are distributed.

INDEX

ABB (Asea Brown Boveri) 103
academic qualifications 421–3
Acquired Rights Directive 533
Adaptation of Working Time
    Directive 254–6
Adnett, N. 255
affirmative action 408–10, 432–3
age discrimination 418–19, 430,
    449
Ahlstrand, B. 70, 78, 346
Allen, J. 27
Allen, M. 99
allowances 363–4
America see United States
Amsterdam Treaty 227, 234–6
Anglo–Irish system 260–1
appraisal 441
Armstrong, M. 345, 346, 354,
    359, 365, 368, 369, 370
Atkinson, J. 423, 466–7
attitude surveys 385
authoritarian personalities 412
automotive industry 124
Ayadurai, D. 308

Back, S. 516
Bacon, R. 511
Baddon, L. 399–400
Bahl, Kamlesh 436
Bailey, J. 325
Bain, G.S. 133, 164
bargained corporatism 188
Baritz, L. 46
Barrell, R. 98, 99
Bartlett, C.A. 102–4
basic pay 361–2
Bassett, P. 23
BAT industries 122
Bean, R. 113
Beardwell, I. 16
Beatson, M. 495
Beaumont, P. 80, 81, 202, 326
Benbow, N. 65
benefits 370–2

Beng, C.S. 194
Berger, T. 15
Blackburn, R.M. 133
Blue Circle 176
Blyton, P. 40, 59, 70, 80, 157,
    315, 379, 482, 483
BMW 342
bonus schemes 364–5
Boyer, R. 104
Braverman, H. 34
British Airways 12–13, 59
British Telecom 536
Brown, W. 313
Burawoy, M. 19
Burnham, J. 62
Burton Group 487
business strategy 346
Bygott, D.W. 443–4

Cannon, D. 537, 538, 539, 544
Carey, A. 33
Carley, M. 125
CBI (Confederation of British
    Industry) 222
CCT (compulsory competitive
    tendering) 531
CEEP (European Centre of Public
    Enterprises) 221, 257
Chamberlain, N.W. 306
Chew, R. 194
Chote, R. 460
Citizen's Charter 515, 531
Civil Rights Act (1964) 418
Civil Service 515, 517
Clark, J. 41, 339, 349, 368,
    472–3
Claydon, T. 80, 81, 190, 468
Clegg, H. 268
Clegg, S. 29–30
co-decision procedure 226–9, 259
Coates, D. 140
Cockburn, C. 38, 40, 157
Colgan, F. 158, 159
collective bargaining 4–6, 7, 125

conjunctive (distributive) bar-
    gaining 319
constraining managerial power
    and authority 307
cooperative (integrative)
    bargaining 319–20
corporate bargaining 316–17
devolution of 316–17
economic contractual terms 306
and employee involvement
    324–6
equality bargaining 444–5
in the European Union (EU)
    258
and joint consultation 302
and labour flexibility 320–4
legislative influences 307–9
and management by agreement
    320
multi-employer arrangements
    310–13, 349
and organisational decision
    making 307
organisational level changes
    316–19
process of 305–6
public sector 350, 362–3
requirements for 302
single-table bargaining 318–19,
    350–1
single-union agreements
    317–18, 350–1
structural framework 310–16
and trade union membership
    302–3
in the water industry 303–45
Collective Redundancies Directive
    245–6
collectivism 76–8, 321, 345–6,
    546, 555–8
liberal collectivism 188
Colling, T. 158, 444
Coloroll 379, 380
commission payments 364–5

commitment 549, 555–8
Committee on International Investment and Multinational Enterprises (IME) 120–1
communicative involvement 393–4
comparative employment theory 41–5
compensation for dismissal 292–4, 296–7
competency-based pay 368–70
competitive advantage 551–5
compulsory competitive tendering (CCT) 531
Confederation of British Industry (CBI) 222
conflict see industrial conflict
conjunctive bargaining 319
consultation procedure 223
contracting-out 511–12
contracts of employment 270–5
    and discrimination 441–2
    employees' duties 272–3
    employers' duties 273–4
    and pay 340
    terms 271
    variation of terms 275
convergence of regulatory systems 260–4
convergence theories 43–5
cooperation procedure 224–5
cooperative bargaining 319–20
core workers 467
core–periphery employment strategy 495–6, 498
corporate bargaining 316–17
corporatist political ideology 187–9
Council of the European Union 219–17
Court of First Instance 219–20
Court of Justice of the European Communities 218–20
Cox, S. 238
Crabb, S. 371
Cressey, P. 246
Cronin, J. 44
Cross, M. 470–1
Crouch, C. 24, 134, 137, 138–9, 154, 189
Cully, M. 163
culture
    national 104, 107–8
    organisational 551–5

Curry, L. 371
Curtis, S. 494
customer care programmes 385

Daniel, W. 340
Deal, T.E. 552
decision making
    European Union (EU) 223–9
    organisational 307
deregulation 58, 59, 460–2
Deutsche Morgan Grenfell 60
devolution of collective bargaining 316–17
Dex, S. 494
Dickens, L. 36, 37, 158, 444
direct discrimination 276–7
disability discrimination 281–3, 419–20, 429
disciplinary procedures 443
discrimination 275–83
    ageism 418–19, 430, 449
    consequences of 409, 410
    and contracts of employment 441–2
    definition 410
    direct/indirect 276–7
    disability discrimination 281–3, 419–20, 429
    and dismissal 443
    educational programmes 430–2
    Equal Pay Act (1970) 275, 279–80
    ethical issues 425–6
    gender roles 413–16
    human capital theory 421–3
    individual prejudices 446–7
    managing diversity 434–7
    national campaigns 432
    and pay 441–2
    political issues 425–6
    positive discrimination 408–10, 432–3
    psychological basis 411–12
    quota setting 408–10, 432–3
    race discrimination 280–1, 416–18, 454–5
    religious 281
    reserve army of labour theory 424–5
    segmented labour market theory 423–4
    sex discrimination 275–8, 413–16, 444

and social attitudes 412–13
    sociological basis 411–12
    victimisation 278
    see also equality; managing equal opportunities
dismissal 283–97
    for breaches of statute 290
    compensation 292–4, 296–7
    and discrimination 443
    fair dismissal 287–91
    and incapacity 287–8
    and lack of qualifications 287–8
    misconduct 288–9
    redundancy 283, 289–90, 294–7
    some other substantial reason 290–1
    unfair dismissal 7, 283, 285–6, 291–4
    wrongful dismissal 283, 284–5
dispute resolution 202–4, 326–7
distributive bargaining 319
Doling, P. 116
dominant values 541–4
Donovan Commission 5, 24–5, 74, 153
Dos Passos, J. 28
Dowling, P. 107
Doz, Y.L. 107, 116
DRG 402–4
Dunkerley, D. 29–30
Dunlop, J. 25, 29
Dunn, S. 320, 475–6
duty of care 274
duty of obedience 272

Ebbinghaus, B. 119
economic growth 24–5
economic policies 336–7
education 418, 421–2
Education Act (1944) 508
Edwards, P. 4, 114, 115, 200, 270, 474
EEC (European Economic Community) 213
Eldridge, J. 16, 25
Elger, T. 471, 473
Ellis, N.D. 320
Elsheikh, F. 164
Eltis, W. 511
employee participation and involvement
    classification and types of 384

communicative involvement 393–4

contingency factors 392–3

cyclical patterns 391–2

financial participation 398–401

impact of power relations and values 389–90

involvement 324–6, 383–5

participation 244–5, 382–3

and pluralism 388

and radicalism 388–9

task centred involvement 396–8

theoretical origins 381–2

and the Trades Union Congress (TUC) 379

and unitarism 387–8

employee relations

context of 7–9

study of 3–7

employees

core workers 467

duty of obedience 272

employee–union relationship 561–2

faithful service 272

peripheral workers 467–8

employers

breaches of trust and confidence 273

duty of care 274

indemnity of employees' expenses 274

payment of wages 273–4

provision of work 274

employment

full employment concept 191

growth of 7

and industrial restructuring 68–71

protection legislation 268–70, 284, 285, 287, 292, 294

psychological contract 344, 558–60

unemployment 190–2, 338–9, 424, 497

see also public sector

employment relationship 5, 74–5

empowerment 324–5, 401

equality

equal opportunities legislation 427–30

equal pay 279–80, 337, 356–8

European Union policy 236–43, 275–6

responsibilities of trade unions 443–6

see also discrimination; managing equal opportunities

equality bargaining 444–5

ethics 425–6

ethnic minorities

qualifications 422

race discrimination 280–1, 416–18, 454–5

trade union membership 158, 160

unemployment levels 424–5

ethnocentric multinational corporations 100–1, 104

ethnocentrism 412

ETUC (European Trade Union Confederation) 119, 149, 220–1, 257

European Centre of Public Enterprises (CEEP) 221, 257

European Commission 216

European Council 217

European Court of Human Rights 219

European Economic Community (EEC) 213

European Foundation for the Improvement of Living and Working Conditions 222

European Parliament 218

European Trade Union Confederation (ETUC) 119, 149, 220–1, 256

European Union (EU)

Amsterdam Treaty 227, 234–6

Anglo–Irish system 260–1

automotive industry 124

co-decision procedure 226–9, 259

and collective bargaining 258

consultation procedure 223

convergence of regulatory systems 260–4

cooperation procedure 224–5

decision making 223–8

Directives 222

Acquired Rights 533

Adaptation of Working Time 254–6

Collective Redundancies 245–6

Equal Pay 240–44, 275–6

Transfer of Undertakings 246–7

Working Time 428

Works Councils 122–8, 213, 247–53, 325–6

employee participation 244–5

employers' organisations 221–2, 257

and equality 237–44, 275–6

institutions 214–20

legislative procedures 7, 222–3, 427

Maastricht Treaty 229

member states 214, 215

Nordic system 261

Protocol Agreement 257, 259

protocol procedure 227–9

qualified majority voting (QMV) principle 224–7

regulations 222

Roman–German system 260, 261–3

Social Chapter 9, 233, 325, 428

Social Charter 231–4

Social Partners 212, 220–1, 227–9, 258, 259–60

social policy 195, 229–34

subsidiarity 229

excellence literature 551

externalisation policies 73–4

fair dismissal 287–91

Fairbrother, P. 154, 524

faithful service 272

Farnham, D. 63, 387

feminism 415–16, 449

feminist theory 6, 36–41, 40–1

Ferner, A. 263, 505

Fernie, S. 252, 379

Fevre, R. 189

financial participation 398–401

Fitt, D. 352, 354

Flanders, A. 4, 140, 305, 306

flexibility 457–69

core workers 467

core–periphery employment strategy 495–6, 498

employee gains and losses 473–5

flexible firm 459, 466–9

flexible specialisation 458–9, 463–4

functional flexibility 467, 469–79
international comparisons
478–9
labour market deregulation
460–2
limits to full flexibility 471–3
numerical flexibility 467,
479–85
origins of the debates 459–60
peripheral workers 467–8
and production technologies
462–3
role of the trade unions 475–8
working-time flexibility 467,
479–85
see also Japanisation; labour
flexibility
flexible firm 459, 466–9
flexible specialisation 458–9,
463–4
flexitime 484–5
Flynn, Commissioner 211–12
Ford 126–7
Ford, Henry 463
foreign direct investment 98, 100,
106
Fox, A. 22, 23, 76, 387
Fraser, Munro 439
Fredman, S. 506
free labour market model 427
free market 186–7, 188
Freeman, R.B. 165
Friedman, A.L. 390
full employment 191
Fullerton, J. 434, 446–7
functional flexibility 467, 469–79
changes in 470–1
employee gains and losses
473–5
international comparisons
478–9
limits to full flexibility 470–3
multiskilling 469
role of the trade unions 475–8
teamworking 469

Gall, G. 318
Geary, J. 366, 367, 383, 469,
473, 492
gender roles 413–16
General Motors 323–4
geocentric multinational
corporations 101

Ghertman, M. 99
Ghoshal, S. 102–4
Giddens, A. 412
Gilbert, K. 357
globalisation 8, 43–5, 97, 460
Gold, M. 260, 261
Gospel, H. 7, 16–17, 62, 63, 72,
142, 149
governments
autonomy of 185–6
government philosophy in the
UK 181–4
impact on employee relations
185, 543–5
policies and strategies 179–80,
185–6
economic 336–7
pay 6, 193–4, 333–6
taxation 337
political ideologies 180, 186–9,
192
role in dispute settlements
202–4
state agencies 180
Grahl, J. 262
Grand Metropolitan 122
greenfield sites 472
grievances 442–3
Griffiths, A. 97
Griffiths, J. 393
Grunfeld, C. 200
Guest, D. 81, 85, 86, 168, 169,
172, 346, 387
Guild Socialism 382, 389
Guinness 122

H-form organisations 71
Hall, L. 341, 359, 371
Hall, M. 230–31, 244, 260, 261
Hamill, J. 112–13
Handy, C. 538
Hannah, L. 68
harassment 442–3
Harbison, F.H. 306
harmonisation of pay 362
Harris, R.I.D. 80
Hastings, S. 358
Hay Method 351
Heath, Edward 6
Heery, E. 174
Hendry, C. 69, 71, 101–2, 102,
103, 359, 368
Herriot, P. 67

Herzberg, F. 343
hierarchy of needs 343
Hill, C. 381
Hillgard, E. 412
Hobsbawn, E. 19, 32, 63
Hodgetts, R.M. 97
Hollinshead, G. 107, 117, 192
Hollway, W. 33
Hoover 198
Hoque, K. 81
hours of work 65–7, 480–2, 483–4
house journal/newspapers 385,
393–4
Huiskamp, R. 325
human capital theory 421–3
human resource management
(HRM) 8, 58–9, 83–6, 345,
555–6
and trade union membership
166
Hussey, R. 308
Hutt, W.H. 200
Hyman, R. 5, 49, 136, 154, 155,
263, 382, 464

Ietto-Gillies, G. 97, 117
IG Metall 176
IME (Committee on International
Investment and Multinational
Enterprises) 120–1
Immigration Acts 417
incentives 364–5
incomes policies 6, 193–4
indexation of pay 519–20
indirect discrimination 277–8
individual prejudices 446–7
individualism 76–8, 321, 322,
345–6, 556–8
market individualism 188
induction 441
industrial conflict 199–204
dispute resolution 202–4, 326–7
strike ballots 155, 157
industrial relations 4–5
definition 4
role of the law 6
voluntarist system 4, 6, 7
Industrial Relations Act (1971)
285, 307
industrial restructuring 68–71
industrial tribunals 428–9
industrialisation 32
integrative bargaining 319–20

internalisation policies 73–4
International Labour Organization
(ILO) 121, 149
internationalisation 8, 43–5, 97,
460
interventionist ideologies 187–9
involvement 324–6, 383–5
see also employee participation
and involvement

Jackson, J.H. 309
Jacobi, O. 312
Japanisation 108–12, 460, 464–6
just-in-time (JIT) 110–11, 464,
465
quality circles 109–10
total quality management 110,
111–12, 385, 386, 396–8
Jewson, N. 432
job enrichment 464
job evaluation 238, 351–3, 358
job security 338
joint consultation 302
Jones, Jack 139
Joseph, M. 64
just-in-time (JIT) 110–11, 464,
465

Kahn-Freund, O. 181
Kandola, R. 434, 446–7
Kanter, R.M. 38
Kay, J. 68
Keenoy, T. 16
Keep, E. 192
Keller, B. 125
Kelly, J. 383
Kennedy, A.A. 551
Kennedy, C. 114
Kessler, I. 322, 367
Kessler, S. 327
Keynesian economics 507–8
Kinnie, N. 344
Kjellberg, A. 326
Kling, S. 366
Kuhn, J.W. 306
Kuhn, T. 15

labour dumping see social dumping
labour flexibility
and collective bargaining 320–4
and decentralisation 316
and organisational performance
320–4

and unemployment 190–2
see also flexibility; Japanisation
labour markets
changes in 537–8
deregulation 460–2
and feminist theory 40–1
free labour market model 427
government involvement
189–90
and pay 338–9, 358–60
reserve army of labour theory
424–5
segmented labour market theory
423–4
Lafarge 122
laissez-faire political ideology
186–7, 188
Lane, C. 60, 63
Lawler, E. 352
Leach, B. 419
Leat, M. 107, 117, 192
Ledwith, S. 158, 159
Lee, M.B. 181
Legge, K. 39, 41, 45, 111, 543,
544, 545, 546
Leggett, C. 308, 311
legislation 180, 268–70
Civil Rights Act (1964) 418
collective bargaining 307–9
disability discrimination 281–3,
419–20, 429
Education Act (1944) 508
employment legislation 268–70,
284, 285, 287, 292, 294
equality 275, 279–80, 337,
356–8, 427–30
European Union procedures 7,
222–3, 427
Immigration Acts 417
Industrial Relations Act (1971)
285, 307
Master and Servants Act (1867)
19, 43
National Health Service Act
(1946) 508
National Insurance Act (1946)
508
Race Relations Act (1976)
280–1
Redundancy Payments Act
(1965) 283, 285, 294
Sex Discrimination Act (1975)
275, 276

trade union 155–6, 165–6,
181–4, 270, 291–2
Wages Act (1986) 361
see also contracts of employment
Levi Strauss 426
Levitt, T. 102
LG Group 93–4, 95
liberal collectivism 188
liberal-feminism 38
Liff, S. 430, 435–6
local authorities 516, 518–19
London Underground 514–15
Low Pay Commission 9, 334,
335, 348
Lowe, D. 344
Lowry, P. 203
Lucio, M.M. 86
Luckman, S. 15
Luthans, F. 97
Lydka, H. 558

M-form organisations 70, 71, 78
Maastricht Treaty 229
McCarthy, W. 193, 320
McCulloch, A. 494
McEnrue, M.P. 446
McIlroy, J. 144, 149, 151, 153,
154, 173
McKenna, F. 19
McLean, H. 399–400
McLoughlin, I. 339
Major, John 428, 515
management 58–68
management by agreement 320
management style 76–8, 346–8,
516
managing diversity 434–7
managing equal opportunities
438–43
appraisal 441
disciplinary procedures 443
dismissal 443
grievances 442–3
harassment 442–3
induction 441
pay systems 441–2
promotion 441
recruitment and selection
439–41
redundancy 443
training and development 441
see also discrimination; equality
Mandel, E. 32

Mangham, I. 549
manufacturing 62, 69
Marchington, M. 74, 75, 77, 78, 79, 80, 82, 346, 392, 393
Marginson, P. 122–3, 496
market individualism 188
marketing 550–51
marketisation of the public sector 513–16
markets
  and the employment relationship 74–5
  product markets 72
  see also labour markets
Marsh, A. 308
Marsh, D. 179
Marxist theory 31–6, 381, 388–9
Maslow, A. 343
Mason, B. 382
Mason, D. 432, 445
Master and Servants Act (1867) 19, 43
Mathias, R.L. 309
Maurice, M. 104
Mayo, E. 28
Members of the European Parliament (MEPs) 218
Members of Parliament 408–10
Menter, I. 513
mergers between trade unions 144–5
Metcalf, D. 251, 379
Miles, R. 158
Mill, John Stuart 381
Millward, N. 8, 79, 84, 85, 146, 165, 166, 170, 254, 340, 349
Milne, S. 117
Milner, S. 302
minimum wage 195–8, 309, 333–6
Mirza, Q. 445–6
misconduct 288–9
modernism 46–8
Monks, J. 148, 537, 561
Moore, R. 308
Morgan, G. 549, 553, 554, 555
Morris, G. 506
Morris, H. 427
motivation theory 343–4
Mueller, F. 124, 128
multi-employer bargaining 310–13, 349
multi-unionism 146–7

multinational corporations
  Bartlett and Ghoshal typology 102–4
  definition 96
  development stages 96
  effect on recipient countries 105–7
  employee relations policies 112–14
  and employment levels 105–6
  ethnocentric 100–1, 104
  and foreign direct investment 98, 106
  geocentric 101
  global structures 102
  influence of 95
  international structures 102–3
  and internationalisation 97
  multidomestics' 102
  and national culture 104, 107–8
  Perlmutter typology 100–2
  polycentric 101, 104
  reasons for investing abroad 99–100
  regiocentric 101
  regulation and control of 120–8
  restructurings 122–3
  and trade unions 114–19
  transnationals 103–4
  United States 96, 112–14
  and world trade 97–8
multiskilling 469
Munro Fraser's five-point plan 439
Murlis, H. 351, 352, 354

national culture 104, 107–8
National Health Service 431–2, 515, 517–18, 532
National Health Service Act (1946) 508
National Insurance Act (1946) 508
National Minimum Wage 195–8, 309, 333–6
National Wages Council see Wages Councils
nationalisation 508–9
neo-unitary theory 20–1
New Labour 8, 58, 87, 184, 196, 253–4, 462
new pay concept 344–5, 346
News International 339

nineteenth century employment practices 3–4, 18–20
non-unionised enterprises 80–3, 170–2
Nordic system 261
Northumbrian Water 303–5
numerical flexibility 467, 479–85
Nuti, D.M. 400

Ogden, S. 303
Ollerearnshaw, S. 430
Opportunity 2000 432, 436
organisational culture 551–5
organisational decision making 307
organisational performance 320–4
organisational structures 70–1
Osborne, K. 486
overtime 364, 482–3

Pain, N. 98, 99
Palmer, G. 7, 16–17, 20, 62, 142, 149
Park, Y. 181
Parker, P. 74, 75, 80
Parsons, T. 26
part-time work 7, 485–91, 498
participation 244–5, 382–3
  see also employee participation and involvement
partnership agreements 87–9, 212
pay
  and business strategy 346
  and discrimination 441–2
  employee/union objectives 341–2
  employer objectives 341
  equal pay 237–44, 275–6, 279–80, 356–8
  government policies 6, 193–4, 333–6
  harmonisation 362
  hierarchies and structures 353–6
  indexation 519–20
  international alignment 360
  job evaluation 239, 351–3, 358
  and labour markets 338–9, 358–60
  legislative framework 337
  and management style 346–8
  and market values 358–60
  minimum wage 195–8, 309, 333–6

and motivation theory 343–4
new pay concept 344–5, 346
and the psychological contract 344
in the public sector 506, 509, 517–20, 531, 532–3
as reinforcement 342–4
as a satisfaction of need 344
soft and hard approaches 347
and technological change 339–40
see also collective bargaining
pay systems composition 360–72
allowances 363–4
basic pay 361–2
benefits 370–2
bonus schemes 364–5
commission payments 364–5
competency-based 368–70
incentives 364–5
overtime 364
performance-related pay 321–2, 367
profit sharing 365–6, 399–400
share ownership schemes 365–6, 398, 400–1
single status initiative 362–3
skills-based 367–8
team-based 370
Pearson, R. 538
Pelletier, J. 165
Pelling, H. 142, 143
pension provision 419
performance-related pay 321–2, 367
peripheral workers 467–8
Perlmutter, H. 100–2
personnel management 59
Peters, T.J. 47
Philpott, J. 334
Phizacklea, A. 158
Pimlott, J. 63, 387
Piore, M. 423, 463
Pirelli 349
pluralism 21–5, 345–6, 388
political ideologies 180, 186–9, 192
Pollard, S. 18, 19
Pollert, A. 469
polycentric multinational corporations 101, 104
Poole, M. 185, 389–90
Porter, M.E. 102

positive discrimination 408–10, 432–3
post-modernism 39–40, 45–8
power
    constraining managerial power 307
    and values 389–90
Prahalad, C.K. 107, 116
prejudices 446–7
print industry 339
Prison Service 526–31
privatisation 58, 59, 511–12
product markets 72
production location 99–100
production technologies 462–3
profit sharing 365–6, 399–400
promotion 441
Prondzynski, F. von 193
Protocol Agreement 257, 259
protocol procedure 227–9
psychological contract 344, 558–60
public sector
    collective bargaining 350, 362–3
    contracting-out 511–12
    employment of women 509
    funding crisis 511
    indexation of pay 519–20
    and Keynesian economics 507–8
    management style 516
    marketisation 513–16
    model employer approach 506, 507
    nationalisation 508–9
    pay determination 506, 509, 517–20, 531, 532–3
    political vetting 509
    privatisation 58, 59, 511–12
    service provision and cost cutting 524–6
    size 69, 70, 506
    and Thatcherism 511
    trade union activity 506–7, 509–10, 512–13, 520–4
    welfare state 507–8
Puchi, W.G. 550
Purcell, J. 70, 76, 78, 124, 128, 322, 346, 367
Pye, A. 550

qualifications, academic 421–3
qualified majority voting (QMV)

principle 224–7
quality circles 109–10, 385
quota setting 408–10, 432–3

race discrimination 280–1, 416–18, 454–5
    see also ethnic minorities
radical-feminism 38–9
radicalism see Marxist theory
railway workers 19
Rainbird, H. 192
Ramsay, H. 390–3
Rank Xerox 426, 435
recruitment and selection 439–41
Reddish, H. 387
Redland 122
redundancy 283, 285, 289–90, 294–7, 443
Reed Elsevier 122
Rees, C. 477
regiocentric multinational corporations 101
regulation of multinational corporations 120–8
regulatory systems 260–4
religious discrimination 281
Renault 245
reserve army of labour theory 424–5
responsible autonomy 325
restructuring of industry 68–71, 68–72
retirement 419
Rexam 402–4
Rhodes, M. 199
Rivest, C. 118, 251
Robbins, S.P. 540, 541
Rodger's seven-point plan 439
Roman–German system 260, 261–3
Rousseau, D.M. 559
Rover 342, 476–7
Rowbotham, S. 36
Royal Mail 386
Rubenstein, M. 442

S-form organisations 71
Sabel, C. 463
Salamon, M. 24
salaries 361, 362
    see also collective bargaining; pay
scapegoating 412

Scarborough, H. 476
Schein, E. 344, 553, 558
Schmid, G. 190
Schneer, J. 44
Schregle, J. 107
Schuler, R. 107, 116
Schulten, T. 123–4, 125, 126, 258
Scott, J. 63
Scott, M. 82
Secker, J. 357
segmented labour market theory
    423–4
selection and recruitment 439–41
self-employment 494–5
sex discrimination 275–8,
    413–16, 444
share ownership schemes 365–6,
    398, 400–1
shift working 483
Singapore 180
Single European Act 224–5, 231
single-table bargaining 318–19,
    350–1
single-union agreements 317–18,
    350–1
Sisson, K. 76, 78, 122–3
skills-based pay 367–8
Skinner, B.F. 342
Sly, F. 160
SmithKline Beecham 435
Social Affairs Council 216–17
Social Chapter 9, 233, 325, 428
Social Charter 231–4
social contract 6
Social Darwinism 18
social dumping 106, 123–4,
    198–9
social justice 194–9, 427
Social Partners 212, 220–1,
    227–9, 258, 259–60
social policy in the European
    Union (EU) 195, 229–34
societal effect theory 104
South Korea 180, 181
Sparrow, P. 368, 369
Spence, A. 494
Spivey, W. 102
staff associations 136–7
state agencies 180
state corporatism 188–9
statism 189
statutory regulation see legislation
stereotyping 412, 448–9

Stevens, C. 327
Storey, J. 84, 110, 346, 387
Streeck, W. 478
stress 67
strikes see industrial conflict
structure of industry 68–72
subsidiarity 228
suggestion schemes 385
systems theory 25–31

Taft–Hartley Act 202
Taiwan 180–1
task centred involvement 396–8
task flexibility see functional
    flexibility
task ownership 324–5
taxation policies 337
Taylor, A.J. 188
Taylor, F. 46
Taylor, R. 309
Teague, P. 260, 262
team briefings 385
team-based pay 370
teamworking 469
technological change 339–40
teleworking 538
temporary work 491–4
Terry, M. 313, 476
Thatcherism 511, 544
theories in employee relations
    11–17
  comparative employment theory
      41–5
  feminist theory 6, 36–41
  Marxist theory 31–6
  modernism 46–8
  neo-unitary theory 20–1
  pluralist theory 21–5
  post-modernism 39–40, 45–8
  systems theory 25–31
  unitary theory 17–21
Thomas, C. 88–9
Thomas, L. 102
Thompson, M. 367, 370
Torrington, D. 341, 359, 371
total quality management 110,
    111–12, 385, 386, 396–8
Towers, B. 199
trade unions
  acceptance of incomes policies
      194
  administration and costs 157–9
  classification of 143–4

and collective bargaining 302–3
development of 141–6
employee-union relationship
    561–2
equal opportunities
    responsibilities 443–6
and flexibility 475–8
function 132–6
future role 79–80, 172–4
internal organisation 151–5
international organisation
    118–19, 148–51
legislation 155–6, 165–6,
    181–4, 270, 291–2
membership and density 3, 4,
    145, 157–69
mergers 144–5
multi-unionism 146–7
and multinational corporations
    114–19
non-unionised enterprises 80–3,
    170–2
partnership agreements 87–9,
    212
power of 139–40
public sector activity 506–7,
    509–10, 512–13, 520–4
rationale for collective employee
    organisation 137–9
and staff associations 136–7
values of 545–7
  see also collective bargaining;
    industrial conflict
Trades Union Congress (TUC)
    147–8, 222, 379
training 61, 441
  discrimination awareness pro-
      grammes 430–1
Transfer of Undertakings Directive
    246–7
transnational corporations 103–4
Turnbull, P. 40, 59, 70, 80, 157,
    379
Tyson, S. 347, 348

U-form organisations 70, 71
unemployment 190–2, 338–9,
    497
  among women 424
  ethnic minority 424–5
unfair dismissal 7, 283, 285–6,
    291–4
Union of Industrial and Employers

Confederations of Europe (UNICE) 221, 257
unitarism 17–21, 345–6, 387–8
United Kingdom
    adoption of EU Directives 192
    British management 60–8
    employment legislation 268–70
    foreign direct investment 98, 100
    government philosophy 181–4
    labour flexibility 459
    manufacturing competitiveness 62
    minority groups 417
United States
    industrial growth 28
    minimum wage 334
    multinational corporations 96, 112–14
    new pay concept 345
    trade union membership 169

values
    changing 540, 551–5
    describing 540
    dominant 541–4
    nature and role of 537, 539–40
    organisational perspective 548–50
    and participation and involvement 389–90
    of trade unions 546–8
    value systems 540
Vickery, G. 478–9
victimisation 278
Virdie, S. 445
virtual organisation 538

Visser, J. 119
Volkswagen 121
voluntarist industrial relations 4, 6, 7
von Bertalanffy, L. 26

Waddington, J. 164, 165, 168
wages 361–2
    see also collective bargaining; pay
Wages Councils 4, 180, 195, 309, 335
Waldeck, R. 430
Wall, S. 97
Wallis, B. 88–9
water industry 303–45
Waterman, R.H. 47
Waters, M. 44
Watson, G. 479, 480
WCL (World Confederation of Labour) 149
welfare state 507–8
Welsh Water 305
Weston, S. 86
Whitfield, K. 193
Whitson, C. 164, 168
Wickens, P. 465
Wilkins, M. 96
Wilkinson, A. 77, 79, 82, 346
Willey, B. 427
Wilson, R.A. 65
Winchester, D. 179, 516
Winnick, David 430
Wolters Kluwer 122
Womack, J. 464–5
women
    academic achievements 421
    feminism 415–16, 449

feminist theory 6, 36–41, 40–1
    membership of trade unions 157–8, 161
    in Parliament 408–10
    participation in the labour force 6, 413–16
    public sector employment 509
    unemployment rate 424
    working mothers 452–3
Wood, S. 467, 468
Woodland, S. 163
work ethic 538–9
workers' cooperatives 382
working conditions 3–4
working hours 65–7, 480–2, 483–4
Working Time Directive 428
working-time flexibility 467, 479–85
    annual hours 65–7, 480–2, 483–4
    flexitime 484–5
    overtime 482–3
    reorganisation of working time 480
    shift working 483
Works Councils 122–8, 213, 247–53, 325–6
World Confederation of Labour (WCL) 149
world trade 97–8
Wrench, J. 445
Wright, M. 320, 474, 475–6
wrongful dismissal 283, 284–5
Wurzburg, G. 478–9

Zurich Insurance 122